D0072143

THE PAPERS OF

WOODROW WILSON

VOLUME 3

1884-1885

SPONSORED BY THE WOODROW WILSON
FOUNDATION
AND PRINCETON UNIVERSITY

THE PAPERS OF
WOODROW
WILSON

ARTHUR S. LINK, *EDITOR*

JOHN WELLS DAVIDSON AND DAVID W. HIRST
ASSOCIATE EDITORS

T. H. VAIL MOTTER, *CONSULTING EDITOR*
JOHN E. LITTLE, *ASSISTANT EDITOR*

Volume 3 · 1884-1885

PRINCETON, NEW JERSEY
PRINCETON UNIVERSITY PRESS
1967

St. Mary's College Library
Winona, Minnesota

Copyright © 1967 by Princeton University Press
All Rights Reserved
L.C. Card 66-10880

Note to scholars: Princeton University Press subscribes to the Resolution on Permissions of the Association of American University Presses, defining what we regard as "fair use" of copyrighted works. This Resolution, intended to encourage scholarly use of university press publications and to avoid unnecessary applications for permission, is obtainable from the Press or from the A.A.U.P. central office. Note, however, that the scholarly apparatus, transcripts of shorthand, and the texts of Wilson documents as they appear in this volume are copyrighted, and the usual rules about the use of copyrighted materials apply.

Printed in the United States of America
by Princeton University Press
Princeton, New Jersey

OC 5030832

923.173
W75p
V.3

13. 50

(Princeton Univ.)

10-20-67

75629

EDITORIAL ADVISORY COMMITTEE

SAMUEL FLAGG BEMIS

KATHARINE E. BRAND

HENRY STEELE COMMAGER

AUGUST HECKSCHER

RICHARD W. LEOPOLD

DAVID C. MEARNS

ARTHUR M. SCHLESINGER, JR.

INTRODUCTION

THIS volume, spanning the period from February 2, 1884, to January 23, 1885, carries Wilson from the beginning of his second semester at The Johns Hopkins University to the eve of the receipt of his first copies of *Congressional Government*.

The documentation for the single year encompassed by this volume is, as the reader will soon discover for himself, amazingly rich and revealing about the Johns Hopkins during one of the great periods of her history, and moreover, about Wilson's widening friendships, intensive study and scholarly writing, and search for his first teaching position. However, the major portion of this volume consists of the almost daily exchange of letters between Wilson and his fiancée, Ellen Louise Axson. All letters between Wilson and Ellen Axson known to exist for this period have been printed in their entirety. They not only record their writers' lives in remarkable detail but also disclose how the "priceless gift" of their love grew and enriched their personalities.

The editorial objectives enumerated in the General Introduction to this series in Volume 1 have remained unchanged, as, indeed, have the editorial methods with one exception. Midway in the second volume, the Editors began the practice of printing information relating to the provenance of a document in a footnote, usually affixed to the editorial heading of the document, instead of running it in after the phrase or sentence describing and giving the location of the document. This new procedure has been followed throughout in the present volume. It would be helpful for readers who have not seen the preceding volume to turn to its Introduction for commentary about certain practices followed in printing Ellen Axson's letters.

The Editors continue to be indebted to the institutions, members of the Editorial Advisory Committee of *The Papers of Woodrow Wilson*, and other individuals mentioned in the acknowledgments section of Volume 1. The Editors express their deep gratitude also to Jean MacLachlan of their staff and Marjorie Putney of Princeton University Press for excellent copyediting; to President Katharine McBride and Professor Arthur P. Dudden of Bryn Mawr College for materials relating to Wilson's appointment to the Bryn Mawr faculty; and to Dr. William D. Hoyt, Jr., for information about the descendants of Nathan Hoyt, Ellen Axson's maternal grandfather.

THE EDITORS

Princeton, New Jersey
April 2, 1967

CONTENTS

Introduction, vii

Illustrations, xiii

Abbreviations and Symbols, xv

The Papers, 1884-1885

Abstracts of Wilson's Two Papers on Congressional Government, 223

Advertisement Concerning the Projected "History of Political Economy in the United States," 172

Agreement Between the Trustees of Bryn Mawr College and Wilson, 597

Editorial Notes
    Ellen's Visit to Wilmington and Her Trip with Woodrow to Washington and New York, 329
    Wilson's Research for a "History of Political Economy in the United States," 447

Letter from Samuel Edward Axson to Ellen Louise Axson, 77

Letters from Wilson to
    Ellen Louise Axson
        Feb. 2–April 27, 1884
            3, 8, 11, 18, 23, 29, 34, 37, 45, 49, 52, 55, 59, 67, 74, 78, 82, 86, 94, 98, 102, 108, 112, 118, 126, 131, 134, 137, 143
        May 1–July 28, 1884
            154, 160, 163, 166, 173, 176, 180, 184, 189, 195, 200, 203, 208, 210, 213, 215, 216, 221, 225, 228, 233, 236, 241, 247, 253, 257, 260
        Aug. 2–Oct. 31, 1884
            268, 274, 281, 288, 292, 300, 308, 311, 318, 329, 330, 331, 335, 337, 338, 342, 344, 346, 348, 353, 355, 359, 362, 365, 367, 369, 371, 374, 378, 381, 385, 388
        Nov. 1, 1884–Jan. 24, 1885
            392, 396, 398, 401, 404, 408, 410, 414, 416, 421, 424, 429, 431, 437, 440, 446, 452, 460, 466, 469, 471, 476, 479, 483, 487, 493, 496, 498, 502, 506, 511, 515, 517, 521, 524, 528, 529, 532, 534, 538, 541, 546, 549, 552, 554, 560, 564, 569, 573, 576, 580, 582, 586, 589, 591, 593, 597, 601, 603, 607, 611, 613, 616, 619, 621, 626, 628, 633
    James W. Bones (drafts), 240, 316, 341
    Robert Bridges, 37, 198, 464, 563
    Richard Heath Dabney, 25
    Houghton, Mifflin & Company, 111, 158
    John Hanson Kennard, Jr., 455
    John Barbee Minor, 150, 159
    Charles Howard Shinn, 373
    Charles Andrew Talcott, 230
    Joseph Ruggles Wilson, 531

Letters to Wilson from
    Herbert Baxter Adams, 529
    Ellen Louise Axson
        Feb. 4–April 29, 1884

6, 15, 30, 38, 46, 57, 63, 75, 83, 90, 97, 105, 115, 128, 133, 140, 149
May 1–July 28, 1884
152, 162, 169, 174, 186, 193, 201, 206, 210, 214, 219, 226, 234, 244, 251, 255, 259, 265
Aug. 4–Oct. 31, 1884
271, 278, 284, 290, 297, 306, 314, 322, 330, 332, 335, 337, 340, 343, 345, 347, 351, 354, 356, 360, 366, 368, 370, 374, 376, 381, 383, 387, 390
Nov. 1, 1884–Jan. 24, 1885
395, 397, 399, 402, 407, 409, 412, 415, 419, 423, 425, 431, 433, 436, 438, 441, 450, 454, 461, 468, 470, 474, 478, 480, 484, 486, 492, 494, 497, 504, 505, 508, 514, 516, 518, 523, 525, 530, 533, 535, 539, 545, 550, 553, 558, 562, 568, 572, 575, 579, 581, 584, 587, 590, 593, 598, 601, 606, 608, 615, 616, 618, 620, 624, 627, 631
James W. Bones, 310, 327, 379, 440
Jessie Bones Brower, 192
Gamaliel Bradford, 21
Robert Bridges, 24, 541, 571
Richard Heath Dabney, 164
William F. Ford, 589
Daniel Coit Gilman, 212
Granville Stanley Hall, 311
Melville R. Hopewell, 33, 338, 435, 483, 520, 574
Houghton, Mifflin & Company, 149, 162, 486
Edward Ingle, 203
John Hanson Kennard, Jr., 62, 139, 205, 388
Marion Wilson Kennedy, 25, 101, 130, 216
John Barbee Minor, 157
Edward Ireland Renick, 22, 52, 54, 102, 318
James E. Rhoads, 501, 513, 596, 613
Albert Shaw, 214, 444, 556
Charles Howard Shinn, 213, 250, 278, 501, 544, 556, 569
Charles Andrew Talcott, 168
C. H. Toncray, 501
Janet Woodrow Wilson, 17, 81, 102, 110, 181, 348, 482, 548, 574
Joseph Ruggles Wilson, 73, 142, 165, 183, 343, 385, 505, 537, 548, 572, 612, 632
Joseph R. Wilson, Jr., 11, 56 (extract), 63, 212, 548
James Woodrow, 134
Hiram Woods, Jr., 209, 326
Memoranda, 214, 362
Minutes of the Johns Hopkins Seminary of Historical and Political Science, 40, 135, 172, 182, 361, 391, 517, 615
Notebooks Described
Classroom Notebooks, 339, 345
Pocket Notebooks, 182, 449
Research Notebook, 449
Notes, Classroom, Described, 359

Notes on a Lecture in Professor Morris's Course on the Philosophy of
    the State, 403
Notes on Professor Ely's Lecture on Bimetallism, 458
Notes on Professor Morris's Lectures on Herbert Spencer, 426, 457
Telegram to Wilson from Ellen Louise Axson, 364
Writings
    A Fragment of a Ditty, 287
    Newsletters from the Johns Hopkins
        I. President Eliot's Views, 42
        II. Johns Hopkins University, 72
        III. Johns Hopkins University, 123
    To E. L. A. on Her Birthday, 178
Index, 635

ILLUSTRATIONS

Following page 296

Johns Hopkins Seminary Room
  Milton S. Eisenhower Library, The Johns Hopkins University

Main Library, Hopkins Hall
  Milton S. Eisenhower Library, The Johns Hopkins University

The Johns Hopkins Glee Club
  Princeton University Library

Ellen Louise Axson
  Princeton University Library

James Woodrow
  Princeton University Library

James W. Bones
  Princeton University Library

Herbert Baxter Adams
  Milton S. Eisenhower Library, The Johns Hopkins University

Richard Theodore Ely
  Milton S. Eisenhower Library, The Johns Hopkins University

Daniel Coit Gilman
  Milton S. Eisenhower Library, The Johns Hopkins University

Basil Lanneau Gildersleeve
  Milton S. Eisenhower Library, The Johns Hopkins University

George Sylvester Morris
  University of Michigan Library

John Franklin Jameson
  Milton S. Eisenhower Library, The Johns Hopkins University

Robert Bridges
  Princeton University Archives

Hiram Woods, Jr.
  Princeton University Archives

Albert Shaw
  Milton S. Eisenhower Library, The Johns Hopkins University

Charles Howard Shinn
  Milton S. Eisenhower Library, The Johns Hopkins University

TEXT ILLUSTRATIONS

From Wilson's shorthand notes taken in Professor Herbert Baxter Adams's course, "The Old German Empire and the Rise of Prussia," 119

From Wilson's shorthand notes taken in Professor Richard T. Ely's advanced course in political economy, 152

From Wilson's shorthand notes taken in Professor Herbert Baxter Adams's course in the history of politics, 339

From Wilson's shorthand notes taken in Professor George Sylvester Morris's course, "The Philosophy of the State," 426

From Wilson's shorthand notes for a "History of Political Economy in the United States," 447

From Wilson's shorthand notes taken in Professor Richard T. Ely's course in finance and taxation, 459

ABBREVIATIONS

ALI	autograph letter initialed
ALS	autograph letter signed
APS	autograph postal signed
att(s).	attached, attachment(s)
ELA	Ellen Louise Axson
ELAhw	Ellen Louise Axson handwriting
enc(s).	enclosure(s), enclosed
env.	envelope
JRW	Joseph Ruggles Wilson
JWW	Janet Woodrow Wilson
TCL	typed copy of letter
tel.	telegram
WW	Woodrow Wilson
WWhw	Woodrow Wilson handwriting or handwritten
WWsh	Woodrow Wilson shorthand
WWT	Woodrow Wilson typewritten
WWTL	Woodrow Wilson typed letter
WWTLS	Woodrow Wilson typed letter signed

ABBREVIATIONS FOR COLLECTIONS AND LIBRARIES

Following the National Union Catalogue of the Library of Congress

DLC	Library of Congress
MdBJ	Library of The Johns Hopkins University
Meyer Coll., DLC	Meyer Collection, Library of Congress
NjP	Princeton University Library
PBm	Bryn Mawr College Library
RSB Coll., DLC	Ray Stannard Baker Collection of Wilsoniana, Library of Congress
ViU	University of Virginia Library
WP, DLC	Woodrow Wilson Papers, Library of Congress
WC, NjP	Woodrow Wilson Collection, Princeton University Library

SYMBOLS

[blank]	blanks in the text
[- - - -]	undecipherable words in text, each dash representing one word
[* *]	undecipherable shorthand, each asterisk representing one shorthand outline
[ ]	word or words in original text which Wilson omitted in copying
〈 〉	matter deleted from manuscript by Wilson and restored by the editors
[Sept. 8, 1884]	publication date of a published writing; also date of a document when date is not part of text
[*Sept. 8, 1884*]	latest composition date of a published writing
[[Sept. 8, 1884]]	delivery date of a speech if publication date differs

THE PAPERS OF
WOODROW WILSON
VOLUME 3
1884-1885

THE PAPERS OF
WOODROW WILSON

To Ellen Louise Axson

My own darling,   Balto., Md., Feb. 2nd 1884

Of course, up here in the silence of my room, I've done a "heap" of thinking since my return:[1] for I have found much to think about, as well as much to do, in getting back into my work; but there is one thing about which I have not dared to give my thoughts leave, and that is *how much I miss you*. I don't want to think about that, because if I did I should inevitably have the blues—and I should be ashamed to have the blues after the privilege I have enjoyed, of carrying joy and comfort to my Ellie. But, then, on the other hand, how is a fellow to escape such thoughts when he sits down to write to you and contrasts this miserable pen and ink business with sweet chats he remembers to have had with you, not seven days ago, when your eyes and sometimes even your lips told him all that was in your heart, and when he found it easy to open up all his secrets to you; or with those wonderful walks in the broad sun-light when his heart was full of the joy of being your companion and of being able to lead your thought away from its sorrow, to dwell on things of hope and of courage! Ah, my darling, if you were happy last week, what must I have been? for I knew that I had been instrumental in bringing the smiles and the colour back again!

Ellie, I want you to make me a promise. Don't show me only your smiles in your letters, but tell me—wont you, my darling?—tell me of everything that perplexes you or makes you sad. You told me last week that I looked at sorrow differently from other people and that I knew how to comfort you better than they. Well, then, my little lady, whenever you need comfort about anything, wont you come to me? You can find no better or surer way of making me happy;—and you could invent no surer or swifter way of making me miserable than by with-holding your *whole* confidence from a mistaken desire to save me pain or anxiety. You know it's a compact, that henceforth we are to be one in hopes and plans and anxieties and sorrows and joys: that was the meaning of my visit; and I'm bent upon keeping you in mind of the fact because I know from experience how hard, how well-nigh impossible, it is to throw off the habit of trying to bear all burdens, small and great, *alone*, with what seems a sort of unselfish devotion. I long to be *practically* all in all to you, my precious little sweet-heart!

Love has many curious effects upon people, but it never had a more unexpected or surprising effect than it has had upon me in making me *prudent* about myself. I used to let small maladies do their worst and torment me to the top of their bent, never thinking of interrupting them by sending medicines in search of them —having a sort of unreasoned confidence in nature's power to turn them out before they had done any serious damage: and so I should probably have done this time, if I had'nt been in love; for there was not much the matter with me and I was getting on well enough. But when I got back and was told that I was looking very badly, and found that the uncomfortable feelings refused to leave me, I bethought me of a dear, loving little lady down in Georgia whom I could serve only by keeping well, and who would be made very unhappy if I were to get real sick: so I did, what I had'nt done for six or eight years; I went to see a physician, and gave him a full history of my small ailments. He assured me that there was not the slightest ground for alarm; that I was suffering from the natural after effects of a harmless disease; and that, if I would delight my palate before each meal with a nauseous mixture he prescribed, I might be sure of comfortable health within a very few days. So you see, my darling, though I can't report myself absolutely well, I can set your mind at rest by the assurance that I'm on the sure road to get so, and that, meantime, I am only slightly out of sorts.

The men at the Hopkins seemed to be very glad to see me back and were all of them very cordial in their greetings—though none of them seem to have taken my absence quite so much to heart as [Charles H.] Shinn in his affectionate kindness would have had me believe. I was missed most, as I expected, by the Glee Club, the remaining first tenor having without me a double burden to carry; and for the coming week I am "booked" for no less than four rehersals. For we expect to give our first concert next week, and we must have as much practice as possible against its coming. I wish you could hear some of the songs we are to sing, especially some of the absurd college songs. Here's a specimen stanza of one of them (to be sung to the tune of "I'm a pilgrim and I'm a stranger")

"I wish I were a hip-po-po-tamus
And could swim the broad Euphrates
                      and eat grass
But oh! I am not; alas! I cannot
Be a hip-po-po, hip-po-po-tamus
    Ch: But I'm a June-bug
        And I'm a fire-fly:
        I can buzz and bump my head
                against the wall."

The other stanzas are of a piece with this one, so that you can imagine how chastly classical the song is as a whole! Why is it that the mere fact of being connected with a college gives grave gentlemen of almost thirty leave to sing in public songs which, under other circumstances, they would not dream of singing? For my part, I rejoice in the chance. The older I get, the more does a boy's spirit seem to possess me and I chafe often not a little under the necessity of having to preserve the dignified demeanor of a man. That's the reason, you see, that I've determined to live at college all my life. Was'nt it odd, Ellie, that I should be restrained and embarrassed by your presence in playing with Eddie and Randolph and the little girls?[2] I was, though, without being able to explain how or why. Probably you would'nt have been much shocked if I had romped and played with them as I felt inclined to do, but something made me shrink from making too great a clown of myself in the presence of a young lady who was supposed to admire me very much.

By the way, I am as much gratified as astonished to learn that I made a favourable impression on that wonderful family at 143 South Broad St.[3] People who are in all respects lovable themselves find it easier than others do to discover admirable traits in others. Their charity covers all defects. Besides, in this particular instance, they were eager to find justification for you.

I trust, my little lady, that you don't neglect your walks nowadays, but take quite as long ones as you took with me—but I know that you will for my sake.

Give my regards to that wonderfully energetic Miss Janie [Porter] when you see her next. I hope she liked me as much on first acquaintance as I liked her.

Give my love to your dear grandparents, to "Uncle Randolph," "Aunt Ella," and to the children one and all—especially to little

Ellen—for I love her both for her own sake and because she loves you so much.

With a heart overflowing with love for my own Ellie,

Your own   Woodrow.

ALS (WC, NjP).

¹ As the last documents in Volume 2 disclose, WW had visited ELA in Savannah during the third week of January 1884. It was a sudden trip, caused by the illness of ELA's father, Samuel Edward Axson, who had been committed to the Georgia state mental hospital at Milledgeville. WW returned to Baltimore, after a visit with his parents in Wilmington, on January 30.

² ELA's younger brother, Edward, and her cousins, Randolph, Jr., Carrie Belle, and Ellen Axson.

³ The address of the manse of the Independent Presbyterian Church. The "wonderful family" included ELA's grandparents, the Rev. and Mrs. I. S. K. Axson; their son, Randolph, and his wife, Ella; and their children, Leila, Carrie Belle, Ellen, Benjamin Palmer, and Randolph, Jr. Edward Axson was visiting.

From Ellen Louise Axson

My darling Woodrow,   Savannah, Feb. 4/84.

I find I have but small allowance of time for writing tonight, owing, first to the urgent demands for having their "pictures took," made by those four small tyrants of mine, and afterwards to a visit from Col. Olmstead.¹ But it is still early enough to write what *you* call a letter—three pages or so! Many thanks for those of last week, and the comparative relief they afforded,—for though I am sorry they don't report more rapid progress, it is a comfort to know that things are not as bad as they might be. Am sorry you were not able to stay longer in Wilmington, but I trust you are all right now, notwithstanding;—my last letter was the one of the 31st, and, taking your promise literally, I suppose I am to conclude that you are therefore "quite well." My poor boy! You will look back on those last two days in Sav. as very wretched ones! You certainly had a hard time; I fear you made *too* great an effort in keeping up so bravely.

Well, as I am being constantly scolded, on all sides, for never thinking to send in any health reports of my own, I must do so now, while I am on the subject of health, and before I forget it. I am perfectly well again, don't cough even once a day now. Dr. Thomas² came in Sat. and formally dismissed the case without even hinting at "cod-liver oil." That tonic of yours has evidently done its work throughly. I am now expecting Rose³ in a day or so, and her coming will serve as a gentle continuation of the invigorating process.

You know, I think you give some very excellent advice in this last letter⁴ and I think too, I shall try and follow it, as far as in me lies. I believe our good Presbyterian ancestors make a mistake in insisting so strongly on the duty of *self-examination*. It is apt to become a morbid habit—to make the conscience *too* sensitive, if such a thing can be. "Know thy-self" may be a very good motto, but there are others still better, for instance "forget thy self." But whatever I may, or may not, be conscious of feeling on any special occasion, I don't think I will be so foolish as to give way to any very real or pungent [?] remorse on the score of "heartlessness." I have always known myself too well for that, and of late my knowledge has been much increased. "It is necessary sometimes to have the heart's great deep broken up, that we may know all that is in it."

Yes, it *is* right to be happy whenever we may—and there is small danger that we will be *too* happy. The Bible, when it tells us to "rejoice evermore," surely means what it says,—means that there shall be evermore something in which to rejoice, and that we should seek and find it.

But oh, it is hard to remember all that when I think of my dear father's "future"! What future is there for one who, at best, *has been* the inmate of an insane asylum? Ah yes, he has a future,— a glorious future! I *can* "rejoice," even now, and when thinking of *him*;—but it is only by looking steadily away from the present, across the dark, the *hopeless*, but, thank God, the narrow tract which lies between, to that wonderful beyond;—remembering that "the sufferings of this present time are not worthy to be compared with the glory which shall be revealed." I *am sure* that the God, whose love is as infinite as His wisdom, has ordered it all for His own great and good purposes; and I want to be not merely *submissive* to his will, but gladly acquiescent.

Surely we *want* His purposes to be fulfilled in us;—we would not, if we could, take matters into our own hands! We ask Him to choose for us, and then—strange contradiction—go mourning all our days because of His choice. We seem to accept, to follow His direction, not freely and joyfully, but only because we *must*. I fear there is not only lack of trust, but *disloyalty* in all this—as though we rendered but a half-hearted allegiance; and that is certainly a very imperfect service which is not a *cheerful* service.

Tuesday morning. It is time that this was being mailed. So I must bring it to a hasty close; not however without stealing a moment to thank you for the picture of the "Princeton man."[5] The young gentleman seemed quite a stranger to me at first, and on that account I was inclined to regard him with disapproval.

But after spending perhaps half an hour getting acquainted I decided that I liked him very much. I suppose it was the mouth that I failed to recognize; the other features are very good—eyes turned rather too much to the light. But the pose is better, and therefore the general contours are stronger and more characteristic, than in the "full face." So it supplements the other very nicely.

I wish we could have had such weather as this while you were here; it is simply glorious, and has been for a week. Almost *too* fine, in fact, for Grandmother seems to think it a sort of sin to stay indoors and lose it all; and consequently I am being dragged out on all occasions, and my work suffers.

The dear old lady has both Aunt Ella and myself altogether in her power. She can *tell* us to "go out" as much as she pleases, and we only laugh and evade; but then she makes a move to go herself, and we are brought speedily to terms, for she is so feeble we are afraid for her to walk out alone. So I really must close and go with her now. She sends you her love. Give my best love to your dear parents. I won't try to tell you how much I appreciate their love and sympathy for me, of which you write, or how much I thank and love them for it. Good-bye, dear love, take care of yourself. Write me soon, and often, how you are; and believe me to be with all my heart,   Your own   Ellie.

ALS (WP, DLC).
    1 Perhaps Charles H. Olmstead of C. H. Olmstead and Co., insurance agents of Savannah.
    2 James G. Thomas, M.D., physician in Savannah and a close friend of the Axsons. See also ELA to WW, Dec. 13 [12], 1884.
    3 Rosalie Anderson of Sewanee, Tenn.
    4 WW to ELA, Jan. 31, 1884, Vol. 2.
    5 WW had sent her his Princeton class picture. See WW to ELA, Jan. 29, 1884, Vol. 2.

To Ellen Louise Axson

My own darling,   Balto., Md., Feb. 5th 1884
    What do you think of a prudent young man who, although already in trouble with his digestive organs, arranges to eat two dinners in one day? Well, I could'nt help it. My friend [Edward] Ingle invited me to dine with him this evening at six o'clock, and because I accepted the invitation should I have refused the dinner offered me by my land-lady at two o'clock? Ingle is the most boyish, but not the least gifted, member of our Seminary[1]— full of jokes and pranks, but also of information and ideas: a sensitive fellow who carries his heart on his sleeve (for the bene-

fit of the proverbial daws) and who is also intensely disagreeable to small Dr. [Herbert B.] Adams because his mind is always ready to be spoken. If I must be quite frank, I'll confess that Ingle bores me much and often. I can't go up to "the Bluntschli"[2] without having him fasten upon me for a confidential talk, with many supplements. If the others of his family are like him, we'll be talked to death (Shinn and I) this evening. By the way, my little lady, in sending your regards to Mr. Shinn, you distinguish him from a very lowly and much despised portion of the human frame only by the use of a capital "S."[3] His name has two n's to it. I gave him your regards, but did not mar his gratification by telling him how you spelled his name.

I had a tremendous surprise the other day in the shape of a letter from Jessie—yes, an eight page letter, written in *green ink*.[4] She gives very little news, except family news. The baby can walk and has two teeth; Lefoy is in trousers, to his intense satisfaction; little Helen is the baby's best nurse; and Marion is reported quite happy at Staunton. Uncle James has given up his commission business and purchased Mr. Eddie Smith's flour mill. "East Rome is now a town and Abe is its mayor. I tell you there is no more whistling now-a-days down at the rail-road, nor stray sheep and pigs walking all over the place."[5]

The letter is full of love and warmest sympathy for you, my darling. She looks upon our engagement just as we do, as a timely, providential blessing, sent in time to solace and support you in your season of deepest sorrow. To me it seems an unmixed blessing for us both. You needed to be given some one who should be entirely yours in heart and life, and who should call forth from you a new love full of hope; and I needed—needed more than anyone but myself can know—the gift of such a love as yours to give me new purpose, new courage, and a new joy in my work. Nobody but myself knows what I gained when I won your love.

You musn't think, my darling, when I write you playful letters, full of absurd verses and other nonsense, as my last was, that I have forgotten your sorrow. That sorrow is mine scarcely less than yours; but it is part of my philosophy, my Christian philosophy, as you know, to endeavour to learn lessons of self-discipline and purification, not lessons of desolation and unhappiness, from the trials that come not through my own fault—to follow, if only afar off, the beautiful example of cheerfulness set by your dear grandparents; and, though my philosophy is immensely superior to my practice, I feel that I am not violating its principles when

I sit down to amuse and divert my little sweetheart: for, if she will but smile and be happy, I am sufficiently blessed and can make shift to be light-hearted myself. You see, the truth of the matter is that happiness consists in living for others—as a great many people have said, but everyone finds out for himself without a definite trial at manufacturing happiness according to some philosopher's receipt. It's all stuff to talk about its being self-sacrifice to live for others: it's positive luxury—albeit a very innocent and respectable luxury—for it makes sorrows light and cares easy to bear. Now, don't laugh! I know that you think this the most amusing part of this letter (not even excepting "Abe's" mayoralty) because it illustrates my tendency to talk big generalities—to drive a six-horse team to even the smallest vehicle of an argument—when what I want to say is plain and simple enough: that I am happy in your love, and happiest when I can believe that I am sending little sunbeams down to you.

I am no more adicted to looking for philosophical principles, however, than is a distinguished Harvard professor who has just left us, after giving us a couple of lectures, and at whom you could not afford to laugh as you do at me: though maybe there *is* this difference in the two cases, that he usually *finds* the principles of which he is in search. I wish that I could live with Dr. Royce for a few months.[6] He is one of the rarest spirits I have met. His is one of those very rare minds which exists in a perfectly lucid atmosphere of thought, having never a cloud on its horizon, seeing everything with a clear and unerring vision. He talked to us the other night at the Seminary, and the dullest fellow at the board listened with delight—I don't mean myself!—because he has the faculty of bringing masses of detail into a single luminous picture where they are grouped with a perfection of perspective and a skill of harmonious arrangement which fill the novice, the would-be historical painter, with despair.

But, my love, it will be late bed-time before I can mail this (for I've dined with Ingle, at the expense of three hours, since I began this much interrupted letter) so you will forgive me for saying good-night. I love you with all my heart.

Love to all.   Your own   Woodrow.

ALS (WC, NjP).

1 The Seminary of Historical and Political Science of The Johns Hopkins University.

2 The Bluntschli Library of the Johns Hopkins.

3 See ELA to WW, Jan. 28, 1884, Vol. 2.

4 Jessie Bones Brower to WW, Jan. 28, 1884, Vol. 2.

5 The members of the Brower-Bones family mentioned in this paragraph were Jessie Bones Brower and her baby, Marion, and stepson, Lefoy; "little" Helen Bones, Jessie's youngest sister; Marion McGraw Bones, another sister, attending the Augusta Female Seminary in Staunton, Va.; James W. Bones, Jessie's father and WW's uncle-in-law; and Abraham T. H. Brower, Jessie's husband.

6 Josiah Royce, eminent American philosopher and long-time professor at Harvard University. The Minutes of the Seminary of Historical and Political Science of The Johns Hopkins University (bound ledger book, MdBJ), Feb. 1, 1884, state that Royce "gave a most interesting account of the development of government in California." This was probably a preliminary report on Royce's work for his *California, From the Conquest in 1846 to the Second Vigilance Committee in San Francisco; a Study of American Character* (Boston and New York, 1886).

From Joseph R. Wilson, Jr.

My darling brother: Wilmington N.C. Feb 5th 1884.

We received your letter, telling us that you had consulted Dr. [Hiram] Woods, [Jr.,] this morning; and were so glad to hear that you were in a fair way to get well again. Father is not quite so well this morning. He is suffering a good deal from his head. Mother is tolerably well, but seems to be feeling languid this morning which is owing to the weather I think. . . .

I am so glad you took a sleeper after all the other night. . . .

Please write soon to me and send me my commission as Vice Admiral. Please print (when you get time) a commodores commission for Ben. And retire him as such.

Mom. and pop. join me in lots and gobs of love. Regards for Mr. Shin.

                    Your loving brother   Joseph.

ALS (WP, DLC) with WWhw notation on env.: "Ans. Feb. 10th 1884."

Two Letters to Ellen Louise Axson

                    Balto., Md., Feb. 7th 1884

You ungrateful little—darling! Because, while I am writing you almost daily in order that you may not be uneasy about my health, I stop short of six or eight pages each time, you complain that I call "three pages or so" a letter! I reckon, miss, that what I write to you aggregates more than eight pages a week— so 'tis a quick argument, ma'am; " 't will away again, from me to you." "To 't again, come." I will confess, though, that in my eyes eight pages from you seem worth any number I could write.

I am *so* glad that my darling is quite well again. That cold had hung on just long enough to make it alarming. I like to believe that my visit was the tonic that worked the cure, and I hope that the tonic supplied by Miss Rose's presence will confirm your good health. You must give her my regards when you see her. I hope to meet her some of these days—maybe after "Mac"[1] and I have both had our hopes fulfilled and you and she are both proportionately miserable in consequence—and become acquainted with her at first hand. Then she and I may be able to find out whether you and "Mac" have been prudent in your choices.

And now it's in order for me too to make my final health report; and I can make one which will, I am sure, be entirely satisfactory. Thanks to Hiram (Dr. Woods), I am completely cured of all my ailments and am as well as I ever was, which is as much as to say, *perfectly* well. You may, therefore, dismiss all anxiety and think of me as in my normal condition, a big, strong creature, eating hearty dinners and capable of a great deal of steady hard work.

I am considerably amused by your comments upon the appearance of the "Princeton man." I conclude, from what you say about the stiff mouth, that you would disapprove very heartily of my shaving off my mustache, as I've sometimes felt inclined to do. You see, when that picture was taken I could'nt "raise" much of a mustache and a clean-shaven face was not only normal but natural. I have myself looked at that photo. with not a little amusement of late, on the one or two occasions when I've come across it either in my own or Woods's "class album." Not that I am better looking now, but because I am *different* looking— so different that the face in the picture seems unfamiliar even to me. Shall I come to see you, next vacation, clean-shaven? If one kind of ugliness is natural to a man, why should he disguise himself in another kind?

You[r] dear grandmother is a very sensible lady, and I am very much obliged to her, for "dragging" you out on fine days. Your work may seem to suffer by the interruption; but if it were not for such indispensable interruptions your work would probably very soon come altogether to a stand-still. I have observed that for me composition is impossible, and that to me constitutional history seems hopelessly obscure, without a great deal of exercise in the open air; and I have been led by observation to adopt the belief that nobody's work can progress very well or go on at all very long without a free use of the same tonic. In a word, my sweet little lady, to be of real use in this world and to serve those one loves, one must be every day for some hours out of doors. When you feel disinclined to go out, remember that, tho' you may not *now* feel the need of exercise, your future useful-ness and happiness depend upon your getting plenty of oxygen and stirring your blood to a free and rapid circulation. Which lecture I submit with a very earnest purpose to one whose health and happiness and well-being are "a' the world to me."

Give my warmest love to your dear grandparents, to delightful "uncle Randolph" and "Aunt Ella," to the boys, and to the sweet little girls; and remember to love me as much as you are loved by

Your own   Woodrow.

P.S. Having read this letter over, I am inclined to volunteer the promise that I wont soon again inflict so much superiorly-wise advice upon you—though, "if you but knew it," this is really as truly and entirely a love letter as any I ever wrote

Lovingly   W.

---

[1] McNeely DuBose, Rosalie Anderson's fiancé. A South Carolinian, he had been graduated from the University of the South in 1880 and in 1884 was a student in the Theological School in Sewanee, from which he was graduated B.D. in 1885. Ordained deacon in 1884 and priest in 1885, he was rector of the Church of the Nativity, Union, S.C., 1885-90.

My precious Ellie,   Balto., Md., Feb. 10th 1884

You are a dear, brave little girl to take your great trouble as you do, with faith and patience and courage. The bright, trustful tone of your letters fills me with a very sweet joy. It does give me such unspeakable comfort, as my thoughts turn, during these quiet Sabbaths, these grave pauses before a new week's work, to the greatest subjects of life, diligence and duty and Christian love and faith, to think that you and I love and confide in and seek to serve the same Saviour, that we are one in these greatest things, as in all things else, and that in that wedded life of ours, to which I look forward so eagerly and for which I long so fer-vently, we shall have that highest joy and strength added to the joy and strength of our love for each other. How can man and wife be truly happy, I wonder, without that most sure and sacred bond of union?

But, my darling, do'nt you look forward to your dear father's future with a little too much despondency? That future do'nt seem to me at all "hopeless." There seem to me to be many reasons for expecting his complete recovery; and if he recover why is there no hope? There are almost innumerable cases like that of Dr. Ben. Palmer's[1] son-in-law, in which restoration to health re-sulted in a permanent return to usefulness. No, no, my darling, do'nt say that there is no hope. If your dear father live to return to health, he will live to resume a happy usefulness; if he do not live to get well, he is sure of a blessed home of peace and rest. Neither alternative is very tragic for him: and, as for ourselves, I am quite sure that, in any event, we shall be happy in caring for him, in smoothing his paths as we may, in ministering to his closing days in any way that is needful and best. That would be an easy work of love. I know that in saying these things I am but expressing your own real thoughts: and that's the reason I say them.

Ellie, do you know that one whispered, timid, monosyllabic confession I drew from you one day in Savannah has been running through my thoughts and putting questions to me ever since? You confessed, to my delight, that your thoughts were prone to go as often and as fondly forward to our married life as mine do. That was a very sweet admission, and you do'nt know how much self-denial I had to force myself to to [sic] keep back the other questions that sprang to my lips, as to *what* you think about that happy future time, what pictures of it your fancy likes to paint, what you like to think of our doing in those coming days. Would you mind telling me *now*, my darling? I am at a safe distance; the pen is apt to tell such secrets with less confusion than a certain shy little tongue I know of; and the telling would delight me beyond measure. Are not those strong and conclusive enough arguments? I do'nt believe that you would hesitate for a moment, if you could know how exceedingly happy it makes me to have you add to the number of those sacred love secrets which belong to us alone—to have you add to the proofs that there are some things which you will confide, and can confide, only to me. Such confidences seem to bring us closer together. But if you would rather keep these particular ones back until I am present to *hear* them, I'm sure that I shall delight in the promise. I'd a thousand times rather hear such confidences than read them!

Give my warmest love to all. I suppose that Miss Rosalie is with you by this time and that you are happy in consequence— I hope so. I'm sure that I should like her for she loves you, and I love you with all my heart.   Your own   Woodrow.

ALS (WP, DLC).

[1] Benjamin M. Palmer, of New Orleans, the distinguished southern Presbyterian clergyman. The son-in-law was Dr. John W. Caldwell, identified at Jan. 8, 1885, note 1.

From Ellen Louise Axson

My darling Woodrow,   Savannah, Feb. 11/84.

Your letters of last week were all safely received, and were most welcome. For the last, giving, as it did, such a satisfactory account of your health, I was especially *grateful*, in spite of the "lecture," and the charges of "ingratitude" of "complaining," &c. preferred against me! No sir I am not complaining of anything! I admit that you treat me very well in the matter of writing; and I appreciate it most highly, because I know that when one has been doing other kinds of writing—or any sort of brain-work—all day, it must be very tiresome to write letters, in addition, especially long ones;—and "three pages or so" does'nt constitute your model invariably, or even frequently. In fact, we both know so well that you have "a good conscience and void of offence" in the matter, that I can afford to be saucy,—can't I?—since you are sure to understand.

As for the "lecture," no post-scriptural apologies are necessary. I receive it with all due meekness—though whether I will be equally docile in following your advice, is more than I know myself—time will show, and circumstances must determine!

I seem to be catching it on all sides. Mrs. Duncan,[1] dropping in as usual before church yesterday, summoned me down stairs, for the express purpose of lecturing me on the subject. And she did give me such a "talking to" as would have done your heart good to hear. "Miss Owens had told her how naughty I was;—how I *would* stay at home and work *all* day"; and she had come to give me some "Christian advice." "For it is as much a Christian duty to take care of one's health as of one's soul";—and with that text she preaches me a regular sermon on my duty to myself, my family, and "someone else," winding up with the *singular* statement that "you don't belong to yourself now you must remember"! So you see you have a valuable ally. She told me to see if you did'nt agree with her; and I laughed, remembering your very "funny" remark about "some *hours* (!)" daily, in the open air. She —Mrs. D.—sends you her warmest regards, and says that she means to take care of me for you. It seems she approves of you very heartily and entirely. What did you do to win that great, warm heart of hers so suddenly?

I made a fair beginning in my effort at reformation, last night, by walking out to Anderson St. church;[2]—you remember it, on the way to Laurel Grove? It was a lovely walk, by-the-way. "If thou would'st view Savannah aright; go visit it by the pale moonlight!" That light seems to be peculiarly in keeping with the character of the place, and I don't believe there is any other city in America with more of an almost solemn beauty than Sav., under it's influence. And we have been having the most perfect nights, for a week past, that I ever saw—the full moon—with the stars too, not keen and cold, but softly bright, like "stars of twilight," and the sky of that tender, dusky violet, with an infinite *depth* to it, peculiar to Southern countries. We went through the Parks and the Extension last night; the former was like an enchanted place—beautiful beyond description.

But if I "go on" much longer, you will think me almost as seriously affected by the moonshine as certain persons whom we had the pleasure of observing while there. It is almost as warm as summer now, and there were scores of people sitting on benches; among them one young man—or perhaps I should say *one couple* —who were "quite too awfully" moonstruck, for he was deliberately sitting, in the bright light, with his arms very much around her! There must be something dangerous about the moon—even my little cousin Leila, gay, restless little chatter-box that she is, grew, under its influence, so pensive, so sentimental in fact, that I could not but laugh at her. It seemed to make her feel, like "Boots at the Holly Tree" Inn, when contemplating the baby lovers, "as if she were in love herself, only she didnt know with whom"!

Are you having this delicious weather in Ba[l]timore too? Here we seem to be dropped into the middle of May. The flowers have burst out in profusion. I drove with Miss Norah Lawton[3] to Boneventure[4] and Thunderbolt[5] today and saw quantities on the way. By-the-way, I must tell you one of Ellen's bright little speeches. Palmer brought me in a handfull of spring flowers a short time ago, and we were all gathered "in a knot," the little ones on my lap, and the three boys hanging over me—as usual,—admiring them, and discussing flowers. "Ellen," said I, "what is your favourite flower?" Oh—*you*! she said, with that indescribably sweet, arch expression, which I never saw on any other baby face. "I am your favourite *flower*?" "Yes." And what sort of flower am I, pray? "Why you're a *daisy*!"—which was very prettily put, if it was slang.

These children including myself are much interested in the "Glee Club" and it's astonishing songs. Randolph in particular, is quite overcome by the poetry and pathos of the specimen given. We all think it "real mean" that you didnt sing some of them for us. You must tell me about the concert. Is it to be before the general public or the college public? I trust it will be a grand success.

No, my darling, I certainly won't think you forget my sorrows, or anything else, because you write me bright cheery letters,—and I should be dull, indeed, if I did not understand and appreciate those letters as much as I enjoy them. I think you *wise*, as well as good and tender; and my confidence in your wisdom, in your power to find and to touch the right chord, will help me to make and keep the promise you desire, viz., to tell you of everything that makes me sad, as well as glad. I will, I dare say, unlearn all my old habits in that regard, at your word. That will indeed be a "curious effect" of love. Even now I am often amazed at myself, at the things I find it in my power to say to you. But love is a great mystery; of that I am more and more persuaded. It is another of those riddles which as the "newspaperman" said "I can't guess, but I'll never give up—no *never*!"

With much love for your dear parents and your brother, and more than tongue can tell for yourself, I am as ever,

Your own   Ellie

ALS (WP, DLC) with WWsh and WWhw research notes on env. Att.: WWhw and WWsh extract from Sidney Lanier, "A Forgotten English Poet," *International Review*, vi (March 1879), 298. See WW to ELA, Feb. 19, 1884.

1 Martha D. B. N. Duncan, wife of William Duncan, and a close friend of the Axsons.

2 Anderson Street Presbyterian Church was a small church located on the northeast corner of Anderson and Barnard streets in Savannah, the Rev. Joseph Washburn, minister. The church had been begun as a mission by the Independent Presbyterian Church in 1868. It is now known by the name of Hull Memorial Presbyterian Church and is located at Bull and Thirty-seventh streets.

3 Daughter of General Alexander R. Lawton of Savannah.

4 Bonaventure was a colonial plantation on the Wilmington River, a few miles from Savannah, famous for its avenues of live oaks draped with Spanish moss. It was acquired by the City of Savannah in the 1850's and used thereafter as a cemetery.

5 One of the earliest Georgia settlements, located just around the bend of the Wilmington River from Bonaventure.

From Janet Woodrow Wilson

My precious Boy—   Wilmington N.C.   Monday—[Feb. 11, 1884]

I have not time to write you at length today—but hope to do so in a day or two. I write now to send you a draft for the payment of taxes. Your father would have saved you the trouble of endorsing, if he had known the proper address. Perhaps it will be better, next time, to give him the exact address, that he may send it direct—and at the same time, save time & trouble. I want to induce him to take the whole property in charge—as it comes in—

leaving the business minutia with you—as you alone have the necessary knowledge of the law.[1]

I will certainly write you in a day or two. I am so thankful to hear that you are in a fair way to be well—and so grateful to Dr Hiram for his help in the matter—thank him for me please. Go to see dear Dr. Wilson & wife[2] when you can, please

Give my warmest love & sympathy to dearest Ellie. She is a brave, sweet girl—I am so grateful that you have secured her love. I would not have you exchange her for the wealthiest and showiest lady of the land.

Good bye darling—for only a day or two—I hope.

Dear papa has not been as well as I would like to see him— but he is so good—so sweet, to me.

Papa & Josie unite in warmest love to our absent darling

Lovingly   Mother

ALS (WP, DLC) with WWhw notation on env.: "Ans. 2/17/84."
  [1] JWW had inherited part of a substantial estate in Nebraska from her brother, William Woodrow. She had engaged WW to manage her share when he began law practice.
  [2] The Rev. Dr. and Mrs. J. Leighton Wilson.

To Ellen Louise Axson

My own darling,   Balto., Md., Feb. 12th 1884

I hope that you are not in the fix I am in: with more work to do than you have time to do well—and work of a kind, at that, which you feel to be barely within reach of your best endeavour, had you abundant time for its prosecution. I am struggling with the second of the series of essays on our constitutional system which I have planned writing,[1] trying to combine simplicity of treatment with multiplicity of detail and breadth of view with narrowness of subject. In a word, I am writing of the organization and practices of Congress and have, on the one hand, to avoid giving to the particulars of the description the dryness and stiffness of a manual of parliamentary law, and, on the other hand, to give colour and significance to the picture by keeping constantly within the view the true relations of these Congressional rules and precedents to the constitutional system of which they are the mechanical centre. Of course, since Congress is both the formative and the motive power in that system, its methods of legislation are vitally connected with the system's operation. But, important as are those Standing Committees which we have made part of our machinery of government, in order to escape the necessity of using some such device as the British Ministry, they are hard to adapt to the requirements of effective literary composition, and great has been my tribulation in the course of my strivings to make them striking and comprehensible figures in a sketch which everybody will find interesting. There's the pinch: to be these three things, entertaining, exact, philosophical. I can't even put the subject on paper as I see it. I've thrown overboard my faith in the old dogma that in order to write clearly one needs nothing more than a clear vision. The seer does not often, or at any rate always, have the gift of expression; and readers delight most, not in a writer who sees, but in one who enables them to see readily and pleasantly.

But what sort of a Valentine is this I am writing! I set out upon the composition of this letter with the intention of making it my Valentine to my precious little sweet-heart. I have'nt sent a Valentine for I do'nt know how long—not since I was a boy: and that's a terribly long time ago; and, now that I feel like renewing the custom, I can't find any in the stores that I would care to send to *you*: for a Valentine is *par excellence* a token of love, and these pictured cards and fluted papers none of them contain just the sort of message I want to send to my Ellie. I can't write verses; but if I could, I would write such as would make her think, when she receives this on St. Valentine's Day, of a lover far away whose love for her runs through all the currents of his life, like sweet music upon the currents of the air, soothing his moments of impatience, stealing away his cares, and filling his thoughts with glad contentment—in short, just such a lover as you would like to hear about. For, you see, supposing myself possessed of the poetical faculty, I could make a very attractive picture even when describing myself, because I know my own faults pretty well and I could leave them all out, idealizing the good traits that might remain. But, since I am not a poet, but a common trudger in prose, I must content myself with *statements*: of which the first shall be, that there's no lover in the land who has more love to send to his sweetheart by St. Valentine than I have to my Ellie. From this it follows, by clear necessity of argument, that she ought to be a very happy little woman, even in the presence of sore trial: for I have heard it said, and verily believe, that love, true love, is very rare in this world of ours; and I know that my love is true: else why has it brought so many new and pure impulses into my life? Besides, to proceed with the argument, the greatness and purity and power of my love unravels a great many mysteries. It explains my Ellie's love for me, and thus becomes the ground of *my* happiness too. For it is not to be believed that that matchless young lady, albeit she *was* intelligent beyond other maidens, would ever have discovered that anything interesting or lovable lay behind my unattractive exterior had it not been for the silent influence of my love for her, which she felt long before she knew what was drawing her towards me. She would not have given her consent so readily to correspond with the gentleman who sat with her in the hammock, had it not been his love that begged the favour. Do'nt you see what an exceedingly satisfactory philosophy this is? It explains why her love for me is increasing, as she confesses it is, strengthening beyond all her thoughts of what was possible. That is evidently because my love for her has grown until it has fairly taken possession of my life, making me sometimes wonder if ever woman was loved as she is: and of course her affections could'nt think of lagging behind, after having once undertaken to keep company with mine.

And how the argument runs, runs *backwards* even! making it plain to be seen that I used to live a very small life when I had nobody to plan for but myself. Of course I used to be lonely, how could I be anything else? It's loneliness itself to look forward to a lonely future. I am lonely now sometimes; but in a very different way. This is only the loneliness of *waiting*: it's only a phase of the impatience to achieve which, my dear mother says, has always been one of my leading traits. What other reason can there be for my feverish haste in driving my constitutional subject so hard towards its complete exposition? It is'nt likely to get old, or to break away from me, or to sink beneath the fatigues of a long journey slowly taken. But I can't go slowly either in work or in love; and, since in the latter I am running toward the great prize of my life, my eager haste must be the more readily excused.

And so this many-sided story of love with its satisfactory philosophy has many threads and cross-threads, plots and counter-plots, beyond the counting or the telling. We'll work it out together: for there's no fun in telling it in separate pieces. We'll *make* the story as we live on for and with each other; and we can make it different from all other stories by making it happy: so that nobody who reads it aright and in God's light will find aught to cry over in the last chapter.

Well! there's one thing you can say of your Valentine with a clear conscience: and that is, that its unique; certainly novel as compared with the ordinary pattern of orthodox Valentines. And yet it has the usual features about it. Though there is no heart *on* it, there *is* a heart *in* it. There's even a picture in it, with poetry beneath it; though not poetry that everybody can read, or a picture that everybody can see. These things will not prove objectionable, however, to *you*, I imagine: for you wont care to show it to everybody, will you? And you'll be satisfied with seeing what's in it yourself, wont you?

As a postscript to my Valentine, here's a quotation from a letter just received from my sweet mother: "Give my warmest love and sympathy to dearest Ellie. She is a brave, sweet girl—I am so grateful that you have secured her love. I would not have you exchange her for the wealthiest and showiest lady of the land."

With all the love of my heart,

Your own   Woodrow.

ALS (WP, DLC).
1 WW was referring to the second chapter of *Congressional Government*. See the Editorial Note, "Congressional Government," Vol. 4.

From Gamaliel Bradford[1]

My dear Sir: Boston Feb. 13 [1884]

I thank you very much for yours of 11th & the article[2] accompanying. I had seen a notice of it & intended reading it. I am always delighted with every fresh recruit, & everybody throws new & different light upon the subject. I have no doubt that the step will be taken sooner or later

Your statement is most powerful and I agree substantially with all of it. The only point about which I should argue would be the constitutional amendments[.][3] These I regard as absolutely impossible. Congress, from its very nature, will be bitterly hostile to the movement[,] will fight it to the last gasp & yield only to overwhelming popular will. But the state legislatures are far more timid & hostile to executive power. It will be *almost* impossible to get it through Congress but to try to get any preliminary action through 27 state legislatures would make squaring the circle look like an easy job.

The first objective point should be, I conceive, to get a resolution of the House inviting the members of the cabinet to seats on the floor for three days in the week just as they now appear before the committees. *I* think that the consequences would gradually develope themselves under our constitution as it is. But if they did not, we should find out what is wanted, & go to the state legislatures with something definite & with definite reasons for it.

But simple as this first step looks, it is of no use to go to Congress for it. It must be reached by outside agitation[.] If some prominent member or senator or still better a cabinet officer would take the stump for it through the country, he could not only carry it within a year or two, but make himself President of the United States besides[.] I have pleaded with a great many of them, but while they see & admit it not one of them has the courage of his opinions

Trusting you will keep on with the good work

I remain, very truly yours   Gaml. Bradford

ALS (WP, DLC).

¹ Gamaliel Bradford, born Boston, Jan. 15, 1831. A.B., Harvard, 1849. Banker. He retired in 1868 and devoted himself to civil service reform and advocacy of more effective national government by giving Cabinet members seats in Congress. Frequent contributor to the New York *Nation* and other periodicals and newspapers. Author of *The Lesson of Popular Government* (2 vols., New York, 1899). Died Aug. 20, 1911. See also the Editorial Note in Vol. 1, "Cabinet Government in the United States."

² "Committee or Cabinet Government?" printed at Jan. 1, 1884, Vol. 2.

³ That is, Wilson's proposal in "Committee or Cabinet Government?" to amend the Constitution to permit the President to appoint his Cabinet from among the membership of Congress and lengthen the presidential term and the terms of members of the House of Representatives.

From Edward Ireland Renick

Treasury Department, First Comptroller's Office,
Dear Wilson: Washington, D.C., Feb'y 14th, 1884.

I am here on a $1200 salary. Got in under Civil Service Act. Began on 11th inst.¹ My duties are purely legal—& no drudgery. The 1st Compt[roller] has large judicial functions—& began in 1880 publishing his opinions. I am, so to speak, his reporter, with large powers of revision &c.

I left Brock Beckwith² in my place with authority & instructions to sell our Code & yr. Form Book. I shall soon make some arrangement about the Brower case.³ Gaddy⁴ is mighty forlorn. I hope now to see you often. If you come here before I go to Balto—call upon me at 1342 N.Y. Avenue—but direct your letters to above heading. . . .

Please write soon & excuse this hasty scrawl.

Yours as ever   Renick

ALS (WP, DLC) with WWhw notation on env.: "Ans. 2/25/84."

¹ Renick, WW's former law partner in Atlanta, had abandoned the practice of law soon after WW did so.

² Perhaps John F. B. Beckwith, of Beckwith and Sims, lawyers in Atlanta.

³ A. T. H. Brower had been involved in a libel suit in which the firm of Renick and Wilson had participated.

⁴ E. M. Gadsden, a lawyer friend of WW and Renick in Atlanta.

To Ellen Louise Axson

My own darling,   Balto., Md., Feby. 14th/84

Do you know that I am a very lone and forlorn individual? I have a dim consciousness that I ought to be ashamed to confess it: for I know very well that I have no right to be disconsolate just because I'm compelled to live here all by myself—that is, without *you* (because I've discovered that for me nowadays loneliness consists in being separated from you)—in view of the sure prospect of obtaining all that my heart desires. But then, you see, content don't lie in prospects when the stubborn fact of the present is that I have, taking my University life "by and large," no companion but one Woodrow Wilson, whom I find an *exceedingly* tiresome fellow. Maybe, if I saw him only occasionally, I might like him well enough, for he tries hard to be agreeable and in some moods is as jolly a companion as I should care to have. But he's with me *all the time*, and he will insist upon worrying me with his tedious literary schemes and pouring into my ears all his petty anxieties, as well as upon entertaining (?) me day in and day out with his odd views of people and things, half cynical and half jocose, but altogether empty. If you notice many ups and downs of mood in my letters, attribute them to his influence over me, and remember that, since I must be always looking at him, I necessarily catch many of his ways. Just that you might have a fair sample of his "aggravating" traits, I'd like to turn him over to you for a little while.

Of course there's Shinn—big-hearted, eccentric, impulsive Shinn—and the other fellows in the house; but I do'nt live and study with them as I do with Wilson, so their influence is'nt to be compared with his. The little card I enclose is from Shinn, as you will see. He found it in some little out-of-the-way book store in some of his characteristic wanderings in the corners of the town, and wants to send it to you as a token of his regard. I never knew a man so delighted as he is in devising little attentions by which to please his friends by proving how constantly they are in his thoughts. Do you remember the reference he made to some love trouble of his, in one of his letters written to me in Savannah? Well, he told me the particulars of it the other day: and I wish I could repeat the story as he told it: for, though I am the only person east of the Rocky Mountains to whom he has confided it, I should be betraying no confidence in telling *you*: for you are mine and all my secrets are yours; but I can't spoil a touchingly pathetic story by a set repetition of it. Suffice it to say, that a young lady of very unusual charms and accomplishments, and seemingly (*he* would not say 'seemingly') possessed of just such graces both in mind and of heart as qualified her for making his life a very happy one, first loved him and then deceived him. That's rather my hard interpretation of the facts than simply a summary of them. Some day I will tell you the particulars, which on his lips bore the colours of a romance, and then you may pity and sympathize and judge for yourself. Just like mine your pity and sympathy will be, I know: and I do'nt think that your judgment will be different.

Have you a copy of Ruskin's "Modern Painters," my darling? An inexpensive edition of the work is published now which I can get, through the Univ. library, at a very small cost; and I am very anxious to send it to you.

Give my love to all the dear family at 143—and to Mrs. Duncan —giving little Ellen (if Carrie wont be jealous) as many kisses as you are willing to be paid for by

Your own   Woodrow.

ALS (WP, DLC). Enc.: C. H. Shinn to ELA, c. Feb. 14, 1884, ALS (WP, DLC).

From Robert Bridges

Dear Tommy: New York Feb 15 '84
Your essay[1] rec'd the other day—for which many thanks. You know my opinion of it of old. Is it reprinted from any magazine?

Heathen[2] is now visiting me. Is recovering from a very severe illness—six weeks on his back.

Pete[3] is now back on the *Post* and gives you his commiseration. Is making "waifs" and has not time to send more.

I have been increasing my college correspondents. Now have fifteen. We want to make a feature of it. I send you one of my circulars—and hope that you will send us an occasional from Johns Hopkins. It is different from other colleges and you need only apply so much of these directions as are apropos. Use your own judgment—which I know will fill the bill. I will send you regular envelopes if you accept.[4]

Remember me to the Cow.[5] Is he engaged as yet? I am in a great hurry—So Good bye

Your friend   Bob Bridges

ALS (WP, DLC) with WWhw notation on env.: "Ans. Feb'y. 20/84." Enc.: circular letter, R. Bridges to "Dear Sir," Feb. 15, 1884, ALS (WP, DLC), requesting recipient to become a college reporter for the New York *Evening Post*.
  1 "Committee or Cabinet Government?"
  2 William B. Lee.

[3] Harold Godwin.
[4] WW did agree to write such college "letters." See WW to R. Bridges, Feb. 20, 1884.
[5] Hiram Woods, Jr.

From Marion Wilson Kennedy

My dearest brother:—   Little Rock, 2/15/84.

Many thanks for your *"Article,"*[1] which was enjoyed *muchly* by us both. How did you ever attain to such a sedate, middle-aged style of composition, brother mine? You write as if further years and longer experience were hardly possible. Your whole *style* expresses the *dignity of age.*

How comes it that neither you nor Ellie have sent us any letters all this while? I sent you both modest little reminders of our existence, in the shape of Christmas Cards, and Ellie sent me a lovely Card. That emboldened me to "write a letter"[2] to the young lady, and there the matter has been dropped. Did she ever speak of receiving a letter from me? I do hope the valuable document was not lost! You see, I was so much excited that I had to blot that exclamation point, by way of emphasis. Please write soon and relieve my anxiety. Just imagine your state of mind if Ellie were to keep *you* waiting *six weeks* for a letter. Would you be "aisy in your moind"? . . .

Good night,   Lovingly your sister   M.

ALS (WP, DLC) with WWhw notation on env.: "Rec'd and Ans. 2/23/84."
[1] "Committee or Cabinet Government?"
[2] Marion Wilson Kennedy to ELA, Dec. 28, 1883, ALS (WP, DLC).

To Richard Heath Dabney

My dear Heath,   Balto., Md., Feby 17th 1884

Your letter of July, after its notable wanderings, many and devious, reached me about two months ago.[1] My impulse was to answer it at once; but, being here under the command of other people, duties have crowded out this pleasure until now. As you see, I am in Baltimore, at "the Hopkins"—not as a "fellow," however, (that was denied me) but simply as a "graduate student." I am sorry to say that I have been altogether disappointed in the department here. Neither the attainments nor the methods of the instructors are what I had a right to expect. Ely (a Heidelberg Ph.D.) is a hard-worker, a conscientious student, and chuck full of the exact data of his subject (like Schönberg's "Handbuch," which is his economic bible);[2] but he moves only by outside impulse and is not fitted for the highest duties of the teacher; whilst Adams, though shrewd and capable enough in a way, works little, save in the prosecution of schemes for his own advancement. By the way, in your letter you mix two Adamses: H. C. Adams (a Ph.D. of this University) who was invited to Cornell, but is now at the University of Michigan—a very capable and learned economist, but much too independent to live while young with President Gilman—and H. *B.* Adams (a Heidelberg doctor) who was a pupil of Bluntschli's, as you say, but a disciple of Machiavelli, as he himself declares, and who, as President Gilman's chief diplomatic agent, is on the high road to preferment, even though his pupils starve, the while, on a very meagre diet of ill-served lectures. You may know that I speak soberly of this man, because I came here to admire and have remained to scoff. There's something very rotten in this state of Denmark, where honours are apt to be conferred by favour; but there can be no question about this being the best place in America to study, because of its freedom and its almost unrivalled facilities, and because one can from here, better than from anywhere else in the country, command an appointment to a professorship. The only choice is between this and Germany: and from the latter, alas! old fellow, I'm practically shut out by reason of my ignorance of German—else I might join you next year! What would I not give to see you again! We could fraternize now in dead earnest: in studies as in everything else! I suppose that it *was* inevitable that I should turn, sooner or later, to a systematic and professional cultivation of history and political science. I was born with that bent in me; and there was no use trying to force nature to unnatural uses. Nature would, indeed, be *most* dutifully served if I could take a special line in my specialty and devote myself mainly to a study of the constitutional history of the United States and of their present actual constitutional system— as contradistinguished from the ideal Constitution of the books and of the lawyer's theories, which latter is only the Constitution of 1789 ornamented with many "wise saws and modern instances." Of course such a study would have to be comparative, lighted by illustrations and parallels, as well as by contrasts, furnished by the present constitutions of Europe and of England. But I don't feel justified in specializing my work in such a way until I have prospect of a chair devoted exclusively to such exposition. Indeed, "there's the rub" all around. Where is a fellow to find a berth? Must he go and teach history, with an incongruous and intolerable mixture of a great many other things, in some college of the South or West? Such would seem to be our inevitable fate, unless we are to aspire so high as to a chair in some of the great institutions of the East, in which a youngster can hardly hope to find a place.

But, besides turning to the study of history and political science, Heath, I've done something else quite as inevitable, and which makes this question of obtaining a chair an exceedingly interesting one: I've fallen in love and *become engaged.* Yes, it's so: I'm bagged! Indeed, having been engaged already five months, I am beginning to feel quite staid and settled! It is wonderful how literally exact the saying is that one *falls* in love. I met a certain Miss Ellen Louise Axson, in Rome, Geo., in April, 1883 and by the middle of the following September I was engaged to her! That's decisive enough action for you! Of course it goes without the saying that I am the most complacently happy man in the "Yew-nighted States." If you care to listen a moment, I will tell you what the unfortunate lady is like. She is the daughter of a Presbyterian minister—and the granddaughter of one too, for the matter of that—and grew up in that best of all schools—for manners, purity and cultivation—a country parsonage. She has devoted the greater part of her time to art—having relieved her father's slender salary of the burden of her own support by portrait drawing and painting which have given her quite a reputation amongst the best people of Georgia—but she is also devoted to reading of the best sort: so that, without any pretense to learning, and without the slightest tinge of pedantry, she has acquired a very remarkable acquaintance with the best literature. If you add to this, the fact that she is in her tastes the most *domestic* of maidens, you will see how well fitted she is to become a *student's* wife. But (as you will readily believe) I can't claim the wisdom of having fallen in love with Miss Axson because I was justified, after a philosophical and dispassionate consideration of her tastes and attainments, in concluding that she would be a proper help-meet for a professor. I fell in love with her for the same reasons that had made the samething easy to several other fellows who were *not* students: because of her beauty, and gentleness and intelligence; because she was irresistibly lovable. Why *she* fell in love with *me* must always remain an impenetrable mystery. I look upon my wonderful success as one of those apparently fortuitous and certainly inestimable blessings which one must content himself with being thankful for and trying to deserve *ex post facto*, as it were, without seeking to understand it— as something sent to strengthen and ennoble me. It makes me very anxious, you see, to get hold of a definite appointment to teach somewhere, at a salary on which two economical people can live comfortably. You can't in reason expect a fellow not to be impatient to possess such a prize.

Is it so, not to change the subject too violently, that Harry Smith[3] is in diplomatic employment in Berlin? So I was told by a student here (T. K. Worthington) who went over to Europe last Summer on the same steamer with the Venables and Miss Leilia Smith. If the dear old boy *is* over there, please give him my warmest love and a cordial ϕ ψ grip for me! I do'nt hear anything nowadays about any of the University (of Va.) boys, even indirectly. I dare say you hear more in Germany. I saw Walter Lefevre, indeed, in Oct. last, on his way to study law under Dr. [John B.] Minor—but ne'er another University acquaintance has come above my horizon. I don't know where Kent *is*, for instance, whether he is still teaching with Coleman in Charleston or not. Enlighten me, if you can. I hate to lose sight of the boys so.

Write to me again as soon as you can, old fellow, and tell me of everything that concerns yourself. In the mean time you may be sure of the love of

Your sincere friend   Woodrow Wilson.

(Even the T. gone from my name now)

ALS (Wilson-Dabney Correspondence, ViU).

[1] R. H. Dabney to WW, July 22, 1883, Vol. 2. This letter, originally sent to Atlanta, had been returned twice to Germany, arriving at Wilmington finally on Dec. 13, 1883.

[2] Wilson was referring to Dr. Ely's lectures in his advanced course in political economy. There is little wonder that Wilson thought that Gustav Friedrich von Schönberg, ed., *Handbuch der politischen Oekonomie* (2 vols., Tübingen, 1882), was Ely's economic bible. Ely, in his lectures in December 1883, had given an elaborate summary of this work, characterizing it as "a collection of monographs written by the ablest living German specialists, representing the high watermark of political economy." Each of the twenty-one authors, Ely went on, "has devoted years to political economy not only but also to some special branch of political economy; and this work contains an answer to the question: what has political economy already done for us?" Transcript of WWsh notes in first, undated, lecture notes in classroom notebook described at Dec. 6, 1883, Vol. 2.

Ray Stannard Baker, *Woodrow Wilson: Life and Letters*, I, 179, published that portion of Wilson's letter referring to Ely, and Ely in his autobiography commented with mild acidity on Wilson's remark. Richard T. Ely, *Ground Under Our Feet* (New York, 1938), p. 111. For all his lack of style as a lecturer, it was Ely, after all, who introduced Wilson to the modern study of economics and (in 1885) to public administration.

[3] Gessner Harrison Smith, who had been at the University of Virginia from 1879 to 1881.

To Ellen Louise Axson

My own darling,   Balto., Md., Feby, 17th/84

The concert, looked forward to so long and with so many misgivings, came off last Thursday evening in "Hopkins Hall"—yes, before the general public—and has been pronounced a great success. I am sincerely glad that the trial is past. There were several "raw hands," besides myself, in the Club—indeed, the majority of us had never before sung in public—and I was by no means sure that we should get through without a break-down: but we did; we even won enthusiastic applause from a very select and critical audience, and we are much "set up" in consequence. It was a hard night's work for me, I can tell you! for I had to sing in every piece, being of the quartette as well as in the chorus. The event of the evening was the "Three Kittens." It is the "Gregorian chant" with these words:

1. "Once on a time, there were three little kittens that lived together in a basket of saw-dust. Said the first little kitten to the second and third little kittens, 'If you don't get out of this, I must!'"

2. Now these three little kittens, such was their state of imperturbability, continued to live together in, &c.
   Said the second little kitten unto the first and third little kittens, 'If you don't' &c."

3. These three little kittens, the audience may be interested to learn, still continued to live in the basket, &c.
   Said the third little kitten unto the first and second little kittens, 'If you don't get out of this, *I shall bust!*'"

Then, while we hummed the tune through again, one of the students (by arrangement) produced, from a place of concealment, a most excellent and irresistibly laughable imitation of the noises of a savage cat fight—which, following upon the solemn absurdity of the chant, completely captivated the audience. As an encore we sang the "Rhinocericus" song of which I sent you a specimen verse, and which seems to have ravished Randolph's heart. Of course *that* was immensely successful. I think the audience was, altogether, well enough pleased to come to our next concert; and there can be no doubt but that we'll sing much better then, because we shall have much more self-confidence now that we have found that we *can* sing in public.

No indeed! we are *not* having by any means beautiful weather here. We've been having nothing but rain, rain, rain—not even big, honest, vigorous, pelting rain, coming down with energy and decision, as if meant to do the earth good; but thin, streaming, penetrating rains, chill drizzles, and damp fogs—not a smile from the sky for weeks together—nothing but heavy frowns or leaden dullness. Of course writing and study can go on indoors all the same, but not with the dash and joy and speed that would attend them if one could but see the clear, cheery sunshine once in a while. My thoughts seem sluggish, and my energies limp, because of the the [sic] oppressive gloom and searching dampness of the weather.

I continue perfectly well, however, and my good spirits don't suffer eclipse. Who would'nt be happy with such a tender and true little sweet-heart as I have! Do you know, Ellie, my love, my darling, that you make me inexpressibly happy when you declare your complete trust in me, in my love and in my power to comfort you and to gladden your life—as you do in your last letter? Your love is my strength, my little lady. It has ennobled and broadened my life more than I can make you believe; and I am giving you in return all the love of which my nature is capable. If you think man's love a treasure, (at least, *this* man's) you are a very rich little maiden, for this man is ready to pour out at your feet all the wealth of his heart—has poured it out, in fact, and is in every thought   Your own   Woodrow.

Love to all—and to Mrs. Duncan, my friend and ally.

ALS (WP, DLC). Enc.: printed program for The Johns Hopkins University Glee Club concert, Feb. 14, 1884.

From Ellen Louise Axson

My darling Woodrow,   Savannah, Feb. 18/84.

I made noble efforts last week, on three or four successive nights, to write you, but something always "came up" to take the pen out of my hand. I wanted especially to tell you of the somewhat more cheering reports we have from Father. We have received several letters from *him*—the first since he left—and they have given us much comfort; they were perfectly lucid, affectionate, and almost cheerful. I meant to send you mine,[1] but some of the others borrowed it;—if I can find it I will enclose it. But, of course, though it is delightful to get such letters from him, we can't attach too much importance to them, since the trouble comes on in paroxysms and he probably writes only in the intervals. The doctors seem to think, however, that he is making some progress. For all your kind, kind words on that subject

I thank you, dearest, with all my heart. I won't attempt the impossible. I won't try to say how much I *love* you for them. And tis true indeed that "love gives me strength, and strength shall help afford."

Yes, Miss Rosalie has come at last, after keeping us on the "qui vive" for a week or so. "Aunt Flo"[2] insisted upon keeping her so long, awaiting Mr. Seay's return, as to seriously affect the tempers of Daisy, Jule[3] & myself. But she finally "arrove" on last Tuesday, and we have been together perhaps half the time since. It will be less difficult to keep my newly formed resolutions about "exercise" while she is here, since it is quite a distance to "20 Habersham St.," and we have never dropped our old habit of escorting each other home after a visit. How well I remember our absurd behavior in old school-days, when I would walk home with her, she would return with me, I again with her, and so on until night caught us, when we would separate at the half-way corner and both "run for it." My dear little "better half" is lovlier than ever, I think. How I wish she had come before you left! She was greatly "aggravated" to find she had just missed you. "All the aunts in Christendom could'nt have kept her if she had known you were here." But she "rests in the hope of seeing you next summer." She says she is in love with you herself from my description. I am going to make her have her picture taken for me —we have never had a decent one of her,—and when I get it, I shall send it you to look at. By-the-way, I have discovered that the little Fraulein in "Check-mated"[4] is very much like *her*: the eyes are hers *exactly*, except that the brows are arched, while Rose' are straight. I suppose it would'nt be *fair* not to report that she discovered, (!) without any prompting on my part, that the picture resembled me!

Speaking of pictures, how you would have laughed if you had been here Saturday at the plotting and scheming which was going on,—with the accompaniment of intense though repressed excitement on the part of Ellen and Leila—all the result of an effort to get possession of Ellen and her "things," and to carry her down town and back without her mother's knowledge. I wanted to get a picture of her in fancy dress for Aunt Ella's birth-day present—not a very disinterested gift, since I have been wanting it for myself so long, to paint; but the birthday makes a very good excuse, and it is fair to kill two birds with one stone.

But Aunt Ella is one who generally knows everything that is going on in which her children are concerned, so we had to employ every variety of stratagem, to accomplish our purpose; and

I flatter myself that we proved our claim to rare genius for "invention and combination"!

Long live that lovable, soft-hearted old "Saint Valentine"! say I, and may he treat every-body as well as he does me. I am altogether *charmed* with "the picture, the poem, and the story"; and I affirm and protest against all opponents that my valentine is the very nicest of all which came to the house that day—some score or so. And by-the-way I had another, a gorgeous one, from someone in Sav!

Please give Mr. Shinn my best thanks for the dainty little card, and the good wishes it bears. What one can I send him in return for them all! "The best wishes that can be forged in his thoughts be servants to him." The card is indeed *very* pretty, and I appreciate his sending it exceedingly. Poor Mr. Shinn! I am very sorry for him. I read his little story with deep interest; but a girl like that should'nt be allowed to spoil a man's life! Do you think so? We will hope he may yet live to thank her for it. Is it a very fresh wound now? Somehow I feel an especially vivid interest in Mr. Shinn, and regard for him, more than for any of your other friends of whom I have heard you speak. I suppose, to go somewhat out of my way in search of a selfish reason, it may be because he has happened to get "mixed up" a little in *our* affairs, and so seems a wee bit my friend as well as yours.

No, my darling, I hav'nt Modern Painters, and it is one of the books which I have always most coveted too; because it is one of those which it is most unsatisfactory, as I have found from experience[,] to take for a week or so from a library. It can only be properly enjoyed and appreciated in the fuller knowledge which comes with possession. I hav'nt forgotten, dearest, that you ask me another question in one of last week's letters; but you will forgive my not sending the answer *now*; you are willing to wait for it, you say. And I will make any promise you wish for an *indefinite* future! But you know very well—do you not?—that it is no lack of confidence which makes me leave *any* question unanswered, or *any* thought unspoken, but only—I don't know what.

Thanks for the little peep you give me into your work, and the tribulations connected therewith. I can almost fancy I see you at it, and I am always *most happy* to be favoured with such a glimpse. I can easily imagine your state of mind over your troublesome, perplexing, but at the same time delightful, and absorbingly interesting task. I am glad to remember that you said, there was, notwithstanding the difficulty, a peculiar fascination about it all, otherwise I should fear you would, like Carlyle, be rendered "desperate"!

But, after all, labour becomes very monotonous and tiresome when unattended by difficulty; does it not? And life itself would be deprived of some of its keenest and most satisfactory pleasures, were there no obstacles to be met and conquered. I notice that the people who grow "weary of living," who find it all "empty, flat, stale and unprofitable["] are the very ones for whom the path-way seems to be made smoothest. So perhaps our hinderances and perplexities, those thorns and brambles, which since the days of Adam, the earth brings forth so abundantly for us all, are but blessings in disguise, another illustration of the truth, that "God in cursing sends us better gifts, than men in benediction."

Do you still keep perfectly well? I trust that "impatience to achieve" is'nt making you out-run your limits of endurance again, but that you have found it wisest to "make haste slowly."

Give my love to your father and mother and all, and with best and truest love for yourself believe me, dearest,

Your own Ellie.

ALS (WP, DLC). Att.: WWhw on separate sheet: "'And what portion can be more blessed than with youth, and health, and strength, to be loved by a virtuous maid, and to love her with all one's heart?" and "'the action of the body is "not" determined by what takes place on the floor.'" WW used most of the first sentence as the opening of his letter to ELA of Feb. 21, 1884.
    [1] S. E. Axson to ELA, Feb. 12 or Feb. 16, 1884, both ALS (WP, DLC).
    [2] Mrs. Seay.
    [3] Sisters of Rosalie Anderson.
    [4] The picture that WW gave her for Christmas in 1883. See WW to ELA, Dec. 18, 1883, and ELA to WW, Dec. 25, 1883, Vol. 2.

From Melville R. Hopewell[1]

Dear Sir   Tekamah, Neb., Feb. 18 1884

Yours of Feb 12th with draft for $68.87 Received. Enclosed you will find County Treasurers receipt for Taxes paid, for 1883[.] I will write you in a few days in reference to the Maria Bones[2] deed.   Yours Truly   M. R. Hopewell
                                        Per D.

ALS (WP, DLC). Enc.: tax receipts dated Aug. 13, 1883, and Feb. 16, 1884.
    [1] Formerly agent of the Estate of William Woodrow, now serving as WW's agent.
    [2] Her quit claim deed, cited in Vol. 2, p. 375n.

To Ellen Louise Axson

My precious Ellie,   Balto., Md., Feby. 19th/84

I was reading, the other night, as a rest from the worry of work, the concluding chapters of a book which I began to read last winter but did not then have time to finish, and which I want to mention to you now in order to express the hope that you have never read it—because I want the pleasure of reading it with you next Summer. It is "Lorna Doone: A Romance of Exmoor," by R.D. Blackmore, and is one of the most charming books you can imagine, for its wonderful reproduction of the quaint, idiomatic, desultory, picturesque style of the written English of the seventeenth century, its refreshing Early-England air, its beauty of description, its striking incidents, and its simple story of pure, whole-souled love. It is'nt a book to read by oneself. It ought to be enjoyed *together* by two people who know a good thing when they see it and I want to enjoy it with my darling. I'll enjoy it all the more for having already read it once; and it will (let me whisper it in your ear)—it will have a fresh beauty in my eyes when read by your side.

Speaking of reading, I am reminded of something else I came across the other day in an essay of Sidney Lanier's[1] (which I happened to hit upon as I was looking through a magazine in search of a very poorly written article on "Self-Government in the Territories").[2] Here it is: "For example, the writer knew, some while ago, a maiden—and one of the brigh[t]est of the time in heart and mind—who for some months was quite seriously possessed with the following idea: *It was impossible*, she would declare, with a very pretty fervor and modesty, and with some show of despair, *that she could ever love a man who loved her, because* forsooth *she knew her own worth to be so small that she could not admire a man with a soul little enough to prize it!*" Did you ever *hear* of such a girl! Now *this* writer knew, no great while ago, a maiden— one of the brigh[t]est and lovliest of that time and of this—who had so humble an opinion as to her own worth that she for a time held back from engaging herself to the man she loved and admired, for fear she was not good enough for him! but she did not refuse to *love* him, and so was not *quite* like Mr. Lanier's interesting acquaintance. I suspect that the latter had simply never met the man she could love; and that my sweet little friend had not found out *then* what a really commonplace fellow her lover was.

Do you know, little lady, that you have said nothing recently in your letters to me about Miss Rosalie Anderson? Did'nt she come

at the time she was expected? I was looking forward with pleasure to the announcement of her arrival, because I knew that you
would be so happy in having her with you, and I was prepared to
be very much comforted by the fact that she was bringing so
much sunshine of love and sympathy into my darling's life.

I was much astonished last week by the receipt of a letter from
Renick,[3] my old partner, written from Washington and telling
me of his recent appointment to a government office. He is legal
secretary to the First Comptroller of the Treasury, and won his
office by competitive examination under the provisions of the new
Civil Service Act. Nothing could have been more unexpected. I
had pictured him as getting on finely in Atlanta, and settled there
for life; but I have selfish reasons for being satisfied with having
him in Washington. In the intervals of earning his twelve hundred dollars, he can send me all sorts of information about the
practical details of government, for use in what I am writing—
as he has generously offered to do. Am I not a mercenary friend?
The fact is, however, that Renick is fitted to be the most valuable
of helpers in such work. He has a perfect genius for asking questions; and no information which he has to impart will be in the
least vague and indefinite. His faculty for gathering exact information is really wonderful: and all his inquiries are prompted
by an enthusiastic liking for *knowing*.

That *was* an exceedingly bright and pretty speach of dear little
Ellen's. It had true wit in it, and was, besides, a witty truth: for
the more I think about it the more I am convinced that you *are*
"a daisy." I hope that you kissed her for that saying and that you
will kiss her, whenever it occurs to you, for *me*, not specially for
that delightful little witticism, but just "on general principles."
I know that she wont object to my kissing her by proxy as often
as I please, *if you be the proxy.*

Of course I remember the Anderson St. Church: for, for some
reason or other, I never forget anything I've seen with you. And
did *you* not feel, my little lady, as you were taking that enchant-
ing walk through the moonlight and laughing at Leila's sentimental reflections that you were in love with somebody? By some
strange law of my nature *I* feel that way under all sorts of skies:
and if the fair maiden I love could but know the smallest part of
the things I am forever thinking of her, she would—she would
see cause to hope that her lover will try to make her life a very
bright and happy one when she has given it into his keeping.

You are very sweet, my darling, to regard my wishes so readily
about the exercise you dislike, but which I am *so* anxious to have

you take. Mrs. Duncan is indeed a valuable ally—but she gave you that excellent advice, my love, because she loves you, not because her special object is to "take care of you for me." Is it so very irksome to you, my lady, to have to take long walks? Don't it make it a *little* easier to do when you do it as a conscious act of love towards me? You are manifesting your love towards me in all that you do for your health. But here I am breaking my promise by slipping into another lecture.

Just when I am hardest pressed by work comes some more, and from a quarter and in a shape least expected. Dr. Ely, our preceptor in political economy, has taken it into his head that it would be a good plan to prepare for publication a history of political economy in the United States, and he conceives that the best method of composition would be the *coöperative*.[4] Wherefore he proposes that he should himself write the chapters on the works of [Mathew] Carey (who began to write sometime in the '30's, and who, as the most important and original of American political economists, would be entitled to about one-third of the little book proposed); that Mr. Dewey, of our Seminary,[5] should write of the economic authors preceding Carey; and that your humble servant should prepare a narrative and critical review of the writings *since* Carey! Alas, Alas! Think of the trash I shall have to read and the work I shall have to do in this new field: For I can't refuse. I came here to advertise myself for a position (as well as to learn what I could) and the best way to do that is to please the professors and get them to push me! Do'nt you pity the poor economists who have written since Carey? I do; but not so much as I pity myself! I hate this thing of serving other men; but it's politic; and the service is honourable.

Give my warmest love to all and remember that I love you with all my heart—that I work because I love you.

Your own   Woodrow.

ALS (WP, DLC).

[1] "A Forgotten English Poet," *International Review*, vi (March 1879), 298.

[2] Decius S. Wade, "Self-Government in the Territories," *International Review*, vi (March 1879), 299-308.

[3] E. I. Renick to WW, Feb. 14, 1884.

[4] The book was to be a "History of Political Economy in the United States." See the public announcement printed at May 10, 1884.

[5] Davis Rich Dewey, born April 7, 1858. A.B., University of Vermont, 1879; Ph.D., the Johns Hopkins, 1886. Assistant Professor of Economics and Statistics, Massachusetts Institute of Technology, 1886-92; professor, same institution, 1893-1933. Managing editor, *American Economic Review*, 1911-40. Author of many books, articles, and state and federal reports. Died Dec. 13, 1942.

To Robert Bridges

Dear Bobby,   Balto., Md., Feby 20th/84
I have time for but a line this evening, being pressed with more urgent spurs than usual in my work; but I must write that line at least in answer to your kind note of last Friday,[1] in order to accept the offered position of Johns Hopkins correspondent of the *Post*. I think that I can send a few notes weekly; and with my first communication I will try to send you a letter. Love to Pete.   As ever,   Yours   Woodrow Wilson

ALS (Meyer Coll., DLC).
[1] R. Bridges to WW, Feb. 15, 1884.

To Ellen Louise Axson

My own darling,   Balto., Md., Feby 21st. 1884
"What portion can be more blessed than with youth, and health, and strength, to be loved by a virtuous maid, and to love her with all one's heart?" It is a blessed portion even when one is compelled to submit to the dismal fate of being separated by several hundred very long miles from the sweet lady of his love— provided she write him such letters as I received to day, full of tender, playful love not only—love which makes the sunlight (which, by-the-way, has at last returned to us) seem more joyous and glorious than is its wont—but also illuminated by the brigh[t]est spirits, which tell of the happiness of the writer and so add to the joy of the receiver. You have good right to be light-hearted, my darling, being in receipt of such encouraging news from your dear father. It is a *great* thing that he is able to write to you. His moments of quiet may be moments of happiness, and so contribute to his entire recovery, if they may be employed in correspondence which makes him feel the unbroken connection with those he loves and of whose love he feels sure. Whenever you write to him, Ellie, please give him my warmest love, assuring him, by as loving messages as you can frame, of my affection and respect for him. For you must remember, Miss, that *he* won my affections before you did. His daughter has *since* made wonderful progress in my esteem; but he has all the time more than held his own: and will some day gain a son who will be a son to him in feeling as well as *"in law."* May that day be hastened! My "impatience to achieve" reaches to other things besides my writing. You do'nt know (yet), my dear little lady, how wilful and headstrong I am, and how I begrudge the time

that leaves you your own mistress. I long to be made your master —only, however, on the very fair and equal terms that, in exchange for the authority over yourself which you relinquish, you shall be constituted supreme mistress of me! That seems to me a fair compact. Besides, having studied constitutions of various sorts, I have not failed to observe that the constitution of the great and ancient State of Matrimony is *Love*: and, when I shall be admitted to a throne under that noble constitution, I shall feel bound to observe its sacred precedents and conform in word and practice to the best principles of government relating to that "limited monarchy," founded, as it is, upon the affection of the subject.

Ah! you shy little maiden! So you decline the easy way of answering a certain question recently propounded, and pledge yourself to answer it in full in the "indefinite future" of next Summer! I am content. What would I *not* rather hear my darling *say* than have her write in cold ink! I know that she thinks me a very formidable, critical creature, for all her love for me (as if she did'nt know that I think everything sweet and perfect that falls from her lips!); and that her heart checks her tongue in its progress of sweet confession even when my arm is about her and she sits quite close to the man who loves her infinitely more than he loves himself: but, "for a' that," her words convey the most precious of all meanings; I can kiss away the confusion from those pretty lips; and—and I am delighted with the present pledge!

Give my love to Miss Rosalie (if I am entitled to send my love to you, I can certainly send it to "your better half.") to your dear grandparents, to Mr. and Mrs. Axson, and all the rest of the household I think of with so much affection, and keep for yourself a portion three times as large as you want from

Your own   Woodrow.

ALS (WP, DLC).

From Ellen Louise Axson

My darling Woodrow,   Savannah, Feb. 21/84.

"Three letters for you, Cousin Ellie," cried little Ellen this morning, "three letters,—one from each sweet-heart!" And so there was—one from you, one from Stockton, and another from Papa. The little lady was correct, as usual. I will enclose the one from Father because you can form a better idea of his present condition from reading it than from anything I can say; and I know how interested you are.

22nd Was interrupted last night, and have had no opportunity since to resume; it is now after ten—no time to begin writing. Yet here I am, seriously entered upon the laborious task of producing a *short* letter! I am sure that you will fervently wish me success in the effort.

Dr. Ely is evidently a clever man, who knows when he has gotten hold of a good thing. I am hence-forth an ardent admirer of his, because he has the good sense to appreciate *you*. How is he likely to do *his* part of the work, by-the-way? Is he a good writer? And who is Mr. Dewey, and what do you think of him? When do you propose to begin the work? Will it involve a vast amount of labour? How long will you probably be engaged upon it?—though that is doubtless a foolish question, as I suppose it is impossible for you to tell. And it is too bad to so overwhelm you with questions of *any* sort. But of course I am deeply interested in this new scheme. And then, you make the most startling announcements as to your work and plans in such a quiet, matter of course manner, that I am constantly left in a comical state of bewilderment, scarcely knowing if I have even "any business" to be so profoundly impressed as I am!

I hope you are not going to be *too* much pressed with work in carrying out your several plans; it would be a poor policy to overtax yourself in your "impatience to achieve"—would it not? But fortunately your constitutional subject "is'nt likely to get old, or to break away from" you; so you are not obliged to ride all your horses at once—three or four abreast, as they do at the circus.

I am truly delighted to hear of the "fortunate combination of circumstances" which has taken Mr. Renick to Washington. That was really a brilliant idea of his; he seems to be that rare character,—the right man, in the right place, at the right time; and I am very glad too that he is so heartily "yours to serve." I am *charmed* too, to learn that your concert was such a grand triumph. There must have been rare fun, as well as good music. *Would'nt* I have been delighted to hear it! When Randolph and I "get a chance" we mean to insist upon a repetition of the whole performance, cat-fight and all,—or perhaps, upon second thought, Randolph might relieve you of that part.

The boys have been wildly excited all day over the prize tournament in honour of Washington's birthday, an addition to the usual drilling and parading which mark the occasion.

The day gains an additional interest—perhaps a stronger—at No. 143. from the fact that it is Ellen's "fête,"—the little lady

is seven today. But the birthdays follow each other so rapidly
in the few weeks past and to come that birth-day cake is really
our daily bread. By-the-way, I think I must send you one of Ellen's pictures to look at. They are *exquisite*; Mr. H. says the
finest picture he has taken in many months, and that she is
the best little subject he ever had—so there *was* profit in all our
labour taken under the sun.

I believe I have already answered your question with regard
to Rose—she *is* here, and I *am* very happy in having her with
me. We see each other constantly, and *walk* together almost
daily.

Begging your pardon, Sir, it isn't my design while "laughing
at Leila's sentimental reflections" to turn witness against myself, and say whether *she* found anything to laugh at in *me*.
You surely don't imagine that moonlight or anything else has
power to work such a spell upon *me*!

But I *must* bring my *short* letter to an end. How are your
father and mother now? Quite well again, I hope, as you have
said nothing about it in the last two or three letters. Please
give them my love. All here send love to you & with as much
as heart can hold from myself believe me, dearest, now and
always   Your own   Ellie.

ALS (WP, DLC). Enc.: S. E. Axson to ELA, Feb. 19, 1884, ALS (WP, DLC).

From the Minutes of the Seminary of Historical and Political Science

Bluntschli Hall, Feby. 22nd, 1884

At ten o'clock, A.M. the Seminary was called to order by Dr.
Adams.

Mr. Gould read the minutes of the last meeting, which were
approved without correction.

Dr. Adams, after announcing the appointments for the next
meeting, introduced Mr. Channing, Instructor in International
law at Harvard University, who favoured the Seminary with
an outline sketch of a paper on *Local Government North and
South*[1] which he had recently prepared and which had won for
him the "Topham Prize"—a prize offered at Harvard for special
original work.

Mr. Channing began by saying that he had been inspired in
the preparation of his paper chiefly by Dr. Adams's monograph
on "The Germanic Origin of New England Towns."[2] He declared that his own views had been formed after as careful an

examination of the local institutions of all the Colonies as was possible with the materials afforded him by the Harvard library, which, though rich in the records of some of the Colonies, is poor in documents concerning others. For purposes of distinctness he would not enter into any discussion of the many minute particulars in which the members of the Northern and Southern groups of Colonies differed amongst themselves as regarded the exact form of their local institutions, but would follow the usual course of taking Massachusetts as the typical representative of the one group and Virginia as the typical representative of the other, comparing and contrasting the local govts. of these two colonies, pointing out their connection with the system of local govt. obtaining in England in the year 1600

In illustration of the fact that the exact form of govt. in the Colonies depended upon economic conditions, upon the form of church govt., and upon the land system, he dwelt at some length on the influences of climate and geographical conditions in determining the character of the settlements in New England and Virginia; upon the social differences arising from the differences in character between the northern and southern colonists; and upon the opposite policies pursued in the matter of land grants in the two sections.

Of ecclesiastical organization he said that the Congregationalism of New England was a form both of church and of social government and necessitated the settlement of the colony in compact, organized communities; whereas the Episcopal organization set up in Va. was specially suited to the rural life adopted by the colonists, and to the other conditions characteristic of Virginian society.

After some discussion of the origin of the New England towns, and of the gradual growth of township, precinct, district, and county organization, he passed on to a consideration of the vestry with a view to emphasizing the fact that, though the vestries both of New Eng. and of Va. were sprung directly from the Eng. vestry of 1600, the former developed into the selectmen who never became permanent officers, whilst the vestry of Va. speedily became a close corporation.

Mr. Channing closed his paper with an interesting tabulated view of the functions of the Eng. parish, the New England town-meeting, and the Virginia vestry.

The paper was received with applause. Dr. Adams said that it represented the first systematic attempt to draw minute comparisons between Eng., New England, and Virginia local institutions, and called attention to the main point of the discussion, which was the continuity of the Eng. parish in the institutions of this country. There was also, Dr. Adams added, a very noticeable continuity of aggrarian institutions, though these were concealed beneath the parochial form.

After expressing the hope that Mr. Channing's article would soon be published, Dr. Adams made some further announcements, and at 11 o'clock the Seminary adjourned.

Woodrow Wilson,   Sect.

WWhw entry, bound ledger book (MdBJ).
    1 Edward Channing, *Town and County Government in the English Colonies of North America*. No. x, Johns Hopkins University Studies in Historical and Political Science, Herbert B. Adams, ed., Vol. 11 (Baltimore, 1884).
    2 Herbert B. Adams, *The Germanic Origin of New England Towns*. No. 11, Johns Hopkins University Studies in Historical and Political Science, Herbert B. Adams, ed., Vol. 1 (Baltimore, 1882-83).

Newsletters from the Johns Hopkins: I

President Eliot's Views[1]

Baltimore, February 22 [1884].

The 22d of February is the anniversary of the birth of the Johns Hopkins University, so that it is in university circles here a day of peculiar interest, marking an important corporate, as well as a notable national event. The day is consequently set apart, of course, for special exercises. On the 22d of February, 1876, President Gilman was inaugurated; and on the occasion of his inauguration President [Charles W.] Eliot, of Harvard, delivered the principal address. This year President Eliot was again present, and again occupied the position of chief speaker, under very different circumstances, however. In 1876 the exercises took place in the Academy of Music, for then the University had no hall of its own; this year they were held in the ample spaces of the gymnasium recently completed. The programme included an opening prayer, a short speech by President Gilman on some of the inside aspects of the life of the University, President Eliot's address, and several Latin songs by the University Glee Club. The audience numbered about 700 people—perhaps as select and appreciative an audience as could be gathered anywhere in the country, and not a movement of impatience did it make, nothing but the deepest interest did it manifest, during the whole hour and a half of President Eliot's address. That address certainly merited every whit of the unusual attention accorded it. It was striking and suggestive from beginning to end, as clear-cut and decisive as President Eliot's own features.

Its subject was "The Degree of Bachelor of Arts as an Evidence of Liberal Education," and its object was to advance that educational reform now in progress whereby the circle of "liberal studies" is to be widened so as to include, besides the Latin, Greek, and mathematics, which were the staples of the sixteenth-century curriculum, those other sciences of later growth and of modern perfection which now command the highest consideration from every one save college trustees and faculties. President Eliot's name has for many years been prominently connected with this reform, and to him as much as to any single man is due the honor of its advancement. It may be safely said that he never advocated it with more power than in this remarkable address. He opened by pointing out that nowhere had reform moved more sluggishly or against greater obstacles than in the alteration of the accepted courses of instruction in institutions of learning. He showed how hardly Greek had obtained admittance to the universities of three hundred years ago; how recent was the perfection of mathematical teaching; how tardily each one of the present staples of college learning had attained to universal use in the educational world. From this he passed on to notice the fact that ever since the canon had gone forth from the teachers of the sixteenth century that certain studies and no others should be considered the "liberal arts" and be imparted as such, no means had been found for gaining recognition for the languages of to-day or for the physical sciences as studies of equal weight and dignity.

Rising in energy of treatment, he presented with the utmost cogency the claims of the English language with its copious and splendid literature, the French and German languages with their treasures of learning and philosophy, history, political economy, and the natural sciences to be admitted to equal rank and dignity in every college curriculum, and to an equality of value as studies preparatory to the degree of Bachelor of Arts with those more honored but no more important ancient and dead languages so long allowed exclusive privilege, and with those mathematics which are dead without their sister sciences.

To realize this reform would, he declared, necessitate a change in educational methods, which must begin at the bottom, with the preparatory schools and academies. It involves an early differentiation of studies. Not all these subjects, each so great in itself, can be mastered thoroughly by a single individual. There must be an early choice of studies, made in the schools by the teachers themselves after a careful examination of the pupil's aptitudes; but made in college by the student himself. Not all, but only a certain proportion, of these studies must be required for a bachelor's degree; but all of them must be put upon the same footing, must be made coördinate and of equal academic value.

The argument of his address President Eliot thus concluded and summed up: "Finally, I step beyond the strict limits of my subject to urge the enlargement of the circle of liberal arts, on the ground that the interests of the higher education and of the institutions which supply that education demand it. Liberal education is not safe and strong in a country in which the great majority of the men who belong to the intellectual professions are not liberally educated. Now, that is just the case in this country. The great majority of the men who are engaged in the practice of law and medicine, in journalism, the public service, and the scientific professions, and in industrial leaderships are not bachelors of arts. Indeed, the only learned profession which contains to-day a large proportion of bachelors of arts is the ministry. This sorry condition of things is doubtless due in part to what may be called the pioneer condition of American society; but I think it is also due to the antiquated state of the common college curriculum and the course of preparatory study at school.

"The execution of the principles which I have advocated would involve considerable changes in the order of school and college studies. Thus, science teaching should begin early in the school course. English should be studied from the beginning of school life to the end of college life; and the order in which the foreign languages are taken up should be for many boys essentially changed. We should in vain expect such changes to be made suddenly. They must be gradually brought about by the pressure of public opinion, by the public opinion of the educated classes taking a gradual effect through educational instrumentalities. Reforms in education always advance slowly; but many of you will live to see this reform accomplished."

During the afternoon the University buildings were thrown open for the inspection of all who wished to look through them, and in the evening a reception was held by the officers of the University, who received the students and their friends, as well as visitors from other cities, in "Hopkins Hall," where refreshments were served and the evening most delightfully spent.

Printed in the New York *Evening Post*, Feb. 23, 1884; editorial headings omitted.
    [1] This is the first of WW's contributions as Johns Hopkins correspondent of the New York *Evening Post*, promised in WW to R. Bridges, Feb. 20, 1884. Others follow at March 8 and April 11, 1884.

To Ellen Louise Axson

My own darling, Balto., Md., Feb'y 24/84

I hope that you want me as much as I want you! that is to say, as *constantly* as I want you. I do'nt know how a fellow whose whole heart is wrapped up in a little sweet-heart of winsomest charms manages to live five or six hundred miles away from her —at least I do'nt know how *this* fellow manages to do it without being overcome by discontent. I am sure that there never was a chap who suffered more than I do because of separation from the chief objects of his love. I do not know, Miss Axson, what your dreams may be as to our married life—though I shall find out from my little sweetheart's own lips (which will at that moment be in great danger) in the "indefinite future" of five months hence!—but this I know, that the days will be much too short for me when I may spend them all with you; so that you must not expect to be allowed any respite after you have *given yourself over* to my society.

I have been dissipating terribly since I last wrote. On Thursday evening I attended a big fraternity supper which lasted away into the wee sma' hours;[1] on Friday morning I helped celebrate the anniversary of the foundation of the University—for the Hopkins, like George Washington, is said to have been born on the 22nd of February; President Gilman having been inaugurated on that day, A.D. 1876—; on Friday evening I went to hear the Concert given by the Princeton Glee Club; on Saturday morning I attended two public lectures; and not till Saturday evening did I get back to my work. Terrible! was it not?

But you were not aware that I was a member of one of the biggest of the much-debated secret, or "Greek-letter," fraternities: were you? Yes, at the University of Virginia, such societies having been prohibited at Princeton, I became a "Phi Kappa Psi." (ΦΚΨ), being thus constituted a "brother" of several thousand college men throughout the country. There is a flourishing chapter of the order here at the Hopkins, and there are, besides, sixty or seventy gentlemen in town who are graduate members (some of them are now grey-headed) so that we had a goodly number at the supper, and there was a very fine "feast of reason and flow of soul." I met a great many interesting fellows whom I had never met before and enjoyed myself thoroughly, although by one o'clock I was pretty tired.

The anniversary exercises at the University consisted of a fine address from Pres. Eliot, of Harvard, a weak and harmless speech by Pres. Gilman, and two Latin songs judiciously administered to the audience by the Glee Club. Pres. Eliot is a man worth seeing and worth hearing. His features are of that striking, clear-cut type wh. bespeaks energy, intelligence, and high purpose, and his address was such as you would have expected from a man of such a mien. His subject was "Liberal Education," and his treatment held a mixed audience of about seven hundred people in the intense silence of eager attention for full an hour and a half.

I am afraid, my darling, that you will find one of the volumes of the edition of Ruskin I sent yesterday rather clumsy. I was rather disappointed in the edition. It was not quite what I expected from the fact that it was the edition being bought by some of our professors here. But it's better than none at all. When we get rich we can get a better.

Give my love to all at 143, to Mrs. D., and to your "better half." I am anxious to see the photo. of the latter—as also the one of little Ellen. I love you with my whole heart and shall ever be

Your own   Woodrow.

ALS (WC, NjP).

[1] It was held in connection with the "First Annual Symposium" of the Maryland Alpha Chapter of the Phi Kappa Psi Fraternity, held at Guy's Hotel, Baltimore, Feb. 21, 1884.

From Ellen Louise Axson

My darling Woodrow,   Savannah, Feb. 25/84.

I am *afraid* I must postpone my regular letter to another night, as it is already so late; and I am so *sleepy*,—though, as you may observe, I don't speak with any certainty on the subject, since for aught I know, this may turn out no shorter than the one of Friday night. The length of my epistles, as well as the matter thereof, seems to be a thing for fate to determine, not I,—and since I can't foresee the result when I begin to write, it is wisest to avoid *attempting* anything like prophesy.

But what do you suppose I have been doing all the evening? Listening to an address by a *woman*! I went out of curiosity, accompanying Grandfather, who with the face of a martyr, went "because his absence would be noticed." We both came back delighted; that is we were forced to admit that, while she "had'nt oughter" be doing it, she certainly did it well. But I have no doubt she is one of the best of the lot. It was Mrs. H. W. Smith who wrote the "Christian's Secret of a Happy Life,"[1] &c. &c. She is a warm, personal friend of Mrs. Green,[2] and I have heard so much of her that I was curious to see her. She has one of the best of faces; and I have no doubt has many very fine qualities—one of them, the finishing touch as it were, being her good taste—her tact. As Grandfather remarked, "she was equally good in what she said and what she did not say."

Many, many thanks, dearest, for the "Modern Painters," which was received today. I can't tell you how delighted I am to own it, or how much I shall enjoy it;—to do so, it would be necessary for me to compute the number of times that I have wished for it heretofore, for that will be the measure of my enjoyment of it in the future. This is a very nice edition too, more complete than the one I was familiar with, in that it has the wood-cuts. And though Ruskin does'nt need the power of association to make his volumes charming, they certainly *have* gained an additional charm from coming as your gift.

No, I have not read "Lorna Doone," and I pledge myself to "touch not, taste not, handle not," until I can enjoy it with you. You have greatly excited my interest in it; and I anticipate a charming treat. Speaking of the "early-England air["]—I picked up a few days ago that old "Harper," which came while you were here, and found myself reading the chapter it contained of "Judith Shakspeare" by Wm. Black.[3] I remember wondering then who had been taking liberties with that name;—but I find it is a greater liberty than I supposed. It seems Judith was Shakspeare's own daughter,—I remember the name now in the will;—the scene is laid at Avon, and the "Swan" himself is one of the principal characters. What do you think of such audacity? It gave me very much the same *shocked* sensation as those books, in which the Bible characters are introduced, marrying and giving in marriage, and talking trite and feeble commonplaces, which are certainly none the less dull for being delivered in a stilted, "antique" style. For instance, "The Prince of the House of David," in which Mary the sister of Martha is engaged to the son of the Widow of Nain, &c. &c.[4] Did you ever read it? *I hav'nt*. Rose is *raving* over another book of that sort now;—"Ben Hur," a new, and *strictly original* life of our Lord,[5] from the cradle to the tomb. It must be peculiarly adapted to the tastes and needs of young "Church women" with a slight tinge of the devotee about them; for Beth [Erwin] too was beside herself about it last summer. She says, Mr. Randall declares in the Augusta Constitutionalist,[6] that it is "the very *best* thing he ever read"! As if such intemperate praise did'nt do a book more harm than good.

Tuesday morning,—I find I have still time to add a few lines to this before closing; as the mail does'nt leave until afternoon.

What do you suppose Rose and I have been doing? Watching, from afar a very curious sight; the operations of the great "French doctor," the Prince of quacks. He has been the leading excitement here for the last three weeks. He came in literally with the sound of the trumpet—in a wonderful gilded chariot, with a whole brass band mounted behind, and himself and his wife seated in front in royal state; she is a pretty little woman, gorgeously arrayed, and is, they say, a better doctor than the husband. For half of every day they are surrounded by dense crowds, numbering thousands—to say nothing of the fine people in carriages on the out-skirts—who are healed of all their deseases instantaneously, free, gratis, for nothing, and always to the sound of music. They make the blind to see, the deaf to hear, and the paralytic to walk; and they pull out teeth by merely touching them so that the people don't even know they are gone! It is the most curious sight I ever witnessed. We did nothing but laugh over it at first, but now, though we certainly don't believe, we are all sorely puzzled. Miss Allie saw two of the doctors watching, and asked them what *they* thought of it. Dr. Charlton[7] said he thought they were making lots of money, and he wished he could make it as fast!—they do that by selling their medicine; the cures are free. Dr. Thomas said he did'nt know what to think, there was evidently *something* in it. The man says, by-the-way, that the doctors of New York paid him I forget how many thousands to leave the place. He is very free with his money, scatters dimes among all the children in the crowd; and when he cures a man enquires what his day's wages are, and if it is necessary for him to "lay up" for three or four days, pays him the full sum for that time, that he may lose nothing. We have been amusing ourselves in the family, trying to induce Grandfather to go and have *his* ears opened. I told him I would go too, if he would, or even lead the way, and let him experiment on me first! The process is very simple; he merely rubs some "Chinese perfume" (!) on the ear. The best of the joke is that Grandfather is strongly tempted to go; says he would, if it could be done in private, but he can't make an exhibition of himself!

But I really must close, for I have some aprons to make today, for Mr Johnson,[8] the missionary, and the heathen Chinee. I shall write him—not the Chinee—a letter, and enclose them,—they are very nearly small enough, and I think they will be almost as serviceable as the famous "blankets and top-boots" were to the Sandwich Islanders. I will give your sweet messages to Papa, my darling, and he will appreciate them as much as I do. I enclose a letter from Dr. Hall[9] to Minnie [Hoyt], which give a fuller report than anything they have ever written us.

All here, including Mrs. Duncan, send you their love. Give mine to your dear parents and brother; and remember, dearest, that I love you better even than you know,

Yours with all my heart,   Ellie.

ALS (WP, DLC).

[1] Hannah Whitall Smith, *The Christian's Secret of a Happy Life* (Chicago, 1883).

[2] Aminta Green, widow of Charles Green, of 353 Park Avenue, Baltimore, an old friend of the Axsons.

[3] William Black's *Judith Shakespeare* (New York, 1884), first appeared in installments in *Harper's New Monthly Magazine* from Jan. 1884 to Nov. 1884. ELA was probably reading the first installment.

[4] J. H. Ingraham, *The Prince of the House of David* (New York, 1855).

[5] Lew Wallace, *Ben-Hur, a Tale of the Christ* (New York, 1880).

[6] James Ryder Randall, editor of the Augusta *Chronicle and Constitutionalist*.

[7] Thomas J. Charlton, M.D., physician in Savannah.

[8] The Rev. James Francis Johnson, Presbyterian missionary in Hangchow, China, 1882-88.

[9] The physician attending S. E. Axson at the Milledgeville asylum. His letter is missing.

To Ellen Louise Axson

My own darling,   Balto., Md., Feb'y 26, 1884

May you never be able to write a short letter to me, and may you often be impelled to write! Ellie, I do'nt believe there's another little lady in the land who can write such charming letters to her lover as you write to me; and I know that there's not a lover in the land who is made happier by such proofs of his lady-love's affection than I am! I'd rather be loved by a certain lass in Savannah whom I know than be famous—and every time a letter from her tells me of her love I feel that it will be easy to become famous. But not by means of the contemplated history of American political economy! I do'nt know, my darling, *what* that will come to. It remains to be seen, of course, whether it will ever be anything more than a plan. We shall have a try at it and see what can be done, the ultimate success depending mainly on Dr. Ely's enterprize and business sense. The Dr's style is not forceful. He has too unerring a scent for the weaker forms and combinations of our tongue ever to achieve any reputation for brilliancy of treatment. But he writes smoothly, clearly, and grammatically and is quite full of encyclopaedic matter and Germanic doctrine. He is the author of a little book, of somewhat the same order as the one proposed, and which has been received with considerable favour. It is entitled "French and German Socialism of Modern Times,"[1] and answers excellently well for a single reading, though hardly able to bear a careful reperusal such as I gave it in preparing for an examination on the subject two or three months ago. Dewey, my proposed co-labourer, is a fine fellow with a clear head and an earnest desire to do good work—probably the best man that Ely could have chosen out of the class, for the preparation of the part assigned him. Yes, my darling, if the work goes on in earnest, it will involve an immense amount of reading, and reading of the sort which is most irksome to me—the reading of books good, bad, and indifferent, of *all* the "literature" that bears upon the subject. It will hardly be possible to accomplish the task this term—in the four months remaining—and some parts of it may have to constitute some part of my *recreation* next summer. If so, I shall have to get you to read me a great deal of your favourite poetry as an antidote. By-the-way, my bonny lassie, do you realize that it is only four months before this "horrid grind" will be over and I will be free to come to see you? I hereby give you four months' warning that it is my fixed and unalterable determination to spend as much of the vacation with you as possible; and I think it my duty, therefore, to advise you to make up your mind to spend at least half the summer in Wilmington. Father and mother are as anxious to have you as I am—if anybody *can* want you as much as I do—and you shall be as much your own mistress there as you could be in your own home. My advice, please observe, is not *altogether* prompted by my natural desire to reconcile my wish to be with the dear home-folks who love and want me so much with my all-controlling wish to be with the fair maiden who has stolen my heart and who is so welcome to it; but that the plan proposed involves many substantial advantages for *you*. Common prudence dictates that you should seek an opportunity to observe me at home where you may see me domesticated and relieved of my "company manners" (if I happen to have any such). How else, pray, can you find out with any degree of certainty whether or not you will find my company endurable when—when you have to put up with it all the time? Of course I mean to be very, very sweet to you all the time; but you are not supposed to know that, and may reasonably expect to catch me now and then in a very ugly temper when you come to watch me in my native haunts, where everybody puts up with me and indulges me to the top of my bent: for nothing tests the temper more thoroughly than does "spoiling." Besides, your visit would be an act of true benevolence to my dear parents, for of course so long as I was at home and away from you I should be very cross and discontented, "sighing like a furnace" and altogether a "tip-top" nuisance. I know, my darling, that you can't tell now *what* you can or cannot do next summer—because you cannot know what there may be to hinder your leaving home—but I am counting on its proving necessary for you to leave Savannah for part of the summer, and I know that you will promise me to do what I have so set my heart upon, *if it is at all possible.* By-the-way, *where* does Miss Rosalie expect to see me next summer? If she has fallen in love with your description of me, it would probably be my wisest plan to avoid her, for I can't possibly satisfy that description, and I am sure that you don't want her to lose faith in the wisdom of your choice. I have something to add to that description, however, which will, haply, fortify her against all possible disappointments on the score of my other qualities: Tell her *that you love me* and that I love you as fervently as "Mc" loves her (you need not say 'more fervently,' though that's my own opinion—for I have crowded as much love into ten months as he has spread through his whole lifetime)[.] By the first statement she will be convinced of my merit, and in the second she will instinctively recognize a bond of sympathy between herself and me.

It was very sweet and thoughtful of you, my precious Ellie, to send me your dear father's letter. I found it intensely interesting as an index of his condition—and exceedingly comforting. My only embarrassment was that I had nothing with which to *compare* it: for it was the only letter of his I ever saw—save those few lines he wrote me sanctioning our engagement, and which I regard as one of my treasures—and I could not tell, therefore, whether he wrote like his former self or not. I could see only that he could scarcely at any time have written more naturally or lucidly, with more perfect self-command. He seems to have been entirely himself when he wrote, and it must be, my darling, that the disease is already measurably losing its hold. It seems to me that we have every reason to be comforted and to hope that he will *soon* be restored to us in perfect health and faculty. I was very much touched by his kind allusion to me. I am *so* thankful that our engagement is a source of happiness to him! Tell him, my love, of my love and admiration for him, whenever you write. What have we to *fear*, my darling, with reference to him when his letters show him so steadfast and unclouded in his love for God and his trust in His Providence? There is light enough in that to drive away all the darkness of the present sorrow.

Don't forget to send me little Ellen's picture, as you promise.

I love that little maiden wonderfully well. Give her a great many kisses for me, and give my love to Dr. and Mrs. Axson, your uncle and aunt, "cousin" Leila, and the dear children—even that rascal Randolph! What message shall I send to you, my peerless little sweetheart? I cannot say more than that *I love you with all my heart* and shall always be   Your own   Woodrow.

Love to Miss Rosalie and Mrs. Duncan.

ALS (WP, DLC).
¹ Richard T. Ely, *French and German Socialism in Modern Times* (New York, 1883).

From Edward Ireland Renick

My dear Wilson: Washington D.C. Feby 28/84.
    Both your letter & the "Day" have come to me. I shall be very glad to help you, and shall gather up carefully all I can, to give you. At present I feel somewhat like the man who makes but 1/19 of the pin—& who knows only how that part of it is done—the difference being that I do not know well even my own especial work as yet. . . .
    [Renick here describes the functions of the First and Second Comptrollers and of the Comptroller of the Currency and the Treasury Department's auditing and quasi-judicial responsibilities and practices.]
    Can I not be told more of your Rome affair? I often think of your enthusiastic account of her who had "brown eyes & read what we read." I have a nice room—4th storey—of a house in which you never see any body or hear a sound. Come over some Sat. & spend it & Sunday with me. Bed, little narrow, but weather cold. Gaddy got a little puppy to comfort him. Mrs [James S.] Turpin breaks up on March 1st—& is coming here. I hope to come to Balto. before long. If you come before you hear again, make for 1342 N.Y. Avenue.   Yours as ever,   Renick

ALS (WP, DLC) with WWhw notation on env.: "Ans. March 3/84."

To Ellen Louise Axson

My own darling,   Balto., Md., Feb'y 28th/84
    Mr. Shinn, who is constantly manifesting great solicitude regarding my entertainment and the advancement of my acquaintance with "light" literature, has just brought me in Henry James's "Bundle of Letters," insisting that I can read them "in a few minutes": for I a few moments ago confessed to him, very in-

discreetly, that I had never read *anything* of James's. But I think —don't you?—that the perusal of this budget of letters "from Miss Miranda Hope, in Paris," &c. may very well be postponed to the present and much more inviting pleasure of writing a letter of my own to my little queen "away down South in Dixie."

Your letter of Monday, with its wonders of lady orators and street healers, reached me this morning—for this is one of the Thursdays about which my weeks revolve—and has lighted up my spirits as all your sweet letters do. I was *very* much interested in and encouraged by the contents of Dr. Hall's note to your cousin. It has about it the oracular reserve peculiar to the opinions of physicians, but shows quite enough of the doctors' hopes to give us reassurance in our hopes.

I consider it very odd, miss, that you should be making aprons "for Mr. Johnson, the missionary," and feel myself growing more and more jealous, the more I think about it, that it has not occurred to you to make *me* some! Besides, consider how you are misleading the poor man! What encouragement may he not find, or imagine that he finds, in *aprons*? How can you have the heart to trifle with his affections in this subtle, insinuating fashion! But the worst of the matter is that you close your letter to *me* in order to make Mr. Johnson's aprons. If you should happen not to hear from me for some weeks, you may know that it is because I've gone to China to intercept that gift and reckon with the missionary—or else that I am sore because of the slight put upon me!

I am delighted that you have not read "Lorna Doone" for I had quite set my heart upon sharing the pleasure you will have in first reading it. In my opinion it is safe to rank amongst our "classics." I suspect that you are quite right in your estimate of "Ben Hur"—for I too have observed that it is most "raved" over amongst Episcopalians of an impressionable type. I have looked into it enough to find that it contains some fine descriptions of the scenery of Judea—rather *too* "fine" indeed, being coloured quite beyond "the modesty of nature"; but excellent samples of a strong style of word-painting such as one would rather read than produce. Mr. Wallace sees much more in nature than nature could reasonably lay claim to possessing; but his nature is a very gorgeous creature, fit enough for the unnatural stage upon which he exhibits her. We dry fellows who write upon constitutional subjects and try to crack nuts of government with our hard heads can but look in amazement at such rhetoric, and count ourselves happy if we escape humiliating awe in its presence. We may not dress our periods in such stately style, but must content ourselves with parading dull facts and talking plain sense. We must eschew "fine writing" and masquerade as men of judgment, men of affairs who can "talk business"—But enough! I've written all this nonsense only to pay you off for the aprons! I love you, all the same, with all my heart and will always be,

                                  Your own   Woodrow.

ALS (WC, NjP).

From Edward Ireland Renick

Dear Wilson: Washington D.C. [c. March 2, 1884]

At the 1st Comptroller's Office I have found a pamphlet containing about 337 pages. It is the "Letter from the Secretary of the Treasury," sent in obedience to sections 3669, 3670 and 3672 of the Revised Statutes, which letter contains estimates of appropriations for the service of the fiscal year ending June 30, 1885.

These estimates are furnished by the several Executive Departments to the Sec'y of the Treas., who transmits them to the House of Representatives. Along with these estimates, he sends statements of the "proceeds of sales of Government property and the expenditures of the moneys appropriated for contingent expenses of the Independent Treasury for the fiscal year 1883."

This letter, I am told, is referred to the Committee on Appropriations alone. The Committee on Rivers & Harbors have referred to it the portion of the report touching upon such matters. As well as I am informed—this is all. There is no conference of the two committees—Ways & Means & Appropriations.

Doubtless Mr. Folger would, if requested, send you a copy of this "letter."

You would much oblige me by telling me anything that you discover of which you have the merest idea that I am ignorant. By accident I pick up such items as the following:

The Home Department was created in 1849; Office of Deputy Comptroller in 1875. I should like to know all such matters. I have been trying to learn all the steps taken before money can be gotten out of the Treasury.

The account or claim is first passed upon by an auditor who certifies a balance to the proper Comptroller, who in turn certifies it to the Secretary of the Treas., who issues a warrant for the amount, which warrant, if authorized by law, is countersigned by the 1st Compt., recorded by the Register of the Treas., and the money upon it paid by the Treas., who takes a receipt therefor. If you have some specific questions, I shall take much pleasure in trying to secure answers to them. I thought I would write what I have written while it was fresh in mind. Hoping to hear soon,   I am as ever,   Yours sincerely   Renick

ALS (WP, DLC) with WWhw notation on env.: "Ans. March 3/84." Enc.: Renick's hw outline of structure of United States Government and list headed "Estimates for 1885."

To Ellen Louise Axson, with Enclosure

My own darling,   Balto., Md., March 2nd/84

I am finding abundant reasons all the time for wishing that you were here, but most of them are selfish reasons, I am afraid, so that it is some relief to my conscience to be able to announce one which is very substantial and at the same time quite unselfish. How I do wish that you could come on (to see Mrs. Green, say!) to see Mr. Walters's art collection![1] The newspaper clipping I enclose describes but a very small part of it and is, besides, miserably written, it seems to me. It is apparently taken for granted by the writer that everyone knows that Mr. Walters's residence and gallery are in Baltimore. There seems to be no question about this collection's being the finest private collection in this country, and I have been assured by a lady of some artistic training that she saw no gallery in Europe more *uniformly* stocked with masterpieces—with more things of beauty and less trash in it—than this. I have not visited it yet, but of course I shall do so, probably more than once, though I shall doubtless enjoy it after a very ignorant fashion. I'll know what is beautiful, but not why it's beautiful. I'll enjoy the play, as Parrot (?) did, but may not be able to tell which is the best actor. Oh that my darling were here! then I could see it through her beautiful eyes and enjoy it tenfold because of her delight! Well, well! this waiting is a dreary, heart-sickening business; but the day's coming, my love, for all it's dragging its pace so slowly, when you and I shall share all our joys—even joys such as these. We'll visit great galleries *some day* together; wont we? In the meantime, though I can't offer to be your convenient, escorting "man around" while you study in the great metropolis, I can promise to be something else to you which I am sure you will think much better.

At present, quite "unbeknownst" to you (though you shall know it now, lest I should lose the credit due me), I am making a fright of myself for your sake. I am letting my hair grow for the sake of the lock you want and made me promise to save for you;

and as my hair is very thick and by no means disposed to submit mildly to conventional forms, I am becoming daily more and more like a mop in appearance. You may imagine how extremely trying it is to me to have this cloud hang upon the manly beauty of which I am so proud: especially in view of the fact that I recently received a call from a very wealthy gentleman who has an attractive daughter and shall have to return his call before I can in good conscience be shorn! Being a provident young gentleman in all things, I must "see this business out," now that I have gone so far in it, because it is much less onerous to raise locks in cool weather than it would be in summer.

I know that you will laugh at the extract I enclose, from my brother's last letter to me: and maybe you will think that I ought to be ashamed of myself for "giving away" the dear boy so heartlessly. But he need not (and I think he *does* not) expect me to keep *anything* from *you*; and, besides, you ought to know, I suppose, (painful as the revelation may be to us) what a fickle and mercenary family you are about to enter. Still, at present, the whole of that family seems to be in love with you, judging from the way they talk.

Give my love to your dear father, Ellie, and to all at 143. As for one little maiden who dwells there, I love and long for her more and more every moment of my life.

Your own   Woodrow.

ALS (WC, NjP).

¹ A large collection of paintings and Oriental bronzes, carvings, enamels, and other *objets d'art* collected by W. T. Walters of Baltimore was placed on exhibit early in March 1884 at the Walters Gallery under the auspices of the Decorative Art Society. Among the paintings were notable examples of various schools and techniques. A detailed description of the exhibition appeared in the New York *Nation*, xxxviii (March 6, 1884), 219-20.

E N C L O S U R E

Extract from Josie's letter:

"You will be, or possibly you will *not* be, surprised to hear that I have given up Katie Reston and have another sweetheart. Katie did not send me any Valentine and seemed to think that she had me all safe and sound no matter what she did, so I gave her up and took Carrie Maffitt, a girl who had showed, or rather *had been* showing her preference for *me*. I have her picture now, and a lock of hair. She has also promised me a hat band, and I did not ask for it either. She is a "hot girl." Don't you make fun of her as you did of Katie Reston."

WWhw (WC, NjP), from J. R. Wilson, Jr., to WW, Feb. 29, 1884, ALS (WP, DLC) with WWhw notation on env.: "Ans. 3/2/84."

From Ellen Louise Axson

My darling Woodrow,   Savannah, Mar. 3/84.

Yours of the 28th, after some little delay I presume, reached me safely this morning;—reached me, too, after rather an unusual fashion. I was down town doing a little shopping for Aunt Ella. At the door of one of the stores I encountered our post-man, who, as soon as he saw me, began fumbling in his package, and finally produced your letter, which he handed me, with a polite smile and bow. Isn't he a jewel of a postman? Sav. is really a model place—it combines the advantages of a city—we *do* have carriers, —and a village,—the carrier knows all about you, and your affairs, and takes a pleasant neighbourly interest in them, like the village post-mistress. It is because the place is of such a convenient size —not very little and not very big. Though it is'nt altogether "Bill Arp's" ideal—"a place too large for gossip, and too small for pestilence, pick-pockets, and professional beggars"!

It *certainly isnt* too large for gossip! I had a remarkable note the other day, from one of the girls who, though quite a good friend of mine, is by no means a confidential friend. She writes to tell me how very glad she is "to hear of my engagement[.]" "The love of a good man is certainly a great blessing. I feel exceedingly happy about this, dear Ellen, and hope you will allow me to share your joy" (!) &c. &c.—in short, "down on your knees and thank God, fasting, for a good man's love"! But the funny part was her writing me so, upon mere rumour! I was rather astonished, though I might have known that it was no secret; for your being here was as good as a picnic,—or even a grand funeral, —to the servants. The children have made so many remarks in which the words "sweet-heart" and "Mr Wilson" play a prominent part, that I, long ago, became convinced that it was time to *break the connection.* It was slightly discomposing. Bold measures were evidently necessary, and, you will wonder at my audacity, but by repeatedly and solemnly asserting that my sweet-heart is named *"Mr. Thomas,"* together with skillful evasions whenever the word "Wilson" is mentioned I have, not convinced them exactly, but puzzled them very considerably. "But," they say, "he *must* be your sweet-heart, because he came to see you"; and then I proceed carefully to demonstrate that there is *nothing* in *that.* It don't amount to *anything*!

It is at Sewanee, Sir, that Rose proposes to see you next summer. She has announced—some few hundred times—that it is her royal will and pleasure that I accompany her home in April, and remain until next *winter*! She sends *you* a cordial invitation to the mountain;—says "if you come *we*"—she & I—"will try and make you think it as delightful as she does herself";—which is saying a great deal, for with her, the sun itself revolves around that particular hill-top. She says she is very much obliged for your message,—sending her your love—but that Mac is ahead of you, after all, for he sends *his* love not only to me but to *you*! Do you know that incorrigible Mac is actually coming *here* this week, to stay as long as Rose does! *Can't* stay away! Did you ever hear of two such simpletons? I *did* think his family could manage to keep him with them through *one* vacation, after being with her steadily, all these years! If it was anyone but Mac I should be highly indignant, feeling that he was infringing upon *my* rights, invading *my* domain. But Mac is "so lovely," that I am really glad he is coming,—he is'nt a spoilsport at all.

I must tell you again how much I appreciate your invitation to Wilmington, my darling. You may be sure that you have my best thanks for it—though *thanks* indeed is all I can send at present. I am altogether at sea, and have no idea whither I am drifting. I shall think it very pleasant if the winds blow me into Wilmington,—and that's all I know about it!

Your letter telling about your "terrible dissipations" has been received, I believe, since I last wrote, as well as the paper containing the synopsis of Pres. Eliot's address. I liked the latter extremely. Wish I could have heard it. Oh dear, how I *do love* fine speaking, and good lectures! It is the most delightful thing in the world, almost. That is one great advantage there is in being a man—one can hear so much more of it!

I am glad you have been having such good times, and that University life is'nt quite "all work and no play." What is the object of the Secret Society? Simply to furnish the *play*? Though perhaps *that* is the secret!

You have my deepest sympathy in the task which lies before you—"the reading of all the literature—good[,] bad and indifferent, which bears upon your subject." I can imagine the weary waste of "documents" over which you must travel. Who is it who says that nine-tenths of all good work is *drudgery*? I hope that is an over-estimate, but the amount of it which historians are probably called upon to endure in collecting materials is something fearful to contemplate. I have often been *awe-struck* when some note or chance remark gave a hint of the stupendous burrowing among mouldy papers and dusty pamphlets, necessary to the making up of half a dozen charming pages, over which one glides so smoothly and easily. Don't you wish you could draw on your "imagination for your facts," like the romancers?

By-the-way, I am curious to know what you think of Henry James, when you finish your "Bundle of Letters"; though I have never read that book, and don't know whether it is a fair specimen of his style. So you did'nt examine "The Portrait of a Lady," when it was "all the rage,"—have never made the acquaintance of "Miss Archer," "the spontaneous young woman from Albany"!

I enclose one of Ellen's "Sir Joshua" pictures;—have but one of the other kind left;—am sorry, for I would like you to see them both. Or stay—I will send both, and if it is'nt too much trouble you can return the one with the large hat. It is that, which Mr Havens thinks so remarkably fine; but, as Carrie Belle says, the other is the "cutest."

I hav'nt induced Rose to sit for her picture yet, though I still hope to succeed with Mac's help, and an occasional word from Grandmother. I never saw an *old* lady who was such a passionate admirer of beauty and grace, as G-mother. It is really difficult for her to *like* a woman who is'nt pretty! She could never altogether fancy Anna [Harris]—though she knew her to be a noble girl,—because she was awkward, and had a rather loud voice. But Rose, with her lovely face, her soft, low voice, and her sweet, gentle manner has stolen her heart completely.

But I *must* close—much against my will. Give much love to your father and mother. You did not tell me whether they are quite well again or no. We have heard nothing special from Papa since I last wrote, but have had pleasant letters from himself.

With truest love, believe me, dearest, to be,

Your own Ellie.

Pray excuse this *horrible* scrawl. I can scarcely make it out myself. It is positively *insulting* to send such a thing to anyone. But you should hear the Bable in which I have been trying to write, and I think you would then understand.

ALS (WP, DLC).

To Ellen Louise Axson

My own darling,   Balto., Md., March 4th/84

I am in a somewhat comical state just now about my work. I have finished the essay upon which I have been at work for the past month[1] and should be about beginning the next essay of the series: but my muse refuses to be forced. She never allows me freedom at the first in any undertaking. She reminds me that the first broadside is half the battle and that it is folly to waste my shot unskilfully at the opening of an action, and so tortures me for days together with debating various plans for the fight. It is my fixed rule to begin with directness, without manoeuvering or ado, and, consequently, I have to devote much care to selecting just the right point of attack in order that the action may become general without loss of time. But this belligerent metaphor is'nt quite what I want, because it represents me as battling *against* my subject rather than *for* it, and because it is much too magnificent. One would suppose, from the tones and the tropes in which I speak of my arduous literary labours that I was writing at least an epic or a system of philosophy, instead of some very commonplace remarks upon a familiar subject. I observe that I am much grander and more impressive when speaking *of* my subject than when speaking *on* it; for, though I have spoken to many of my companions about my work, only one of them understands just what it is. I discovered, only a few minutes ago, that one of them thought that I was engaged in writing a *history* of the Constitution; and I suppose that even a dear little lady away off in the far South, who knows all the secrets of my heart, will smile in puzzled amusement when she reads what I have written: for, you see, the one man who sees into my plan *has heard me read my first essay.* I must talk very big and do very little to have given everybody so exaggerated an idea of the scope of my studies. I am much too young an eagle to try the long flight they expect to see me take. I am content for the present to explore the native mountain in the immediate neighbourhood of the nest, reserving the pleasures of distant explorations to a time of stronger wings and longer pinion. I guess that the truth of the matter is, that I have spoken so knowingly of several distant peaks, which can barely be descried on a clear morning from the crag just over the nest that my innocent companions have concluded that I must have often been far abroad. Indeed, I sometimes *feel* like a hum*bug* rather than a royal bird. Your noisy humbug is a great braggart, tho.' he can never look the sun in the face or beat a tireless flight through the free air of the high heavens. It must be worth while to be a genuine eagle, born with an eagle's spirit. It's something, in the first place, to begin life on a mountain-top where the eye is not stopped in its view by your neighbor's stupid, square brick house with its chintz curtains at the windows. There's education in a "birds-eye" view. Then, too, its better to swing in independent flight from top to top than to be all your life flocking and nest-building and chat-tering with innumerable commonplace little birds in the branches of a tree which is, even at its highest twig, very near the ground after all. The only difficulty is that when you want company there are not eagles enough to make it. It's all well enough to make notable passages over wide continents and see noble stretches of the world, but it's lonely to do it all alone, and after it's done, no-body's the better but yourself. Eagle life is very selfish, as I heard many an aged eagle confess, with a sigh because he had'nt had a hand in dropping leaves upon the sleeping babes in the wood. It must be right chilly up on the dizzy crags when one gets old and feels his feathers growing thin! The war-horse that carries his spurred and belted rider to the field no doubt rejoices to smell the battle afar off and runs a short career of glorious excitement; but I suspect that his old age is not blessed with as pleasant and goodly memories as are the last days of some sturdy servant of the plow who can look back over long seasons of golden harvests. And so it is with the eagle: there's no one to bury him, and no work interrupted when he dies. He's been a great, mayhap a famous, traveller; but travelling do'nt hasten the millennium. The fact of the matter is, that it's hard to find anything to do when one lives away from the haunts of ordinary birds, and I shall be glad to recount my pedigree to my fellows and demonstrate my right (as well as the necessity that is laid upon me) to perform very humble tasks in the economy of the bird universe. And yet one can't help recurring regretfully to the advantages of wings built for long flights. How much one could see. He might make easy stages to the South and study Southern life and customs. What could be more diverting than to see two maidens, each look-ing in her beauty like the other's other self, giving the brightness of their eyes, meant to speak love, not to follow farces, all morn-ing to the taking performances—and their pretty ears meant to hear love, to the conned deceptions—of a notable quack. I've been told that such things may now and then be seen, by a bird who's there in season, in a city of the South. But then, when one comes to think of it, it's easy enough to see similar scenes elsewhere. Have I not seen a young man of my acquaintance stand for an hour or more listening to street quacks whom he despised, but whom he suffered to amuse him? He did not have charms that might have been better employed, as did the maidens of the story, and so was not wasting them, but he might have been laughed at by his friends had they seen him. Moreover, an eagle might be better engaged than in spying out young ladies much wiser than himself, at whom he could not afford to laugh. It is to be suspected that, instead of being amused by the sight of those two lovely maidens, he would only be vexed and discontented—because he was not a man—a young and handsome man—who could stand by their side and make their beauty his own for a season: for I have heard many things of one of those fair damsels which would make any bird of sense wish himself a man a thousand times a day, if he might win her favour. Doubtless she is a great force in this world: for it has always stood as one of the primal truths that the love of a pure woman can make and unmake kingdoms—or, at least, make or unmake *men*—and do not men move kingdoms? What would the world be like if Woodrow were not loved by his matchless Ellie, and Ellie were not loved by

Her own   Woodrow?

ALS (WC, NjP).
1 The second chapter of *Congressional Government*.

From John Hanson Kennard, Jr.[1]

My dear Wilson,   New Orleans, La., March 5th 1884.
. . . I am still desolé over my withdrawal from our seminary and after the delightful compliment you paid me in your letter I am more anxious than ever to be with you. . . .[2] I shall never cease to regret that I missed that course of constitutional reading with you; for although I shall try and read the books you have so kindly mentioned it will not by any means be the same thing as reading with you. I am sure you will make a hit with your His. of Amer. P. E.[3] and shall look forward to the publication of the work with much interest. I expect, however, the the [sic] book will be kangaroo in its character, viz; all its strength will lie in its tail, i.e., in the last chapters. . . .

Remember me most kindly to Shinn. I hope you will allow this poor letter to serve as one of the links in the chain that is, I hope, to hold us together until we meet again.

Very sincerely,   Your friend   J. H. Kennard Jr.

ALS (WP, DLC).
1 John Hanson Kennard, Jr., lawyer. Born, Wilkinson County, Miss., 1862; attended Roanoke College; B.A., University of Louisiana, 1882; student at The Johns Hopkins University, first term, 1883-84; LL.B., Tulane University, 1886. Practiced law in New Orleans, 1886-98. President Southern League of Building and Loan Associations, 1891-97; president Interstate League of Building and Loan Associations, 1894-98; moved to New York in Dec. 1897 as editor *Savings and Loan Review*. Admitted to New York bar 1905 and practiced in New York until death on March 7, 1939.
2 See J. H. Kennard, Jr., to WW, Feb. 14, 1884, ALS (WP, DLC) with WWhw notation on env.: "Ans. 2/24/84." In this letter, Kennard told of his withdrawal from the Johns Hopkins.
3 The projected "History of Political Economy in the United States."

From Joseph R. Wilson, Jr.

My dearest brother: Wilmington N.C. March 5th 84.

I received you[r] sweet letter yesterday morning, and was *so* glad to get it.

Our debating club at it's meeting last evening decided to have a public debate at the end of the session—(the last of May)[.] There is to be a President's address, an oration, a declamation, and then the debate—with three members on each side. It is to be on the stage in the hall up at Miss Bradleys school. I am President *now*, and was elected President for the night of our public debate,—so *I* will have to deliver the President's address. I would like to give a history of the society from the time it was organized up to the present time—giving the objects of it &c. *Please help me.* . . .

I do not change my sweet-hearts so often because I am fickle, but because I find they wont have *me*, and I am *certainly* not going to have a girl who wont have *me*. Carrie Maffitt reciprocates my feelings towards her. I know she does because she said she loved me. *I* said *I* loved *her,* and so *she* said the same thing about *me*. You are very much mistaken if you think that I am going to let *you* get ahead of *me* in courting. Not a bit of it. I have Carrie's picture, a lock of hair, and she lent me one of her rings. I am all "hot" and dont you forget it. . . .

Mama and Papa join me in more love than words can express. Love for Miss Ellie.   Your loving brother   Joseph.

Did you receive papa's enclosure mailed last Saturday?[1]

ALS (WP, DLC) with WWhw notation on env.: "Ans. March 9th/84."
  [1] A check for $50, enclosed in JRW to WW, March 3, 1884, ALS (WP, DLC).

From Ellen Louise Axson

My darling Woodrow,   Savannah March 7/84.

I have come to the conclusion that, though there are a dozen other things, which I probably ought to be doing, I *must* write to you tonight;—primarily, to thank you for the delightful little book received yesterday; and, in the second place to console myself for the sight which I have recently witnessed,—Rose and Mac vanishing around the street corner together!

First about the book, which made a nice little surprise for me, yesterday and about which, by-the-way, you[r] letter of today says nothing. I read the greater part of it last night, enjoyed it extremely, and am *so* much obliged to you for it. One charm about these lectures, I think, is the delightful glimpse they give of Ruskin himself, in his old age.

I had read none of his recent writings, and I see a decided change since the days of the "Modern Painters": while losing none of his early enthusiasm, he has grown much softer, more genial, less intolerant. While loving his old friends no less, he seems to have added many new ones to his list. Nothing could be prettier or more graceful than some of his allusions to younger artists, especially since we know that, like everything Ruskin says, they have the nobler virtue of perfect sincerity.

I do indeed heartily echo your wish that I might see the Walters collection. I have heard of it often—in my "Art Treasures of America" it takes a prominent place. You must tell me what you think of it, and whose pictures you like best. Mrs. Green is here now, came last Friday, will remain two weeks. Will the exhibition last so long? Perhaps I might run up for a day or so, with her! Grandmother called on her, day before yesterday,—she had heard of you, was very curious about you, and wanted to interview me on the subject. I hav'nt seen her alone yet,—dare say, she will scold me for not volunteering the desired information, long ago.

By-the-way, I have a good joke on you! one too good to keep, though it includes others much more terrible upon myself. Tuesday afternoon I called for Rose, & found her in a great glee over a visit she had just received from Mrs. Olmstead. The latter excited her mirth, in the first place, by enquiring if she knew me. And then those three people,—for Mrs. Anderson[1] too was included,—had the shocking audacity to discuss me, at large. Mrs. Olmstead said she didnt believe I would ever marry,—she never saw a girl who seemed to shrink so from all that sort of thing. "But," she added, rather anxiously, "I met a young *minister*—a Mr. Wilson, at the Doctor's a few weeks ago; he seemed to be staying there; Mrs. Axson brought him in and introduced him— and I took a *perfect antipathy* to him, for I saw he was in love with Ellie. I can't bear to think of her marrying a minister and settling down to that narrow, prosy life (!). But I *can't* think there is anything in it." I must explain that Mrs. Olmstead, though a very lovely lady, is'nt quite so heavenly-minded as her husband,—and it seems that I am a "spirituelle" creature, who should be favoured by fortune with a brighter existence than the Manse affords! "But *ain't* folks funny?" You didn't know you had made enemies, as well as friends, in Sav.—did you? However, I hope Rose made it all right,—for she carefully explained that she had heard of you, and you were *not* a minister,—a statement which was received at first with incredulity, Mrs. O. being so positive that you *must* be one. At all events, Mrs. Duncan's enthusiastic friendship ought to atone. She calls you *her* Mr. Wilson,—says she has adopted you. By-the-way, I am going tomorrow, if I can, to see a famous portrait of her as a young girl. You know, she was exquisitely beautiful; and they say the college boys in Athens *kissed* this picture so much, that they *wore the lips entirely away*!

I *did* enjoy the extract from Josie's letter immensely, though, as you fore-see, I *am* shocked to discover such fickleness to be one of your family traits. Is it common to *all* the members of the family? I enquire with deep anxiety, because I bethink me that neither did *I* send out any valentines this year!

Am sorry you are going through such an ordeal "raising" that "lock." I assure you, I appreciate your efforts most highly, though I did'nt design subjecting you to any such severe test. But I am doing something for you too, Sir, something per-fectly *aw*-ful!—far beyond "raising locks," but I shan't tell you what it is. And yet it *is* a shame that "I should lose the credit due me"! Well then, I am slowly and steadily cutting off both my arms, at the shoulders,—I am *sawing* them off—an eighth of an inch a day. What do you think of that as a proof of affection?

I think it is perhaps fortunate that your muse does'nt permit you to proceed in full career,—an unbroken gallop,—from essay to essay. Probably she would be wiser still if she insisted upon an interval of complete rest,—upon your forgetting all about it, as it were, as judicious ministers forget, on Monday, that there is such a thing as sermon-writing. Have you selected a general title for your essays? Perhaps that, if well-chosen, would serve to explain their nature. I was amused at myself the other day, when trying to tell Rose about your work. I am perfectly clear in my own mind that I knew *exactly* what I was talking about, yet I am disposed to think that I gave some very absurd, some rather paradoxical definitions. And then when asked what it was "called," I could'nt say.

I have specially enjoyed, not only the *ideas* of today's letter, but the imagery in which they were clothed, because you must know that I have birds "on the brain" just at present—and you seem to be in somewhat the same condition! I have just finished reading a book lent me by Mr. Strider,—"The Bird," by Jules Michelet, with two hundred illustrations by Giacomelli. Two of the bird's best friends have thus, as you see, united to do him honour, and it is pre-eminently a labour of love. The drawings

are little gems—they have all the dainty grace which marks Giacomelli's work, and are, beside, exquisite specimens of the English style in wood-engraving with its careful finished workmanship[,] its extreme delicacy of execution.

And Michelet writes about bird life and character so charmingly, so lovingly, dwelling with such tenderness on its joys and
sorrows, it's patient, courageous, watchful love, that really I
would almost as soon kill a baby now as one of these "little children of nature"! His subject is "the Winged Life"—"that strange,
delicate, mighty dream of God." He would tell us something of it's
glory and its pathos; he seeks to give us a glimpse into a nature
"at once above and below our own,"—"the animal nature on the
borders of the life of the angels." But how I rave! What I meant
to say was that Michelet is very unorthodox on the eagle question, and what is more, has the hardihood to publish his heresy
to all the world. He does'nt admit the divine right of the eagle to
reign king of the air; in these pages, he is dethroned, and the
nightingale, and the swallow, reign in his stead. Because in the
bird kingdom rank is not to be decided by brute strength, in which
the mightiest is surpassed by so many other creatures, the real
strength of the bird lies in his powers of song and flight, and the
one who excels in those respects is indeed the royal bird. I am
sure I don't know why I trouble myself to write all this, or you
to read it, yet I am strongly tempted to give you the benefit of one
of his paragraphs on this subject. You may decide for yourself
whether to accept it as consolation for *not* being an eagle, or as a
malicious thrust based on the assumption that you *are* one!
"Whatever pleasure," he says,—["]our personal instincts of violence, our admiration of strength may cause us to take in these
winged robbers, it is impossible to misread in their deathlike
masks the baseness of their nature. The pitifully flattened skull
is the degrading sign of these murderers." . . . "These birds of
prey with their small brains offer a striking contrast to the
plainly intelligent species, which we find among the smaller birds.
The head of the former is only a *beak*; that of the latter has a
face. What comparison can be made between these brute giants
and the intelligent, all-human bird, the robin redbreast. . . . As
for their 'courage' what occasion have they to display it, since
they encounter none but weaker enemies? Enemies? no, victims!
When the rigour of the season, or hunger, drives their young to
emigrate, it leads to the beak of these dull tyrants countless
numbers of innocents, superior in every sense to their murderers; it prodigalizes the birds which are artists, and singers, and

architects, as a prey to these vulgar assassins; and for the eagle and the buzzard provides a banquet of *nightingales*![″]

But enough of all this,—I told you at the beginning that I was daft about birds, at present, and now you must admit that I have proven it.

I am sorry to say that those two maidens, so well described by you, were less fortunate than you suppose—they heard nothing of the great healer's eloquence. They only passed by on the other side while that good Samaritan performed his mission,—or rather they lingered at the door of a store & took a general survey of the scene—the multitude, and it's presiding genius. They could hear not a sound, except music, though they *did* see, a great way off, the chariot and horses, the purple and gold, and—no, I won't vouch for "the fine linen."

We have some little invalids here just now—Ellen fell down, last week, and did not *break* her collarbone exactly,—there is no displacement,—but the Dr. says "*cracked* it badly." It has given her a good deal of pain, and she must wear her arm in a sling for several weeks. Eddie too is unwell,—has a severe cough,— & a curious one too, he coughs incessantly at night, and not a particle during the day. However he seems, and I hope is, better now. Last night he coughed with every breath,—*nothing* could control it: He coughed most of the time in his sleep, but I did'nt close my eyes until five; and as I opened them again at seven, it would perhaps be well to bring this note to an end!

Give much love to your father and mother. I will tell you, in strict confidence, a little discovery of mine, it is this—I love you with all my heart. Mrs. Olmstead would look with wonder in her eyes could she know how entirely "the little proud Wild-heart" is tamed,—how willingly "it abandons liberty for love"!

Good-night, my darling, I am now and always,

Your own Ellie.

ALS (WP, DLC).

[1] Mother of Rosalie, Julie, and Daisy. See also ELA to WW, May 26, 1884, n.1.

To Ellen Louise Axson

My sweet Ellie,   Balto., Md., March 8th/84

That *must* have been an exceedingly refreshing note from the young lady who wished to share your joy in having won "the love of a good man"! That's really an excellent joke—for wit consists in large part of the *unexpected*. As I re-read, a few minutes ago, what you had to say about it in your letter I could'nt help forming the wish that you had mentioned the dear girl's name. How pleased she would have been to receive a letter from a good man, thanking her for having exhibited his character in a new light and for having pointed out so clearly his services to womankind. For you must confess that, to you no less than to me, hers was an entirely new and original view of the case, one which would never have occurred to you, had it not been for her suggestion. It is not uncommon for such new lights to appear to eccentric, unpractical persons—and this delightful young person is evidently extremely unpractical, for I cannot see exactly how she is to be allowed to *share* your joy so long as bigamy is forbidden by the law of the land—not to mention other obstacles which might occur to her upon reflection[.] It can scarcely be consistent with so exemplary a young lady's conception of "a good man" that he should love more than one woman at a time!

So Miss Rose wants to take you off to Sewanee for the next half year, does she? Well, my darling, that would be a very delightful programme for you; but I am selfish enough to regard rather ruefully any such plan of appropriation on her part: for I could'nt possibly take advantage of her generous invitation for more than a few days. You know "Mac." and are used to him, and so are quite safe from having your sport marred by his presence; but Miss Rose *do'nt* know *me*, is *not* used to me, and would have to treat me as a stranger and a guest. Even "Mac.," I imagine, would be a little in your way if both he and Miss Rose were your guests and all your plans with her, for all the day and for every day, had to include him. In short, I would *feel* that I was in the way, whether I was or not,—But I'm talking nonsense, and selfish nonsense at that! I'll promise to do what I can to conform to any plans my darling may choose to make; and I'll not let my shyness or my pride stand in the way of their making. I shall be happiest in the arrangement which will give you most pleasure. I know how much you love to be with Miss Rose, and I'll try not to be jealous if she takes you off to herself. At any rate, I appreciate her invitation very highly indeed, and I am quite sure that, if you and she conspired, you could easily make me think Sewanee the most delightful place on the continent.

I have not been at all well for the past two or three days. A long spell of the worst sort of weather has debarred me from taking my usual exercise, so that I have been literally "under the weather." I sat down on Thursday afternoon to write you a letter, according to my wont, and did succeed in writing about a page; but what I wrote read as badly as I felt, so I gave over the effort, concluding that it would be kinder to disappoint you by withholding the letter you expected than by inflicting upon you such a doleful epistle as I might be able to compose under the circumstances. Besides, I was just then further disturbed by anticipations of what was in store for me that evening. I could not forget the announcements which I had seen on the bulletin-boards at the University: "Thursday, March 6th. There will be a meeting this evening at eight o'clock of the Hopkins Debating Club. Subject: Comparative value of classics and science in a liberal education. For the classics: Mr. Hodges; for the sciences: Mr. Woods.[1] *Mr. Woodrow Wilson has consented to act as critic of the discussion.*" Yes, Mr. Woodrow Wilson *had* been indiscreet enough to consent to do that very thing! The "Hopkins Debating Club" is composed almost entirely of undergraduates, and was ready to believe, upon the representations of some misinformed person, that I was capable of giving it "points," and setting it a fashion in the proper methods of debate, professing to "know of my experience and ability in such exercises." According to contract, therefore, I dragged myself around to the meeting, feeling much more conscious of possessing a body than of possessing a mind, and after the discussion had been concluded—very creditably to both sides—I made a fifteen-minute speech which was most enthusiastically received, but which, I am sure, contained much more entertainment than instruction. I knew that the real purpose in inviting me had been, not to profit by my "experience and ability in such exercises," so much as to get a speech out of me: so I put in just enough criticism to keep myself in countenance, and for the rest contented myself and *them*, strange to say, with rambling remarks on "things in general." It was a very ridiculous position to be put into, and I felt afterwards that the chief cause for gratification on my part was that I had, in a measure, prevented the society itself from seeing how ridiculous it was. There's nothing like acting a farce as if it were tragedy!—if the audience be not so judicious as to grieve.

My darling, I am ever so much obliged for that exquisite picture of dear little Ellen. It is one of the prettiest pictures I ever saw; and I quite agree with Carrie Belle in thinking it much the "cutest" of the two. I shall prize it very highly. You had promised only that you would send me Ellen's photo. to *look* at, and I am, therefore, specially glad to be permitted to *keep* one of the two you sent—and that the one I should have chosen.

I can't say that I think Henry James's "Bundle of Letters" more than *clever*. The conception might have been anyone's: private letters written from the same boarding house in Paris by two Yankee girls of very pronounced types, by a Boston "aesthete" of the most extravagant sort, by an unsophisticated English maiden, by a conceited, shallow Frenchman, and by a ponderous German. There is, of course, very considerable skill of style in the execution of the plan; but each of the letter-writers personifies only what may be said to be everybody's ideas as to the different national characteristics. The German is what we all suppose a German student to be without having seen him, the Boston youth is just a little bigger ass than young Bostonians are supposed to be by those who laugh at Boston, the New England girls have the hard, angular, unattractive characteristics usually supposed to be typical of women of their nativity, &c, &c. Any clever, observant, satirical, cynical traveller who had hobnobbed with numberless representatives of various nationalities might have wiled away his leisure by writing such letters as these, and could have published them without fear of being suspected of possessing anything more than a surface acquaintance with human nature. Mr. James's *art* in these letters is admirable, but the pictures are commonplace—one is not certain that they are not meant for caricatures. I can imagine Macaulay writing such fictitious letters for the amusement of his dear sister Hannah; but I cannot imagine his publishing them as serious literary work, as part of his contribution to literature—though sister Hannah's son[2] would doubtless have spread them before the public without hesitation. But—"being as how" I have very uncompromising opinions of my own as to the sort of literary work that is worth while, and am nothing if [not] critical, I'd better let you off from any further expression of my views upon this very popular bit of Mr. James's writing.

It do'nt look at present as if we were going to have any Spring here at all. We are still having genuine winter weather of the most intensely disagreeable sort—just such as we have had for the past four months, in a word. I think it's quite safe to say that we have not had, on an average, more than two bright days out of every ten since the first of November, which is a pretty dismal record. When the sunny days do come back I shall hardly know what to do with myself. My spirits will be sure to run riot after so long repression. One's mind may grow well enough, but one's heart stands still in this chill northern climate. Dull, sunless seasons full of storms have less power over a great city than over rural neighbourhoods, no doubt; but even in the city their spell is powerful. They can make life dreary anywhere.

Yes, my sweet little lady, mother and father were quite well when I last heard from them. They always send their warmest love to you—so do sisters, too, whenever they write. I heard from sister Marion just the other day.

I *am* so glad that your dear father continues able to write to you. Give him my love always, my darling, when you write to him. Give my love to Dr. and Mrs. Axson, to "uncle Randolph" and "aunt Ella," and to Miss Leila and the children. Will you give little Ellen a kiss from "Mr. Thomas"? (Oh, you sly little dissembler, you!)

I find that the University term closes the *first* week in June—are you glad? Only three months, and *then*

> "who is this, by the half-open'd door,
> Whose figure casts a shadow on the floor?
> The sweet brown eyes—the soft, fawn-colour'd hair—
> The cheeks that still their modest colour wear—
> The lovely lips, with their arch smile that tells
> The unconquered joy in which her spirit dwells—
> Ah! they bend nearer—
> Sweet lips, this way!"

Biding those three months' going,

> "We are apart; yet day by day,
> I bid my heart more constant be.
> I bid it keep the world away,
> And grow a home for only thee
> Nor fear but thy love likewise grows,
> Like mine, each day, more tried, more true."[3]

—Which is more poetry than has been quoted, at one sitting, this twelvemonth gone, by   Your own   Woodrow.

ALS (WP, DLC).
[1] James S. Hodges, A.B., J.H.U., '86; Allen C. Woods, A.B., J.H.U., '86.
[2] George Otto Trevelyan.
[3] Freely paraphrased from Matthew Arnold's "Switzerland" group. See WW to ELA, March 18, 1884.

Newsletters from the Johns Hopkins: II

Johns Hopkins University.

Baltimore, March 8 [1884].

One of the chief characteristics of the Johns Hopkins University is the amount of work which is carried on under its auspices outside of its regular class work and lecture courses. There are generally in progress several courses of public lectures by scholars from other institutions, and in each department of study there are "seminaries" or societies for the prosecution of original work by advanced students. Work akin in method to the laboratory work of the physicist is carried on in the Greek, the English, the Historical, and other "seminaries."

The latest creation in this line is the Archaeological Society, which has not yet quite perfected its organization, but which has been far enough developed to show its peculiar and original form. It is to consist of an inner "circle" of some ten or twelve skilled archaeologists, and of an outer and much larger circle of "associate" members. The members of the inner "circle" are to do the real work of the society, conduct original research, and prepare papers and reports upon all relevant topics, to the reading of which the "circle" of associates are to be audience. The regular members, in a word, are to study and instruct; the associates, to listen and be instructed. The prime object of the society is to develop interest in archaeological study, and, with this in view, one of the most enthusiastic members of its inner "circle" has drawn about him several small groups of students for the purpose of guiding them in the study of such specific subjects as Romanesque architecture, the art remains of particular centuries, etc. The active membership of the society is made up of some of the most highly-trained classical scholars of the University staff of instructors, and some very excellent work may, of course, be confidently expected. In the meantime, we are about to have a course of lectures on archaeology, which will be open to the public.

The most interesting of the recent public lecture courses is that, just closed, upon English Literature, by Professor Hiram Corson, of Cornell. Professor Corson has devoted most of his lectures (eighteen of the twenty he has delivered) to the poetry and prose of the Restoration period. Dryden was made the central figure of the lectures, and special consideration was given to his use of Shakspere's materials in manufacturing a drama suited to the tastes of the later and degenerate time. The other adapters and emendators of Shakspere were also examined at some length, and with much sharpness of ridicule. Professor Corson rejects the view that the degeneracy of the Restoration drama was due to Puritan influence, tracing its beginnings back to times long anterior to the days of Puritan supremacy. Sheridan was included in the lecturer's treatment of the Restoration school. The two concluding lectures of the course were upon Chaucer.

A course of a very different sort is that recently begun upon educational topics. A very large number of the advanced students at the University are preparing themselves for the duties of teachers, and this course has been planned as a sort of normal school feature of university instruction. It was opened by two lectures by President Gilman on the leading features of collegiate and university methods in this country and abroad, and it will be continued by the leading teachers of the several departments with the object of acquainting the students who attend with the latest and best methods of instruction in the several branches of study. It is, in short, to be a course in pedagogics. These lectures are not open to the public, but only to those students who have secured tickets by special application.

In addition to this course, which is understood to be under the direction of Dr. G. Stanley Hall,[1] Dr. Hall himself is announced to give a series of public lectures in Hopkins Hall upon educational topics of general interest, such as the modern and best means of teaching the deaf, dumb, and blind, etc. And so the attention of the University is taken up until some new course shall be announced. We live upon a diet of great and ever-increasing variety.

Printed in the New York *Evening Post*, March 10, 1884; editorial headings omitted.

[1] Granville Stanley Hall, psychologist, philosopher, and educator, born in Ashfield, Mass., Feb. 1, 1844. Educated at Williams College (B.A., 1867; A.M., 1870); Union Theological Seminary, 1867-68; Harvard University (Ph.D., 1878). Studied in Germany, 1868-71 and 1878-80. Taught literature and philosophy, Antioch College, 1872-76; Instructor in English, Harvard University, 1876-78; Professor of Psychology and Pedagogics, The Johns Hopkins University, 1883-88; President and Professor of Psychology, Clark University, 1888-1919. Founder, *American Journal of Psychology*, 1887, and *Pedagogical Seminary*, 1892; founder and first president, American Psychological Association, 1891. Author of many books. Died April 24, 1924.

From Joseph Ruggles Wilson

My dearest Son—   [Wilmington, N.C.] Mar 10 84

Have you a catalogue, or circular, or anything issued by Texas University which gives the names of its Trustees? I have no knowledge as to any one of them. It is possible that, had I the list, there would [be] a name or two which would be of use. I should think that, in Johns H. library or reading room there must be such a Cat. Meanwhile, see Leighton Wilson and confer with him. Also write to yr uncle James [Woodrow] telling him precisely what you want, and in some such terms as in your last letter to me. When I shall have gotten some Trustee names I will write to Dr. [Benjamin M.] Palmer and get him to use his influence with one or more of them. But don't set yr heart upon this matter, upon this merely possible chance. It may be that you and I will have to organize a school somewhere for ourselves! I think we could make it go. I have thought of it a good deal, although with my mind looking through a mist.

Can you not obtain a strong letter from yr. own faculty, recommending you as you desire? Also, from Dr. McCosh?

It will be better to have all recommendation letters put into yr own hands that, at the right time, they may [be] sent on in a bunch.

We are all well, my darling and if we were ever so sick would be strong in our love for you   Your affectionate F.

ALS (WP, DLC) with WWhw notation on env.: "Ans. 3/16/84."

To Ellen Louise Axson

My own darling,   Balto., Md., March 10th/84

I am quite sure that if Mrs. Olmstead could have seen my actions after receiving your letter this morning she would have concluded that I was adicted to opera *bouffe* rather than to preaching. I executed a dance and song quite in the approved Italian manner, sending my heels as high as my notes. Is it *really* possible that you may "run up, for a day or so," with Mrs. Green? The Walters gallery is to be open every Wednesday till the end of April, so that there's plenty of time. Ah, my darling, you do'nt know what a thrill that little sentence in your letter sent through me! It's too good to be true. If you will come, you will not only see the Walters collection, but you will make me the happiest man on the continent besides. If there is anyone in Baltimore whom you would like to see, I'll promise that you shall see him, to your heart's content. When I wrote about it, I scarcely dared to hope that my darling might come. That "day or so" will make my work so easy that the first of June will be here before the inspiration is gone! This is not just the best season to see Baltimore but it will never again seem so beautiful to me after I have seen it once with you. I will try, till you see it again with me some day, to remember it as you saw it! My darling, if it be at all possible, fulfil your half-made promise!

I will write again to-morrow, of course[.] I am dashing off this note only that it may, beyond all peradventure, reach you before Mrs. Green's departure: for I gather from your note that she will leave at the end of this week.

This delightful letter of yours, which I have already read several times since its arrival a few minutes ago, suggests a great many things that I want to say in reply; but I must not say them now. I can say, at this writing, only what I have said several times before, but what I have never said satisfactorily, and what is never an old story, because its truth is renewed every moment of my life and grows bigger every day, that my heart and life are yours and that your love is more precious to me than aught else in the world. Will you really come to see—the Walters collection, and   Your own   Woodrow?

ALS (WC, NjP).

From Ellen Louise Axson, with Enclosure

My darling Woodrow,   Savannah, Mar. 10/84.

I enclose another letter from Papa, principally because it is the easiest method of conveying to you certain messages it contains; but also because I think it indicates some improvement in his condition. It is one of the brighter letters we have received from him. He seems to dwell less on himself and to take more interest in other things which is a great point gained. You perceive he is much impressed by the Ely-Wilson-Dewey scheme! And I am inclined Sir, to think, though you may treat the matter indifferently, regarding it as more of a "bore" than anything else, that it will be of decided benefit to you. It is an "evidence of ability," which everyone is capable of understanding, at a glance, and willing to accept without question. A first-class professor, you see, must know what he is about, and it is so much less trouble to accept his opinions than to form them for one's-self. Who cares unnecessarily to exercise their own powers of discrimination and appreciation? Here is a learned professor, whose judgement has already been given in a very tangible shape!

I have been trying to find the "Overland" for Jan. here, but have not succeeded as yet. I wanted Anna and Beth to see a certain article[1] in it, which I [am] sure would interest and please them extremely, and was rather afraid to trust my copy away from me. Anna, especially, will be glad to read it, for various reasons,

Ever since she first heard that you were a student of constitutional history and political economy, she has professed the most intense anxiety to know you[r] exact attitude in politics, your views on various points, and especially "how you stand on the tariff question."

When your letter telling of the "Free Trade Club" in Atlanta,[2] enlightened me on that point,—to some extent—I meant to write at once and relieve her mind, but I am sorry to say I have been very culpably negligent in the matter!

I must tell you of a little compliment paid you the other day,— and if you don't like it you can skip it. Rose, looking over my "Jean Ingelow," came upon some lines which you may have heard.[3] They begin "A mouth for mastery," &c. "Ellie," said she, "did you mark this for Mr. Wilson's sake?" I admitted the soft impeachment. "Yes," she said, "I knew it;—I recognized them." "Recognized them! What do you mean?" "Why," said she, "I think they are so true of him; at least they are an excellent description of that photograph!" "Out of the mouth of two witnesses shall every word be confirmed."

I really ought to stop at the foot of this page—but I don't mean to,—for I said I would not sit up late tonight, and I was *so* tired I didn't begin writing until after nine. I have laid in my supply of exercise for the whole week today—have "taken in" both town and country. I wish you could have been with us this morning where

> "Deep in the lonely woods the jasmine burns
> It's fragrant lamps, and turns
> Into a royal court, with green festoons
> The banks of dark lagoons."—Timrod.[4]

To go "jasmine-hunting" is the favourite amusement in this beautiful spring weather;—though in truth, that mal-treated word "hunting" is even more than usually inappropriate in this case, when all the world seems covered with them. We came home covered with them ourselves—clothed with them, as with a garment—a trailing garment at that. But if you care for them half as much as I, all this is enough to make you home-sick. *How* I do love them! the beautiful, beautiful flowers! They seem to breathe the very spirit of the South!

This afternoon we, that is Janie, Rose, Leila and myself, went on another expedition, viz., to take a lesson in "Art needle-work." I hav'nt enough to do you know, nor has Janie, with her twenty-five scholars, so we take this up to kill time. So behold us all deep in the mysteries of Kinsington stich and French knot, arrasene—

and—but I spare you. My head has been turned over all these things since I saw the marvels of the Woman's Decorative Art rooms in New York, so when the opportunity offered, I was obliged to get "a wrinkle or two."

I think on the whole that with domestic, missionary, and art needlework, and my "batch of generals" I should manage to escape "ennui"—dont you? I am making a sort of portrait gallery of heros—Gen. Lawton and Mrs. Gen. L., Gen. Jackson and two of Mrs. Jackson, and Gen. Gilmer![5]

But I must make an effort to close here, without finishing the sheet, as a sort of atonement for my treatment of you on Friday night. Did you not think me literally "inebriated with the exuberance of my own verbosity"? But when my garrulous mood is on me I have no mercy, whatever.

Give much love to your father[,] mother and all. Do you know, Sir, that when you send your love to "all the family at 143," you are sending it to a strange young lady! And my feelings are very much hurt about it too! Miss Willie Law,[6] Aunt Ella's sister has been here for two or three weeks. She is a great acquisition, for she [is] a most lovely woman. She is the only unmarried one among the *eleven* sisters, and the others of course are always battling over her[.] Aunt E. was victor in the last skirmish, and hopes now to keep her through the spring.

Good-night, dearest, With truest love, Your own   Ellie.

ALS (WP, DLC) with WWhw pencil notation, "Revised Statutes 3669, 3670, 3672," on verso of env.

  1 "Committee or Cabinet Government?" Anna and Beth were Anna Harris and Elizabeth Adams Erwin.

  2 WW to ELA, Dec. 11, 1883, Vol. 2.

  3 They were from Jean Ingelow, "Laurance." ELA's copy could have been any of several editions published in England and the United States between 1863 and 1884.

  4 From Henry Timrod, "Spring."

  5 Generals Alexander Robert Lawton, Henry Rootes Jackson, and Jeremy Francis Gilmer; Mrs. Lawton and Mrs. Jackson.

  6 Of Greenville, S. C.

E N C L O S U R E

Samuel Edward Axson to Ellen Louise Axson

My darling Daughter   Asylum near Milledgeville Mch 6:84
    . . . I have something from your letter that is *not little*—but exceptionally great. I allude to the honors that have been placed upon the youthful brow of *Your* Woodrow & *mine* by his professor in selecting him to assist him in the writing of his forth com-

ing book[.] Congratulate him for me when you write, and tell him that I am as proud of him as his Ellie is—and that my love for him is as genuine as my admiration is exalted. We shall not be anymore disappointed in the expectations we have of *great* things in connection with his ready pen—than in the *good* things in connexion with his noble heart which we have already seen. shall we? . . .   I am yr loving father   SEA

ALI (WP, DLC).

To Ellen Louise Axson

My own darling,   Balto., Md., March 11th/84
   I was infinitely amused by your report of what Mrs. Olmstead had to say about me. Just after reading your letter I undertook to shave myself, but took an unconscionably long time to complete the operation, because every now and then that delicious joke would take hold of me and shake me so that it made it absolutely necessary to hold off the razor until the convulsion was over. Why the dear, venomous lady! She hates with a spontaneity worthy of a more generous emotion. I never dreamed that she could be harbouring such feelings when she was saying her courteous adieux that evening. I am quite used to being taken for a minister. There seems to be something about the cut of my jib that leads a great many people to conclude that I am a missionary craft of some sort—though I could myself never discover what it is. But then it was very unreasonable of Mrs. O. to take such a violent dislike to me. It was quite natural that Dr. Axson should be entertaining a young minister, and that young minister could not be blamed for being in love with you. The only serious question, from Mrs. O's standpoint, was, whether or not you were in love with him. As to that, Mrs. O seems to have been kept sufficiently in the dark to enable her to hope for the best. I quite admire her for her feelings about the matter: they showed her love and admiration for you, and so long as she loves you in so earnest a fashion I must insist upon being unable to give her anything but my heartiest friendship in return for as much "decided antipathy" as she can bestow upon me. Mrs. O. does not seem, however, to be a very skilful reader of character. How did she come to believe so firmly, in spite of the ominous apparition of the young minister, that you would "shrink so" from marrying and "all that sort of thing"? This is really the most exquisite part of the joke! If she had known my darling as well as she might, she could have guessed, at least, the existence of that precious

store of sweet, overflowing love which you had had so long in keeping for the man of your choice—as an unspeakable gift to fill his
life with gladness and strength, and would have seen that your
happiness could never be complete until you had found some one
whom you thought worthy of the gift. As to the absolute worthi-
ness of the recipient, she should have reflected that even a young
minister might perchance have sense enough to appreciate you,
and that no man whom you loved, however much he had fallen
short before he won you, could fail to have a dash of nobility and
a new elevation of purpose given him by the discovery of your
love for him and your trust in him, unless he had an incredibly
small soul. Argal, I should like to meet Mrs. Olmstead again.

I am so glad, my darling, that you enjoyed the little volume of
Ruskin's lectures which I sent you. Do you like the portrait? I
do, very much. It is a face of so much placid power. I have never
read much of Ruskin—only enough to know that his wonderful
prose has a great fascination for me—but I have read sufficient to
enable me to appreciate what you say about the changes which
have come since "Modern Painters" was written. I too had noticed
the greater gentleness and tolerance of his later judgments. Age
has mellowed him—has, too, made him broader and more catholic
in his sympathies. If he could have begun in such a temper, he
would have been betrayed into much fewer extravagances.

I received another letter, the other day, from Josie,[1] containing
a passage about his love affairs with "little Miss Maffitt" which
was even more remarkable than the one I sent you. I am tempted
to copy it too: but I really mus'nt betray the dear boy any further.
I must, however, transcribe this one sentence for your sake: "I
do not change my sweet-hearts so often because I am fickle, but
because I find they wont have *me*, and I am *certainly* not going
to have a girl who wont have *me*." I had protested against his
numerous changes on the ground that Wilmington was a comparatively small place and that at such a rate there was serious
danger of the supply of sweet-hearts not holding out. The above
is his justification of his policy, and is, I think, quite satisfactory.
It relieves the family, at any rate, of the suspicion of fickleness
which caused you such "deep anxiety," and shows that the neglect
to send a valentine was serious only as a symptom—one symptom
among many—of the fatal indifference of the now discarded Miss
Reston.

You have greatly mystified me on the score of the "proof of
affection" which you have put in competition with my *lock* raising! What can you mean by saying that you are "cutting off both

your arms, at the shoulders"? The only thing that I can imagine is, that you are wearing *braces* to make you stand up straight—is that it? Well, that *is* an heroic proof of affection, my little sweetheart, if that's what you are doing, for it must be supremely uncomfortable. But it's worth while, if you can't stand up straight without them. I believe that I have already confided to you the secret that I think your figure as pretty as any I ever saw: and it would certainly be a sad pity to spoil it with a stoop. Yours was a *tendency* to stoop rather than a genuine stoop; and if you should ever develop a fondness for walking with a certain tall man, even that tendency would probably be driven out by the desire to look your companion in the face as you walked and talked. At any rate, he would insist upon seeing your eyes occasionally, and that would help things.

I think that M. Michelet has disposed of me on the eagle question. He was taking the orthodox naturalist's view, I the orthodox literary view. It must be that I was led to sympathize with the eagle, in part, because of the predominance of *beak* in my physiognomy!

Unconsciously, you have asked me a very hard question when you inquire what I am going to call my series of constitutional studies. An appropriate title—one which is brief and at the same time sufficiently distinctive—is just what I have not yet been able to find. I might call them "committee government," since they concern chiefly the way in which Congress controls the policy of all branches of the government through its committees; but at least one of the series is to concern the organization and powers of the executive departments, and such a title would not suggest such a chapter. I do'nt want to bring the word Constitution into the title either, because I am describing the system which has grown up *about* the Constitution—a system made out of judicial decisions, statutes, and unwritten precedents—rather than the Constitution itself. "The Government of the Union" is the best I have thought of yet: but it is altogether too vague. Maybe I can find just the name I want when the series is done and the christening can no longer be postponed.

I was *very* much distressed to hear of dear little Ellen's severe accident and of Eddie's distressing cough. I sincerely hope that they are both much better by this time.

I am quite well again. I was completely cured of my ailments by a single sentence in a letter: "perhaps I might run up for a day or so with her!" I could'nt manage to feel a bit sick after reading that. My darling coming to Baltimore! Ellie, maybe if

Mrs. Olmstead could have seen the wealth of love that is in my heart for my matchless "little proud Wild-heart," she would not have wondered that you were willing to "abandon liberty for love," and would have seen some reason to hope that even in a manse you might find a little happiness.

Love to your dear father, to Mrs. Duncan, to all at 143, and to Miss R. from   Your own   Woodrow.

ALS (WC, NjP).
   [1] J. R. Wilson, Jr., to WW, March 5, 1884.

From Janet Woodrow Wilson

My darling Son,   Thursday—Wilmington, N.C. March 13th 84

I did not mean to say what Josie's wording of my message made me say. The truth is I have gotten into a terrible habit with regard to my correspondence—I have not written to anybody for *weeks*. . . . As one week after another has passed without carrying you any thing from me, I have taken great comfort in the knowledge that you were receiving your loved Ellie's sweet loving letters. That is all I meant by my message dear. I think I have resolution enough, however, to enable me to overcome my present habit—and I can safely promise you a note each week—from this time on. In spite of appearances, I am sure you know that I am as dependent upon writing to you as you are upon receiving what I write. For I cannot be satisfied without talking to you sometimes—even though I hear from you regularly, I dont express myself very clearly—but you will understand what I mean.

Your father wishes me to ask you to get *all possible particulars* as to the opening you have written about as soon as you can. It might spoil all to make application at the wrong time. . . .

This is an *introductory* note only! You see I must write *several* notes—apologizing for my neglect.

We all love you dearly—but I need not tell you that. We look eagerly for the letters you faithfully send—whether you hear from us or no. It is very good in you not to make any fuss about our neglect. Mrs. Dr. Moore is here. She tells me that her sister and brother-in law called to see you. She had a letter from her sister saying that they were at home the evening you called—but the servant supposed you called upon the *daughter*—who was out. They were very sorry about the mistake for they have taken a fancy to you. Papa & Josie, join me in unbounded love to you, darling. Good bye till next week

Lovingly Your   Mother

ALS (WP, DLC) with WWhw bibliographical references on env.

To Ellen Louise Axson

My own darling,   Balto., Md., March 13th/84

It would really be too bad to withhold from Miss Anna and Mrs. Beth. the pleasure of reading my article, lately published in the "Overland," so I send you some of the extra copies forwarded me from the far-off office of that excellent journal, having duly put my autograph upon them in the style most fashionable amongst distinguished authors. I should have forwarded copies direct to your two friends had I not been so selfish as to wish to throw upon you the responsibility of the infliction. Pray conceal from them the fact that I aided and abetted you in this enterprise!

I quite agree with you, my pet, in thinking that "the Ely-Wilson-Dewey scheme" will be of very considerable advantage to me, *if it come to a prosperous issue.* But, you see, that is still problematical. The plan may be said to be still more or less in the air; and, even after the proposed book is written, it is by no means certain that the publishers will like it, being known to be such a shy race, and so much more intent upon guaging *saleability* than *readability* and intrinsic merit. I must finish the third of my constitutional essays (the one upon which I am now at work) before I can give my serious attention to the American economists, and it, therefore, still remains to be seen what success I can count upon in my own part of the proposed treatise. I have made light of the scheme in my letters because I have always been much impressed with the wisdom of that homely proverb which counsels us against counting chickens before they are hatched.

Why, my precious little sweet-heart, this letter of your dear father's which you have sent me is more than encouraging: it is gladdening. It really looks now as if he were hoping to get entirely well much sooner than I had thought at all possible[.] I cannot express my pleasure at those passages of the letter which concern myself. Surely it ought to make a man nobler and better to be loved and admired so much beyond his deserts by those whom he most honours and whose opinions he values most highly! It is very sweet and thoughtful of you to send me such letters to read—and it is especially gratifying to me as a proof that you realize how sincere and *loving* my interest in your dear father's case is.

But, little lady, you evidently do'nt realize the danger you run of *spoiling* me by telling me of all the compliments you hear paid me—putting in only an occasional Mrs. Olmstead by way of mild antidote. Just reflect how unbearably conceited I am likely to be made by this treatment, which for the present seemeth to be delightful but may in the end prove to be grievous. I have, however, this defence, that I am utterly unable to see the justness of most of the remarks you report—firmly believing, for instance, with reference to Miss Rose's very pretty and gratifying compliment, that my mirror, which is big and candid, is a much safer guide than Motes's photograph—and am forced to ascribe them to the blind partiality of friendship.

Your letter of to-day says nothing more of the possible visit to the Walters collection, my darling. Can it be that you were only joking when you said you might come up with Mrs. Green? If so, there are some castles in the air of my building which will come to very disastrous ruin. I can't help hoping, though, until I know that Mrs. G. has left Sav. without you.

Give my warmest love to your dear father, and to all at 143—except Miss Law!—remembering that I love you beyond compare and am altogether   Your own   Woodrow.

ALS (WC, NjP).

From Ellen Louise Axson

My darling Woodrow,   Savannah, Mar. 13/84.

"If you have tears, prepare to shed them now"!—that is to say when the enclosed picture meets your gaze. I was showing Janie how to tint the other day, and while looking for cast-away pictures to experiment upon, came across this,—which I did'nt know I had with me;—so we tinted it too. And now I feel that duty demands I should not deprive you of the entertainment which the sight of it will afford you;—only I *beg of you, don't* look at it *too long*! It always reminds me of Mr. Wright's[1] remark about a friend of ours in Rome, who, in some amateur performance, was the hero of a farce,—"*so* obliging in him to make such a fool of himself, merely to gratify us"! But then I had no idea they would carry the joke so far. I thought it would end with the "proof"; but to my horror received from Concord, some time after, this finished picture. And now, after keeping it carefully concealed so long, I am "so obliging" as to still further expose myself by putting it on exhibition for your benefit! The picture is made still more preposterous by the perfectly white hair, which all the "liquid colour" it will hold can bring to nothing but flaxen!

My darling, since the receipt of your sweet note of the tenth, I have suffered not a few twinges of conscience because of the idle words which occasioned it. I will anticipate the appointed day of judgement and hasten to "give an account thereof." Though indeed my going to Baltimore is something so entirely out of the range of possibilities, that it never occurred to me that you could take me seriously. It is indeed "too good to be true." I could as well speak of "running up" to the North Pole "for a day or so." "All the same," I appreciate no less your delightful note on the subject, and your earnestly expressed wish to have me there. It is possible that "wish was father to the thought," as with me it was doubtless father of my "foolish jesting" with regard to it. Yet bearing in mind the delightful fact that "the University term closes the first week in June," and remembering too the other fact that it is not yet so *very* long since the twenty-seventh of Jan. it would, I admit, be unreasonable to sigh for the unattainable.

By the way, I must express my appreciation of you[r] amiable conduct with regard to plans for the summer. In the present state of affairs, I suppose it would be a waste of time to discuss Rose's scheme, or any-body else's, further than to thank you for that rash promise of conformity to any plan I might "choose to make." Perhaps Carrie Belle is right after all in her estimate of your character. Looking up at your picture tonight, she suddenly said with much emphasis "that's who I like," and when I smiled down upon her approvingly, she made the following remarkable statement, "I'll tell you one [reason] why I like him, 'cause whatever you tell him to do—he *doos*!" What do you think of that? They say children are instinctively right in their judgement of character; but her decision *has* been rather a revelation to me—though perhaps that is only because I never tried "*telling*" you to do anything!

I am *so* sorry to hear that you have been unwell; *do* hope it is nothing serious, and that the cure you announce proved permanent. Am *very* glad that Mr. Wilson the critic was so enthusiastically received. I envy the Hopkins Debating Club—lucky fellows that they are! I am *wild* to hear you speak! perfectly frantic! You would'nt treat me as Mac does Rose, would you? She has never heard him preach, though everyone else at Sewanee has. He won't let her. We used to make him utterly wretched when I was in Sewanee by threatening to go "anyhow." But his case was very different, because, I dare say, he is a poor speaker.

I think you *might* have sent me the passages from Josie's letter. I should'nt think he would care! and I find them extremely edifying as well as entertaining. The insight which they afford into the workings of the masculine mind in such matters gives them great value, and renders them worthy of profound study!

I was intensely amused at over-hearing Palmer, Randolph and Eddie discussing matrimony the other night. They seem to have very throughly matured opinions on the subject. And I am happy to add that their views are such as do them credit, they show a spirit of manly independence—and honourable pride[.] They are evidently high-toned young gentlemen, for it was unanimously resolved that they would *never* marry a rich girl—"not for *nothin*"! they would—terrible alternative!—do without getting married first! I don't know where our boys get such "high and mighty notions." Stockton[2] is even worse. He remarks of something or other that it would be almost as bad as for him "to marry a rich wife and live off of her money, and of all the contemptible things under the sun, I do think that is the most so!"

I *meant* you to be "mystified" as to that "proof of affection," but you have guessed! However my powers of endurance—or perhaps my affection—have almost given out. My experience on last Sunday was a little too much for me. I don't find such things conducive to a devotional frame of mind. Our Sunday-school lesson was the chapter which tells of St Paul in the stocks at Phillipi, and I felt that I had gained some new lights on the subject. I was especially impressed by the fact that he "sang praises" under those circumstances.

I do like the portrait of Ruskin extremely; age has improved him in personal appearance as well as in other respects. This picture is much more attractive than another I have, taken in earlier life,—the beard has perhaps something to do with it; it seems to suit his style. I am glad you like Ruskin,—perhaps you will read to me parts of "Modern Painters," some of these days.

By-the-way, who is the author of the poetry quoted in one of this weeks letters? Good-night, dearest. All send love—Ellen and Eddie are almost well again.

With best love I am, my darling as ever.

Your own   Ellie.

I neglected to mention that I think of moving over to London for a day or so to see the spring exhibitions at the Burlington House and the Grosvenor. Don't you think it would be a good plan?

ALS (WC, NjP).
  [1] James Wright, of Tallulah, Georgia, one of Ellen's former suitors.
  [2] [Isaac] Stockton [Keith] Axson, II, brother of ELA.

Two Letters to Ellen Louise Axson

My own darling,   Balto., Md., March 16th/84

This is one of the first unclouded, gloriously bright and genially warm days we've had for many a long week: Nature must be aware (for *no* one is too small for Nature's sympathy) that on another Sabbath day just six months ago a little maiden's heart was made glad, and a certain man's life made strong and full of joy, by a pledge which revealed to each a sweet secret and bound them together by the holiest of all ties; and that it is fitting that she should smile when her children are happy. However that may be, the sun *is* shining gloriously to-day, and my heart is full of happy thoughts such as I cannot tell of my peerless little queen, to whom I have sworn life-long allegiance. I do'nt think that the most forbidding skies could make me think to-day anything but joyous and propitious, and, if you'll excuse me, Miss, for making so bold, I am going to write you a regular love letter before the sun goes down. You must admit that a little variety of subject is agreeable in correspondence and that there can be no impropriety in allowing me now and again to write of my feelings towards you. I have, it is true, once or twice said something in my letters about my admiration for you and my desire to see more of you in the future; but such indirect statements do small justice to my real feelings. It would probably be impossible for me to convey to you any adequate idea of the part you have played in my thoughts during the nine months which have elapsed since we met in the little parlour in Rome, or, rather, since the time I saw you first in the church:—for I have discovered, some time since, that I am made much as other men are, and I shrewdly suspect that I should have contented myself with calling on the good minister whom I loved and admired, without asking after his daughter, had I not seen her that day in the church and found in her glorious brown eyes some promise of what I had been searching my small world for: a sunny, loving heart and a quick, earnest, thoughtful mind. At any rate, I wanted to see that face again. I had seen a great many beautiful faces before, but it seemed to me that I had never seen any beauty which filled me with such a longing desire to find out what was behind it as came over me when I thought about the face of the little lady they told me was the pastor's daughter. And, after I had found out that she could make good the promise of her eyes!—what else could I do but fall in love with her? I could not mistake my own symptoms, for one of them at least was altogether novel to my experience. Was I not conscious of admiring the very failings of this shy little lady? and did I not feel that for the first time I had met some one whom it was quite beyond me to criticise? Every other young lady I had known I had been quite able to disapprove of in some points; but here was an enchantress who completely disarmed my critical faculty and made me feel as if my whole life had somehow got concentrated in the desire to win her and be with her always! Surely you will concede that that was a psychological phenomenon of the first magnitude, which I could not well neglect; and will forgive me for saying that I love you passionately and that you are the only woman in the world that I could marry.

Yes, my darling, to-day I renew the declaration I made six months ago—and renew with all the added love that has come with the sweet intercourse of the intervening time. If I was yours then, much more am I now, Your own Woodrow.

My hopes are still trembling in the balance about the visit to the Walters galleries! Wont you come?

My own darling, Balto., Md., March 18th/84
I do'nt know why I should have taken your unmeant promise to come to Baltimore so seriously, unless it was because it seemed to be in answer to my suggestion that you should come, and was expressed so soberly that it seemed to contain a half-formed resolve to do what I had not before thought of as possible: and it occurred to me that, by taking it as a promise, I might help to make it a *full* resolve. There seemed to me to be at least a possibility that something might come of it. However, I admit that it was extraordinarily stupid of me to misunderstand you so strangely. I am not usually so slow of comprehension: and my stupidity in this instance has certainly brought its own punishment. There are some men, you know, who set their hearts upon an object often very impetuously and unreasonably and then refuse to *see* even the most obvious obstacles: when the inevitable disappointment comes upon them they deserve to be laughed at rather than pitied.

I do'nt know exactly what to say about the remarkable picture you sent me. It looks enough like you, my darling, to make me think it very pretty; but of course a smiling picture is always very absurd, and *this* one makes me a little indignant, because the smile is (how could it be otherwise?) so mechanical and unnatural—such a travesty on my darling's genuine smiles, which are so bright and winning. I *did* shed tears over this wonderful Concord production, not tears of grief, however, but tears forced by over-much laughing. It is delightfully comical!—and yet *not* 'delightfully' either, because, despite the premeditated, determined smile, which is too evidently made to order, it is your face, the sweetest face in the world, and the longer I look at it the less comic it seems: my love drives out the laughter. You see the quandary I am in: I think the face lovely notwithstanding the smile, and I am put out with the smile only because it is enough like your real smiles to be provoking. It's just a mild caricature. I don't wonder that you were surprised and chagrined that the picture was printed—no artist could approve of it—but I'm glad now that it was, and I shall prize this copy of it.

So you "envy the Hopkins Debating Club," and are *"wild* to hear me speak"? But reflect! These young gentlemen do'nt know what good speaking is. Of course I speak better than most of *them* do: I've had vastly more practice and have taken pains to train myself; but that's not saying that I speak well. Moreover, I must disappoint you by telling you that I entirely sympathize with "Mac." in being violently opposed to having my sweetheart hear me speak in public. I've frequently felt sorry for young ministers on the special ground that they could'nt in conscience refuse to let their wives go to church and so *must* sooner or later face the ordeal of preaching before the person whom they loved most in all the world. I have never yet been persuaded to speak where there was any possibility of my parents' hearing me. The only ones of my relatives who have heard me are uncle James Bones, who slipped in on me at the University of Va. when I had to speak as the representative "orator" of the literary society—before an immense audience wh. would only have inspired me had he not been in it—and Jimmie Woodrow (Jas. W., jr.)[1] who was at the University with me: and, if I could have my own way about the matter, they would continue to be the only ones! You see, my little lady, it's all *vanity.* "Mac." and I wish our lady-loves to have as high an opinion of us as possible, and are conscious that we do'nt show off to the best advantage when we are speaking in public. I want you always to be proud of me and I cannot be expected to stand in the way of my own wish by letting you hear me speak.

Of course I do'nt mean that I intend always to avoid letting you hear me speak. I mean simply that I will do nothing to make an occasion for you. I am so constituted that I should probably speak better in your presence than under any other circumstances, both because of the inspiration which would come from the knowledge that I had the complete, the loving sympathy of at least one of my audience—an inestimable aid which none but the speaker can appreciate—and because I should be impelled to put forth my utmost efforts to gratify you by doing well. But there is, on such occasions, a terrible wear and tear on the speaker which I attribute to the fact that he feels that he has someone else besides himself to carry through the race: that there is a heart beating as intensely as his own for his success. There is absolute joy in facing and conquering a hostile audience for example or thawing out a cold one if the speaker feels that the hisses of the one or the critical stare of the other is hurting no one but himself; while, on the other hand, he finds himself sensitive to all the movements of even the most friendly audience if he knows that there's someone present who cares more than he does when or how much he is applauded. Do you see what I mean? The very intensity of his sympathy with that loved auditor distracts his thoughts. It is as if he were both orator and audience.

I was immensely amused by dear little Carrie Belle's description of my character: and I may say that I was gratified too; for, though I can't say that I admire a man who does everything he is told to do, I am quite sure that I have no sympathy with one who does not do what he is bid by children and by those whom he loves, when to do it contributes to their happiness without at all interfering with his duty—when the only sacrifice is a sacrifice of his own comfort or convenience[.] As for my promise to conform to any plans you may make for the Summer, I am afraid that I cannot claim any very great amiability on its account. The only unselfish feature I can find in it is that, if the Sewanee plan prevails, my stay with you would, as I said last week, necessarily be brief. I should be apt to follow you, if possible, wherever you might go—for I am, strange to say, conscious of a consuming desire to see my darling—and the only way in which my happiness could be affected would be by the existence of circumstances which would regulate the length of time we might be together. The only thing I feel inclined to insist upon is, that you consult only your own happiness—I should doubt my love for you, were I not conscious of preferring that to my own indulgence. It is you whom I love, my darling, not myself—and I love you beyond all compare.

The quotations in my last week's letter, about which you ask, were from Matthew Arnold—with here and there an adaptation to make the lines suit my purpose. Did you like them?

That spray of yellow jasmine you enclosed in your letter last week, together with the account of your jasmine hunt, *did* make me homesick. I long to get into the Southern woods once more: they contain so much that I love—and with you to wander through them with me I could be supremely happy.

Am I to conclude, Miss, when you send me "love from all" that you include Miss Law. If I am to receive such messages from her, it is very hard lines that I should be forbidden to send my love in return. Until this point is settled, you may give my love to all the rest, and keep for yourself as much as ever you can appropriate, for I am altogether   Your own   Woodrow.

ALS (WC, NjP).
¹ James Hamilton Woodrow, son of Dr. James Woodrow.

Two Letters from Ellen Louise Axson

My dearest Woodrow,   [Savannah, March 18, 1884]

We had a house full of company here last night, who stayed so late, and left me so exhausted, physically and mentally, that it was impossible for me to write even a *note*. I send a hasty line this morning to explain—havn't time for more until tonight, or perhaps until tomorrow night, as I will be at the Gilberts this evening. You see, its against my principles to waste day-light, writing letters. Especially at present, while my hands are so full, I must *paint* while it is called day. I am doing a "plaque" for Mr. Johnson the Missionary—also a panel for Mr. J. the M.—likewise a cherub's head—likewise some pin-cushions, &c. &c. all for Mr. J. the M.! So you will readily perceive that I hav'nt any time to waste on *you*! It is a missionary *fair*, you understand. We have had a series of them, every class in the Sunday-school has one, and now it is my turn. Every class of girls, I should say, the boys are, as usual, drones in the bee-hive. They are poor creatures, are they not? Can't do anything! I don't know what they were made for!

Poor Mr. Johnson, this church has undertaken to support him; and they seem to have made up their minds that he is to be sustained upon *ice-cream*! I am afraid he won't find it very nourishing. I don't know why the church fathers can't put their hands in their pockets, like little men, and turn over the money without all this foolishness. It don't seem quite the orthodox way of doing church work. But poor human nature must be beguiled into doing it's duty; and it seems to be the part of the women to present those duties, especially that hardest one of benevolence, in the form of sugar-coated pills.

But I am writing too much. I will close in haste, or I will not catch this mail; so good-bye for the present.

I love you, my darling, with all my heart, and am yours *forever*. It was six months on Sunday since that bright September day when I first awoke to that strange fact,—*very* strange it seemed then, but now—already—become so entirely a part of me, a very law of my being, that I could almost believe it had always been.

Your own   Ellie.

My darling Woodrow,   Savannah Mar. 19/84.

Many thanks for the copies of "Committee or Cabinet Government" which came safely to hand last week. It was *very* good in you to send them, and I am really *delighted* to get them. Now I am much perplexed to decide which of some half a dozen or so of my friends has the best right to the third copy. I think I must make them pass it around;—I shall make Anna's copy serve Agnes [Tedcastle] and Minnie [Hoyt], too, since they are all, thanks to me, good friends together. I never rest until I make all my friends love each other as well as me. Those three did'nt *want* to do so, but I coerced them, and now they are sworn friends and cronys. Even that unmanageable Anna, who, like yourself, is "nothing if not critical," has meekly joined the mutual admiration society, and now can almost rival me in "raving" over them all, including Rose and Beth.

I had long letters, by the way, from both Agnes and Anna a few day ago. The latter wants to know "how Mr. T. Woodrow W. is conducting himself?" Agnes gives a little Rome news, which however you have probably heard. Mr. Bones has leased his house for two years to Mr. Reynolds the banker, and Marion will remain for that length of time at Staunton.[1]

Agnes writes begging me to visit them this Summer; and to-day I had a still more urgent letter on the same subject from *Mr.* Tedcastle. What do you say to that plan? I dare say it would suit you better than my Sewanee, Morganton, or Gainsville invitations! Janie, who is to be married the first of June, is very anxious for me to wait here until then, but I hardly think I can. Dear old Helen,[2] who has been here ever since you left, leaves this week, and Janie seems to think we are both deserting her in her extremity. We [–] Helen and I [–] spent last evening with the Gilberts; and Mrs. G. passed her time, as usual, embracing us both at once,—she has ample room in her capacious arms,—and saying how *very* happy she was to have "*both* her pets back again" and how *very* sad she was not to be able to keep us! If Northan people are undemonstrative, the Gilberts must be the exception which proves the rule, for I never saw anyone so warm-hearted.

I wonder if there is very much, after all, in these theories about "national characteristics," which we hear so much about. I am inclined to think that a typical *American* at least, isn't a very common specimen; and I have seen a number of Irishmen who were everything an Irishman is supposed *not* to be. Mr. Killough (Helen's husband[)] is a striking instance of that. I think he is without exception the *calmest* person I ever saw. He would make a splendid soldier, for *nothing* excites him, *nothing* "throws him off his balance." I think he could hear the trump of doom without the quivering of an eye-lid. As Janie says, he has "less enthusiasm" than anyone she ever saw. I don't know how Helen, who is on the other extreme, adapts herself to him. I should feel like a bird doomed to be all my life beating my wings against a stone wall. But he is a noble fellow, and I like him extremely,—a grave, earnest, faithful man, having in their fullest development "the instincts of labour and patience,"—and the soul of honnour too! Do you think it true that "if man were constant, he were perfect"?(!) If so Mr. K. is certainly perfect! I don't think I ever heard of such a case. It is just ten years ago since he first addressed her, and was rejected; and he has repeated the operation at very frequent intervals through all these years—and always, until a year ago, with the same result! And Helen says it was literally true that she did not care for him *in the least* during all that time;—though now she is "perfectly devoted" to him. Don't you think he is a phenomenon? Really I should think a man would find it difficult to reconcile that sort of thing with proper self-respect. Yet he certainly effected it, for that very quality of self-respect is one of his most conspicuous traits;—he is self-reliant and to be relied upon.

We had a great deal of fun at the Porters this morning over a *love-letter* which Clark [Porter] had *found* on the street. It was written in *1856* to Miss Gertrude Dillon of Sav., by a student at some college called "Clairvaux." It was written in an exquisite hand, but was a very singular composition, and excited a great many speculations as to the circumstances of the case in the Porter conclave. It began and ended with "Dearest"—but otherwise did'nt sound much like a love-letter,—at least so it struck me,—and I regret to add that I was so unwise as to express that opinion openly, and so raise quite a laugh at my expense!

I am sorry that the weather continues so persistently and depressingly bad with you. How strange it is to read of such experiences in the midst of our perpetual sunshine. Last week the weather was perfect and the moon-lit nights glorious! What! Is it really a *month* since I was last writing sentiment about moonshine and enchanted gardens! "How tempus *does* fugit"! But I did better still this month. I took, not a walk, but a long drive of fourteen miles in the moonlight! The Gilberts took me with some friends of theirs from Concord, the two sons and one daughter-in-law of Senator Rollins[3] of N.H.,—*very* nice people—out to Montgomery, the prettiest of our little salt-water resorts. We drove out in the morning—a carriage full and a buggy—dined at the fine new hotel they have just built and came back by moonlight;—and *that* was the delicious part of it. I never had just such a ride,—an exquisite night, soft an[d] balmy, the air fragrant with jasmine, a narrow woodland road, and the effects of light now on the pines, and then on the old moss-wreathed oaks, altogether indescribable.

I trust that the bright promise of last Sunday is being fulfilled, and that you too will have some bright weather now. I should imagine that even in Baltimore, ere this, the winter is past "and the time of the singing of birds is come."

I hope you are no longer "under the weather," but are entirely well again. How is it? And how does essay No. 3 progress?

We have not heard from father for over a week now, and are a little anxious in consequence, but I trust without cause,—he has never written regularly.

I had a sad letter from Beth the other day. Her uncle Captain Tate at whose pleasant country home I visited while in Morganton, has lost his mind from *intemperance*. I was deeply shocked. I knew he *drank*,—as does every-one else in Morganton,—but had no idea he went to any excess. Beth writes that he is quite violent, but his wife, very much against the judgment of her friends, refuses to let him go to the Asylum. Poor desolate woman, when I think of her sorrows—of those *five* little graves, and then of *this*, I feel as though I am just learning the meaning of *sympathy*. Even our trouble seems small indeed compared with hers; for what sorrows *can* be compared with those which come from *sin*? Those are the things which it seems to me it would be *impossible* to bear, because there is [no?] place for *faith*,—it all seems the work, not of God, but of the evil one. The one secret of happiness in this life is an abiding *trust* in Gods wise and tender providence. It seems to me that without that trust there would be nothing to save us from despair. But how can one see the finger of God in this? He is not the author of sin.

Your sweet little anniversary letter came safely to hand on yesterday. I won't try to say how welcome it was, or how often I have read it, but you may be sure, my darling, that it was properly appreciated,—and that I love you now, and will always love you, "with my uttermost power." And so, dearest, good-night.

Your own   Ellie.

ALS (WP, DLC) with WWhw and WWsh notes for *Congressional Government* on env. of second letter.
¹ Marion Bones was at the Augusta Female Seminary there.
² Helen Porter Killough, a girlhood friend who was soon to move to Hoboken, N.J., was a sister of Janie Porter. ELA wrote of visiting Helen Killough in ELA to WW, Oct. 8, 1884.
³ Edward H. Rollins, United States Representative from New Hampshire, 1861-67, and United States Senator, 1877-83.

To Ellen Louise Axson

My own darling,   Balto., Md., March 23/84

It makes me very weary with this hurry of study and work under dull leaden skies which forbid one's finding joy in anything, and in a chill, damp atmosphere which drives out comfort, to hear of the glorious weather you are having, the delightful moonlit nights, &c., but this sort of thing can't last much longer even here, and I am sure that I am made of tough enough fibre to stand the siege. Only, there's no harm in saying that I wish I were well out of it. The mischief of the matter is, that I am quite well and in good spirits and so can't justify myself in complaining—except that I am beset by the worry of having more work to do than there's time to do it in.

"Essay No. 3" is coming on quite prosperously, "an' thank you kindly, Miss," now that it's fairly under way. Its tale is a very simple one, fortunately, without many threads to the plot, and can be told directly and rapidly, so that two or three days will, I hope, see it completed, with the just addition of its moral. Then I shall be free—all too late—to read up for three big examinations which are to close the term as with a sort of salvo—to make us feel that we have gotten a proper "send-off" for our vacation.

According to present appearances, it will be hard to find you when that vacation comes. Unless you are firmly to accept *one* of your numerous invitations, resolutely shutting your ears to all the rest, you will lead me quite a chase next Summer, Miss. I am not going to be drawn into expressing any preference in the matter of your choice—my interests being manifestly so much on the side of my and dear mother's plan, to get my darling to visit my own loved home, to allow me conscientiously to take a brief in any other case. As long as there's a chance of my having you for a little while all to myself, you can't reasonably expect me to advocate any other invitation. Besides, I want *you* to make the choice. My part shall be simply to acquiesce without anything more said.

I see that I shall have to do something in this Johnson matter! It's terrible on my nerves to have you member of a church which is bound to constant interest in him and work for him! It is true that China is a long way off and that the danger of the young missionary's coming over with the idea of insisting on a contribution in the shape of a member of the congregation, besides the contributions of money which satisfy only his bodily wants, is on that account remote; but I am anxious to visit China anyhow.

As the end of the term approaches I begin to be very much perplexed about *my* plans. Father will be at home only during the first half of the Summer—and that is a fact which, viewed from one standpoint argues the desirability of my spending the early part of my vacation at home, and, viewed from another standpoint, points to the latter part of the season as the best time for my stay there. In favour of the first course is my desire to be with father—for it is both education and pleasure to be with him—and to help him, as I have usually done, in the preparation of the Assembly's *Minutes*; and in favour of the second, the equally strong desire not to leave mother and Josie alone in uninteresting Wilmington—indeed, I do'nt see how I can do *that*, when dear mother will *want* me so much and feel that she's going to lose me for good and aye so soon. It looks as if there were a *third* standpoint from which it is easy to see conclusive arguments why I should spend *both* halves of the Summer at home. With both affection and duty pulling me homewards and an irresistible and consuming love drawing me *you*-wards, I halt in some distress amongst a great many possible plans. You see, I shall have to make up my mind upon the various questions involved without any assistance; for the dear home-folks are as unselfish as I should like to be, and wont assert their claims upon me, much as they want me. I'd be likely to take some very definite determination anyhow, however; because it's not my way to let things drift—only, I do'nt just yet see how I am going to do both what I would and what I ought. When one sees one's way clear to the right thing it's easy enough to do it: but *groping* is an uneasy business! You are indispensable to my happiness, my precious little darling, and I literally live for the time when you will be mine and we can be *always* together; but I am quite sure that, if it were necessary for the performance of my duty and the proof of my love towards my dear parents to give you only a small part of my vacation, I could do it—if you would love me the while, as I know you would, with full confidence that I would rather be with you than with anyone else in the world; and provided, of course, that it was a mere question of duty *versus* pleasure, that you did not *need* me: for I am as much yours now as the marriage ceremony can make me. I could like "Mac." as much as you do, Ellie, if he had not shown himself so weakly self-indulgent in following Miss Rose to Savannah. If I understand the circumstances of the case aright, that was not manly of him!

But why should I be writing all this so solemnly? It all goes without the saying; and certainly my little lady do'nt need to be told that I ought to give a generous portion of my vacation to the dear homefolks, and that I shall give it willingly, even if my selfish heart does all the while yearn for her. Man is a queer compound of love and selfishness—at least *this* man is.

I recently made a great "find," namely, a Presbyterian church where there is first rate preaching[1]—first rate by the Baltimore standard, which is not very high or exacting—and plenty of pretty girls. I am now a regular attendant upon its services. One do'nt often find attractive orthodoxy in the pulpit and beauty in the pews, so that I am specially gratified because of this discovery. See the advantage of a strict training in doctrine! No amount of beauty in the damsels of an Episcopalian or Methodist or Baptist church could have led me off; but beauty in one's own church may be admired weekly with a conscience void of offense. By-the-way my orthodoxy has stood still another test. I was invited a short time since to join the finest choir in town; but it was a Methodist choir, and I declined. True, I did not care to join *any* choir; but of course the controlling motive in this case was connected with the question of doctrine. Should I be asked to sing in a Presbyterian choir, I could easily find some other, equally creditable, reason for saying 'nay': for Presbyterian choirs should be of the best.

Give my love to all at 143—save Miss Law—to your dear father, to Mrs. Duncan, and to—well to yourself: for, to tell the truth, I love you with all my heart, and am irretrievably because willingly and in every thought   Your own   Woodrow.

ALS (WC, NjP).
[1] The First Presbyterian Church of Baltimore, the Rev. Dr. James T. Leftwich, minister.

From Ellen Louise Axson

My darling Woodrow,   Savannah, Mar. 24/84.

I don't believe that you with all your constitutional studies and writings, your class meetings and seminary meetings[,] your essays and criticisms, have, after all, half the trouble that I find in getting a "chance" to write letters! For all those matters are altogether under your own control. You can say to one "go," and it goeth, to another "come," and it cometh. What are they compared to five unruly children, whom no power on earth can repress, or convince that I am not always and altogether theirs to command? Who begin before tea is well over, clamouring for stories or games, reading or drawing,—who pin me down if I attempt to rise, "head me off["] in the hall, way-lay me on the stairs, and pound at my door, if I am so fortunate as to gain the stronghold of my room, until—totally subdued by numbers—and noise,—I surrender at discretion, and am borne off in triumph to do their bidding. That is the history of every night,—that is of every night on which some scheme of my own inspires me with courage to attempt rebellion;—at other times I am meekly submissive from the first. You would laugh at some of our amusements;—but it seems a party of wide-awake children can sometimes extract more entertainment from "reding, riteing, and ritthmatic" than from a "true-true" game. Sometimes we have impromptu spelling-bees almost as uproarious as that famous Western specimen described by "truthful James." Then again we are absorbed in maps, or grow hilarious over "capitals and chief cities." On other nights we will make astonishing discoveries in mathematical science,—and that is perhaps the best fun of all, especially when "Cousin Nell" gets hopelessly stranded in trying to answer her own questions. And sometimes we have grand "memory-matches" in which I don't fail to cover myself with glory. Do you think you could learn a page of *poetry! perfectly* in seven minutes, before an audience of five children, all gazing breathlessly at the clock, and telling off the fatal moments, as surely, solemnly, one by one, they drop into the dread abyss of time?

But it is just like me to write three pages of apology for not being able to write *at all*! I started out to say that I would try to practice self-denial in the matter of writing tonight, since it was so late when I began;—for after the children had dismissed me I was obliged to paint for awhile—you see to what straits I am reduced,—so that now it is after eleven. And Rose and I have taken exercise enough today to be grateful for the "sweet restorer." Rose

—alas—leaves on Thursday, and we have been shopping on the strength of that fact. What do you suppose she bought as a present for Mac? If you guess I'll—I'll give you one too! But you will be obliged to "give it up," so I will tell you,—a *carpenter's plane*! It seems that Rose went shopping with him, and Mac, who is blessed with a "turn for mechanics," had that on his list of purchases; but having spent all his money "buying presents" ! was obliged to come back without it! So Rose undertakes to supply the deficiency. I wish you could see that pair, as I see them;—they are too deliciously funny for anything. And yet in some respects they are very much like brother and sister,—Rose says she wishes they were.

So you *do* sympathize with Mac, and are ["]violently opposed to my hearing you speak." I think that is down-right cruelty—yet I shan't accept it as the death-blow to my hopes! I do see what you mean—I understand and appreciate it;—yet all the same I would'nt scruple to follow your Uncle James' example and "slip in on" you, if I had the opportunity. The temptation would be irresistible, even overpowering my regard for your feeling, though I might be considerate enough to go in disguise!

But I must close, though much against my will for I feel as though I had scarcely begun. Yet it is well for you that I must, for I am too tired to write anything approaching *sense*. Many thanks dearest, for the dainty little Easter card received on Saturday. With truest love I am as ever

Yours with all my heart   Ellie

Kindest regards to Mr. Shinn.

ALS (WP, DLC).

To Ellen Louise Axson

My own darling,   Balto., Md., March 25th/84

It's delightful to turn aside for a little while from the labours of "Essay No. 3" and talk to my little sweet-heart, even if I do have to talk with a clumsy pen and can't hear any answering words from her until the mood in which I write has grown old. I think, by-the-way, that I can promise some improvement in the style of my correspondence by the time another week sets in: for by that time essay-writing will have been put temporarily aside and I can bring *fresh* powers, instead of rather jaded ones, as now, to the composition of these epistles. It's no small matter, let me assure you, to walk through a letter with the light step proper to it after treading for hours together through the big fields of constitutional disquisition in the heavy boots of formal discourse and (assumed) learning! So that, if you find me ponderous and staid in my letters, you must not wonder at the natural effects of habit. Now I should remark in this connection that heaviness and formality are qualities which I sedulously seek to avoid in *all* my writing, but that I have at hand evidence of the fact that I *do'nt* escape them. Sister Marion, for instance, says in her last letter,[1] after thanking me for the copy of "Committee or Cabinet Government" which I had sent her, "How did you ever attain to such a sedate, middle-aged style of composition, brother mine? You write as if further years and longer experience were hardly possible. Your whole *style* expresses the *dignity of age*" (The underscorings are her own)[.] Alas! alas!! I suppose that that dear sister of mine really thought that she was saying nothing but what was altogether complimentary and calculated to gratify the author of the "middle-aged" style. But I am as much shocked as if she had said that mine was the style of the middle ages instead of that of the middle-aged. What I am shocked at is, not the fact—for I knew that quite well before—but the *visibility* of the fact to uncritical eyes. The style of that particular article is, I know, more terribly "sedate" and stiff than most of my writing, because there a big subject is packed into a very narrow space: but why should Mrs. Kennedy, a Christian woman, remind me of the fact? You see, when a fellow is ambitious to acquire a crisp, fast-moving, brilliant, hard-hitting style—a way of putting things that will be very delightful to the palate of those who agree with him, but very acid to the taste of those who do not—he can't help wincing a little bit under the treatment of those adjectives "sedate" and "middle-aged"! I like wisdom, but I like it *strong*; I like it militant, not mild and owl-eyed.

Coming from church last Sunday night I overheard one side of a conversation between two ladies which may interest you. I was walking more rapidly than most of the dispersing congregation, and, as I strode along disguised in my rubber overcoat (for it was raining, as usual), I stepped in front of two ladies just in time to hear one of them say: "Did you notice that young man, with glasses, sitting over there under the gallery? He had side-whiskers and wore a long coat. You'd hardly call his hair black, but it was quite dark—not a bad-looking fellow: nor particularly good-looking either." "Well, what about him?" "Why he's the same one we saw out in the park—" and then I passed on and the ladies turned the corner, leaving me to reflect that *I* had been sitting quite apart under the gallery, and to congratulate myself that, though "not particularly good-looking," I was considered not very "bad-looking." What do you think of that for a description, in impartial negatives, of your humble servant? These gossiping ladies were not quite as complimentary as you and Miss Rose (*per* Jean Ingelow), but I suspect that they were much nearer the hard facts of the case.

Our Glee Club is looking forward to two rare disciplinary exercises—disciplinary to the patience of its members. On Thursday evening next we are to sing at "The Two-Hundred-and-fiftieth Anniversary of the Founding of Maryland." There is to be a great deal of tiresome speech-making, by tireless speakers, on this interesting occasion and we are to sing that dignified and patriotic, but none the less fatiguing, "America" and that other national air, good for the throats of a brass band but not so good for the human voice, "The Star-spangled Banner." We had not a little difficulty in learning the latter, at our rehearsal last night, because four members of the Club ("one of whom I was which") had never heard it before, and it is by no means easy to acquire. I hope that our audience of Thursday evening will not suffer as much at our hands as we suffered at the hands of the songs we are going to sing for them!

The other disciplinary exercise is to be an entertainment for the benefit of a "free kindergarten," in which a lady elocutionist is to play the principal rôle and we are expected to lift our voices in her support. What this thing is coming to it is beyond human ken to divine. Presently we will be travelling with the apostles of the "Woman's Christian Temperance Union," and singing at the polls wherever voting is to be done on a "prohibition amendment" to a State Constitution! It is considered the "proper thing" to sing only under some charitable "auspices."

That was a good joke on you, my darling incautious little lady, about the love-letter which Clark Porter found on the street. I do'nt know what this strayed letter contained—though it was old enough to have gotten *cold*—but I should like very much indeed to learn how you think a love-letter ought to "sound." I have often been puzzled on that point: for, "being as how" the letters I write to you are written *for* you, to suit you, that is, and not myself, I have tried to put myself in your place, as far as my imagination could accomplish the feat, and to conceive just such a letter as you would most enjoy. But such an operation is, as you must see, necessarily a very imperfect one, and a candid expression of your views upon the subject would be delightful. There is one view of the case from which I have derived considerable comfort, and that is, that my way of making love, inasmuch as it was successful with you, must as regards yourself be the right way. That certainly seems unimpeachable logic; but it is, nevertheless, unsatisfactory: for, when a fellow wants to tell his love in delicate forms of wooing words which will steal his lady's heart afresh with every syllable without making her conscious that it is being stolen anew, he is naturally dissatisfied with the blunt, passionate declarations that are the best things his clumsy pen can stumble upon. See how impotent my art is! I venture to say that you are not aware, Miss Axson, that there's a thrill of love in every line I write to you: I want you to see it between the lines, but I dare say you do'nt. So now I'm going to tell you how my letters to you are composed. They are composed with the strongest impulse to put '*I love you*' in every line—because that is what I'm thinking all the while as I write—but with only an occasional moment of license given to the impulse—commonplaces and indifferent topics being forced to the front meantime. But I can tell you at the *end* of my letter—can't I?—that I love you with all my heart and will always be   Your own   Woodrow.

ALS (WC, NjP).
  [1] Marion Wilson Kennedy to WW, Feb. 15, 1884.

From Marion Wilson Kennedy

My dearest brother:—   Little Rock, 3/28/84.
    The news you gave us of dear Ellie's trouble was quite a shock to us. We had heard nothing from home since just after Christmas, and have not heard anything yet, except a letter from Josie this week, full of his "girl" and his "*bycicle club*." Neither Father nor Mother was mentioned even in his whole letter, I believe. I must confess, I feel right badly treated by the home folks—but must not complain, I suppose. Have received three whole letters from them since they went home in the fall! . . .
    This brings me back to Ellie again. How nice it was that you could go to the dear child, and what a comfort it must have been to her, I can imagine. She has indeed a heavy burden to bear, and I need not urge *you* to continue to help her all in your power. You *will* do that. Give her my warmest love and heartiest sympathies. We so often think of her, and speak of her as already one of ourselves. I do hope the day when she becomes so, in name, is not far distant. . . .
                              Lovingly your sister,   Marion.
ALS (WP, DLC).

From Janet Woodrow Wilson

My precious Son,   Wilmington, N.C. March 28th '84
    . . . We were so sorry to hear that you have been bothered once
more by that very troublesome "midst" of yours. How do you account for these attacks? Is it from any unusual diet? If so it would
be worth while to avoid the special cause. However, I am sure you
do not care about eating, enough to expose yourself to suffering. . . .   Lovingly Yours, *Mother*

ALS (WP, DLC).

From Edward Ireland Renick

My dear Wilson: [Washington] 29 Mar 84
    When I tell you that our whole bureau has been required to
work two hours extra each day for the three past weeks, & will be
required to do so for some time to come, you will forgive me for
not having sent the information which I promised to try to obtain, & will indulge me a little. I am not able to call a moment
my own before 6 P.M. & after that I am fit for nothing. In an hour
I could tell you more than I could write in a night–& I hope soon
to see you. A recent article in the Nation (do you get it?) gave
a very true account of the workings of these departments.[1] The
clerks–especially what are known as the Chief Clerks of each
bureau–furnish the Sec'y of Treas. with his figures; they get them
from a knowledge of each year's expenditures. They go often
before the Cong. Committees–being sent for.
    Gaddy stood Civil Service exam. in Atlanta 2 weeks since. Mrs
Turpin is here now for that purpose. Hope both will get appointed.
Please excuse this, I am so tired.   Yours as ever   Renick

ALS (WP, DLC) with WWhw ciphering on env.
    1 Renick probably referred to W. B. K., "Letter to the Editor: Heads of Bureaux
in Civil-Service Reform," New York *Nation*, xxxviii (March 20, 1884), 255-56,
describing the degree to which bureau heads depended upon subordinate officers and clerks.

To Ellen Louise Axson

My little queen,   Balto., Md., March 30th/84
    If you are at all observant of the habits of animals, you will
perhaps have noticed that, though for many months I was in the
habit of writing a letter to a certain fair maiden every Thursday
—so that she might think, during the singing in church, of a Sunday, of the love messages she read the day before—I have for a

week or two past departed from the practice—leaving the aforesaid maiden to think about the voices in the choir, about the tenor
to her left, or about anything suggested at the moment; and it
must have occurred to you that there was probably some explanation of the fact, very few animals abandoning fixed custom without imperative reasons for so doing. The reason in this case was
neither more nor less than press of work. As the end of the term
draws near the work accumulates because of the approaching
examinations. On last Thursday my Caligraph was going all day
long, as it was also on Friday and Saturday: for "essay No. 3" was
finished on Wednesday evening and had then to be copied in the
fair hand of my machine. Copying is a terribly tedious business
—especially copying one's own work; and the copying of these
three essays is by no means a small job: there will be about one
hundred and seventy pages of—of *caligraphiscript*—by the time I
have copied the forty pages that remain: and you can imagine the
effect upon my spirits of this task of grinding off hour after hour
the sentences of which I am now so tired—of spending a whole
day with the style which is so disgusting to me. It is very unnatural, I know, to have such feelings towards my own offspring,
but I can't like it. I am comforting myself, as Lycias did, with the
reflection that others into whose hands these essays come will
probably read them only once and so escape the contempt bred by
familiarity. But I am wandering from my original text which was
the Thursday letters, about which I was speaking with the intention of adding the promise that, if you have missed them, I will
resume them, now that the back of the copying job is broken, if
you will be a real good girl and write to me at all sorts of odd
times when you think I wont be expecting a letter.

I do'nt wonder that you find it so hard to find time to write if
you are in the habit of giving up all your evenings to those jolly
games with the children. I believe that it has been observed to
be very generally the case that an independence which is very
seldom asserted, and, even when asserted, is prone to "surrender
at discretion" when pressed, is sure to be little better than none at
all: and I am quite certain that the least conclusive argument for
not serving children on some particular evening—they being the
judges—is that you have served them on every other evening.
How I wish I could look on at those gay spelling-bees and memory
matches! Of course I could'nt think of taking part: it would be
temerity to enter a contest with a young lady who can learn a
whole page of poetry perfectly in seven minutes! I could'nt learn
the words of a page of anything, prose or poetry, in seven min-

utes—I should be doing well to do it in *seventy*. The hardest work I ever had to do was to memorize my own speeches when I was adicted, at college, to the silly practice of committing them to memory. In spite of the most diligent preparation, I generally forgot whole sentences after I got on the stage and had to extemporize after all in some main passage of the "effort."

So you would go to hear me speak, if the opportunity offered, even if you had to go in disguise! Ah, you rash little maiden! You do'nt know what you would be risking: the trouble of a disguise would hardly be repaid by hearing a poor speech. Besides, the only speaking I am likely to do for some years to come will, probably, be done in the class-room, where the only audience will be young men—and I am inclined to think that for you a young gentleman's suit would hardly be a disguise. I could tell you a better device than disguise for obtaining an opportunity to hear me speak! If you—but I am not bound to disclose plans for my own defeat.

I am *very* sorry that Miss Rose has gone away, my darling. It made me very happy to know that she was with you: for I have'nt forgotten the light that used to come into yours [*sic*] eyes whenever you spoke of "Rose," the love-light that used to make me almost jealous; and I used to like to think of your having your dearest friend so near you—though "Mac" must have spoiled the arrangement just a little bit. By-the-way, when is "Mac" to become a full-fledged "priest" and take a charge? We must not fail, during some one of our Summer vacations, to search out the Rev. "Mac." and "sample" his preaching. I trust that he will attain to a somewhat higher standard in the pulpit than is reached by most "rectors." The incentive to effort in that direction is certainly great enough: for my observation is that to preach with the slightest touch of eloquence in that church is to win a bishopric— so the good preaching be but sustained by steadiness of character and salted with orthodoxy.

I hear Dr. Leftwich (formerly in Atlanta) every Sabbath now, and find *his* preaching a very curious study. It often—as, for instance, this morning—furnishes a notable illustration of how manner may overcome matter in speaking. Dr. L. has a good voice for informing men, but a very poor one for persuading or moving them. He speaks of the flight of the mists before the face of the morning in the cool, dispassionate, colourless cadences natural in the statement of a mathematical proportion but quite flat and discordant in the harmonies of public speech. *He* is often moved by what he is saying, but his congregation never is, because their [there] is no sympathetic vibration in his voice as he says it, only the measured, inflexible tones of the passionless logician. This is partly explained by the fact that his preference is evidently for the dry, skeleton syllogism rather than for warmer, more vital forms of speech. He cannot be an orator, because oratory is an *imaginative* art—and it can move people only by persuading, not by convincing, them. The woman who said that she could not believe any man to be an orator who did not send a chill down her back made a very sensible remark. She recognized in certain physical sensations, because she could not recognize in the effects produced upon her mind, the operations of those forces which—which men like Dr. L. do not possess.

The singing at the Maryland anniversary was very highly praised. The boys insist that *I* won the *encore* on the "Star Spangled Banner" by a telling high note at the end of the last stanza.

Give my love to your dear father, and to all at 143.

I love you with all my heart and am altogether

Your own   Woodrow.

ALS (WC, NjP).

From Ellen Louise Axson

My darling Woodrow,   Savannah, Mar. 31/84.

What hour of the night do you suppose it is Sir? Why, just half past eleven! Is'nt that a pretty time to be beginning a serious composition like the present? It seems as though Monday nights are fated. I shall be obliged to change my day for writing if this thing continues. We had a room full of "company" tonight, and a "regular spread," as the boys would say,—so I couldn't write. But I had a "lovely"! time, all the same, for Mr. Strider[1] and I got off in the corner by ourselves, and talked poetry and pictures *all* the evening. Mr. Strider is *awfully* nice! I am quite captivated by him;—and he's captivated by *me* too! He *says* he is; and "if he says so, it's *so,* if it *ain't* so," because he is a *preacher*! I mean to set my cap for him, and cut out Lucy Green, and Mary Harding and all the rest. Just *think* how much fun I might have, if it hadnt gotten out that I was *engaged*! But someone will be sure to tell him all too soon, and cut short our nice little flirtation. Really it *is* a good thing that I am so well protected by yourself against him, else I *might* have lost my heart, and then I suppose I should have been a blighted being, after all, notwithstanding my serious objections. But Mr. Strider can't for a moment be weighed in the balances with *you*, my darling,—because, you see, he is a *small* man—does'nt weigh more than 120 or so!

I *was* much entertained by your account of yourself "as others see you." You wish to know what I think of it? I think that while, on the one hand, it by no means falsifies my "Jean Ingelow" description, on the other hand, it affords striking evidence of the truth of my *Wordsworth* description,—the first part of it at least! You didnt know I had such a description? It was for the benefit of some questioner to whom I preferred giving short answers and few particulars,—so I informed them that you, as well as Coleridge, were "a *noticeable* man with large grey eyes."

I am glad that "No. 3." is coming on so well, and will so soon be finished,—or probably *is*, already. For I presume the non-arrival of my Saturday's letter was the result of your being so deeply engrossed in adding the final flourishes. I trust you will find sufficient relief from your labours, in preparing for "three big examinations[");—but of *course* you will, for don't the wise folk tell us that "change of occupation" is all that is necessary, in the way of rest and recreation!

Of course, my darling, it is right for you to spend your vacation with your dear parents, who need you so much, and of course I will continue "to love you the while, with full confidence" &c. I trust I am not so abominably selfish as to say anything else. If you find it best not to come *at all* you must not mind me, but do it. I won't murmur. On the contrary, Sir, I will immediately proceed to convince myself that I don't *want* to see you *in the least*—would much rather *not*! "for that is my way." I have been obliged so often to give up things I had set my heart upon, that now I don't mind it much; one thing suits me almost as well as another. If I can get what I want I am in perfect ecstasies—it is the very grandest, most delightful thing that ever happened,— but if I can't get it—oh, it is nothing! nothing! only sour grapes! I wouldn't have it so if I could! Query, how does it please your lordship to have yourself, or your visits rather, likened unto *sour grapes*?

By the way, I must defend poor, dear Mac. What could I have said to give you such a wrong impression of him? He has no parents, no near relatives save one brother. There is therefore no one who has a better right to his time than Rose, for of course his host of Uncles, Aunts, and cousins—for he seems to be related to half the people in Carolina—can present no imperative claim. If he chose to spend part of his vacation here, basking in the sunshine of the Forest City, there was no reason why he should not.

Just think what a delightful offer I had the other day,—to go to Fla., take quite an extensive tour, and return, free, gratis, for nothing! Wouldn't that have been charming? Mr. Fleming Superintendent of the road, and a friend of ours, invited Grandfather, Grandmother, and myself to go, and made every effort to induce G.-father to accept,—but he said he had'nt the time. By the way, perhaps you would like to hear the end of that famous *fair*, which has intruded itself once of [or] twice into my letters. It came off on Friday and was a brilliant success. We are much elated, because we cleared $80.00, $30.00 more than any other class, and $60.00 more than some of them. But we are not satisfied yet, but have taken it into our heads to make it a hundred, and so we will, if Dr. Wilson (J. L.) will only give us time; he has already been dunning us for it.

I am shocked at Mrs. Kennedy's unchristian—nay, *inhuman* [—] treatment of you! But I have no doubt she meant well, and in our dealings with each other, our *motives* after all, are of chief importance. And then reflect;—would it have pleased you better if she had said that the style gave evidence of the *extreme youth* of the writer? Just think what many poor fellows struggling with all the crudities of college-boy compositions, would give for a style which seemed to be—even though it really was *not*!—the result of matured thought, of profound wisdom and experience. *Every-one* thinks your style remarkable—clear, strong, vigorous,— full of force and brilliancy, and at the same time highly finish[ed], graceful, smoothly-flowing. And if you add *dignity* to all your other fine qualities, why, so much the better. You don't really think it incompatible with the rest, do you? And by-the-way, though I have only a line left—for I *can't* begin a third sheet now —I must reassure you on the "love-letter" question. Yours *sound exactly* as I think they ought, and they suit me marvellously well. In fact, Sir, you may consider that your efforts at adapting yourself to my capacities have met with most gratifying success! And now my darling I must say good-bye. With all the love that you want—more perhaps than I care to tell.

I am as ever   Your own   Ellie.

Please excuse this *fearful* scrawl.

ALS (WP, DLC).
  ¹ The Rev. J. P. Strider, pastor, First Presbyterian Church, Savannah.

To Ellen Louise Axson

My own darling,   Balto., Md., April 1st/84

About the dark integument enclosed I have several remarks to make. It is not quite long enough to hang oneself with, but it is quite visible enough to serve as a fair specimen of the head from which it came. Again, one [on] the one hand, it is an astonishingly small product of two months' persistent culture, though it beyond all doubt represents locks long enough to get into their unhappy owner's ears and abundant enough to give him a desperately poetical aspect. Possibly, if I could have managed to get a better view of the top of my head, I might have secured more than I did, and might have cut less ragged edges to what I did get; but, fortunately, the value of this gift depends neither upon its size nor upon the mechanical skill with which it is prepared. It has no intrinsic beauty or worth, as have the beautiful silken strands you gave me; but it may serve as an emblem of the greater gift I have already made you, the gift of myself, and I hope that in that capacity my darling will prize it as something more than an ordinary lock of hair.

Ellie, I wonder if you can guess with what thoughts the opening of this new month fills my mind? This is, you know, the anniversary month of our first meeting. I would give a great deal if I could remember the exact date of that call I made upon your dear father when I got him to call in his daughter that I might be introduced to her; for that was a notable date in my history. The year that has elapsed since then has been fuller of blessings for me than any other of my life-time: for not only has it brought me your love, my darling, the inestimable gift for which, until then, my life seemed to be as it were in waiting, but it has also blessed me with the privilege of being your comforter in a time of terrible sorrow, a privilege which has bound us together in a new way.

I am quite aware, Miss, that I have already several times gone over the events of a year ago in my letters, and that a severe standard of criticism would exclude too constant repetition from correspondence, as from other more formal and less desultory forms of composition, but I am ever and again rehearsing those events in my memory, and, finding that I do'nt tire of them myself, am bold to believe that you do not either. If I am mistaken—why, skip the next page or so. I should reflect, however, that those events had a significance for me which was, probably, very different from the significance which they had for you. You look back only upon scenes and conversations, I recall novel and very vivid *feelings*; for you it was a time of a pleasant new acquaintanceship, for me it was a time of astonishing self-revelation. It took you all that time to find out that you had met someone "whom you *could* love," but it did not take me half that time to find out that I had met someone whom I did love, simply because I could'nt help loving her. In short, you were irresistible, while I was only interesting. Consequently, I have much the best of the recollection: for the *tragic* part of my feelings during that season is no more painful to recall now than would be labour that had been crowned with complete accomplishment. Of course, I had no sooner found you out and fallen in love with you than I began to be tormented by the fear suggested by my brief opportunity of seeing you, the fear that I should not be able to win you. You see it *was* a tragic business, my little lady. Had I not found the maiden of whom I had been dreaming whenever I had built in the air the home for which I hoped and lived? and was I not about to leave for good and aye the State in which she lived, possibly to leave also forever the very circle of her acquaintanceship. If she had not promised, as we talked in the hammock, that she would write to me, I should have gone home the next day with the heaviest heart ever man had—not defeated, for I should have sought her out again, come what might, but sorely disheartened: for aught I knew she might have turned missionary before I could see her again. Whenever I call you *my* Ellie, *my* darling it is with a little reminiscent thrill of the feeling of that time, with the consciousness of the most passionate wish of a life-time fulfilled, of an all-absorbing determination carried out. Speaking of that resolution reminds me of the associations which cluster in my mind about my first meeting with your cousin, Miss Minnie Hoyt. I must have seemed to her very awkward just then, because I was really confused. I had just made a great discovery which so filled me with conflicting emotions that I did not hear your words of introduction until I was almost to the rail-road on my way home. Then it gradually dawned on my understanding that I had been presented to "Miss Hoyt, your cousin"—but that ray of enlightenment did not disturb the reflections whose predominance had at first excluded it, nor did it prevent their proceeding to their natural issue, the resolution which I presently stood still to utter: "I'll win that little lady, or—break my heart!" You were probably quite unconscious, during that twilight hour, of the plans—no, not the plans, but the purposes—which were forming in the heart of the young gentleman who had just been your escort. This possessive pronoun, *my* precious little sweetheart, is, you observe, the lineal descendant of that resolution. We will divide the honours thus: the conquest was yours, the victory mine. Some of these days, you will learn, I trust, the sort of love that went to make up that determination. I can't tell now *what* I should have done if you had said me nay: there's no telling what a man will do when he knows that his happiness and the success of his life's work depend on winning in the suit! It would doubtless have depended, in my case, on the tone of the refusal. If it had meant plainly, unmistakably, that you did not love me *at all*, I should probably have accepted the decision as final, fatal as it would have been to me: for I have not Mr. Killough's disposition. My pride would have forbidden my doing as he did: and I question, besides, the value of love won as he won Miss Porter's: that is, I question its value *for me*. I should not like to be loved, like a Newfoundland dog, for my faithfulness: I should want to be loved first, on trust, with a spontaneous, irresistible love, and prove my faithfulness afterwards. The love which is manufactured, so to speak, by perseverence, is only sublimed friendship, not the love of natural selection. But, however this point may be, this I know, that what I want is *your* love—and its possession is what this wonderful year has brought me:—the rest I can tell you when—well, another time.

Love to your dear father and to all at 143, and a whole heartful for yourself from   Your own   Woodrow.

ALS (WC, NjP).

From Janet Woodrow Wilson

My precious boy,   [Wilmington, N.C.] Wednesday—April 2nd 84

Your most welcome letter to Josie, was received this morning. I am *so sorry* that you are so over-worked, my darling—I am not sure that it will pay. I will enclose your allowance—with the *plus* you [say] you are in need of. I trust that miserable humbug will not be able to neutralize your efforts[1]—for if anybody deserves to succeed *you do*. . . .

Take care of yourself my precious boy. You know *health* is the first consideration.

Love unbounded from us each one.

                    Most lovingly Yours   Mother.

P.S. omitted. ALS (WP, DLC) with WWhw and WWsh notation on env.
   [1] One can only speculate about this reference. Professor Adams had probably just asked Wilson to read part of *Congressional Government* to the Historical

Seminary, for Wilson did read the introduction on May 9, 1884. It is most likely Wilson had been writing his mother in the same vein he had used to Ellen (letter printed at Jan. 1, 1884, Vol. 2), saying, of Adams: "I seldom talk with my chief professor nowadays . . . because I have found him possessed of a very quick faculty of *acquisition* and prone to use as his own any original material which one may inadvertently lay before him."

To Houghton, Mifflin & Company

Dear Sirs,   Balto., Md., April 4th/84

I send you, by express, today some *mss.* which speaks for itself, but for which I must speak a word or two.

After spending much time for a number of years in a study of the practical side of modern constitutions, I have attempted a sketch of our federal government in those particulars of internal organization which seem to me clearly functional, and therefore essential to a proper study of our constitutional system. We cannot measure Congress by the standard of its duties unless we know its means of performing those duties; and it has been the object of my studies to make those means clear to my own mind, as it has been the object of my writing to make them visible to others.

As a constitutional study, the subject is, as you will perceive, a new one. Not that I have brought out any hitherto unseen facts; I have simply grouped facts which have not before stood together, and thus given them the setting of a new treatment. I have modelled my work chiefly on Mr. Bagehot's essays on the English Constitution, though I have been guided in some points of treatment by the method followed in some of the better volumes of Macmillan's admirable "English Citizen Series."

The three essays I send you evidently go but part of the way through the subject suggested by their general title. Outside of the introductory portion, which traces the steps by which the federal has overshadowed State power and by which Congress has overshadowed the other branches of the national govt., they concern only the House of Representatives which is but half of Congress, though, as I think, the greater half: they should be supplemented by essays upon the distinctive features and influence of the Senate, and upon the dependence and independence of the Pres. and the executive departments.

My proposition, then, is this: If you approve of the parts I send, and would publish the whole as a small volume, provided the parts to be written should come up to the sample, I shall set out upon the completion of the plan indicated as soon as possible. In what I have yet to write I should wish to say a good deal about the conditions imposed upon public life—i.e. upon the development of statesmanship—by the Committee system of Congressional govt., and a good deal about the *caucus*—especially the *legislative* caucus—as a resultant of our peculiar constitutional system—in short, to speak philosophically about some of the greater influences of the Committee system upon the tone and fashion of national politics.

My excuse for adopting this plan of sending only an instalment of my work is that other engagements forbid my giving my whole time to this study, and I should not feel justified in devoting valuable leisure to it unless I could be assured of its publication in case it should all be well done.

I could not promise to complete the additional essays I have sketched very shortly because for some time to come I shall be busy in fulfilling an engagement to assist Dr. Ely, of the Johns Hopkins University, in preparing a brief history of American political economy.

I hope that you will think it worth while to read all that is in these three essays which I send; but, if you must make a selection, I should like to call your attention to the third essay as embodying an entirely new treatment of our financial administration.

Hoping to hear from you soon and favourably, I am

Yrs. Very Respty,   Woodrow Wilson

ALS (WP, DLC).

To Ellen Louise Axson

My own darling,   Balto., Md., April 6th/84

You are a delightfully humble young woman! In assuring me of my success in "adapting myself," in letter writing, "to your capacities," your tone is such as to make it quite certain that you meant to speak of your *in*capacities—but I suspect, Miss, that you say such things *to me* because you know that it is quite safe. You can wear this dress of modest faculty amongst your friends, just as Mrs. A.T. Stewart[1] can afford to wear plain gowns where she is known. But, for a' that, I'd have you understand, Miss, that it was'nt your generous dowry of all the best gifts of womanly wit that brought me to your feet—I share to the full Stockton's aversion from marrying for wealth. I should'nt have come courting you if it had'nt been for something else that you possess: a capacity for loving which is—as great as mine (I did'nt know how infinite mine was until I loved you!)

"As the dawn loves the sunlight I love thee."

By the way, quoting poetry reminds me that I ran off some verses from the author of this pretty line on my caligraph the other day for the purpose of submitting them to your judgment, my sweet lady; for I suppose that you have not seen them, inasmuch as they are from a poet whose fancy is not quite pure enough to make his productions safe reading, his most exquisite verses having neighbour verses whose seductive music does not quite suffice to purify the thought which is its burden[2]

It was just like you, my darling, just like my sweet, unselfish little love, to say what you did about my Summer plans: it was just what I expected that you would say—except, Miss, that it almost took my breath away to be promised that you would set about convincing yourself, with every prospect of success, that you did'nt *want* to see me! My not coming to see you at all is, however, by no means a likely contingency, let me assure you. In the first place, *I* could'nt stand it, if you could. In the second place, it wont be necessary. And, in the third place, I know beforehand just what my sweet mother will do about the matter: she wont *let* me stay at home on her account. She will invent arguments of the greatest cogency why I should not; she will convince me that I would contribute to her happiness by going and make her miserable by staying; if necessary, she will go away herself—over to Columbia to see sister Annie, maybe—in order to force my departure. I believe that the dear lady once wrote to you that *I* was unselfish; did'nt she? Who could'nt or would'nt serve acceptably a mother who made absolutely no exactions and offered on her part nothing but affection and self-sacrifice! Still, it's only too evident in what direction her heart is set in regard to the plans for next Summer. She will be sorely disappointed if she does not have us *both* with her for a part of the time. This is from her last letter (and there's been a parallel passage in each of her letters for the last four months): "How is dear Ellie? and how is her dear father? Give my best love to the dear girl—I do hope she will be able to come to us in the Summer. Tell her I love her very dearly."

I beg "Mac's" pardon, my love. I misunderstood; you have entirely exculpated him. He did exactly what he should have done—exactly what I would have done—and would have been a gander to do otherwise. Is not that the "amende honorable"?

Ellie, in my various sojourns away from home I have of course been in all sorts of churches and heard all sorts of preachers and

I have come to the conclusion after this rather wide experience that one of the most conclusive proofs of the vitality and truth of the gospel is that it has not been killed by the preachers—which emphatic and extravagant statement I make in remembrance of the sermon I heard this morning from the Rev. Dr. Patton of Princeton Seminary.[3] Dr. Patton was called to Princeton, from Chicago, after I had left college, so that I had never seen him; but I had heard of him as a man of unusual power and when I learned that he was to preach in town to-day I of course went to hear him. As soon as I saw him I was disappointed: a tall, lean, spare-visaged man, with narrow, knit brow and a mouth set to the taste of vinegar. As soon as I heard him I was grieved: the angular wrists and darting forefingers developed in his delivery made me nervous, his didactic manner made me antagonistic, and his rasping voice, together with his niggardly treatment of the vowels of the language made me indignant and amused by turns. The communion was to be administered, and he chose for his text the suggestive words "This do in remembrance of me"; but instead of giving his text such an exposition as would serve for a spiritual preparation for the solemnities of the sacrament, he entered, with true professional instinct, upon a discussion of the institution of the Lord's Supper as an evidence of the divinity of Christ, and laboured with abundant supererogation to demonstrate its appropriateness and serviceableness. Fortunately, he could not destroy my enjoyment of the service, but if anything could have destroyed it, that sermon could. You see the fact is, my little sweetheart, that such preaching disgusts me: so perhaps I better not say anything more about Dr. Patton.

Do you suppose that I have given over the habit I once before confessed to, of dreaming about my future home as I sit alone in my room on these quiet Sabbath afternoons? Not a bit of it. I venture to say that on these particular occasions you are the most thought about young lady and I the most serenely happy young man in the country: and I am ready to make a bargain with you: if you will continue to love me more than you love anybody else in the world, I will covenant and agree to make you one of these days the happiest wife in three kingdoms! Do you think that I can fulfil the contract?

Give my warmest love to your dear father and to all at 143, as well as to Mrs. Duncan. Good-bye, my darling. I love you more than tongue can tell or you can guess, and am

Your own Woodrow.

ALS (WP, DLC).

¹ Widow of Alexander T. Stewart, the famous New York merchant and philanthropist.

² These, as WW to ELA, April 22, 1884, reveals, were from Swinburne's "Tristram of Lyonesse." Wilson typed them on a separate sheet, now missing.

³ Francis Landey Patton, born Warwick, Bermuda, Jan. 22, 1843. Educated at Knox College of the University of Toronto, and Princeton Theological Seminary, from which he was graduated in 1865. Ordained, 1865. Pastor, Eightyfourth Street Presbyterian Church, New York, 1865-67; Nyack, N.Y., Presbyterian Church, 1867-70; and South Church, Brooklyn, 1871. Cyrus H. McCormick Professor, Presbyterian Theological Seminary of the Northwest (now McCormick Seminary), 1872-81; pastor, Jefferson Park Church, Chicago, 1874-81; editor, Chicago *Interior*, 1873-76; Moderator, General Assembly, Presbyterian Church in the United States of America, 1878. Stuart Professor of the Relations of Philosophy and Science to the Christian Religion, Princeton Theological Seminary, 1881-88; lecturer on ethics, College of New Jersey, 1883-84; Stuart Professor of Ethics and the Philosophy of Religion, College of New Jersey, 1884-1913; President, College of New Jersey and Princeton University, 1888-1902; President and Professor of the Philosophy of Religion, Princeton Theological Seminary, 1902-13. Died Nov. 25, 1932.

From Ellen Louise Axson

My darling Woodrow,   Savannah, April 7/84.

Many thanks for the "dark integument" enclosed in your last. It is a gift of whose value you, Sir, are not the proper judge,—but *I* know;—and I shall prize it more than I can tell, both as an emblem of that greater gift, and for it's own sake;—for, excuse me—I think it *has* great intrinsic beauty; and worth too. Is it not the product of two months patient, self-sacrificing effort?

By-the-way, where, oh where, is the promised Saturday's letter? It hasn't come yet. You see with what confidence you have inspired me. I came home on Sat. in the greatest haste when I thought mail-time had arrived, and flew up stairs, absolutely certain that I should find a letter there awaiting me. But perhaps you were waiting to learn from me whether I had "missed" them! However, I am not complaining; you treat me a great deal better than I deserve, my darling. I am certainly not disposed to murmur after that letter of last Thursday. I admit that it ought to last me five days,—and so it has. I have read it—well, I don't know *how* many times, and not only read it, but—I could'nt help it—have occasionally kissed it, as well as the—But if I *am* a goose, there is no reason why I should publish the fact, is there?—and so prove myself doubly foolish.

You and I seem to have been, to some extent, thinking the same thoughts last Tuesday, both agreeing even in trying to fix *a certain date* with accuracy. It was almost exactly a year ago today, for the day upon which I saw you first was the first Sunday in April; whether that call of which you speak, was made on Mon., Tue., or Wed., I can't remember—can you?

How fortunate it is for us that we are creatures of such endlessly varying moods; that our eyes are not turned forever, Sphinx-like, in one direction,—that even in the very limitations of our nature, of our powers of endurance there is provided relief,—reaction against suffering. How otherwise could I, all my sorrows and perplexities apparently lulled to rest, all my burdens cast away, spend a whole day in as pleasant a reverie as if I had nothing to think of but love. That is a wonderful power of yours, my darling, which can enable my thoughts to dwell on *this* year of all others in *happy* retrospect. But you don't need to have me tell you now that you have made my happiness this year, a happiness as great, as matchless in my experience as the sorrow which followed so hard upon it.

I am not sure that you have so much the best of those recollections, after all. True, mine don't seem to have the clearness and definiteness which belong to yours; they all seem to refer to some strange, sweet, shadowy dreamland, and are therefore singularly hard to put into words; but that seems to be the result, not of the absence of feeling, but of it's being altogether a matter of feeling, or attended only by very vague, unformed thoughts. Language is a clumsy tool, at best, capable perhaps in the hands of a good workman of expressing *thoughts* with accuracy, but wholly powerless to deal with the more delicate forms of feeling. There, I suppose, we must fall back upon the original mode of expression. To speak and "to hear with eyes is part of love's rare wit"; and I assure you that when I first heard that language from the eyes I love, I felt *something*,—I don't know, and so won't *try* to say what.

Ah those dear eyes! How well I know the look of them! Methinks I see them now, with the eyes of my heart. Strange—is it not—that, being thus gifted with the inner vision, I should so long to see them in the other, every-day fashion! But we are hard to satisfy, we "humans." It takes a whole council of great powers—*imagination*, and reason, and philosophy, to say nothing of religion, to give some people a small share of the one poor little virtue of contentment!

I have finally decided what to do with myself for the next month or so, at least. I am going to Rome, the first of May, to stay with Agnes while Mr. Tedcastle is away. I don't want to go; it will be a "scramble" to get my work finished by that time, and I wanted to go to Gainsville, on my way up, and get a peep at the baby and Auntie.[1] But Mr. T. has written three letters and Agnes two *volumes* on the subject, urging, entreating, nay, *com-*

manding me to come. I *must* "strain a point,"—they "need me
so,"—so there seems nothing for it, but to go. So I will spend May
there, run up to Gainsville in June, then back to Rome, chiefly
to see Stockton, who will probably spend his vacation there, and
finally proceed to Sewanee early in July. At least, that is the present plan; the terrible state of suspense, in which we are constantly kept, renders it almost impossible for me to make very
definite plans. I think it would be better if we could make up our
minds that there is likely to be no great change, one way or the
other, for some time to come. But that seems impossible because
his condition *does* vary so from week to week,—now he is a great
deal better, then much worse; and I seem to be almost paralyzed
by the uncertainty, the constant fear of "something happening."
I can't tell what to do,—which way to turn.

I am glad the anniversary singing proved such a grand success, and that you won such glory on the occasion. Your fame as
a tenor bids fair to keep pace with your fame as a political economist! How I would like to have been there! By-the-way, I *must*
know about that device for hearing you speak! An [i.e., If] you
love me, tell me; my heart is set upon hearing you; and moreover you have now aroused my *curiosity* with regard to the
scheme in question. Don't you know it is positively dangerous
to work too much upon a woman's curiosity? The strain might
prove fatal!

I hope you are having more cheerful weather than you have
been reporting for some time past. Surely, though "Spring comes
slowly up that way," it must have reached you at last. The "month
of roses" has fully come with us, and I hope that, there, it is at
least the month of violets. Savannah is most beautiful now,—it
is always fairest at this season. It's greatest beauty, after all is it's
children. I don't think there can be so many lovely little people
in any other place; at any rate, one does'nt see so much of them
elsewhere;—one does'nt see whole regiments of them at once,
camped out in the squares, or drawn up on dress review. In this
delicious climate they, of course, live out of doors. And in the
parks where they most do congregate, one would fancy they were
holding a perpetual "baby-show." You missed that exhibition
when you were here, because it was very cold weather and they
were safely housed.

By-the-way, I must tell you about the funny little friend I
have just made. As I was walking down the street, I noticed
several yards in front of me, a group composed of a nurse rolling
a baby-carriage while a handsome, sturdy little three-year-old

trudged beside. By and by he chanced to look around, and catching sight of me, he paused, regarded me solemnly for a moment with big black eyes, and then startled me by deliberately turning back, and, without saying a word, taking my hand and walking with me, down the street. I tried to engage him in conversation and discover who he was, but he only talked a gibberish, which the nurse said was Spanish. He attended me for quite a distance, and then, having reached his crossing, he gravely held up his mouth to be kissed, and so went on his way, and I saw him no more.

I am finishing this on Tuesday morning—having been interrupted as usual last night.

Your letter has just been handed me, but, of course, I have no time now to write more in answer to it—except on *one* point. That is to thank you and your dear mother again for your kind invitation. But you know I told you that I did not think I would be able to go. It is impossible, my darling, for reasons too numerous to mention,—one of the most important being that Grandmother and Aunt Ella are strongly opposed to the scheme. But you must *try* and make your mother understand just how deeply I appreciate her kindness. With best love to them all, and a heartfull for yourself, I am as ever your own   Ellie.

ALS (WP, DLC).

¹ ELA's baby sister Margaret ("Maggie" or "Madge") was living with Aunt Louisa, Mrs. Warren A. Brown.

Two Letters to Ellen Louise Axson

Balto., Md., April 8th/84

No, my precious little sweetheart, I *do'nt* think that *dignity* is incompatible with fine qualities of style; on the contrary I think it essential: for even a playful, jocose writer must have dignity —else he is a clown, "kindly making a fool of himself for other people's amusement." But you will observe that "middle-aged sedateness" has a mild, featureless aspect quite apart from the finer qualities of dignity. By some curious law, the word sedate is always associated in my mind with the word *dapper*. It suggests negative characteristics which are in sharp contrast with that dignity of demeanor which may keep company even with jollity and is inseparable from power[.] But, how high little Mrs. Kennedy's eyebrows would go, were she to hear these fine discriminations drawn from her innocent remark as a text! The next time she undertook to write any comments upon the style of her captious younger brother she would probably write in blank, sending him a generous list of synonymes from which to choose the adjectives he might prefer, with a request to return the rest in good order.

As I was standing quite absentmindedly before a picture in the Walters gallery, last Wednesday, I was startled by hearing a lady just by my side say to her companion: "That looks like a street in Savannah." I turned so suddenly to look into her face that she seemed a little annoyed, returning my gaze with the air of one who would say "Pray, mind your own business." I have'nt an idea who she was: my first thought was that it might be Mrs. Green; but, without any means of knowing what Mrs. Green looks like, I concluded that she was not a small, slender person with prominent nose and angular jaws; and certainly the little placid-faced lady, in long, close-fitting gray coat, who accompanied the possessor of the Roman nose could not be Mrs. Green, for she was much too young. So I admitted to myself the fact that there *might* be people in Baltimore besides Mrs. G. who had seen Savannah and could fancy that they could discover likenesses to its streets in pictures whose only suggestion of a street was a row of gaunt trees.

From Wilson's shorthand notes taken in Professor Herbert Baxter Adams's course, "The Old German Empire and the Rise of Prussia"

Yes, I spent several hours last Wednesday in Mr. Walters' gallery, and shall spend at least as many more there next week. I thought of you during those hours more than I did of the wonderful paintings by which I was surrounded, I think. What would I not have given to have you with me! Of course I can't describe the collection; I can't even tell you which I liked best, for the styles and subjects were so different and so various that one could not make any definite selection of one or two "best." I can tell you, however, something about the three pictures over which I spent the most time, returning to them again and again: they were Alma Tadema's *Sappho*, de Neuville's "Attack at Dawn," and Dagnan-Bouveret's "An Accident." The three had a common characteristic in their realism and perfection of detail: but in everything else they are as different as possible. In de Neuville's picture "a detachment of Mobiles and Turcos of the army of Bourbaki, retreating on Switzerland, is surprised at daybreak by a Prussian column in a village of the Jura." The surprised irregulars are pouring from a narrow door-way in the dark street of the village; one of their number, sooner aroused than the rest, has his trumpet to his lips summoning his sleeping companions in arms with a few notes of hasty call; some are firing an ineffective shot or two at the close ranks of Prussians advancing through the grey mists of the chill morning; all are dazed and in consternation; and the bleak, frost-crusted snow, the dim, waning light of the quaint, square, swinging street lamp, together with the more lurid light that gleams from the door-way and the darting, vivid flashes of the guns, convey a sense of the cold cheerless air of a winter dawn and of the hurry and terror of the surprise which I cannot but regard as very wonderful. De Neuville's skill in painting snow—especially crisp, icy snow—and flame are exemplified in another picture in the collection which contains a wretched group of outposts crouching around a slim pitiful blaze in snow-filled trenches.

The "Accident" is a wonderful study of *faces*. A smart young doctor is binding up the wounded hand of a pale peasant lad, whose mother is crying quietly behind her apron in the corner, while is [*sic*] stolid, calmly helpful grand'am stands critically watching the bandaging, not at all dismayed by the basin of bloody water which stands by on a chair, tho' more sympathetic than the heavy clown who looks on with lack-lustre eyes from the bench behind the table. The physician's back is turned, so that his face cannot be seen; but the poor, terrified, suffering little patient has a countenance with everything in it: an almost comical, but withal pitiful, conflict between resolute pride and the acutest pain, his eyes not yet quite rid of the first fright of the mishap.

I think that I lingered longer over Sappho than over either of the others, tho' there is very little in the picture about which one can tell. A young poet has visited Sappho on her island of Lesbos and sings to her and her maidens in the orchestra of a white marble theatre overlooking the sea. The wonder of the picture is in its colour, in the pose of the figures, in the marvellous imitation of the surface and weather-stains of the marble, in the sympathy displayed with the antique life. I will send you the description of it which Mr. Walters has had printed in his pretty little catalogue. It's quite as good (!) as I could write.

The Easter card I send by the same mail that is to carry this is, as you will see, from Mr. Shinn. He was sending off some cards the other day, and asked me to send you this one with his compliments.

I was delighted to hear that the fair was such a success, my darling. If you have any trouble with Dr. Leighton Wilson, send me as your agent and I'll "manage" him. I love you with all my heart   Your own   Woodrow.

My own darling,   Balto., Md., April 11th/84

I ought to beg your pardon for having disappointed you about the Saturday letters—for you will not get one *this* week either—but when a fellow puts an 'if' to a promise he is of course bound in self-respect to stick to the condition. No, little sweetheart, that was only my *excuse*, not the real, controlling reason. The reason was that your letters did not come at the usual time. The immediate inspiration of my Thursday letters has been the receipt of certain other letters which generally reach me on that day; but last week your letter did not come until very late in the day, after the hour when I have usually found time to write, and this week your letter, not starting till Wednesday morning, was delayed in its coming till to-day, Friday—so that both times I have been without my accustomed inspiration not only, but a little bit sick at heart with disappointment as well—in no condition to write a letter to anybody. But, since my darling thinks so much of her Saturday letters, I promise, without an 'if', to write hereafter at least a few lines every Thursday, whether your letter comes or not.

That was a strangely sweet letter I received this morning, my darling; and yet it has left me in low spirits. It is *not* easy to give up the hope upon which I have been living for the last seven-month—the hope of spending the greater part of the Summer with you—and yet it looks now as if that hope were slipping away. I have seen for some time, of course, that there was no chance of getting you to visit Wilmington. I have been reiterating the invitation of late for the purpose of calling forth your *reasons* for not wishing to go; and now that the reason has been given I am as much in the dark as ever. I find it hard to believe that your Grandmother and Aunt could regard your visiting my home as *improper*. Dear mother would be considerably surprised to learn that a plan which originated with her was so thought of; and I am quite sure that, in the old country at least, such visits are usually considered not only proper but *customary*, when other circumstances permit: so that there must be other grounds for their opposition. There are other grounds which are sufficient. There is not quite enough difference of climate between Savannah and Wilmington to make it certain that it would be beneficial to your health to spend much of the Summer in the latter; and, besides, I have all along been quite conscious that the plan of having you there was a very selfish one on my part—Wilmington being, perhaps, the dullest and most uninteresting place on all the Atlantic coast, though busy with trade and full of nice people.

Your plans for the Summer, my darling, are exceedingly attractive and I am heartily glad that you have been able to lay them so. I am specially glad that you are to get off so soon, though it *will* cost you a preliminary scramble with your work to get ready for your departure. I know how delighted Miss Rose will be at the latter part of the programme, and how Jessie [Bones Brower] will rejoice when she hears of the first part. For my part, I need not tell you, my precious one, I shall be happy to think that you are with your dearest friends.

So you are impatient to hear what the device is by means of which you might get a chance to hear me speak, are you? Why, little lady, I should think that, if you were to try real hard, you might possibly *guess* what it is; but, I know that stress of curiosity *is* dangerous, and that the simplest things are often the things which are hardest to guess, so I will tell you: If a certain little lady were to come to me and put her arms around my neck and kiss me, I am quite sure that I should consent to anything she might ask. Is not that easier than disguising?

But I mus'nt take any more time for writing to-day. I wish I could kiss you, my darling, for that sweet letter just received. It brought tears of joy to my eyes, little sweetheart, so full was it of what I prize more than my own life and all the world besides —your love. I can match it with as great for I am, more entirely than you can realize,   Your own   Woodrow

P.S. Love to your dear father and to all at #143.

ALS (WC, NjP).

Newsletters from the Johns Hopkins: III

Johns Hopkins University.

Baltimore, April 11 [1884].

The Johns Hopkins University is nothing if not up to the times. Last week Professor J. Rendel Harris, lecturer on New Testament Greek, gave three admirable discourses of a semi-public nature, on the lately published Bryennios manuscript, "The Teaching of the Apostles." Professor Harris is thoroughly well versed in church history, and has a fresh familiarity with the writings of the fathers which cannot but stimulate those who come in contact with him, so that he was able to impart not only great instruction, but to furnish real entertainment as well to the company of university men and city divines who assembled in Bently Hall to hear his comments upon the remarkable manuscript which has been exciting so much interest for a few weeks past among both churchmen and lay scholars. Professor Harris's conclusions, founded both upon internal evidences and upon the quotations from and references to the work contained in the writings of churchmen from Irenaeus down, are that the book belongs to the Jewish wing of the early Church, having probably been written somewhere upon the northeastern shores of the Mediterranean, most likely in the immediate neighborhood of Antioch, and that it is unquestionably of very great antiquity, belonging in all likelihood to the closing years of the first or the opening years of the second century.

Professor Harris recently contributed to the proceedings of the Historical Seminary a very notable paper upon "The Paschal Scandal"; that is, upon the history of the stories which have fired in great part the late Jewish persecutions in Russia[1] He pointed out, and established from abundant historical proof, the remarkable fact that some of the most atrocious of the recent massacres of Jews in Europe had resulted from popular belief in scandals identical with those which were set afoot against the Christians in the second century. Every father of the second century was busy with rebutting the charge that human flesh was eaten at the Paschal feasts. After the Church had thrown off these suspicions, they were inherited by the unorthodox minority, by the Montanists and Jews, and later, in the sixth century, by the Jews and Manicheists—always by the unorthodox. In the stories of the twelfth century each country furnishes a saint to the supposed barbarous sacrifices of the Jews, though the Prioress in Chaucer borrows her tale of St. Hugh, not from Lincoln, but from the East —from Asia. It is by these same suspicions that the Jews of to-day are pursued in Europe by idle tales which were invented first in the second century, which have been again and again refuted ever since, but which are still a vital persecuting force.

It is understood that Professor Harris will next year have charge of the classes in Church History.

There have been many interesting features in the work of the Historical Seminary during the past two or three weeks. The department recently received a most valuable donation from the widow of the late Dr. Francis Lieber in the shape of the most important of the manuscripts left by her husband. They include the original manuscripts of some and the revisions of most of his books, together with the first drafts of his decisions in the cases arising under the Mexican Commission of 1868, in which he acted as umpire, and upon which he was engaged at the time of his death in 1872. The anniversary of Dr. Lieber's birth recurring just after the receipt of this interesting gift, a meeting of the Historical Seminary was called for the evening of that day [March 18], and a couple of hours were devoted to a review, by President Gilman and several of the advanced students of the department, of the history of the works represented by the manuscripts, and comments upon the methods of study and revision indicated by them.[2] At Dr. Adams's request, Mr. Edward A. Freeman has sent the Seminary some of his own MSS., with promise of more.[3]

One of the most interesting of the papers recently read to the Seminary was one by Mr. Talcott Williams, of the Philadelphia *Press*, upon the history of Tammany Hall and New York city politics.[4] The first number of the new series of "studies" in historical and political science is a double number for the months of January and February, containing Dr. Adams's interesting papers upon "Methods of Historical Study."[5] These papers have been prepared with great care. They discuss not only the methods of historical study in vogue at the Johns Hopkins, but also the chief features of instruction in such branches at the chief universities of Europe and at those American colleges which have undertaken thorough courses in history and political economy. They may be taken to represent the very latest and best ideas upon the proper functions and modes of university and college teaching in these branches. The next number of the series, which will soon be issued, will contain Dr. Ely's paper upon the past and present of political economy—a striking review of recent developments in the mode of pursuing that science, and of present phases of thought in its several departments.

The Historical Seminary has lately undertaken, in coöperation with the Seminary of Modern Languages, some interesting lines of study in folk lore.[6]

The public lectures upon archaeology, which were brought to a close on Wednesday last by Dr. Gildersleeve in a lecture on the relations between plastic and literary art, are considered to have been a great success. They have had the attraction of variety which so many like courses lack. Dr. Emerson's part in the course was the only old-fashioned part, the only part which dealt with the better known of the artistic remains of Greece; Mr. Clark and Mr. W. J. Stillman spoke almost exclusively of recent discoveries and excavations in which they had themselves taken part, and their audiences thus received the impression, always a pleasant one, of coming into contact with work which is in actual progress. The entire course was well attended and much enjoyed.[7]

The training in the new gymnasium under Dr. Hartwell[8] goes quietly and steadily on, but is not meant to lead up to exhibitions of skill; its only purpose is to furnish exercise and secure symmetrical physical development.

The spring recess began on the 10th and will continue until the 17th.

Printed in the New York *Evening Post*, April 15, 1884; editorial headings omitted.

[1] The Seminary Minutes for March 7, 1884, record that Harris read a paper entitled "The Development of the Passover Scandal."

[2] Apparently a special ceremony. It was not recorded in the Seminary Minutes.

[3] Edward A. Freeman, Regius Professor of Modern History, Oxford University, 1884-92, and author of many books on English history and government. Freeman exhibited special interest in the work of the Historical Seminary. During a visit to America in the autumn of 1881, he spoke several times before the Seminary and contributed *An Introduction to American Institutional History*, to the first volume of the Johns Hopkins University Studies in Historical and Political Science. No mention of the "MSS." to which WW alludes appears in the Seminary Minutes preceding the date of WW's report. For later references to Freeman's contributions, see the Seminary Minutes, Oct. 10 and 17, 1884.

[4] For a long account of Williams's paper, see Seminary Minutes, March 28, 1884.

[5] Herbert B. Adams, *Methods of Historical Study*, Johns Hopkins University Studies in Historical and Political Science, Vol. II (Baltimore, 1884).

[6] Probably a reference to a discussion in the Historical Seminary on April 4,

1884, of a paper, "Old Teutonic Life in Beowulf," presented by a Mr. Johnan of the English Seminary, six members of which attended the Historical Seminary on this date.

7 Basil L. Gildersleeve was a noted philologist and Professor of Greek at The Johns Hopkins University, 1876-1915. Alfred Emerson was Fellow in Greek at the Johns Hopkins, 1882-84, Joseph T. Clarke of Boston, had been in charge of the expedition of the Archaeological Institute of America to Assos, in Asia Minor, in 1881-83. William James Stillman was an artist, archaeologist, journalist, and diplomat.

8 Edward M. Hartwell, Ph.D., M.D., Instructor and Associate in Physical Culture, The Johns Hopkins University, 1882-90.

To Ellen Louise Axson

Baltimore, Md., Easter Sabbath [April 13], 1884

Ellie, my darling, if I have made happiness for you during the year just passed, what do you suppose you have done for me! You have a very enviable lot in this world, little sweetheart: it is to make other people happy. What would your dear mother have done without your companionship, my pet? You were everything to her: and after her death you were all in all to your dear father —are so still—his comfort and his pride, his brave, loving, sunny-tempered, Christian daughter. Not many people, my darling, have brightened the lives of those about them as you have. As for me! —you have given me everything—your love—and have made me happier than in all my happy life I ever dreamed of being. Of course I'm not satisfied—I wont be until you are my "very own" —I can't for the life of me conquer the discontent which fills me because of the necessity of temporary separation from you—I seem to *need* you, my darling, and I regard with impatience every circumstance which stands in the way of our seeing each other. But all that is not saying that I am *unhappy*. Very far from it! I have but to *wait* to have all my dearest hopes fulfilled: and the man who could'nt be happy under such circumstances would'nt be worth loving, little lady. So you see, Miss, what tremendous forces you have set at work. You have the making or the marring of another life besides your own! It behooves you to be very careful in the use of your power: for what might'nt you do with the plain, quiet gentleman whom you have appropriated?

I am so glad, my darling, that your plans for the Summer are complete and that they promise you such long stays with the friends you love most. I shall envy Mrs. Tedcastle and Miss Rose, but as long as they are contributing to your pleasure they are sure of my affectionate regard all the same. It is very wise, I think, to make your arrangements without reference to any possible changes in your dear father's condition—Oh, my poor little girl!

Try, my darling, to think of the possibilities of his case as little as you can. "Take no *anxious* thought for the morrow." Let us try to make our trust in God a real trust that will enable us to look forward without fear, in full confidence of ourselves one day seeing the mercy and the wisdom of the present dispensation. When there is anything to be done it is a *sin* to be passive; but when there is something to be endured, it is a duty for us to compel our hearts to be still in the presence of the doings of the Almighty. I *hope* for the best in this matter—I think that there is reason to expect an eventual perfect recovery—but if hope is to be excluded in the end, let us pray God to give us strength and faith sufficient for that day. I know what you must suffer, because of the suspense and the anxiety, and oh, my darling, I do so long to share the burden with you, to know that my love is your sufficient human support! I would give my life for you, little sweetheart; and I feel this sorrow almost as keenly as you do. You may imagine, therefore, the supreme delight with which I read the sweet, loving letter you wrote me last week, in which you told me that I *had* made even this past year a year of happiness for you! You could have made no greater contribution to my joy than that sentence contained. Strange that we should ever have thought it *chance* that brought us together in Asheville!

Dear mother and I have been trying to persuade father to go over to the Pan-Presbyterian Council which meets soon in England.[1] He is a delegate elect not only, but member of one of the most important committees appointed by the Philadelphia Council to report at this meeting, besides which his health is just now in a state which seems to make some such trip imperative. But it is hard to get him to consent. He has always underestimated his own abilities in a most provoking manner, and cannot yet be convinced that his services in the Council would be of any value. We do not despair of success, however: how could he withstand the convincing, nay, *compelling* arguments which his elder son's letters have latterly contained! To stay would be sinning against reason! I shall be delighted if he can be persuaded: he needs both the change and the rest: and he has never been across the water, having been all these years postponing the trip in expectation of the never-coming time when he could take us all with him.

But I mus'nt write any more this afternoon, my love. Good-bye: a score of kisses—if you don't want them all give some to dear little Ellen. Do you really suppose, Miss, that I think you a "goose" for kissing my letter and its contents? I'll tell you what I think of that when I see you. I'm much too far off to tell you now. Ah, my darling, do you know—can you guess one-half—how much you are wanted and needed by   Your own   Woodrow?

ALS (WC, NjP).
1 The third General Council of the World Presbyterian Alliance met, actually, in Belfast on June 24, 1884. JRW had been elected a delegate to the Council by the General Assembly of the southern Presbyterian Church in 1876. As WW's letters subsequently disclose, he did not succeed in persuading his father to attend.

From Ellen Louise Axson

My darling Woodrow,   Savannah, April 15, 1884.

I was'nt aware that you added to your various other accomplishments, that of *art-critic*, yet it seems you are a "first-rate" one. I was deeply impressed, as well as charmed, by your description of the three pictures, and am exceedingly dubious as to the one in the catalogue being "as good as you could write." I have seen an engraving of one of the three, "The Accident," and am therefore prepared to form an intelligent judgement as to the merits of your description! For I suppose that, being a picture which depends for it's value on *expression* rather than colour or tone, one can get a very good idea of it from the engraving. It is indeed a marvellous study of expression—a complete triumph, I should say. I don't see how it could be improved upon—that is, how *that* subject could be treated more successfully or effectively.

Well Sir, if I hav'nt seen the Walters gallery, the finest collection in the United States, I am ahead of you on one point at least. I've *something* to boast of,—for I just *know* I've seen the *worst* collection in the afore-said States! They are the productions of Mr. R. W. Habersham of Augusta. I never imagined anything so excruciating! They—but I won't expatiate upon them!—poor old man! But there is one singular fact about them. Whatever the subject of the picture, whether drawn from history, mythology or the realm of pure fancy,—they are generally, by-the-way, very murderous in their character—the hero is always the artist *himself*! There is over and over, the same long white beard, small, watery light eyes, and narrow forehead. He came two or three times and insisted upon our going to see them. And now he seems determined that I *shall* take lessons from him, whether or no;— has begun a large composition to serve as an object lesson for me, he says, and I am to go daily and observe it in it's several stages. You would have laughed could you have seen me, a little while ago, struggling over the composition of a note, which would offend neither him nor my own conscience;—gravely informing him how much I regretted *not* "that circumstances would prevent my availing myself of his kind offer" but that I regretted *the circumstances* which prevented,—&c. The poor old man really thinks he is the greatest artist of the age. Ah well! I hope that whatever he has lost by that self-satisfaction, he has at least gained some sort of happiness. I have often envied people who have a good opinion of themselves,—it must be such a pleasant, comfortable feeling. How often in other times, have I looked out upon earth and sky and found them very good; and then, finding my satisfaction destroyed by an unutterable self-disgust, have thought, with some longing, that if I could only be in half as good a humour with myself as I was with things in general, I would certainly be the happiest creature in the world. But I take it all back. I don't crave the joys of self-complacency, if their possession will not only make me supremely ridiculous, but, worse still, deprive me of every impulse toward progress—destroy my last forlorn hope of attaining to better things.

I fully endorse all you say about Dr. Patton. I heard him in New York, and was almost as much repelled as you seem to have been. In accent he was to me so unintelligible, in voice and manner so disagreeable, and in matter so metaphysical, that I came away anything but edified. But I concluded that it was my own fault, that my lack of appreciation was simply another evidence of my natural stupidity and need of "culture"! I thought perhaps that accent and manner was the correct thing at Princeton, and *universal* among "Princeton men"!

It is well that you enlightened me as to the device for hearing you speak, for certainly I should never have "guessed" it. Many thanks—for relieving my curiosity, at least. As for the information, I will lay it away in my memory, and in case you drive me to desperation about the speaking, I *might,* as a last resort, be so cruel as to practice upon you the secret charm, which, like a very Sampson or Merlin, you have revealed.

Grandmother, my darling, could not with very good grace object to my going to Wilmington on the grounds you first suggest, since she literally *made* Mama come down and spend the whole winter here while she was engaged to Father! The climate of course is a principal drawback to the visit in her eyes. But her opposition is only one of many reasons which render it impracticable.

By-the-way, do you know that you are supposed to be in Sav. now? I can only account for it from the fact that I was out, two or three times, driving and walking, with Mr McKee, a young man from Rome,—or rather a young man from New York, who has been in Rome for a time, and is now going home by way of Sav. You are not *at all* alike, but perhaps if one should give a general description of his height, colouring, shape of his face &c., there might *seem* to be some resemblance.

Please give my warmest thanks to Mr. Shinn for the beautiful Easter card. Tell him he doesnt know with what pleasure I received it, or how much I appreciate it. Many thanks to yourself for the *exquisite* lines from Swinburne. No, I had never seen them before. I think them *perfectly beautiful,* some of them have been haunting me ever since.

But I must close now, for I have gotten to be an early bird, of late, and I must not burn the candle at both ends;—have been for the last two weeks going regularly to "morning prayers," almost to the Park. It is a case in which virtue is it's own reward, for at that hour the walk is delicious. If you could see me at half past six, in my solitary progress up Bull St., you would certainly think me the most erratic young person you had ever encountered, for I cross and recross the street *at every corner,*—for the purpose of getting better views up and down the avenue. Sav is very fair in the morning light, with the level sunbeams gleaming on wet leaves, glancing here and there between the trees, and beyond them all, ending the vista with a splendour of misty gold.

All here send love and with just as much as you want from myself believe me as ever   Your own   Ellie.

I have an impression that the appear. of these compositions of mine grows steadily "wusser and wusser"! Why don't you make a great fuss about it, and say you consider yourself *insulted* to have such things forwarded you? It might have a salutary effect on me! But pray excuse me this time, for I am *so* tired I hardly know what I *am* writing.

ALS (WP, DLC) with WWsh notes for *Congressional Government* on env.

From Marion Wilson Kennedy

My dearest Brother;—   Little Rock, 4/15/84.

I feel quite confused in mind at present, owing partly to the fact that there are three whole letters, from *home folks,* all waiting for answers at the same time. Something altogether novel in my recent experience. . . . Oh, my dear boy, I was actually on the point of forgetting the very thing that has been uppermost in my mind for several days past. What would you think of a Professorship in "Arkansas Industrial University"? The salary for each chair is $1700.00 a year. It seems to us that this would be an unusually good time, and the chance an unusually favorable one to make a reputation for oneself, as well as for the University. You know, Gen. Hill[1] has just resigned, and the probability is that the faculty will be entirely reorganized before openning in the Fall. If you think well of the plan, please let Ross[2] know as soon as convenient. Fayetteville, where the University now is, is in the mountains of upper Arkansas, and in not only a beautiful but very healthy portion of country. You need fear no malaria there. Judging from the apparent comfort in which the Presbyterian minister's family lives there on a little more than $500.00 a year, I think living must be quite reasonable in Fayetteville. That place is in easy access by rail now, and so is much more attractive than it was a little more than a year ago. What do you think? I will write a note to Father by the same mail that takes this to you, and will ask him to let you know his opinion of the offer. I do not think there is much doubt of it being easily obtained for you. Ross has several friends on the Board of Trustees, and would certainly feel no hesitation in suggesting your name, feeling that the favor would by no means be all on one side. Don't fail to let us hear from you as soon as possible. . . .

With warmest love from us both to yourself and to dear Ellie, if you should *happen* to write to her.

Lovingly y'r sis.   Marion

ALS (WP, DLC) with WWhw notation on env.: "Ans. April 23rd 1884."
  [1] Daniel Harvey Hill, former Confederate general, president of the University of Arkansas, 1877-84.
  [2] The Rev. Anderson Ross Kennedy, Marion's husband.

To Ellen Louise Axson

My own darling,   Balto., Md., April 15, '84

Many and most loving thanks for the beautiful Easter card which came yesterday, to prove what I would rather have proof of than of anything else in the world, that my darling is thinking of her far-off lover who spends so much of his time in thinking of her. I should have valued one of the ordinary cards of the season (such as I sent you) if it had come from you, how much more, then, this one which is so far from the ordinary! You are a more faithful observer of the times and seasons than I am. Your card came at the proper date: being an Easter card, it waited till Easter to put in its appearance; whereas I, innocent youth, forgot to plan any such conjunction in sending the only card I sent out. My mind, as well as I can recollect, operated somewhat in this way: Seeing some pretty cards in a window and being in the habit of associating pretty things with a little maiden who loves such, it occurred to me, in the most natural manner possible, as it occurs to me every day about things which I have not the money to buy, that I should like to send one of them to that little maiden, and, nothing in this instance preventing, I suited action to the thought, not reflecting until some time afterwards that those particular cards were intended for a particular season which was still some weeks distant, and that, therefore, I was decidedly "previous." You had a great advantage over me in being able to think of more than one thing at a time, in being able to think both of me and of Easter. I have, however, I must tell you in all candour, Miss, a very grave suspicion about the motives which prompted you to send this card, and to make it so beautiful. I have not forgotten the pretty trepidation with which you were led to regard your failure to send me a Valentine in view of the fatal consequences which resulted from a similar failure on the part of young damsel in whom my respected younger brother was till then much interested.

Mrs. Perkins, be it related, is none other than the wife of Mr. Perkins, who is a Johns Hopkins student boarding at No. 8 Mc-Culloh St., and Mrs. Perkins is an amateur artist—a *very* amateur artist, indeed (not to say a very *im*ateur artist). Not that this is all that Mrs. Perkins is: she is, besides, a college woman, a graduate of Wellesley, versed in several languages and on speaking terms with one or two sciences (albeit she keeps neither her person nor her room tidy and will certainly convince her husband of the necessity of a divorce when she undertakes to keep house for him). All this, however, is only by the way; I began with the intention of saying that Mrs. Perkins, having acquainted her friends in the city with the fact that she is an artist, receives many curtesies as such and is quite kind in letting us all into the benefits thereof (which ought, of course, to make me very much ashamed of having made the remarks I have just made about her failure to harmonize Greek roots and cleanliness, but which, for some reason, has failed of its natural effect)[.] The other evening, therefore, we (that is, the "No. 8 crowd["]) all went, in her suite, to the art loan exhibition at the "Wednesday Club" rooms. It was an exhibition of "home talent"—and *such* an exhibition. Some of the pictures, of course, were really worth looking at: but most of them were fearfully and wonderfully daubed. The Baltimore artist, I judge from this exhibition, confines himself for the most part to portrait painting, and with very remarkable results. Either his "subjects" are very homely and he sticks with unflinching candour to their native disproportions, or he has a most whimsical rogue of a brush! Why there was a portrait there of one young damsel who, if she be really like that, could make her fortune in a museum as a "living skeleton." The number of full-length, life-size "dudes" in the collection was very noticeable and very deplorable. I hoped that there was a Mrs. Dieterich and that she was there; for by all odds the best portraits were by Mr. Dieterich—some strong faces of elderly subjects and some exquisite children's faces—especially a little beauty—the loving mother of a doll—in water colours. I could'nt quite make out what most of the landscapes were about. But really I must stop this: it would pain the Baltimore artists to know that I thought such things of their productions, and Mrs. Perkins might read these terrible sentiments in my face when I go down to supper if if [sic] I were to dwell on them any longer now.

If I should be accused of ill feeling towards artists I can disprove it by the fact that there is one artist in the world, whom I could name, an I would, whom I love with all my heart. The only painters I dislike are those which do dishonour to that which she loves. By-the-way, Miss, I hope you don't know much about the Constitution of the United States for I know marvellously little about art and if you know *both* subjects how am I to be the head of the house?

With love unspeakable,   Your own   Woodrow.

ALS (WC, NjP).

From Ellen Louise Axson

Savannah, April 15/84.

I was obliged to deny myself the pleasure of writing last night, my darling, because having been out all the evening. I found I could only do it by sitting up to a late hour; and as I have been rather overdoing *that*, in the last month or so, I decided it would be wiser to wait quietly until tonight. I have engagements which prevent my writing more than a line this morning—especially as this must be mailed at once, to avoid the danger of being delayed, as were my last two letters. Am sorry they failed to reach you on time—don't know how it happened,—there must be some change in the hours for collecting the mail. So goodbye for the present. With truest love   Your own   Ellie

ALS (WP, DLC).

From James Woodrow

My dear Woodrow: Columbia, S.C., April 16th, 1884.

I received your letter some days ago, and at once went to work to find out who the Texas Directors or Regents are. I have been very busy, so that I have not written to you; and I now write merely to tell you that your letter came; and that I approve of your plan and will heartily do whatever I can to further it.

I will write more fully as soon as I can.

Your affectionate Uncle,   James Woodrow.

ALS (WP, DLC).

To Ellen Louise Axson

My own darling,   Balto., Md., April 17th/84

You were quite right to postpone your writing rather than do it at the expense of any part of your night's rest. It is always a very trying disappointment to me not to receive a letter from my darling at the time I expect it—and a note merely stays any anxiety I might feel, without lightening the disappointment very much—but I would a thousand times rather be disappointed than have you sit up beyond bed-time to write. I am quite sure that I care much more for your happiness and well-being than for my own gratification—which is just another way of saying what I have, I believe, said several times already: that I love you.

I am not feeling very well to-day, being somewhat the worse for the wear of overwork—or, rather, perhaps I should say, of over*worry* about my work; but, fortunately, there are only about six weeks remaining of the University term and I'll soon be free to recuperate at my leisure—though it's just a bit comical to think of recuperating on the diet of German upon which I expect to subsist during the vacation[1]

Shinn is in New York, looking up a journalistic position. He wants to get to work as soon as the term here is over, and if he can get on the staff of a good paper in New York, he will be content to turn his back upon the West for some years. He is still very sore, poor fellow, about that sad love affair of his, and wants to keep away from the old scenes until he has rooted out all the pains of the experience. He's quite right, I think, under the circumstances, for I imagine, from what he has innocently told me of the lady, that she would not help to make it easy for him, were he to return to her neighbourhood. I sincerely hope that he will get a position of the sort he wants. I never knew a man who seemed more plainly cut out for journalism than he, and I am quite sure that, with half a chance, he could make for himself a very solid reputation in editorial circles in a comparatively short time. Above all things else, Shinn is versatile, and it is just that quality that makes the brilliant journalist. I rec'd an eminently characteristic epistle from the ardent Westerner this morning, wh. I enclose for your amusement, explaining that the "H. G." referred to is Harold Godwin, a Princeton class-mate of mine.

I must remark, incidentally, in closing, that I love you, my precious little sweetheart, more than you know, being persuaded that there is no sweeter maiden [in] the world, and none who can confer more happiness upon   Your own   Woodrow.

Love to your dear father and to all at 143., not forgetting *Mrs. D.*

ALS (WC, NjP). Enc.: C. H. Shinn to WW, c. April 15, 1884, ALS (WP, DLC).
    1 This reference seems to date the beginning of WW's serious study of German.

From the Minutes of the Seminary of Historical and Political Science

Bluntschli Library April 18, 1884.

Seminary called to order at 8:10 P.M. by the President Dr. Adams. . . .

Mr. *Wilson* reported upon the *"Banker's Magazine"* for March and April. He referred to an article on "American Forests" as being ludicrously out of tune with the times in its optimistic view of our forests. An article on *"Banking in France"* was also commented upon and commended for its style of condensing and conveying information. The banking customs of France were compared with those of England. An article on the "Legal Tender Decision" was characterized as "colorless." Prof. James' article on *Studies* in *"Comparative Finance"*[1] was criticised as lacking in imaginative treatment and summed up as "good material but not a good study". . . .

The rest of the evening was devoted to the consideration of the *Educational Bill* recently passed by the U.S. Senate.[2]

Dr. *Adams* opened the matter by explaining our connection with education in general, and our consequent interest in this important educational measure, and remarked that the fact that the Bill had won its way by sheer force of argument, from its first position of comparative contempt to its final passage, should be regarded as a strong point in favor of its wisdom and expediency.

Mr. Ramage was the first speaker in favor of the Bill. Considered it worthy of support for three reasons:

(1) Because it is just
(2)   "   " " expedient and wise
(3)   "   " " constitutional.

Contrasted the educational facilities of the South before the War with those of the present time. Thought the Ante-Bellum denominational colleges of the South compared favorably with Yale and Harvard at that time. Laid special stress upon the duty of the F[e]deral government to assist the South in educating the negroes because the South is unable to do it unaided, and because the influence of the Southern states in the Electoral College renders it necessary to the safety of the Federal government itself, that the negroes should be educated.

Also spoke of the dangerous position of the South itself, threatened as it was by "a black wave with a white foam."

Mr. *Shaw* took the negative side of the question and traced the history of the present measure to the alarm raised by the census of 1880, which gave statistics, that *seemed* to prove the inability of the South to educate their people. He denied this thesis with great emphasis and distinctness. He declared it absurd to suppose that any people, living as they do at the South, should be economically unable to give their people a common school education. His economic argument was close and cogent. Mr. Shaw also showed the injustice of the national government's putting such a premium upon the negligence and moral dirilictness of those states, that had not provided good common schools.

Mr. *Wilson* next spoke at considerable length and with great clearness and force against the Bill. He confined himself principally to a strenuous argument to prove that the principle contained in this Bill was both *unconstitutional*: and *politically inexpedient*. The federal government should not in any way interfere with, or become responsible for common school education. Justice, Wisdom, and the Constitution all agreed in leaving this whole matter entirely with the respective states.

Mr. *Dewey J.*[3] favored the Bill. He wished to direct attention to the facts of education in the South, and gave some statistics from the census of 1880, which seemed to show, by the increasing percentage of illiteracy at different periods of life, a retrograde movement in education. Said that history proved that educational advance always came from *above*, and asked with considerable iteration and emphatic eagerness whether this question of education was not, in reality, a *federal* question. Having elicited no response, he sat down.

A motion was made during the progress of the debate to extend the session of the Seminary one hour. The discussion was quite interesting but it is impossible to give a complete report.

Drs. *Adams* and *Jameson*, and Messrs. Alden, Dewey D., Ingle, Yager & others interjected some questions and remarks. *Papers* by Mssrs. John Johnson and Arthur Yager were announced for next meeting.

Adjournment 11. P.M.   Arthur Yager   Secretary.

[1] Edmund J. James, "Comparative Methods in Finance," *Banker's Magazine*, XXXVIII (April 1884), 757-64.

[2] The Senate had passed the education, or Blair common school, bill on April 7, 1884. Introduced by Senator Henry W. Blair, Republican, of New Hampshire, this measure provided for the appropriation of $77,000,000 for educational purposes to be distributed among the states in proportion to their number of illiterates.

[3] John Dewey, the philosopher, who took his Ph.D. at the Johns Hopkins in 1884 and was a brother of Davis R. Dewey.

To Ellen Louise Axson

My own darling,   Balto., Md., April 20th/84

There *are* some orators in the world after all! I had heard one or two, but so long ago, and with so many disappointments intervening, that I had almost lost faith in the existence of such beings. I used to long to hear some man whom I would, because I must, recognize as an orator; I anticipated the coming of such a man as a revelation of power: but I used almost to despair because of repeated disappointments. I heard a man once, a man renowned for eloquence—so renowned that John Bright called our noble English language *his* language, and Chatham's—and my heart almost stood still as my attention tip-toed to catch the first possible glimpse of his power:—a tall, stately man who trod the stage with straightened figure and erect head like one conscious of a right to command men. His voice, too, when first it reached the ear, satisfied because of its full sonorous quality, its strength, and its melody. But it never woke; it never left its first easy, leisurely pace; it lingered, finally it *droned.* What could be the matter? Had the man no life: did he always tire with that ponderous, monotonous cadence? Had his voice always that dull rebound when it struck the shallow bottom of that sluggish tone? No: he was repeating a memorized lecture, and so was a mere automaton, not giving us of his life—and not actor or poet enough to be kindled by old, familiar, oft-told sentiments. What a mistake—what a suicidal mistake! Did he not know that the only fire which is the fire of true oratory is the fire of the orator's own *life*? Unless he gives his audience of himself, unless the audience now and again catch sight of the native, unartificial fires which burn in his heart of hearts—and who could help watching and noting and thrilling at *such* a sight?—his finest phrases will fall cold and dead. *They* have no life apart from *his*. What kindles an audience is no such enigmatical thing as "personal magnetism," though it is something quite as mysterious, perhaps: it is contact with the orator's own inmost life—with his very soul. They have seen and touched his spirit; they have for the moment partaken of his power. His heart has gone out into theirs, and the life of their sympathy has entered into him.

It is such thoughts as these, my little sweet heart, which dash my amusement with *sadness* when I hear you declare your desire to hear *me* speak. I shrink from it most of all because of my unwillingness to have you so sorely disappointed as you will be: for not till I have rid myself of the accursed bonds of *self-consciousness* can I be an orator. Imagine a true poet self-conscious while writing his divinest verse, or a true painter self-conscious while painting some broad breezy expanse of moorland alight with the first glow of the morning sun! Oratory has much in common with both poetry and painting. The one thing that mars Thackeray, as it seems to me, is his self-consciousness. Self-consciousness is restraint; it shuts in the native forces and makes of the would-be orator at best only an actor!

But why am I filling my letter with these so commonplace reflections—what brought on this attack, do you say? Why nothing, except that I have again heard Dr. [Joseph T.] Duryea, the conjurer who used to conjure with my spirit when I was a boy at Princeton, and who is one of the true orators of the pulpit—as unlike colourless, disagreeable Dr. Patton as the athlete in his full vigor is unlike the skeleton which the anatomist rattles before his pupils.

I have been suffering my one-time delight in base-ball—which was my chief solace ten or twelve years ago—to draw me out as a witness to the splendid games which one can see here at this season between the "crack" professional nines of the country: at least I've been to see *two* such games; one I witnessed yesterday afternoon. Just before dinner my friend, Dr. Woods, met me on the street, and, after inspecting me critically, lectured me for "working myself to death," declaring that I looked about to break down, if I was not sick already; and so carried me off *vi et armis* to dinner, and after dinner to a ball game. His brother and sister, and a young lady who is visiting the latter, went with us, so that we had a jolly time. I like good company as much as I enjoy a good game of baseball, and, having both, I was *immensely content*, so to speak, though it was marvellously like wasting time, considering all I have to do before the close of the term.

Have you fixed upon an exact date yet for your departure for Rome, my little lady? It will seem quite natural to address my letters to Mr. Tedcastle's care, "Rome Geo." How I wish I could follow them and deliver their messages in person! You must promise, Miss, to write me an extra quota of letters when your vacation begins, and fill them chuck full of love messages, else how am I to stand the separation much longer? It seems to me, by the way, Miss, that you are looking forward to the continuation of that separation with a remarkable amount of philosophy! How am I to know, pray, that you care when you do'nt say so? It's a legitimate *inference*, I admit, from certain other facts, and from expressions you have used; but is a chap to live on inferences?

With unbounded love,   Your own   Woodrow.

ALS (WC, NjP).

From John Hanson Kennard, Jr.

My dear Wilson,   New Orleans, La., April 20th, 1884.

On my return from the country three days ago your letter was awaiting me,[1] and I was delighted to get it I assure you. I can hardly account for the strength of my attachment to the J.H.U. and every thing about it. Probably much of the feeling is owing to the magnificent opportunities I saw afforded by the Univ. and to the friendships I began in it. Of course I agree with you as to the incompetency of our beloved instructor [H. B. Adams]; but the Univ. itself offers so much in the way of general culture, and you are so much in the stream of educational work that it seems now to me, who can not be there, that the Johns Hopkins is the ne plus ultra of universities. . . .

If any of my class mates ask after me give them my kindest regards, especially to Shinn and Sato.

Write soon.

Sincerely your friend,   J. H. Kennard Jr.

ALS (WP, DLC) with WWhw bibliographical references and notation on env.: "Ans. May 20th/84."

[1] WW's letter, which is missing, was apparently a reply to J. H. Kennard, Jr., to WW, March 5, 1884.

From Ellen Louise Axson

My darling Woodrow,   Savannah April 21/84.

Many thanks for the beautiful and interesting little catalogue, which, together with the "Saturday letter," I found awaiting me on my return from the country today. I have just been looking over it, with much pleasure, and am more than ever convinced that Mr. Walters has a splendid collection. How did you like the famous Gerôme, "The Duel after the Masquerade"? I have seen engravings of it, and it seems to be a work of terrible power. And what did you think of "The Hemicycle"? How I wish I could have seen the "Millets," and "Corots," and the sketches (apparently) of Mariano Fortuny! Did you like the "St Sebastian[']? I think the Baltimore artists showed considerable courage to give their exhibition of home talent now, while the masters have the floor, —should think they would have waited and avoided the vivid contrast. They must have formed an excellent foil to some of those great pictures.

By-the-way, I am shocked, grieved, and mortified that *you*—a deciple of learning—should deliberately go to work to put a *premium upon ignorance*, first by your unappreciative and even satirical remarks concerning your gifted friend, Mrs. Perkins, and then by your rashly expressed "hope" that I don't know much about the Constitution! Who would have anticipated such conduct in a *professor*! But then you don't profess to teach women. I begin to wonder whether you deny them the "right" to be "on speaking terms" with sciences and constitutions! However, it is a matter in which I have no personal interest, and I dare say Mrs. P. can take care of herself. I must add that your wishes are abundantly gratified, for the depth of my ignorance as to the Constitution of the United States is simply unfathomable. I am sorry you are being so overweighted by your work, and am *very* sorry you are not feeling well. I *hope* those remaining six weeks will not prove too great a strain. What a pity it is, that the hardest work in colleges, the preparing for examinations, should always come in the spring when one is least inclined for it. I believe the Sewanee [the University of the South's] plan of ending the year at Xmas is the best.

I have been "awfully" busy too—yet in spite of that fact I ran away and took a three days vacation! That is, I *went* on business and *stayed* for pleasure, for I was so fascinated that I could'nt get away. I went to "Richmond," the old family home of the Clays. Mr. Tom [C.] Clay, the present owner, married Aunt Ella's sister, the fairest of the fair "Miss Laws."[1] She is as good, and bright, and lovely as she is beautiful; in fact an ideal woman—an ideal *Southern* woman of the most exquisite type. He is, not perhaps as *ideal*, but certainly a *typical* Southerner;—and a delightful specimen. He has all the Southern prejudices, in excellent condition, —is, in spirit, as much a slave-holder as he ever was, has no use for Yankees, or for Yankee capital "to develop the resources of the country"; indeed he would, on general principles, prefer that those resources *should'nt* be developed. He regards with almost the impatience of the savage the inroads of civilization. He loves his forest solitudes with a passionate love, and would wish them to remain forever untouched. He knows all about trees and flowers and birds; and he hunts and fishes, and reads old books, plants his rice, watches over his negros, worships his wife, (or treats her as though he did) and in all respects lives as much as possible as his father did before him. Indeed, he lives by tradition; and as he was taught so will he teach his boys—"to ride, to shoot, and to tell the truth." He is, of course, a charming host and a delightful companion,—being a thorough wag, an inimitable mimic, and full of enthusiasm for many things, especially poetry and the wild woods;—and, by way of conclusion, he is a noble, Christian gentleman.

How I wish you could see Richmond! I can't say how often I wished for you while there. The place, it's inmates, and their life upon it, is all one beautiful, noble, pathetic poem. I never saw such majestic desolation. The situation is lovely in the extreme. Behind the house, a few yards only from the door, runs the broad and limpid Ogeechee, making a great curve half round the place. There is a bold bluff over hung with superb trees, and, at this season, all aglow with flowers. Indeed the whole place is a tangle of trailing vines and flowers, as wild as the forest itself, yet unlike it; for over nothing can the hand of man pass without leaving its trace,—without giving an impression of sadness, of ruin, which nature untouched never makes us feel. And such avenues of moss-draped oaks and cedars! Boneventure[2] itself almost sinks into insignificance. There are some six or eight of them—all leading no-whither, for everything was destroyed by the war. The house itself was burnt by Sherman, one ivy-covered chimney only remaining to mark the spot. They live in one of the old outhouses, —a dwelling which would be extremely uncomfortable in any other climate. The interior is marked by those odd contrasts with which we have grown so familiar;—rough walls and scanty furniture, with many valuable old heirlooms, and the finest of damask and silver. Indeed it is a very one-sided poverty, this! They live sumptuously every day in that pine cottage; whatever else they may want, there is no lack of rich and delicate food, where earth and air and water bring forth so abundantly. It is altogether the most complete, as well as beautiful, expression of our Southern tragedy I ever saw; and after all it is *not* a tragedy. There is small place for that, in the home where that lovely woman lives and labours, and which she glorifies with the light of love. It is a dignified poverty, yet, in her case especially, worn lightly and with a frank and careless grace. There is about her and [an] indescribable, soft gaiety, an almost girlish winsomeness and grace, combined with deep earnestness, high courage, and patient, steady effort. For years she has struggled bravely to educate her boys— to ensure their going to college; and first to, herself, prepare them for it; sitting up night after night to study that she may be competent.

However, I did not intend to fill my whole letter with this one subject; but you will excuse me, for perhaps you can guess how all this has worked upon my imagination and sympathies. The younger brother, [R.] Habersham Clay, has married a rich girl, and his inheritance, Strathy Hall,[3] his mother's old ancestral home, has risen, like a phenix from its ashes; and is a beautiful and exquisitely tasteful place; yet it was odd to see how commonplace and uninteresting appeared its smooth lawns and trim gardens, it's inlaid floors and tiled chimneys, it's rosewood and plush, beside the noble wreck at Richmond.

I am *so* glad your father thinks of going to Europe; have no doubt it will be the very thing for his health. I do hope you will succeed in pursuading him.

Well, I *must* close though I have so much to say that I feel as though I had scarcely *begun*—thanks to letting one subject run away with me.

With a whole heartful of love I remain

Yours forever   Ellie.

ALS (WP, DLC).
[1] Caroline Matilda Law Clay. The "Miss Laws" were daughters of Judge William Law, a prominent lawyer of Savannah.
[2] See ELA to WW, Feb. 11, 1884, n. 4.
[3] A colonial plantation located in nearby Bryan County.

From Joseph Ruggles Wilson

Dearest Woodrow—   [Wilmington, N.C.] Ap 22 [1884]

I am just from Presbytery,[1] & find yrs of the 16th on my table. Of course I will introduce Mr. Inglis (not "English") when he shall have come along and reported. So—it is "a Mr. *Sadler* you are pleading for"—Ah—'hum—yes—I suppose so.

I have received a note from Marion Kennedy, in which she lifts to view what I regard as a fine chance in yr behalf. She says that she has advised you of the same. Don't hesitate to send on recommendations to Ross—and at once.

As to the Texas U'y., the names of Trustees—are these still un-get-at-a-ble? It is rumored that [Robert Lewis] Dabney would like to quit there, and return to Virginia!

I am sorry, dearest one, that yr. heart is so set upon my going to Belfast:—for it is *almost* certain that I *cannot* go. The [General] Ass'y will not adjourn before 1st June: and I would have to sail about the 10th or earlier[.] The *minutes*—meanwhile—have to be published, and by me. I am fearful too, of the ocean! The Council, besides, is a great bore, and it gives literally no chance for conspicuousness—for all its proceedings are cut & dried, and its debators chosen, beforehand. There are other reasons:—*Expense* is one.

In great haste but with great affection   Your   F.

All send lots of love.

P.S. Dear Mother handed me the catalogue of T. Un'y, since I wrote the above. There seems to be *no* room for you. English Professor & Assistant being already at work, & Dabney political science. I don't know *one* of the Regents.

ALS (WP, DLC) with WWhw notation on env.: "Ans. April 23/84."
  1 The Presbytery of Wilmington met at Clinton, N.C., April 16-19, 1884.

Three Letters to Ellen Louise Axson

My own darling,   Balto., April 22nd, 1884

I have copied for your delectation a few more passages from Swinburne's "Tristram of Lyonesse." I am bent upon having you enjoy with me these exquisite bits of fancy and music, tho' I'm driven to copying for the purpose, Shinn's copy of the poem being the only one to which I have access. Were it mine, I could put it aside to read with you in the golden coming days when we shall be together. The passages are all taken from the first part of the poem ("The Sailing of the Swallow") wh. tells how,

> "About the middle music of the spring
> Came from the castled shore of Ireland's king
> A fair ship stoutly sailing, eastward bound
> And south by Wales and all its wonders round

To the loud rocks and ringing reaches home
That take the wild wrath of the Cornish foam,

*   *   *   *   *   *   *   *

To the wind-hollowed heights and gusty bays
Of sheer Tintagel, fair with famous days,"

bearing Iseult, under Tristram's charge, to wed Mark, Tintagel's king. I am sure that you will agree with me in saying that nothing could surpass the beauty and vividness of the description contained in the longest of the quotations, where the storm brews and breaks and again gives place to the sun, leaving the sweet girl, "shining like all April in one day," to throw her wraps aside in the returned smiles of the scene and make that artless, playful, sweetest speech, "I too have heart then, I was not afraid." I can imagine some of poor Tristram's thoughts as he looked and listened. It is not related what he said.

I have been putting this wonderful verse of Swinburne's to the use which I generally make poetry serve in my mental economy: to prepare me for composition. I had a speech to make at the Seminary the other night, on the Blair Educational Bill, which Dr. Adams insisted upon having discussed, and so I read Swinburne. From Shakspere, or from any finely figurative writing I get a stimulus for extemporaneous expression, with either my tongue or my pen, such as I can get in no other way and from no other source. It sets my mind aglow, seeming to make it nimble and strong, with a joyous strength fit for doing at its best any work it is capable of doing at all. But, for the matter of that, I think that the proper office of all books—even of those dreary compendia which supply one with the innumerable facts of life and science—is to stimulate the mind. The man who reads everything is like the man who eats everything: he can digest nothing; and the penalty for cramming one's mind with other men's thoughts is to have no thoughts of one's own. Only that which enables one to do his own thinking is of real value: which is my explanation of the fact that there are to be found in history so many great thinkers and great leaders who did little reading of books—if you reckon reading by volumes—but much reading of men and of their own times. "A little learning *is* a dangerous thing," but so is too much learning also. Reason and understanding are the only things one cannot have to[o] much of. A man can hardly have too much strength; but he can develop one set of muscles to the exclusion of others till they become clumsy and unwieldy: and he can certainly wear too many clothes.

But this is a dreadful habit I'm falling into, of loading my letters to my precious little sweetheart with so much cheap philosophy. It is not because I think that you have done anything to deserve punishment, my darling—on the contrary, you've done nothing but make me happy—but because I'm naturally a very foolish fellow who likes to pour his commonplace thoughts out at the ears of those who love him and wont laugh at him. What a dreadful time you will have when you shall have put yourself at my disposal in such matters! Do you think, Miss, that you will have the courage to promise to "obey" a man who will be forever insisting upon your hearing his views of the world many times every day—a man of restless, unappeasable ambition to produce something worthy of the world's reading, and bent, meantime, upon compelling you to hear and pass judgment upon what he does in the progress of the adventure? But I wont frighten you: because I am only too well convinced that without my Ellie's loving aid and companionship I shall never do any of the great things of which my ambition has dreamed! My darling!

> "Thy soul is shed into me with thy breath
>   And in my heart each heart-beat of thee saith
>   How in thy life the lifesprings of me lie,
>   Even one life to be gathered of one death
>   In me and thee, though day may live and die."

I have just had a letter from sister Marion in which she asks "what I would think of a chair in Arkansas Industrial University." Of course I can't say until I hear more of the *character* of the chair, which she *thinks* might just at this time be easily secured for her interesting brother; but I shall write for further particulars. What would my darling think of a home amidst the pretty mountain lands of upper Arkansas? Ellie, listen! I love you with all my heart! Love to all at 143, and to your dear father, from

Your own   Woodrow.

My own darling,   Balto., Md., April 24th/84
I do'nt wonder that you filled your whole letter with "Richmond"; having just returned from it, how could your mind fail to be full of recollections of *such* a place! I would have given *anything* to be with you on that visit, not only for love's sake, because I long to be with *you* anywhere, but also for my profession's and my imagination's sake. The picture you painted of that home went straight to my heart. Far removed as my sym-

pathies are from the *prejudices* of such men as Mr. Clay, they are altogether with the men themselves: my heart goes with them, though my judgment holds back from their opinions. One who has seen "Richmond" and "Strathy Hall" has seen the old and the new South: most of the nobility of life and feeling is in the former, but the thrift of progress, the hope and the only feasible approach to a new nobility is represented by the latter. I should have liked to have gone with you to Richmond, therefore, not only that I might know Mr. and Mrs. Clay for their own sakes, but that I might realize by actual sight what, hitherto, I have realized only in imagination, the old Southern country life. Such homes are very few nowadays, because such inmates are very rare, and to miss knowing them is to lose our only chance of *knowing* the history of our own birth-land. Mr. Clay *cannot* reproduce himself in his sons, however; time will move too fast for him, and there is a sad danger that he will give them only the worst, not the best, of himself.

If you have given me a complete picture of Mrs. Clay, my little lady, I shall be inclined to admit that you *do* know an "ideal" when you see it, and shall begin to hope (since you applied that word to me once on a time—before you knew me as well as you do now) that there is something better in myself than I had supposed! And the best thing you told me about Mr. C. was what you said about his treatment of his wife. I have all my life long sought to cherish that chivalrous, almost worshipful, regard for woman which seems to me the truest badge of nobility in man— and which languishes in true men (or, at least, is in danger of languishing) only when certain damsels who think only of balls and the fashions, or certain dames who think only of marrying off their daughters, come into one's circle. Such women have to be tolerated with a strained, self-compelled courtesy; and one has to reserve his strong, passionate *love* for such noble women as Mrs. Clay and my precious little queen. Upon the last named person I have centred all the love of which I am capable, together with all the ardour of devotion for her sex that has been one of the chief inspirations of my youth. Are you content with that confession from   Your own   Woodrow?

My own darling,   Balto., Md., April 27th/84

I know very little about Mr. James Payn—indeed, the only thing from his pen I ever remember reading was an article on "Sham Admiration in Literature"—but that article was admirably sensible in its advocacy of genuine, as opposed to fashionable, opinion, and the little extract I enclose confirms me in the conclusion that he is a gentleman of eminent sense, whose heart is altogether in the right place.[1] Some of these days when I have to write, from a very tall pinnacle of fame (ahem!) *my* autobiography just think of the volumes it will contain about a certain young lady with lovely shy brown eyes (a lady who is young *now*, that is, but probably wont be then: though I should like to make a bet of anything you please that those lovely eyes will always retain their youth of love and beauty, and will always be bright with the inarticulate speech of the heart which, if I know it aright, will grow younger instead of older); and wont the famous (?) author have to readjust the judgments of the world by letting them into the secret of how much of his success has been built by the loving hands of a helping wife! I suspect that an attempt on my part to write an autobiography would end in my writing your biography, my little sweetheart: for I wont *have* any life apart from yours!

In case, my dear Miss Axson, you may have in your possession "any literary matter which you may be able and willing to contribute," you will please give due attention to the enclosed circular.[2]

It looks very much as if that unmanageable father of mine were going to slip through my hands after all in the matter of attendance on the great P-P. Council. He says that he cannot go on account of his duties as Stated Clerk of the General Assembly and editor of its Minutes. I have now played my last card in offering to edit the Minutes for him. I am very much afraid *that's* "no go," however; because, though I've served a pretty thorough apprenticeship as his assistant in the editing of the Minutes, I do'nt think he would feel altogether safe in leaving the whole job to me—even if I could convince him that he would be treating the Assembly quite right in doing so. I am bitterly disappointed; I had set my heart on his going.

My friend Dr. Woods is fairly radiant nowadays: he too is engaged to be married—and to an exceptionally fine girl, too.[3] He talks about the matter with a very puzzling emphasis, having said to me more than once: "Well, old man, it *does* feel good to be engaged"—as if *I* had said that "it felt good"! Ah! the rascal do'nt know how fortunate he is: for does he not live in the same city with his lady-love? What would you think, my little lady, if we poor separated creatures could live, during this period of waiting, within four blocks of each other and catch at least a glimpse of each other every day? But, let me tell you, as a profound secret, that I do'nt really envy the Dr. even his fortunate situation in this regard: for, great as is the admiration I entertain for Miss Laura Hall, I can't see any comparison between the prize for which the Dr. is striving and that which is before me; and there seems to me to be a peculiar fitness in my having to go through a severer discipline of waiting than any one else.

You will probably hear with deep regret that the great Johns Hopkins University Glee Club met last evening to disband for the season: though it will doubtless comfort you to know that the last act of its life was an act of benevolence. One week ago it sang in the Methodist church at Woodberry (a thriving suburb of Balto.) for the benefit of the "Woodberry Workingmen's Library and Reading Room." I wish you could have seen the audience! It was composed for the most part of factory people—of factory girls, truth to tell—and of course such a handsome set of young men as the Club took immensely with such auditors. The "classical" pieces, and even the milder sort of college songs, did not rouse much enthusiasm, it is true; but the "three kittens" and the "Hip-po-pot-a-mus" went straight to their hearts, and will long be of sweet savour in their memories. After the concert we were treated to a very nice supper and came back to town in our four-horse 'bus in such high and musical humour that we doubtless made many peaceful citizens turn uneasily in their beds, as we went roaring and rattling thro'. the quiet streets.

Do'nt forget, my darling, to answer my question about the "Arkansas Industrial University." It really begins to look as if I might go out there, if I am to judge from what sister Marion says in a letter received to-day[4]—though the prospects are at most probabilities, not certainties.

Give my warmest love to your dear father and to Stockton when you write, as well as to all at 143, keeping for your sweet self just as much as ever you want from

Your own   Woodrow.

ALS (WC, NjP).
  [1] The "little extract" is missing. James Payn was an English writer and editor, author of many novels and essays.
  [2] The "enclosed circular" is missing. It was an advertisement for materials relating to the history of American political economy, similar to the one printed at May 10, 1884.
  [3] Laura Hall, daughter of Robert C. Hall of 257 Madison Avenue, Baltimore. Wilson visited frequently in the Hall home. Woods married Laura Hall on October 28, 1886.
  [4] Marion W. Kennedy to WW, April 25, 1884, ALS (WP, DLC).

From Houghton, Mifflin & Company[1]

Dear Sir: Boston, 28 April 1884

We have read with real interest the *ms* which you forwarded to us. We do not like in any case to make conditional promise of publication, and we cannot well decide on this *ms* in its present incomplete state. So far as the essays go they seem to us to be good in themselves and to have elements of interest for the public. If we had your entire work before us we could undoubtedly speak with positiveness. We can only say that if the rest is as good as this, we hope you will send it to us and allow us to consider the question of publication. Farther than that we cannot go, and we beg you will take this letter as evidence of our sincere interest, and of not a little confidence in your ability to produce an interesting and acceptable book.

Yours truly   Houghton, Mifflin Co.

Shall we return you the *ms*?

ALS (WP, DLC).
  [1] The author of this letter, unknown to Wilson, was Horace Elisha Scudder, who wrote the letter without signing or initialing it. Scudder also wrote the letter to Wilson of May 5, 1884, and, presumably, the letter of Nov. 26, 1884, although the only extant copy is one that Wilson made. Scudder was born in Boston, Oct. 16, 1838, and was graduated from Williams College in 1858. He was associated with Henry O. Houghton, the publisher, 1864-80, and was an editor at Houghton, Mifflin & Co., 1880-1902, and editor of the *Atlantic Monthly,* 1891-98. Author of many works of history and fiction, he died in Cambridge, Mass., on Jan. 11, 1902.

From Ellen Louise Axson

My darling Woodrow,   Sav. April 29/84.

Once again my Monday night has been stolen away, and once again I am forced to postpone my regular letter. I should be fully convinced that it was time to change the night, if I was to remain longer in Sav. But I daresay that in that calm retreat—East Rome, (or—I beg their pardon—*Etowah City!*) I shall be able to pursue the even tenor of my way, unmolested. Then I will try to atone for past irregularities;—though as for writing "an extra quota of letters" as a vacation amusement, I sincerely hope I shant have any "vacation." But at present I am so *very* busy that the most pressing question is to decide what I can best afford to leave undone. When I write at all it is on the principle which guided the old farmer, who had so much work to do that he couldn't decide what to do first,—so he went a'fishing!

I am very, *very* sorry to hear that you are trying to break yourself down with over-work. I have been *distressed* all the week at the state of affairs revealed by the remarks of your friend Dr. Woods. I hope he will fairly *persecute* you with base-ball games, &c. I have been informed by one in whom I have great confidence that "*too* much *learning* is a dangerous thing,"—it don't pay for itself. I have also been creditably informed that one of the best evidences of a well-disciplined mind is the ability to know just when you have worked enough, and heroically to act upon that knowledge, whatever the temptation to the contrary. I say 'heroically,' because I think it is the very hardest thing in the world to do. If things are going smoothly one is fascinated, and wants to "go on forever"; and if they are not going smoothly—why then it is harder than ever to leave, before one has conquered. How often have I worked on and on, in a half feverish, and wholly ineffective fashion, though I knew it was almost a sin to do it, just because I had'nt *self-control* enough to do otherwise. I *do* hope this next letter,—today's—will tell me that you are feeling better, and have decided to show yourself some mercy.

I should think you would find the mountain lands of upper Arkansas a very pleasant home. But as I know nothing whatever about it, of course, I hav'nt much to *say* on the subject—have only like yourself, to wait and *hear* more of the facts. Would the Industrial University expect to take you *now*, or wait 'till they can get you!—that is, until you finish your course at Baltimore? By-the-way what *is* an *Industrial* University? I would have you understand, Sir, that this is'nt a *note* of apology, as you might imagine from the first page, but a *letter* and must serve the purpose of one, until tomorrow night—for I am going to a grand wedding tonight. The bride is Jacqueline Prince, Gen Jackson's niece and adopted daughter.

Give much love to your dear parents. All here send love. I leave on Tuesday night—a week from today. Good-bye; take care of yourself, my darling—and believe me

Yours with all my heart   Ellie.

ALS (WP, DLC).

To John Barbee Minor

My dear Sir,   Balto., Md., Apr. 29th/84

As a former pupil of yours, and because I lay great store by your possible counsel and aid, I take the liberty of addressing you on a subject of some delicacy. For the past year I have been pursuing studies in history and political science here at the Johns Hopkins University, with a view to fitting myself for a professorship in those branches. After spending some months at my home in recuperating from the sickness which was the immediate cause of my withdrawal from the University of Va., I went to Atlanta, Geo., and practiced law there, with moderate success, in partnership with Mr. E. I. Renick, whom you doubtless remember as one of your pupils. At the end of one year, however, I concluded to give up the practice and come here for the course of study which I have since been pursuing. It was, I now know, inevitable that I should make this change sooner or later. Ever since before I entered your classes—ever since the middle of my college course, indeed—my tastes have set very strongly in the direction of the study of history and political science, my main ambition having long been to become an authoritative writer upon constitutional history, administration, and non-partisan politics. My mistake of plan was, not in studying law, and in studying where I would be most thoroughly grounded in the principles of the common law —for such preparation for my present studies was simply invaluable—but in entering upon the practice with the hope that I could add to congenial occupations at the bar the studies of a writer on historical and state questions. I suspected from the first that my chosen course was not the wisest; a few months of actual trial of the experiment sufficed to convince me of its folly; and I have turned with satisfied conscience and renewed hope to the profession in which I can, I am sure, do to the best advantage, the work for which I am fitted both by taste and acquirement.

I hope that you will pardon me for having troubled you with this rather tedious chapter of my personal history: I have given it merely in order to enable you to understand what might otherwise have seemed to you like vacillation in the course I have followed, and to introduce the chief matter of the letter, which is the request—made with great hesitation—that you will, if perfectly agreeable and convenient, put into writing such an estimate of my character and abilities as you can vouchsafe under the circumstances, and as you would be willing to have me use in pressing my candidacy for any chair that may offer. Influential friends of mine in Arkansas are desirous of securing a place for me in the "Industrial University" of that State and I am anxious to add to letters from my instructors here such other letters as I may be able to obtain through the kindness of my instructors at Princeton and the Univ. of Virginia.

I have hesitated some time about asking this so considerable favour of you, and have finally made bold to do so principally because I know that you will deal perfectly frankly with me in the matter, refusing my request if for any reason you see fit to do so.

Be kind enough to present my kindest regards to your daughters. Their society contributed more than they know or I can say towards making my stay at a University delightful, as your instruction contributed everything towards training me in thorough and efficient methods of study.

Hoping that your health continues strong, I remain

Respectfully and gratefully yrs.   Woodrow Wilson

ALS (Minor Papers, ViU).

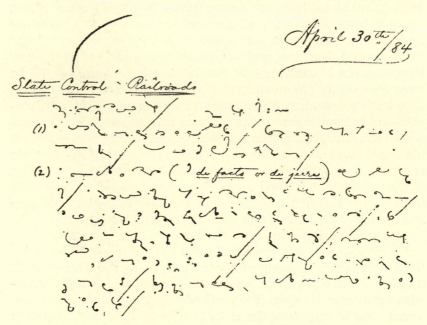

From Wilson's shorthand notes taken in Professor Richard T. Ely's advanced course in political economy

From Ellen Louise Axson

My darling Woodrow,   Savannah May 1st 1884.

Yours of the 27th, with it's very interesting enclosures, came safely to hand this morning much to my relief,—for you must know, that I had been foolish enough to get up a regular panic over the non-appearance of my usual Tuesday letter. I found nothing better to do than to connect that fact with the ominous words of your medical man, and leap to the conclusion that you *had* "broken down" and were very ill. "How much suffering has been caused us by those troubles which never came to pass"! I was in a perfect quiver the whole morning with the dread lest today's letter too should fail, and my fears be thereby confirmed. And as the hour for the mail drew near, and then passed—for the mail was late—my hand trembled so violently that, though I continued to try, I could not draw at all. How silly and cheap it makes one feel to have caused such a commotion about nothing! It all seems so utterly unfounded afterwards, that you wonder how you *could* have been such a simpleton. But "trifles light as air are to the"—anxious—["]confirmations strong as proofs of holy writ." Though I did'nt give myself credit for so much ingenuity in devising means for torturing myself. I am not usually in the habit of borrowing trouble. But I suppose it would scarcely be possible for one to pass through all that I have suffered without losing something of the childish "confidence in events." I hope by-the-way that my fears *were altogether* without cause. You say nothing about your health, but I judge all is well, as you speak of having been to the club the night before. *Are* you quite well?

So you are actually started on your history!—these circulars look like business. I wish you the greatest success, and pleasure, in it. Is it to be your vacation work as you proposed?

May 2

I was interrupted last night, as usual, my darling; and as I have only a moment's time now for writing, and see no prospect ahead of me for being able to make even another *attempt* this week, I will close this scrawl at once, and let it go—though it does'nt deserve to be sent. I really am in a tight place—a thousand and one things demanding my attention at once—and there are guests in the house too. Miss Carrie (or rather Mrs. Clay) is here from Richmond, with her youngest boy,—my little sweet-heart. The latter, a little seven year old, conceived what one might call a *frantic* passion for me when I was in Bryan. So after I left he was so anxious to come to town that a week ago his mother sent him, and yesterday followed herself. He has'nt been in, for six years before, though it is only an hours ride on the cars. He is one of the lovliest and most beautiful boys I ever saw, and his artless compliments and love-making are *too* funny and pretty. I never saw such a chivalrous little soul; he is "a verrie parfait gentil knight." In fact I fell in love with *him* too. You see, I am getting faster and faster. We made even better time than that recorded in my last "affaire du coeur"—he was my accepted lover in three days. He almost convulsed his father soon after my arrival at Richmond by enquiring with deep anxiety if I was *his* cousin as well as Randolph's; "because," he said, "I want her for my sweet-heart, and you know, if she is my cousin, I can't have her."

I am *so* sorry you have failed to prevail upon your father to attend the council. A trip to Europe would be the best thing in the world for him. I really think it gave Grandfather a new lease of life.

What does your sister write you about the Arkansas scheme. Does she tell you what manner of "chair" it is? And is it the sort you want? Where is the University situated? Is it near Little Rock? You ask my opinion about it. As I said before I don't know any of the facts, so I can't have a very intelligent opinion, but of course if *you* like it, so do *I*, very much indeed.

Your little cutting from Payn is very nice;—and your remarks thereupon, my dear Sir, give rise to a new and somewhat startling train of thought. It suggests possible consequences of having to do with men of genius which had'nt occurred to me before!

By-the-way, you should have seen how "struck" this family looked when I showed them your circular. True, I had told them what you proposed doing, but I presume they did'nt realize that you were such a great man *already*!

But I really must close or I will miss this mail too. Good-bye my darling—once again, *take care of yourself*.

With all my heart,   Your own Ellie.

ALS (WP, DLC).

Two Letters to Ellen Louise Axson

My own darling,   Balto., Md., May 1st/1884

I must say that my sweet little lady-love is the most tantalizing young woman of my acquaintance. I ask her what she would think of the mountain lands of upper Arkansas as a home—for *herself* of course—and she replies: "I should think *you* would find the mountain lands of upper Arkansas a very pleasant home"! Am I to understand, then, Miss, that you have no personal interest in the matter, but intend to marry me without binding yourself to live with me? I had supposed, in my innocence, that in choosing a home for myself I should be choosing a home for you, and so turned to you to learn what you would think of the prospect of going away beyond the Mississippi, far away from both your home and mine: but, if I am not to have your companionship, I am quite indifferent as to what sort of place I go to.

There's not much to tell about the Arkansas institution: it is much like all the other Southern and western colleges. It is called "Industrial" because its chief endowment consists of a large quantity of land granted that State by Congress, as other public lands were granted other States, for the partial endowment of mechanical and Industrial schools; and it justifies its name, I believe, by furnishing to a portion of its students a certain amount of instruction in the industrial arts. The University of California was founded in the same way by similar grants of land from Congress, though its courses of study, like those of the Arkansas University, are very much like those pursued elsewhere. Like the University of California, too, the Arkansas institution is *co-educational*, admitting women to its classes, and even to its faculty.

Of course not all these features are aggreeable to my tastes; but the same features are common to all the new and most of the old colleges below the very first rank—are found, indeed, in some of the very first—and one must face the fact that it is impossible, as it is undesirable, to start at the top, in just such a berth as one could wish for. Such places have to be won from the foot-hold of places lower down: and any foot-hold even is extremely hard to find: for very few colleges care as yet as much as they should for good teachers of history and political economy—though everything is now tending in the direction of a much greater demand for such in the near future—and a good offer is not to be despised whencesoever it comes. The offer from the Arkansas University *is* a good one for a beginner in the professorial field, though it is by no means superlative. Sister Marion says: "The salary is $1,700.00 a year. It seems to us that this would be an unusually good time, and the chance an unusually favourable one, to make a reputation for oneself, as well as for the University." The probability (which is still not a certainty) of there being a vacancy for me arises from the fact that the President of the Univ. has just resigned and an entire reorganization of the faculty is expected, in consequence, before the opening in the Autumn. There are some eight or ten professors, besides the faculty of the medical school which forms a distinct branch of the University. The existence of this technical school in addition to the academic departments would seem to justify, partially at least, the assumption of the name "university," though the courses pursued in the latter departments are scarcely university courses.

In short, taking the circumstances all together, as far as I have learned them, the opportunity seems quite as favourable as any other that is likely to offer, and my only desire now is to learn what my darling thinks of the case, so far as it has anything positive about it. If the vacancy expected should occur, bro. Ross seems quite sure of his ability to secure it for me; and, if the chair be given me, I should doubtless be expected to enter upon its duties next September. That would, of course, break in upon the plans which I have so far had: but no great harm would result. A man learns best what he is under the immediate necessity of teaching, of making his own in order that he may impart it fresh to others, and I could study more effectively in Arkansas, consequently, than in Baltimore (except that I would not have there the splendid libraries of Balto.). The chief advantage in being at the Hopkins, for one in my situation, is not more that it's one of the best places for study than that it's the best place from which to seek a professorship: and my original plan was to work here two years, at the most, in case a professorship did not sooner offer.

I should not mind how long I had to study here and wait for "something to turn up," were it not for a single circumstance, which is that, strange as it may seem, *I want you*—with a longing whose intensity sometimes seems like to break my heart.

Pardon this tedious *business* letter, my darling: my excuse for it is that its subject concerns you as much as it does me: and, if you know how to find it, this epistle contains as much love as any I ever wrote. You are "a' the world to me," and I am

Your own   Woodrow.

My precious little queen,   Balto., Md., May 1st/84

I am driven to the comical and, in my experience, unprecedented necessity of writing a brief supplement to the letter I mailed scarcely an hour ago. So full was I of the Arkansas business, that I neglected to say anything to dispel the anxiety about my health which appears in my darling's note of this morning. I am not *quite* well, but I am lightening my work, and there's no danger of my being really sick: so that my little sweetheart must not distress herself about me. It's rather *worry* than work that hurts me; and, if I can get my plans for some time ahead satisfactorily adjusted with your loving approval, and can induce you to promise that our wedding may come as soon after such adjustment as possible, there will be small chance for worry to hold dominion over me longer. I want to make my first appointment the immediate starting-point for the winning of a better appointment by doing my best work in it; but I know that I can't

do my best in any work which I may have to do without you: so
that the beginning of my real career waits upon you—hangs upon
the sacrifice you may be willing to make in my behalf, provided
it be a sacrifice to marry   Your own   Woodrow.

P.S. I must really protest, Miss Axson, against your laughing at
me for pleading so earnestly on the strength of what is at most
only a possibility. It's a very earnest matter with
                                   Yours lovingly   W.
ALS (WC, NjP).

From John Barbee Minor

Dear Mr. Wilson,   University of Virginia, May 1 1884.
    Your's of 29 recd, and I hasten to comply with your request,
inclosing the testimonial desired herewith.
    There must be a difference of tastes in order to make a world,
and I acquiesce in the necessity therefor. I cant forbear some
natural surprise however,—*natural*, having regard to my own pursuits in life,—that one shd prefer to wander through the interminable mazes of political speculation, rather than to move, with
measured pace, amidst the nicely adjusted parterres, and the
well-defined squares of municipal jurisprudence.
    But at all events I heartily wish you as much satisfaction as
can possibly attend the cultivation of the field you have chosen;
and trust that in respect to that most important political topic
to us, the structure of the Federal Government and its relations
to the States, you will find abundant reason to hold a middle
course between the affected *practicalism* of New England con-
solidation on the one side, and the subtle and delusive theories of
Calhoun on the other.
    If this last expression shocks you, submit to the *jar* with as
much philosophy as you can command until you can inquire
and think for yourself, and I am persuaded that at length you
will think it not mis-applied.
    Give me leave to suggest that you will do well to forbear to form
final conclusions upon any topics of practical application in what
is called political science, until you have an opportunity to look
at them all around,—*tota re perspecta*, as counsellor Pleydell says.
You cannot confide in the ingenuousness of *political* any more
than of *theological* theorizers. You must verify the citations of
both with scrupulous care, or else will be betrayed into very
devious paths.

The young ladies desire their thanks for your kind message, and beg to be cordially remembered to you; and both they and I hope that you will find it not impossible to include the University ere long, in your journeyings to and fro. Be assured that a hearty welcome will always await you at our house.

With much regard, I remain
Very truly yours,   John B. Minor.

ALS (WP, DLC) with WWhw notation on env.: "Ans. May 4/84." The enclosed testimonial is missing.

To Houghton, Mifflin & Company

Dear Sirs,   Balto., Md., May 2nd/84

Your pleasant letter of April 28th was duly received yesterday. Allow me to thank you for having given my *ms* so careful a reading, and to express my satisfaction at the results. You have, I am sure, given me as explicit and as favourable an answer as I had any right to expect under the circumstances; and you may rest assured that I shall push the completion of my work as rapidly as possible, in order that I may be able to submit the additional essays to you before the end of the year. The portions remaining to be written will, I confidently expect, be the most interesting, because the broadest and least technical, chapters of the subject; and, if I have secured your interest by the parts submitted, I am the more hopeful of satisfying you with what I have yet to write.

In the mean time, I will leave with you the *ms* of parts II and III, which will probably need very little addition or alteration, asking you to return only the *introductory* chapter to which should be added some references to the recent *legal tender decision*[1] and a brief commentary upon the Constitutional phases of the "Blair Educational Bill"—in case it should become law. That chapter, indeed, is one which will not be complete till it's too late for anything to happen affecting its conclusions before its final publication.

My address will remain unchanged until the first of June.
Very truly yours,   Woodrow Wilson

ALS (WP, DLC). Endorsed "H. E. S[cudder]."

1 WW was referring to the Supreme Court's decision of March 3, 1884, in the case of Juilliard *v.* Greenman, which upheld the power of Congress to make United States notes legal tender. He incorporated the reference in note 2, p. 33, of *Congressional Government*. This reference in turn was based upon an extract of the core of the decision, which he copied presumably at about the time that he wrote this letter. His extract bears the WWhw caption, "Legal-tender Case: March 3rd 1884," and is on a loose page tucked into his bound notebook, "Index Rerum," described in Vol. 1, pp. 84-85.

To John Barbee Minor

My dear Sir: Balto., Md., May 2, 1884

Your exceedingly kind letter of the 1st was received this morning, and afforded me very keen gratification. I value your cordial endorsement more than any other I could receive: and your advice no less. Though I have an abundant portion of human nature, I think that I should have valued your advice even if it had not accorded so nearly with my own views. I have studied many of the questions which immediately concern the structure of the Federal Government and its relations to the States with considerable thoroughness, and the more deeply I look into them the more am I inclined to that middle course which you commend.

It seems to me that the preservation of the proper balance between the central and the State governments depends, in the first instance, upon the control vouchsafed to public opinion by the structure of Congress, by the machinery of legislation; and I venture to send you a paper of mine,[1] prepared last summer and printed some months ago in the "Overland Monthly" of San Francisco, in which I have set forth pretty fully some of my conclusions with regard to federal legislative methods. So long as Congress is unmanageable, its parties irresponsible and its practices practically secret, it will be impossible to check the course of aggression which has for so many years past characterized its action at all points where its jurisdiction touches that of the States.

You may possibly regard the opinions expressed in my article as of the number of those too hasty final conclusions against which you warn me: but I *have* looked at the questions involved "all around." Beginning before my graduation at Princeton, and issuing first, in 1879, in an article on "Cabinet Govt. in the United States" in the *International Review*,[2] my investigations of the legislative methods of Congress have led me finally, during the past few months, to undertake the preparation of a series of essays in which, without advocating any specific reform, I seek to give a clear picture of the actual workings of Congress, and of the rest of the federal machinery as related to Congress. About half of my work is completed and correspondence with a publishing house in Boston, to whom I submitted the part completed, leads me to hope that it may eventually be printed in book form, when I shall take great pleasure in sending it to you in further justification of what I now send.

Again thanking you for your kindness, I remain, with sincere regard,   Very truly Yours,   Wood. Wilson

ALS (Minor Papers, ViU).
  ¹ "Committee or Cabinet Government?"
  ² Printed at Aug. 1, 1879, Vol. 1.

Two Letters to Ellen Louise Axson

Balto., Md., May 4th 1884

I hope that my darling will not answer hastily the questions contained in my last letter. Of course this Arkansas matter is as yet wholly "in the air"; it may, and possibly will, come to nothing, and I have suspected, since I wrote last Thursday, that I was hardly justified in troubling you by building on so slim a foundation the request that you would decide, conditionally at least, so grave a matter. My inclination now is to beg that you will withhold your reply until I see you in vacation: for you can hardly know, little lady, how much depends upon that reply. The first year of my work in a professorship will be the critical year: and the conditions of that work are within your control: a fact which need not frighten my darling at all, but which will, I hope, make her slow to decide contrary to my wishes, and dispose her to wait till she can consult me in person before she comes to any final conclusion. Since I *have* made this Arkansas possibility a text, however, I will explain fully my own views and feelings in the matter. The first year of my work will be the most trying because I will have to pass it amongst strangers, who, besides receiving me without sympathy, will watch me, as a youth and a novice charged with important duties, with constant criticism: it will be the season when my situation, my standing, will be altogether *a-making*; and, though I have no fears as to the final result, I long to have the support of your love and companionship from the very start. They would be simply invaluable to me, saving the *wear* and *tear* of the trial. Now, I know that my darling loves me well enough to interpose no objections on her own account, but does she think that her duties to others stand in the way? You know—don't you, my little sweetheart?—that our marriage would'nt at all change your relations to Eddie, if you should want still to keep him with you.

But enough of this for the present! I wanted only to give you plenty of time to think about it, in case there should be any immediate change in my plans: I am quite willing to trust all to your heart's dictates.

Besides, you will be just about to start for Rome when this reaches you and will be too busy even to read it (?), may-be. May God keep my darling on her journey! Try to think of me, if you please, Miss, just a little, as the cars speed you northwards: and when you reach your destination give my regards to Mrs. T[edcastle]—if you should still be thinking of me then!—and my warmest love to all at "Oakdene."[1] I love you, Ellie, more than you will ever know. Love to all at #143. and to Mrs. D.

Your own   Woodrow.

P.S. I am feeling better even than when I wrote last. Lovingly, W.

[1] The Brower home in East Rome, or Etowah City, Georgia.

My own darling   Balto., Md., May 5th 1884,

It strikes me that, since it happens that I love with all my heart a certain little lady who is just about to leave home, it might not be amiss to send a little note to meet her at her destination: for, mayhap, she will be glad to see it; and, besides, I have on my mind this morning a special message I want to send her. I want to send her a kiss for some words I read this morning: "of course if *you* like it, so do *I*, very much indeed." You could have said nothing sweeter, my darling—nothing surer to go deep into my heart: for that saying was just like my little sweetheart, and anything just like her is sweet beyond compare in my estimation.

I am *so* sorry, my darling, that my neglect to write as usual on last Sabbath caused you so much anxiety. It was *very* thoughtless of me to make such a gap in my correspondence just after having told you of Dr. Woods' fears—but you may be sure, my precious, that, if I were to fall really ill, you should be the first to learn of it. My silence *did* mean that I was feeling badly—but there was nothing at all serious the matter and I am *quite* well now.

But I did not intend to make a letter of this: I will write as usual to-morrow. This is intended only to remind you that there is someone who loves you beyond all bounds, and who is thinking of you and wishing for you all the time. Will you let me send you *this* time "a score of kisses" with the boundless love of

Your own   Woodrow

P.S. Eddie is with you, is'nt he? Give my love to him, to my future *big* brother, Stockton, and to your dear father, when you write, as well as my sincerest regards to Mrs Tedcastle. You have given me no news of your father recently, my darling: do you hear nothing favourable? Will any parts of Rome remind you of

Yours lovingly   W.?

ALS (WC, NjP).

From Houghton, Mifflin & Company

Dear Sir: Boston, 5 May 1884
    We send you as you request the first Essay on Congressional Government, retaining the rest of your *ms*, subject to your order.
                            Truly yours
                            Houghton, Mifflin & Co   S[cudder].
ALS (WP, DLC).

From Ellen Louise Axson

My darling Woodrow,   Savannah May 6/84
    I declared to myself, yesterday afternoon, that *nothing* should prevent my writing at night. I would do it, if it was necessary to sit up all night for the purpose. But after I had been occupied, first with friends, and then with packing, until twelve o'clock, I found it was "no go";—that is, I would not be able to do more than I would have time for this morning,—write the few *necessary* lines in answer to your last letters.
    The discovery that you are not anxious to remain longer in Baltimore, my darling, alters very materially my impression as to the Arkansas scheme. If you want a professorship now, there is, of course, no reason why you should not take this one,—so far as I can see, no ground even for *hesitation*, which would not be very inadequate and foolish. You may trust me to think "nothing *dismal*, at any rate," of "the prospect of going away beyond the Mississippi."
    I scarcely know what to say of the matter as it affects me. Perhaps it is'nt necessary for me to say anything now. If I had only myself to think of, I would not, dearest, hesitate for a moment to do anything you wished. But how can I think of such things in the midst of this terrible suspense about Papa? How can I tell when or where he might need me? And my boys too need me now. I must work for them for awhile. Why, Sir, I also am bestirring myself to obtain a *professor-ship* (ahem) and with some prospect of success. I wish to teach drawing and painting in a school. I think I can make more at that than at the crayon portraits,—at any rate it is more to be depended upon,—and then I can do the portraits too, "after hours."
    But I won't begin to discuss any of these matters now,—hav'nt time,—will, of course, write soon after reaching Rome. I leave tonight, reach there tomorrow at dinner-time. All here send there best love. Grandmother received a letter from Mrs. Duncan a day

or so ago, and she sent her love to you;—she has been in Marietta for some weeks. Grandmother is curious to know what sort of a *climate* they have in Ark! Whether very hot, very cold, or neither or both? And if there is much of that special horror,—*malaria*? Good-bye for the present. Ah, I *do* love you very, very dearly, my darling! I am *not* "afraid to say how much."

Your own   Ellie.

ALS (WP, DLC). Enc.: clipping of Frances Anne Kemble's poem, "Absence."

To Ellen Louise Axson

My own darling,   Baltimore, May 6th 1884

   As I read over again that sweet letter of yours which came yesterday I can't help charging myself with cruel thoughtlessness in having left you in suspense about my health after writing of Dr. Woods's apprehensions—"the ominous words of my medical man." I should'nt have given you cause for anxiety, in the first place, by repeating the Dr.'s warning: that was the *stupid* part of the performance; but the fact of the matter is that I have of late gotten so into the habit of telling you everything, as though you were but another part of myself, that I am in constant danger of falling, inadvertently, into mistakes such as this recent one, by telling my darling what will only give her pain without bringing any compensating advantage to either of us. Forgive me, my little sweetheart! I'll try not to be so stupid again.

   It's really very reckless of you, Miss, to carry on so *many* flirtations as you do; you scarcely give me time to forget your conquest of Mr. Strider before acquainting me with your later affair with minute, infatuated Mr. Clay: the redeeming feature of the case being that you confess all to me. Did you never reflect, Miss, that you are making a terribly long record of broken hearts? As far as I can ascertain, pretty much every eligible young man who has been permitted to become well acquainted with you has fallen in love with you! I am thankful that *I* am not responsible for so much damage! I *did*, however, have something very dreadful happen to me the other night. I was out calling with a couple of young ladies upon two other young ladies (you see I am not so indiscreet as to *name* my conquests!) and one of the latter actually called me "a sweet thing." *Was*'nt that dreadful!

   You must give my warmest regards, my little lady, to Miss Anna Harris and to your cousin, Miss Hoyt. I feel as if they were both of them *my* special friends—and I sincerely hope that they will be some of these days: for do'nt you think that they can be persuaded to visit us when we have a home of our own?

I have had several quiet laughs all to myself, my darling, trying to picture the consternation (?) with which you would be reading the contents of my last few letters; and yet I have'nt felt much like laughing either: for never in my life did I write anything with so full a heart and so earnest a purpose as I had when I wrote those letters. If I were sure of my prize so soon as I had secured an appointment—well, I am sure that my darling will do anything she can to make me happy—for she said so—and I am supremely happy in that knowledge. I love you with all my heart.

Your own   Woodrow.

ALS (WC, NjP).

From Richard Heath Dabney

My dear Tommy: Berlin—May 6th 1884.

If I were not a lazy reprobate, I should have long since hastened to write to you and offer you my hearty congratulations for having secured the heart of so charming a young lady as, from your interesting description, I judge Miss Axson to be. However, I hope you will not think that I mean to disparage her charms when I say that, if I knew her, I should feel very much inclined to write and congratulate her also on her prospective husband. For, however rich a prize she may prove for you, I am very certain that the gain will be, by no means, all on one side. . . .

I am sorry you have been so much disappointed in the courses at Johns Hopkins, but after all I don't think it makes much difference whether a fellow hears good lectures or not; for pretty much all the results of modern science are contained in a printed form in books. Practically, I think we could get along, (now that we are men, and have gone to work in earnest on a profession,) about as well without any lectures at all and without being at any University. Still there are some considerable advantages in being at a University. One is, that a man has a better chance of getting a place to teach, if he is connected with a centre of learning, than if he pursues his studies privately. I am not one of those who imagine that they have accomplished their mission on earth when they have succeeded in having Ph.D. or some other caudal appendage tacked to their names. . . .

I agree with you perfectly in not wishing to have to teach History along with half a dozen other subjects at some one-horse, or perhaps half-horse college, but still, I don't think it is good to specialize too much at first. Excessive specialization is, I think, one of the evils of modern science. . . .

Yours sincerely,   R. H. Dabney.

Postscript.

I don't know whether I ever told you that my grandfather and some of my aunts are living in Baltimore. Their address is 98 *John* street, or, as it is sometimes called, *Mount Royal Avenue*. It would please me very much if you would call on them, provided you can find the time, and have the inclination to spend an hour occasionally with a family who will be delighted to see you and who will treat you without any stiffness or useless ceremony. . . .   Sincerely yours,   R. H. Dabney.

ALS (WP, DLC) with WWhw notation on env.: "Ans. Feby 14, 1885."

From Joseph Ruggles Wilson

My dearest Woodrow—   Wilmington, May 6, 1884—

Please find enclosed my check for $50.00. And so much for one item of business

As to the second item—that touching the land out yonder, your mother wishes you to be the judge—knowing that you will better know how to provide against *risks* than either she or I. So far as we can understand the matter presented in Mr. Dorsey's missive[,] Messrs Munger & Pease¹ have two payments yet to make—one for $2,875, another for $1,020 for which you have their notes. They wish to pay the first at once, asking permission to borrow $1,500 (to enable them to do so) on a 1st mortgage on the property, and then to replace their note for the second with a second mortgage, to your credit, payable in a year. You can tell whether it be wise to suffer such a replacement—and, if you consent, whether you are more likely to get the $1,020 thus at the end of another year than to collect it when the note falls due.

As to the third item—the Arkansas affair. What a few days ago was reasonable certainty is now it appears a complicated uncertainty[.] At any rate you do well to send on your docs. Something satisfactory may come from it. You need only to get a foothold—a start—and the rest will go by itself.

The other day I received a letter from Joseph W. Martin Esq., a Little Rock lawyer who signs himself "Chairman Ex Com. A.I.U." In this letter I am told that "the Board will meet June 12th to elect a successor to Gen D. H. Hill, with a salary of say $3000.00. We want a good strong man, firm in his religious convictions—of good scholarship; and above all—no, not above all, but is exceedingly important—a man of fine executive ability combining the suaviter in modo with the fortiter in re. . . . . Can't you put me in communication with such a man? A layman preferred."

Now I have a great mind to send him *your* name: or, if he will not have this, *my own*. At any rate, I will get him not to fix upon any one until he and I shall meet at Vicksburg, where Mr. Martin is to be present as a member of [the General] Assembly. *If* we could both be in the same institution—but it is too good to think about.

We are all well, except yr dear mother who has been fighting for many days with dysentery—the battle having at last turned, we hope, in her favor.

I need not say that we all love you greatly—and are anxious to have you fix the date of yr return to our welcoming arms.

Affectionately   Your   Father.

ALS (WP, DLC) with WWhw notation on env.: "Ans. May 9th 1884." Enc.: George W. E. Dorsey to [JRW], April 28, 1884, ALS (WP, DLC).
    1 Dorsey was an agent for properties coming to JWW from the Estate of William Woodrow. William T. Munger and Charles H. Pease are among those who gave notes in part settlement for JWW's share of land from the Estate of William Woodrow, as shown in the indentures printed at June 27, 1883, Vol. 2.

To Ellen Louise Axson

My own darling,   Balto., May 8th, 1884

There could have been nothing sweeter than your note of Tuesday, with its loving, confiding messages about my plans. My darling! You always return just the answers that my heart desires!

But I must say, my little sweetheart, that the hint you give of your own plans frightens me. Of course the mere chance of my securing a position at once ought not to be allowed to stand in the way of your taking a position as teacher of drawing, and I should oppose nothing that seemed to you and your family either wise or needful in a matter like this; but you could hardly make an engagement of the kind you speak of for less than a year and the prospect of having all possibility of our marriage absolutely excluded for so long a time would be to me like consignment to a prison-cell for a twelvemonth!

Of course it goes without the saying, my darling, that I had not forgotten your dear father in sketching possible plans: *everything* must depend upon his condition; my whole object was to prepare you for what I *might* be in a position to ask you to do, provided it were at all possible, under all the circumstances. As for your brothers—"your boys"—my darling, it is part of my strongest purpose and dearest hope to stand in your place towards them as regards money matters—to espouse your duties as well as your sweet self; and the sooner I can relieve you of the necessity of thinking of such things as a teacher's position the happier will I be. The only thing, therefore, for us to think of after I shall have obtained a place with adequate salary will be your dear father's condition: nothing else shall stand in the way of that union which will perfect our happiness, and by perfecting our happiness add to our usefulness.

You must admit, my little sweetheart, that I have very fair powers of description to have enabled sister Marion to read so clearly the character of a certain little lady whom she had never seen. Of course I knew how much and how frankly—how like a true and unaffected woman—my darling loved me, and how she would count it only part of her loyalty to truth, and to me, to avow the full extent of that love and to confess her readiness to join with me in rejoicing over any circumstance that promised to hasten the time of our marriage; but I did not know that I had succeeded so well in giving others so just a conception of her true character.[1] Why what would our love be worth to each other, my pet, if we could not freely declare it! and what a farce our engagement would be if either of us felt constrained to conceal the fact that we were wishing for its consummation!

I think it very probable, dearest, that your dear father, were he consulted on the matter, would wish our marriage to come as soon as possible, knowing, of course, that it would in no way take you away from the boys, but would only add to your life someone who would love them and care for them to the full extent of his ability as if they were his own brothers by blood: for that was just the interpretation I put upon a passage (which I read more than once or twice) in one of his letters wh. you sent me.[2] In language that touched and gratified me not a little, he expressed his thankfulness for the fact that, though he was so mysteriously taken away from you, he could safely commit you to my love and care. And certainly, since he does trust me, nothing could be more natural than that he should wish for our early marriage in order that his darling daughter, who has been the light and joy of his life, should have some one to lean upon, some one to share her burdens—should they be accounted burdens. You can imagine, therefore, my precious one, how anxiously I await the issue of this Arkansas affair. Here is at least a chance of winning you at once: and I confess that I am a good deal frightened at the possibility that, should the desired vacancy open up for me beyond the Mississippi as is expected, an engagement on your part to teach should have put you for a time beyond my reach. Still, I do'nt offer this as an objection; because I sincerely honour your determination in the matter, and would not have you postpone your chance to mine, which is still only a chance. Since you say that you have "some prospect of success," you must have picked out your school: would it take you away from home, or is it in Savannah? Would it be necessary to promise your services unconditionally for a fixed term? You see, my love, how deeply exercised I am about the whole question!

Those are beautiful verses of Frances Kemble's that you sent me with your tacit endorsement: they are more than beautiful, for they contain just the sort of philosophy that I like and just the tone of love that seems to me truest and best: they are exquisite, the sweetest love verses I ever read—and I read them as from you.

It is hardly necessary, I imagine, after writing the preceding pages, to say anything of what my heart is all the day full of, my love for you: but maybe you are not tired of hearing me say that I love you unspeakably. You are all the world to me. I long for you all the time. Love to all at "Oakdene" and kindest regards to Mrs. T., with also much love to your dear father, to Eddie, and to Stockton, from   Your own   Woodrow.

ALS (WC, NjP).
    ¹ Marion had written: "How perfectly charming it would be to know that Ross had been able to aid you in getting into a suitable position for taking unto yourself such a wife as the dear little girl who will, I should not wonder!—be quite glad too. Would she acknowledge as much? I imagine she is one of those brave women who, knowing, modestly too, that she gives as much as is given when she gives her heart into your keeping, is not at all afraid to let you see how completely you have possession of it." Marion W. Kennedy to WW, April 25, 1884, ALS (WP, DLC).
    ² Axson mentioned Wilson favorably in several letters to ELA, but Wilson is probably referring to S. E. Axson to ELA, Feb. 16, 1884, ALS (WP, DLC), in which Axson wrote that Wilson was "a noble fellow, quite deserving I think of the accomplished girl we have consented for him to have one of these days."

From Charles Andrew Talcott

My dear Tommy:—   Utica, N.Y. May 8th 1884
    For some reason or other I am a very tardy correspondent. If you will take the trouble to recall the past you will find that I have called your attention to this fact several times before. I am *very* late in acknowledging your pamphlet on Cabinet Government.¹ It is not certainly because I did not enjoy it or thoroughly appreciate its strength. I did, both,—and took a just pride, not the

first time either, in my friendship with its author. You have doubt-less seen how Judge Story refers to the subject in his Commentaries;[2] from his language in sections 871 & 872 I rather inferred that he was inclined towards your opinion. I think the chief difficulty which the subject presents is the tendency there would be to increase the influence of the Executive department. Still, there is no doubt that the Executive influence is strong now and as Story puts it, is [sic] "is compelled to resort to secret & unseen influence, to private interviews & private arrangements, to accomplish its own *appropriate* purposes, instead of proposing and sustaining its own duties & measures by a bold & manly appeal to the nation in the face of its representatives." In my judgment it would take a longer period than is allotted to the life of one man to convince the American people that it is best to make any change in the Constitutional *organization* of the government. . . .

I hope you will let me hear from you soon. Although silent my thoughts turn to you often & I can assure you that not a whit of the old time regard & esteem has been lost in the lapse of these years. I never hear from any of the fellows and any news you send would be gladly received.

Sincerely as Ever   Charles A. Talcott

ALS (WP, DLC) with WWhw notation on env.: "Ans. July 5th/84."
  [1] "Committee or Cabinet Government?"
  [2] Joseph Story, *Commentaries on the Constitution of the United States* . . . (2 Vols., Boston, 1873).

From Ellen Louise Axson

My darling Woodrow,   East Rome [Ga.], May 9/84.

It is odd with what peculiar sensations I write that new old direction at the head of this page. Five months is a short time, and yet it seems almost as strange as sad to be once again in Rome. Still, though I so dreaded coming, I am rather glad to be here after all,—to be in Agnes' home, at least,—at the old window, looking out on the morning sunlight and the quiet hills I know so well. I doubt if I shall find it equally pleasant to walk the streets again, or, especially, to sit again in the church.

But enough of all this. I reached Rome Wed., after a very pleasant journey—find Agnes and all friends well, and everything going on very much as usual. Mr. Bones is looking very well indeed: he called yesterday morning at eight o'clock. I regret to say that I had just opened my eyes! so I did'nt see him. He called again at night, and I again regret to say that he found Mr. Wright here, so I scarcely feel that I have seen him yet as I would like. I suppose you know that Mr. Brower is in Chicago in business, and will probably remain permanently;—if he does so decide, Jessie will go in the fall. I daresay it will be a good move for them, but *so* hard for Mr. Bones. I had heard nothing about it all,—was much surprised Friday night. I hav'nt seen Jessie yet,—was just starting over this afternoon when visitors were announced. Indeed I think Agnes must have advertised my coming somewhat extensively. I have had nothing but company since the first hour after my arrival. Most of my special friends have been here—including those faithful swains, Messrs. Wright, Thornwell and Baker! Mr. W. called at four yesterday afternoon, (being unable, as he said longer "to restrain his impatience" to see me) and stayed until *ten* at night, thanks to Agnes who was malicious enough to ask him to spend the evening. I could have "*pulverized*" her for it, as Randolph says.

What do you think he brought me, by-the-way? A *letter from you*! Imagine my surprise at receiving it from his hands. It seems that Mr. Roe, book-keeper at McWilliams, is charged with the duty of getting the mail out, during Mr. Tedcastle's absence, and being a friend of Mr. Wrights, he, knowing he was about starting over, made him his messenger.

I had a comical time with Mr. W.—he had been hearing some reports about me, it seems, and attacked me on the subject with more warmth than discretion. He made nothing out of me then, —yet he did gain his point in the course of the evening, for he asked me, a-pro-pos of some other case, if I did not think "engagements" ought to be 'announced'? He was still Englishman enough to think it the only *right* way. It kept girls out of mischief! "There were some persons, at least, whom they ought always to tell;—this custom of concealment caused them often to be very *unkind* and *unjust* to other gentlemen,—indeed to do them incalculable harm." He added that if he should discover that a young lady, to whom he had been "paying attentions which she could not fail to understand, had, all the time, been engaged, he would lose respect for her." Whereupon I was so "scared" that I would have told him my secret in the next breath if I had'nt thought it would be too pointed; but I certainly shall, when I next see him. After all, there is a good deal in what he says. It is better to be honest and straight-forward in such matters as well as in all others, though it does lead to disagreeable consequences. If one remembers the good rule, "put yourself in his place," one perceives that not to be candid in certain cases is to be very selfish.

Yet I certainly don't admit that all one's gentlemen friends have a *right* to one's secrets, simply because of certain "attentions" which whatever they may "mean" by them, hundreds of gentlemen have paid girls without meaning anything at all. But what in the world am I writing all this to *you* for? I am merely thinking aloud, and I doubt not you will be more bored than edified by my "thoughts."

I have received three sweet little letters from you this week, my darling, none of which have been answered, except by my heart. So now I must turn back for a moment to the first, and the matter of which it treats. That seems a very reasonable request of yours, dearest, that I should not answer your questions hastily,— that I should decide nothing until I see you—a *very* reasonable request to one so predisposed to do whatever you wish. Yet what am I to do? There are matters, which, if *I* don't decide them as soon as possible, bid fair to decide *themselves*, not at all in my favour. I ought to be making every exertion to get a situation for next year; and I ought to do it at once, because schools make their arrangements for the coming year before the June commencements. For instance, I hear that Mrs Caldwell's[1] art teacher has resigned [at the Rome Female College], and I ought to go immediately and apply for the place,—but I hav'nt done it. I have also a splendid letter from Mrs. Bacon the artist to a friend of hers at the head of a teacher's agency in New York, which I should send on at once,—but I hav'nt done it,—simply because it is so hard for me to disregard your request "to decide nothing until I see you." If I take these steps, and anything comes of it, things *will* be "decided" you see for a year. But I *must* take them at once, because for the sake of others, you know, it would'nt be right for me to let things drift. Dr. Mack,[2] who is very kindly exerting himself to get me a position, wrote me the other day about an opening in the Charlotte school,[3] which I must see about as soon as possible. But I will say no more about all these little perplexities and uncertainties now; I am sure that, however it turns out, it will all be *right*.

What is your idea, my darling, about your visit? Would you prefer to make it *here*, at the beginning of your vacation—would you like me to remain until you come? Or would it suit you better to make it later in the summer at Sewanee? I am *so* glad you are better again. And if you *please* Sir *don't* make yourself sick with "worry," whatever you do—nothing pays so badly. We know that everything is *sure* to be for the best. Yet I understand your case and sympathize most deeply in it. Uncertainty—suspense—*is*

harder to bear patiently than most positive evils. Good-bye my
darling   With truest love   Your own Ellie.

ALS (WP, DLC).
  ¹ Probably Kate Pearson Caldwell, wife of Dr. Samuel Craighead Caldwell,
then a professor at the college and soon to succeed his father, the Rev. John
McK. Madison Caldwell, as president. However, "Mrs Caldwell" may have been
Caroline E. Livy Caldwell, wife of the elder Caldwell.
  ² The Rev. Dr. Joseph B. Mack, pastor, First Presbyterian Church, Columbia,
S. C., 1878-81; financial agent, Columbia Theological Seminary and Davidson
College, 1881-88. See WW to ELA, June 26, 1884, where WW was constrained to
speak out bitterly against "my darling's friend," and ELA's reply of July 3, 1884.
  ³ Probably the Charlotte Female College.

From the Minutes of the Seminary of Historical and Political Science

Friday, May 8th [9] 1884.

Meeting called to order at 8.10 P.M., Dr. Adams in the chair.
Minutes of the previous meeting read & corrected. Absent, Mess.
Dewey, Ramage, Randall, Rich, Shinn & Wilhelm. The principal
paper of the evening was by Mr. Wilson who read the introduction
to his work on Representative Government.

Dr. Adams expressed a desire to have at least one more of Mr.
Wilson's papers this year especially if he were to leave us for the
frontier. His studies on the national government were of advantage here, as this subject has long been intended to be a part
of the work on institutions undertaken in this department. Mr.
Wilson's work is better than anything in that line that has been
done heretofore in the Seminary. Another year it would be good
to bring forward in the "Historical Studies." Von Holst has promised to write an introduction for a series of national studies. . . .

Seminary adjourned at 10.10 P.M.

[Walter B. Scaife, Secretary]

An Advertisement

[May 10, 1884]

Announcement is made that Dr. Richard T. Ely, of Johns Hopkins University, in coöperation with two members of his advanced
class, Mr. Davis R. Dewey, A.B. (University of Vermont), and
Mr. Woodrow Wilson, A.M. (Princeton College), is now preparing a History of Political Economy in the United States, and that
they would be obliged for any books, pamphlets, brochures, magazine articles, speeches, etc., etc., which might be of assistance in
their work.

Printed in the Philadelphia *American*, VIII (May 10, 1884), 74.

To Ellen Louise Axson

My own darling,   Balto., Md., May 11th 1884

Is Rome looking just as it did in the glad days of last Spring when I was there making the acquaintance of a certain very captivating young lady? Can you see from Mrs. Tedcastle's the bare-topped hill we once toiled at climbing, and in climbing which you took effective steps towards consummating the theft of a poor fellow's heart? Have you ridden out on that lovely picnic road, or do you intend walking down to the big rock by the river? I'd rather have my darling go to such spots than have her dwell on the sad memories with which, for her, the whole neighbourhood must be peopled; For, after all, my little sweetheart, our lives are but just begun and our thoughts must be for those things which carry us on towards the future; and it makes me *very* happy to know that my Ellie is'nt given to brooding over things which are past mending, but is full of the hope which honours God and of the love that makes her sweet life a light to bless and cheer all to whom that love is given! 'Tis impossible, Miss, that, by any indirection even, you should have gotten any of the Law blood into your veins, but it seems to me that that charming description you gave me of Mrs. Clay is but a picture of your elder self, that is to be, in its colours of devoted love, of cares lightly borne, of beauty and joyous, girlish winsomeness. The fact is, I suppose, that you did not need to seek these things for yourself amongst the Laws, but got them quite naturally (and of course without any personal credit!) from your lovely mother. You see, I really can't be too particular about not spoiling you, and so must assure you that, though I know you possessed of all these qualities which make me love you to distraction, I do not suspect you of having *originated* them!

I have heard nothing further from Arkansas. It will probably be some weeks before there is anything to report. The trustees of the University meet, I believe, in the early part of June; and we must, of course, wait upon them for a solution of the question, whether or not the desired vacancy is to be made.

Of course you will have seen Jessie and the rest of the "Oak-dene" household before this reaches you, and will have reported that I have been behaving myself as well as could have been expected under the circumstances. Give them all my love.

It may please you to know, Miss Axson, that I love you *infinitely* more than I did this time last year, that I love you, indeed, with a wholeness and singleness of heart which ought to satisfy any reasonable, or, for that matter, any *un*reasonable damsel.

                                        Your own   Woodrow.

Regards to Mrs. T.

ALS (WC, NjP).

From Ellen Louise Axson

My darling Woodrow,   Rome [Ga.] May 12/84

It is so late now that I will scarcely be able to finish this to-night, but I will at least *begin* at the right time; and bring it to a conclusion tomorrow morning, since it will reach you just as soon by that plan. I find it equally impossible either to slip away from the circle here in the evening, or to write letters to certain persons—in their midst. So I will wait until morning, when there will be fewer difficulties in the way of my gaining a place of refuge.

I don't believe I mentioned that I found other guests here, Agnes' Aunt from Fla., with her little son, and her niece, a pretty girl from Dover Del. They have all stopped for a short visit on their way to Delaware. The aunt is a woman about whom I have heard a great deal, and have had a great deal of curiosity. She is the lady, who during the war, while quite a young girl, shot one Yankee dead in his tracks, and arrested another. She actually made him—I am sure I don't know how—hand over to her his gun, pistols &c.; and then she marched him before her, two miles, to the Confederate camp. And that is scarcely more than a specimen of her adventures. I was rather surprised to find this heroine an exceedingly quiet person, with a *very* low voice, and a gentle, subdued manner. One would never suspect any smouldering fire beneath that surface; and there is certainly nothing masculine about her—a very small, somewhat faded brunette, retaining however traces of past beauty. She seems to be an remarkably unselfish, *helpful* sort of person. By the way, it is a curious fact that, notwithstanding her antipathy to Yankees, she married a handsome, dashing major in their army almost before the war was over, and in the face of violent opposition from her family. Indeed, her brothers wanted to kill him, and she had hard work to save his life; they being quite as much at home with the rifle as herself. But as his nationality was his only offence, they have finally forgiven him, and are very good friends.

Yes, I have seen Jessie and the baby[1] and all. The baby is per-fectly lovely, and Jessie is looking very well,—*so* much better than she did last fall. But she is in a state bordering on despair over Mr. Brower's absence. It is really funny to hear her lamentations; they made me open my eyes, for Jessie has such a matter-of-fact way of expressing herself, that I never suspected her of so much sentiment. It is really settled that they are to go to Chicago; that is, he is there already—has made his arrangements, and Jessie will join him in the autumn. He had a fine position offered him in the large business in which his brothers are interested, the manufacture of printing-presses. But of course you have heard all about it. Jessie says Mr. B. finds it harder to leave his enemies than his friends, it is a great trial to him to even *seem* to be giving up the fight. I hav'nt had a "real good talk" with Mr. Bones yet, thanks to Mr. Wright;—but he told me Sunday that he would come again soon,—he didnt count that visit, as he had long ago given up trying to "sit out" young men. Mr. Wright and I, by-the-way, had an "explanation" last night, and a miserable time generally. I tried *very* hard to manage so that he should'nt feel humiliated (and that is the principal thing, you know,—it is wounded pride, not wounded love, that throws them into such a "state.") If he had let things remain as I left them when I had made my little speech, he might have retreated with flying colours. But instead of that he must needs keep saying exactly the wrong thing, getting himself more and more deeply involved and making it infinitely more unpleasant for himself, besides leaving me sick at heart. How any woman can *enjoy* being "made love to" by more than one man, passes my comprehension. I don't see the fun of it. But he did have the grace to say that I had done no wrong in the matter, &c. &c.

You must not let yourself get too much "exercised," dearest, over that school question. I am so far from seeing a satisfactory way out of my difficulties, that it may be *impossible* to settle matters before your arrival, however much I try. Indeed we are very nearly in the same predicament,—it would be hard to say whose fate for the coming year is likely to be settled first. I think it probable that if I wish I can get the place here at the college. But there are serious objections. In fact I know too much about it. I would *prefer* going to some other school, where, not knowing what to expect, I could at least have the satisfaction of *hoping* that all would be well.

That was a very, very sweet and noble letter of yours, my darling, that of last Saturday. My heart was very full, as I read, and is yet too full for me to *try* to say what I think of it—and you. But you are *too* good by half! And if you insist upon making light of such substantial obstacles as my boys,—then, sir, it is my place to see to it that you *don't* make a perfect Atlas of yourself. Such a rashly generous youth needs someone to look after his interests. Though, of course, as Aunt Ella says, I can't expect people to wait until Eddie is grown and married! And he, dear little fellow, is mine, "to have and to hold."

I have not written about Papa because, as you supposed, I had nothing good to tell. We have had no letters from him since those you saw. We hear but little from the doctors—they have always been very reticent in giving us—in Sav.—an opinion; we only knew he had been much worse for a time. But Uncle Will[iam D. Hoyt] has shown me, since my return, a letter, which he has recently received from Dr. Hall, giving a full report. His condition has been almost as bad as at first, the doctor says, but is now better. But the case, as it develops itself, is much more serious than they at first supposed. The symptoms are bad, and they can give little or no hope of his ever recovering. I hardly dare to send that word to Sav. Poor Grandmother! She always seemed so hopeful, so much more hopeful than I. But perhaps she was not; perhaps we were *all* only pretending to hope for each others sake. I can't tell. May God help us all, and comfort us, not with false hope, but with *true* faith.

I am, my darling, yours with all my heart,   Ellie.

ALS (WP, DLC) with WWhw notation and figures on env.
¹ Jessie's baby, Marion.

To Ellen Louise Axson, with Enclosure

My own darling,   Balto., Md., May 13th/84

I had completed a birthday letter to you, in rhymed and metrical prose, before your letter reached me this morning (you will doubtless be puzzled, by-the-way, as *I* am in looking back upon it, to decide what induced me to adopt the *form* of poetry: I can only say, that my *mood* was poetical, though it did not produce *in kind*); but the contents of your letter demand an immediate reply—which I proceed to cast into this *un*metrical form. I must confess, my little sweetheart, that your letter has given me a terrible case of the "blues." It almost breaks my heart to think that there is not now at hand any means of preventing the consummation of an arrangement which will take my darling away from me and will separate her from her friends, to enter upon trials such as she dreams not of, and such as it should be my duty to relieve her from! And, though I dare not stand in the way of what she esteems her duty, this thing shall not be done if I can prevent it. My darling, listen! you must promise me that you will take no final step (such as the definite *acceptance* of a position— no application is final) in this matter *for one week from this date—before*, i.e., *the 20th of May*. For my sake, my darling, sacrifice everything but a last or an only chance, rather than do anything final before that date!

I cannot help regretting, Ellie, that you did not tell me earlier of these plans of yours. From what you have said, I conclude that they have been on foot for some time. They mean something very serious to me: and more time to think and arrange about them would have been invaluable, saving several very miserable days. Of course I do not say these things, which will distress you, to upbraid you for not having consulted me: for I know that my darling was led to do as she did through no motives but such as went hand in hand with her love for me; I say them only to urge upon you the absolute necessity of letting me into all your counsels, if you would save me from infinite pain and anxiety.

An extract from brother Ross's (Mr Kennedy's) letter,[1] received yesterday, will open up to you the exact state of affairs in Arkansas. "The probabilities are so strong in the direction" of a reorganization of the faculty "as to amount almost to a *certainty*," and, if reorganization comes, bro. R. is "quite sanguine of getting what we want." Indeed, he "thinks it quite certain, in that event, that he can manage to get the chairs readjusted to meet my wish." The only drawback to the situation is that the final resolution of the trustees with reference to reorganization cannot be reached before the first week in June, and the elections that would result upon reorganization could not be held before July or August. So that we must use what patience we can in the matter, contenting ourselves with the favourableness of the prospect. The edge of my interest in the affair has been considerably dulled by the thought that no immediate success may be able to hasten the realization of my dearest hopes; but there will be no resulting abatement in my zeal in any undertaking that promises to put me in a position to marry my darling so soon as God will.

That's rather an odd philosophy of yours, Miss, that, whatever comes of this will be *"right"*: it is almost too near to saying that "whatever is is right," wh. is very far from being true. I have full faith in the right ordering of Providence; but we cannot be too careful in seeing to it that we do our duty, not only, but that we do it *in the wisest way*. A false step on our part would not be right because it belonged to the general fore-ordained order of events.

I[t] makes me very indignant to think of what that fellow Wright dared to say to my darling! He ought to have had sense enough to know that he had received a final dismissal. He certainly has *no* right to know of your engagement, and there can be no good reason for telling him of it unless by so doing you can get finally rid of him and of his impertinence[.]

But this wont do: to be finding fault with so many things in a letter which is to reach my little sweetheart on her birthday: to be writing all sorts of cross things when there's nothing in my heart but unspeakable love for my darling, to whom I am writing! Will you let me send you twenty-four kisses, my darling, for to-day's greeting. The fifteenth of a certain month of May did more for my happiness than all the other days of my life-time put together and I shall take the privilege of bringing this twenty-four-fold pledge of the fact to you some of these days. Meantime, imagine them, if you care to, in your heart: would you walk out of your way for any part of them *now*, little sweetheart?

You must be on the look out, my pet, for a little package I sent you by express to-day. I am afraid that it wont reach you on the 15th, as I was so stupid as to make the mistake of supposing that express-matter would go in just the same time as mail-matter.

Remember, not before the 20th![2]

I love you, my darling, I love you with all my heart, and am altogether   Your own   Woodrow.

ALS (WC, NjP).
    [1] A. R. Kennedy to WW, May 8, 1884, ALS (WP, DLC) with WWhw notation on env.: "Ans. May 20th, 1884."
    [2] Double underscoring by WW.

ENCLOSURE

To E.L.A. on Her Birthday

May 15, 1884

I cannot tell, my lady fair,
What thine own thoughts may be
When that thou comest once again
Thy natal day to see;

But this I know, and fain would tell
Close at thy listening ear,
That God has given few gifts more blest
Than this thy closing year.

Bright as thy frank and laughing eyes
Should be this blest May-day,
And radiant as thy loving smile
Its sun's flower-kissing ray.

Thy sorrows past are hallowed all
By deeds of duteous love;
They speak to thee of gladness given
To that dear one above.

They testify of love's glad care
For duties thou did'st bear
To make thy home again as bright
As when her form was there.

That home was stricken, not in wrath
For sin, or shame, or wrong,
But that in God our trust might stand
And in his strength be strong.

Why should'st thou not thy birthday hail
With joy and hope and mirth?
How sad so'eer thy life has been
God smiled upon thy birth.

For thee he sent to blessings bear
Of love and sympathy,
To show to us the beauty rare
Of brave work's majesty.

He sent thee to make bright the lives
And ease the arduous part
Of those to whom thou wast to bring
Thy purity of heart.

He gave to thee in largess free
Not only beauty's charm,
But all the graces that win man
And stay him from his harm.

Thou art thyself his chiefest gift
To him to whom 'tis given
To see in thy sweet, trusting eyes
The love for which he's striven.

If that thou think'st it good to be
On such blest missions sent,

Can'st thou not smile e'en o'er the year
That's been so sadly spent?

This fair May-day sure seems to me
A rose without its thorn;
For can there be aught ill in this,
The day when thou wast born?

Until I saw thy winsome face
And love-light in thine eyes,
I had not known the fairest forms
Born 'neath these May-day skies.

But now I can believe that this,
The hey-day of the Spring,
Is fairest month in Nature's round
For that it thee did bring!
                                        W.W.

WWhw (WC, NjP).

To Ellen Louise Axson

My own darling,   Balto., Md., May 15th/84

As you may imagine, I have not been able altogether to escape worry in the presence of the anxious uncertainty just now attending both your plans and my own: for it would cause me infinite distress should you be compelled to carry out your idea of seeking a situation as teacher for the year to come; but I trust that before the 20th I shall have an alternative plan to suggest which will disentangle us both from present perplexities and relieve me from the strain of anxiety which has during the last few days been giving me several headaches a day. If the certain advices for which I eagerly look do'nt come, I shall have to bear the bitter disappointment as best I can and school myself to patience. I do hope, my darling, that you will not have found it necessary to take any step which you cannot retrace before I have had time to write again—before the 20th!

I was profoundly surprised to hear of cousin Abe's having gone to Chicago. I had heard absolutely nothing from Rome, except now and again a bit of news through you, since February. What *will* poor uncle James do, if Jessie is taken away from him? Give them all "lots" of love from me, and tell Jessie, if you please, my pet, that her cousin away off in Baltimore would really like to hear the particulars of this contemplated change.

I can hardly say yet, my darling, *what* my idea is about my visit to you: just at this writing I have ideas with reference to only one particular concern. As soon as I get home I can begin to plan my movements with some certainty, but until then I can't plan them at all.

If you will consult the first page of this letter, little lady, you will perceive that it was written on the 15th; but let me tell you, Miss, that I have'nt thought about you a bit more than usual to-day: for I think of you pretty much all the time, quite regardless of dates. But, though there was no difference of intensity, there was a difference of kind in my thoughts[.] I have been wondering what *your* thoughts have been to-day. Wont you tell me, my darling? The world has changed a great deal for both of us since your last birthday: I suppose, for instance, that you did'nt think of *me* at all on your last birthday (I didn't know even when your birthday came) whereas you *may* have thought of me once or twice to-day? Yes, my darling, I know how much; and I am coming soon to tell you what I have been thinking of you! Warmest love to your dear father, and Ed. and Stockton, and regards to Mr. T. I love you unspeakably.   Your own   Woodrow.

ALS (WC, NjP).

From Janet Woodrow Wilson

My precious Son,   Wilmington, N.C. May 15th 84
    Yours of the 13th was received this morning—and has distressed me not a little.

My most anxious wish in your behalf, for some time, has been, that you might secure such a position as might enable you to marry the sweet girl who is now your promised wife—*at the earliest possible day*. You know how we love you, and how anxiously we desire your happiness. You know, too, that your nobly generous father would not hesitate to make any *possible* sacrifice to secure that happiness. But *would this plan* that your propose, lead to happiness. I *think not*. Supposing our hopes should be disappointed—that you should fail to secure a permanent home for our dear Ellie? I think it would be far kinder to allow her to take such a position as she proposes—than to take her to B[altimore] to join you in your anxieties for the future. Besides, I do not think, dear, that *she would consent* to occupy such a position. Of the two conditions, I think she would be happier in occupying, for a short while, such a position as she proposes. And, my darling, you must consider *her* feelings, first of all

Now, what I would advise is this. Of course you have kept her advised of everything with regard to your prospects—"chances." So, I would beg her to make no *definite* arrangement, while these are undecided. It is a long while yet till the fall sessions shall open—so that she *need* not make any contract for some time. Of course you will be frank—and beg her not to commit herself, until your fate for the coming year is decided. Believe me, this is the only true plan for your, and her, happiness. To marry in the manner you suggest would only lead to anxiety and unhappiness.

Can I do anything to induce dear Ellie to visit us this summer? I will write to Mrs. Axson—or anything *anything*—to bring the dear girl here.

I write with a heavy heart—for I fear my letter will be only a disappointment to my darling boy.

Josie joins me in love unbounded to you.

Yours *most* lovingly   Mother

ALS (WP, DLC).

Pocket Notebook

[c. May 16, 1884]

Inscribed (WWhw) on first page following cover stamped by Baltimore stationer and 1884 calendar: list of names and addresses beginning with "T. Alexis Berry."

Contents:
  (a) WWhw memorandum of receipt of $10.90 for "hay and herding lease," dated May 16, 1884.
  (b) WWhw partial draft of letter to James W. Bones, printed at July 12, 1884.
  (c) Various WWhw notes on and extracts from Bagehot.
  (d) Fragment of a WWhw ditty, printed at Aug. 12, 1884.
  (e) Miscellaneous brief WWhw and WWsh memoranda and scribbling.

Pocket notebook (WP, DLC).

From the Minutes of the Seminary of Historical and Political Science

Bluntschli Library, May 16, '84.

The Seminary was called to order by Dr. Adams at 8:15 P.M. Absent Messers. Ramage, Fisher, Rich and Worthington.

Mr. Scaife read the minutes of the previous meeting.

The paper of the evening was by Mr. Wilson who read a second chapter from his study on Congressional Government, giving a very able and instructive account of the inner workings of the

House of Representatives, through its standing committees. The duties and powers of its Speaker were discussed, and interesting comparisons were drawn between the House of Rep. and the House of Commons, and the French Assembly. . . .

The Seminary adjourned at 10.05.

W. P. Holcomb, Sec.

From Joseph Ruggles Wilson

My darling Son—   Vicksburg, May 17, '84[1]

I have not sent you the telegram you desired, for I dared not. It was, certainly, necessary for me to think over the matter you so warmly present, and as naturally as warmly. My conclusion is reached. It leads me to do what will hurt you; i.e., to advise against the precipitancy to which your heart inclines—your *heart* rather than your judgment I must believe. For, would it be wise to involve that dear girl in a relationship wherein she would be constrained to feel her dependence upon your mother and me— because you and she would be constrained to draw all your support from us—or nearly all—for an indefinite period. My first impulse was—yes—marry at once—bring your loved one home—let us be one family—and get on together as best we may. But w'd I thus be dealing with my noble son in a noble way? Better counsel him to wait still longer, and until he has something of his own to lay at the feet of his bride. Darling, my heart bleeds at penning such words. And I am sure you will forgive them.

The Arkansas matter I have almost no faith in. The principal elector is here—a member of Assembly—and he has not approached me on the subject, or given me an opportunity to approach him. Failing here you will have only a possible fellowship to fall back upon—and is not that withdrawn in the event of the *marriage* of its incumbent?

That sweet Ellie—I admire her resolution to engage in teaching for the support of her brothers. It is heroic. Imitate her, my son, in the sacrifice she is making for independence. If as you say her constitution is frail—too frail to undergo the wear an tear of a year's school life—then she is too frail to marry at all, and would do wrong to do so. But I cannot write more, with these tears in my eyes and these yearnings in my heart for you both. You want *the truth*—for by nothing less can you stand, as in nothing less can you be happy.

If, however, contrary to my advise, you should decide to marry, be sure of one thing—she and you will be as welcome to your home as possible—for whatever I have shall be cheerfully and ungrudgingly yours, so far as you will permit or need.

Besides, after you tell your mother all—let *her* say what is best.

I hardly dare to send this letter, my own dearest boy for I feel that you must almost *hate* me for my interposition. God grant the contrary. But I am compelled to do *right* come what may.

Your affectionate   Father.

ALS (WP, DLC) with WWhw notation on env.: "Ans. May 21/84."
    [1] JRW was attending the General Assembly of the southern Presbyterian Church, which met in the Vicksburg, Miss., Presbyterian Church, May 15-24, 1884.

To Ellen Louise Axson

My precious little sweetheart,   Balto., Md., May 17th/84

My somewhat mysterious insistence upon delay till the 20th must have puzzled you not a little, and I ought to explain at once, in order not to leave you to the useless making of all sorts of conjectures as to what wild scheme your impulsive, unmanageable lover has in hand now. This is the whole of the mystery, then, my darling: I was in hopes that certain letters I was expecting would contain more definite news than I have yet had about the progress of my schemes for a settlement next year, and that I could ask you to forego your own projects for something more definite than an "if." But, alas! little lady, I have learned nothing more than I knew before and can no longer plead for any delay. This last manoeuvre of a wilful man bent upon having his own way has proved a dismal failure: and, if the fuss he made about it and the interruptions of plan it may have cost have not distressed my darling, no harm has been done. You see, Miss, if you *will* go and engage yourself to an intense individual who takes everything to heart so deeply, you must nerve yourself to abide many extraordinary vagaries with patient allowance until you can take him in hand and teach him more moderate ways.

I have enough faith in my prospects for next year to be just a little bit glad to hear that yours promise very small things as yet. That sounds like a very heartless thing to say, I am afraid: for I know just how you feel about your work; but I know that *you* will not miss my meaning. I *dread* seeing you undertake a teacher's duties, because I know quite enough of the conditions of such a situation as you seek to wish most earnestly to keep my darling from its wearing, harassing trials. I know how bravely and nobly you would bear all the annoyances that would lie in the path of such duty—because I know how bravely and nobly you *have* worked in the past. You have'nt dreamed yet, Miss, how great an admiration I have for the little heroine who loves me. But I can see no reason for wishing to see additional burdens cast upon you, which, though they cannot break your spirit, may break your health and so mar for good and aye your happiness. Besides, little lady, I have some ambition stowed away in odd corners of my heart. I have never yet been of any use to any one: I have yet to become a bread-winner; and I should find unspeakable delight in taking upon my own shoulders the burdens you have had to carry. The reward would be two-fold. It would, in the first place, be *yourself*—and you can't form an approximate guess, Miss, as to how much that means to me—and, in the second place, the novel indulgence of affording substantial aid to those near and dear to me. I am quite willing that you should think the proposition a "noble" one—I confess myself quite ready to tolerate the very nicest things you can think of me—and I cannot object to your calling me "rashly generous"—for I have stoutly determined to let you call me what names you will—but I must insist upon being allowed to think of it as just what it is, a self-indulgent purpose from which I will not be retarded even by hard names such as "Atlas" and the like. "Aunt Ella" never said a truer thing than that you "can't expect people to wait until Eddie is grown and married"—at least, if *I* am the "people" she had in mind. I don't recollect, Miss, ever having shown any special antipathy towards that dear brown little chap—indeed I had tricked myself into the belief that I could love him quite as much as my brother as you love him as yours—and, even were I *not* disposed to love him, were he as great a rascal as he could "stick," I would take a half dozen like him to obtain a certain incomparable prize to which he is attached! So you see how necessary it is that you should make up your mind that, if my slow-going plans ever lead me into a decent salary, the very kindest thing you can do for me is to let me have my own way in this matter.

My darling, how can I tell you any part of my feelings about the sad news from your dear father. Oh, my heart is *so* heavy when I think of the terrible sorrow which my sweet, brave, Christian darling has to bear, and I do so fervently long to be with her at this time when she needs my love and comfort most! May God bless and keep and strengthen you, my love! Does it help you at all to know how much I love you? It would be an immense comfort to me to think that it did!

I am sincerely glad for your sake that you have had a full explanation with Mr. Wright, and I earnestly hope that it will shield you from any further attentions from him.

Wont you be glad to know, my pet, that my year's work will be over by next Tuesday afternoon? After that day only the collection of some material for the writing I hope to do this vacation will delay my departure for home. My spirits are rapidly rising at the prospect—for I never stood in sorer need of home rest, and I am, in consequence, positively home-sick. I see no reason now why I should not start within about a week. I can give you the exact date, maybe, in my next letter.

Give my warmest love to all at "Oakdene" and tell me all you can about their plans, if you cannot persuade them to write to me, for I know nothing but what your letters have contained.

How did you spend your birthday, little lady? I hope that it was a bright, happy day and that you managed to think once or twice of the love borne you by

Your own   Woodrow.

ALS (WC, NjP).

From Ellen Louise Axson

My darling Woodrow,   East Rome [Ga.] May 19/84

I made a futile attempt at writing on last Friday night,—being anxious to lose no time in thanking you for the beautiful gift, which reached me on that day,—but I was interrupted by Mr. Thornwell, and have had no opportunity since to resume. So that, after all my good intentions, I have postponed writing until the usual time.

I am *so* much obliged to you, dearest, for your *lovely* little gift; it is just as dainty and pretty as can be, indeed altogether charming,—one of it's charms, not it's least, being the "little buds of blue" with the dear old meaning that they bear. No fear but that I will heed their message well. Really, your treatment of me is almost enough to reconcile me to *having* birthdays! Who would forego the occasion which gives rise to so many delightful attentions, actually inspiring one's friends to write *poetry* in one's honour! Many thanks, dearest, for that too. The subject matter, indeed, is such that I don't dare hazard an opinion as to it's merits. In fact I am more than dubious as to the truth of most of the statements it contains, but those things, of course, are merely poetical licenses; one shouldn't subject a work of the imagination to so narrow a standard,—to so mean a test! Yes, I had a very bright and pleasant birthday; one that passed off most

satisfactorily; that is to say, I forgot altogether that it *was* my
birthday until there came to me a message from a far-away
friend, to give me a *pleasant* reminder, and to turn my thoughts
into the happiest possible channel. I freely admit that I have no
business to forget my birthday,—to make light of such a catastrophe! I should try to realize what it means to be twenty-four
years old. Indeed I *must* try to learn the art of growing old gracefully,—to avoid doing things unbecoming my age and dignity;
and of course the first step is to see and appreciate the facts of
the case. But that I fear I have never done;—true, I sometimes
feel awfully old,—sixty-four at least;—and then again I feel fourteen; but *never* just what I am—a mature young woman of four
and twenty. But there were other matters in that birthday letter,
which urged me to an immediate answer. My darling! You make
me love you more every day,—you find a hundred different ways
in which to do it! I can't tell you how deeply I appreciate your
tenderness and thoughtfulness. How full of both was the letter
which came today! But you must not let yourself be thus "careful
and troubled about many things," dearest. There is nothing so
dreadful in teaching; indeed, it is excellent discipline—'twill do
me good. And I *am* sure that it will all be well in the end. Beware,
Sir, how you try to pursuade me to the contrary; for if I once
lose faith in all things working together for good, I will, that very
hour, lie down and die!

No, the delay of a few days in the prosecution of my plans has
made no difference,—no harm whatever has been done.

As for me, there are so many arguments for and against every
course that I don't know what I want, and, worse still, I don't
know what I *ought* to want! And as there seems no way of finding out, and if I did find out, no way of attaining to it, I have about
reached a quiescent frame of mind, and have decided "in whatsoever state I am therewith to be content." Though in truth I am
not very tranquil when I think of you so harassed about it all,
actually getting up head-aches on the strength of it! How glad
I am that you are going "home" so soon! I was surprised, as
well as delighted, to learn *how* soon, for I thought the term did
not end until June. Isnt it over sooner than you expected? And
by-the-way the announcement has, for one small reason, *startled*
me too, bringing my sins to mind. When Mrs. Green was in
Sav. she told me, over, and over, and over, that I must "send you
to see her.["] I said "Yes'm," very meekly, but I hav'nt done it, you
see, some unaccountable shyness has prevented. I don't by any
means propose to "send" you now, especially when your time is

so short, and your hands probably so full. But I merely mention the matter to say that if you *have* time, and care to go, she will be glad to see you;—that is if she has'nt altogether lost patience with me because of my delinquencies in this and other respects, notably letter-writing. I think that altogether I have treated Mrs. Green rather shabbily as concerns you; but it really was'nt my fault. Of course, I had no objection to telling her anything she wished to know, but I didnt propose to take a whole roomful into my confidence, and I never saw her alone;—there were always such crowds there, her time being so short. She attacked me several times openly, at the dining table and elsewhere, but of course I had no idea what she was talking about. So though she asked many questions about you, she left altogether unenlightened, knowing only that you were in Baltimore at the "J.H.," and that she wanted to see you.

What a *splendid* notice of your lecture that is, you sent me![1] I am perfectly carried away by it. It is so different from many of those things, which get all the facts hopelessly mixed, and then pile on the adjectives of praise in the most indiscriminate, stupid fashion. But this is so just, and true and appreciative, and well put. It quite overwhelmed me. I have been in a very vacillating state ever since I received it. I am wild for them to see it in Sav., so I take it out and prepare to send it, but then I am *so* afraid the precious thing will be lost that I change my mind and put it back; —and by and by return and repeat the process—and so on indefinitely. So you have decided to present your papers as lectures before the Academy![2] I remember you were doubtful about it. I dare say it is an excellent plan, to let them have a taste of them at any rate. Is it the history of Political Economy that you are busy collecting materials for now or the essays? Is Mr. Renick helping you as he proposed? What is Mr. Shinn doing now; did he succeed in New York? I hav'nt heard anything of him since the comical note, with it's many post-scripts.

We are alone here now—Agnes[,] Eddie and I. The soldier's wife and the pretty little brunette left on Sat. night. Mr. Tedcastle will be back "next week," to quote Agnes, who remarked about a dozen times on Sat., "now, *tomorrow* I can say, 'Arthur will be back *next* week,' and that will seem *so* much nearer!["] I believe I am glad he is coming. His presence will afford an occasional welcome interruption to the discourses about him. But it was a subject on which I *did* need to be enlightened, for though I liked him very much, I had no idea he was such an angel in disguise. "You know there are very few men like Arthur this side of heaven,"—so says Mrs. Arthur. If I had a wife I should forbid her—ah! I beg her pardon,—I should respectfully *suggest* to her not to make me ridiculous by perpetual praise. Dear old Agnes! She is just as sweet and good "as they are made";—it is a shame for me to laugh at her—but then I don't mean anything by it. But I have reached the end of this sheet and really *must not* begin another.

Give love to your parents, to Josie, and all. Agnes sends her kindest regards.

Goodnight. I love you, dearest, more than tongue can tell, "infinitely more that I did this time last year"!

Your own Ellie.

Mrs. Green's address is *353 Park Avenue*.

ALS (WP, DLC).

¹ As the extracts from the Minutes of the Historical Seminary have shown, Wilson read chapters from *Congressional Government* to the members on May 9 and 16, 1884. As the only newspaper "notice" yet found was a purely factual mention in the Baltimore *Sun*, May 17, 1884, the *"splendid* notice" that Woodrow sent Ellen must have been an extract made by him of the high praise bestowed by Professor Adams and recorded in the Minutes of the Seminary for May 9, q.v.

² That is, the Seminary of Historical and Political Science.

Two Letters to Ellen Louise Axson

My own darling,   Balto., Md., May 20th, 1884

You may direct your next letter to the care of the Rev. Dr. Joseph R. Wilson, Wilmington, N.C. I expect to leave this borough on the afternoon of Monday, the 26th, and to reach home early Tuesday morning, much before the hour at which my interesting younger brother, the Capt. of the Wilmington Bicycle Club, is accustomed to rise, but not earlier than he *will* rise when it is necessary to take the buggy down to the station to fetch his elder brother, from the University. Dear father is away at the Assembly, of course, and I expect to reach home before he does, in good season to go myself to the station to meet him.

I find that dear mother is extremely reluctant to give up the idea, which she has been cherishing all winter, of having you with us in Wilmington a little while this summer. In her last letter she returns to the project—though I had told her of your decision—and says, "Can I do anything to induce dear Ellie to visit us this summer? I will write to Mrs. Axson—or anything, *anything* —to bring the dear girl here." Are you not dismayed, little lady, to find the Wilson family so set in their determination to have their own way?

I am, like most helpless individuals of my sex, quite aghast at the amount of packing I have to do before I get away. Of course, since it is uncertain whether or not I shall return to Balto. next year, I have to pack up all my properties, books and all, ready for shipment, in case shipment becomes necessary. By the time this letter reaches you, therefore, you may imagine me in the toils of this great undertaking. I can doubtless pack my big box and my two trunks in a single day—but what a day that will be! Do'nt you wish you were here to help me? I do'nt. I would give any-thing in the world to have my darling here but I would'nt let her take a hand in such packing as I have to do. She might sit by and give me advice, and laugh at me, to her heart's content (such an arrangement would certainly be to *my* heart's content) but she should'nt break her back over the trunks and the heavy books.

My first plan was to pack up at once and get off as soon as lec-tures came to a close, but I concluded that it would'nt be decent to run away before making a round of parting calls on the dozen or so old and new friends whom I have found and made in Balti-more. Such calling will, therefore, be my chief occupation for the next day or two. There are some old Augusta friends of father's living here upon whom I have not called at all—having carefully concealed from them my presence in town with a view to keep-ing as much out of society and as close to my studies as possible—and of course upon these people I do'nt dare to call now. It would be too late to make my peace with them.

What do you do with yourself nowadays, my darling? Are you as busy with your drawing as ever; and do you ride out every day with Mrs. Tedcastle as you used to do last Autumn when you were staying with her? Since Mr. Tedcastle is away from home, I sup-pose my little sweetheart do'nt use the twilight now as she did then—lingering on the piazza thinking of "people" while Mrs. T. drives into town to fetch her husband home from business. Of course you see a great deal of your cousin [Minnie Hoyt] and of Miss Anna Harris.

I wish I *could* tell you, my love, what to expect about my visit. If one could shape his own ways quite irrespective of duty, it would be easy to say when I would go to see the little lady who is "a' the world to me," but, as it is, I can decide nothing at all about it yet awhile. There are embarrassments about my going to Rome as well as about my going to Sewanee. I know that Jessie must have her little house already full beyond the point of con-venience and comfort and I am naturally disinclined to impose

upon her hospitality, genuinely glad though I know she would be
to have me come and stay *ad libitum*. I have already told you how
I feel about accepting Miss Anderson's cordial and generous invitation. I do'nt want to make her sacrifice her enjoyment of your
visit to her by a too-generous entertainment of a troublesome
man who would be all the time engrossing your attention. But,
whatever the obstacles, see you I will before the vacation is gone,
if it be but for a half hour in which I may hear you say once
more that you love me and get another kiss from those sweet lips.
I *could'nt* go all the summer through without seeing you if I were
to try: and if I do'nt make you a long visit, it will be only because
I am busy with plans for that best of all times, the time when I
shall come and beg my darling to go with me to a little home of
our own where she may learn the full meaning of my love for her.

Now that the session's work is over, I am getting back my
light spirits and my perfect health with the return of leisure and
the consequent absence of the strain of a big burden of work.

I love you with all my heart.

Your own   Woodrow.

My own darling,   Balto., Md., May 25th/84
Packing and paying parting calls (most trying of all duties)
have altogether upset my usual ways and have prevented my writing to my darling at the usual times: but I know that she understands and is not afraid that I *forgot* to write to her.

Your sweet letter that reached me Friday made me very happy,
my precious. I am so glad that you liked the little present I sent
you, and that your birthday passed so happily. Yes, you *are* a
dreadfully mature young woman—and yet to see you one would'nt
suppose that you were very aged. There's lots of joy and love in
those sweet eyes of yours—if my memory does not betray me—
and a roundness and bloom as of youth in those pretty cheeks.
Altogether one who was disposed to be deceived would think that
they had found in my Ellie a maiden in that hey-day of youth
in which maidens, when they have any charms at all, are most
irresistible. But the fact remains that you are four and twenty—
an age which even I, who am considerably more than seven and
twenty, must admit to be very advanced.

Do you really think, my precious mature little sweetheart, that
I was trying to persuade you that all things do *not* work together
for good? I would as soon try to persuade you that there is no God.
I meant only that your little piece of philosophy, as you put it in

one of your letters, would justify one in letting things drift, in the assurance that they would drift to a happy result. I was simply expressing, too awkwardly, no doubt, my idea of *how* all things work together for good—through the careful performance of our duty.

Do you think that you *can* safely wait until I see you before deciding the question of seeking a teacher's position? I do *so* hope that you can—though I would not ask it or advise it, if it seems either imprudent or unwise to do so. "Until I see you"! My darling! how I do long for that time, how fiercely impatient I am for its coming! I love you so much that I can't do without you much longer. It is wonderful what progress we have made since Sept. in becoming acquainted with each other. So many things, and so many sweet words of your own have opened up your heart to me that I feel as if we were already wedded—and, let me tell you a secret, Miss, which you must not breathe to a soul: the more I see of that loving heart of yours the more impossible does it seem that I could live without its love.

I presume we are intimate enough acquaintances to warrant my using a *pencil* when my ink is poured out and my inkstand packed up?

Off for home to-morrow—to reach there Tuesday morning

Love to Ed. and all at Oakdene. Regards to doting Mrs. Arthur. With a heartful of love for Ellie,

Your own   Woodrow.

ALS (WC, NjP).

From Jessie Bones Brower

Dear Cousin Woodrow,   East Rome. Ga. 25 May 1884

I received your paper containing the very complimentary notice of your articles about a week ago,[1] & it is needless to say that we were all very proud of you Sir. I of course sent the paper on to Abe & he wants to know just when & where all the articles are to appear, so that he can read every one. We all knew that you were going to make a brilliant mark in the world some day, but had not expected it so soon.

Well, to change the subject but to another pleasant topic of conversation, we are all enjoying a certain young ladies visit to Rome, & by the way as I expect her to spend a part of her time with me couldn't you make it convenient to happen along at that time? We should enjoy a visit from you exceedingly but it is not altogether from selfish motives that I want you. I dont imagine it would be disagreeable to either of the parties most concerned. I declare Cousin Woodrow you are a fortunate man to have secured such a prize, for I declare a lovelier vision in the shape of women flesh I never saw than Ellie Lou is this summer. She is *perfectly* beautiful, as as [sic] lovable as she is beautiful. You certainly must make it convenient to happen along wont you? But I know you will come if it be possible. . . .

Hoping to hear from you soon saying that you will soon be with us, I am as ever,

Your affectionate cousin,   Jessie B. Brower.

P.S. omitted. ALS (WP, DLC) with WWhw notation on env.: "*Ans.*"
   [1] See ELA to WW, May 25, 1884, n.1.

From Ellen Louise Axson

My darling Woodrow,   East Rome [Ga.], May 26/84.

And so you are actually homeward bound tonight, and tomorrow's sun in it[s] rising will, God willing, smile upon your "welcome home." "Oh fortunate, oh happy youth,"—you little know now how fortunate. I am *so* glad that you have escaped from your burden of work so early, and before you were quite worn out. Do you mean to begin again immediately upon your writing, or to take a real holiday for a time like a sensible man?

Mr. Bones has just left, having taken tea with us. He seems very happy at the prospect of having Marion [McGraw Bones] with him again soon. *Her* holiday begins next week. I should think he would be sorely tempted to make it a perpetual holiday, for he will need her badly when Jessie leaves. It is fully determined that they are to go in the autumn; she only remains through the summer, she says, that she may not lose the fruit of their labour on garden and farm.

And by-the-way, she charged me with a message for you last Tuesday, which, as it happens, works in very well by way of answer to your last letter. She said she had been trying to write you, and still intended to do so; but in the meantime, while she is waiting for a convenient season for writing, she will prefer her request through me. It is that you will be sure and make her a visit this summer. She seems to have any amount of room, for she confided to me a grand scheme she had concocted which was to have her friend Miss Hunter, and you, and Marion, and me, and I won't venture to say how many more, all with her during "the encampment" about the first of July. But I shan't be here then,—even had I intended to remain so long, I would feel disposed to fly if I thought there was any danger of coming into contact with one of those dreadful things. I always objected seriously to them, and now I have indeed little heart for it all. But I rather think we would have a pleasanter time here than at Sewanee, because there is such a large family there in the summer,—the Dr. & his wife, Clarence & Daisy, Jack & Julie, Mac & Rose and The Prodigy and his mother;[1] to say nothing of the whole Quintard family, who might as well live in the same house. True, you ought to be there to protect me from The Prodigy for he is a most terrible lady-killer. He has broken scores of hearts, and there are dozens of beauties & heiresses dying of love for him now. But, as I was saying, we should have no peace there; for the Family is as formidable in character as it is in number; it almost passes belief that Rose should have lived through all they have made her suffer. Mr. King (Clarence) & Mr. McRae (Jack) are the most dreadful teases I ever saw; and in such different ways too. Mr. King has reduced teasing to a fine art. One scarcely objects to being teased by him, he does it in such a delicate and at the same time exquisitely comical fashion. He is so full of humour of the sly, covert kind, and his expression is such a study—so odd, so quizzical, so altogether inimitable! It is a sort of wit that I appreciate very keenly, and I would almost rather be his victim than miss the sport. "Jack" on the contrary is one of those great, rolicking fellows, always laughing at one, saying impudent things; playing practical jokes, and being outrageously tormenting,—only he is so good-natured, one can't get "mad" with him. I never saw a greater contrast than in those two brothers[-in-law] of Rose's. In every respect, Mr. McRae is the typical handsome animal—a splendid creature, except that he is rather *too* large—ugh! His hands are so fat but he has a large well-formed head covered with a mass of curly blond hair, big blue eyes, a fresh ruddy complexion, and very symmetrical features. And when you have said that, you have said about all, for the spiritual part of him is sadly undeveloped. Yet he is a throughly good fellow, a fair average specimen of a man,—one of the sort that are turned off by the gross.

But Mr. King is unique. He has a face which was certainly not constructed upon any approved model of either beauty of [or] strength, but which is full of interest and attraction, at least to those who know him. There is an odd charm about the face and the man to me—and to many others, for he has the gift of winning hearts. He is emphatically a *gentle*man. There is an almost womanly tenderness about him; and he is supposed to be the most devoted son and husband in Sav. But I have already given these two quite an absurdly large share of my letter, so I will cut short my description of Mr. King short. By-the-way he is very tall, and very thin, and very pale, which makes the external contrast between the two really ludicrous.

Yes, I spend my time in very much the same old way. I have only done one picture though, as yet: there are others which are weighing on my mind & which I would like to be doing, but the "spring sewing" was also weighing on me, so for the last two weeks the machine and I have been having a trial of strength. We drive occasionally, but not every day as we did last fall. Mr. T. is not here to keep Agnes up to the mark, you see. It is too ridiculous to see how that man watches Agnes! Every night he has a budget of questions to ask—has she taken a walk or drive?— has she taken a *nap* &c. &c.; and if she has'nt he looks "so sorry," that she is as penitent as a little child. But when he is away she relapses somewhat.

Give much love to your mother, to your father, when he returns, and to Josie. Also give your dear mother my most heartfelt thanks for her repeated kindness. I would be glad indeed to thank her in person—but that is impossible, I am afraid. I hope you find her, and your father too, quite well. But now I *must* close, though "I wouldn't choose to." I give you joy, dearest, in your home-coming, and hope you will have a very happy vacation. With truest love believe me as ever   Your own Ellie

ALS (WP, DLC).
    ¹ Dr. and Mrs. H. M. Anderson of Sewanee, Tenn.; their daughters Daisy, Julie, and Rosalie or Rose; Daisy's husband, Clarence King; Julie's husband, Jack McRae; and Rosalie's fiancé, McNeely DuBose. The "Prodigy" was the Rev. Thomas Frank Gailor, identified at July 28, 1884. His mother was Mrs. Frank M. (Charlotte Moffett) Gailor. Dr. Anderson was a physician in Sewanee.

Two Letters to Ellen Louise Axson

My own darling,   Wilmington, N.C. May 28 [1884]
    A change in through schedules both kept me in Baltimore some hours beyond the time at which I expected to start for home and, by keeping me on the cars all day yesterday (Tuesday), cheated me out of writing to you at the usual time. If I had known before-hand the new arrangements about through trains, I would have planned so that my darling might have her letter at the usual time come what might—for I hold it to be an incontrovertible principle that it is much better to inconvenience myself than to disappoint her.

I reached home last night between ten and eleven o'clock, having left Balto. a little before ten in the morning. I *tried* to start on Monday afternoon. Trusting the schedule in the morning's paper, I sent my trunks down to the train that took me last January to Savannah, and followed them down under the escort of four University friends who divided my hand luggage amongst them and insisted upon relieving me of all responsibility save that of walking straight and smilingly in their midst. And then, after all this ceremonious preparation for departure, I did not depart. I was informed that, by a recent change, "the 3.20" was no longer a through train, and that I would have to wait till next morning if I did not want to spend the night in Washington or Richmond. So back I marched with my escort, feeling, as one of my friends suggested, "as if I had been down to see myself off."

I hope that the delay which this "regular" letter has suffered has caused my little sweetheart no anxiety

I find dear mother very far from well. She has been all winter suffering first one and then another result of her last year's illness. I have been trying to persuade her to go away from home for at least a portion of the Summer; but she has many good reasons for not wishing to do so. The fatigue of fixing the house to be left and the still greater fatigue of putting it again in order after returning from a long absence make her dread both what must precede and what must follow a "summering" away from home. The chains of housekeeping bind her fast. Then, too, besides all this, she finds more comfort at home than elsewhere, and the climate of Wilmington is in the summer everything that could be desired. It is quite a resort nowadays even for families from the upper part of the State. If it were malarial or debilitating, I could get her way from it; but, since it is everything that could be desired, she wont be dragged away merely for the sake of a change.

I have settled down with the comfortable determination to take what we used to call at college "a solid loaf" for a few days before getting at the work I have set myself. It is to be on *my* subject, on Congressional government, not on the history of political economy. I shall leave that until it is definitely determined whether or not I am to return to the Hopkins: for, if I do'nt go back to Balto. I shall of course resign my part of that job to some one else who can work with Ely on the ground. One could not carry on the studies necessary to such work away from the great libraries of a big city without immense expense.

Yes, I *did* get away from Balto a couple of weeks earlier than I had expected. The last ten days of the "semester" are taken up with the examinations of the undergraduates, it seems, all lectures closing about three weeks before the "final day." Maybe my darling will be glad to learn that her sweetheart won this session the highest honours open to him. President Gilman told me just before I left, as I was bidding him good-bye, that I was to be offered a fellowship for next year. A fellowship carries with it a stipend of $500.00, besides various valuable privileges, and the twenty fellowships given in the several departments (there are two in ours) are competed for very sharply every year not only by the best men in the University but even by honour-men of the German universities: so that they are regarded as the great prizes. I have the additional satisfaction of knowing that I was picked out by both the faculty and the students of our Seminary as having full title to the appointment. All of which goes to prove, however, that I was the least unworthy, not the most worthy. Complete success, such as I have had at the Hopkins, has the odd effect upon me of humiliating rather than exalting me: for I can't help knowing how much less worthy and capable I am than I am thought to be. I am not so clever at deceiving myself as I am at deceiving college companions—and Roman girls. You need'nt scold me, Miss, for not telling you that I was a candidate for a fellowship. I did'nt want my darling to be disappointed in case I did not succeed, so I said nothing about it. It's satisfactory to have a fellowship awaiting one if professorships be not offered as desired.

I love you, my precious Ellie, oh so dearly!—with a love that ought to satisfy any reasonable maiden. Mother and Josie send you lots of love. Father is not yet back from the Assembly. I'll write again as soon as I get a little bit rested. I'm too tired and stupid to write any more just now—but never so out of sorts that I can't think loving thoughts of the little lady who's all the world to me.   Your own   Woodrow

Wilmington [N.C.], May 29th/84

What would I not give to be able to come at once and take my sweet, brave darling away from her work, that I might work for her. I *am* working for her now—I have been working for her all winter—but unhappily it has been, and is yet, only work that will pay in the future. My darling's letter of this morning lets out a secret which it did not mean to let out: that my precious Ellie was scarcely strong enough for the two week's trial of strength with the sewing-machine and that the arrears of other work weighing on her mind have taken their usual bouyant, playful mood from her spirits. You were very tired when you wrote that letter, darling. Are you glad that I have "escaped from my burden of work" "before I was quite worn out"—why, little lady, I was in no danger of being worn out by work—not half so much in danger of it as is a certain little maiden whom I know and love—and I am about to take a thorough rest—for work on the "Minutes" [of the General Assembly] wont amount to much—and intend writing, when I begin upon my vacation's task, at such an easy pace that the occupation will serve as a mere recreation. It's easy to rest at home—and I think, begging your pardon, Miss, that I· *do* know how fortunate I am in the privileges and love of that home. But, then, I know this besides, and my heart is full of it, that I shan't be happy till I have made a home, equally full of love and privilege, for my darling. I know that she is not *un*happy now—she is much too brave and trustful a Christian for that—but then it seems to me that, maybe, I shall have a chance, some of these days, to lighten a little bit the burdens which she now carries marvellously as if they were privileges, and to complete the number of my own blessings by serving her at *our* home. I am an impatient, unreasonable chap to be so constantly chafing under the slow progress of time which is in allwise hands? Not a bit of it. I am only wishing out loud, in order that I may *not* chafe—as I would if I had to keep all these things to myself. I am only suffering my love for a certain young lady to have its full, free, and natural bent in expression, because I somehow have a shrewd suspicion that the ears into which these things are poured will hear them with allowance and receive them into a responsive heart whose thoughts will send smiles, and not frowns or tears, to the face I would give half a kingdom to see.

Dear mother and "Dode" send a heartful of love. More anon
from   Your own   Woodrow.

ALS (WC, NjP).

To Robert Bridges

My dear Bobby,   Wilmington, N.C., May 31st., 1884.
"If wishes were horses," I should have ridden over half a dozen times to see you before leaving Baltimore, and if thoughts were letters, many a mail would long ere this have brought you the

heaviest sort of epistles from me; but I have discovered that slavery has not been abolished in this country—at least not in Maryland—having been myself detained in the most wearing bondage in the city of Baltimore. Now, however, both leisure and business invite me to write.

I worked myself sick at the Hopkins and so had to neglect, towards the last, the correspondence I undertook for the Post;[1] and finally I had to leave before the "final day" had come around to be reported. I took the liberty, therefore, of putting the interests of the Post in the hands of a University classmate of mine, Edward Ingle by name, who has had a good deal of experience in reporting and will, consequently, I am sure, do quite as well by you as I could.[2] So much for the business: now for the news of myself, which you may like to hear. I have done as hard a year's work at the Hopkins as I shall ever do anywhere, and have won as great rewards as they had to bestow. None of the appointments for next year have been as yet officially announced—that is part of the ceremony reserved for "final day"—but President Gilman told me just before I left that I was to be offered a fellowship in history for next year. I have had my eye for some time past on a professorship of history and political economy in an Arkansas college, but if things do not turn out as favourably as I hope in that direction, I shall of course accept with thanks the $500 and the various privileges of the fellowship, very well content with so much good fortune.

I am just now taking a solid loaf of the most luxurious kind; but in a week or so I expect to tackle again the constitutional writing which I began at the Hopkins; though, as you may guess, there is no telling how soon I shall fly the track to go to see a certain charming young lady in Georgia in whom I am somewhat interested. Courtship beats constitutional questions any day, old fellow, if you would only believe it.

I not only enjoyed but admired the "Ferry" poem very much indeed, Bobby.[3] Both its transitions of thought and its tricks of verse are exceedingly happy. I can't help being glad that you return now and then to verse. You can put as much into it as any man I know, even if the mechanical part of it does cost you labour—which nobody but yourself sees. I wish you would let me know something more of your literary plans. Are you working at anything outside the office? I hope that you are. Give Pete loads of love from me. Tell the dear old fellow that, if I get a professorship next Autumn, I wont be far behind him in getting married.

Give my warmest regards to any of the boys you may see, and keep for yourself a new portion of the old love of

Your sincere friend   Woodrow Wilson

WWTLS (Meyer Coll., DLC).
  [1] Printed at Feb. 22, 1884; March 8, 1884; and April 11, 1884.
  [2] The report from the Johns Hopkins printed in the New York *Evening Post*, June 24, 1884, was probably written by Ingle. WW was not its author.
  [3] "Over the Ferry," reprinted in R. Bridges, *Bramble Brae* (New York, 1902).

To Ellen Louise Axson

Wilmington, N.C., June 1st [1884]

Oh, my precious Ellie, my poor stricken darling! how shall I tell you the things that are in my heart to-day! Miss Hoyt's note with its so sad message[1] came this morning, and ever since it came my heart has been aching as if it would break—not for *him*, my darling: for surely it was a blessed, gracious release from the sorrows and terrors of his condition; but for you, and for Stockton and Eddie. The very fact that you did not write to me yourself, but got your cousin to write for you, indicates, in a way that frightens me, the effect the news, coming, as it did, so suddenly and without warning, must have had upon you. Try to bear up, my darling. Remember how many there are left who love you and to whom your love is all in all. Your dear father, however sad or tragic his death may have been, is happy now. His Saviour, we may be sure, did not desert his servant at the supreme moment; and it is a joy to think that he is now reunited to the sweet, noble mother who went before him.[2] She escaped altogether, in God's mercy, the tragedy of insanity which clouded his last months; and now he has escaped it too and is gone to a joyful rest. It is altogether best for him, my pet: and as for us, have we not each other—have we not, above all things else, the blessed privilege of living for the service of God, in a glad performance of duty. Oh, my darling! I love you, and my heart is almost broken at thought of your unspeakable sorrow!

My first impulse upon receiving the note this morning was to go to you at once; but I must think of you, not of myself in this matter, and of course just now—in the absence of any public announcement of our engagement—my coming would cause you only embarrassment. Tell me, then, darling, just what you want me to do. I am ready to come at once if you want me and think it wise and best that I should come. I long to come, but will wait to learn your wish: for I want to come for your comfort, not for my own indulgence. Write as soon as ever you can, darling, for I shall be sick at heart till I hear: and write your whole mind without reserve. May I come, or may I not?

It seems to me, little lady, that this last blow draws us closer together than ever. Are we not now all in all to each other, as far as this life is concerned? I would stand in the stead of those you have lost, filling up to overflowing with purest love your cup of earthly joy.

Father, mother and Josie send you fullest love and warmest sympathy—and I, my peerless little sweetheart, am more than ever   Your own   Woodrow.

ALS (WC, NjP).
¹ Minnie Hoyt to WW, May 29, 1884, ALS (WP, DLC), saying that ELA had asked her to write him of the death of S. E. Axson on May 28, 1884.
² Margaret Hoyt Axson, ELA's mother, who died on November 4, 1881.

From Ellen Louise Axson

My darling Woodrow,   Rome [Ga.] June 2/84

I suppose you have, ere this, received Minnie's note of Thursday, and so know of the new sorrow which has fallen upon us. Yet, it is even so:—my dear father passed quietly away on Wednesday night. He seems to have sunk rapidly at the last; we had no warning whatever except that terrible letter to Uncle Will, which was indeed the best preparation for this which we could have had. God has been very merciful to him. He *has* "been pleased to deliver him." He has "made haste to help him." Yet I don't know that it made it much easier for me. One may think they have no hope, but when death ends all they discover that they had. And it seems to me that the terrible sense of desolation—of emptiness of heart and hands,—of a part of one's self having been forever torn away, is all the greater when that which we have lost has been an ever-present, anxious, sorrowful thought, an all-engrossing care. And then it is so hard, so hard, that people should think and say—to me too—that "it is better so"! Oh my dear, dear, father, the best, the purest, truest man I ever knew:—so useful too! One who lived so well, and did his work so faithfully and earnestly,—better that *he* should die than live! What an end to such a life! What a dreadful, hopeless tragedy it would seem, if we did not know that his true life has but begun; that the other is a probation, which, seen in God's light, is "but for a moment," and is followed by "a far more exceeding and eternal weight of glory."

June 3rd   You see, I am not as brave as I thought I was, dearest. I thought that I would heed the counsels of my friends, break through my old reserve on such matters, and to you, though to you alone, "give sorrow words"; but I could not bear it. I will not try again today.

I am *so* glad, so *very* glad, and *proud*, my darling, that you have taken the scholarship. No indeed, I won't scold about not having heard of it before, for it is too delightful to receive it as a complete surprise. What a *splendid* man you are, to be sure! What an "extra-special" man! You bring forward such various proofs of that fact, and in such rapid succession, that you quite take my breath away. I am struck dumb with awe. How long do you retain the scholarship[?] For one year only, or as long as you stay at the University? How gratifying that you should have been the choice of both professors and students! Certainly, your year in Baltimore has been a complete triumph, or rather a series of triumphs. My darling, are you *very sure* that you are wise to think of going elsewhere next year? Of course I can't pretend to judge in the matter, since I can't know *all* the circumstances, but the first thought which strikes me, and outsiders too, in view of the honnours you have won, is that it would be "*such* a pity" for you to give them all up so soon,—before you have reaped the advantages. You have made a place for yourself there,—have gained distinction. Is it well for you to drop out of it *now*, and go so far away, where you would be no more a living *presence*, but only a *voice*?—not that even—only the echo of a voice. In short, won't you win your laurels sooner,—wont you find it easier to gain your proper place in the literary world, if you remain longer in that great centre of thought and work? Then you say that if you leave, you must resign your work with Dr. Ely; and it seems to me that *that* too is *a pity*. Would not that work be a great advantage to you?—a very valuable introduction to the general public? That is just the sort of fact, you know, by which it (the general public!) is most easily influenced,—most profoundly impressed. And again if you remain, you will have *all* you[r] time for study, and for the work you like best, and which is of the first importance, whereas if you went away, you would be for a time almost engrossed by other things, "getting into harness," adjusting yourself to your new position, to the duties of a professor. I fear you would find at first little time for your own special work,—unless you overdid it all and half killed yourself. And that would be another danger of the situation. I know what you have said, that you have or *may* have a good opening, and that if you let it pass, you may not find another just when you want it. But perhaps there is no great danger of that. And what if you *are* obliged to wait, you can *afford* to wait if you have scholarships, &c., and you will have all the more time for uninterrup[t]ed work and study.

I hope you will pardon my saying so much on matters which I probably know nothing about; but then I *must* say how the situation strikes me. And I am *so* anxious that you should decide on that course which will be wisest "in the long run." And especially that you should be unbiased in your decision by any considerations in which *I* am involved. But I am sure it is unnecessary for me to say that. *Of course* you *can't* be so weak as to refuse to see what is *best* to be done and to *do* it, simply because there is something else which as it happens you would *like* to do, but which can *just as well* wait. Indeed you *must* leave me out, in forming your judgement, for I have now a positive offer of a place as art teacher which I must decide upon in a few days. And you know I told you how I felt about it, and that I would'nt be justified in letting things drift.

I am *so* sorry, and disappointed, to learn that your dear mother is still not strong. I wish you could devise some change—some plan—that would build her up. Give my warm love to her, and to your father and Josie, and keep for yourself "just as much as you want." My darling! You are indeed now "all the world to me." As ever   Your own Ellie.

ALS (WP, DLC)

From Edward Ingle

Dear Wilson: Johns Hopkins University Baltimore June 2/84

Allow an unsuccessful candidate to congratulate you upon having received the appointment of fellow in the University. You might have told me before you left Baltimore. I am
                              Your friend   Edw. Ingle.

ALS (WP, DLC) with WWhw notation on env.: "*Ans.*"

To Ellen Louise Axson

My own darling,   Wilmington [N.C.], June 3rd/84

I wish I knew some words to write to my darling that would carry comfort and gladness into the midst of her sorrow—what would I not give to see her smile, with a sweet light of love and hope and trusting assurance in the dear eyes I so earnestly love! —but I am *such* an awkward, dull fellow when I try to express what I *feel*. When I feel strongly I want to do everything and say nothing. I am sure that my precious Ellie loves and trusts God as

earnestly and truly as I do—as implicitly as did the noble mother
and father who are now safe in the enjoyment of an unspeakable
reward—and that she is bearing the burden of her present sorrow
with a sweet Christian patience which needs no word of mine to
strengthen it. But, then, I know also that, though it has no thought
of rebellion or of complaint, her heart is almost broken by the
repeated blows which it has received, and oh! I would give my life
so gladly to save her from pain. The simple hope that my love is
now a solace to her fills me with purer, keener joy than I ever
knew before! If she lets me come to her—if she will but open her
heart wholly to me, and cry in my arms, that I may kiss the tears
away—But how uselessly I am talking! You *know*, my darling, how
passionately I love you, and what I would be to you now, if you
can and will let me be your nearest and only sufficient earthly
comforter. I do'nt know what to write, but I trust my darling to
read my heart. I am awaiting your answer to my last letter with
an impatience which you can understand if you want me to come
as much as I want to come!

I received a letter from Jessie the other day, my pet, which was
just full of you. Jessie loves you very dearly and admires you so
much that she is afraid that I am not sufficiently impressed with
a sense of my exceeding good fortune in having won the promise
of your hand. I answered her letter at once, reassuring her on
that important point—and promising to do, what now I have to
confess to you: to tell her something which I would conceal from
you, the exact date of the visit I expected very soon to make her.
I wanted to take my little lady-love by surprise, though of course
I should have told her that I was coming very soon. I little suspected how soon such play would be driven out of my head by
news that made me sick at heart! My poor little darling! Does it
hurt you, pet, to have me talk of these indifferent matters? Of
course my device is very transparent, but suffer it nevertheless:
I want to make you think of me—of something away from yourself—if you will be so good. I can tell you one or two amusing happenings which will in the telling enable both of us to forget the
ache at our hearts, maybe. On last Thursday evening—the second
evening after my return home—I went to prayer-meeting with
dear mother and "Dode" and found it necessary to do yeoman's
service in the singing[.] The usual leader was absent and without
some imperative action on the part of some one with a strong
voice the tunes would have gone helplessly to pieces. The organist
very soon began to stagger under the embarrassment of hearing
a different "time" observed in each pew—the dragging and hur-

rying becoming most distressing as they reached the rear seats— so I struck in on the "air" with all the accumulated energy of long Glee Club training, and really managed to rally the forces to some sort of coöperation. But here's the funny part of the story: After the meeting was over I was cordially thanked by a lady with an exceedingly weak, almost inaudible, voice for *having helped her out*. I was sufficiently rewarded for having shouted myself hoarse—for who would not do that much to serve amiable Mrs. Willard?

My other story is amusing in quite another way. Just before I left "the Hopkins" Prof. Stanley Hall, Prof. "of Psychology and Pedagogy" sought an interview with me. Prof. Hall is an exceedingly interesting and able man who studies the mind by a method original with himself: by seeking to learn the mental history of innumerable children and young men; and when I heard that he wanted to see *me*, I supposed that I was to be a *subject*: an impression which was confirmed by the first part of our interview. But no; I was mistaken. Dr. Hall had seen and been struck by the "thesis"[1] which I had handed in with my application for a fellowship and wanted to know if I would assist him next year in drilling the undergraduates in the fundamental principles of *Logic* and *Psychology*! I laughed in the good doctor's face, assuring him that my only qualifications were a sound understanding and no knowledge. It was like a metaphysician to find a promising assistant in the author of three essays on Congressional govt.! But enough of these: I can't laugh at them myself for thinking of my sweet Ellie's sorrow. My darling, I love you with all my heart: And, let me tell you, little lady, there are three other people in this house who love you very dearly. I am altogether

Your own   Woodrow.

ALS (WC, NjP).

[1] WW had submitted the first three chapters of *Congressional Government* with his application for a fellowship.

From John Hanson Kennard, Jr.

My dear Wilson,   New Orleans, La. June 3 188[4]

Well pleased was I indeed to hear that you had come through so well on your examinations and my heart yearned to be with all my old classmates at such a critical time. But as your last and most welcome letter indicates, you are now free, and are doubtless treading your native heath in company with your fiancée. . . .

I hope you may get your position at the "Industrial Univ. of Arkansas," for I am sure you would use it but as a stepping stone to higher things. I am sure you would not find yourself at all out of the world, and you could tie yourself with a band of ink to all the educational centres of the country.

I hope you are going to be a statesman. I am sure you are fitted for it, and the country stands in great need of statesmen and not "terriers." Worthington, you know, is to follow that profession, and had I the income I would do the same. Who knows, we three may yet meet in Congress. . . .

I shall always expect to hear from you unless you get too busy to write. Though we may never meet again, I shall always be glad that we did meet for I am sure I have gained a friend, and a friend is rare in these days. Excuse melancholy.

Good bye.   Sincerely your friend,   J. H. Kennard Jr.

ALS (WP, DLC) with WWhw notation on env.: "Ans. July 2nd, 1884," and other WWhw and WWsh notations.

From Ellen Louise Axson

My darling Woodrow,   East Rome [Ga.], June 5/84.

Your sweet letter of Tuesday reached me this morning, and calls for an immediate answer. I fear you wonder why I have not sooner replyed to the one *received* on Tuesday. I have delayed writing because I felt some hesitation as to what I ought to say. Of course I want you to come, my darling. I *always* want you, —but I did'nt want to *say* "come," for I was exceedingly averse to being again the cause of your taking a hasty, inconvenient journey—upsetting all your plans, interrupting your work, &c. I prefer you to come when it suits you best,—that is, I suppose, the time when you *originally* planned to come; for glad as I would be to see you now, I can safely promise that I will be just as glad to see you then. But your letter of today, in which you disclose the secret that you had intended to come *soon*, makes it less difficult for me to say how glad I will be to see you now.

There are certain reasons which would tend to make your visit more satisfactory now than later. The last part of my stay in Rome will be a turmoil of packing and breaking up, and selling out. We are only waiting for our present tenants to leave the house, which they will do as soon as their own, here in East Rome, is completed. As they rent the house furnished, I can of course do nothing until then. So I am, at present, quietly waiting, and could therefore get the full benefit of your visit. But I reiterate, come when it bests suits you. You will be equally welcome should you "come in the evening or come in the morning, come when you're looked for or come without warning."

I am very glad that you will now have the opportunity of meeting Stockton. He is of course here; there were but two weeks before his school closed, so that it was unnecessary for him to go back. He will spend his vacation with Uncle Rob [Robert Hoyt], going to Davidson in the fall. The dear boy is wonderfully improved in many respects. I never saw any one grow so suddenly out of boyhood into (almost) manhood; he is only seventeen tomorrow,—his birthday. He is a noble fellow,—and I am happy to say that I am by no means the only one who thinks so. He took a splendid stand at school;—and by the way his teacher says would probably have taken the speaker's medal if he had remained to the close. It rested altogether between himself and one other.

I think that your story, in which Prof. Stanley Hall figures, if amusing, is, also very interesting and pleasant. Are you sure that it deserves to be treated as nothing more than a joke? Are you quite confidant that you are incapable of teaching "Pedagogy"?

How is your dear mother now? I hope she grows better. Has your father returned? Give my best love to all. Marion Bones returned today, and they are all very happy over it. I hav'nt seen her yet.

I heard from Sav. today;—Grandmother is much better than she was; she was much prostrated at first,—having been quite feeble before the blow came. Grandfather returned to Sav that same day, she needed him so much; he was only here four hours; but Uncle Randolph remained over. Grandfather seems quite well, and bears his sorrow as he has always borne everything, with perfect calmness and *cheerfulness*. He appears to live above all the storms of this world.

I don't know what I wrote or tried to write—last Monday night, dearest. But I fear I said things which I ought not to have said, and which perhaps gave you unnecessary pain on my account. But I could not help it. I had been wounded, nay, *tortured* almost past endurance that afternoon by one of my comforters. Oh, how can people presume as they do, to pry into the providence of God! They call this a "judgement," and that a "reward," and the other "a special answer to prayer" as calmly and confidently as if they were omniscient themselves, or had been present at His counsels. I *know* it is all right, and I not only know it but *feel* it with all my heart. Not for a moment would I wish it other than as He wills. Sometimes when I think what it means to be in God's hands, under His direction I scarcely dare to ask for any earthly good, lest taking me at my word, He should give me *my* will rather than His. Is it not better to trust Him altogether,—to wait quietly and let Him decide? But I don't trust because I understand; I know that "The end will tell, the dear Lord ordereth all things well." And in the meantime, I think I can employ myself better than in trying to explain what I don't know anything about. Why, this *friend* related to me, at great length, how, on the Sunday before, that Wed. night had been appointed as a time of special prayer for Papa; and it had been discovered that just as they were in the act of prayer, he began to sink; which was considered a striking and wonderful instance of *direct answer* to *prayer*. I was asked again and again if I did not think so, and if I was not "thankful"!

But why should I speak of these things, or think of them? Oh I am so very, very tired, of thinking principally! I sometimes wish I could go to sleep and never, never wake again.

But what am I saying! May God forgive me—and you too, my darling. You see what comes of your rash request that I should "write you all my mind, without reserve["]! There are things which it is bad enough to *think*, without framing into words. But you must not be troubled, for I know that this is only a reaction, partly physical, from a long strain. I shall be better in a few days, indeed I am better now. Goodbye my darling. Believe me I love you more than words can tell.   Your own Ellie.

ALS (WP, DLC).

To Ellen Louise Axson

My own darling,   Wilmington, N.C., June 5 [1884].

If you could have seen my face after I had read a letter which came to me from Rome this morning, you probably would not have guessed that the letter was from my sweetheart, for I am afraid that my face was very long and perplexed. Both the news and the arguments contained in that epistle weighed upon me and troubled me. The news that you had actually been offered a position as art teacher and must accept it in a few days came upon me like a sentence to imprisonment; and the arguments in favour of my returning next year to Baltimore, coming as they did, from the person whom I love best, and therefore honour most, in all the world, opened again, wide, the question with which I have earnestly struggled for many a week past, and had well-nigh settled: whether I ought to prefer Arkansas to Balto.—should I have an opportunity to choose. All that you say, my darling, is very true: and it is all the more forcible because it is so sweet and disinterested:

but I *am* now "*very* sure" that it would be altogether wisest—for reasons which I will explain to you fully when I see you—for me to go to Arkansas—to a professorship anywhere—if I can. Besides, little lady, I had about decided to give up that work with Ely in any event. I *must* be true to myself; and I am not properly equipped for the task Ely would have me undertake. I could write something altogether *readable*, doubtless; but it would not be thorough or profound; and no chance of getting my name before the public shall tempt me to do what I should some day regard as beneath my reputation, as weakly done. Ely would probably be quite content with something superficial—possibly I could easily satisfy him; but I want to satisfy my own conscience first of all: and I have something all my own, which is thoroughly and conscientiously done, as far as it goes, and which is much worthier of publication and much surer to aid me to a solid reputation than would be my part of the projected history of American Political Economy.

My darling, your suffering is mine. My heart bleeds as yours does at thought of the loss of your noble father: and, my pet, I wish you *would* put away your reserve with me in this thing and in all others, that I might *feel* and know that I am all the world to you. If you would "give sorrow words" which would be for my ears only I might bear some part of your burden and that sorrow *would* lose its *sting*. I love you unspeakably: and all here love you.

Your own   Woodrow.

ALS (WC, NjP).

From Hiram Woods, Jr.

Dear Tommy,   Baltimore, June 6, 1884.

I want to drop you a line of congratulation on your appointment to a fellowship. The "American" of this A.M. says you received an appointment.[1] I am not surprised at your getting it. . . . Remember me to your Father. Don't spend too much time in Georgia. See if you can't be heroic enough to leave the charming society which you have doubtless enjoyed before this, and devote your Summer to the consideration of the profundity of Adams and the honest candor of the President, of the Foundation.

Your perspiring friend,   Hiram

ALS (WP, DLC) with WWhw notation on env.: "Ans. July 2/84."

[1] The *Baltimore American*, June 6, 1884, in a report of The Johns Hopkins University commencement exercises, listed the names of eighteen men appointed fellows for the academic year 1884-85, including "W. Wilson, of Wilmington, N.C., history."

To Ellen Louise Axson

My own darling,   Wilmington [N.C.], June 8th/84

I will start for Rome to-morrow evening, just twenty-four hours behind this letter. I would start this evening were it not Sunday. You may make your mind quite easy, my precious, unselfish little sweetheart, about my wish and plan and convenience in the matter. I can come now without disjointing any important arrangement or disturbing any work that cannot as well be done when I come back: so that there is no reason at all why I should not take my body where my heart has been this long time past. I am coming right away with a heart full of joy that I can take love and comfort to my darling.

Good-bye, precious, till—to-morrow. Be as glad to see me as you can! I love you unspeakably.   Your own   Woodrow.

ALS (WC, NjP).

From Ellen Louise Axson

My darling Woodrow,   East Rome [Ga.] June 9/84.

I am almost rash enough to hope that this letter will miss you, —that ere it reaches Wilmington, you will be *Rome*-ward bound. But perhaps that is too much to expect. At any rate, the mere possibility must not prevent my fulfilling my Monday night's engagement. But the thought that you are coming, and *soon,* has the effect of making me even more impatient than usual with this slow medium of pen and ink. And it has also the very singular effect of leaving me with nothing to say,—or rather to *write.* The subjects to be treated are legion; but each one, as it occurs to me, is in turn rejected, because "he is coming soon, and I can discuss it so much more satisfactorily then,—why *begin* on it now?" The vexed question of Arkansas versus Baltimore certainly comes under that catagory. So I will permit it to rest for the present;—especially since I can't even conjecture what those "reasons" can be, which are strong enough to overbalance the statement of the case which you admit is "very true," and "forcible." But I *will* add, en passant,—because it is barely possible that I will find myself with somewhat less of the courage of my convictions when your eyes meet mine,—that they must needs be *very good reasons indeed* to convince my advisers here. They are, each and severally, strongly on the Baltimore side. (Now *don't* say it is none of their business, or that the above sounds too much as though they were giving, not me, but *you* gratuitous advice!

because they did'nt mean it that way.) I believe every *dispassionate* judge would give the same opinion. Uncle Will (my second father,—always) says *he* thinks you ought *by no means* to marry soon; and that if you continue to do the sort of work you are *now* doing, you will have no difficulty about finding a place when the time comes. He says that our American young men of talent will have made a great advance when they learn the noble *patience* of the German student. So you see, Sir, you must learn "to labour (not only) but to wait"! But enough of this. I said I would myself "wait" until you came, before discussing it further, and I am not keeping my promise.

I have seen Marion Bones, of course, and she is lovlier than ever. I believe she is (almost) the most beautiful little creature I ever saw,—and *so* sweet! How is it that you did'nt fall in love with her? "seeing as how" you don't share my prejudice against pressing "first" cousins into that sort of service! Mr. Bones is much concerned at the prospect of Marion's "coming out" in Rome. He says he don't believe in borrowing trouble, but it is truly distressing to think of her being associated with such young men—"the condition of affairs among them is most lamentable," he has "seen nothing approaching it in any other place; there is an equal lack of manners, morals, education and brains!" Not a very inviting prospect for our little beauty! But at any rate we won't insult her by even *fearing* that she will find her "fate" among them.

By-the-way, Jessie, in her turn, disclosed the secret already revealed by yourself, viz. that you were soon to be here. So that, even if you had not discovered it, 'twould doubtless have all come out;—and it would have served you right. Cruel youth! Don't you know that nine-tenths of the pleasure of life lies in anticipation? Would you deny me all those delights? You don't know how everyday and all day long, since your letter came, my heart has sung to itself that one sweet refrain—"He is coming, he is coming!" It is the last thought at night; and in the morning it returns with the first gleam of consciousness, before ever my eyes are opened. "He is coming—coming!" I think the birds must sing it at my window! What else could remind me always so early? It even precedes that other—"a letter today," which has grown to be my waking thought on three days in every week.

While we are on the subject of "singing!", by-the-way, I will give you a song for your *own self*; it is Mr. Tedcastle's favourite,—I heard him just now pass through the house, chanting it in a loud but lugubrious tone of voice,—

"Oh dear me, and my dear too
If it wasn't for me what would my dear do!"

Ah, dearest what indeed would I do without you? You are my very
life! If it is, as you say, a "joy" to you to know that your love is a
solace to me, then you should be glad indeed, for that love can
transform the world for me,—can turn darkness into light.

Many thanks, dear, for the sweet flowers in your last letter.
Give warm love to your father & mother and "Dode." Goodbye for
the present. See [Chapter] III John, 13 & 14 verses! God grant it
may be "shortly"! Again "good night" and once again "I love you."
Your own Ellie.

ALS (WP, DLC).

From Joseph R. Wilson, Jr., with Enclosure

My dearest brother: Wilmington, N.C. June 11th 84.
    I enclose a circular received from Baltimore this morning,
which will interest you very much.

We are all well, and miss you very much, and on *our* account
wish that it was about time for you to come home again.

How did you find Miss Ellie? Is she staying with cousin Jessie?
Be sure and give her my love. How is cousin Jessie and uncle
James and his family? Give them a great deal of love, please.
Tell Marion that I have given up all hopes of ever hearing from
her again, as she has been owing me a letter for about two or
three months. Now brother please dont forget to give these messages and answer these questions. Tell Miss Ellie not to take up
so much of your time as to make you forget everything else. . . .

Mother and father join me in send[ing] a great deal of love to
Uncle James, cousin Jessie, Marion, Helen, Miss Ellie, and any
one else that may be there that we ought to send our love to.

Be sure and write *very soon* to
Your loving brother   Joseph.

ALS (WP, DLC).

E N C L O S U R E

From Daniel Coit Gilman

Sir: Baltimore, June 2, 1884
    The Trustees of the Johns Hopkins University, at a meeting held
this day, have appointed you a Fellow of this University, for the
period of one year from September 1, 1884.

Please signify your acceptance of the office.

D C Gilman

President of the Johns Hopkins University.

Printed form LS with hw insertions (WP, DLC).

Two Letters from Charles Howard Shinn

Dear old "Chum"   Brooklyn—June 13 [1884]

Woodrow, my dear, I hope you flourish these days. As for me, I never knew how dear Baltimore was till I settled down in this Norland city & ee'n began the heady-brothey-struggle. Nor do I think I appreciated our jovial life. Now I make amends by thinking of you every week-day & hour—as of no one else in the whole crowd. . . .

How nice it is that every one of us who sat about that table rec'd recognition of some sort—! Hurrah for J.H.U. and your fellowship! Everyone is rejoiced. *You* was intended in your cradle for a Fellow at J.H.U. How happy that fair and womanly woman away off in the heart of Southland has been over it all! . . .

I want to know all about the Ark[ansas] case & news in all ways. Sometimes I get blue—for tho' I'm not melancholy by nature —I like—I do confess it—I like *certainties*. And I dont love continual change—such as the past few years have been. I want to crystalize a bit. . . .

Adios—with love and remembrance ever—   C. H. Shinn.

ALS (WP, DLC) with WWhw notation on env.: "Ans. June 28th 1884."

Dear Woodrow—   Brooklyn. N.Y. [June 14, 1884]

A letter today rec'd from my sister [Milicent] reports a crisis in Overland[1] affairs. Tis a long & sad story, & she a heroine. Think we can tide over, & get capital interested in it at last. But I want you to send *at once* one or two or three mss. of suitable articles from your old stores—don't fail . . and I'll do something tremendous for you . . some day soon. Saw Bridges today & we had a long chat about W.W.—   With love,   C. H. S.

ALI (WP, DLC).

[1] The *Overland Monthly* of San Francisco, published by the Shinn family.

To Ellen Louise Axson

[East Rome, Ga., c. June 16, 1884]

I was coming in to beg you to take a walk, even at hazard of more rain; but, as Miss H.[1] is still with you that plan must go and I must wait till to-morrow, if I can—for I must sing &c. with Cousin Abe[2] this evening. Could you happen to wish to make a visit this evening to Oakdene.   yrs   W.

ALI (WP, DLC).
  [1] Probably Minnie Hoyt.
  [2] Abraham T. H. Brower.

From Albert Shaw[1]

My Dear Colonel: Staten Island, Tuesday, June 17./84.
    Not much of a letter this morning: only a paragraph congratulating you on the honest fulfillment by the authorities of the Johns Hopkins of their obvious duty in the bestowal of Fellowships in our department. Shinn tells me you halt between two pleasant possibilities—that you know not which of two proffered crowns to accept. The "Arkansas Traveler" is a fascinating tune; but so also is "Maryland, my Maryland." I only hope that whichever choice you make, it may go thundering down the slopes of time that you chose wisely and prospered very greatly. And I suspect that it will. . . .
    I hope you'll feel in the mood, some balmy morning, to drop me a line.   Yours truly   Albert Shaw.

P.S. omitted. ALS (WP, DLC) with WWhw notation on env.: "Ans. June 30th/ 84."
    [1] A member of the Seminary of Historical and Political Science, Jan.–May, 1884. Born, Shandon, Ohio, July 23, 1857. A.B., Grinnell College, 1879, A.M., 1882; Ph.D., The Johns Hopkins University, 1884. Many honorary degrees. Established the *Review of Reviews* in 1891, and edited it until 1937. Author of many biographies and books on business and government. Edited the first collection of Wilson's public papers. Served on many commissions and public bodies. Died June 25, 1947.

A Memorandum

                                        [c. June 18, 1884]
    Best checks a mixture of elements. Senate valuable in proportion as and because it is undemocratic—just as the Brit system is perfect in proportion as it is unroyal—a republic with an aristocracy, and a stable throne for a centre—central pillar.

WWhw memorandum on verso of env. of J. R. Wilson, Jr., to WW, June 16, 1884, ALS (WP, DLC).

From Ellen Louise Axson

My dearest Woodrow,   [East Rome, Ga., c. June 18, 1884]
    I am so very, *very* sorry that you are unwell today; earnestly hope you *may* be "all right" this afternoon, but if, as is most

probable, you are not, be sure *not* to come over and expose your-self to this "beastly" weather, as Mr. T. calls it. Yours with much sympathy and truest love,   Ellie.

By-the-way, I wonder if Mr. Bones business with me is so im-portant that he will expect me this morning, rain or no rain?

ALS (WP, DLC).

To Ellen Louise Axson

My own darling,   Wilmington, N.C., June 25th   1884

I reached home this morning safe and sound, after a less irk-some journey than I had expected to have. Most of the hours of actual travel were bridged over with sleep, and during the com-paratively few daylight hours of Monday afternoon and Tuesday morning I managed to do without inconvenience what I had not done on the cars for many a long day before: I read and so wiled the time away. And, let me tell you a horrible secret, I did not have the blues at leaving you as deeply as I had anticipated. I'm a queer chap even in my own view—and can never forecast what my mood will be under any given circumstances. I felt a sort of quiet, deep-running contentment all my journey through because along with the intense desire to be back with my darling again, never to leave her, there came the feeling that my visit, too brief as it was, had done me ever so much good, having given me new joy in my love and fresh vigour in my work, and that the new assurance of your love that the delightful intercourse of those two weeks had given me was a new source of strength and patience. You could believe in my love, my pet, my little beauty, if you could know what wonders of joy it works in me. It wont let me be sad, even though it does make me long with all the ardour that is in me for the time when we shall meet not to separate.

But this is not telling you of my journey, which was all I meant to report upon in the few lines I can write to-day.

I reached Columbia yesterday about noon and stayed with sis-ter [Annie Wilson Howe] until a little after ten at night: of course I enjoyed immensely even that little visit. Little Jessie [Howe] is better, and as sweet and gay as if she were quite well, but the doctors are still quite anxious. It is pitiful to see the lovely little thing hobbling about on crutches—though she seems to regard that mode of locomotion as a huge joke—except when she would like to run after the boys.

I find dear mother much better—to my sincerest delight. She is still weak, however, and I come from Columbia armed with what she will be the first to acknowledge the strongest possible argument for a trip: namely, "brother George's" opinion that she ought to take one. I shall be sure to make the most of a strong position. I've been deep in *Minute* "proof" already and shall be getting constantly deeper.

Give warmest love to all at Oakdene and to Eddie and Stockton—and regards to Mrs. T., Miss Minnie, Mr. T., and all. I appreciated so much Stockton's coming to the station to see me off.

I love you with all my heart and am, if possible, more than ever

Your own   Woodrow.

ALS (WC, NjP).

From Marion Wilson Kennedy

My dearest brother—   Little Rock, 6/25/84.

Your letter was especially welcome, for several reasons. It contained the first line of news we have had from home, since Father wrote us from Vicksburg. We have felt *very* anxious consequently, as Father mentioned Mother's state of health as his reason for not making us a visit this year. Then, we had heard nothing as to Ellie's movements, or of yours, either. It did not take any great amount of brightness to imagine that you and she were together somewhere, if that were at all possible. I do feel so sorry for the poor child. She has had a hard experience during the past three or four years. We have been dreadfully disappointed about the University here, as to the action of the Board. They only elected professors to fill the two vacancies, Mathematics and the Normal department. In fact, I do not *know* certainly that those chairs were filled, but no other chairs were created, as was hoped, and your tastes would not suit *those*. . . . Ross will, however, write you all about the matter. We are truly delighted at your latest successes, but not at all surprised. You have always succeeded in your efforts. . . .

Ross joins me in warmest love to all—

Lovingly y'r sister,   Marion

P.S. omitted. ALS (WP, DLC) with WWhw notation on env.: "Ans. July 5/84" and other WWhw notations.

To Ellen Louise Axson

My own darling,   Wilmington [N.C.], June 26th [1884]

The attack on uncle James Woodrow which I predicted has begun,[1] and very much in the way—though not from the quarter—

I expected. I know that you agree with me on the subject, and I am sure that you will be pained to find Dr. Mack leading the ignorant outcry, in a letter which I must unite with uncle James in calling impertinent, audacious, and wicked.[2] It *must* be reckoned wicked to bring upon God's church such reproach of spite and bigotry. The "neglect of the sanctuary" referred to in the letter was uncle James's failure to attend church regularly during Dr. Mack's ministry in Columbia. Uncle James, like myself and a great many of the Columbia congregation, found Dr. Mack's preaching exceedingly uninstructive—and was fain (very unwisely, but with no want of love for Christ and his gospel) to content himself on Sabbath's with private worship at home; though he of course saw to it that his children should be unfailing in their attendance upon public services. I had supposed that Dr. Mack was above the littleness of feeling spite because of uncle James's slight of his ministrations; though I knew that he had not been above making a most ridiculous attack upon father because I had been taken away from Davidson and sent to Princeton. He and father were some years ago associated on the Board of Trustees of Davidson, and at one of the meetings of the Board Dr. Mack tried, in the most offensive, ungentlemanly manner to *silence* father as unworthy of any voice in the management of the college because he had been untrue to it in taking me away and sending me to the hated North, where I could learn more. Memories of such conduct on Dr. Mack's part—conduct which showed him to be built on a very mean plan—made me wince a little on the one or two occasions when I have heard you express admiration for his character—but such matters were petty at most, and I let what you said pass, rather than seem to dislike my darling's friend—because I can overlook very big faults in any one she may like; but I did not then think Dr. Mack capable of such work as this attack upon uncle James—made in the very spirit which (as I have often told you) I most despise. There is something almost amusing in the request that uncle James should confess himself unchristian by resigning before any action has been taken by anybody but Dr. M.! If Dr. M. would but wait and read uncle James's views when they appear, as they will, in print, he would find Dr. Woodrow quite as good a Christian as he—only more conversant with the indisputable facts of science. If uncle J. is to be read out of the Seminary, Dr. McCosh ought to be driven out of the church, and all private members like myself ought to withdraw without waiting for the expulsion which should follow belief in evolution. If the brethren of the Mississippi Valley have so pre-

carious a hold upon their faith in God that they are afraid to have
their sons hear aught of modern scientific belief, by all means let
them drive Dr. Woodrow to the wall[.]

But I have discussed all of this with you already; why trouble
you with it any further! The only reason I have had for saying so
much about it was that it has, during the past few days, had so
large a place in my thoughts—and I set such store by your sympathy, my darling, in *everything*.

I have been as busy as possible all day with the Minutes, and
have found very little time, so far for making a beginning on
essay No. 4—on the Senate. Last night I wrote a few pages of introduction—enough to get me fairly started—and that's no small
part of the task, you know: to set out prosperously.

What would I not give to be reading *Lorna Doone* to a certain
little lady whose mere presence makes me happy! Are you not
afraid that you will forget the first part of the quaint story before
we can get on with it? But maybe it wont be so long after all. I
have a sort of happy presentiment that we wont be so long
separated as we have been in the past. If we both go North in the
Autumn, there is no reason why we should not go together part
of the way: and Balto. is much nearer to New York than it is to
Savannah! Or if, on the other hand,—but that 'if,' though the
more glorious of the two, is too doubtful as yet to build any
definite hopes upon.

Do'nt be alarmed at my apparent determination to write to
you every day, little sweetheart. I would *like* only too well to send
you a little note every day—if only to say that I love you—but I
have'nt time for that extravagant indulgence; and I am writing
to-day, close upon the heels of yesterday's letter, because, as you
must admit, Thursday is one of my "regular" days for penning a
word or two for the eye of my Eileen, and I *must* be faithful to an
innocent habit!

I must not go beyond this page, however, because dear mother
is waiting for her ride.

Good-bye, my precious darling. Love to S. and E. and regards
to Mr. and Mrs. T. I've been thinking about you every waking
minute since I left, and want you as much as I love you,

                              Your own   Woodrow.

ALS (WC, NjP).
    1 Wilson was referring to the attacks against Dr. Woodrow for his recent de-
fense of the Darwinian evolutionary hypothesis. These attacks would soon culminate in one of the most notorious battles in the nineteenth-century war between
science and religion.
    Dr. Woodrow, a geologist, chemist, and theologian, had been Perkins Professor
of Natural Science in Connection with Revelation at the Columbia Theological
Seminary since 1861. (See the biographical note at March 14, 1874, Vol. I.)

His inaugural lecture at the Seminary and his article in the *Southern Presby-terian Review*, XVI (April 1863), 549-69, stirred some suspicions on account of their assertion that there was not and could not be any conflict between scrip-tural revelation and scientific truth. Dr. Woodrow made additional enemies by an article in the *Southern Presbyterian Review* of July 1873 attacking the emi-nent conservative, the Rev. Dr. Robert Lewis Dabney, then professor at the Union Theological Seminary in Richmond, for alleged ignorance of modern science. However, the controversy that would culminate in Dr. Woodrow's re-moval from the Perkins chair began only after he revealed his conversion to the Darwinian hypothesis in an address before the Alumni Association and Board of Directors of the Columbia Theological Seminary on May 7, 1884. This ad-dress was given in response to a request of the Board of Directors who had be-come disturbed by rumors that Dr. Woodrow was unsound on evolution. The address is printed under the title "Evolution" in the *Southern Presbyterian Re-view*, XXV (July 1884), 341-68.

This was the beginning of a long and complicated struggle, the course of which will be followed in letters and notes in this and subsequent volumes. For a careful review of the case, see Clement Eaton, "Professor James Woodrow and the Freedom of Teaching in the South," *Journal of Southern History*, XXVIII (February 1962), 3-17.

2 J. B. Mack to W. E. Boggs, June 4, 1884, TCL (WP, DLC).

From Ellen Louise Axson

My darling Woodrow,   Rome [Ga.], June 28, 1884.

You remember that I promised to write you this week,—and I therefore proceed to do it, for I *always* keep my promises! True, some persons might be as unreasonable as to think that one was obeying the letter rather than the spirit of said promise in writing at eleven o'clock Saturday night. But I can't be responsible for what people *think*! Indeed, I have had *such* a week of it, that writ-ing to you seemed like all the other pleasures of life, "a thing to dream of not to" do;—something forever out of reach, a blessed memory only! You know, the Cranes were moving when you left; and on the same day that they finished moving out, we moved in; or rather we plunged in, head over ears. Such a task as it is! And the books are the worst of all. I didnt suppose anything could make the sight of books so hateful to me. I feel rather spiteful in thinking of the authors! They might have been better employed. I am even inclined to agree with Uncle Rob, that—say—three volumes would contain all that was worth saying in the whole lot. But such experiences teach one several useful lessons—among others the undesirableness of riches,—of dragging about with one too much "impedimenta,"—in short, of playing, in the journey of life, the part of the laden donkey, whose own share in his burden is only a cabbage leaf or so, to satisfy the need of the moment. I am convinced that I have too many "things" entirely. I would rather like to be an Arab, with all my worldly possessions hanging from my saddle bow.

But I didnt mean to indulge in such a tirade;—"out of the

abundance of the heart the mouth speaketh." We will now change the subject. I am indeed delighted to hear that you found your mother so much better. You could not have given me better news. I am very glad, too, that you have a good prospect of getting her away, for though the climate of Wilmington is, *of course,* very good, that of "Arden Park" [near Asheville, N.C.] is, I must believe, even "gooder"—as Willie[1] says. Then too, it will ensure, for a time, complete freedom from care,—domestic duties, &c. For of course *she* can and does leave her cares behind her,—does'nt feel obliged like some housekeepers to carry her house on her back.

I was, too, very glad to know that you had so pleasant a journey, and that you had'nt "the blues." That's right, and I will try to follow your good example. Indeed, I don't think that *any* thought of *you,*—even the thought that you are not *here,*—has power to give me the blues. I am so glad that you are *somewhere*!

The joy it gives me "to love, and be loved by you" is too deep and entire to be affected, *beyond measure*, by accident of time and place. And yet I *do* miss you *so* much! More than I ever did before. What shall I do with all the days and hours "that must be counted ere I see thy face"? Don't you think I am unreasonable to begin thinking already about the next time? It certainly is'nt because thoughts of the last time have been exhausted, or have lost their charm. But perhaps I am a little like certain children I know who about a week after Xmas, begin to lament that they must start their calculations all over again—that they can no longer say it is one, or a dozen, days away, but three hundred and sixty! They find the pleasures of anticipation at a discount. But for all that—even though I do refuse to be *altogether* satisfied,—your visit, dear love, made, and is still making, me *very happy*. If it "did good" to you, what do you suppose it accomplished for me, whose need of something to do me good was, at that time, so much greater.

But I must write no more, at present, for it grows late and I have earned my night's repose. Will write on Monday night as usual, unless circumstances *imperatively* forbid. My address now is care Dr. W. D. Hoyt. Minnie sends her warm regards, and so does Stockton—or rather his love,—to be accurate. Much love to your dear parents and Josie, and for yourself, my darling, *all my heart*.   Your own   "Eileen"

Excuse this *fearful* scrawl, I am too tired to know what I am about.

ALS (WC, NjP).
[1] Ellen's first cousin, William Dana Hoyt, the four-year-old son of Dr. W. D. Hoyt.

To Ellen Louise Axson

My own darling, Wilmington [N.C.], June 29/84

The question as between Arkansas and Baltimore has been decided for me—and in a way which would—three weeks ago at least—have given you unqualified satisfaction. The Board of Trustees decided *not to reorganize* the faculty: so that I did not even become a candidate. There was nothing to become a candidate for; and the whole scheme is as though it had not been. This news came to me yesterday morning,[1] and I had to sit down at once, with as good a grace as I could assume, and write to dear President Gilman that I would accept the fellowship and pay my respects to him in due season, at the opening of the next "semester" of "the Greatest Educational Show on Earth."

And now, Miss, are you satisfied? For my part, I am deeply disappointed, because I firmly believe that the sooner I get to work in the faculty of some comparatively small college, with my darling for my helpmeet and loving companion, the sooner I shall reach usefulness and achieve the highest success. As things stand, I can go back to the unrivalled advantages of the Hopkins and write and study at pleasure, but *not* to my *heart's content*: for *that* depends upon my having some *certainty* before—some certainty of such an opening, it matters little whether it be great or small, as will open up to me with promise the career I have chosen. The indefinite postponement of our marriage is, for me, one of the greatest elements of the disappointment. It seems to me that I can wait for anything more patiently than for that! I am not talking mere lover's sentiment, my darling, when I say that my life, and consequently my success, is bound up in you, and that I cannot live or work at my best until I have, not your love only, but your self, your companionship, as well. I never had a more earnest conviction than this. Before I knew you—before I loved anybody—I realized that my real career waited on my possession of a home and a loving wife of my own; and since you came into my life to brighten and bless it that feeling has grown into a conviction.

And now, little lady, what do *you* think of the whole matter? Are you altogether gratified? No; I know you are not, my pet, because I know how much you love me, and how sincerely you wish what I wish. I know that it was nothing but love for me which led you to advocate my return to Baltimore. But I have a selfish desire to learn from your own pen that you are just a little bit disappointed at *knowing* that our engagement must be indefinitely prolonged—that you feel your need of me as much as I feel my need of you. Wont you indulge an unreasonable man by making free confession of all your feelings on this head?

Will you be going to New York now beyond a peradventure?[2] When does the session open at Cooper Institute?[3] Not before the end of September, I suppose? I have a request to urge, Eileen, my precious darling: believe me, all my heart is in it, and I make it, therefore, without any apology for returning to a matter about which you have already expressed what would seem to be a final judgment and decision. I could not beg even a friend with such persistent reiteration: but I can beg *you* without any loss of dignity to reconsider your refusal to visit Wilmington. It will not be necessary for me to start for Baltimore, probably, before the last week in September, and what I want to beg of you, my love, (in case the session at Cooper Institute does not begin early in the month) is that you will spend Sept., or, at any rate, the greater part of it, with us, and then let me escort you northward. There is nothing here, dearest, from which even your bashfulness need shrink; nothing but love and love's consideration: and I think that you would face a great deal more than a transient embarassment for my sake. I cannot leave home at all, consistently with duty, until I leave for Baltimore. The work on the *Minutes* is to continue till the time for dear father's vacation, and *then* both he and "Dode" go away—the latter to Bingham's school,[4] whose sessions open July 30th. Dear mother's heart will be almost broken at having to give up her second boy. It pains me not a little to think how lonely she will be next winter without him! Father will doubtless return home about the middle of Sept., as usual: and meantime we have set our hearts on having you come to us. Can you refuse? Am I to see nothing of you till I seek you out in New York many months hence, in some brief interval of my work at the Hopkins?

There is no prospect of getting dear mother away this summer. She is considerably better than she was, and unless she gets positively sick she wont hear of a trip: If you could see how much *she* wants you to come, you would be as much gratified as you would be persuaded!

I have left myself scarcely any space for speaking of the extracts enclosed: but they explain themselves: the one is the *St. L. Presbyterian*'s copy of uncle J's editorial in the *Southern Presbyterian*, the other the same paper's editorial comment.[5]

With unbounded love,   Your own   Woodrow.

My darling, dont let anything short of absolute necessity prevent your consenting to what I ask. You don't know what your refusal would cost me.   Yrs.   W.

ALS (WC, NjP).
  [1] See Marion W. Kennedy to WW, June 25, 1884.
  [2] Ellen had decided to go to New York in the autumn to study art, and she obviously had discussed her plans with WW.
  [3] Actually she had decided to attend the Art Students' League in New York. See ELA to WW, July 7, 1884.
  [4] A private school founded by William Bingham in 1793 and located at this time in Mebaneville, N.C. Robert Bingham, the fourth headmaster, moved the institution to Asheville, N.C., in 1891.
  [5] WW was referring to the editorial, "The General Assembly and the Perkins Professor," in the Columbia *Southern Presbyterian*, June 19, 1884, reprinted in the *Saint Louis Presbyterian*, June 27, 1884.

An Abstract

                                              [c. July 1, 1884]

Congressional Government. By Woodrow Wilson.
[Abstract of two papers read before the Seminary of Historical and Political Science, May 9 and 16, 1884].

These two papers constitute the first two essays of an extended study of Congressional as contrasted with Parliamentary government. In the first paper, which is introductory to the more special and technical chapters which follow it, those tendencies of constitutional construction, those precedents of actual governmental practice, those phases of national thought upon questions of administration, those conditions of society, and those indications of future development were brought together which have caused the original, ideal balances of the theory of the Constitution to give place in the actual conduct of the federal government to a constitutional system, which, much broader, even in principles, than the Constitution itself—though still resting firmly upon that Constitution as its foundation,—knows the federal government, not as a power coördinate with the State governments, but as a power greater than they, both actually and potentially, and Congress as supreme director of national policy, to the overshadowing of both the prerogatives of the Executive and the privileges of the Judiciary. Under such a system Congress is, of course, properly the central figure of constitutional study. To know its methods of procedure and its ways and means of overseeing and directing the course of affairs is to know the most essential machinery of our national government; and, in order to know these things, one must see Congress from the inside.

In the second paper this inside view of Congress was exhibited in a sketch of that device of organization whereby the House of Representatives divides its work, and its functions of deliberation, amongst more than forty Standing Committees to whom go, as of course, all bills introduced, from whom emanate all the propositions that are vouchsafed consideration or advanced to action, and in whose hands, consequently, are the direction of business and the control both of debate and of conclusion. The peculiarities of this plan of Committee government were emphasized by extended contrasts with that other system of government, called "parliamentary," in which the powers given the Committee of the House of Representatives are conferred upon ministers who are also the advisers of the Executives;—a system which may be said to be the prevailing governmental fashion of the world. Of this system the British House of Commons is, of course, the parent type, though for the purposes of this essay, and for the sake of more varied illustration, the French constitution was put by the side of the British as a leading example of that plan whereby the heads of the Executive departments are made the leaders of the legislative majority, thereby securing a government characterized by free debate and a well-defined party policy. Parliamentary government is direct party government, Congressional government, indirect; in the one, responsibility rests upon a compact ministry all of one party, in the other, upon a disintegrate ministry of Committees which are made up of members of both parties and all factions, and which, unlike the ministry of the other system, do not come into direct contact with the practical affairs of administration. In the one the best, the picked men, lead; in the other, all, the weakest as well as the best, have a hand in leading, every member of the House being a member of one or other of the Standing Committees. In Congressional government, moreover, the decisive contests of legislation take place in the privacy of Committee rooms, whilst under Parliamentary government those contests of necessity take place in public, upon the floor of the legislative body. Unlike, however, as these two systems are, they are kin in representing a common effort to set up some such "legislative commission" as J. S. Mill proposed, whereby a numerous assembly, itself radically unfit to make good laws, can get good laws made. We have more than forty such commissions; Great Britain, only one.

Reprint (WP, DLC) with WWhw notation at bottom of page: "J.H.U. Circular, July, 1884." Brackets in text.

To Ellen Louise Axson

My precious little sweetheart,   Wilmington [N.C.], July 1st/84

I am not feeling at all well to-day, and so must content myself with only a few lines to my darling—I wish I knew how and where to find contentment when I get no lines at all *from* her. She promised to write to me last week—and would have done so without a promise, I'm sure, if something unusual had not prevented —and I am desperately uneasy as to the cause of her silence. I sincerely hope that she is not sick. If I were quite well myself, I could probably throw off anxiety: but my weak condition inclines me to admit apprehension—and apprehension stands in the way of my getting well.

We are having terrible weather here—the weather of my first week's stay in Rome intensified: and it is this fact which may be taken to account for my sickness, doubtless. When there were rains in Georgia this section was in sunshine, but now its skies are leaden and its streams are swollen; and the end is not yet.

I am delighted to be able to report that dear mother is *decidedly* better—considerably better than she was last weak, and my fears on her account are, for the time at least, much lightened. If I could only keep well myself, I might be able to quicken her recovery still more by contributing to her ease and amusement.

I have neglected to ask you, my darling, to give my warmest regards to your uncle "Will" and his wife[1] and to tell them that I regretted very much indeed not being able to call on them before I left. What with my unlucky sickness and much hastened departure, I had, very much against my will, to forego the visit I intended making them and which I was sincerely disappointed at being cheated out of.

I do hope, my pet, that you are well, and that the Cranes have made way for the work you want to do at the house. How much I wish I were there to help you in the packing! *Please* be very careful of yourself, darling, and do'nt try to do too much at once—don't overtask your strength. I am so glad that you have Stockton to help you! I know that he will relieve you of as much of the work as possible. Give him my love, please, and kiss Eddie for me

Do'nt be alarmed at my sickness, little lady: it is not very serious. I shall conquer it and be none the worse.

I love you, I love you, I love you

Your own   Woodrow.

Regards to Mr. and Mrs. T[edcastle]. and to Miss M[innie Hoyt].
and Miss A[nna]. H[arris].

ALS (WC, NjP).
  ¹ "Aunt Florence," Mrs. William D. Hoyt.

From Ellen Louise Axson

My darling Woodrow,   Rome [Ga.], July 3rd 1884.

Here it is, Thursday morning, the time when my "regular" letter should reach you, and I am just sitting down to write it!
What will you think of me?—that I am a naughty little girl? No,
I am sure you won't have any "hard thoughts" of me because of
it—for you know right well, that if I had done as I *wished*—I would
have written several times,—and I hope, above all else, that you
won't have any *anxious* thoughts;—doubtless you will *not*, for my
last letter, by *it's* tardy arrival no less than by *it's* contents, will
sufficiently explain all deviations from the even tenor of my way.
In fact, I have been in such a turmoil "from early morn to set of
sun" that it was impossible to write more than a postal card,—
and I don't send them to *you*! Of course I *expected* to write at
night but I had the bad taste to wind up each days operations
with "*such* a head-ache" that I positively *could* not accomplish it,
—don't let that worry you, by-the-way,—it is nothing whatever but
fatigue, the weather being so intensely hot, and I perhaps not
quite as strong as usual. But we are now almost through with
our task, have done all that we can do with our own hands, and
are "only waiting" on men and events; that is the most tedious
part of it; I wish I could be half a dozen men, several horses,
and a dray, so that I could "go ahead" and be done with it. The
town is so crazy over the encampment, that, for neither love nor
money, can we get a soul to work for us. Stockton and I have
been having rather a dreary time of it, working all alone, day
after day, in the dismantled home. I think my last task has been
the worst of all—the looking over old letters and papers. It forced
me to do what I am always trying upon principle *not* to do—to
dwell in the past,—to draw constant heart-breaking comparisons
between *now* and *then*. I thought at first I could not bear it—that
I must burn them all at once, but it seemed necessary, so I forced
myself to go through with it. I have now almost finished, and
while the house is so quiet, Stockton even away,—he has gone
over to Mr. Tedcastle's to pack *my* books,—I will lay them aside
and at last write to you.

By-the-way, I have just been reading what was perhaps the

first letter I ever wrote—or rather dictated. It was written in
1862 and begins thusly—["]My dear little Papa, Dis is a bad 'ittle
dirl, she hollow and ty, and steam." In the midst of my sad task
I hav'nt failed to derive an odd sort of amusement from reading
these reminiscences of the time when I was "a blessing," "a
treasure," "a sunbeam," "the lovliest little creature in the world,"
in short *the* baby"! If I had time I would give you some choice
extracts. Here is the last, written in 1862. I just came across it a
few moments ago. "Ellie's sympathies have been much excited
in behalf of the poor soldiers since I have been making this coat.
She comes up to me every now and then and says, 'Mama you
sewing poor solies toat? poor soly do to seep in the wain,'—which
means 'rain.' Then she begins 'poor Bobbo do to seep in de wain,'
and goes through the list of her acquaintances,—poor Dorcy do
to seep—&c, poor tousin Charlie—poor *little* Charlie, poor Marion
&c. &c., and her little voice expresses as much compassion as if
she knew all about it." But *why,* when I have so much to say to
you, and so little time—*why* will I waste that little with this sort
of padding!

I was more sorry than I can say to read the letter from Dr.
Mack enclosed in your last. What a strangely unjust, *unworthy*
way he has chosen to accomplish his purpose, even supposing that purpose *were* altogether what he *imagines,* "the good
of the Seminary." I am *afraid* the letter shows, not only narrow prejudices but a *very* bad spirit,—still one always likes to attribute to people as good a motive as possible, and I can't bear to
think, unless I am *obliged* to, that he was actuated by anything
so intensely small and mean as personal spite. With men of violent prejudices, you know, opinions are so apt to degenerate into
passions. But I don't know anything about it. I think it *perfectly
outrageous* that Dr. Woodrow should be so treated,—whatever the
motive. I hope it won't do him any harm at any rate; and I don't
suppose it will, after his article is published, and people understand the matter more perfectly. I read his editorial (?) on the
subject Sunday. I will send back Dr. Mack's letter in my next,—
hav'nt it with me, here.

I have been variously interrupted, since writing the above, and
must now make haste to finish, or my letter won't "get off." What
do you think that wretch, my cousin Minnie, "went and did"?
Why she brought Mr. John Stephens[1] to call on me *here,*—in this
bare house, where there is scarcely a chair to sit upon,—and me a
perfect fright! And I was to see him at tea *anyhow;*—am sure I
could have dispensed with the pleasure until then. I had occasion

to see her alone just before they left, and you may be sure I embraced the opportunity to give her a piece of my mind. How do you suppose the little hypocrite tried to defend herself, and sooth[e] me? By saying that her "express object" in bringing him was to let him see "how pretty you are 'just so,' that your lovliness!! don't depend upon your being 'fixed up' "!! Was'nt that an ingenious invention for escaping my wrath?

Another interruption! nothing *but* interruptions! and now my time is up, this *must* be mailed at once. Your *two* letters, of the 30th [29th] and the 1st, just received. I will *try* and answer to-morrow, my darling, I *must* not wait, great as is the temptation, or my letter will be delayed still another day, and you will be still more anxious. I am *so* distressed, dearest, to learn that you continue so unwell, or rather that you are, I fear from this letter, a great deal worse. I am afraid you are seriously out of sorts, and I can't help being unhappy about it.

As for the other matter, it was *such* a difficult question to decide, that I can't help being rather glad it has been decided *providentially*; we will always be so much surer that it is all for the best, than we could possibly have been, if it had been left for us to choose. At the same time—but of this more anon—I *must* stop. Am *so* glad your mother is better, and I hope—how I *do* hope!—that you will soon follow her example.

Love to all, and for your dear self as much as heart can hold. Believe me, dear love, now and forever,

Your own Ellie.

ALS (WP, DLC).
¹ Nephew of Alexander H. Stephens.

To Ellen Louise Axson

My own darling,   Wilmington [N.C.], July 3rd/84

I am feeling *very much* better to-day. If we could only have decent weather, and if I could only have frequent letters from my precious little sweetheart, I am quite sure that I could quickly get entirely well, and stay so: for it is a noteworthy fact that a very marked improvement in my health set in yesterday morning when I received and read that sweet letter you wrote so late Saturday night, and did not mail till Monday, and it is exceedingly probable that if your usual Monday letter had come to-day the cure would have been complete. The fact is, little lady, that the blues which I so strangely escaped on my journey homeward, were only postponing their visit, and there is nothing I now find it so hard to endure as separation from you. If you don't write to me as often as possible, you will be contributing towards making the burden all the heavier. This is not of the nature of a complaint, but simply a plea for indulgence

Sometimes I wonder, my darling, what I should do if you did not love me. My knowledge of your love cures me of many a mental complaint. Often when I get thoroughly disgusted with myself, because I can't write as I would, or because of some new discovery of weakness or ignorance, I say to myself: "No matter, Ellie loves me; and so long as she loves me and I do the best I can at mending my shortcomings, I shall be happy and shall have all the success that's good for me. I'm all right so long as I have her." You can't imagine, sweetheart, what an amazingly cheering effect such thoughts have upon somebody you love!

If the packing began early last week you must be within sight of the end of your big task by this time. That's "a consummation devoutly to be wished!" I shall be delighted to hear that you are through, the hateful books safely boxed and the "things" ready for their mistress to leave them when she will—provided you shall not have overworked yourself in bringing about such a happy state of affairs. It's *too* bad that I had to leave just when I did—just when I might have been of some useful importance. For I *could* have helped you a little bit: could'nt I? True, the several hours' work I do here on the *Minutes* every day is of considerable use; but I have a very insistent wish to be of use to *you*!

Did I tell you that I found a very pleasant letter from [Albert] Shaw awaiting me on my arrival at home? He writes to congratulate me "on the honest fulfillment by the authorities of the Johns Hopkins of their obvious duty in the bestowal of Fellowships in our department." He had seen Shinn in N. York and has a great many complimentary things to say about him, which would gratify Miss Minnie immensely. I wish I could let her read the passage.

I've been struggling with my correspondence ever since I got back, but have'nt yet been able, even by daily efforts, to catch up with it. I was dreadfully in arrears, and shall have to rattle away at my "caligraph" several days more before my conscience is finally eased. You see, there's one great disadvantage I labour under when I am at home. I am supposed by the dear folks here to be such a facile letter-writer that I am charged with the conduct of all the family correspondence. I write to sisters for the family: I hope that they regard me as a good representative.

The essay on the Senate ("No 4") is not running on so easily or so fast as it would were I feeling quite well; but every day sees some advance in it, and the slow, laboured pace is doubtless friendly to *thoroughness*. I shall be quite satisfied if I can complete it by the end of this month.

Now that I am sure that I am going back to the University I find myself wondering how I shall find a way out of my agreement with Dr. Ely about the history of American political economy. If I free my hands of my own peculiar work, by finishing the greater part of the remainder of it this summer, as I expect to do, what good reason can I give for not undertaking the reading necessary to fit myself for the work I thoughtlessly consented to do for him? It will look like bad faith. If I had not returned to Baltimore, it would have been *necessary* to resign the task: but now it is by no means easy to get out of it. I shall have to wait and have a full, candid consultation with the little doctor before making any final resolution in the matter. May-be he can show me how I can do what he wants without doing sham work, all talk no knowledge. I wont do what I can't do honestly, even to keep peace with Dr. Ely.

I am waiting with very intense anxiety, my darling, to hear what you will say to my proposal with reference to the last weeks of the vacation. It will be a very bitter disappointment to me if you refuse—and dear mother will take it terribly to heart.

Love to Eddie and Stockton and sincere regards to Miss M. and the rest of the family. How shall I express my love for you, my matchless little queen! I love you more than my own life, my darling.   Your own   Woodrow.

ALS (WC, NjP).

To Charles Andrew Talcott

My dear Charlie,   Wilmington, North Carolina, July 5th., 1884.

The wanderings of your letter[1] in its search after me indicate how much there is to tell you of myself and my movements since you last heard from me. It is now more than a year since I left Atlanta for good and aye. After staying there a year waiting for practice and getting wee bits of it now and then, I concluded to act, before it was too late, on the conviction which had been growing on me ever since I began my law course but which I had been very slow to allow. I had to confess that all along the practice of law had been secondary, only something by the way, in my ambition. My tastes and what I had of talent all lay in the direction of studies in political science and a career either as a politician or as a writer on politics. It was out of the question, as

I very soon found, to succeed at the bar with such ambitions always in the foreground; and it was impossible, as I believed and still believe, to go actively into politics and keep my profession too. As I had no independent fortune to fall back upon for support should politics fail me after it had deprived me of my practice, I saw that my only proper course was to give up all idea of an active political career and, turning to the other almost equally attractive alternative of spending my best energies in the higher sort of writing on questions of politics and statecraft, to seek some profession which would offer more legitimate opportunities for such work than were to be found in a law office. Manifestly the only place for me was a professorship. But I was not equipped as I should like to be for such a post: so I left Atlanta and spent last year at the Johns Hopkins University in Baltimore taking the graduate courses in history and political science. It was from there that I sent you the little pamphlet on "Committee or Cabinet Government?" My year was a very successful one in point of University honours, for the writing I did there won me an appointment as fellow in the department, which means free tuition and a stipend of $500 for the coming winter. Of course my object is to get established as soon as possible as professor of history and political science in some reputable college big enough to give me some latitude in my work, and that wish can be soonest and most surely realized by making for myself a brilliant record at "the Hopkins" which is becoming a sort of employment agency for the faculties of the country. With the splendid libraries at hand in Baltimore there is every facility for work that one could desire, but you will not be surprised to learn that I am very anxious to get out of the preparatory stage, out of the pupil stage, and set up for myself in the real work of my life

I am the more anxious on this head because, quite unbeknownst to thee, Charlie, I have engaged myself to a little Georgia girl whom I am immoderately eager to take into partnership. The only thing that stands in the way of this "consummation devoutly to be wished" is an adequate salary: hence my extreme interest in securing that ne plus ultra. You did'nt think it of me, did you, Charlie? Well, to tell you the truth, I would'nt ha' thought it of myself. I did'nt do it of malice aforethought; I had no idea of doing such a thing until I met the young lassie aforesaid away up in one of the northwestern counties of Georgia, and then I did it in spite of myself and in the teeth of all discretion. And the worst part about it is that I am not the least bit sorry for it; on the contrary, I so much approve of myself for the act that I wish I could induce my friends to do likewise. I verily believe that it pays, old fellow. Did you ever think seriously on the subject?

I need'nt tell you how much good it did me to hear from you again, Charlie. I wish that the practice of the law were productive of the milk of human kindness, so that you might be moved to write to me oftener. The worst feature of the case is that I can't get mad with you about it. My liking for you somehow struck in so deep that you might come down and kick me and I would be more than apt to take it in good part. Seriously, old fellow, it's a sore trial to me not to hear from you oftener. I want to keep as close to you as the facilities of the mail will allow, against the time for which I am all the while wishing when we can see something of each other, after the first straits of making a living are passed.

Of course I saw a great deal of the "Cow" while I was in Baltimore last winter. She is as gay and as whole-souled as ever, though not quite so skittish as of yore. The practice of medicine, like the practice of law, lingers, she tells me, waiting for the gray hairs which a fellow don't expect to get until he is tired of waiting. The dear old animal has, like myself, for several months been an engaged man—and a splendid girl it is that is booked to share his lot with him.

I came very near catching a sight of both Ridge and "Dan'l"[2] in Baltimore. The former made a flying visit to the city quite unheralded and so found everybody out. The latter stepped down from Harford Co. to act as one of the Vice-Presidents of a Republican State Convention, but got out of town before I knew that he was in it.

Of the rest of the fellows I have little authentic news, except that I saw by a New York paper that Pete was married in Bath, England, to Miss Marquand,[3] and that I know Bob to be alive but too outrageously busy to send a fellow more than a semi-occasional scrawled line of wonderful penmanship.

I shall return to Baltimore about the first of October. My address there will be "Office Johns Hopkins University," simply. Until then I expect to be at home here. Write as soon and as often as you can to

Your sincere friend,   Woodrow Wilson

WWTLS (photostat in RSB Coll., DLC).
  [1] C. A. Talcott to WW, May 8, 1884.
  [2] Jacob Ridgeway Wright and J. Edwin Webster.
  [3] Harold Godwin married Elisabeth, daughter of Henry G. Marquand, benefactor of Princeton, and sister of Allan Marquand, College of New Jersey, '74,

long Professor of Art and Architecture there, and of Henry Marquand, College of New Jersey, '78.

To Ellen Louise Axson

My own darling,   Wilmington [N.C.], July 6th/84

Judging from what Marion [Bones] says, in a letter to Josie, about the state of the weather in north Georgia, I am afraid that you have been a good deal hindered in your work at the house by the incissant rains, that is, if you are moving the things out as well as packing them up. I have been thinking of that work every day, and a great many times every day, wondering as to its stages and hoping soon to hear of its satisfactory conclusion. It is wonderful how persistently my heart stays with a darling little maiden several hundred miles away, longing to know all of her in-comings and all of her out-goings, almost chafing because it cannot know everything that passes with her! And yet it is'nt wonderful either. At any rate I don't wonder at it, because I happen to know that that same little maiden is the most lovable in the whole world.

There's no news to tell you, my darling—except that I am quite well again—for my life runs on with little variation from day to day:—and even if there were any news to tell I don't think that I would tell it in this letter: because it seems to me, when I sit down on Sabbath afternoon to have my usual talk with my own Ellie, that there is only one subject about which it is *appropriate* to write, and that I ought to obey my instinct to postpone all other topics till some other day. I want to speak of nothing but my boundless love for her. And, surely, if one were looking for *sacred* subjects, it would be hard to find one more sacred than the love of a true-hearted, manly man for his betrothed. Since I know that, if ever I did aught that was true, my love for my queen, my precious Eileen, is pure and of the very stuff of the heart, I esteem it a good Sabbath subject. I am quite aware that I do not confine my attention to it to the hours of Sabbath: but when I've been spoiled by having indulgent ears to listen to what I am always repeating about it and by knowing that there is a pair of lovely eyes that will grow the brighter at reading what I have to write about it, no matter how often I may repeat my phrases or reiterate the heads of my discourse. Ah, my darling, you have not won, in winning me, the love of the best man in the world—or even in your own little world—but you have won as true, as trusting, as unbounded love as ever man gave.

Love to all and for yourself—   Your own   Woodrow.

ALS (WC, NjP).

From Ellen Louise Axson

My darling Woodrow,   Rome [Ga.], July 7, 1884.

If thoughts and words were one,—if as they say of pure spirits,
the deed could always follow the wish to do, how many letters I
would have written you since last Thursday! It seems strange
that all my thinking since then has not proved an irrisistible
power *forcing* me to write in spite of circumstances. All that I
can say about it is that it was a case in which the spirit truly was
willing but the flesh was weak. But now I am all right again, and
the work, which at one time, owing to various back-sets, seemed
likely to "go on forever," is actually *finished*; and I mean to do
better as to my letter writing. I really must make a noble effort,
and acquire the useful art of writing *short* letters, so that,
whether people are satisfied or not, they, at least, need not be
anxious. I am so *very* sorry that you were made to suffer anxiety
on my account. Am I *really* to believe that your not hearing has
such an effect upon your spirits? Somehow I can't "take it in"
that *my* letters *could* make such a difference to anyone! However,
you *are* better, be the cause what it may, and I am *so* happy to
hear it. If I could only be sure that it is a permanent improvement! if I could but know that you were *well* and likely to remain
so! I don't know that I was ever more relieved than by those first
words of your Saturday's letter—"*very much* better." You see instead of coming at dinner-time, as usual, it did'nt reach me until
night, which gave me time to get up a first-class panic; for I
knew that after your last letter, you would be sure to write soon
again, if you were able.

So I must say what I think of the conclusion of the Arkansas
matter! must let you know whether or not I am "altogether gratified"? My darling, you have yourself answered the question—I *do*
love you with my whole heart and I *do* wish what you wish! Won't
that do? or shall I say still more? Well then, I *do* miss you always
—I *need* you always—and—I am *not* ["]altogether gratified"! And
your arguments had almost persuaded me that you would gain
more by going, than by staying in Baltimore,—that you would
really work to better advantage. I say I was *almost* persuaded,
but not quite; for you know you would have relinquished a great
deal in leaving just now. When I look at that side of the question,
as of course I do *altogether* now, I am *most content*. I am sure
that things have turned out for the best, that it will simply end
in your reaping the benefits of *both* plans,—those of Baltimore
now, and of the smaller college a little later. That plan is not

abandoned, but simply postponed; and though a year, or two, or three may seem very long now, we know how swiftly time flies; they will be gone before we dream of it. In short, it has been decided that you are to have the *whole* instead of *a part*, as you in your impatience would have chosen. And then you will always be spared the fear of having made a mistake. I think that fear would always have haunted me more or less; the pros and cons were so nicely balanced;—the case was so difficult to decide, and at the same time of such serious consequence. But now it has been submitted to a judge who *never makes mistakes*, who can see the end from the beginning. "When we observe what mistakes we mortals make when we have our own way, it seems strange that we should be so fond of it"—I believe I am beginning at last to realize that, a little, to be somewhat less wise in my own conceit; for I don't seem to care half as much about my own way as I used to.

Yes, I suppose I will be going to New York now, beyond a peradventure. That is the present plan at any rate. The fall session at the [Art Students'] *League*; (not *Cooper's*,—I would'nt care to go *there*.) begins the first Monday in Oct. Oh, dear me, *why* will you propose such delightful plans as that Wilmington visit, with the Northward journey at it's close? I am so tempted and tantalized by the thought of it, that it positively makes me unhappy. You can have no idea how hard it is for me to say "no"—hard, because I would, for some reasons so much like to do it, and harder still—much harder—because you wish it. And yet I *must* say it, because I gave Grandmother my solemn promise not to go. Even if I had not promised I could'nt think of going when she is so violently opposed to it. She talked and *talked* and *talked* to me about it, over and over again, none less earnestly and pleadingly because she met with no opposition; for I only laughed and said, "Why Grandmother I have no idea of going, I must admit I would like to,—but still—I can't." But she was a wise old lady, she knew that whether I had the idea then or not, it might *possibly* be instilled into my mind. She knew, what I did not suspect then but now perceive, how all-powerful you are; that a few earnest words from you would make me not only yield my point, but literally change my mind. So she didn't rest until she made me promise, "upon my honnour," not to go, under any circumstances. Her opposition is the *only* thing *now* which prevents my doing as you wish; but of course you see yourself that it would be impossible under the circumstances for me to go. Please give your dear mother my love, and tell her I thank her with all my heart both for her invitation and her desire to have me. I would be *so* glad to see her and your father as well as yourself. I am delighted to hear that she continues to improve. Good night, my dear one. Remember that I love you "with the smiles, tears, breath of all my life"—that however much we may be separated I am always and altogether   Your own   Ellie.

ALS (WP, DLC).

Three Letters to Ellen Louise Axson

My own darling,   Wilmington [N.C.], July 8th/84

If anything were needed to fill up the cup of my happiness in the possession of your love, such letters as that sweet one you wrote in the bare house on a Thursday morning would more than serve the purpose. My delight is complete when you write to me in that way—with a natural, unrestrained, absolutely free out-pouring of anything and everything that happens to be uppermost in your mind or heart at the time, without thought of how it may sound, because it is for your very nearest and dearest friend to read. It's almost like being there with you as you look over the old letters, with now a smile and again an ache at the heart. There's nowhere I should rather be than with my darling as a wit-ness of and a participant in her everyday life, and letters like that one seem in a way to admit me to that happiness.

You make one grave mistake, Miss, in speaking of the contents of some of those old letters of the far-away war time: you refer to the time when you were "a blessing" and "a treasure" as a time *past*: whereas I wish to assure you that there is, to my certain knowledge, at least one person in the world who thinks you these things, and more too, *now*, in the present year of grace;—a verita-ble "sunbeam" in his life ("as the dawn loves the sunlight I love thee"), "the lovliest creature in the world": and the same person who holds these opinions as self-evident truths did not fail to feel very envious of one Mr. John Stephens because the said Mr. S. had had the privilege of seeing you "just so," in careless working garb, whilst he (the jealous complainant) never saw you any way but "fixed up." I have an idea, all mine own, that in an old dress, a big apron all awry, and handkerchief headdress you would look sweet enough to—not to eat, for no one could see you at any time without wanting above all things else to *keep* you—nor to kiss, for, whatever your costume, the temptation to kiss you is hardly re-sistible—but to kiss and *hug and* keep, one and all—too sweet not to be appropriated, peaceably if might be, but forcibly if must be. I don't know what may have been your costume when Mr. Stephens saw you—I conclude, from the fact that he did not carry you off, that you were not arrayed in the way I have described (or that Miss Minnie had influence enough over him to restrain him); but I've made up my mind, that, some of these days when I get you into my power, you shall trick yourself out in that very way and let me kiss you until I get tired. But, ah me! it don't pay to be dreaming such dreams at this hour of our day: I must change the subject to keep up my spirits!

You mus'nt take it so much to heart when I am sick, my little sweetheart. I've never been seriously ill in my life, and I certainly was not this time: and now I am perfectly well again. Whenever I write to you that I am unwell I am inclined to reproach myself afterwards for having told you anything about it: and yet I tell you such things *on principle*; for, much as it distresses me to hear that my darling has brought on terrible headaches by overwork or that she is in any way the least bit unwell, I am sure that I should be much more unhappy if I thought that she did or would conceal such things from me: and so I try to do as I would be done by. Be sure, therefore, that I will tell you all, and don't be unhappy about my casual ailments—tho', on second thought, I don't believe that I should like you to be altogether indifferent, Miss Eileen.

I am glad, my darling, that you agree with me so entirely about Dr. Mack's conduct in regard to the Perkins Professorship —I knew that you would. I'll withdraw the imputation of personal spite, if you wish me to, as not proven, though I think it not much below the stature of some other motives which Dr. M. has clearly discovered. I am going to send you uncle James's article, which is just out in the S. *Presbyterian Review*.[1] Don't read it, little lady, if you are not interested, but give it to "uncle Will"— though I think that you will find the piece as readable as I found it, and that you will be glad to know just what uncle James has to say, that you may judge for yourself as to the character and motives of the attack upon him.

You were a naughty little girl to work yourself into those head- aches: that was the naughty part of your conduct, and not your failure to write to me—though, truth to tell, I find it nowadays, as always, a terribly unhappy business to have to wait many days for a letter from you. I am *so* glad that the work at the house is over! for it *is* over by this time, I suppose. I hope that my darling will take a real rest now—wont you, pet?

And now allow me to remark for the *severalth* time, Miss Eileen, that I love you with all my heart. My warm regards to your uncle and aunt, to Miss M., and all the family—and much love to Stockton and Eddie. There's not a moment when I am not consciously   Your own   Woodrow.

ALS (WP, DLC).
    [1] "Evolution," cited in WW to ELA, June 26, 1884, n. 1.

My own darling,   Wilmington [N.C.], July 10th/84
    I wish that I could help being anxious and unhappy when Thursday comes without bringing the accustomed letter from my darling; but I can't. Here I am forlorn and uneasy because all Thursday's mails have come in without fetching the letter for which I am waiting. May-be it would help matters if I could get vexed with my little sweetheart for not having written: but I can't do that for the life of me. I never think of blaming her—because I know she's not to blame—I only wonder what's the matter.
    I have'nt sent you a copy of the *S.P. Review* yet, dearest, because father has loaned his and I have to send to Columbia for another.
    Have your plans taken any more definite shape as to dates, my pet, now that the packing and house-clearing are disposed of? I suppose that you will soon be off for Gainesville, wont you? It's not very long before our little circle here will be breaking up. "Dode" must be in Mebaneville, at "Bingham's" by the 30th of this month, and father will be setting out on his usual vacation trip about the middle of August, if not sooner, to be gone for six weeks or so: so that from that time till the latter part of September dear mother and I will be here holding the position all alone. It would'nt require very much "cheek"—would it, little lady?—to come to see us two, who would make you feel happy and at home before you had been here ten minutes. I don't believe that you *can* refuse *this* invitation, therefore I'll neither urge it further, nor allow myself to be tortured by thoughts of the disappointment, should your visit in any way be prevented.
    After I had finished and sealed my last letter to Miss Eileen, mother asked me if I had sent you her love, and was inclined to make a few remarks when she found that I had not—until I told her that if you did not know by this time, without the aid of reminding messages, that she and father and "Dode" loved you very dearly, it was not for want of telling, but because you did'nt want to know. The truth of the matter was that I am al-

ways very selfish when writing to you, thinking of no one's love
for you but my own, and, consequently, forgetting to speak of
anything but the things which directly affect only us two. I take
it as a matter of course that everyone who knows anything about
you loves you—because I don't see how they could help it: and I
forget that you may not be disposed to take it so for granted.

Love to Stockton and Eddie and warmest regards to your uncle
and his family. I love you more every day—I don't know where
it will end: but if you can stand it, so can

Your own   Woodrow.

ALS (WP, DLC).

My own darling,   Wilmington [N.C.], July 11, 1884
I know that you will be very much puzzled to know *why* your
letter, written at the usual time, did not get here on Thursday: so
I must write you just a line or two, to say that it *did*, but by the
night mail which was not delivered till this morning—your letters
having, of late, been very stupidly sent around by *Charleston*—
and to say, if I can, what I think about your refusal to come to
Wilmington. First of all, my darling, let me say that *you* did perfectly right, that you could not, as you say, have done otherwise
under the circumstances. It would not have been becoming in
you to disregard your grandmother's wishes, so expressed and
urged. Unless her opposition can be overcome, the visit must,
of course, be foregone and I must bear the cruel disappointment
as best I can. But I had no conception before of the character or
intensity of her disapproval: and I must confess that I am very
deeply hurt by it—no less so than dear mother is. For, since custom sanctions your visit, there must seem to Mrs. Axson to be in
this instance some personal, or at least some *special*, reasons
which forbid it, and I can't help noticing that you have all along
forborne to give the arguments by which she has enforced her
objections—except that you have mentioned the altogether in-
sufficient and mistaken plea of climate. I speak thus plainly, my
darling, because I am above all things anxious, if I am wrong
on this point, to be set right. I sincerely trust that the admiration
which Mrs. Axson has expressed for me does not stop short of
confidence in me: and if I could imagine any other reasons for
her violent opposition, I should be only too glad and eager to
do so.

Mother has to-day written to Mrs. Axson[1] begging her to reconsider he[r] decision in the matter: and I hope that her request

will be of some avail—I can't see, indeed, how it can fail to be. And it would not do any harm—would it, little sweetheart, for you to write to your grandmother and ask her to reconsider the question and release you from that extraordinary promise. The circumstances have altogether changed since that promise was extracted: and I know that you will do what you can to save mother the chagrin of losing this which may be her only chance of having you with her before we are married.

I *am quite* well, my darling—except that what you were compelled to say in your letter has deprived me of my appetite for the time being and brought on a throbbing headache.

So you *were* made sick by your work, and my anxiety was not groundless, after all. Ah, my darling, I am *so* sorry—though you do comfort me by saying that you were "all right" again at the time you wrote. Please take care of yourself, my precious Eileen. When you are tempted to overwork yourself, or to do other like indiscreet things, think of me. What would I do without you, my love! You are in very truth all the world to me: and without you life would be, for me, nothing better than mechanical work done under the whips of duty.

I love you! I love you with all my heart, and it becomes daily a greater joy to me to be   Your own   Woodrow

P.S. I send uncle James's article in the proof sheet[, the] only form in which I can get it without waiting [a long] time.
                                        Yrs. lovingly   W

ALS (WC, NjP). Postscript torn.
¹ JWW to Rebecca Randolph Axson, July 11, 1884, ALS (WP, DLC).

Draft of a Letter to James W. Bones

[Wilmington, N.C., July 12, 1884]

Of course under the circumstances disclosed by your letter of the 10th,¹ recd this morning, mother consents to the loan of $1,000 out of the Munger and Pease funds. The delay already caused has pretty much upset our first plans and any further plans we may wish to form must now wait upon you. I write this at once to authorize the loan, in order that the mortgagee's impatience may be stayed, and shall wait to hear from you later as to rate of interest on the loan and as to the arrangements you expect to make for its repayment. We are sincerely & unqualifiedly sorry that you have been put in such straits in this matter—and we are of course as glad as we can be under the circumstances that we are in a position to help you. Let me hear from you again, please, as soon as possible about the details of the loan &c.

All join mee in love to you and to all at Oakdene

In haste   Yrs aff

WWhwL (partial draft) in pocket notebook described at May 16, 1884. WW's entry in his account book, described in note 4 at March 21, 1882, Vol. 2, reads "July 12 Loan to J.W. Bones 1000.00."
  1 Missing.

Two Letters to Ellen Louise Axson

My own darling,   Wilmington [N.C.] July 13th/84

So you "can't 'take it in' that *your* letters *could* make such a difference to anyone," can't realize that anybody's life stops for want of a letter from you, and want to know if you're "*really* to believe that my not hearing has such an effect upon my spirits"? Well, you *are* a little goose—a very desirable and surpassingly lovable little goose, with whom one would wish to live all his life, but a goose for all that, about some things. *In primis*, about *yourself*, not to *know* how much you are to some people, and notably to a particular person not necessary to mention. The simple truth, Miss, in my case, is that if the intervals between your letters be long—and how long a few days seem now!—or if a letter confidently expected at a particular time is in the least bit delayed, everything in my arrangements gets off its hinges: I can't write a single sentence about the Senate, can't be decently sure of an appetite—am a nuisance to myself, and doubtless to everybody about me. This is the plain, uncoloured truth, my darling, and I, therefore, assure you that you *are* to believe that your letters have *every*thing to do with my spirits.

Is it not a little interesting to note, my precious Ellie, that we are so intimately connected in heart that our lives are already inseparable? that what you do determines what I shall do? If you write frequent letters full of love and hope, the Senate gets on famously; if you write infrequently, not a step will the essay-writing budge! The idea of your asking if you were really to believe it! Has'nt the little lady I love imagination enough to put herself in my place and judge of my feelings by her own? Have the character and regularity of my letters nothing to do with the state of her feelings?

Yes, my darling, I am *quite* well again, and have been so for some days; but that fact does not give me half the satisfaction I derive from knowing that that wearing work at the house is finished and my little sweetheart consequently free to rest and

recuperate. Sometimes, when I am specially disgusted with myself, I think that the only difference the state of my health makes,
whether it be good or bad, is the difference it makes to *her,* and
to the dear ones here who love me so amazingly beyond my
deserts. I am taking absurdly good care of myself now, under
dear mother's prescriptions of indulgence, but I have an excellent
end in view: I am improving myself against the time of your
coming, so that I may have all the energy possible to devote to
your entertainment:—for, now that I know that my Eileen's own
heart is for coming in September, I count her visit assured, because I don't believe that Mrs. Axson can under the present circumstances continue her opposition. Having met her, I find it
impossible to believe that she will deliberately wound our feelings
without cause, or continue to put such a slight upon us.

Do you want me to say that I am content with your expressions
of feeling and opinion concerning the abrupt conclusion of the
Arkansas scheme? No, I wont say that, but that I am "altogether
gratified." Who would'nt be delighted with such assurances as
you have written about it! You have said just what I most wished
to hear you say about it. Ellie, my matchless little sweetheart, do
you know that, when you allow yourself to be demonstrative, as
I have so often coaxed you to be, and to say, as you know how
to say so sweetly, what your feelings are towards me and as regards our coming life together, you find a way to thrill me with
a joy of happiness such as no one else in the world can or could
make me know?

Since you repel with some contempt the idea that it was to
"Cooper's" you had intended to go, I perceive that I have repeated the, with me, not uncommon performance of displaying
ignorance. I, in my innocence, had supposed that Cooper's Institute was the best school of the kind in the country, that it was
to the art student pretty much what the Hopkins is to the student
of the sciences; and I must confess, with all contrition, that I
don't know what the League is. Take pity on my ignorance,
dearest, and tell me all about the latter. I want to know for the
sake of knowing, as well as because it is at the League that
you are to study. It's wonderful, is'nt it?—how closely the limits
of men's—at least of some men's—information coincides with the
limits of their own practical concerns and occupations! But until
you broached to me your conditional plan for spending next
winter in New York, which took me so much by surprise the day
you made that sweet promise, I had never heard of the League.

The enclosed editorial (from the *N.C. Presbyterian*)[1] is, doubtless, a fair sample of the sort of examination to which the views of the Perkins Professor will be subjected. If Dr. Dabney's logic with reference to evolution is like his logic with reference to Geology, maybe it is inexorable as an unjust judge is, in refusing to listen to reason—or inexorable in quoting the poets.

Father, mother, and "Dode" send you lovingest messages, my darling. Give my love to S. and E. and my warmest regards to Miss M. and the rest of the family. To my precious little sweetheart you may give thoughts of unbounded love from

Her own   Woodrow.

1 WW was referring to an editorial entitled "Dr. Woodrow on Evolution," Wilmington *North Carolina Presbyterian*, July 9, 1884. This editorial took note of Dr. Woodrow's article on evolution in the *Southern Presbyterian Review* of July 1884 and remarked that, while Dr. Woodrow was unassailable on the ground of heresy, his views would hardly be acceptable to the Board of Directors of the Columbia Theological Seminary or to the General Assembly of the southern Presbyterian Church. The editorial concluded as follows:
"We prefer the views of Dr. Dabney, founded as they are on eternal truth and constructed on the principles of inexorable logic.
"In the words of Dr. Dabney: 'These speculations are mischievous in that they present to minds already degraded, and in love with their own degradation, a pretext for their materialism, godlessness and sensuality. The scheme can never prevail among mankind. The self-respect, the conscience, and the consciousness of men, will usually present a sufficient protest and refutation. . . .'"
The Dabney quotation is from Robert Lewis Dabney, *Syllabus and Notes of the Course of Systematic and Polemic Theology* (2nd edn., St. Louis, 1878), p. 32.

My sweet Eileen,   Wilmington [N.C.], July 13th/84
Hurrah! I knew Mrs. Axson, after all, better than you did, my darling. You may imagine the delight with which I heard dear mother read the enclosed! I went down to the P. O. to mail the letter to my sweetheart which I finished about half an hour ago, and brought from the office this delightful note from Mrs. Axson, in which the dear lady actually expresses the *wish* that you should visit us! My darling, I can't tell you how happy this has made me, both because it dispels my perplexity as to Mrs. Axson's reasons for not wishing you to come, and because it assures us of having you with us during propitious Sept. What strides I can take to-morrow in essay "No. 4"! How impossible it will be for headaches to come or for appetite to go: for Sept. is coming! My darling, I am not only glad, but *thankful*. I was beginning to look forward to the year at Baltimore with weary anxiety: but now my own precious little sweetheart is to be given me beforehand to cheer me: and she will give us a generous portion, if not all, of Sept.—wont she? The time will be gold to me, and its length will measure my preparation for successful work next year!

Mother sends her love, my pet; and I wish you could have seen

the delight in her face when she read your grandmother's letter—
a release from the promise indeed!

In unbounded love and excited haste,

Your own   Woodrow

ALS (WC, NjP). Enc. in second letter: Rebecca Randolph Axson to JWW, July
12, 1884, ALS (WP, DLC).

From Ellen Louise Axson

My darling Woodrow,   Rome [Ga.], July 14/84.
Your two letters of the 10th and 11th both came to hand yesterday. I was very glad to receive the extra letter, though very
sorry for the mental disquietude on your part of which it was
the result. I myself, dearest, have been and am still not a little
disturbed and perplexed by it all. I hardly know what to say or to
do about it. Indeed I have from the first laboured under very
peculiar embarrassments in this matter, as perhaps you can
imagine, if you remember some of your own remarks on the
subject! especially those which brought in your mother and her
view of the case.

But now, I see it is best for me to "speak plainly," as you say,
since otherwise, you will attach undue importance to Grandmother's objections. You must not take those objections so seriously, my darling. Above all I beseech you not to speak of being
"hurt" by it. There is no ground for that on either your part or
your mother's. How *could* you think there are any "personal
reasons" in her mind, forbidding it! You don't know how much
she admires and *loves* you. No, it is not a personal matter, nor is
it in the *slightest* degree a question of *propriety*. It seems to be
altogether a matter involving *local* differences in social customs.
You and your mother say that "custom (in England) sanctions
it." Grandmother thinks that custom (in Sav.) don't! You remember saying that the ideas and manners of social life in
Charlston and Sav. were something altogether unique. Well,
those ideas are Grandmother's; and her's was the Charlston of
the old regime too; she is even more "particular" than the younger
generation,—she is equal to a French duenna. I believe they say
those "notions" *are* an importation from France. I think she was
led to express herself more decidedly on the subject because of a
little comedy, which was being enacted at the time in Sav. I suppose you don't remember a little discussion, which took place at
the dining table the Sunday you were in Sav. about a certain "girl
in blue" in one of the Stoddard pews. I remember it because it

was the first appearance before the Sav. public of the fair heroine
of the play. It turned out that Charley Green, the grandson of
Mr. Chas Green and Mr. John Stoddard, Sen.[,] had become engaged to "the girl in blue" and she had come down from Wisconsin to visit them,—and "thereby hangs a tale." Suffice it to say
that she was being much laughed at and talked about; and it
had its effect upon Grandmother; she did'nt want me subjected
to similar remark. I laughed at her a great deal about it, telling
her that she could'nt say anything because she had invited Mama
to spend a winter in Sav. under similar circumstances; but she
said, that was very different, because Little Auntie and Mama
were school-mates and devoted friends before she had ever seen
Papa, and besides *he was'nt there*!—which to be sure did make a
slight difference!—suggests the play of Hamlet with Hamlet left
out!

But though I laugh at this complication as much as I am able,
I assure you it has been no joke to me. You can readily conceive
that, between you and Grandmother, I found it a delicate matter
to deal with. I hope you won't make it harder for me by taking
any false view of it. Indeed, I *know* you won't misunderstand me,
and I don't think you will misunderstand her. Above all, I implore
you to drop the idea that anyone thinks it would'nt be "proper"
for me to go—you remember, you used that word. None of the
four persons concerned would be likely either to wish anything
improper, or to differ very materially as to what comes under
that head. There is a great difference between matters of *etiquette*, which vary continually with time and place and person
and matters of true propriety. I can of course write to her and get
a release from my promise. I know exactly what she would say,—
"do just as you please, of course! *I* have no authority in the matter"; but then she would never be *convinced*. You see, it is'nt a
subject one can argue with her about, it is only a matter of feeling. Old people don't change their minds easily, especially in cases
which involve their early prejudices. But your mother's having
written alters the case materially. I don't see myself how she can
do anything but consent—what she will *think* is another matter.
I will write at once and find out and let that decide me.

I am very sorry to hear about that head-ache, my love. I hope it
was of short duration. If I were a man I would'nt condescend
to get up a head-ache on any girl's account! *Heart*-aches now are a
different thing. I think I would confine myself to them; they are
less serious!

I am perfectly well,—hav'nt been at all sick, only had a series of head-aches while at work, the combined effect of the heat and fatigue, but was quite well as soon as the work was over; except that I was rather "used up" last Sunday week. I was very busy again last week, but in such a different way that it was the best sort of rest. I am spending a few days in china painting with Mrs. Nance at the college. She does it more exquisitely than any amateur I ever saw. I never felt any desire to learn it until I saw her work—had seen so much daubing on china that I was rather disgusted. But then, when I thought of teaching I felt that I laboured under a disadvantage, in not understanding it; for it is the popular craze, and there are twenty persons wishing to study it for one who cares for crayon. We have been having a very pleasant time together, Bessie Caldwell,[1] Miss Fannie, Annie Lester and myself. It seemed like old times to be once more at work in the old school-room. I don't know even yet exactly when I will leave Rome; have added an extra week to my visit on account of these lessons, then I must finish one more portrait, so I probably won't get off before the first of next week. It seems hard to get away—for many reasons; so many people are insisting that they "have claims" upon me, that I see no course open to me save "repudiation"—unless I can effect a compromise. I was "all about in spots" last week, spending one night here, and another there, which explains why I did not turn over that new leaf, and write you a second letter, as I certainly proposed doing. Since I *will* insist upon spending the whole day at work, society demands that I should, with as good a grace as possible, devote my evenings, at least, to making myself agreeable.

Yet I did very much want to send an answer of some sort to that sweet letter of last Sunday. I don't believe anyone else ever wrote such letters, as my darling. Each one seems to steal my heart afresh, and make me love you more than the last. Are you not afraid you will make me love you *too* much? I am not—I don't think one *can* love too much; it seems to me that one does really "desecrate the sacred God-word, love" in speaking of it as though it were a luxury, which might become a snare by being indulged overmuch. How can there be too much of that which is best of all. It seems to me that whatever in our life below is least of the earth, earthy,—most pure, and good, and holy, most closely allied to heaven is included in that word.

> "What know we of the saints above
> But that they sing, and that they love?"

At any rate, I am sure, my darling, that I can't love you more than you deserve to be loved of me. Ah, dear heart, you have not won in winning me the best, the brightest, or the fairest; but you have won a love as true, as tender and trusting as ever *woman* gave! Give much love for me to all your household, and especially to your dear mother—I do love her very deeply. And dear, you must beg her for me, not to be vexed or hurt with me or mine for being so "contrary." Good-night my love,—again and once again I *love you*, and am forever,   Your own   Ellie.

Hurrah for Cleveland! Are you very much pleased that the Convention did'nt "blunder as usual"?[2] What did you think of that letter in last week's "Nation" about "a Third Party"?[3]

ALS (WP, DLC).
  [1] Of the family identified at May 9, 1884, n. 1, as connected with the Rome Female College.
  [2] The Democratic national convention in Chicago had just nominated Governor Grover Cleveland of New York for President.
  [3] G. B., "A Third Party," New York *Nation*, xxxix (July 3, 1884), 10-11. "G. B." was probably Gamaliel Bradford.

Two Letters to Ellen Louise Axson

My own darling,   Wilmington [N.C.], July 15th/84
    I wonder if you can really realize how happy I have been made by the assurance that with September would come what I have been longing for ever since I could connect your plans with mine: my darling's visit to my home? During the two days which have elapsed since Mrs. Axson's very cordial little note came, the whole house has changed its appearance for me. I find myself, as I go from one room to another, connecting you with all the familiar objects, and fancying beforehand the associations they will hereafter have with your visit: just as the most vivid impressions of mother's little room at Arden Park that remain in my memory now recall it to me as it looked while you sat in it and I wandered restlessly in and out, wondering how I was going to make you understand how much I loved you.[1] Please, Miss, don't delay *very* long about writing to tell us when you will come. I know that Miss Rose will forgive you if you cut short your visit to her just a little so as to come here the sooner; because she will understand that she would certainly do as much for "Mac.," if he had a home which she had never seen. Or, if you can't say just when you will come, at least write at once to say that you are coming, that I may hear repeated, as it were from your own lips, the assurance which has already made me so happy.

It has turned out as I said: Essay "No. 4" *has* progressed famously since your grandmother's little note came, and I am now
within at least hailing distance—so to speak—of its end. I did not
know myself how my heart had been set upon having you come to
visit us until I had reason to be sure that my wish was to be
gratified. *Then* there was such a rise in my spirits and in my anticipations for the year at Baltimore as I had not thought possible. See what a big part you are playing in my Baltimore career,
young lady! You assured my success last year beforehand by confessing your love for me, and now you are about to assure my
success next year by proving your love for me. You are a truly
delightful little person—my good genius! When you come we can
plan the best way for making New York and Baltimore very close
together. We'll organize an inter-State Love League (of two members only, in order that it may be of manageable size) which will
be as much better than the Art League as—as love is better than
art. I'll draw up a Constitution in true legal form, and then we
can make by-laws at our leisure as they become necessary.

But enough for this time—you'll get tired of so many letters on
the same subject! All send you their love, my precious little sweetheart—and I love you and long for you more and more every day.
You are my own matchless darling, and I am
                                   Your own   Woodrow.

¹ A reference to WW's and ELA's visit to Arden Park, N.C., on Sept. 15, 1883.
See the Editorial Note, "The Engagement," Vol. 2.

My own darling,   Wilmington [N.C.], July 17th/84
I have no complaint to make of the P.O. authorities as to the
carrying of your last letter. It came on the briefest schedule time
—a fact which has put me in the best possible humour. The arguments which it contains make very evident what I was beginning
to suspect: that we have been talking somewhat at cross purposes
because we were using the word *'propriety'* in two very different
senses. I meant by it nothing more than *social* right and wrong
(i.e. the biddings and forbiddings of etiquette, of the *conventions*
of society) whilst you give the word a very much higher and
graver significance as standing for the greater distinctions between moral right and wrong. There would not, I take it, be anything morally wrong in a woman's being with a man of honour
and purity under any circumstances; but it is easy to imagine a
great many circumstances under which it would be in the highest
degree *improper* for her to be with him, as giving rise to scandal.
Of course, my darling, I don't misunderstand either your position

or Mrs Axson's now (though I *did* misunderstand hers at first)[.]
Your explanation has taken all the sting out of her opposition;
but you can easily see *how* I was hurt by it. I was assured that it
was not with her in the least a question of *propriety*—though it
now turns out that, as I understand that word, it was *altogether*
a question of propriety—and I was naturally at a loss to imagine
what other reason there could possibly be that was not special or
personal. I was at first quite prepared to learn that Mrs. Axson
had acquired those extreme notions of propriety which I knew
to be peculiar to Charleston: but I was told that it was not that at
all, and so I was at sea and in distress. The only reason that I
could have understood was repudiated.

No indeed, my darling, I am not likely to have any hard thoughts
about dear Mrs. Axson—in no case could I have felt anything more
than a very keen sorrow that she should be so far from a true
knowledge of me or mine—and in *this* case I was simply mistaken
—and no harm done! Especially since Mrs. Axson has been so
sweet as to waive her objections and say that, under the circumstances, she would *like* to have you come! That's the delightful
last act of the tragi-comedy.

You are mistaken, my little mischief, in your parenthetical
statement of my argument. I did *refer* to English custom, but I
by no means based my requests upon it, but upon my own observation—so please you—of American custom. I wish we *were*
governed in social matters by sensible English practices, but we
are not, and I am not quite so foolish as to seek protection from
the sanction of customs which live beyond sea. Yes, little sweetheart, I *have* an indistinct recollection of the references to the
" 'girl in blue' in one of the Stoddard pews"—I have the special
reason of *embarrassment*, which notably strains the attention to
a very tense pitch, for recollecting everything that was said at the
table while I was in Savannah. But the talk which improper conduct excited has nothing to do with our case, my pet, and so "the
girl in blue" ought not to be suffered to do any more mischief than
she is already answerable for.

There is one more thing I want to say, my love, before I leave
this subject and that is that I have had a part in the matter which
I was sometimes afraid would lead Mrs. Axson to misunderstand
me. I have been doing the pleading for this visit, and, though I
pleaded for dear mother and in her name, I have of course been
open to the suspicion of using her desire to see you as a decent cover
for my desire to have you come to see me. Since it was impossible
for me to go to see you again this Summer, why should not dear

mother choose this time to press her invitation for my sake? There would be nothing wrong in the scheme: and yet I should not like to be suspected of it. I am free to confess that your visit will be, and *do*, everything for me, and that without it I should be altogether unhappy: but at the same time I am quite sure that my eagerness in pressing dear mother's invitation has not been a selfish eagerness. Mother has had her heart set on your visit from the first. She longs to have you come and your coming in September will give her your companionship at the time when she and you can enjoy each other's company most keenly and get to know each other most agreeably—and at a time, besides, when she will most *need* you: when father is away and her baby—the only child left her at home, for some years past—for the first time away at school. If it were possible, and necessary to secure your coming, I would gladly go away to accomplish it—both for dear mother's sake and your own. I'd rather be the grave-digger than not be in the play at all.

Excuse me for having taken up the whole of another letter with discussing a question that's settled: but there were some points which really seemed to need straightening. The matter *is* settled, is'nt it, my darling? Of course I see that Mrs. Axson is *not convinced*: but she has given something more than her consent to your coming[.] She must mean what she says when she declares that she wants you to come; and we are counting on the visit.

My precious Ellie! I wish I could give you a score of kisses for all the sweet, loving things you say in this letter! All—the very most—I can ask of you, is that you will love me as much as you are loved by   Your own   Woodrow.

ALS (WC, NjP).

From Charles Howard Shinn

Dear Woodrow—   Brooklyn. N.Y. 7/18 [1884]

My only excuse for this long delay is that I have wished to wait until I could give a definite acc't of myself—& of my prospects

Your letter did me a world of good. It was one of the best letters I ever had in my life—so affectionate, and good & interesting. I do hope that all your plans will come out as you hope for—& that Miss Axson may be in N.Y. this winter. Then you come in some time & I'll go back to Balto. for a few days with you—I look forward to it all with the greatest delight. . . .

With love & trust—   Chas H Shinn.

ALS (WP, DLC) with WWhw notation on env.: "Ans. Aug. 13/84" and WWsh draft of opening lines of his reply. WW to ELA, July 28, 1884, includes an additional extract from Shinn's letter.

From Ellen Louise Axson

My darling Woodrow,   Rome [Ga.], July 19, 1884.

Your "Thursday letter" I have, at last, gotten my hands upon, after much tribulation on its account. I spent last night at Uncle Will's, and the letter came here, to Uncle Rob's, where I have been for a week past; Stockton, who came down to tea, forgot to bring it,—forgot it again this morning. Then I came up expressly to get it—and Stockton was out and the letter not to be found. But I have it at last, and have just finished reading it—for the "severalth" time. It is really surprising that I should receive any letters, or get any mailed—with uncles and brother all so unreliable. Uncle Will handed me on Sunday a *business* letter from Uncle Randolph, with one for Mr. Bones enclosed, which he had carried in his pocket, I don't know how many weeks; it was written some time last month. Then I wrote to Auntie [Louisa Brown] and Rose at the house, while packing—the same day that I wrote to you—and turned them over to Stockton's tender mercies. On last Friday he chanced upon them in his pocket and concluded he "might as well" mail them. And now hear the conclusion of the whole matter—they have just been returned to me, both of them, because I had put them in the *wrong envelopes*! So I don't know whether Stockton or I have proved ourselves most *distracted* by the packing. The worst of it was that the one to Rose I had "begun in the middle" without addressing anyone, so that Auntie read it almost to the end before finding out that it was not intended for her;—though she must have been sorely puzzled by the contents. You may be sure I re-read said contents with deep interest for the purpose of discovering to what extent I had betrayed my follies and frivolities to the good lady;—but I believe there was'nt more than my average and indispensable proportion of foolishness. True, there was some raving about *you*, which made me feel a little warm as I read, and which must have proved singularly edifying to her, since I have never mentioned to her your existence!

Your Tuesday letters however came promptly to hand, with Grandmother's enclosed. They, of course, settle the point under discussion, my darling,—I will see you all in Sept.—and I am truly glad that it has been so satisfactorily and pleasantly settled. I *deeply* appreciate your mother's kind interest in the matter,—her writing to Grandmother &c. And I doubt not you will make me feel "at home and happy" there,—happy, indeed! My heart already leaps within me at the thought of seeing you again so much sooner than I had hoped. I would gladly pass through very much worse ordeals than that to content my Love,—especially when the prize for me is the sight of his dear face.

I would have answered your letters that (Tuesday) night, but to tell the truth I was so completely mystified by Grandmother's note that I preferred to wait until I, too, had a letter from her. I could'nt have read that note over oftener if it had been from you; and I read it very much as I read yours; first hastily, and then almost *spelling* it, word for word, as I went along. You see, I was trying to read between the lines, and discover the true inwardness of it all. Minnie, who was spending the night here, found a great deal of amusement at my expense, because, every few minutes in the course of the evening, I would take out that letter and laboriously read over those enigmatical sentences. "Certainly—I—did—not—wish—to leave—on Ellens mind—the impression—that I—would make any opposition" &c. ["]To hope—she will not—allow—her grandmother's opinion—to influence her"!

So all that talking I was not to regard as "opposition," but merely as an expression of "opinion," by which I was not to be at all influenced! But then was that promise so seriously asked, and as seriously given, not expected to "leave any *impression*" on my mind? But however that may be, she *is* convinced,—thanks to your mother. I received a very pleasant letter from her tonight, *advising* me to go; so "all's well that ends well." I can't tell yet exactly when I will reach Wilmington, but I will surely go as soon in Sept. as possible. Grandfather and Grandmother will be in Gainsville the last of August, or first of Sept, and my movements will be determined by their's, as of course I must see them before I go North. I think now of going to Sewanee first of all—next week —in order that my visit to G. may fit in better with their's.

But I really must close; for this light is *dreadful*,—a chandelier almost against the ceiling,—it is making even *my* eyes ache,—and it is twelve o'clock. I think it has been *months* since I have been able to *begin* a letter to you before eleven at night,—except those that I write in deserted houses.

By-the-way, be sure not to tell anyone that I am going to Wilmington, it is to be a profound secret. I mean "to fold my tent like the Arabs, and as silently steal away." I did try to tell Jessie and the rest last night, but it was impossible. Best love to all the household and for your dear self a love better than the best,

              With truest love   Your own Ellie.

ALS (WP, DLC). Enc.: Rebecca R. Axson to ELA, July 12, 1884, ALS (WP, DLC).

To Ellen Louise Axson

Wilmington [N.C.], July 20th/84

I quite agree with you, my precious little sweetheart, as to the proper bearing of a man towards certain bodily ailments, and, therefore, being a man, I *don't* "condescend to get up a headache on any girl's account"—*that* would be too bad! But the fact of the matter is that I have of late made the notable discovery that a headache does not have to be *gotten up* but is a free-gift of circumstances: and these circumstances are a part of my discovery —just as gunpowder may be said to be a part of the discovery of the fact that it is explosive. I have discovered that I am so wrapped up in a certain little maiden who loves me, and has promised to prove her love for me by the best proof conceivable, that separation from her keeps me in a state of mild irritation which may at any time be made violent to the stirring up of otherwise unaccountable pains by the addition of any weight of disappointment not inevitable. This, you observe, is a really very profound philosophical analysis of the case and quite excludes the theory of a headache being *gotten up* on account of any girl. For, besides demonstrating the natural and inevitable character of the headache, it discloses the fact that it comes, not on "*any* girl's account," but on a *particular* girl's account—and that the only girl on whose account it *could* come. It further remains to be pointed out that it has long been known that love—the love felt by a true man for his promised wife—is quite out of the line of men's other experiences and has, consequently, a way, and a sway, all its own: so that it is probable that "if you were a man," as I am, and were in love to the depth that I am, you would have radically different views as to the manliness of such headaches as those in question. Moreover, it should be remarked—though probably this has already occurred to you—that my confessing to these headaches, was but offering circumstantial proof of a fact to which I have frequently had occasion to call your attention, but which cannot be too much emphasized, namely that my love for the maiden aforesaid is as genuine, as "sure enough," as any she ever dreamed of exciting. Nor is this departing from the observance of philosopical statement. It is quite in keeping with the universally recognized tenets of what may be called the philosophy of human nature that I should fall in love with this very maiden—and that desperately and with all the strength of my nature: for I found in her the loving, sympath[et]ic, trusting heart that, if given to me, would ensure my happiness, and the gifts of mind which, if possessed by my wife, would ensure the success of my work, as far as success lay in me at all! All of which brings us back to the old story which it shall be our delight to continue telling each other for the rest of our lives. *I love you; I love you with all my heart*—What more could I say!

Love from all to you, my darling: and from me love to E. and S. and warmest regards to your uncle and family.

Does it make you happy to know that I am

Your own   Woodrow.

Appendix:

I am so sorry, my darling, that you will not be here in time to hear father preach! In order that you may have a decent excuse for saying that you are sorry too, I am going to give a sample from this morning's sermon. I can't give you the sermon's *spirit* without giving you its *self*; but I give you a sentence or two from its least significant, that is to say its descriptive, parts (the only parts which are *separable*) as affording some hint of the power of expression that gave it its extraordinary strength. The text was the opening words of the psalm of praise composed by Moses just after the Red Sea had been crossed, "The Lord is my strength and my song." "Then you perceive the movement of yonder cloud which sinks in darkness between pursuing and pursued—you hear at the same time the swell of a rising wind, the breath of Jehovah, which resembles the rush of a tempest—and, *its* work done, you behold a double wall of water with that wide road of dryness between, which is soon echoing to the hurrying feet of the fugitives—whom, by-and-by, you see gathered, still trembling but no longer terrified, upon the plains beyond, having now nothing to look back upon, except the sweep of those reassembling waves which, with the first sobbings of a saved people's deliverance, lift to the skies the last screamings of a lost people's despair."

Here's the other sentence I've chosen (and I've *stolen* both "unbeknownst" to the author): "I have beheld upon the expiring Christian's writhing features the soft tokens of a *heart* at rest amid waves of fiery pain, and have heard from the Christian's pallid lips the breathings of a sweet content amid the very gaspings of keenest distress—and then have seen him fade away from the world of sin and sorrow—and yet of pleasing ties, so hard to break—leaving on the reposeful face—of *clay*—a light such as the setting summer sun sometimes permits to linger for a while upon the hill-top that looks towards the coming morning."

ALS (WP, DLC).

From Ellen Louise Axson

My darling Woodrow,   Rome [Ga.], July 21/84.

The probability, at present, is, that I have now written for the last time that word "Rome" at the head of my letters to you[.] I believe, or hope at least, that I will get off on next Thursday. I can't remember whether or not I told you that I think of going to Sewanee first, in order that my visit to Gainsville may fall in with Grandfather's. They expect to be there and at Mount Airy the first of Sept.; and of course I am exceedingly anxious to meet them there. I feel as though I *must* see something of them, before going away for so long a time.

But even yet I am not *sure* that I will leave Gainville for the last. Having only thought of the plan last week, I am still waiting for letters from Gainsville on the subject, which will decide me. I am only certain at present that I will go *somewhere* on Thursday.

I was out a[t] Jessie's on last Thursday evening, and we all, Marion and I especially, grew greatly excited over a charming scheme of Mr. Bones for turning our journey into a pleasure trip. You know Jessie leaves on Thursday and if I go to Sewanee, we will travel together as far as Chatanooga, which was of course my reason for choosing that day. Mr. Bones will accompany her that far on her way, and his plan is that Marion should go too, and that we three should remain over and spend a day on Lookout. Would'nt that be splendid? I have always been so anxious to see that view from Lookout,—have already made three unsuccessful efforts to get there; and I earnestly hope that this won't share the fate of the others.

I found Jessie of course in the midst of the packing confusion. They are fortunate in having the depot so near. They have chartered a car, which stands always there, so that whenever they finish with a box or an article of furniture, they can send it over and "be done with it." They have also been so fortunate as to rent the place as it stands, as a dairy farm, so that Jessie was spared the trouble of selling off the stock, &c. by piece-meal. I never know whether to tell you news of them or not; it seems as though you would hear it all from *them*; and yet I judge from what Jessie says, that you very probably *don't*. She tells me that she "has'nt heard a word from you since you left." How shocking! I had an idea that you were a better correspondent! Since you *do* hear so little directly from them, I must tell you of their very characteristic adventure of last Wed. They went, on that afternoon, several miles up the Silver creek road to find a good bathing place. Their equipage was the *dump-cart*, and Jessie was the driver. They had all the children packed into it, together with a varied assortment of other articles—old clothes, &c. You can readily imagine the catastrophe,—on the way back the staple slipped, and they were all unceremoniously tumbled out in a heap! The horse, in it's fright, began to back, and some of them, the baby particularly, had a very narrow escape,—but it *was* an escape, they were *altogether* unhurt. Then the horse began to run, and kept it up for a quarter of a mile or more, with Jessie running too at full speed at his side, pulling at the reins. At last, after she had turned him against a steep bank, and he had gone up and down it half a dozen times or more, she managed to stop him, and they gradually collected their scattered forces. The ground, farther than the eye could reach, was strown with fragments of the wreck consisting, as aforesaid, chiefly of old clothes. Of course, since it turned out so well, it is the best joke of the season—though indeed it might have been something very serious.

Well, Mr. Baker has been here tonight, to make his farewell visit, and as he left after eleven, it now grows quite late, so that I must try to make my letter short,—especially as it has just occurred to me that I *must* write you again before I leave in order to tell you positively where to direct your next. What do you suppose I am writing with now? Alex. Stephens gold pen! the one he used constantly for years, with which he wrote his histories &c. When Mr. John Stephens was here, several weeks ago, he drove Minnie perfectly wild with delight by bestowing it upon her. I never saw a girl so beside herself over a gift. It certainly is an interesting relic, and he was "awfully good" to give it to her. That is a singular friendship between Mr. Stephens and Minnie. He makes the greatest possible a-do over her, is always begging that he may "adopt" her, writes to her frequently, comes up expressly to see her and take her home with him,—and considers her as altogether the cleverest, sweetest[,] most wonderful girl of the period. As a young man Mr. S. was desperately in love with Aunt Florence—was a rejected suitor of her's—and a laughable feature of the case is, that, even now, Uncle Will don't seem to fancy him much or to "relish" his affection for Minnie. But if *his* wife doesn't mind it I don't see why Uncle Will should, and she seems fully to share that affection. Of course, you know that the Mr. S. I mean is the nephew of "the great commoner.["]

Many thanks for the paper on Evolution.[1] We found it extremely interesting, and of course very "satisfactory" as to Dr. Woodrows position. I was of course anxious to see it,—was, when you mentioned it, just about sending for the Review. It is an old friend which I don't see, since last fall. So Dr. Mack proposes going into print with *his* side! What a little busy-body he is![2]

I intended to answer your questions about the "League," in this letter, but must postpone it now, until the next,—am so busy all day that I need some sleep at night. Have finished my lessons in china-painting,—graduated!—and am now at Uncle Will's again. Have been at my crayon-work all day, while the others sewed, and Stockton read to the assembled family "Alice through the Looking Glass"!

Give my warmest love to your mother and father and "Dode" and for yourself, dear love, the whole heart of

Your own Ellie.

ALS (WP, DLC).

¹ James Woodrow, "Evolution," *Southern Presbyterian Review*, xxv (July 1884), 341-68.

² J. B. Mack, "The Other Side," Richmond *Central Presbyterian*, July 9, 1884. In this article, Dr. Mack reviewed the Woodrow controversy to date and argued that the resolution adopted by the Alumni Association of the Columbia Theological Seminary, thanking Dr. Woodrow for his address on May 7, 1884, was only *pro forma* and not an endorsement.

To Ellen Louise Axson

Wilmington [N.C.], July 22nd/84

How can I tell you, my precious Ellie, my darling, what was in my heart as I read the letter that came this morning, or how shall I sing to you the music that has been in my heart ever since I read it! If I could tell you, it would seem, here on this featureless paper, only a repetition of what I have already told you so often: though my love for you never seems to *me* twice the same. It is constantly changing, in one sense, with the fresh accessions that come every day—changing in degree and (so to speak) in *consciousness*, while remaining always the same in kind. My darling is coming! I am sure that there is more eloquence in those four words than in all the books I ever read—how much more than in any I shall ever be able to write! If I could put as much joy and delight for others into a volume as those words bring to me, I should be easily immortal! Ah, my matchless little sweetheart, I love you more than words can tell, and am happy beyond measure in the knowledge that you are actually coming to my home—that the wish that has so long been uppermost in my heart is really to be fulfilled! But there is no use in trying to put these thoughts into writing—I am so glad that I don't *need* to put them into writing—that my darling *knows* how much I love her and how supreme my joy is when I can have her with me—how indispensable she is to me. If you are glad that you are coming—and I know that you are, for you love me and have *said* that you are glad—translate your gladness into an expression of my gratification at the prospect, and try to imagine how glad *I* am!

I don't wonder, little lady, that you were sorely puzzled by that Delphic note of your grandmother's! It *was* "a sticker," as the boys say, and I expended not a little thought upon that portion of it which said that nothing had been meant by the persistent importunities which were employed to extract that promise. But one thing was plain, and that was that she had changed her mind and meant what she said—whatever had been the means of her conversion. She would'nt, I knew, say anything but just exactly what she thought: and I was content to acknowledge that it was none of my business how she *came* to think it. Doubtless, now that she can see the "girl in blue" in proper perspective, her view of the proprieties is softened and she is willing to have her heart tell her what is best for *you*.

I really think that there is probably less risk of being subjected to remark of any sort in Wilmington and in our house than in any other place I know of. The people here are not unusually given to gossip, I believe; and I know that they have been impressed with the fact that we are proud beyond most folks and will not brook any interference, even of comment, with our private, family concerns.

My darling, my head is full of plans as to what we shall do when you come; but maybe the best plans will be those which we shall make together after you get here. Mother sends her warmest love, my pet—as do father and "Dode" too—but mother is most immediately interested in the visit, as the others will be away, and so sends a special message of love because of the delightful turn things have taken. She will be almost as glad to see you as I will.

That *was* a comical mistake about the letters to Miss Rose and "Auntie"! You dear reckless little girl, you! So you "rave" in your letters about *me*, do you? How many pennies would I not give to read some of the things you write about me! for you know, Miss, that the things one says *about* another are often more instructive that [than] the things one says *to* that person. I suppose that you'll have to be discreet now and make a clean breast of it to Auntie" (?)

This is the first chance I have had, little sweetheart, to echo your "Hurrah for Cleveland!" I felt like giving "three times three, and a tiger" when the news first reached me from Chicago. It was a splendid nomination—the one I had been devoutly wishing for—and I believe that the ticket will be elected in splendid style. The Democrats actually did the very wisest thing that they could have done! That means something unusual, like an overwhelming victory. The party, though, I am troubled to see, has not been able to come quite up to the good sense of the Convention. There is coldness in many quarters as to the nomination, and here and there actual disaffection! But the tremendous Republican bolt ought to make up for that!

No, ma'am, I did not see the article in the *Nation*:[1] but the name of it promises just what I want: or, rather I want two new parties—not a third. Two *big* ones, two *real* parties, are enough—more are factional—like the screaming French parties.

I know that you will be glad to learn, my darling, that the "Senate" ("Essay No 4") is completed—and half copied, half *caligraphed*. I *thought* it was done some time ago: but found that it had to be recast in the ordering of the parts, and, consequently, in many details of the treatment. I hope to have No. 5 finished and No. 6 under way by the time you come.

Warmest love to E. and to S. (tell him beware! if he ever forget to mail a letter to *me*!). Regards to Miss M. and all. You are all the world to me, and I am altogether Your own   Woodrow.

ALS (WP, DLC).
[1] See ELA to WW, July 14, 1884, n. 3.

From Ellen Louise Axson

Rome [Ga.] July 24/84.

It is just half an hour, my darling, before I leave for *Sewanee*, so as you may imagine I have time only for a line. We spend tonight on Lookout Mountain—reach Sewanee Friday.

My address there is care Dr. H. M. Anderson.

Love to all.   Yours with all my heart.   Ellie.

ALS (WP, DLC).

Two Letters to Ellen Louise Axson

My own darling,   Wilmington [N.C.], July 26th/84

I am glad that you decided to go first to Sewanee, because I know how much you love Miss Rose (and "Mac"!) and how much pleasure you will derive from being again with her (and him!). Give my love to Miss Rose, and to "Mac" too, if you please. On the whole, I believe that I am not jealous of him, though he *has* won the affections of both his own sweetheart and mine. I am inclined to think that, if I knew him, I should like him immensely myself—almost as much as I should like and admire his lady-love. It would be only poetic justice if I could make her fall in love with me!

You have not told me, little lady, whether or not you are going to spend your days at Sewanee at the easel: but if you are, I am afraid that I stand a poor chance for getting as many letters as I want: because of course, with that houseful of people, your evenings till late bed-time must be *sociably* spent, and I must insist that you rob yourself of no more sleep in order to write to me. It would make me nothing less than supremely unhappy to be deprived of your sweet letters, but I should rather do without them (which is saying all that I can say) than have you write them after eleven o'clock at night. I have been *very* much distressed to think that you have been making a habit, lately, of doing so. I care a vast deal more for your health, my darling, than for my own gratification, and I *beg* of you not to be so imprudent. It is very sweet of you, but very wrong of you all the same, to make such sacrifice of your health for my sake.

The scheme of a trip to Lookout Mountain *was* happily conceived and I am delighted, my darling, that you were able to carry it out. That must have been a jolly crowd that left Rome on Thursday: it is interesting to me to reflect that with that little company went away what was all of Rome, for me. With both Auntie's and Jessie's homes in other people's hands, and my little sweetheart gone for good and aye, there is nothing in Rome that I know—and *nobody* that belongs to me, except Marion and uncle James who will *board* as if they did not *belong* there! Still, I may tell you, my precious Eileen, if you will promise me that it shall be one of our secrets, that there are some spots about Rome which no change can rob of the beauty they have in my eyes, because they are hallowed by associations with my earliest acquaintance with a young lady—whom I would describe, if I did not know how skeptical you are with regard to my judgment in the matter of feminine charms, and how prone you are to blush—who, at first quite unconsciously to herself, taught me some of the most astonishing lessons I ever learned: amongst other things, the difference between admiration and love, and how a man who thinks that his whole soul is given to doing honest thinking and finding useful work to do may suddenly discover that his success, his everything, depends upon his winning the love of a gentle little maiden with shy brown eyes and sunny smile who lets him catch now and again a glimpse of a character which wins him in spite of himself.

By-the-way, my dreams during the last two nights have been full of visions of that same little maiden with the brown eyes. Strange that she should be in my thoughts so constantly, is'nt it? And she was a delightfully imperious young lady in my dreams, too. We were I don't know where, but in some place where we were together all the time—some place that was new and strange to me, but where she knew everybody—and she managed me according to her own sweet will, taking me to see people whom I did not want to meet, coaxing me with amazing, and yet (to me) delightful, facility out of all wish for independence of thought or action—in short chaining me in the most grateful slavery ever dreamed of! It made me downright cross to wake out of those dreams. The lovely little woman has *bewitched* me! If I could be near her now for a moment, I know what I should tell her. I should look into those eyes that have told me so many sweet secrets that have made me grave and glad by turns—grave at thought of the responsibility they laid upon me, and glad at thought of the happiness of which they assured me—and should admonish her to remember, in the midst of the many gay friends who are lavishing their love upon her, the love of a quiet, homely man away off by the Atlantic—the love of one whose life is wrapped up in hers. I am not afraid that she will forget it: but I should give the admonition all the same, because I prize above all things the privilege which is mine of telling her of my love for her. That privilege is the earnest of her trust in me, her love for me, and I would not exchange it for all the honours that seem to me the greatest in the world.

Well! Well!—there were several things I meant to tell you about in this letter—but here "Ive been and" used up all my time and my space after my usual fashion, in inventing new ways of renewing declarations of my love! The simple truth is, my little queen, that that love so fills my heart that it *will* out when I am writing to you. I hope, Miss, that you don't object? and that you will indulge me in the confession that I am　　　Your own　Woodrow.

P.S. To relieve "Dode's" anxiety lest you should not recognize the "Original" of the picture he sent you to-day, I will say that you behold in it the "counterfeit presentment" of Mr. Joseph R. Wilson, jr., in the uniform of the Wilmington Bicycle Club., and that the "wheel" beside him is his Celebrated Columbia, No. 52.[1] I trust that you are properly grateful both for his gift and my explanation.　　　　　　　　　Lovingly Yours,　Woodrow

P.S. No. 2. Father and Mother wish to add their love to that of the "Original."　　　　　　　　　Lovingly,　W.

[1] This photograph is reproduced in Vol. 2. For "Dode's" own joyful account of getting the bicycle, see Joseph R. Wilson, Jr., to WW, Oct. 22, 1883, Vol. 2.

My own darling,　　　　　　Wilmington [N.C.], July 28th/84
　　Do you think that a certain young lady can get along for a few days without the usual letters from her lover? I must be out of town until about Thursday evening, and it is extremely unlikely that I shall be able to write while I am away—much as I shall certainly *want* to write. I am going to escort "Dode" to Bingham's School, at Mebaneville, and, as I am going as special commissioner to superintend the business of his entrance and see him comfortably "fixed" in his new quarters, I shall probably find plenty to keep me busy. This will be the dear youngster's first long good-bye to home, and as I have a keen enough recollection of how I felt when I had to say a like good-bye, upon setting out for Davidson, I am very anxious to be as much of a comfort and aid to him as possible. I believe, however, that the separation will be a keener trial to dear mother than it will be to "Dode." Not that he has'nt a passionate love for home: but, like all high-strung youngsters, he looks forward with relish to the adventures to be had at a big boarding school. For mother, on the other hand, his going away seems the first part of what must be a final separation from the last child left her. How I wish that my work lay where I could be with her! It does seem very hard that she should rear us only to lose us, only, as it were, for the *purpose* of losing us! But we will make her have a good time in September, anyhow— wont we? And, in the meantime, I'll get "Dode" happily ensconced, as cadet recruit.
　　I received a long and exceedingly interesting letter from Shinn the other day, little sweetheart.[1] Since I can't read you the whole

of it, I will quote the part which concerns you: for part of it does concern you. "I don't think I ought to write you so long a letter as this," he says. "I swear, I know you wont read it. I believe you've gone to Georgia again to see that lovely lady[.] (It's a solemn fact—though you may'nt believe it—that my regard and liking and friendship for your betrothed, merely from seeing her picture and hearing bits about her, have become very strong indeed. I never before felt so much about one as if I had known them—as if they were first cousins at least—if not—well—long-lost, newly-found, sisters. Don't laugh at this outburst—it's my Texan blood—it's the streak of gush, I suppose—only it don't seem gush to me—and therefore I contest it is not gush—but fact.)"—Of which I have'nt the slightest doubt, my dear fellow!

The dear, ugly, whole-souled chap has been having what must, under the circumstances, be called a wonderful success with his "outside work." He has been paying his expenses with his earnings ever since his first week in New York, and the newspaper men tell him that the like has'nt been done there for many a year by a man without any backing. Hurrah for the plucky old Californian! That foolish, deceitful girl out yonder on the Pacific coast did him a wondrously good turn when she threw away the best chance of her life and drove him across the continent. He has a magnificent faculty for getting on in the world—and New York is for him the best world to get along in. It's just the place to appreciate his peculiar talents, his versatile capacity for turning his hand with almost uniform success to any sort of literary work that is likely to find a market. And what exalts his work is that he don't do it as a *hack*, but with a perennial interest and enthusiasm. He has a quick, ready adaptivity and a *young heart*: which latter possession seems to me indispensable to any one who has *general* literary, journalistic, work to do—work unconnected with any great lines of original thought or with any great cause. Shinn, as he says himself, cannot construct; but he has really first-class powers of *interpretation*. In a word, he was born just at the right time: in the age of journalism.

That *is* an odd, almost a romantic, friendship between Miss Minnie and Mr. John Stephens. Does Miss Minnie admire him as much as he admires her? By-the-way, you have not reported what impression you made upon Mr. Stephens in your packing attire. I have no doubt as to the truth of the matter: but I should like to know what he said. I have a very strong desire that Miss Minnie should meet Shinn: he is so *entirely* unlike other men that she might be induced, upon full acquaintance with him, to renounce her resolution against the sex. But, alas! Shinn is *deaf*, and could'nt, I'm sure, understand a word Miss Minnie might say!

All right, my darling, if you wish it, mum shall be the word about your visit to Wilmington. It shall be a private benefit for the chief actors. But, you don't mean to say that you have formed the rash resolve to keep it a secret from Miss Rose, and that it is from her that you are going to silently steal away! You will prove yourself a most wonderful young woman if you manage to hide the whole plan from her, despite all-day companionship and nightly confidences.

Our work—father's and mine—on the Minutes of the Assembly is at last done, after many a hot week of tedious, vexatious labour over the proof-sheets: so that when I get back from Mebaneville my hands will be quite free for my essay on the Executive (No. 5) which must then be undertaken, and I can, probably, push its composition as fast as I am eager to push it. If I could but write about fifty *per cent.* better than I have yet been able to write—if I could come nearer to the standard of my master, Bagehot—all of this work would be a supreme delight to me. Even as it is, I take real pleasure in it, and shall be sorry when the series of essays is completed. There is a keen satisfaction always in the act of creation—no matter how humble the scale of the creation or how small the thing created. If one is developing his own ideas, what he writes seems peculiarly his own. It is wrapped up in a possessive pronoun. One regards it with an affection like in kind, though inferior in degree, to the love a mother has for her child— even when it is acknowledged, as it is by some sensible mothers, that the offspring is not beautiful. This, at any rate, is my way of accounting for my enthusiasm in doing work which does not win my entire approval after it is done. The literary workman has'nt the satisfaction vouchsafed to the faithful craftsman— to Stradivarius—the satisfaction of knowing that the product of his hand is perfect of its kind: but his, none the less, is the satisfaction of faithful workmanship—of knowing that he is doing his best: that he is thinking truthfully and doing all he can to give perfect expression to the truth.

Herein, you perceive, my precious little sweetheart, may be said to lie one of the secrets of the delight I derive from the privilege, of which I make such diligent use, of writing to you. There is one truth always uppermost in my mind, nowadays, and that is the truth that *I love you.* I am forever trying to find some new expression for that truth, in order that I may come nearer to an *adequate* expression of it. I know that I shall never find that latter—because I know how much bigger the fact is than the biggest burden that words can carry—but I like to try, all the same. Maybe, by accumulations of expression, so to speak, I may get you to understand some part of the feeling I have for my Ellie, my little queen. Being too far away from you to speak to your heart by *actions,* I *must,* in order to content myself, try to send you words that will find their way to your heart—messages of love that will find a glad welcome there in that heart whose riches have been given to me—and all of whose riches (so selfish am I) are needed to satisfy me!

We leave for Mebaneville at 9 o'clock tomorrow morning. I shall want to hurry back to get your first letter from Sewanee. Sincerest regards to Miss R. All here send warmest love. You know how much to keep as from   Your own   Woodrow.

ALS (WP, DLC).
¹ C. H. Shinn to WW, July 18, 1884.

From Ellen Louise Axson

My darling Woodrow,   Sewanee [Tenn.], July 28/84.

Your last letter—that of the 22nd—was handed me at the depot, last Thursday afternoon, just as I had begun almost to despair of getting it before I left. For we *did* leave on Thursday, after all, and I *have* been to Lookout at last. In fact, we carried out our programme so exactly, that my statement as to what we *intended* doing will serve very well as an account of what we *did* do. We started with quite a large party, Uncle Will, little Will [Hoyt], and Bessie Caldwell going with us as far as Kingston. We left Jessie and the children at "Boyce's," six miles from Chat.—Mr Brower joined her some twenty-five miles farther up the road. The rest of us, Mr. B. and Marion, Stockton, Minnie & Florence Hoyt, went on to the city, where we immediately engaged a carriage and buggy and started for the mountain,—which we reached at eleven that night. Notwithstanding the fact that Mr. Bones & Marion had only two hours sleep the night before, and I, four hours, we, of course, got up at four the next morning and walked a mile to see the sunrise. But the sun, I am sorry to say, failed to follow our good example—*he did'nt* rise. After sitting on the rocks, in a bank of fog, for an hour or so waiting for him, we accepted our fate, and straggled back, a rather damp and discouraged looking crowd. But by and by, while we were at breakfast, the sun came out gloriously, and things began to look more cheerful. When we finally reached "the Point" the fog had almost vanished, and the view was magnificent beyond description. Have you ever been there? I think it must be, as Mr. Bones says, one of the finest views in America. It was certainly grander and more extensive than any which I have seen before—even than those never-to-be-forgotten ones from "Mount Willard" and "Richmond Hill." It transported me to the seventh heaven, where I remained the rest of the day. We came down from the mountain in time for Mr. Bones to attend to some business, and for me to make a call on "dear old Janie."[1] Then at half past one I took leave of our pleasant little party and started for Sewanee,—they leaving for Rome very soon after.

I reached the mountain safely just at tea-time,—found my dear Rose, and all my friends well, and have been having a very "good time" ever since. This is commencement week at the University [of the South]; in fact the "speaking" began the night I reached here, and I gave sufficiently strong evidence of my interest by attending,—though I fear my motive was'nt so much a thirst for knowledge on my own account, as a wish to prevent Rose from missing such an improving occasion. The place is crowded with visitors of all sorts,—young men and maidens, old men and children[.] There are a dozen Bishops, to begin with, while as to the lesser clergy—their name is legion! You should have seen the procession yesterday. They had on gowns of every colour under heaven—purple and red, and blue and pink. Then there were the choristers in white, and the gownsmen in black, to say nothing of the rest of the boys in all the "pomp and circumstance of war." Oh it was most imposing!

You know everything here is modeled after the English Universities, and these gorgeous gowns and "hoods" represent different ranks and degrees as they exist at *Oxford*!

We had a splendid sermon, by the-way, from Bishop McLaren of Chicago,[2]—a noble argument with a most eloquent conclusion. Just think! he was a Presbyterian until a few years ago! Is'nt it *too* bad that he should be lost to us? Still they needed him more than we, and I fear they could'nt have gotten him by any other process,—for they don't train such preachers in their church.

I wish you could see "the Prodigy"![3] How you would laugh! I don't see how he can be such a lady-killer,—he is anything but handsome, and *I* should'nt call him "fascinating." Besides he is so exactly the ideal (Irish) Roman Catholic priest that I should feel it was a sin to fall in love with him. He has a round, rosy face, which expresses great self-satisfaction, and love of good cheer. There is a comical twist to the corners of his mouth, and a merry twinkle in his eye, and he has an endless fund of rather bright small talk. I hav'nt heard him rise to any other sort, so far. But I have no doubt he is very clever. He is professor of Eclesiastical Polity and Church History, and also of English Literature in the University proper. His mother is a curiosity. She has the strongest possible Irish brogue; is related to various "peers of high degree["] in the "ould counthrey," but she is too modest to allow any hint of her aristocratic connections to become apparent in her own manners, speech, or person. She is, however, a devoted mother, has worked long and well with her needle to educate her only child,—and has given him the best advantages which *the Church* affords. Happy mother!—she has gained the desire of her heart! —and may she live yet to see him a *"Bishop*["]!

I found quite a delightful surprise awaiting me here,—Cousin Hattie (Ewing) and Cousin Allie (Truehcart)[4] Uncle Tom's two daughters are here for the summer. I dare say you have heard me hold forth on the subject of those two lovely cousins of mine. Allie, I saw two years ago in New York, but I hav'nt seen Hattie, our favourite, since her marriage; so the meeting was a great treat.

Your letter and the picture of "Dode" have just reached me,— while in the act of writing. The picture is excellent and I am *so* glad to have it; I appreciate very highly his sending it,—and am also sufficiently "grateful" for your explanation! True, I did'nt need an introduction to Mr. J. R. Wilson, Jr., but I am happy to be presented to his better half (!) "Columbia No. 52."

No, I have brought no crayon work with me to Sewanee. My time is so short, and there are always so many "distractions" here, that I knew if I did it would be a mere form,—so I will try to heed your injunctions and write at reasonable hours. No fear but that I will also heed that other "admonition," my darling; there is no power at Sewanee, or in the world, that could make me forget for a moment that dear friend by the Atlantic. I too have been dreaming of *you* constantly of late; and it has been *such* a treat, for I so seldom dream except when I am sick or in trouble;—and as they are not "pleasant dreams," you of course don't appear in them.

I am very glad that "No 4" is off your mind,—and hands too,— caligraphed and all! I suppose you are deep in "No 5" now; what is its subject? I hope you are feeling stronger now,—have seen the last of those head aches &c. How is it? You say nothing about your health in these last letters.

Give much love to all. Rose sends her love (and Mac's!) She

thinks it "too bad" that you failed to come to Sewanee. "You should have given her an opportunity to fall in love with you."

Good-bye dearest, I love you more than words can tell, and am forever,   Your own Eileen.

ALS (WP, DLC) with WWhw on env.: "the main principle—the govt. of the people—upon which it is founded."
     ¹ Janie Porter, "our own girl, Papa's 'adopted daughter,'" as Ellen wrote WW on Nov. 12, 1883, Vol. 2, married Samuel Chandler, one of two sons of Col. Milton Chandler, of Decatur, Ga., in June 1884. See ELA to WW, Nov. 12, 1883, and Dec. 31, 1883, both in Vol. 2; and ELA to WW, March 19, 1884.
     ² The Rt. Rev. Dr. William E. McLaren, Protestant Episcopal Bishop of Illinois.
     ³ Thomas Frank Gailor, born Jackson, Miss., Sept. 17, 1856. A.B., Racine (Wis.) College, 1876; S.T.B., General Theological Seminary, 1879. Numerous honorary degrees, including an S.T.D. from Columbia University, 1891, and a D.D. from Oxford University in 1920. Ordained deacon, 1879; priest, 1880. Rector, Church of the Messiah, Pulaski, Tenn., 1879-82. Professor of Ecclesiastical Polity and Church History, University of the South, 1882-90; Vice-Chancellor, 1890-93. Co-Adjutor Bishop of Tennessee, 1893-98; Bishop of Tennessee, 1898-1935. Chancellor and President of Board of Trustees, University of the South, 1908-35. Chairman, House of Bishops, Protestant Episcopal Church, 1916-22; Presiding Bishop, 1919-25; president, National Council, Protestant Episcopal Church, 1922-25. Author of many books, including *Some Memories* (Kingsport, Tenn., 1937), published posthumously. Died Oct. 3, 1935.
     ⁴ Harriet Hoyt Ewing and Alice Hoyt Truehart were two of the daughters of the Rev. Thomas A. Hoyt of Philadelphia and his first wife, Mary Harrison.

Two Letters to Ellen Louise Axson

My own darling,   Wilmington [N.C.], Aug. 2nd/84
     I got back from Bingham's on Thursday night and am just now beginning to recover my spirits. It was terribly hard to have to leave "Dode" away off there amongst strangers, to shift for himself, though I believe that the excitement, the novelty of the situation, and his passionate love for the society of other boys made the experience less trying to the dear chap than it was to me. He has a wonderful faculty for making friends which converts strangers into familiar acquaintances in an amazingly short time—so that he wont be long homesick. But it made me sick at heart to have to leave him. I was, so to speak, vicariously homesick, because there came back to me with painful vividness my own feelings when, more than ten years ago, I was left at Davidson. Still, I was some months (four months) younger then than Josie is now, and much more sensitive than he has ever been to the embarrassments of being thrown amongst unsympathetic strangers—for a Freshman is commonly understood not to receive very loving consideration from the young gentlemen whom he meets at college.

     Bingham's school is about a mile from Mebaneville and in Mebaneville there is no inn, so we were entertained at Major

Bingham's while I stayed, Mrs. Bingham hospitably insisting that
Josie should not go into his quarters in "barracks" as long as he
could be with me. I never was more kindly treated anywhere.
Mrs. Bingham is a thoroughly likeable lady, and her two daughters add very agreeable manners to great good looks. They exerted
themselves to make my stay a pleasant one, and I, of course, as
you must yourself admit, Miss, it was my duty to do, made myself as "fascinating" as I possibly could—being rewarded with the
assurance, given directly by Mrs. Bingham, and conveyed indirectly through "Dode," to whom one of the young ladies confided
the fact, that I had quite charmed the family. An immense conquest, you see: three ladies in two days—and two of them young,
handsome, and unmarried! Don't you think it dangerous that I
should be loose, allowed to play havoc amongst the hearts of
young ladies who have no means of knowing that I am engaged?
Strange that I should have been cast down instead of elated yesterday after such a triumphant progress: and all because there
was not the letter I wanted and had been thinking about all the
time I was away amongst those I found awaiting me when I
returned! Somebody kept a letter written on the 28th until the
30th before mailing it and the P.O. authorities here were kind
enough to hold it, for the two cents due, all day yesterday without
notification: so that dear mother was asking me every now and
then if I was feeling unwell! All her anxiety passed away after
the letter was delivered. There are a great many coincidences
which are hard to explain, are there not?

So you have been dreaming constantly of me of late, have you,
little sweetheart? And pray, Miss, *what* have you been dreaming?
What will you take to tell me some of those dreams? Since you
dream so seldom, there must have been something very special
to make you dream and something very special for you to dream
about.

And "the Prodigy" is a comical prodigy after all, with nothing
fascinating about him! Your description of him is very vivid and
very amusing. It is rendered the more amusing by the fact that
you seem to have experienced a little relief at finding him less
irresistible than he was reputed to be. Did my little sweetheart
expect to find it dangerous to come within his influence? Now
that you have discovered how harmless he is, you ought to feel
sorry for him, because I very seriously doubt whether he has
experienced the same relief upon seeing you that you felt upon
seeing him. You mus'nt make it too hard for him: and beware,
little lady; maybe his fascination manifests itself in his conversa-

tion, so that he is, like John Wilkes, "only half an hour behind the handsomest man" in the world.

Yes, my darling, I am feeling quite well and like myself now. I have'nt been saying anything about my health in my recent letters because there was not so much as a single ache to report. I am so seldom sick even with petty ailments, and my few pains last winter in Baltimore and during the early weeks of this vacation were something so unusual that I gave them more notice than they deserved. I am free from worry now, and worry is my principal enemy. When you come next month, I promise that you shall find me light-hearted and as fat as I have yet found out how to be.

The thought that my darling is coming *next month* acts as a wonderful tonic whenever I begin to feel a little bit depressed because this, that, or the other thing goes wrong! I should not be surprised if the last part of essay No. 5 should prove to be by all odds the best part of the whole series—unless I can manage to write a portion of No. 6 while you are here—because as September approaches my spirits will rise, and it will be strange if my pen don't catch some of the colour reflected from them. The more I see of other women nowadays, my precious Eileen, the more vividly do I realize the fact that you are the only woman in the world that I can love—that you are the one person in all the world whose love is indispensable to me. You *are* all the world to me!

Father and mother send warmest love to my darling. Love to Miss Rose and to "Mac." For yourself keep all that is greatest in the love of   Your own   Woodrow.

Wilmington [N.C.], Aug. 3/84

Partly for the sake of getting back into the convenient round of my old programme, and partly because of a private liking (which you may have discerned) for writing to you, my own darling, during those quiet afternoon hours when one seems to realize, with a sort of solemn impulse of preparation, that the duties of a new week are at hand—the hours of Sabbath pause— I am going to write just a little love-letter to the sweetest little woman in the world. It's hard for me not to be *always* writing love-letters to that irresistible little sweetheart of mine: because my love for her seems all the time fairly to fill my thoughts to overflowing and I feel as if I *must* tell it to someone: and whom *can* I tell—to whom would I tell it—but to herself? It is *hers*, and

I sha'nt make it common by talking about it to other people. And yet how can I tell my precious little heart-keeper anything more about my boundless love for her? I am overwhelmed with a very comical sense of embarrassment whenever I think of the countless love-letters I have written her already! If she has kept all of them, how it must puzzle her to find a place to stow them all away! Does she stack them, I wonder, or bale them? Fortunately I know a secret of hers which makes me sure that she wont get tired of having me write the same things again and again. After all, my pet, the chief delight for us is in *possessing* each other's love, in having this love to talk about, and not in talking about it in new ways. In my private opinion, you are the lovliest woman in the world: but that's not what makes me happy. I am happy because I am loved by the lovliest woman in the world. She has never been able to give any satisfactory account of *why* she loves me: but she has demonstrated it without explanation; and that clears away all sorts of difficulties I used to look forward to. It would have been impossible for me to live at my best without love: but how was I to make the right woman love me? Until the right woman came along and just fell in love with me "plain so," without any reason, *that* was what used to make me anxious. I still don't understand how it came about, but I know that my darling loves me, and I know that she is the right woman because I am ready to spend all my life for her if I may spend it with her.

Well! this *is* a rambling, disjointed epistle I have suffered myself to write: but you don't mind indulging me in such occasionally, do you? The long and short of the matter is that you are unspeakably dear to me, and that I could'nt, if I would, be anything but   Your own   Woodrow.

ALS (WP, DLC).

From Ellen Louise Axson

My darling Woodrow,   Sewanee [Tenn.], Aug. 4, 1884.

Sewanee, as I have before observed to you, is a truly charming place, the life here is "ideal" and "idyllic"—and all that sort of thing! One of it's greatest charms is that it is so delightfully "out of the world." But "heaven upon earth's and [an] empty boast,"— I find there are certain drawbacks to being out of the world; not the smallest being the various delays and irregularities connected with trains and mails. I know that my last week's letter—the only one which, in spite of my efforts I managed to write,—was very much delayed in reaching you,—for it seems that letters written Monday night don't leave the mountain until Wed. morning; so today I will begin betimes, and *perhaps* I will have an opportunity of sending to the "station" before night. Your last reached me promptly however last Wed. Yes I have managed to get along *after* a *fashion* without the usual letters but am *very* glad the "few days" are almost past, and that you are probably again in Wilmington. How soon Josie's school opens, by-the-way! To begin the first of Aug. is what these boys here would call very "hard lines." I can imagine that his leaving *is* a very keen trial for your mother;—am glad you are to be with her for two good months longer. I suppose that your father too, having finished the Minutes will soon be off for his vacation. I am *very* glad that task is done and you are free for more congenial labour. I hope you may have just as much pleasure in writing about the "Executive" as other people will have in reading what you write. We—readers—will attribute our pleasure to whatever cause we choose, and of course we will allow you the same privilege. I have no doubt—

9 P.M.—My plans for writing this morning, as you see came to grief,—was interrupted by visitors who detained me until dinner time. Immediately after dinner the whole family party, with René,[1] started off in a hack for "the Rift," and the "Cascade," a very beautiful, though rough ride of six or eight miles. We returned by moon-light, reaching home only an hour ago. I had seen most of the "sights" about Sewanee three years ago, but these were new to me, and they are simply magnificent. I never saw a place more wildly beautiful than the great ravine into which this "bridal veil" is flung;—and the heavy rains of late have made the veil itself even more than usually fine. Altogether we have had a wonderful afternoon. It was so delightful to have it all to ourselves. We are going to picnic at another beautiful place on Thursday—Lost Cove,—but we are to go with a "party," a gentleman for each girl, and that is *so* tiresome,—it spoils everything. I had expected to leave on Thursday, as the two weeks to which I limited myself when I came, end then. But Rose takes my leaving so *very* much to heart, that I think I will be *obliged* to add another week to my visit. She was quite outraged with *you* when she first found that her visit was to be cut short, after that fashion. But I told her you had already pleaded for forgiveness on the ground that she would, no doubt, do as much for Mac; that seemed to touch and soften her heart. She said that she supposed she *must* forgive you, but that she has a *great deal* to forgive! She added yesterday that whenever she thinks of it she "gets mad

all over again, and then is obliged to forgive again." It *is* rather hard on her, after pleading so earnestly for *six* months! and being promised *two*, at least, to have it cut down to two weeks. She is perpetually sighing over that charming "studio" she has fitted up for this occasion, and "*all* our plans"! You would laugh at those same "plans,"—we had enough to fill a dozen summers. Rose and I were *always* famous schemers when together; the things which we are always going to do, and to read, and paint and study together are like the sands of the sea-shore for number. And, she adds pathetically, "this is our last chance"!—these are the last times. For all of *us*, in many ways, "the old order changeth giving place to new." She will be leaving Sewanee next year, and Réné leaves this fall; she and Mr. Beckwith[2] will be married in Oct. How strange it seems to look away beyond these short changeful years to those of the old, far-away time, that were so long and peaceful, and that seemed to stretch on and on before us in endless vista,—when it seemed a life-time from Xmas to Xmas, and "nothing ever happened"! You see Sat. was Rose's birthday, and that is almost like having another myself; it conspired with other things to set us to thinking, and "remembering." Twenty-four years is a long time to look back upon!—and the eighteen during which we have loved each other have given us endless memories in common.

But enough of all this. According to Mr. Gailor (the Prodigy[)] my memories should extend still farther into the dim past. He informed me the other day that he had a picture of me, which was published in some magazine—I forget what—in *1856*; *he* "had treasured it for twenty years"! I asked him if the publisher had remembered to give the name; he said "no" it was called "Sunshine" or something of that sort, but it was me, all the same.

I was very much pleased with the extract from Mr. Shinn's letter. I have often wondered at my own interest in, and friendship for Mr. Shinn,—so much warmer and more personal than that which I felt for any of your other friends,—and it is satisfactory to know that my feelings are properly reciprocated! It would be humiliating to me if the regard were all on one side. Am truly delighted to hear of his success in New York. He does indeed seem to have found his right place and vocation. The ball has, for once, rolled into the round, not the square hole,—a spectacle always gratifying to one's sense of the fitness of things, even when one feels no special interest in the ball.

We anticipate quite a treat tomorrow,—we are going to hear a lecture from Prof. Gildersleeve on Homer. He is to lecture here for five or six weeks; and twice a week, the ladies are invited. He delivered the first of the series today; Mac and Mr. [Robert] Ewing were delighted, and even Mr. Gailor expressed some approval. I heard him make a short presentation speech on commencement day, in which however I conclude he was out of his element, for it was very poor. By-the-way they conferred some degree upon him—"D.C.L." I believe—and the ceremonies upon the occasion were very imposing. You should have seen him kneeling before the old chancellor, while the vice-chancellor solemnly arrayed him in his "robes"; of course he was only one of many. Ah, we had grand doings here all last week! I must say, without intending any unkind reflections on my good friends that a great deal of it seemed, to Presbyterian ideas, decidedly childish. I am having a delightful visit here however. I don't believe there is a lovlier family anywhere than this; their home-life is really charming. One great advantage they have is that they all sing so delightfully. I don't believe any other one thing adds so much to the pleasure of the home circle. Then the place is most beautiful, and the "society" as everyone knows "unrivalled"!—the only objection being too much young man! I always thought myself totally indifferent to *them*, but I begin to suspect that I must once upon a time have liked them a *little*, because now I like them *less*,—perhaps I cared nothing then, and now less than nothing,—"now all men else seem to me like shadows"! However they are very nice young men indeed—gentlemen, all of them, very different from the Romans; and some of them are well worth talking to. But how fortunate it is that the people we chat with and smile upon can't read our thoughts. They would be rather surprised to know how often they and their possible sweethearts were being pitied and sympathized with, because they are "so different from somebody." "There is none like him, none!" No[,] all of them put together wouldn't make *one* like him! My love to your dear parents. Good-night, dearest. Remember that I am always and altogether   Your own   Eileen.

ALS (WP, DLC).
  1 Réné Fairbanks, a girlhood friend of Rosalie Anderson.
  2 A clergyman of Atlanta who, according to ELA to WW, Dec. 17, 1883, Vol. 2, was engaged to Miss Fairbanks.

Two Letters to Ellen Louise Axson

My own darling,[1]   Wilmington [N.C.], August 5/84
    I had been hoping to have a second letter from Sewanee ere this, but none has come: so I must swallow my disappointment

as best I can and do what I can this afternoon to write away my
low spirits. The prescription is generally a successful one: because if there is anything that can conquer my "blues," it is my
love for you. By talking about it I can always talk myself into
a good humour, at least, if not into absolutely gay spirits. It's
odd, is'nt it, that my love should have two such opposite effects
—making me "blue" when I don't hear from you as often as it
prompts me to desire, and happy so soon as I manage to forget
my temporary cause of discomfiture and fix my thoughts anew
on the little maiden who is the author of all the trouble? But so
it is. I *can't* think of her and be unhappy, though I am sometimes distressed at not receiving more frequent proofs that she
is thinking of me. So, you see, it's the old story of *selfishness*. So
long as I can keep myself and my own selfish desires out of view
and think only of her, whom I love more than I love myself, I am
all right; but once let me get to dwelling on what Mr. Woodrow
Wilson would like to have, for the sake of his own private gratification, and of course I am discontented. This, then, is the service
which writing to you does me: It brings me back to (what I hope
is) my natural self: the self which loves you without a particle
of self-interest. It is only when I have other things to worry me
that I need thus to recall myself, however, so that you need not
suppose, little sweetheart, that I often allow my spirits to sink
whenever you are prevented from writing frequently. I go upon
the noble principle of trying not to be selfish more than a small
portion of the time.

At last the movement of the political campaign has reached
Wilmington, and to-night we are to have our first ratification
meeting. North Carolina is to elect a governor, as well as Con-
gressmen and presidential electors: and to-night there will be
presented the really edifying spectacle of the present governor,
Jarvis, speaking in favour of the successor who is to supercede
him.[2] I am going to attend, of course, because all politics may be
said to be "in my line" and a fellow can generally learn something from campaign speakers, even from poor speakers—something of human nature at least.

Mother and father send their warmest love to you, my darling. Give my love to Miss Rose and "Mac.," and remember, my
precious Eileen, that "I do love nothing in the world so well as
you."   Your own   Woodrow.

1 There is a WWhw partial draft of the next-to-the-last paragraph of this letter
in the pocket notebook described at May 16, 1884, as well as most of the final
sentence in the preceding paragraph, about selfishness.
2 The Governor, Thomas J. Jarvis, was superseded by Alfred M. Scales, who
served in 1885-89.

My own darling,   Wilmington [N.C.], Aug., 7th/84

I sincerely hope that you are having no such continuous rains at Sewanee as we have been having here. It would be hard to imagine anything more dreary or depressing than the weather we have had to endure for the last few weeks. Rain, rain, rain—until even the sand can absorb no more; until the dull dampness seems to have entered our very systems and to have made our minds as sodden as the soil! I would defy anyone of ordinary sensibilities to keep up gay spirits for days together when nature is so persistently forbidding.

The rain did hold off long enough to allow the open-air mass-meeting of Tuesday evening, of which I spoke in my last, to assume the proportions of a big success. A thunder-storm did linger most of the time on the horizon, giving us a lurid back-ground of incessant lightning against which to view the fire-works displayed in front of the speaking-stands but [by] the enthusiastic committee of arrangements: but it did not intrude itself upon us to dampen the ardour of the occasion, so that, barring the interruptions made at my elbow by some silly girls who were conspicuously out of place in such a crowd, not only because of its nature but also because of their desperate ignorance of the matters the speakers were talking about, I enjoyed the speech-making and the scene to the top of my bent. Gov. Jarvis, who made the principal address of the evening, was admirable. I had expected a good deal from him; but I received more than I had expected. In the first place, he *looked* like a man, which is almost half the battle with a public speaker; in the second place, he had the *voice* of a man, full, round, and sonorous; and in the third place, he spoke the words of a man, earnest, moderate, eminently sensible. The principle draw-back was the audience, which was big and dull. It applauded the stock sentiments, and let most that was *fresh* as well as eloquent go without any manifestation of approval. It cheered the name of Gov. Cleveland, but let the great principles which his name represents pass without any show of a cordial greeting. In other words, it was not an *intelligent* audience: and Governor Jarvis therefore deserved the greater credit for preferring to dwell on arguments which were worthy to be applauded rather than upon sentiments which were sure of applause, besides showing himself well trained for his task by compelling a hearing to be given to the least entertaining sides of the questions at issue. He is not an orator, but he seemed to me to illustrate the advantages which the powerful speaker, even if he be without unusual talents, must always possess over the forceful editor, even if the latter be endowed with genius. The well-commanded voice, the manly bearing, the earnest manner of the capable speaker trick men into listening with pleasure, and into continuing to listen willingly despite the fatigue of hours of standing in wet streets, to things which they would not think of reading in print, even though they could read them in half the time. Those people who talk about the press having superseded oratory simply shut their eyes to the plain evidences to the contrary exhibited in all parts of the world every day to those who have more than one eye. I never yet read a great speech without regretting that I had not heard it; and I never knew anyone who did not feel the same way about it. I have read nearly all the published speeches of John Bright—and each one of them is better than the best of editorials—but does that compensate me for never having been within sound of the voice of the greatest of living English orators? But hold on, my dear Woodrow! all this argument you are rushing into may be very good, but it is altogether gratuitous. There's nobody on the other side. You may reserve your strength against the time when you may be gainsaid by somebody! Let's have a little peace and quiet in a *letter*!

The fact is, my precious little sweetheart, that I dare not usually touch upon any subject outside of ourselves, in my letters, for fear of being betrayed into a tedious discourse. I know that whatever I might write would be leniently judged by a certain little maiden whom I love (I sometimes think, indeed, that maybe it would be better for me if my productions were none of them ever to be subjected to any severer light than the light of her loving eyes), but that don't excuse me for being prolix and stupid.

I had an idea that the session at Sewanee continued all summer and that the principal vacation, and therefore the Commencement season, came in the winter, so that I was a good deal surprised to learn that you had happened upon the closing exercises. That many-coloured, much-arrayed procession must have seemed to the unecclesiastical spectator "a regular circus"—a truly remarkable exhibition to be given free of charge. It must be Sewanee, and not the Johns Hopkins, that is "the greatest educational show on earth."

It *was* a pity, my darling, that I could not give Miss Rose "a chance to fall in love with me" (and that was an exceedingly sweet speech for her to make); but then she ought to be obliged to me for relieving her of the responsibility of wasting an opportunity. Give my love to her, please, and to "Mac." Mother and father send warmest love to you, my pet; and as for myself, what can I send more than you have, the whole heart of

　　　　　　　　　　　　　　　　Your own　Woodrow.

P.S. I have had but one letter from Sewanee yet. I sincerely hope that nothing is wrong. Lovingly, W.

ALS (WC, NjP).

From Charles Howard Shinn

Dear Woodrow—　　　　　　　　　　Brooklyn N.Y. 8/9 [1884]

Just as a matter of dignity I want to know who is the debtor in the letter way? I wrote you—abt. *Overland* & Co. You answered most charmingly and did my heart's heart good like a medicine. Then I waited till I could have some news that was "worth while" and at last I wrote you a league long, ocean-torrent of words. And I think you were drowned, or swept out to sea, or are sitting on the rocks waiting for dry weather. All I want to know—is where I left off in my romance of "A Bohemian in N.Y."

I have little time today for a long letter. I love to think of you every day—no one else of them all grew so near my sense of satisfactoriness as you—all in all—up & down, through & through—and you know that. I want you to do great things—you and that brave beauty of the South.

I *am* surprised however that you haven't applauded my political progress. [Albert] Shaw & a dozen others pitch into me so & my father is desperate over it. I have a 20 page letter from him to answer—all politics. . . .

If you don't write me soon—I swear you shall never have that rail road pass to the Pacific Coast that I was going to get you in a few years from now!

Bridges—Marquand[1] & Harold Godwin all kind & pleasant fellows. They have a whole "slather" of fatted calves penned up waiting for your arrival in N.Y.

　　　　　　　　　　Love to all & sundry,　C. H. Shinn.

ALS (WP, DLC) with WWhw notation on env.: "Ans Aug. 13/84."
　[1] Henry Marquand, who worked on the New York *Commercial Advertiser* with Harold Godwin.

From Ellen Louise Axson

My darling Woodrow,　　　　　Sewanee [Tenn.], Aug. 9 1884.

I am so sorry that my letter was again delayed; though, knowing the ways of the mountain, I must say that it was "just as I expected." You are so good and *"lovely"* about it—and everything!—that you really make me feel conscience-smitten in the matter; though I did write at my regular time, and your letters of this week were also twenty-four hours behind-hand. Ah me! If I were only in my own home, living my own life, as in the "long still days of yore," we would see if you did not receive frequent proofs that someone was thinking of you! As it is, I fear you must sometimes take it for granted. In all the months since I have loved you, I have, you know, been obliged to do what I *must*, not what I would. If "circumstances won't accommodate us," you remember, "we must accommodate ourselves to circumstances." But after all, I don't believe you need any "proof." You *know*—do you not?—that I am thinking of you *all the* time? If thoughts were words—winged words—how soon I could prove it! You would receive enough manuscript to crush you, in place of the sheet or so, which I have been trying so constantly to find time for writing since receiving your "Thursday letter" yesterday.

It seems to me I am kept as busily engaged, *playing* here, as I am kept, elsewhere, at work. I am not without a glow of virtuous self-satisfaction as I think of the way in which our time passes[.] I really must send our record to Grandmother and dear Uncle Will;—it would do their hearts good. They have "laboured with me["] so faithfully and constantly, lo, these many years, about "taking more exercise," that I think they must be as tired of the word "exercise" as I myself. But, for once, I believe they would be satisfied; we spend about half of every day taking long walks and drives. You will be interested to learn that this delicious mountain air is doing me a world of good. I have gotten back to my normal weight,—115 pounds;—so am both *fat* and rosy,—in fact I am growing very improvident with those roses—I have of late months been in the habit of wearing them only for *your* benefit, but now I flaunt them all the time.

This climate is assuredly invigorating—just think, I walked *seven* miles on Wed. afternoon, and was'nt even tired!—and yesterday we *climbed* four or five, in search of the "Bridal Veil." Such a scramble I never had! It was delightful. Both times we were with large "walking-parties,"—the most popular amusement here. Yesterday the party consisted of five girls and *seven* young high church clergyman! The atmosphere here is almost *too* pure and elevated for a little heretic like myself to breathe with comfort.

Yes, the session at Sewanee *does* continue all summer, but they have "commencement" in the *middle* of the year—instead of at the end! They had vacation this week, but school begins again on Monday. Indeed, Dr. Gildersleeve's lectures went on without regard to the holidays. I have heard the two which were open to ladies, and liked them exceedingly,—though there was very little in them, after all. He was *so* afraid of getting beyond *our* depth that he scarcely skimmed the surface of his subject. He was constantly informing us that he couldn't do this or the other "because of the nature of my audience." But they were quite charming in their way. We were invited to meet him at "five o'clock tea" on Thursday at the Hodgson's[1]—the Vice' chancellors—liked him very much. He informed me, by the way, that I was "a cousin of his"! through my grandfather, who was also one of his oldest friends. I didn't like to embarrass him by asking him to trace the relation-ship.

Am sorry you are having such gloomy, depressing weather; it rained here too, most of last week, but has been charming for ten-days past,—clear and cool.

But I must not scribble any more now, for it is "after eleven," and besides I started out to write a short letter, and I must do it. And then too I must leave room for Mr. McRae's document. He came to me today for your address—he wants to write to you, because he thinks you "ought to know how things are going here"! I told him that if he wished I would save him trouble, by enclosing his note. So he will have ready for me—and you,—tomorrow, "a detailed account of all my flirtations"![2]

Love to all the household. Remember darling that whatever there may be without to amuse or divert, deep down in her heart of hearts your little love thinks *ever* of *you.*

Your own Eileen.

So you got into mischief up at Bingham's, and left desolation in your track! Poor girls! You "must'nt make it too hard for them"! I have no doubt they are very nice girls especially if they resemble their mother. I have heard all about her, from some one who *ought* to know her—if he don't—her husband. I remember his keeping me—and I fear the other occupants of a sleeping-car,—awake until twelve o'clock one night, while he raved about her, and gave me all the details of his love story. He thought her the "ideal woman"; and then he delivered to me, in full, a lecture which he had lately prepared on that time-honoured subject. It was very entertaining. And by-the-way he was to send me the manuscript, to "criticise"—but it never came!

ALS (WP, DLC).

1 The Rev. Dr. Telfair Hodgson, former rector of Trinity Church, Hoboken, N.J., elected Dean of the Theological Department, University of the South, in 1879 and Vice-Chancellor and Executive Head of the University in 1880.

2 As will appear in ELA to WW, Sept. 1, 1884, Jack McRae never wrote his letter to Wilson.

To Ellen Louise Axson

My own darling,   Wilmington [N.C.], Aug. 10th/84

I conclude from what you say in your letter of the 4th, about your plans as to the length of your stay at Sewanee, that this is about the last letter I should address to you there: so that I must wait until I learn to whose care I should consign letters addressed to Gainesville. The schedule of mails at "the mountain" must have resulted in a rather ridiculous grouping of the epistles I have sent thither. If they reached you in pairs, their arrival must have illustrated very forcibly the one-sided arrangement which has so often made me secretly heart-sick, in spite of the fact that I was writing out of the fulness of my heart—not because I was constrained by a promise but because I was constrained by love— the arrangement whereby I have been writing three letters to your one. Of course I have all along understood perfectly the circumstances which made it altogether proper and equitable that I indulge my darling in that way and I have done it gladly—indeed I don't know that I *could* have written less frequently if I had tried; but my delight in writing to my precious little sweetheart has not made the intervals between her letters seem any shorter: I believe that it has, on the contrary, made them seem longer. When one is pouring his heart out into the ears of one whom he loves, the fact that he can explain and excuse tardy and infrequent reciprocations does not make the delays any the less distressing and hard to bear. And so with the letter-writing: my heart has never had even a thought of rebellion against its mistress because of the short diet of love-messages upon which she felt obliged to keep it, but it has, nevertheless, had many an ache and many a downcast mood because of its apparently barren expenditure of its overmastering affection for that same irresistible little mistress, whose tyranny was so sweet to bear even when felt the most. Then, too, I have sometimes had a shrewd suspicion, little lady, that *maybe*, if the number of letters you were to receive depended on the number of letters you wrote, you would find odd moments, before unnoticed, turning up in which just a little message from your heart, if not a big letter, might be written to somebody. I don't believe in "*counting*" letters: that's ungracious and ungenerous, and I *could'nt* do it if I would: but neither do I believe in a plan which will permit one to *count on* unearned letters, because, whatever may be the reason for such a plan, it must make one of the correspondents unhappy quite independently of good reason. After all, it does seem as if an interchange of letters—letter answering letter—were the best arrangement for those whose hearts wait on each other's expressions of love—who can live apart from each other only because they may have constant assurance of each other's welfare and affection. Of course you understand me well enough, my darling, to know that this is nothing like a *complaint*: it is only a candid confession, such as I felt I ought to make, of the conclusions which have been forced upon me by the fact that I have for some time past, quite in the teeth of my natural disposition, been subject to an extraordinary depression of spirits, which would give place always to my usual light-heartedness whenever your letters came, but return as the week lengthened which was to bring another letter. I have been quite ashamed of the weakness, but I could not wink the cause, and I am fully satisfied that the cause was a very adequate one; for, ever since I became acquainted with a certain little maiden, I have been absolutely dependent upon her for supplies of good spirits—I have been listening for words of love from her, and have been depressed when they were withheld.

Indeed, it's scandalous, Miss, that you should so monopolize the thoughts of a youth who pretends to be busy with very great subjects quite remote from love. You carry his thoughts about with you from place to place in the most arbitrary manner imaginable, and how is he to command his forces for the completion of solemnly philosophical essays on questions of practical politics. True, No. 5, on the Executive, is (reckoning according to the number of topics proposed to be discussed under its rather broad roof) a little more than half done, and this week will probably see its first draft completed; but then might it not have been finished *now* if you had'nt been jealous of the two hours *per* day which it has been claiming. Ah! my little queen, I wonder if the goods monopolized ever rejoiced so in the power of the monopolist as my love has rejoiced in being engrossed, to the ousting of all other images—womanly or other—by you, its life and its joy! I *almost* make a goose of myself—can you believe it?—whenever I think of the precious maiden who loves me. My heart has been waiting for her ever since it could wait for anybody, and now she has come and is mine!

So the coming of Miss Rose's birthday again reminded you of

your very advanced age, did it? Well, that must be accounted a very grave drawback to an otherwise joyous occasion; for I hold it a great mistake for people of declining years to dwell too much upon the past. In my own case, for instance, how depressing to look back upon the spent pleasures of a stretch of years even more terrible for length than those dread twenty-four! Still, we should reflect, reverend madam, that there are yet, probably, several years left us, and that the experiences of the past have been meant to serve as lamps to our feet.

But, seriously, my darling, there are not many people who have been blessed with such cloudless, unbroken friendships as yours: and I can conceive of nothing more beautiful or enviable than such memories as must cluster around that delightful eighteen-years companionship with Miss Rose. Such things seem to me to furnish notable proof that *maybe* you are both well worth loving. I am ready to believe that "Mac." is as far from having made a mistake as I am, though I am glad beyond all expression (don't tell Miss Rose this part) that our risks have been adjusted, and our investments of fortune made, as they have been.

I had a very pleasant surprise last night in the shape of a call from one of my Johns Hopkins Glee-Club-mates—not the livliest and most enjoyable member of the crowd, nor the one I was most intimately associated with, but a very clever, likeable fellow of cordial feelings and an interesting ballast of sense, though rather too eager to seem to know more than the rest of mankind. He was passing through only, on what would seem to be a rather unseasonable visit to Florida, so that I got only a glimpse of him.

I am not surprised that you did not admire Dr. Gildersleeve's presentation speech, for that is *not* his forte. Nothing that requires ease and grace is attainable by Prof. G.; but he is strong in knowledge and in enthusiasm in the pursuit of his own special branches, as well as in the study of good literature, in whatever shape or language found, and I am quite sure that you must have been rewarded in attending his lectures on Homer—provided his manner did not distract you. He is unquestionably a great scholar, but I do not know that he has ever been seriously accused of being a great lecturer: though his style is, in whatever he has published, strong in the best and purest English idioms. His command of *language* is undoubted; but a command of language does not always or necessarily give one the command of an audience—who must be approached through their *ears*.

I am surprised that so dignified a man as Professor Gildersleeve should have gone through all those rather grotesque cere-

monies for the sake of a degree from an institution less celebrated and widely-known than himself.

Father leaves for Saratoga to-morrow morning, to be gone five
Sabbaths.

Be sure to write me as soon as possible, my darling, about
your movements, your Gainesville address, &c. I shall be very
anxious to hear.

I am sincerely glad for Miss Rose's sake, and for yours, that
you extended your visit to her—tho.' if the week you give her is
to be subtracted from the September visit, I know somebody
whose disappointment will be more poignant than even Miss
Rose could have felt. It was very sweet of her—and quite like her,
as I have learned to know her—to admit my plea as readily as
she did: for I know as well as she can what it is to give you up
after having been with you, and it *is* hard, *very* hard, that she
should be cut off with so short a visit. But what would become of
me, if you were to give her the two months promised!

Little lady, you wont linger many days after the first of September, will you? Remember next year's work in Baltimore, and
how much you can add to it by every day of your stay here! Will
those days add anything to anybody's work at the League? If so,
the sooner you come the better.

Love to Miss Rose and "Mac." Mother and father send best
love; and I have simply no heart for anybody else but you, my
own Eileen. I shall not be quite happy until all your visits may
be made in the company of　　　　Your own　Woodrow.

ALS (WC, NjP).

From Ellen Louise Axson

My darling Woodrow,　　　　Sewanee [Tenn.] Aug 11, 1884.

I have been thinking of you very constantly all this afternoon,
and wishing—ah, *how* much!—that you were with us;—that would
have been the one thing necessary to complete my satisfaction,
for we have been having what I call a "real good time,"—just the
sort of "time" that I enjoy most of all. The day was *so* delicious
that we felt as though we couldn't spend *any* of it indoors. So
early in the afternoon, Rose and I betook ourselves to "Morgan
Steep," where we remained until sunset, reading "Aurora Leigh,"
embroidering, and "drinking it in." Would you like to have been
there? Or does the idea of "Aurora" make you feel "*tired*"?
Though of course we wouldn't have subjected *you* to such an infliction. Morgan Steep is one of the most charming "points" about

Sewanee, and the road to it is *lovely*. It is a mass of granite capping a precipice almost as bold as that at Lookout, and commanding a glorious view of valley and mountains. It is surrounded on all sides with the lovliest little nooks and dells—"shady coverts"—'gainst the ["] hot season,"—and far down at the base of the precipice, but quite accessible, is one of the wildest and most picturesque of those ravines in which Sewanee so abounds. Altogether an ideal spot. We had planned to *live* there and at Proctor's Hall, this summer; but there is always so much a'-doing, that, so far from carrying out that scheme, this is the first time we have even visited it. But now that the exhibitions are all over, and things at the University have quieted down, I hope we will have more time. Those "exhibitions" were not as interesting as they might have been, because the standard among the speakers is so wretchedly low. I believe I was more pleased with the "games" than any of the rest of it,—the prize contests in running, vaulting, throwing &c. I had never seen anything of the sort before, and it seemed marvellous to me to see people springing nine feet into the air;—and apparently without effort too;—some of the boys seemed to fly over like birds. These games are a new feature here; they were introduced by "the Prodigy," who himself takes part in some of them. I think that is one reason for the hero-worship of which he is the object among the boys. He certainly has wonderful influence over them, and he uses it well, I think. It is wonderful that the poor man isn't altogether *unbearable* with so many people conspiring to ruin him. The boys, as I said, worship at his shrine because he is such a "good fellow," the old men because he is "a brilliant fellow—fine scholar—rising man—splendid preacher—sure to be a Bishop"!!—and the girls for some *inscrutable* reason, probably his "conversation"—which *is* rather extraordinary, by-the-way. Sir, how *dare* you intimate that *I* was in any danger from "his Reverence," or that I apprehended any danger? No, I assure you that the feeling with which I first beheld him was not one of "releif," on my own account, but of surprise on other people's; for I certainly didn't expect to find in this all-conquering hero a realization of those waggish, frolicing young priests, who figure so conspicuously in modern French pictures. Though, to do him justice, there is no lack of earnestness about him when one knows him better, he is not what I should have imagined the feminine ideal, even among high-church damsels. But he seems to have been the centre of innumerable matrimonial schemes. At present, all the old ladies are trying to marry him to a Baltimore girl, Miss Pullain, who is spending the summer here. She is a lovely woman, and I should think they would succeed. But Mr. Gailor, with all his Irish impulsiveness has been wonderfully discreet. He has not only "never been in love," but, stranger still, he has never been *suspected* or *accused* of being in love. So that now he has the reputation of being a hardened wretch—either utterly heartless or "wedded to his books." But I think I have given you quite a sufficient dose of Sewanee gossip,—have no doubt you are ready to cry for mercy.

How *can* you call such an interesting letter as that last of yours "prolix" or "stupid"! The *word*—and your use of it—were certainly the *only stupid* things about it! Don't you *know* my darling, that, more than anything else, I enjoy hearing of what interests you, —that I want to know the things that fill your *mind* as well as heart,—in short that I have, like yourself, a curiosity to know "what you are thinking about"! I would have been rather glad to occupy the place of one of those "silly girls," and listen to that fine speech. That is one thing for which I envy men very often,— their opportunities for hearing good speaking,—their monopoly —almost—of that most thrilling and exciting of pleasures. I am glad they let us go to church at least! The world will indeed be turned upside down, and human nature itself will be changed when "editorials" will be able to contend against the magic of the voice. Editors, charm they never so wisely, can't make our hearts burn within like the true master of assemblys.

But I must make haste to close, because this is the morning for Dr Gildersleeve's address on "Sappho," and as I have a chance, for once in a way, to hear a "speech," I must be prompt to embrace it. I am closing this, as you see, in the morning as I was kept up late last night by visitors, and my letter would not, in any event, leave before tomorrow. Mr. McRae hasn't yet prepared that report of his, for me to enclose. Am sorry if I have unwittingly excited in you a curiosity, which I will be unable to satisfy—Mr. McRae being the only person in the world who knows anything about the "flirtations" in question. You can direct this week's letters to Sewanee, and after that send them to the care of Mr. *W. A Brown* Gainsville, Ga. I *will* leave on next Monday, whatever the consequences. I never had such a struggle to get away from a place. I am afraid my friends here don't speed the parting guest. Goodbye, dear heart, let me tell you a secret,—"the more I see of other men—nowadays the more vividly do I realize the fact that you are the only man in the world that I can love" and also that I *do* love you from the bottom of my heart.

As ever   Your own Eileen.

ALS (WP, DLC).

A Fragment of a Ditty

[c. Aug. 12, 1884]

4   We get our learning served in bits
    Of German literature
    With now and then an Eng word
    Our ears to reassure.

5   Oh we don't care a wee bit oath
    For other colleges
    They don't know what true flourish is
    They're mere apologies.

6   But now you'll think that we're stuck up
    Because we go to Johns
    Hopkins where we can get the latest kinks
    To obfuscate the dons.

7. But then you see we're too polite
    To tell you all we know
    We'll just throw out a hint or two
    And give you time to grow.

8   Now don't you feel a little proud
    Within your secret heart
    That you may live in Baltimore
    With us to take a part

9. As for ourselves we're very glad
    To bring you to the light
    And after giving you this treat—
    To bow and say good-night.

Encore:

Oh please don't make us sing again
The song that we've just sung
For if the office found us out
We'd certainly be hung

Be kind enough to keep it dark
That we've told you anything
But what the sucking baby knows
And trusting angels sing.

WWhw in pocket notebook described at May 16, 1884. On the next page of this notebook, WW jotted the following: "You did'nt know, brer Rabbit, that I was a 'pote,' did you? I wrote last evening a 'pōme' of 15, 4-line stanzas! Think of it! I do not despair, however, altogether of my sanity."

To Ellen Louise Axson

My precious Ellie,   Wilmington [N.C.], Aug. 13th/84

You have'nt told me what your Gainesville address is to be, and it's too late to send another letter to Sewanee, but I *must* answer the sweet letter I received this morning without delay, so I have hunted up what *was* to have been your Gainesville address last summer and am going to venture this to the care of Mr. Warren A. Brown.

Yes, my darling, I *do know* that you love me with all your heart and that you are, consequently, thinking about me all the time. If I doubted that, I don't know what would become of me! It is'nt that, it is'nt doubts—as I said in my last—that make it so hard for me, in spite of will and heart to be unselfish, to do without letters from you as frequent as my letters to you. As I said then, so I say again, that it's only a trial of myself and never a doubt of you that has convinced me that I had better not write so many times oftener than you do. I have understood the 'must' in your case *perfectly*—I would'nt have asked my darling to do otherwise than she has done. I love and trust her with all my heart and am *sure* that she would make any sacrifice for me. But the fact still remains that, writing, as I do whenever I write to you, with my whole heart aglow, I can't help longing for and half expecting a reply, though I *know* that none is coming. I don't know that I can make you see what I mean: but it has been impressed upon me by the stern fact of continued low spirits. There are *some* things, however, which I *can* tell you without obscurity; as, for instance, that I *delight* in writing to my darling, never having *grudged* a single line I've written, and that her love-letters have been and are precious beyond measure to me!

> "Warmed by her hand and shadowed by her hair
>   As close she leaned and poured her heart through thee,
>   Whereof the articulate throbs accompany
>   The smooth black stream that makes thy whiteness fair,—
>   Sweet fluttering sheet, even of her breath aware,—
>   Oh let thy silent song disclose to me
>   That soul wherewith her lips and eyes agree
>   Like married music in Love's answering air.

> "Fain had I watched her when, at some fond thought,
>   Her bosom to the writing closlier pressed,
>   And her breast's secrets peered into her breast;
>   When, through eyes raised an instant, her soul sought

My soul, and from the sudden confluence caught
The words that made her love the lovliest."

.   .   .   .

"Thou lovely and beloved, thou my love;
  Whose kiss seems still the first; whose summoning eyes,
  Even now, as for our love-world's new sunrise,
  Shed very dawn; whose voice, attuned above
  All modulation of the deep-bowered dove,
  Is like a hand laid softly on the soul;
  Whose hand is like a sweet voice to control
  Those worn tired brows it hath the keeping of:—

"What word can answer to thy word,—what gaze
  To thine, which now absorbs within its sphere
  My worshipping face, till I am mirrored there
  Light-circled in a heaven of deep-drawn rays?
  What clasp, what kiss mine inmost heart can prove,
  O lovely and beloved, O my love?"[1]

I am so glad to know, my pet, that your stay at Sewanee was so full of the delights, not only of the companionships you love, but also of the scenery and the exercise you love—rambles to lovely nooks and invigorating climbs amidst wild surroundings—as well as amidst the *mild* surroundings, quite out of keeping with nature, of youthful high-church divines! And it *is* good news indeed that you have been getting both "*fat* and rosy." You mus'nt dare, Miss, to put in your appearance here on the first of September with the humiliating confession that you went to Gainesville to *work*, and so to lose both flesh and colour. We'll guarantee to keep you in both here, even if Wilmington *is* a dull, uninteresting place. I have understood that a certain young lady loves the water almost, if not quite, as much as she loves the mountains and valleys: and we can take her on the water here to her heart's content.

What became of Mr. McRae's letter with its account of "all your flirtations"? Were you frightened into destroying it after receiving it to be enclosed in yours. The fact that you offered to be the sender of it was very reassuring, but is not the fact that it is missing and you do not attempt to account for its non-appearance a very suspicious one? Or did Mr. McRae repent? I beg that you will explain: because you can easily conceive what my state of mind must be!

I can almost imagine that I heard that lecture of Dr. Gildersleeve's with its considerate references to "the character of his audience." You unquestionably heard the real and only Dr. G. He always treats a mixed audience just that way, if I am to judge from the occasions when I was mixed with one under his ministrations. He tantalizes such a gathering—quite as capable, often, of intellectual enjoyment as the special students for whom he presumably reserves his unreserved utterances—with glimpses of the pleasure and entertainment he *might* give them—an he would.

What do the original people at Sewanee "commence" in the middle of their term?

Father left on Monday last, as he expected to do, for Saratoga, and will be back again in season to see you before we start north to our "schooling."

Dear mother sends you a heartful of love, my darling. As for myself, I continue to love and *need* you more and more every day. Without you and your sweet love, the world would be drear and desolate for   Your own   Woodrow.

ALS (WC, NjP).
¹ Dante Gabriel Rossetti, *The House of Life*, sonnets, "The Love-letter," and "Mid-rapture."

From Ellen Louise Axson

My darling Woodrow,   Sewanee [Tenn.] Aug. 15 1884.

I have been on a picnic today at Keith's Palisades, eleven miles up the road, and am therefore, at this present writing, exceedingly sleepy and stupid,—so much so indeed, that I doubt if you will be able either to read or comprehend what I *do* write. But it is Friday night—your last, reached me Wed. night, and I can delay no longer sending a few lines, at least, in answer to it—though indeed *my* last, though sent before it's arrival, was, almost, a sufficient reply. I am very, *very* sorry that I have been the means of rendering my darling in any degree "unhappy" or "depressed." Though indeed, as I look back, I scarcely see how I *could* have behaved better. I assure you my trouble was want of opportunity, not want of will. How often have I felt almost irresistibly tempted to write, but have denied myself because I thought it was my *duty*! Even if I cared to try, it would be impossible for me to make you understand, dear, the great and constant pressure which I have been under for many months. I have been obliged to count every minute,—I dare say you would laugh as much as Aunt Ella or Agnes if you knew anything of my endless elaborate contrivances for saving time, for "working things in" or for making them dove-tail each other, so that there may be no waste minutes between. Of course, my difficulties and embarrassments have, all along, been rendered many times greater by the fact that I was a "visitor"—*obliged* to perform, with as good a grace as possible, the "social duties" which that position involves, subjected to all sorts of interruptions both from within (the family) and without,—and, in short, preyed upon by endless circumstances over which I had no control. I have been literally *forced* to write all my letters, to everyone, late at night,—and I am sure that, from my heart, I pity the recipients of those epistles, which, with tired hand and head, I pen at those uncanny hours. What wonder that regard for them, even more than for myself, disposes me to reduce their number to a minimum;—though when *every* letter that I write means another night's sleep curtailed of its fair proportions, regard for myself has a good deal to do with it too!

But it is after eleven now, by the way,—and besides I think I have perhaps dwelt enough on the subject. I wish I could close the discussion by solemnly promising to do better in the future; but I fear I can't even do that. It is a sin, you know, to promise where you are not *sure* you can perform, so I will only say that I will *try* to do better—I will do the best I can! It is not only many a day since "old Leisure died," for me, but, at present, there are no signs of a resurrection; indeed I doubt if I ever see his face again. Though, to be frank, my acquaintance with him was always so slight, owing partly to to [*sic*] circumstances, and partly to my disposition, that he might very easily pass by without my knowledge.

I wish you could have been with us today, on this the last and best of our mountain excursions. We had a glorious day, in every respect. We went in a hack first to Monteagle, the watering-place eight miles from here, where is situated the Southern "Chatauqua." The assembly grounds are very attractive, and the thing is much more throughly organized than I had supposed. We went principally to hear an oration on "Burns" by Mr. Wallace Bruce, (!) a lecturer whose fame has reached Sewanee. If there is anything in a name his treatment of Scotch subjects ought to be *sympathetic*, at least,—and so it was. The address was by no means remarkable, but it was a very graceful eulogy on Burns, varied by numerous charmingly rendered extracts from his poems. After leaving Monteagle, we went on to "Fairmount[,]" the "church-school" which is for the girls what Sewanee is for the boys of the "low country"; and after that we drove three miles farther to "Keith's Palisades,["] where we took our dinner. This place is the most famous of all on the mountain; and though somewhat inaccessible from Sewanee, it is fully worth a day's journey. I won't, —at this hour especially—attempt a description of that great stronghold of nature;—indeed it is *indescribable*. It was the grandest place I had ever seen, not even excepting the "Notch" in the Franconia mountains. I believe I gave you my schedule for the next week or so in my last. I still expect to leave for Gainsville on Mon. Give much love to your mother. Rose sends hers to you —indeed she *always* does. And remember, dear, that I love you, love you, *love* you with *all my heart*.   Your own Ellie.

Rose says tell you she "does *wish* you had been with us today,["] and you *must* come to Swanee "*next* summer." I won't write next Monday night because I will be on a "sleeper," but will write as soon as I can.

ALS (WP, DLC).

Two Letters to Ellen Louise Axson

My own darling,   Wilmington [N.C.], Aug. 16th/84

I was *too* smart by half—was'nt I?—in taking if [*sic*] for granted that you would literally add but one week to your stay in Sewanee and upon strength of that conclusion beginning to address my letters to Gainsville ahead of time? Calculating that your departure would be on a Thursday, and suspecting that you would cheat yourself of several letters by not letting me know what your Gainsville address would be until you should be upon the very eve of that departure, I turned to a very graceful epistle beginning "Dear Mr. Wilson" (how long ago seems the time when that was written!) which said that letters sent to you at Gainsville to the care of Mr. Warren A Brown would reach you; but whose P.S. explained that the contemplated visit must await the event of your cousin's relapse; and determined to prove my great sagacity by being before-hand with the aforesaid instructions, that you might be glad to see a letter already come for you when you reached your destination![1] But vaulting ambition again oe'rleaped itself, and I succeeded only in cheating you of a letter which *should* have found you in Sewanee. For *this* letter, I take it, *would* miss you if it sought you there—unless I have miscalculated the connections of the irritating "mountain" mails—and so I send it with a clear conscience to join its waiting predecessor in the hands of Mr. Brown. I am the more chagrined at my so clever mistake because it caused a seeming silence to follow significantly upon that last letter I sent to Sewanee, in which I must have seemed, when interpreted by the silence ensuing, to repudiate finally the existing arrangement as to our correspondence. No! my darling, I have no real fear of having been so misunderstood by you! If you can't understand me, who can? I know that you read what I write in love as pure and unquestioning as that in which it was written. If I can't talk with absolute freedom and frankness to you, I will seal my lips to everybody! I am only afraid that you did not at the time understand why no letters came after Wednesday, and that you were made a little anxious by my clever anticipation of facts.

Dear mother and I have been leading an exceedingly quiet life since father left on last Monday—except that she has undertaken some rather extensive house cleaning, of which her housewifely habits were cheated last summer because of her illness and her absence from home. For the matter of that, though, our life was quiet enough before father left—except that his ever-active mind keeps the minds of those about him alive with all sorts of interests which they would not of themselves be likely to hit upon, and astir with all sorts of topics which it needs a mind like his to suggest. He makes me his *intellectual* companion when I am at home, and the life he stirs up in my brain is worth a whole year's course at "the Hopkins." Without him, therefore, our life is *narrower*, rather than quieter: and you may guess, from what I have said, why it is that we miss him as grievously as we do.

When are you coming to us, my darling? You have not named any definite time yet and I am miserably uneasy about any possible postponement of your coming that you may be planning. The time is too precious to make me willing to lose a single day of September: and I shall be cruelly disappointed if you are planning to make your visit here a short one—shorter than four weeks. I dare'nt think of the possibility of that!

My present diversion is dentistry—not practicing it, but being practiced upon by it! I have had so much work of the kind done in my head, at one time and another, that I had supposed myself hardened to its most ingenious tortures; but I find that there are some things to wh. one cannot become accustomed, encounter them as he may. He can bear them, but he cannot *grin* and bear them.

Do you know, little lady, I am inclined to think from what you say of Mr. Gailor in your last letter (and I may remark, parenthetically, that you devote a little more than one-fourth of that letter to the discussion of that gentleman!) that he is a much finer and more interesting man than you were at first disposed to allow, while suffering from the effects of your disappointment in the matter of his personal appearance, and that he is, if not within half an hour, at least within half a fortnight of the handsomest man in the world. Above all else I like what you say about his earnestness. If he is earnest *and* open-minded—ready to receive the truth—nay eager to search it out—and quick and courageous to declare it, he is a man made to succeed, and deserving of success, in anything. I should like to meet him. I could enjoy him: because as a man who does not shine in conversation, I should not be at all nervous about being *out*shone.

Yes indeed! I *should* have liked more than I can say to be on "Morgan's Steep" that Monday afternoon: but I should have liked best to be there *unobserved*, to see and hear those sweet maidens who sat there bent on occupation which it would have been a shame to interrupt—a selfish wish, I allow, because one of those maidens wanted me, but a self-sacrificing wish after all, because by being unseen I should have missed the smile that makes me glad—and the love-light from my Eileen's eyes. But, whether sefishly or not, I have a strong desire to be with her and feast my eyes upon her when she does not know of my presence—and especially when she is in such companionship as that which she was rejoicing in on "Morgan's Steep." The only thing is, that, were I to see her as she would certainly appear then, I fear I should not be able to keep in hiding long—for force of something that would impel me to—to announce myself.

I have just finished reading aloud to dear mother the portion of "Lorna Doone" which I read to you in East Rome, so that when you come I can read the rest of it aloud to both of you, if that be agreeable. Have you forgotten yet the part you heard? I never knew dear mother so delighted with a story. Of late years she has grown very weary of novels, and only the best and the most unusual can enlist her interest; but "Lorna Doone" has quite captivated her. Certainly there are very few novels any part of which I could get my own consent to read three times: but each time I read "Lorna Doone" I am charmed anew by some beauty before unseen.

Did you ever read or hear of a comical romance called "Vice Versa"? Introduced to Mr. F. Anstey through that remarkable production, I liked him well enough to venture upon the perusal of his later "Giant's Robe,"[2] and now, being in the midst of the book, I am half glad, half sorry that I ever commenced it. That it is powerful in plot and style and absorbingly interesting only

brings home the nearer to one's heart the pain of its tragic incidents. It is full of that which is infinitely worse than the tragedy
of murder and blood-shed, the tragedy of fraud and of misplaced
love and trust; and I nowadays read so few novels that this one
has affected me most potently, even to the troubling of my
dreams. It is much too well done. It don't seem like a fiction.

I have taken to novel reading as the invalid takes to a tonic.
It is as nearly the opposite intellectual employment to that upon
which I have been engaged in writing my essays as I can hit
upon and so affords me the best rest and diversion. My mind has
for the last six or eight weeks been so constantly a-stretch, without relaxation, concerning the subjects of my essays that the
work was beginning to tell upon me: hence the antidote. You love
to hear "what I am thinking about"—do you, my little enchantress? But, besides yourself, I think chiefly about these dry constitutional matters with which my work deals: you would'nt like
to have a letter full of them, would you?

Dear mother sends warmest love and is getting very impatient
to see you. I love you with all my heart, my precious Eileen.

Your own   Woodrow.

ALS (WP, DLC).
  ¹ ELA to WW, July 31, 1883, Vol. 2.
  ² F. Anstey [Thomas Anstey Guthrie], *Vice Versa, or A Lesson to Fathers* (New York, 1882), and *The Giant's Robe* (New York, 1881).

My own darling,   Wilmington [N.C.], Aug. 20th/84
I received your letter of Friday (the 15th) this morning. The
"mountain" mails had kept it until it masqueraded as a Monday
letter.

I am sorry that you put yourself to such pains to explain and
apologize in answer to what I had said about our correspondence.
I hoped that I had made it plain that I was speaking for myself,
not *against you*. I trust you and believe in your love for me too
entirely to fear that you will ever be wilfully remiss towards me.
I was simply confessing, not exacting.

I find myself exceedingly tired to-night. For the past three days
I have been hard at work helping dear mother in the most fatiguing of all manual labour, the labour of house-renovating; so
that I have fairly earned the right of being stupid even beyond
my wont. My only excuse for undertaking letter-writing while in
such a plight is that I shall probably have no time for it to-morrow.

I went this afternoon to consult a friend of ours who is high
authority in rail-road matters as to the best and least expensive

route from Gainesville to Wilmington, my darling, but I left him scarcely any wiser than when I sought him. There are four several routes which might be taken: one through Charlotte, Greensboro, Raleigh, Goldsboro, &c—as quick as any, but long and therefore probably more expensive—; another, through Atlanta, Augusta, Columbia, &c—doubtless the best, if you could make connection in Atlanta with the train that leaves for Augusta in the morning about eight or nine o'clock—; a third, through Greenville, Columbia, &c—about which I know next to nothing—; and, lastly, a fourth, to Charlotte and thence direct to Wilmington by the "Carolina Central." The chief drawback to this last is the terrible road, the "Central," on which you would have to spend the night—safe enough, like most roads not in the direct lines of through travel, but rough and tedious. Still it brings you by what would probably be the shortest way and there are, I learn, comfortable sleepers on which one can lose consciousness of the tedium of a slow ride through a country best traversed in the night. My authority, Mr. Riach, the rail-road friend aforementioned, seemed to think that one could'nt do better in coming from Gainesville than to endure the "Central." You will doubtless get competent advice at your own end of the distance, however, which will make your choice of routes easy: only be sure to let me know beforehand which way you will take, that I may be on hand at the right time and at the right station, to meet the train which is to bring me my darling.

No, Miss, you have *not* told me your programme "for the next week or so"—would that you had: because, as I more than intimated in my last letters, everything depends, for me, upon what that programme may happen to be.

Will you see Stockton in Gainesville? Since Davidson opens on the 11th, I suppose that he will be in Gainesville before the 1st, if he is to be there at all before his vacation is over? If you do see him, give him a great deal of love from me. I hope—and expect—that he will have the most successful of courses at college, and I can wish him no better fortune than to have a class such as will make his four years work with them years of enjoyment such as my jolly classmates made for me. I would esteem it a real compliment if he would write to me from college when he finds time.

Where is Eddie? You have not mentioned the dear youngster since you left Rome. I suppose that he was to join you—or, rather, that he did join you—on your way from Sewanee to Gainesville.

You must not forget to tell me, little sweetheart, about the

Johns Hopkins Seminary Room

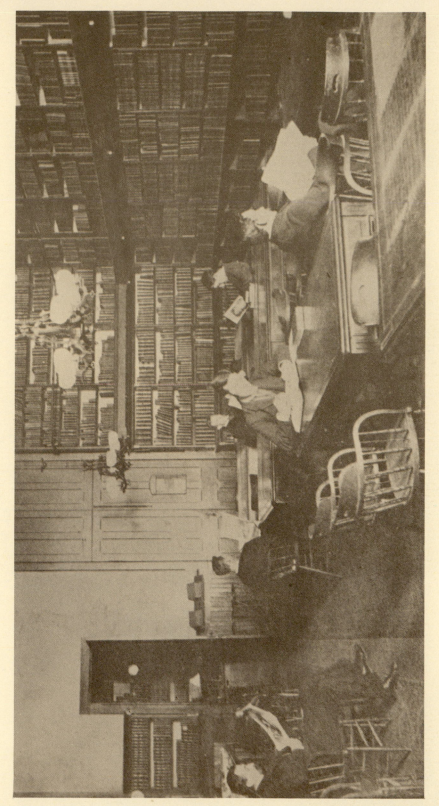

Main Library, Hopkins Hall

The Johns Hopkins Glee Club

Ellen Louise Axson

James W. Bones

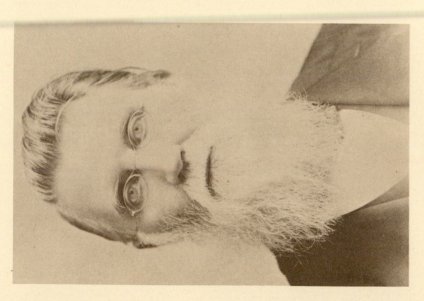

James Woodrow

Richard Theodore Ely

Herbert Baxter Adams

Daniel Coit Gilman

Basil Lanneau Gildersleeve

George Sylvester Morris

John Franklin Jameson

Robert Bridges

Hiram Woods, Jr.

Albert Shaw

Charles Howard Shinn

families you are visiting in Gainesville: for you know I know nothing about them! I have, for instance, not the most remote idea who Mr. Warren A Brown is—or whether you are now visiting the aunt to whom you inadvertently sent the letter you had intended for Miss Rose. You have told me very little about the relationships in that part of the country, and, as those relationships are some day to be mine too, I am naturally anxious to be fortified against any too egregious mistakes into wh. I might be betrayed

But, however near and dear little Maggie [Margaret Axson] and all the rest at G. may be to you, my precious Eileen, I hope that they can't keep you from setting your face in this direction *very* soon.

> "What of the heart without her? Nay, poor heart,
> Of thee what word remains ere speech be still?
> A wayfarer by barren ways and chill,
> Steep ways and weary, without her thou art,
> Where the long cloud, the long wood's counterpart,
> Sheds double[d] darkness up the laboring hill."[1]

Dear mother sends word of a love impatient for your coming. I love you inexpressibly, my darling, and am altogether

Your own   Woodrow.

ALS (WC, NjP).
[1] Rossetti, *The House of Life,* sestet from the sonnet, "Without Her."

From Ellen Louise Axson

My darling Woodrow,   Gainsville [Ga.] Aug. 20/84

You see that I have at last torn myself away from the dear mountain, overcome all the obstacles to my progress, and am safely landed in Gainsville. I reached this interesting village yesterday morning, after a very prosperous journey. I find all the family "well an' doin' well,"—the Grandparents perhaps a *little* more feeble than when I last saw them. But the boys and little Maggie are looking splendidly. She is a perfect little beauty. I think she grows prettier all the time, and I am sure she grows sweeter, and more interesting. She is really a remarkable looking child,—she has the most beautiful mouth I ever saw, with such lovely brown eyes and fair hair; and she has one of the brightest, most expressive faces I ever saw; she reminds me of Ellen. But after all she is'nt half as *good* and sweet as my dear little model boy, Eddie. Dear me! how glad I am to see the child again! I don't know what I will do, all winter, without him. The merry little scamp is so affectionate and tender-hearted, with all his boyish-ness, that I miss him quite as much as if, like Ellen, he were always at my side or in my lap.

I had the pleasure of finding my *cousin* Ed,[1] here too—I thought he had gone long ago. He is Auntie's only son, and the only "big" cousin I have of "the other sex." He is a dear boy,—a very "Hoyt"—Uncle Will all over again—clever, ambitious, warm-hearted, quick-tempered, impulsive! I hav'nt seen him before since he was a college boy. He is now a *very* rising young lawyer of twenty-six, and quite a dashing youth withal. He has a dashing "turn-out" at any rate; he *drove* over from Athens—his home—that he might have the use of it here. The horse is a perfect beauty, and he goes like the wind. It is glorious to ride behind him; we took a drive yesterday afternoon, of course, and again this morning before breakfast. Ed gave up,—he says,—a very charming trip to Ashe-ville &c. which he was to take with a party in order to come here and meet me. So he thinks, I ought to be "very good to him" and "do everything he wishes" to make up; and, of course, I promised I would try; so I began by forcing my self to get up and drive at the heathenish hour of five. But it was delicious after I really waked.

I found your sweet letter of the 16th awaiting me here; the other I did receive at Sewanee after all; it was forwarded, and reached me three or four hours before I left. Many thanks for both. No, dear, I was in no danger of misunderstanding your seeming silence. Your love claims for itself, and makes good too, the right to put it's own constructions on everything. The only motives which we can understand are those which have their origin in love. You don't need for me to tell you, my darling, what your letters have been to me in all these long months that have passed; how they have helped me to bear things—how it has comforted me merely to *expect* them—to know that they were *coming,* always so true to their day. But I would not be unreasonable about them, and above all I don't *want* you to write when it is not a pleasure, but only an effort—a task. So, dearest, write just when and how you will, and only so often as "it seemeth good to you." I promise that while I will be more than glad when they do come I won't complain when they don't. I dare say you are having a quiet time, with those two who, as you tell me, are the "livliest" members of the household away at once. How is Josie getting on at school, by-the-way? Is he as much pleased as he expected to be? Stockton seems to be very much charmed with Josie's picture. I have found him several times studying it intently. His school begins the *thirteenth* of Sept., and my idea is to leave Gainsville for Wilmington with him. I was surprised to find, dear, from this last letter, that you really expected me the *first* of the month. That will be impossible, for many reasons; in the first place I "came to Gainsville to *work*"—I have two or three portraits and ever so many other things to do here; and then, sir, I think it would be bad on your account for me to spend the *whole* month! Hav'nt you been telling me all along how busy you are? And if you waste as much time on me, while I am there, as you propose, just think what an interruption I would be! But I have not *postponed* my visit at all, for I said from the first—in Rome—that I would try and go to N.C. some time between the tenth and fifteenth.

I am *very* glad that your father will return while I am with you, so that I will have the pleasure of seeing him too. We are trying to persuade Grandfather to go on to Saratoga in a week or so; he needs a more decided change than this, and we are sure that is the very place of all others for him. But the journey is trying, especially to Grandmother, and they can't bear separation.

I read that absurd little thing "Vice Versa" while at Sewanee. This later work must be of a very different style, from your account. That was a very lovely poem, by-the-way, in your last,—indeed peculiarly "lovely"! That much abused word is obviously appropriate in this case, at least, for reasons evident on the face of it—it is used so often in the poem itself. Who is the author?

I am *very* sorry to hear that you have been overworking yourself again, and have been obliged to turn to novel-reading *as a tonic*. I *hope* you have not *seriously* overtaxed yourself; the weather is rather too warm for such experiments.

I am sorry to say that Mr. McRae's document was not forthcoming. He was, as he would put it, "too mortal lazy" to get it up. But I will reassure you on the subject. I hav'nt done any serious mischief. The chief cause of complaint against me was that I was sailing under false colours,—in other words that I didn't stamp "engaged" on my forehead. I am *so* glad that *you* consider that a secret to which other men have no right; your convictions serve to strengthen mine, you see! For I myself was foolish enough to feel, at the last, a faint little twinge of conscience on that score! I was'nt at all concerned to find in "his Reverence" a growing tendency toward getting me off in corners, for the purpose of exchanging confidences about Wordsworth and Carlyle, Tennyson and Ruskin, and making long quotations from the same. Nor,—knowing how well able he had proved to protect himself against the other sex,—did I feel any compunctions when he informed me that I have been a *"revelation*! to him"! &c. &c. But it did seem too bad to let him go with me all the way to Cowan—the "Kingston" of Sewanee—and endure with me the inevitable waiting there[.] But then I could'nt push him off the train at the last moment and say, "you must'nt do this, because I am 'engaged' "! But Mr. McRae, now that he has no longer the fear of me before his eyes, will soon tell the secret, and make all right. He has been suffering tortures all this time in his efforts to keep the secret. After all, perhaps my only fault was that I *did not* flirt with him, since all his *friends* agree that "there never was a man who needed more to be taught a lesson"! and that they "would give *anything* to see him fall desperately in love, and 'get the mitten' "![2] He certainly *hasn't* fallen desperately in love, nor has he any "mittens" that I know of. But I must stop, or you will accuse me of devoting the fourth of another letter to the poor "Prodigy." But I *did* do him injustice in my first, and it was only fair that I should atone. All that I said then was true, but it was a very one-sided, superficial view; he *is* an interesting man,—a *very positive* character,—his faults and virtues are equally conspicuous. I paid very little attention to him most of the time, because I didnt like his attitude toward women; but he likes the same books I like, and, with his Irish enthusiasm, he likes them so *intensely,* and talks about them so well, that sometimes I *would* grow interested and all aglow even in spite of myself. But enough! this is *positively* the last time I will mention Mr. G. Give warmest love to your dear mother and believe me dear heart,

Yours always and altogether   Eileen.

ALS (WP, DLC).

    1 Edward Thomas Brown, first cousin of ELA and son of Warren A. and Louisa C. Hoyt Brown. Born near Gainesville, Ga., Jan. 7, 1859. After brief attendance at Davidson College, he studied law privately and was admitted to the Georgia bar in 1878. Practiced in Athens, Ga., and was mayor of the town 1890-92. He later practiced law in Atlanta and Washington. Chairman of the Georgia Democratic State Committee, 1900-1904. Died in Washington, March 10, 1933.
    2 An expression meaning to be dismissed or rejected.

To Ellen Louise Axson

Wilmington [N.C.], Aug. 23/84

It would be very difficult for me to describe exactly, my darling, the sensations with which I read that letter of yours which told me this morning that you were not coming, and had never had any thought of coming, before the middle of September. Of course you had intended to tell me at first, when you formed your plans, that you could not be here before "some time between the tenth and fifteenth"—and doubtless, having thought about the telling, you were persuaded that you had told—but the only mention of a time which your letters have contained was this, in the first letter that *promised* the visit (July 19): "I can't tell exactly when I will reach Wilmington, but I will surely go as soon in Sept. as possible"—and upon that sentence, which was followed by one which spoke of the seeing of the dear grandparents in Gainsvillle in the latter part of August as the only duty likely to cause delay, I have built hopes and plans which I must try now not to recall, but to forget as quickly and completely as may be. It was these hopes and plans, indeed, which kept me so strenuously at work on my writing—till essay No. 5 was completed the other evening. I was pressing myself, even with rather too cruel spurs sometimes, so that my work might be done before the first of September. What did it matter if I *did* drive myself a little too hard now: was I not clearing the way for a whole month of rest and joy which would more than recruit me for the winter's work ahead? So long as I must do without you, hard work is my best recreation and my only complete diversion. It wears me out less than the passionate impatience at separation from you which must come with ease or idleness. So I shall plunge into it again till the middle of Sept. comes, trusting to those cruelly brief last weeks to give me such vacation as may be needed for the months at the Hopkins which must come so soon—though I had intended to spare myself by reserving this concluding essay for the first month of the University term. It wont be so bad, after all! My writing brings you to me in a certain sense, because it is all *consciously* done for you. If these essays, which have all been composed largely for your sake, should be published, the triumph shall belong to your love: and if they should go no further for the present than the University Seminary, the consolation for the fact that the publishers do not see any money in them shall be that your love is independent of success of that sort—that it is for *me* and not for my books! No. 6, then, shall be begun on Monday, and, if you will promise to give your heart to the enterprize by keeping its author and his work constantly in your loving thoughts, it shall be a success beyond all its predecessors!

We were not expecting you to put aside your work to come to us, my darling—I knew too well how devoted, or incorrigible, you were in your attention to your drawing to think of that. We were hoping that you would look upon your coming here as a visit to home-folks, not to strangers, and we had planned giving you a special room which you might use exclusively as a studio. How we were going to fix it up matters not now: but according to a notion of my own which I am sure, Miss, that you would have considered strikingly original. But enough of this! I had made up my mind not to talk about the plans which have been crowding around that fond mistake of mine which has already cost me so much. You will say that the wish was father to the thought and will laugh at me for taking so much for granted—No: I hope you wont laugh at me; and I know that you would not if you could realize what a terribly passionate matter love is with me—how it magnifies little disappointments into ordeals almost tragic and makes contentment absolutely impossible where you are not. It makes me tremble sometimes to recognize the strength of my own passion. What fools those very perspicacious people have been who have judged me by my cold exterior and have imagined my feelings as temperate as my reason. They would be surprised and shocked, doubtless, to see me offer up my life for that which I believe or for her whom I love! It would be *so* hard to believe that they were mistaken!

I am sorry, my little sweetheart, that you thought "Vice Versa" merely "ridiculous." It seemed to me something very different: a very grotesque, extravagant conception, of course, but much too well done to be laughed *at*. One *must* laugh *with* it: it is irresistibly amusing; but do you see no art in it? do you think it unworthy of a serious literary workman? I am anxious to be of your mind in such matters, so that I am quite open to be convinced by you.

You must'nt think, little lady, that I really had any serious objection to your devoting a fourth part of as many letters as you might please to discussing the character of Mr. Gailor. I can see no good reason why you should eschew all further mention of him, if you find him interesting; and I am certainly not at all surprised that his ardent admiration of and brilliant talk about your favourite authors should have repeatedly thawed your dislike for some of his other qualities. I am not at all inclined to be frightened by the fictions Mr. McRae was going to construct because you were attracted by "his Reverence's" ability to talk better than anyone you had met before about *our* best friends. I *believe* in friendships between the sexes; and, though I may claim the liberty of reserving my opinion about the probabilities as to Mr. Gailor's feelings towards a young lady of whose charms I have had some experience, I should be inclined to look upon Mr. McRae's stories of *flirtation* as something quite different from a *joke,* however I might choose to seem to him to receive them. Our love for each other, my darling, is much too sacred a thing to make me tolerant of such impertinences as Mr. McR. pretended to be contemplating. Although I feel free myself, *because* of our perfect confidence in each other, to rally you about the men about whom you speak, and to warn you to beware of the charms of certain "Prodigies," it angers me that anyone else should dare to do so! I have always regarded teasing as of doubtful gentility when ventured by any but one's nearest relatives and dearest intimates: and I am quite sure that some people who have teased me have thought me curt and disagreeable. I enjoy your sweet, coy thrusts, loving you the more for them—and I know that you will not refuse me a kiss because I take this occasion to express my sincere pity for Mr. Gailor—; but that anyone else should *dare* to accuse my own Eileen of flirting, though the accusation be intended only in joke, makes my blood considerably warmer than is his wont! It is playing with that which belongs to our most sacred confidences. I acknowledge that it would be surpassingly silly to manifest *openly* one's resentment against such liberties; because teasing is too easy, and therefore too common amongst those who are capable of no more refined wit, not to be arrogated as a privilege by the merest acquaintances. But one may have one's private opinion, and may protect oneself by an icy exterior which may cool adjacent impertinence. Father may tease me: but not Mrs. Sibley! I am making a poor out at saying what I wanted to say: probably the plainest statement of my meaning is this, that when I cease to trust you I will go and hang myself; and when I cease to resent any jokes which affect our love for each other, I shall have ceased to be my natural self. I was'nt laughing at Mr. McR. when I was cross-examining you as to what had become of the "document."

Ah, my darling, how much I love you! You are in very truth all the world to me. It often seems to me that now, so long as we are awaiting the consummation of our love, I am living in a sort of period of *intermission*, in which I am constrained to be content with the satisfactions of duty done, against the coming of the time when my *love* shall be satisfied, and rewarded for its waiting. Not that the performance of duty is in any sense or degree distasteful. My duty towards my dear parents, for instance, which has kept me so long away from you at a time when vacation and the warmest desires of my heart invited me to go to you, has been very sweet in the performance because of my intense love for them: I *would* not escape *that* duty, if I could! But, all the same, you are infinitely dearer to me than they even (though

I once thought it incredible that I should ever love anyone more than I love them) and nothing short of the *possession* of my darling will ever secure me complete happiness: so that all my work in the meantime must lack that without which it is at best imperfect, your constant presence and sympathy. To win you for my own has been my one inspiring thought ever since I knew you for what you are—even since

"I saw her upon nearer view,
A Spirit, yet a Woman too!
Her household motions light and free,
And steps of virgin-liberty;
A countenance in which did meet
Sweet records, promises as sweet;
A Creature not too bright or good
For human nature's daily food;
For transient sorrows, simple wiles,
Praise, blame, love, kisses, tears, and smiles.

"And now I see with eye serene
The very pulse of the machine;
A Being breathing thoughtful breath,
A traveller between life and death;
The reason firm, the temperate will,
Endurance, foresight, strength, and skill;
A perfect Woman, nobly planned,
To warn, to comfort, and command;
And yet a Spirit still, and bright
With something of angelic light."[1]

And yet of course even now, while my hopes still stop short of their best fulfilment, my student's "pensive citadel" is no *prison* to me. Dear mother seems to think, or fear, that it *is*, sometimes when her anxious eye detects lines a little too rigid or too indicative of fatigue in my face, and tries to drag me away from my writing, apprehending, apparently, that too much thinking will suit ill with my digestion. She is inclined to say (will you think it sacrilege if I change and appropriate the lines?)

"Why, Woodrow, all your spirits flown,
Thus for the length of half a day,
Why, Woodrow, sit you thus alone,
And dream your time away?

"Where are your books?—that light bequeathed
To Beings else forlorn and blind!

Up! up! and drink the spirit breathed
From dead men to their kind."[2]

It was in the spirit of some such advice from the sweet lady
who watches over me so tenderly, that I undertook to turn aside
for the sake of the tonic of novel reading—though I cannot claim
that novels contain exactly the sort of spirit which Wordsworth
meant.

But I had no idea, when I sat down to this letter, of inflicting
so tedious an epistle upon my sweet Eileen. I have been writing
on and on for my own indulgence, not too regardful of your comfort,—somewhat in the temper of "Cousin Ed." who would have
you do whatever he wishes to make up for what he gave up for
your sake. Suffering under a keen disappointment, of which you
have been the innocent cause, I am inclined to be quite ruthless
in compelling you to read an interminable effusion in which I
try to work my way back to good spirits by dint of talking to you
about myself. I hope that the circumstances will so soften your
heart as to make endurance somewhat less difficult! May-be you
will be disposed to draw this moral from the length of this letter:
that this is what comes of my not writing at stated times as I
used to. I let my feelings &c. *accumulate*, so to speak, until by
very reason of having been pent up so long they sport themselves
beyond all bounds of moderation when finally they are let out.
By-the-way, Miss, how did you ever get the notion into your head
that it could ever be a "*task*" for me to write a letter to you? From
the fact that some of my letters have been so stupid that they
must have been perfunctorily written? You certainly could not
have gotten it legitimately from anything I ever said—unless I
have unconsciously fallen to misrepresenting myself. The truth
is that the only hard thing about it is to keep *from* writing whenever an hour of leisure invites me to send you word of the love
which is constantly springing up anew in my heart. Why I have
ever declined such invitations is a psychological phenomenon
which I have failed to make intelligible to you, but which (and
I'm sure my darling knows this) has no denial of love in it!

I can readily believe that little Maggie is as beautiful and as
attractive as you say, my pet. Is there no tradition that you looked
much the same way when you were a baby—the first time I fell
in love with you?[3] I would give a great deal to see her as she is
now. Is she entirely given away—deeded in fee simple—so that
there is no chance of her ever coming to live with us one of these
days, when we shall have a place to live ourselves? Give Eddie

a great deal of love from me, my darling. I am *so* sorry that you must give him up for the winter! I am glad that Stockton is with you—and will be with you so long—though I must be forgiven for envying him the happiness!

Give my warmest love to Dr. and Mrs. Axson (and dear mother's too) and my sincere regards to the rest of the family ("Cousin Ed." included) if they will allow you so to introduce me, and keep for yourself the unbounded love of

Your own　Woodrow.

The poetry about which you ask—that which I quoted and you admired—is by Rossetti. W.

ALS (WP, DLC).
¹ From Wordsworth's "She Was a Phantom of Delight."
² Adapted by WW from Wordsworth's "Expostulation and Reply."
³ There was a story in the Wilson family that Woodrow, as a boy of seven in Augusta, had held baby Ellen in his arms during a visit between the Wilsons and the Axsons.

From Ellen Louise Axson

My darling Woodrow,　　　　　　Gainsville [Ga.] Aug. 25/84

I have managed to slip away, in order to write to you while that demoralized family below stairs, from Uncle Warren down to Maggie, is in a state of uproar over some primitive game of cards. It is truly shocking to see those tender feet so early led astray, but never-the-less, there is Maggie, dancing about as wild with delight as Eddie, because "Uncle Warren is an 'old maid' "! —a transformation which I had supposed would affect all right-minded persons most painfully. But I fear these youngsters are of as depraved a disposition as the precocious villain in "Vice Versa,"—as much inclined to gloat over the downfall of their elders; even when the "elder" in question is their own dear old play-fellow,—"Nuty." And, by-the way you wanted to know something about "Uncle Warren" and the rest. Yes, he is "Auntie's" husband;—a dear, kind, soft-hearted man,—one whose character may be as briefly described as Richter's,¹ for he too "loves God and little children." Auntie is Mama's only sister,—the one for whose sake I was given my middle name. She is a very noble woman—indeed her goodness is something phenomenal; and she is as wise and kind as she is good. I wish you knew her. She has two splendid girls. Loula, two years younger than I, and Minnie who is Stockton's age. They are two of the nicest girls I ever knew; indeed their list of virtues and accomplishments is almost too long to begin upon now. I will tell you all about them when

I see you. Ed, of whom I believe I spoke in my last, is her only son. I wish you could meet him too—he is *wild* to meet you. How delightful it would be if you were only here to go with us to Tallulah [Falls] this week! Have you ever been? I have been *so* anxious to go all my life; and now I believe I really am. Stockton, Ed and I, and perhaps Loula, will go up the latter part of the week. I am very glad that Ed think[s] *he* is necessary to my safety at "Tallulah the Terrible," for he will be good company, as well as a good *guard.* He is a very tall, strong, broad-shouldered fellow,—and is indeed good to have around at such places, not for his strength alone, but still more for that instinct for *"protecting,"* which he posesses in such large degree. It seems really an "instinct" with him to take care of *all* women and young children; while as for those he loves, "he might not beteem the winds of heaven, visit their face too roughly["]! In fact, quite a chivalrous youth! He will never say anything unkind or critical of any of us—we are all *lovely*—he *pretends* to think! Stockton came to Auntie's with Eddie a few days after I left Rome for Sewanee—has been here ever since. We four are for the first time in our lives at table together. It seems very sad that we should be so separated. No use grieving about it—'tis true! but one can no more help that, than one can help the separation. I almost cry myself to sleep every night because I can't have Maggie; she is the dearest, *baddest,* most bewitching little creature I know. We will each be in a different place this winter. Eddie and I, and perhaps Stockton are going, in a week or so, to make Uncle Henry[2] a short visit, at Maysville on the Athens road; and then we will leave Eddie for the winter.

You were right, it seems, about Stockton's school;—it does open on the *eleventh*; and Prof. Blake[3] writes that he *must* be there by the tenth. So he leaves on the ninth—two weeks from tomorrow. That is sooner than I expected, and I am not at all sure that I will be able to start with him, I have *so* much to do and the visit to Uncle Henry to work in too. But I mean to try very vigorously to be ready. I have one advantage in the fact that, after my long rest, I feel as "fresh as a daisy," and able to work to some purpose. I have already—since Thursday morning begun and finished one portrait, and have another well in hand;—and have been out once, and generally twice, everyday too,—to drive with Ed, and to the hotel to see Grandmother.

If I don't go with Stockton, I will leave on the next Monday, and reach Wilmington on the 16th of Sept.—of all days in the year![4] That would be rather nice, don't *you* think so, dear? "Quite a coincidence." But it will be much pleasanter for Stockton and I to travel together, not to mention *other* inducements to an early start! so I will leave on the 9th if I *possibly* can! Many thanks for your information about roads; I have as yet made no enquiries at this end; but think I will take the "Central." Of course, will write you later on those points.

Stockton appreciated your kind messages very much indeed. He sends a great deal of love to you, and says he will be glad to write to you from college[.] Maggie also sends love,—having been put up to it by that bad girl Loula, who, having tired of her cards, has been seeking fresh amusement, teasing me—hanging over my shoulder, and rendering letter-writing a hopeless task.

So you are seeking relaxation from "the cares of state" by plunging into a house-cleaning frolic! Perhaps it is an excellent idea, they say it rests the mind to get the body throughly tired. How about the essays, by-the-way? I judge that since finishing No. 5 you have been resting on your oars.

Give much love to your dear mother—and just a little to her son. Good-night my love,—how I wish I could *say* goodnight. But I *feel* very close to you tonight—almost as if I could clasp hands across the distance[.] I wonder if it is because you are thinking about me.   Yours forever   Eileen.

ALS (WP, DLC).
  ¹ Perhaps the German author, "Jean Paul" Richter.
  ² The Rev. Henry Francis Hoyt, maternal uncle of ELA.
  ³ John R. Blake, of Davidson College.
  ⁴ The anniversary of their engagement.

To Ellen Louise Axson

Wilmington [N.C.], Aug. 26/84

You may have observed, Miss Axson (if you have not, you *will* have observed it before you see the last of me) that I am given to abrupt and somewhat disconcerting departures from the true paths of the philosophy in conformity with which it is my dearest desire to live. The chiefest tenet of that philosophy is that life is not worth living unless it be lived for others: and yet how often am I chagrined to find myself acting very devotedly and earnestly for myself alone, in most astounding denial of just that head of the creed! Mayhap I can call to your mind an illustration adequate to establish the point. Did you not receive a few days since a voluminous epistle which had about it, besides its length, this notable feature, that its writer had allowed not a little sadness to creep into it—sadness doubtless natural in a person of passionate loves and hatreds, but sadness for all that? Well, supposing that person to hold the philosophy of which I speak, is it not manifest that in so writing he departed from his faith? Assuredly the only proper object of a love-letter—it is natural, if not quite a matter of course, to conclude that so long a letter, to *you, was* a love-letter—is to carry joy unalloyed to the dear one who is to receive it: and to thrust his own selfish disappointments into such a letter should be quite out of the question for a lover who is persuaded of this creed, which I declare to be the only one worthy of a lover who would be worthy of the one he loves. But enough of the illustration. As for myself, I am the more surprised when I turn aside from the consistent practice of this philosophy because in ordinary moods I am fully aware that, even selfishly speaking, its practice is the best policy—though I remember saying once, in half-earnest, to a young lady that it was wisest to be exacting in this world where people were prone to do only what was *demanded* of them, as of right. No policy can be best which does not go hand in hand with an approving conscience, because success without contentment must be small gain. As a matter of fact, too, I *am* content to know, for instance, that my little sweetheart is with those who love her, where she can be happy, where the hours run as fast and as joyously as "cousin Ed's" horse, where there is work to satisfy diligent hands and companionship to comfort a loving heart—*provided* I may be sure, the while, that she would *rather* be where I am than anywhere else in the world, because I am there, did duty permit: that her thoughts and her love and her desires are all for me, that she is glad because she is living toward the time for which her heart waits, the time when she shall be mine for life, forever: and I *do* know that. It is because I know that that I am in all I do and think

Her own   Woodrow.

Written a few minutes afterwards:

In looking over this letter, I am constrained to recognize the fact that it is really scandalous. You have enough love talked to you to spoil all the least spoilable lasses in a kingdom! My next letter shall be all about the stupidest news of the town: about Sound parties and fires, political meetings and base-ball games, market prices and novelties in ship-rigging. Or else it shall be redolent with all the most pungent thoughts of certain (would-be) famous essays now again in progress. Look out for it with fear and trembling! Until then try to love me as much as I love you, for I am, all the same,   Your own   Woodrow.

ALS (WC, NjP).

From James W. Bones

Dear Woodrow   Rome Ga Aug 28/84

On my return from a short business trip I find your letters of 23d & 25th awaiting me. Their tone surprises & pains me a good deal, written as they are to one who is so much your senior & who is bound to you & your parents by such close & tender ties. I have been far from intending to be inattentive to your mothers interests. Her kindness in consenting to the loan of $1000. in order to get the mortgage settled was gratefully appreciated. The delay in putting the matter in proper shape has been due to the strong hope I have had that Dorsey would make a sale which would enable me to refund the money due your mother promptly. This hope he has been holding out to me but you see what he says in a letter inclosed[.] I also asked him if possible to advance me $1000. on $3000. of my land notes offering to pay 1% per month interest but you see what his reply is. Another cause of my delay has been the absence of an expected statement from Dorsey as to how I stand with him. He sent me the note & mortgage cancelled some days since & promised to send me statement but it has not yet come. I have tried to borrow money here but it has been impossible so terribly stringent has the financial situation been. Under all these circumstances I cannot fix a definite time for the payment of the loan but am perfectly willing to give a note with 8% int to be paid as rapidly as possible. In this connection it may be as well to call your attention to the fact that in consequence of the error made last summer in our division, in counting as an asset of the estate 80 acres valued @ $12.50 per acre which had been previously sold & credited on my cash a/c; & to which I called your attention this summer during your visit[,] your mother is indebted to your Aunts estate $500. You will also remember that when we made the division the taxes payable for 1883 were not included & were left to future settlement between us. The amt therefore due your mother will be reduced by these matters & will make the indebtedness to her less than $500.

As to the charge by Dorsey for one half the commissions on the sale to Munger & Pease he is correct. When those sales were made there was no cash payment & the payment of the commission was postponed. This fact I overlooked entirely last summer & was reminded of it only recently. I thus directed him to divide the amount between us which was the correct thing to do.

We get pleasant letters from Jessie[.] She & the children are well & pleased with their new home. I hope your father will give them a call. Marion & my mother are both well. We are boarding pleasantly at Miss Bowies. We will leave for Staunton next Friday (tomorrow) week. With warmest love to your mother

Your affec Uncle J W Bones

ALS (WP, DLC) with WWhw notation on env.: "Ans. Sept. 2/84."

From Granville Stanley Hall

My Dear Sir: W. Somerville, Mass. Aug. 29 [1884]

After our interview[1] I felt still more anxious you should think favorably of the proposition we talked over, & the matter has been kept open to the present time in the hope that you might see your way to it if we could talk it over again. I am not surprised so much as sincerely respectful of your decision. I read almost by chance your thesis & should have felt my self most happy with the stimulus of such a co-worker.

Ever respectfully yours G Stanley Hall

ALS (WP, DLC).
[1] See WW to ELA, June 3, 1884.

To Ellen Louise Axson

My own darling,   Wilmington [N.C.], Aug. 31st/84

I need not tell you,—I *cannot* tell you—how much I hope that you *will* be able to start with Stockton: for, sweet and fitting as would be the "coincidence" of being reunited on that best day of all the year,—*our* New Year's day,—the 16th, it costs me not a little to see your visit, which will at best be so short, cut still shorter by *any* delay. My heart is sick with longing for you, my precious Eileen: and yet I should not like to see you pay the price of too hard work in order to get away before the 15th. I am afraid, as it is, that you are presuming too rashly upon the store of strength and spirits laid up at Sewanee and are overtaxing even your wonderful working powers. I must beg you, darling, *not* to overwork yourself, even for my sake; and I shall trust you to come at the earliest possible moment. I wonder if you want to see me (even at the expense of the visit which you seem still to dread a little) as much as I want to see you? If so, you must be forlorn beyond your wont, my dear light-hearted little sweetheart.

I am *so* glad, my pet, that you have at last had the opportunity you have so long desired of visiting Tallulah,—and that you were able to make up so delightful a little party for the trip. That you were quite satisfied with that party, Miss, was conclusively attested by the significant fact that you sent me that very pretty invitation to join the excursion much too late to leave me any chance of accepting. Well, I'm of a forgiving nature, and so am neither jealous nor offended, but hope with all my heart that my love derived even more delight than she expected from her sight of the Falls and their wild surroundings. How I wish I *could* have gone with you, Ellie, my queen; for I have never seen Tallulah and it is well worth while seeing grand scenery for the first time, or any time, *with you*. Much as my heart is filled and my mind exalted by the beauties of nature, I am of too slow or too reticent a nature to make much *manifestation* of my feelings: my delight does not come to my eyes and to my lips as yours does to your sweet eyes and lips, and to me your sympathetic enjoyment would be worth many times more than all my own! My heart is full of you and your joy would be sweeter to me than my own. One of my favourite forecasts of the future anticipates the opportunities we may have, when we shall be—free to go where we please without chaperon, of visiting places which will satisfy my darling's love of the beauties and grandeurs of God's splendid creation. Then we shall—but stop! I've been forgetting the post-scriptural promise of my last letter! And yet, maybe t'would be a heartless thing to write you a prosy epistle, full of dull news and commonplace comment upon it, such as I write to those correspondents—that is to *all*, save one—whom I will not permit to know me except in my company garb, set down to entertain a guest, strenuous in insisting upon topics of passing interest,—even joining Gordon in the Soudan rather than let the conversation flag,—but never vouchsafing more than a glimpse of the thoughts and impulses and affections which are part and parcel of myself, and so sacred, not because they are great and rare, but because they are private, personal, not current upon the vulgar tongue of the world.

Then, too, the specifications of that promise were ill-advised, because I am never so inconsiderate as to write to *any* of my correspondents about Wilmington. To do so would be to invite indignation from the person to whom I wrote, because of the bore, and to risk the indignation of any Wilmingtonian to whose knowledge what I had said might unluckily come. I write from a *Post Office*,—rather than from a *place* bearing description. And, if the place wont bear description, the people certainly will not. At least they don't *provoke* description. There is not enough striking individuality about them to furnish picturesque material. Too many of them are like my friend, the book-seller, and my five-minute acquaintance, the librarian. The other day I wanted to verify my recollection of a passage in Buckle and,—as there is, strangely enough, no copy of his works in the house,—went down to the chief book-store to see if I could find there a copy of the 'History.'[1] Mr. H., the book-seller, had never heard either of the book or of its authors name. He insisted upon calling poor Henry "Bockle," and wished to know if his book had appeared recently! I left him abruptly, lest I should too plainly betray my inordinate admiration for him, and went up to the public library, to search there for the work, or for any traces of a knowledge of it. The handsome young damsel in charge there heard my inquiries with a smile of ill-concealed incredulity as to the existence of any such work,—much as if I had asked for 'Snooks on the Moon-Beam." They had, she said, no history of civilization but *Guizotte's* (so she persisted in pronouncing the honoured name of poor dead M. Guizot). It was like being told that the library contained no work on *art* save a history of idol-worship, and that, so far as was known to my informant, that was the only work upon art extant!

Of course not all Wilmingtonians are like this hardened book-seller and that unhappy girl. Like every town of its size it has its portion of culture and scholarship. But then I find that one is constantly liable to chilling experiences such as the one I have just detailed,—which was scarcely less trying to the nerves than a New York earthquake. And it cannot reasonably be expected that I should love to dwell long upon the qualities, whatever they be, of people who are continually putting me to the trouble of making courteous, smiling answer to the question whether I have "commenced practicing yet." I generally try to say "Oh, no" with the tone of one who gives the reply expected to those who ask if he has undertaken something much beyond his age.

Dear mother makes *pastoral* calls, and I make some or none according to my mood. I write after breakfast, drive before supper, and after supper generally read aloud while dear mother sews or embroiders. Between the morning writing and the afternoon driving, I attend to father's business letters and to my own correspondence, and, for the rest, follow my own devices quite diligently. Although we have *one* excellent road, we have *no* good streets; but dear mother is very fond of her gentle little mare and we go as regularly as possible over the same route, which supplies us with plenty of fresh, sea-scented air, but with no fresh scenery. Nellie's jog-trot (Nellie is the mare) is what you would easily recognize as a violent anti-climax to the paces of "Cousin Ed's" dashing nag; but the little animal is a model "lady's-horse," and the dear lady who owns and constantly drives her could hardly do without her faithful services. Her daily rides in the buggy give her just the recreation and exercise she needs after her busy house-keeping. This driving, however, is declared, or rather decreed, *not* exercise enough for me, her big son, and I am urged to inflict upon myself various walks and gymnastic performances which I grumblingly regard as much too big a price to pay for the privilege of devoting my mornings to study. And yet a chap *does* need some powerful antidote when [he] takes original composition in large doses. There is not, I take it, *half* as much wear and tear in mastering the contents of a score of books as in writing *one*. At least I'm sure that no amount of reading taxes me so severely as I am taxed by two or three hours of concentration upon my writing.

Good-bye, sweetheart. Give my love to the dear Grandparents and to Eddie and Stockton. Kiss Maggie for me as often as she will let you. My sincere regards to *all* at "Uncle Warren's."

> "How many times do I love *thee*, dear?
> Tell me how many thoughts there be
> In the atmosphere
> Of a new-fall'n year,
> Whose white and sable hours appear
> The latest flake of Eternity:—
> So many times do I love thee, dear.["][2]

Your own   Woodrow

ALS (WC, NjP).

  [1] Henry T. Buckle, *History of Civilization in England* (2 vols., London, 1857-61).

  [2] From Thomas Lovell Beddoes, "Song from 'Torrismond.'"

From Ellen Louise Axson

My darling Woodrow,   Gainsville [Ga.] Sept. 1   84.

I am afraid a certain young gentleman of my acquaintance is just a little of a hypocrite! What do you think about it yourself? How else than as hypocrisy, shall I characterize those profuse apologies for the length of his letters into which he sometimes falls; he can't pretend that he does'nt know how precious every word of those letters are to their happy recipient. They are never long enough for her;—no I won't say that either, for that would suggest a possible improvement in them, whereas they are *altogether perfect*; and besides it would indicate dissatisfaction on my part; and I am opposed upon principle to being dissatisfied with *anything*—oftener than I can help! You would have thought your "long letter" appreciated, if you could have seen how often and how long I pored over it. I took it with me to the falls, and read it at every odd moment during those three days, until finally, Loula, in despair, stole it away from me, thereby reducing me to the verge of desperation. I don't appreciate practical jokes, of that sort, any more highly than do you the *teasing*.

And, by-the-way, while I think of it, I must say just one little word for poor Mr. McRae! You understand, of course, that he never meant to tease *you*, nor to prepare any "document" at all; —it was only through *my* mischief that you heard anything about it. He was merely (not teasing) but joking with *me*; with whom his acquaintance, *he* felt, *was* sufficient to justify it, especially as he knew that I would never "take the trouble to get mad"! Mr. McRae's fun is always perfectly good-natured;—knowing so well as I did that he *meant nothing* by his charges, and also that there *was* nothing whatever in them, it never *occurred* to me to take offence. It would have been giving by far too much weight to a little "chaff." Yet on general principles, I quite agree with you on the subject of "teasing."

You notice that I am a day behind time in writing this week; and even now I must, if possible, send only a "few lines." Uncle Henry and his Fannie[1] are here for a day and a half only; and I have not been able to find a moment for writing, night or day. These girls won't let me! They follow me up if I try to slip off, and fill the whole house with their presence and their chatter. Indeed, their hours here are so few, that I suppose correspondence ought to be suspended while they last. But I will try to make up for it the latter part of the week. I cant even tell you now about our trip to Tallulah. Oh, how I *wish* you had been with us! It was *glorious*!

And now a word about the time of my departure. I had finished all the work which it was necessary for me to do here, and thought I would be ready to start on Tuesday. But my plans have all come to grief again; and because of something for which I can't grieve, either. Grandfather has decided to stay a week longer than he expected; they can't bear the idea of my leaving them so soon, and of course, I can't think of doing it. I dread the parting exceedingly, at any time, because, in Grandmother's case, I cannot but fear that it is the last. So I will remain until the 15th, I think; though if I can't get the schedules to work well for a Monday leave-taking, I *may* start on Friday, the 12th. Will write you again after I have studied the time-tables. This delay in Gainsville is particularly unfortunate for me, because I will be here all this week without any work. I had another portrait to do, but no stretcher; so acting on the suggestion in your letter, I ordered it sent to Wilmington, rather than here, thinking thereby to *secure* my "early start." And now behold!—I have *both* the shortened visit, *and* the work to do in Wilmington! Too bad! but it can't be helped. Good night, dear heart, will write again *very* soon. Your sweet letter of the 26th I found awaiting me on my return from Tallulah—the one for which you apologize was very, *very* sweet too, if it was "sad,"—"and I would that my tongue could utter the thoughts it aroused in me." Much love to your dear mother and for yourself the whole heart of

Your own   Eileen.

ALS (WP, DLC).
¹ Frances Hoyt, daughter of ELA's Uncle Henry by his first wife, Mary Frances Hines.

Draft of a Letter to James W. Bones

Wilmington, North Carolina, September 2nd., 1884.
My dear uncle James,

I have received your letter of the 28th. of August. Allow me to say that in my opinion you had no cause to feel pained by anything in my letter, and that I, on the other hand, have reason to feel indignant that you should see fit so to address me. I am, and have always been, quite as sensible of the tender ties subsisting between us as you can be, and I have never done or said anything in which those ties were ignored. I have, on the contrary, always been respectful and regardful of your feelings. But considerations of seniority have no proper place in business transactions, and there has already been too much sentiment in the management of the affairs of the estate to admit of straightforward, business-like dealings between the parties interested.

Since I became connected with the management of the estate my interference has been treated, by both yourself and Dorsey, so much as something to be tolerated rather than respected that it has been impossible for me to perform my duties satisfactorily either to myself or to those to whom I am responsible. In the matter of this loan I have thus far waited altogether in vain for anything more than an *indirect* and *inferential* acknowledgement of it. Of course we did not require or expect its immediate repayment; but we did expect its prompt and formal acknowledgement and securement. It required, however, repeated urgings from me to get from you any answer at all to my letter acquainting you with mother's assent to the arrangement. I appreciate and honour your desire to repay the loan at once, but I cannot understand how your efforts in that direction should have stood in the way of your doing the only thing I asked, namely, telling me what you purposed doing to secure us against risk.

The matter of the taxes, again, illustrates very well the extraordinary difficulties and embarrassments under which I have laboured. At the time at which we made the arrangement about them of which you speak you promised to let me know their amount and to send me a copy of the tax-receiver's receipt so soon as you should have paid them, upon the understanding that I was to square the account with you at once. But from that time to the moment when I received your letter of the 28th I heard not a single word about them. I forgot to speak about them to you when I was in Rome; but I took it for granted that the matter had been neglected by the Nebraska men and that the taxes were still unpaid. I was about to write to Nebraska to inquire about them.

As for the oversight about a certain eighty acres included by mistake in the deeds of partition, that matter is no more in shape to be settled now than it was when I was in Rome and it was still in abeyance. Because here again I am unwilling, and indeed unauthorized, to move without business accuracy and form. It is indispensable that, for the sake of my own stewardship, I should know the exact description of the tract in question and the date and terms of the deed to uncle Thomas, in order that I may identify the tran[s]action with the item to which you refer in your accounts, of which I took a copy with your permission, and which formed the principal basis of the division.

I am sure, too, that you will agree with me in thinking that your note should, in the first instance, be for the amount of the loan, unreduced by these unsettled balances. I am not in any way responsible for the delay about the taxes or for the mistake about the land, & and [sic] I cannot see the propriety in mixing transactions so entirely dissociated. By reducing your note to the estimated amount of the unsettled balance you would in effect be claiming interest, for the time to elapse before the payment of the note, on sums which we have all along been ready to pay, so soon as the claim should be made certain, and which were unpaid through no fault of ours. Still, to avoid inconvenient conplications of account, I am quite willing to consent to the reduction in the principal of the note, after these other claims shall have been definitely identified and established as I have suggested.

I trust that you will understand this letter in the spirit in which I have written it, a spirit of entire candour and respect.

I know of no other way to express myself about matters of business.

I am very glad indeed that you are going to accompany dear Marion to Staunton. Give her a great deal of love from us both to carry thither with her.

Respectfully and Sincerely yours,   Woodrow Wilson

WWTL (draft) with WWhw emendations (WP, DLC).

From Edward Ireland Renick

My dear Wilson,   Washington, D.C., Sept 4, 1884.

Will you return to the "Johns" as a "fellow" next term? Gaddy, who is now a $1200 clerk here in the P.O., says that he heard so. You know poor Robt. Boylston[1] is dead? I have married— as you may have heard—Mrs Turpin, who with her children are now with me here—& anxious like myself to see you if you pass our way. . . .

I am about to dispose of our "Code of Ga," & will remit your part when obtained. Please let us hear from you soon—

Ever yours,   Renick

P.S. omitted. ALS (WP, DLC) with WWhw notation on env.: "Ans Oct. 14/84."
    [1] Son of Mrs. J. Reid (Hester) Boylston, with whom WW boarded during most of his stay in Atlanta.

To Ellen Louise Axson

My own darling,   Wilmington [N.C.], Sept. 6th/84

The news that your arrival must *certainly* be postponed till the 16th has stung me with another pang of the disappointment which I find it increasingly hard to bear, because I had allowed myself to hope that you would, after all, come, for my sake, with Stockton, on the 13th: but of course I have nothing to say against your decision,—though I must confess, Miss, that the extreme cheerfulness with which you acquiesce in the necessity for the delay quite takes my breath away.

I am, unhappily, a comparatively idle person just at present. The last essay of the series, so long and so tediously talked about, was completed some days ago. It is a little shorter than its predecessors, being merely a sort of concluding summary of the series, and I made such a desperate spurt in its composition that it was finished long before I had expected: for I had intended to use it as a diversion till you should arrive. But I could not spin it out for the sake of keeping my mind vigourously employed: and the

immense lot of copying now remaining to be done is tedious drudgery rather than engrossing work. I have to make *two* copies of
Nos. 5 and 6, as I did of the others: and that means an almost
endless grinding at the caligraph.

I am delighted beyond measure, my little sweetheart, to know
that you enjoy my letters so much,—even the longest and poorest
of them: but I was, none the less, not hypocritical when I sought
to excuse their bad qualities. It is only another proof of the blindness of love,—to which I owe so much,—that you think all or any
of them "absolutely perfect." Their chief merit, so far as I can
see, is that they are *genuine*, that they reflect truly, and without
attempt at withholding anything, the mood in which they are
written. Then, too, there can be no doubt about their being inspired by a boundless, passionate love for my precious little
queen.

Give my love to Stockton, please, my pet, before he gets off,
and tell him that I shan't forget his promise to write to me from
college.

I have'nt told you, have I, that there is an old Davidson class-
mate of mine living here now? Will. [William B.] Phillips (son of
Rev. Dr. [Charles] Phillips, then professor at Davidson, but now
at Chapel Hill.) was one of the most boisterous boys, and yet one
of the hardest students in college. Since I knew him as a class-
mate, he has made a thorough practical study of chemistry, and
he is now doing well here as chemist for a flourishing guano company whose works are just outside of town—far enough away to
prevent their being a nuisance to town noses. He is married,—has
been married for some two or three years,—but just now he is
practically a bachelor, his wife having been away almost ever
since I came home, and I have been having the full benefit of his
companionship. I am so much of a stranger in Wilmington that
I have made no friendships amongst the young men of the town,
and "Bill's" presence has, consequently, been a real comfort to
me. Not that he is a very companionable fellow,—he is too self-
conscious and too stiff for that,—but he is cultured and well-in-
formed, jolly and talkative, and infinitely more agreeable than
any one else I am likely to meet in these parts. By saying that he is
'stiff,' I mean partly that his speech is rather too carefully laboured, but principally that he is noticeably cautious about committing himself to any view in which he is not sure of a backing.
He has what I have often wondered that any really intelligent person should possess, a vigilant fear of showing ignorance of *anything*. I can understand the shame which would lead a man to

avoid confusing a want of information upon any subject which he professed to have studied; but it is not so easy to comprehend the blush which confesses ignorance as to other matters. One could wish, and should strive, to make his knowledge as wide as human interests, but it is no disgrace to him if there be thousands even of ordinary things, outside his life and thoughts, which he does not know. And, what's more, if one don't confess ignorance, he shuts himself out from one of the most useful and most pleasant ways of learning. I should much rather learn from a man, who had made his knowledge his own, than from the books from which he got it. What he knows one can't find out for himself, because one can't meet the people or undergo the experiences that have contributed to make up the sum of his knowledge. By making an interrogation point of oneself one can gain much of the world's knowledge by proxy, laying all men under tribute of information. It even pays to feign ignorance sometimes of the very points one esteems himself most familiar with,—for the sake of getting at, not what people *know*, but what they *think*. They are sure to think something different,—in tone and in point-of-view, if not in substance,—from your own thoughts, if they think at all; and new views are new lights, often disclosing the ruts into which one's own thinking has unconsciously settled. But, dear me! what a digression! I've wandered a long way from Bill Phillips! Well, no matter!—he's gone off to-day to join Mrs. P.— and so is wandering far from me.

I received a short letter from Renick (my whilom law-partner) this morning, which, short as it was, startled me with news both distressing and amusing. The news which especially distressed me was that Robt. Boylston, the oldest and most promising son of the lady with whom I boarded in Atlanta, is *dead*. I saw him in June when I passed through on my way to Rome and he was in the best of health and spirits. Renick writes under the impression that I had already heard the sad tidings, and so gives no particulars.

The other piece of news, which I have called 'amusing,' but which is quite as startling,—and, perhaps I should say, quite as distressing,—as the news of young Boylston's death, is that Renick himself is married, to the lady with whom we boarded after leaving Mrs. Boylston's. Mrs. Turpin was a widow,—was a widow when Mr. Turpin won her: for death had first of all deprived her of a husband in taking away Mr. Evans. "Mc" Evans, her son by her first marriage, lived with her when I boarded with them, and I am quite sure that he must have been at least twenty-three or twenty-four when he died, which was only a few months after I left Atlanta: so that a very moderate, considerate estimate would make his mother now about forty years of age!

Well, you know, Renick obtained a clerkship in Washington, by examination under the new Civil Service Law, and after his success in that direction the ardour for like employment seems to have spread amongst his friends. Mrs. Turpin was sick of the struggle of professional boarding-house keeping and wanted some surer means of supporting her two children (an Evans daughter, at school in New York, and a Turpin son, worrying her life out of her in Atlanta): so she sold out all she had and sought *her* fortunes in Washington, an applicant for government employ-ment. Since she went to the capital I had heard nothing of her or of Renick till his letter of this morning dumbfounded me with this incredible announcement: "I have married—as you may have heard—Mrs. Turpin, who with her children are now with me here —and anxious like myself to see you if you pass our way." That's all,—not another word about it, his newly-married bliss—the joys of third-husband-hood! As I "may have heard"! Why, my dear fellow, I hardly believe the evidence of your own statement, made in your own so well-known handwriting! Nobody but Renick him-self could have made me credit such an astounding, sad, ridicu-lous, breath-depriving, outrageous piece of intelligence! I don't know that I altogether believe it now. If Mrs. Turpin were *beau-tiful*,—but she is not even good-looking; if she were fascinating, —but she is barely interesting (for a few moments at a time); if she were—ah, maybe *that* was it! She was in distress—in a big city, without money or chance of self-support, and with no friend save Renick. But not even *that*, combined wth Renick's constitu-tional folly and weakness about woman can explain his action in marrying her, unless we eliminate his *sense* from the problem. He could have kept her out of absolute want and helped her to reach friends or obtain employment without *marrying* her. No ecstacy of chivalry could necessitate that. Are we to believe that he was in love with the woman, or supposed he was? There's no telling! I can believe anything as soon as that he has ruined his life and burdened it as well by marrying a woman quite old enough to have been his mother. I did not think that Renick *could* make such a fool of himself, even about a woman!

I will write to Gadsden and ask *him* the particulars. Have I made you familiar with dear old "Gaddy's" name? He was my other Atlanta chum, and a stirling, splendid fellow he is,—quite as trustworthy and likeable as he is thin and eccentric. He is one of the celebrated South Carolina family. He too is in Washington City now, in the Post Office department: and he probably knows the inside history of the Renick-Turpin match. It must be worth knowing,—but I have already given you quite enough [of] it. My mind was so full of it that I *had* to write off some of my excitement and indignation about it!

Please, my darling, don't put off your coming again! I have actually had, during the last two or three days a wild, unreasoning fear that something would happen to prevent your visit *altogether*! If you could only come right away, I should feel no fears about my winter in Baltimore: as it is I sometimes fear that I have worked too long and too constantly this summer and that I have left myself too little vacation to recruit me for the pull just ahead of me. There is a little maiden whose voice and whose presence have in them a magic which fills me with the ease of mind and the joy of heart which are the only things that can rest a man of my disposition—and there's no magic in the world, but hers, can do it.

Give my love to your grand-parents, Eileen, and to Eddie and Maggie, and my kindest regards to all the rest.

> "How many times do I love, again?
> Tell me how many beads there are
>   In a silver chain
>   Of evening rain
> Unravelled from the tumbling main
> And threading the eye of a yellow star:—
> So many times do I love thee, again."[1]

Your own   Woodrow.

ALS (WP, DLC).
[1] From Thomas Lovell Beddoes, "Song from 'Torrismond.' "

From Ellen Louise Axson

My darling Woodrow,   Gainsville [Ga.] Sept 8/84

I will give you credit for being *very* patient in truth, if you have not grumbled a bit, at the short allowance of writing which I did last week. I myself was impatient over it, I must confess; but it was unavoidable; for I have been ill for the last five days, with quite a sharp little attack of fever,—some of the *Rome* malaria, the doctor says, cropping out at this late day;—he indignantly denys the possibility of my having become possessed of it *here*. But the fever is broken now, and I will be all right in a day or so. I am sitting up for the first time today; and in honnour thereof will drop you a line to tell you what I am about;—though I am every moment expecting someone to come in, with amazement and horror in face and voice, and take my pen from me,—they have already gone through with that little comedy with my needle.

But the fact is Stockton has just left ten minutes ago—left for a whole year, and I am so desperately blue over the parting that I *must do* something to mend matters; and what remedy so effectual as a talk, or even a few words, with *you*? Ah, darling, you don't know what a comfort it is merely to *think* about you. It helps one bear pain and weariness, as well as greater troubles.

What would I do, dear, without that one, sweet thought, ever present—ever making itself *felt* deep down below all lighter or heavier thoughts? I have often wondered what I would do without it but I cannot tell—I can't even *imagine*—so much a part of myself has it become. When, in the night, "the old sorrow wakes and cries," what else has *power* to lull it to rest? Alas, not even thoughts of heaven; they mingle with it, soften and soothe. But there is something else, which, whether rightly or wrongly, has proved itself able, many and many a time, to *banish* it altogether, —to turn sorrow into gladness. And so I will not count myself unhappy, "though fallen on evil days,"—God has so strangely, so tenderly "tempered the wind to the shorn lamb."

Sept. 9. You see, I was interrupted, as I expected; so this morning I will take advantage of an improved state of affairs to add a little to my "few lines." I am decidedly stronger today,—surrounding articles have almost ceased to fly about in that erratic and startling fashion, whenever my over-reaching pride tempts me to rise to the full dignity of my five feet, three! I am so well, that I think of running over to Uncle Henry's on Thursday—and running back on Sat—and running to Wilmington on Monday according to agreement! This little illness has broken up my *visit* to Uncle H. but I must go over to take Eddie—and give Aunt Emma[1] a lecture as to the proper treatment of his case—I wonder what she would say to such an impudent speech;—but I mean to give it to her in shape of *hints* and suggestions,—sugar coated pills! I dread to find myself at the mercy of her voice,—open to an attack in person, about my "treatment of them,"—her messages have been enough. That room, which has been ready and waiting for me *three* months, is a silent witness against me. But I tell her it would be too improvident to exhaust all my welcomes at once;—I am saving her for next time.

So if I am well enough, and of course I shall be if I have no relapse,—I will leave here on Monday afternoon[,] reach Charlotte early in the morning, make close connexion there, on the *Carolina Central*, and reach Wilmington, I suppose, Tuesday night. I can't find out how long it takes to travel from Charlotte to Wil. Am sorry I can't spend Monday night as I expected, on the C.C., but it seems I can only make connections by leaving here in the afternoon. Is that all that is necessary? I shall be so hurried this week that I *may* not write again—unless I *must*, to say that I am unable to leave!

And so you have finished all the essays! I give you joy! Don't you "feel good" over it; or do you feel lonely, as though you had parted from an old friend? I am *very* glad it is done, though I hope you hav'nt over-worked yourself in the doing. Am sorry you have that immense mass of copying; I can imagine how it must make you feel. To copy one's own work of any sort, is the most boring, uninspiring thing I ever tried to do. What a pity someone else can't do that part of it! I am glad at any rate that you are not going to have double work during the first months of the term. But after all you will probably find something else to take it's place,—perhaps let Dr. Ely claim you for his own.

That was a very pleasant picture you give of your own and your mother's life in Wil. As for the sketch of your good neighbours! fie, for shame! You are worse than I am about Rome;—but then no one in Rome ever asked me if I had "begun practicing yet"! That *is rich*! You poor martyr! I fancy I see you making that sententious! felicitous,!! perspicacious!!! reply.

Poor, poor Mr. Renick! What a *dreadful* thing this marriage is! Amusing! Yes, but none the less a tragedy. How *could* it have happened? It would require an even broader and deeper knowledge of human nature than my cousin Ed (*says* he) possesses to explain it. It is one of those cases which turn one's thoughts involuntarily to old Brabantio's theory—"witch-craft"! Of course *she* married *him*—but how? The old *wretch*!

By the way, your allusions to your Atlanta friends remind me that I had a gem of the first water to send you, which I herewith enclose.[2] Did you ever see such powers of description? Why can't *you* write like that? What a graphic, poetical sketch of Miss Mayrant! don't you feel like hiding your diminished head when you think of your efforts in that direction? You failed even to *hint* that she was "supple and subtile"!

Another interruption! Will I ever get this letter finished (someone tampered with the ink during one such interval and behold the washed-out result!) This time it is a telegram from Ed, who wants to know when I leave,—he wants to get another peep at me before. After our return from Tallulah, he went to Athens, to attend court. I have missed his protection sadly, for Loula is distressingly popular, and the young men are distressing in other ways. Ed and I had a standing engagement with each other; and we would hide on some veranda, while the circle in the parlour followed their own devices. Do you suppose that if you had received your invitation to Tallulah in time you would have accepted? If I thought that, I fear I should tear my hair "over spilled milk" too. If you could only have been there! It was the grándest place I ever saw. I never had such an experience before. I don't think I have told you about it. We started early Friday morning to make all "the descents"[.] There are three falls, you know, "Tempesta," Hurricane, and "Oceana." We went to "Oceana" first, the lowest and smallest—stood on the rock over which the water fell, and then amused ourselves, for a time, on the rocks below the fall, by the "whirlpool,"—to which, it is said, they have never found a bottom. It was bright when we started, but while there the sky began to be clouded. Finally we started back toward "Hurricane," climbing up and down the crags, always as near the water as possible. When we reached the top of the precipice, the others turned back to the hotel, but Ed and I went on. We hung by a tree just over "Hurricane," within six inches of it. That was *glorious*, we felt almost a *part* of it. One gets so much more idea of the awful *power* of the falling waters when close to them. In the meantime the skys had grown very dark, and when we finally found ourselves opposite "Tempesta," at the edge of the cliff, we had the grandest spectacle I ever saw. Over the whole visible face of the sky, stretched the cloud, black and lurid, but its most intense blackness was just behind the white, foaming, raging mass of waters. And there was the strangest, most beautiful light over everything. To describe those "toppled crags," and shadowy granite walls, and gleaming waters, as they showed under it, would be a task for a poet, not for me.

We watched as long as we dared, and then went down the ladders, which at that point are hung from the cliff; an iron rod is drilled into the rock, and from it they are suspended. It had begun to rain by that time, but we were now at the bottom of the fall, and the rocks were so wet and slippery, and the spray so heavy, that it made little difference whether it rained or not. We skirted the rapids,—after it's first great leap, the river makes a sharp turn, as it does at Niagara,—and finally reached "the tower" at the base of the fall,—in the midst of the waters as it were—just as the storm broke in earnest. We rushed up the various flights of stairs, and reached the top in time to see it all. Oh it was wonderful—it was majestic beyond description, both the sight, and the sound, when the voice of the thunder mingled with the voice of many waters, making one mighty music!

I would not have missed it for the world,—was never so beside myself with rapture in my life. We stayed there about an hour, when the storm passed, and we made the other small descents—to Ladore and the rapids;—we were so wet anyhow, that we could'nt be wetter, so we concluded we might as well go through with it;—and finally reached the hotel just in time for dinner. The people had had a panic there,—thought they were going to have a cyclone.

More light on the subject of my schedule &c.! The agent was *all wrong.* I leave G. at ten o'clock Monday *morning,* reach Charlotte at 8.45 P.M., make close connection there, and reach Wilmington at 7 *o'clock* Tuesday morning,—just as I expected at first. Just think how many beautiful things I have seen this summer; and now I am to wind up with the *sea,*—which I do indeed "love almost if not quite as well as the mountains." It is very pleasant to think that I am once more "to watch the crisping ripples on the beach,—and tender curving lines of creamy spray." And it [is] pleasant too,—just a little—to think that I am to see *somebody* once again, and soon ah, *soon!*

Did you see the notice of Dr. Woodrow and the "Evolution" affair, in the "Nation"?[3] Very good—part of it! He "is not a young man, nor eccentric, but an acknowledged teacher of teachers, and has temperately spoken his mature thoughts upon a subject which has been his especial study, and upon which he was expected to speak." That's well and strongly expressed;—is'nt it?

Give *much* love to your dear mother, take as much as you want for yourself and believe me   Yours forever   Eileen.

ALS (WP, DLC).
  1 Emily A. Roberts Hoyt was the second wife of ELA's Uncle Henry.
  2 The enclosure, describing Wilson's friend, Kate D. Mayrant, is missing.
  3 "Notes," New York *Nation,* XXXIX (Aug. 21, 1884), 157-58.

From Hiram Woods, Jr.

My Dear Tommy,   Baltimore, Sep. 10, 1884.

Your good letter was duly received. With all due respect to your printing machine, and in spite of my unbounded admiration for the inventor's skill, I prefer vastly your own hand-writing in personal correspondence. There's a sort of sitting-on-the-United-States-Senate air about your machine writing which makes your letters more the production of that wonderful creature a "fellow" of the *foundation*," than of T.W.W. Hence—etc. Quod erat demonstrandum. . . .

Will be delighted to see you in Oct. If your fair young lady comes by way of Balto. I shall hope to meet her.

Yours As Ever,   Hiram Woods, Jr.

ALS (WP, DLC).

From James W. Bones

My dear Woodrow   Rome Ga Sept 16th 1884

On my return recently from Staunton to which place I accompanied Marion & took a brief rest from work I found yours of 2d awaiting me. I cannot but think your letter displays an uncalled for amount of feeling but I will not argue the matter with you. I am not aware of having had any disposition since you took charge of your mothers affairs to consider your connection with the management of the estate as an interference. I have had no feeling on the subject but one of gladness that you had relieved me of the responsibility of her portion. It was always a pleasure to me to serve her whom I loved & still love so dearly & it would have continued to be a pleasure. But I felt that life was uncertain & that it was better in every way that you should take my place. It is probable that I was spoiled by the long continued confidence placed in me by your mother & not having done anything so far as I knew to forfeit that trust I have felt perhaps too much the change which has taken place since her son has taken charge of her affairs. If then I have failed to act towards you in a "straight-forward business like manner," in the slightest degree I beg to apologize[.] Henceforward I shall be careful that *sentiment* finds no place in any business that may come before us. I do reproach myself for not having more promptly acknowledged your mothers kindness in helping me to pay off the mortgage[.] I endeavored some time since to explain my remissness & to apologize for it & can now only renew my expressions of regret for my short comings in that matter.

In regard to the 80 acres erroneously included as an asset last summer in our division viz W½ NW¼ sec. 1.17.7 I inclose a letter of Mr Dorseys on the subject & also a list of the lands originally in Township 17, of those sold, & those unsold at time of our division. This list I wrote for after your last visit to us. The 200 acres (including the 80 in question[)] were deeded to your Uncle Thomas under these circumstances. While I was at Fremont in spring of 1880 a party offerred $2000. cash for 160 acres of your Uncles land near town. I wrote him & found he did not wish to sell prefering to keep his land as a permanent investment. He consented however to exchange his 160 acres @ $12½ per acre for 200 acres of ours @ $10. per acre. This was a fair exchange at the time as his land was more valuable than ours to that extent on account of location, quality of land &c. I sold his land on June 1st 1880, & received the $2000. & credited the estate that amount as you will see by reference to your copy of my cash a/c. I also charged the commission paid Dors[e]y for negociating this sale along with some others same date. How it was both Dors[e]y & I failed to get proper entry on our lists I cannot imagine unless it was my mistake in confounding the number of acres viz 160. & 200. in marking off & transferring from our list of lands to your uncle Thomas' list. It was a mere clerical mistake. The estate got the $2000. & the 200 acres as named on the paper sent you were deeded June 9th to your uncle to replace the 160 acres of his sold. If you desire further confirmation of these statements you can write to your Uncle Thomas & he will doubtless send you a certified copy of his deed. We have been paying the taxes on this 80 since the sale & I know your Uncle will cheerfully refund the amount as soon as I write him on the subject which I will do at once.

In regard to the taxes paid in 1883 but not included in our settlement, in moving to Jessie's last Fall I left some papers, including the tax receipts inclosed, in a draw[er] of my book case which was packed away in the attic along with other furniture. There was some trouble in getting at the book case & I kept putting the matter off until it passed entirely out of my mind. When you were here this summer I looked among my papers at my office, but could not find them. Since receiving your letter I remembered where they were & got them out. I am thus particular to show you that I had no intention of annoying you. I did not wish to ask you for the money until I could send the receipts as vouchers; I can see no impropriety in mixing up this tax matter & the 80 acre matter in arranging the $1000. due your mother. She is clearly indebted to your Aunts estate for her half of the 80 erroneously counted as an asset last summer @ 12½ per acre by $500. & her half of the 1883 taxes. This 80 would have been cash to me this summer in paying the mortgage & had it belonged to the estate there would have been no occasion for your mother lending the $1000.

I hope my dear Woodrow I have now placed all before you in a business like way, without any sentiment. Such near friends & relations as we are cannot afford to indulge in unpleasant feelings. If I have done wrong in any way I am willing to confess my fault. Let us make a fresh beginning & I feel sure we will conduct our business affairs more pleasantly in future.

With warmest love to your dear mother & father, the latter of whom has I hope returned home greatly benefitted[,] I remain   Your affc Uncle   James W. Bones

P.S. omitted. ALS (WP, DLC), attached to WW to J. W. Bones, Oct. 9, 1884. Encs.: three tax receipts and hw list of land tracts.

To Ellen Louise Axson

For Eileen   [Wilmington, N. C., Sept. 16, 1884]

You probably can think, my darling, of some associations connected with this day which will make my desire to give you something which may serve as a memento seem a very natural one. Looking for a present such as I would *want* to give you is, in Wilmington, like looking for a rose on a desert: but if you will *use* this portfolio, I shall be satisfied. The paper will, of course, be consumed in the using, but the portfolio may last a little while to remind you of the love of your own

                                            Woodrow.

ALS (WC, NjP).

EDITORIAL NOTE

ELLEN'S VISIT TO WILMINGTON AND HER TRIP WITH WOODROW TO WASHINGTON AND NEW YORK

The preceding document suggests that Ellen Axson carried out the plans she had outlined in her letter of September 8, 1884, and reached Wilmington for her visit to the Wilsons early on the morning of September 16, thus enabling Woodrow to present the portfolio to her on the anniversary of the day which it commemorated.

Ellen and Woodrow left Wilmington on October 1. Arriving at Washington that night, they found hotel accommodations[1] and spent the following day seeing the sights of the capital, among them, the Corcoran Gallery of Art.[2] They boarded a sleeper for New York late that same day, October 2. The next morning Woodrow accompanied Ellen to her boarding house at 60 Clinton Place, which she may have selected earlier on the advice of friends or because she had known it during her previous stay in the city. Woodrow met several of the

[1] See WW to ELA, Oct. 5, 1884.
[2] See ELA to WW, Nov. 15, 1884.

other occupants and no doubt remained at least for lunch with Ellen.[3] In the late afternoon he sought out his friends, Charles H. Shinn and Harold Godwin, and visited with them for several hours, probably through the dinner hour.[4] He left for Baltimore at some time that same night, October 3.[5]

[3] As ELA to WW, Oct. 4, 1884, suggests.
[4] See WW to Robert Bridges, Nov. 19, 1884.
[5] He seems to have taken a night train and to have arrived at Baltimore early in the morning of October 4. See WW to ELA, Oct. 4 and 5, 1884.

To Ellen Louise Axson

My own darling,   Balto., Oct. 4th 1884
    I cannot tell you how desperately heavy-hearted I have been ever since I left my precious little sweetheart in those dreary quarters amidst those horrid people. As yet I have much too much time to think about it. How I do hope that you will soon have news to tell me of a pleasant change in immediate prospect! I am quite well, though dreadfully weary. I am just about to begin unpacking. When I get at my writing materials, I shall have a better chance, as well as more time, to let my own familiar pen run on again of its master's boundless love for his Eileen.
    Goodbye till to-morrow. God bless you, my darling. Shall I come back to you? Do you need me?
                                    Your own   Woodrow.
ALS (WP, DLC).

From Ellen Louise Axson

                        [60 Clinton Place,] New York, Oct. 4, 84.
    "I wish you a very good morning," my darling, and hope you are feeling well and bright on this bright day. I am happy to say that the sunshine has had its due effect on us,—things seem much more cheerful,—even the dining-room looks better. And by the way, the dinner last night *was* somewhat better than the other meals. It consisted—I believe you are interested in the details of this affair!—of soup, fish and potatoes; and the second course was very decently cooked! I did'nt go down to breakfast, but the girls say it was quite a tolerable *yankee* meal. So I think they will try and put up with things here,—I would do it myself, without hesitation, if I were in their place;—of course, they can let the people severely alone. They say they *can't* pay more than this, and they are sure they can't do better at this price. The "Christian Home" is infinitely worse; I wish I had time to tell you about it—it is *too absurd*! Eva McNulty[1] has board there for

a week, so I will remain here for a week too. By that time I will know better what to do, and this is a good safe place from which to look about.

I did nothing about making a change this morning. Mr. Marvin was with us, you know, and on his account I was ashamed to make enquiries at the League; and I hadn't time to go to Cousin Ben's;[2] am going this afternoon if possible[.] The gentleman at the League, Mr. Davis, I suppose, was very pleasant indeed; showed us about the place[,] gave us full directions, &c. So we will be ready to "pitch in" Monday morning. We have been all the morning on the street getting our drawing materials and doing some other little shopping; and we have just finished lunch— for which we had excellent appetites. Good bye for the present darling. The girls want me to hurry out with them so I must close. Will write fully as soon as possible. Oh, my love, my love, how I *do* miss you—and how I *do* love you.

Your own   Ellie.

Please dear write me at *once* what my hotel bill was, that I may send it. Events followed each other so quickly after we left the house, that I forgot all about it, and it makes me feel *so* humiliated.

ALS (WP, DLC).

[1] Eva McNulty, a friend of ELA from Savannah.

[2] Benjamin K. Bliss, widower, who kept a seed store at 34 Barclay St. and lived at 133 E. 35th St., New York. His connection with Ellen was through Margaret Bliss, who married Ellen's grandfather, the Rev. Dr. Nathan Hoyt.

To Ellen Louise Axson

My own darling,   Balto., Oct. 5th 1884

I am afraid that you don't have any Sunday mail-delivery and that this letter will, consequently, be paired with the one I wrote yesterday, so that you will have been kept from Friday till Monday without word from me. I wish that you could be a *man* during your stay in New York (though I would'nt for the world and more than all that's in it have you remain one longer than that!) so that you could go down to the P.O. for your letter on Sunday, as I did for mine this morning, and have the other unrestricted opportunities of action which men, and men only, can have. I was genuinely unhappy until your letter came; but the very sight of it this morning brightened me up, and the contents of it have done much toward bringing back my wonted light spirits. It is *something* that things are not quite so bad at No. 60 as they seemed at first, and I trust that my darling will soon be in better, more cheerful and comfortable quarters: tho' I still have some serious misgivings about your boarding *alone*.

I am almost settled again in my little den and am beginning to rally from the loneliness and homesickness which rode me with cruel spurs all day yesterday, riding on even into my last night's sleep. I called on President Gilman and Dr. Adams yesterday, a few hours after my arrival, and was very pleasantly, almost cordially, received by them both. There are, I learn, a great many new men in our department, but the seven or eight "old men" who have returned suffice to make one feel at home in "the Bluntschli."

If I were not afraid of vexing you, my proud little lady, I would decline to obey your injunction to write you "at once" what your hotel bill was; because that is a debt which would not spoil by keeping. But I *promised* to let you share the travelling expenses, did'nt I? Well, your part of the hotel bill was $2.25 and your sleeping car berth to New York cost $2.00, so that I spent for you $4.25. Now, my darling, send this just when it may be most convenient, because I do'nt need it at all, and shall be very much distressed if you put yourself out to be punctilious with me in such a matter.

Oh! how my heart longs for you, my pet, my precious, matchless Eileen, my own little sweetheart! I love you even beyond my heart's power of computation. Your love is everything to

Your own   Woodrow.

ALS (WP, DLC).

From Ellen Louise Axson

My darling Woodrow,   New York Oct 5 1884

I thought I would be able to write my Sunday letter early in the day, so that you would get it sooner. But I could not content myself with "a line" today, and up to this time I have had no time for more. The half past six o'clock programme is suspended on Sundays, we are allowed to sleep late, and we did it. We had scarcely finished breakfast before it was time to get ready for church. Mr. Marvin Jr., "Cousin Walter's" old bachelor brother, called for us, and took us to their pew in the Madison Ave. Dutch Reformed church. Dr. Reed[1] is the pastor, and we liked him very much indeed. I think I will attend there frequently; though it is a long journey, almost up to Central Park. It was a simple but impressive gospel sermon, and he has a *very* pleasant voice and manner; there is something very attractive in his clear, crisp accent, and easy, almost conversational style. After church the young Marvin boy—have forgotten his name—escorted me to Cousin Ben's, where I was to dine. We had early dinner, then went, at four o'clock, to communion at their church, Dr. Park-hurst's;[2] after which Theodore[3] brought me back to Clinton Place; —so there you have the history of the day. I had a very pleasant time at Cousin Ben's. I believe I like them better when I don't stay with them. I found my way there yesterday afternoon, and was quite warmly welcomed by Clara.[4] Cousin Ben is absent, has gone to Boston to see his *lady-love*; it is a shame though to misapply those words in that fashion; the old simpleton is about sixty-five, and the lady is fifty! They are to be married a month from today. She is a distant cousin of his, and of mine too, they inform me. Clara likes the lady, and is altogether pleased with the match, because it sets her free. She has been engaged a long time to a gentleman living in Bordeaux; but her father was quite de-pendant on her, and she could'nt leave to go so far away. Now she will be married in Dec., and go at once to France—the man, Mr. Andrews, is an importer of wines! The family is larger than when I was here last, for the oldest son who lives in Cal. is here on a visit with his wife, and the youngest, Theodore, who was then in Europe, is now at home. Oh, he is *such* a curiosity! He has a craze on the subject of art,—is quite a collector, and spends all his time exhibiting his treasures and expatiating on their merits. He is a comical looking little fellow, and when he is dancing around, "placing" his pictures in different lights, and explaining what solemn depths of expression there is in this face, and what exstatic joy in that, while the others fulfill their mission of "keeping him down" by hinting that it is colic or cholera morbus from which the saints in question are suffering, the scene is rich, I assure you! By the way, before I leave the sub-ject of my cousins, I must inform you that I had a splendid din-ner! five courses, and I did justice to all. They have promised to find me a place to board if they can, and if I wish. I want to see what I can do at the League first. Our board here is five dol-lars, by the way, for this room—four & a half up stairs—which makes me more willing than ever to pay seven, elsewhere. Eva McNulty has applied here for board without success—no room. I would really feel mean beyond measure about keeping her away from Annie, even if I liked this place. Eva says if she can't make a change she is going to take the steamer this week and go back to Sav. Her place is beyond endurance, the rooms are very small, and there are five in each; one of her room-mates clerks at

Macy's, one is a sewing girl, and one is a factory girl; and she says they are *perfectly horrible* in manners, conversation, and everything else. As for the rules and restrictions—there [*sic*] name is legion; they are not even allowed to have their trunks in their rooms, but must keep them in the basement. Our place is ideal, by comparison. By the way, we have discovered one nice looking girl among the forty-three here; she seems to be a perfect lady, has nothing to do with the noisy crowd about her, in fact appears to enjoy herself even less than we do, for I should judge she was entirely alone. She is a tall, slender, pale brunette, and *so* pretty. We are quite interested in her; but we have never heard her speak yet. When we do, it is possible we may be rudely disillusioned. Well, I believe I have told you everything that has happened, or that I have done, so far, except that I went shopping yesterday afternoon again, and bought me "a love" of a cloak, one that would keep me warm in Greenland. There is one thing which I am sorry to say has *not* happened yet, I have not heard from you —was hoping that I should today, but I suppose that was unreasonable. But I am anxious to hear that you are in a peaceful frame of mind, and not worrying yourself into head-aches. I'll venture to say that you have taken my little troubles twice as much to heart as I myself, you dear, foolish boy. I think that the power of controlling one's thoughts is as useful an accomplishment as one can have—the power, I mean, of dismissing a disagreeable thought as soon as you have had enough of it, and of summoning what you will to take it's place. I believe I am beginning to acquire that power. When I grow tired of trying to plan and scheme, of my abortive attempts to look through that stone wall called "tomorrow," I use a certain spell that I possess, and the scene changes. But then it is no credit to me. I am only fortunate in having a talisman powerful enough to lay any ghost; and that talisman, dear love, is no other than your name. I can— and I *do*—think of you always my darling and find comfort and joy in the the [*sic*] thought. So you see how much you help your little sweetheart, even when you are away down in Balt. But I *must* close now, I have been scrawling abominably—fear it will take you *hours* to make this out.

Good night my darling I love love *love* you!

Your own   Eileen.

ALS (WP, DLC).

1 The Rev. Dr. Edward A. Reed.

2 The Rev. Dr. Charles H. Parkhurst, minister of the Madison Square Presbyterian Church since 1880 and a leader in the crusade against Tammany Hall in the 1890's.

3 Theodore Bliss, son of Benjamin.

4 Clara Bliss, daughter of Benjamin.

To Ellen Louise Axson

My own darling, Balto., Oct. 6th/84

If you are at work at the League this morning, you have the advantage of me. I find that all my duties at the University have been bunched in the middle of the week, being grouped on Wednesdays, Thursdays, and Fridays,[1] and that I shall have Mondays, Tuesdays, and Saturdays to use as I please—an exceedingly satisfactory arrangement, since work without interruption is the only sort that can have thought in it—but for the present an irksome fact because it keeps me waiting when I would be working off the rest of my loneliness and low spirits. I shall occupy myself, however, with writing a letter of consummate tact (!) to the publishers to whom my essays are to go first, and with getting my *ms.* into shape for being sent. There need be no lack of something to do.

Oh, my pet, how much I love you, and how desperately I miss you! I think of you all the time, and all my thought is dominated by the hope that you are finding pleasant arrangements and congenial people at the League, and that light is breaking upon your perplexities about boarding. With love unspeakable,

Your own Woodrow.

I am quite well. Regards to Miss Lester and Miss Young.

ALS (WC, NjP).

[1] Wilson did not make, or keep, a schedule of his courses at the Johns Hopkins during the academic year 1884-85, but his classroom notebooks and other evidence reveal that he was attending (a) the Seminary of Historical and Political Science, which met once a week for two hours throughout the year under Prof. Adams; (b) Finance and Taxation, two lectures a week throughout the year by Dr. Ely; (c) Principles and Historical Growth of Commerce, one lecture a week during the first semester by Dr. Ely; (d) Methods of Administration in England, Germany, and France, one lecture a week during the second semester by Dr. Ely; (e) Education, one lecture a week throughout the year by Prof. Hall; (f) History of Politics, three lectures a week throughout the year by Prof. Adams; (g) Modern European Politics (what Wilson called "Modern Constitutions"), one lecture a week throughout the year by Prof. Adams; and (h) Philosophy of the State, one lecture a week during the first semester by Dr. George S. Morris, Lecturer on the History of Philosophy.

Wilson's classroom notebooks for Adams's, Ely's, and Morris's courses are described at Oct. 8 and 10, 1884. Wilson's incomplete notes on Hall's lectures are described at Oct. 16, 1884. As these notebooks and WW to ELA, May 23, 1885, Vol. 4, all reveal, Wilson attended lectures only during the early weeks of the second semester, although he continued to attend the Historical Seminary until the end of the term.

From Ellen Louise Axson

My darling Woodrow, New York, Oct. 6/84.

We have all been so busy tonight exchanging notes as to the day's experiences, that the evening has passed before we knew it; so that now if I don't make haste to write my note, I will be left in the dark, as we were on Sat. night. We had a call too from Mr. Marvin this evening, and besides all that a grand "political excitement" over a great Republican demonstration in the street just outside of the door;—you remember we are near one of their headquarters. We have been very much entertained by the novel sight,—the gay processions and the fire-works, the music and speaking and cheering—especially as the cheering was quite as loud for Grover Cleveland as for "Jim Blaine"! We girls have a great deal of fun over our political differences,—Florence being a hopeless Republican. That is one respect in which I believe we excel most of you men,—viz. the power of keeping our temper during such discussions. But I suppose it is because we don't take "politics" seriously enough.

But I must stick to *really serious* matters now, and waste no more of these few short minutes! We all began our work today, Florence at the Kindergarten and Annie & I at the League; Florence is disgusted and Annie and I are equally delighted,—somewhat to our own surprise, for we expected anything rather than to *enjoy* the first few days, among strange people, strange methods, &c. True, we are all at sea about our work, for instead of crayon, they use charcoal entirely,—a material which is handled very differently from crayon, and which we know nothing about; but we have so many companions in misery, that it is rather funny than otherwise, and I think we shall like it very much. We have a nice-looking and pleasant class of about twenty girls, and half a dozen young men, and we have two large bright cheerful studios for the antique department. They are on the third floor;—the portrait and woman's life class and the offices are on the fourth, and the men's life and painting classes have two splendid studios, with sky-light, in the fifth floor. Our teacher is Mr. George De Forest Brush! We hav'nt seen him yet, he does'nt make his appearance until Thursday. Your thrice welcome letters reached me this morning. I won't *try* to tell you how glad I was to get them. Am delighted to hear such good reports from you, and trust you are going to have a delightful winter at the "Johnny Hop." But I *must* say goodbye darling,—you see how well nigh impossible it is for me to write a "few lines." I love you, dearest, more than tongue can tell, and am always and altogether

Your own   Eileen.

I enclose the four, twenty-five, in this, trust it will reach you safely,—I don't know how to get a money order here.

ALS (WP, DLC).

To Ellen Louise Axson

My own darling,   Baltimore, Md., Oct. 7/84

I have just received your sweet letter of Sunday and it has put me in the best of spirits. It is everything to me to know that my darling is getting along happily in the great city, that she has found friends who are ready to give her cordial help. If she be comfortable and content I can't *help* being happy.

I have just finished preparing my *ms.* to be sent to Boston and am about to start out for the express office. Then I shall be free to turn to my University work, until the *ms.* is returned and has to be sent to some other publishing house!

I hope, my pet, that this is the fourth letter of mine that has *reached* you (?). I have *written* four, such as they were. There's no news for me to tell, such as the particular's about your peculiar cousin and about the delights of the "Christian Home" which made your letter so interesting. But I can put into mine that which makes yours so cheering and delightful to me, unbounded love.

Regards to the young ladies. I am well and love you beyond all imaginings, my precious.   Your own   Woodrow.

ALS (WC, NjP).

From Ellen Louise Axson

My darling Woodrow,   New York, Oct. 7/84.

Your note of the 6th—yesterday—came safely to hand this morning, and the package of envelopes this afternoon;[1] many thanks for the latter—or indeed for *both*; it certainly *is* charming to hear every day, and to get the letters so soon after they are written too; they reach me just after breakfast every morning.

I am very glad to hear of the satisfactory adjustment of matters at the "U"! Those three uninterrupted days will indeed be great gain;—I hope they won't give you very much work to do "out of school hours" so that you may be able to get the full benefit of them. I wish you much success in your venture with the Boston publishers, my darling,—would like to read that graceful epistle.

We are in very good spirits today at No. 60;—we have an addition to our family by the way. We have taken Eva in with us. Four girls is a goodly number for one room—only one window too,—but there was nothing else to be done, her situation was desperate. It is pleasanter for Florence, at least, for they attend the same school, and as it is a long walk, they feel much more comfortable now that they can take it together.

Just think what a terrible enterprise I have entered upon; I am going over to Hoboken tomorrow, to find Helen's[2] home. Florence is going with me; Grandmother sent me the address yesterday morning, and I have been trying ever since to gather up my courage for the undertaking. If we could only take a cab and drive to the door! but there is that wretched ferry between! However, Mr. Marvin has given us full directions and I have no doubt but that we will find the place. Helen has never been well since that first attack, her disease is galloping consumption, and the Dr. gives them no hope; the end is expected any day. The change to this severe climate seems to have at once developed in her the family trouble. What a pity that she came! And yet I suppose we ought not to think of it in that way, for God rules in everything. Good-night, my darling, these girls are chattering so that I *can't* write, and will try no longer. Believe me dear love
Yours with all my heart   Ellie.

ALS (WP, DLC).

[1] WW had sent ELA a supply of stamped envelopes addressed to him on his Caligraph.

[2] Helen Porter Killough.

From Melville R. Hopewell

Dear Sir   Tekamah [Neb.] 10/8/84

Yours of 1st Recd—I have prepared Release of Mortgage, and forwarded to Jas. W Bones for Execution on its Return; think I will be able to Remit you the Jack col[lection]—or most of it.
Truly &c *M. R. Hopewell*

APS (WP, DLC).

To Ellen Louise Axson

My own darling,   Balto., Md., Oct. 8th/84

The result of grouping our ex[er]cises in the middle of the week is that when we are busy we are busy "sure enough." The lectures have been coming in such rapid succession to-day that this is the first opportunity I've found for the duty which is altogether a duty of love and delight, and the lectures still to come warn me that I must be exceeding brief even now.

I have just received and devoured your note of Monday. I am *so* glad, my precious little sweetheart, so *overjoyed* that your work at the League has begun so pleasantly and promises to be so much to your satisfaction. I can be *altogether* content now, if only you get suited and settled in the matter of board.

I saw our new class this morning for the first time—unremarkable men for the most part, but one or two whom I shall *have* to describe to you anon.

I am quite well and love you as not even yourself will believe.

Your own   Woodrow.

P.S. The order for $4.25 came safely to hand, you cruel, provokingly proud and prompt little darling, and I suppose I must say 'thank you.'   Lovingly,   W.

Always regards to the young ladies.

ALS (WC, NjP).

From Wilson's shorthand notes taken in Professor Herbert Baxter Adams's course in the history of politics

Three Classroom Notebooks

[Oct. 8, 1884-Feb. 18, 1885]

Inscribed on cover (WWhw): "History of Politics *Adams*"

Contents:

WWsh and WWhw notes and bibliographies taken in Professor Herbert Baxter Adams's course in the history of politics, Oct. 8, 1884-Feb. 18, 1885. Notes for Oct. 8 and 15, 1884, on loose sheets. Includes WW's notes taken on reports by various students. They also indicate that WW reported on Walter Bagehot on Jan. 28, 1885.

❖

[Oct. 8, 1884-March 18, 1885]

Inscribed on cover (WWhw): "Finance *Ely*"

Contents:

WWsh and WWhw notes and bibliographies taken in Dr. Richard T. Ely's course in finance and taxation, Oct. 8, 1884-March 18, 1885. Notes for Oct. 8 and 15, 1884, on loose sheets. A transcript of Wilson's notes on Ely's lecture on bimetallism of Nov. 19, 1884, is printed at this date.

✧

[Oct. 8, 1884-Jan. 28, 1885]

Inscribed on inside of cover (WWhw): *"Woodrow Wilson"* and on page 1 (WWhw): "For earlier lectures see leaves in back of book. *Oct. 22, 1884.*"

Contents:

WWsh and WWhw notes and bibliographies taken in Dr. George S. Morris's course in the philosophy of the state, Oct. 8, 1884-Jan. 28, 1885. Notes for Oct. 8 and 15 and Dec. 3, 1884, on loose sheets. Transcripts of Wilson's notes on lectures on Herbert Spencer are printed at Nov. 5, 12, and 19, 1884.

Student notebooks (WP, DLC).

From Ellen Louise Axson

My darling Woodrow,   New York, Oct. 8/84.

Well here am I, again able to report myself safe, and well and not *lost!*—at least we were only lost a short time. We succeeded, on the whole, very well in finding our way to Hoboken, and I think I will be able to go alone next time. Am very glad I went to-day for Janie [Porter Chandler] leaves tonight; Helen has rallied since last week, and the doctor now thinks she will live several weeks, perhaps several months; but oh, she looks *dreadfully!*— not in the least like herself,—she is a perfect skeleton; and is of course altogether helpless, can't move herself, or speak above a whisper. But she talks just like her dear old self, and is so peaceful and *so lovely*. She still has a faint touch of her old bright manner. Dear girl, she was pointing out to me some of the handsome things about her room, pictures, bronzes &c.,—her *wedding presents*. Could anything be sadder than the whole story of her life? And poor Mr. Killough! I like him *so* much; he is a noble fellow, has shown himself singularly so, throughout it all. He is a splendid nurse,—so gentle and quiet and calm. They have been sitting up every night for weeks, and Janie is completely broken down. She has taken a violent cold which has settled on her lungs so she is going home tonight. I hardly see how she can bear to do it, but it seems necessary. They have a very fine professional nurse now.

But why should I write you all these details, about one whom you have never seen? Only, I suppose, because I can *think* of nothing else just now, and it begins to grow natural to tell you everything, and anything, I am thinking. But though I know you are interested in my friend, darling, it isn't necessary to draw any more largely on your sympathies now. Oh, dear love, how I wish I could see you tonight. I am *so* heavy-hearted—I think I will go to sleep and try to *dream* about you by way of finding comfort. Good night, darling,

With all the love of my heart   Your own   Ellie.

ALS (WP, DLC) with WWhw and WWsh notation on env.

Draft of a Letter to James W. Bones

Dear uncle James,   Balto., Md., Oct. 9/84.

Your last letter to me reached Wilmington so shortly before my departure for this place that I have not till now found it possible to give it the careful attention I desired. At last, however, I can reply.

I have noted, upon examining the papers several facts which seem to have escaped your notice. First as regards the eighty acres (W½ N.W. ¼, 1. 17. 7.) erroneously included in the deed of partition. At the time of the exchange with uncle Thomas, the Woodrow estate gave him 200 acres @ 10 dollars per acre for 160 acres at $12.50 per acre. The latter was then sold and credited. That's settled. But 80 acres of that 200 deeded to uncle Thomas remained upon our list (though it does not appear in the copy of the list which I took with all care and now have before me) and it was this 80 (valued at $10, not $12.50, per acre) which got by mistake into our deed of partition. It appears, then, that by this error Auntie's estate lost $400.00, not $500.00. None of the land adjoining this 80 acres, in 1-17-7 is valued at more than $10.00.

Next as to the taxes. $12.18 was paid on E½ N.W¼, 11-17-8, which is neither upon my copy of the list of Dodge lands, nor upon my carefully-made copy of the map. So, again $24.36 was paid on N.W. ¼ 12-17-8 which appears neither upon the list nor upon the map. Both these tracks, however, are marked on the map as *formerly* owned by the estate. As to E½ N.E ¼ 11-17-8, there is some doubt. It is credited to the estate on the map, but *not* on the list. It would seem, therefore, that $48.72 (or at least $36.54) had been erroneously paid in taxes.

The resulting deduction in the $1,000 owed mother by yourself would, accordingly, be either $479.13 or $473.04—depending on whether E½ N.E ¼ 11-17-8 should be paid for or not. If the *map* be right, there is another mistake unremedied, because the settlement was made on the basis of the list which says nothing of this tract.

Let me hear from you, please, as soon as possible about these matters.

WWhwL (draft) (WP, DLC). Atts: J. W. Bones to WW, Sept. 16, 1884; J. W. Bones to WW, Oct. 28, 1884.

To Ellen Louise Axson

My own darling,   Balto., Md., Oct. 9th/84

The world has been going so hard with poor little Dr. Ely—since his marriage[1]—that he is ill, in his bed, to-day and I am unexpectedly left with an hour at my disposal which I had thought to spend with him.

I thought that my little sweetheart would find hearing from her lover everyday while she is in the great, lonely city a very comforting arrangement—worth even the trouble of writing daily to him; and so I am delighted to have my anticipations fulfilled by her confession, that it "*is* charming." You dear little witch! And what do you suppose it is to me to have a note every morning from you? Why, the most I *can* say is, that it makes this lonely, anxious life not only endurable but full of a quiet, abiding joy! I love you, my Eileen: you are all the world to me!

I havent made any visits yet—except to friend Woods' office—because I have had so many small things to engage my hours "out of school." Last night, for instance, I sat up till mid-night looking over maps, land-lists, and tax-receipts by way of accompaniment to a business letter which I was writing to uncle James Bones, calling his attention to several errors which had resulted from his want of care and exactness.

I sent Shinn your address yesterday. I supposed that he had noted it when I directed the flowers for him, and I certainly mentioned it to him several times in conversation; but a letter from him followed me almost immediately from New York, begging to be informed what it was. You may, therefore, expect a call from him very soon, I suppose. Remember that he is quite deaf, my pet.

How is your acquaintance with charcoal progressing, my little artist? I am as much interested in the details of your League experiences as you can be yourself.

I am quite well—though foolish enough to have a slight headache, which I shall try to walk off by carrying this letter to the Post Office. With love unbounded,   Your own   Woodrow.

ALS (WC, NjP).
1 Ely had married Anna Morris Anderson of Richmond, Va., on June 25, 1884.

From Ellen Louise Axson

My darling Woodrow,   New York, Oct. 9/84.
Florence has just been reading aloud to us her letter home; and I am so pleased with it that I don't think I can do better than copy it entire. It runs as follows—"Dear family,—The light is *very* bad tonight,—can't write at all,—all well—good night!" In fact the light is *uncommonly* bad; it jumps from the floor to the ceiling every second, and our heads feel as though they were jumping with it; there is nothing to do but to shut our eyes and talk, or to go to bed. So good night, my darling. Yours with all my heart.
                                                  Eileen.
We *are* "all well and and [*sic*] doing well."

ALS (WP, DLC).

From Joseph Ruggles Wilson

My dearest Woodrow   Wilmington [N.C.] Oct 9, 1884
Dr. Palmer writes, in a letter received this morning: "8 of the Directors (of S.W.U.)[1] cordially support the nomination; 2 acquiesce in it; one has not been heard from yet; and one opposes, viz *J. H. Bryson*[2] for whose opposition you will not (continues Dr P.) find it difficult to account. . . . I think it probable the Ex. Committee will extend to you a formal invitation, to be ratified by the Board at their next meeting in June. The election is substantively made already, and only lacks the outward form to be given when the Board shall meet."
This intelligence has greatly excited your dear mother & myself as you may easily guess. I write at once to our darling son & faithful friend, to tell him what will be so pleasant to his ears too.
We were glad to get your telegram & letter, and to know that yr. trip passed off well[.] We do hope that dear Ellie (whom we both paternally & maternally love—big) will soon get suited as to boarding, &c.
With great love   Your affc   Father

ALS (WP, DLC).

[1] South-Western Presbyterian University, Clarksville, Tenn.

[2] The Rev. Dr. John H. Bryson, pastor of the Huntsville, Ala., Presbyterian Church. Dr. Bryson, in 1873, had accepted a call to the pastorate of the First Presbyterian Church of Columbia, S.C., after the Session of that church had decided to terminate JRW's services as Stated Supply. See WW to ELA, Oct. 12, 1884, n.2.

To Ellen Louise Axson

My own darling,   *Bluntschli Library* [Baltimore] Oct. 10th, 1884

I must write my note this morning from my place here at the "Seminary" table in between lecture times, for want of a better place and opportunity.

I have just received your account of your visit to Hoboken, my pet, and have been very much distressed by your account of poor Mrs. Killough's touching condition. I am *glad*, my love, that you told me all about it, because I want to hear about everything which affects you or concerns your friends. Your friends are mine already—I love them through you, because you do.

Little Dr. Ely is well to-day and I am awaiting the hour of his lecture, which is to distress me till dinner time. If he would speak out like a man, it would be endurable, but *dribbling* is distracting to a chap of my intense disposition.

Have you seen Master Brush, your preceptor, yet? I am curious to learn his characteristics, good, bad, or indifferent.

To-night comes the second Seminary meeting of the "semester." The first one I missed—a circumstance which I regret only because Dr. Adams occupied a large part of the time in discoursing on the life, adventures, achievements, and talents of our one-time chum and co-worker, Chas. H. Shinn. Shinn's success has greatly impressed Adams—all success commands his instant homage—and the discourse was a eulogy.[1] To-night we are to cogitate solid economic subjects.[2]

I am quite well and kept in excellent spirits by thought of your love for me and consciousness of my unbounded love for you. What would I not give for five minutes of your presence every day. Your letters are the next best thing, and have already become indispensable to me.

In haste, love, and repentence for this scrawl,

Your own   Woodrow.

ALS (WC, NjP).

[1] The Minutes of the Seminary of Historical and Political Science, Oct. 3, 1884, briefly mention a letter from Shinn and an abstract of his forthcoming book, *Land Laws of Mining Districts.*

[2] The main paper of the evening was "Pennsylvania State Finance and Taxation," by Thomas K. Worthington. The Seminary Minutes, Oct. 10, 1884, give a long summary.

Two Classroom Notebooks

[Oct. 10, 1884-Feb. 27, 1885]

Inscribed on cover (WWhw): "Modern Constitutions, *Adams*"

Contents:

WWsh and WWhw notes and bibliographies taken in Professor Herbert Baxter Adams's course in modern European politics, Oct. 10, 1884-Feb. 27, 1885. Notes for Oct. 10, 1884, on loose sheets.

✧

[Oct. 10, 1884-Feb. 27, 1885]

Inscribed on cover (WWhw): "*Commerce Ely*" and "*Administration Ely*"

Contents:

(a) WWsh and WWhw notes taken in Dr. Richard T. Ely's course in the principles and historical growth of commerce, Oct. 10-Dec. 12, 1884. Notes for Oct. 10, 1884, on loose sheets.

(b) WWsh and WWhw notes taken in Dr. Ely's course in Administration, c. Jan. 9-Feb. 27, 1885.

Student notebooks (WP, DLC).

From Ellen Louise Axson

My darling Woodrow,   [New York] Oct. 10/84

As the light is better tonight, and the girls are all busy writing, too, and therefore comparatively quiet, I hope I will be able to write *my* note with somewhat less difficulty than usual. Such a set of chatterboxes you never saw! We waste the whole evening generally, because we won't let each other alone,—there is so much to tell about the day's experiences, and the sayings and doings of the people at the League and the Kinder-garten. But we *enjoy* our evenings at any rate, and we "get on" remarkably well together. If you could look in on us you would find us very cosy and comfortable. Our room, in spite of it's dingy furniture, looks quite pretty and homelike, now that we have scattered about it our books and pictures, and odd[s] and ends—and have given it a few other "womanly touches." The pleasantest feature of the room is the central feature, the round table with it's crimson cover, and pretty drop light; and when we are gathered about it,—Annie and I "sketching," Florence generally, and all of us talking at once, we almost forget that we are strangers in a strange land. By the way, I never told you what a good friend we have found in the house, in the person of the house-maid, Katie. She is a bright, merry and *exceedingly* pretty Irish girl; just as pleasant and cheery and kind-hearted as she can be; and she has taken a great fancy to us apparently, she is certainly very good to us. She is the only person except the landlady with whom we are on speaking terms. I hav'nt been in the parlour since you left except to look in the directory.

And by the way, I will be *delighted* to see Mr. Shinn as you know, but what in the world am I to do if he comes at night? How can I talk to him—a deaf man—in that room with the forty shop-girls? The hubbub would be stilled for once, and they would be all ears instead of tongues. The girls have been laughing over the scene in anticipation all day. I hope he will either come in the *day*, or not come at all until I move. I have said nothing about moving lately, because I was tired of the subject,—and have no doubt you are equally so. I *could* fill up every letter with that business in it's various stages! I could and would have left before this, but I am waiting for the other girls to decide what they will do, —and they change their minds every hour. But I won't begin on the subject now at the end of my sheet. My acquaintance with charcoal is progressing satisfactorily, I believe,—at least Mr. Brush's verdict is quite favourable; and I like it very much indeed. When I get time I must tell you something about Mr. Brush and some of the other League notables. Goodnight darling—take good care of yourself. I don't like those frequent head-aches *at all*. There must be some reason for them. Give my best love to your dear parents. I fully intended to write myself before this but have been waiting to "get settled[.]" While I was giving an account of myself I wanted it to be a *good* one, you know. With all my heart

Your own Eileen.

ALS (WP, DLC).

To Ellen Louise Axson

My own darling, Balto., Md., Oct. 11th/84

I am too much distressed this morning to know how to write such a note to my darling as she would like to read. I have not had a single line from home since we left, and my mind is full of all sorts of vague fears and forebodings—such a silence never occurred before: and, though it may mean nothing serious, it *may* mean a great deal that is serious. If I don't hear this afternoon, I shall telegraph to know if anything is the matter; though of course, when I reason about the thing, I am sure that they would have let me know immediately if there was any alarming trouble keeping them from writing as usual. You see what a desperately nervous and anxious chap I am about those I love. I can get up alarms and worries at the shortest notice—especially when I am feeling as I am to-day, weak and nervous on my own account. I shall get to work on some of the vast masses of reading I have to do, and *work* myself back to myself and my usual self's senses! This is Saturday—one of the days given us to follow our own plans, and of course the only natural plan is work.

You probably wont get this note until its successor, of to-morrow, joins it—and my knowledge of that fact must explain my having written it is [in] such a key: I hope to hear from home this afternoon and then send after it a laughing companion which will not let it dampen your Monday spirits.

You may rest assured of this, my little queen, that, however miserable I may be at times, I never fail to derive profound joy from your love, and cannot in any mood or any extremity be anything but with all my heart's love,   Your own   Woodrow.

ALS (WC, NjP).

From Ellen Louise Axson

My darling Woodrow,   New York, Oct 11/84

I don't think the mail boxes are emptied on Sunday, and therefore this will probably not reach you before Tuesday; so as I expect to write again tomorrow, and that too will reach you on Tuesday, I will let you off with a line tonight. It isn't necessary to double on you, and besides as it is Sat. night, I am very busy and a little tired too. We have taken a long tramp this afternoon, shopping and looking at boarding houses. By the way, I think we have found a jewel of a house now, if the girls can only go to it—but of that more anon. Speaking of our shopping—we found ourselves in rather a comical predicament. We wanted some salt and *whiskey* to keep our hair from falling, and I wanted some cubeb [medicinal] *cigarettes* for my cold. Nice purchases for young ladies! were they not? When we reached the store our courage failed us entirely, we *couldn't* ask for both at the same place, so we came home without the whiskey.

I have just been interrupted in my writing for a quarter of an hour or so, by an animated discussion as to churches and our programme with regard to them tomorrow and throughout the winter. F[lorence] and Annie are in favour of "Grace Church" [Grace Episcopal Chapel] tomorrow and a new one every Sunday; but I don't fancy being a wanderer on the face of the earth in any more senses than I can help. The first Pres.—Dr. Paxton's[1]—

is just around the corner. Do you know anything about him. Who was the minister your father said I must hear—the best in N Y?

I *must* say "goodnight," love. Am *so* glad to hear you are quite well again. Am sorry you missed the eulogy on Mr Shinn. I think that was quite "nice" in Dr Adams. Much love to your parents. I love you darling with all my heart, and as much as your heart can wish.   Your own Ellie.

ALS (WP, DLC).
¹ The Rev. Dr. William Miller Paxton, pastor of the First Presbyterian Church of New York from 1866 to 1883. Dr. Paxton, unknown to ELA, had retired in 1883 and was living in Princeton, N.J.

From Janet Woodrow Wilson

My precious boy,   Wilmington, N.C. Saturday Oct. 11, '84.

Yours of the 9th reached me this morning. I have just put up the partition deed—or deeds. There being the three together, I thought it best to send them all—since I was not sure whether you wanted all or not. . . .

How is dear Ellie? I am so glad that she came to us—for now I am *sure* you will be happy in each other. She is very lovely, I think—so intelligent & every way attractive. I trust it may not be long before you shall have your dear little girl all to yourself.

Your father has written you as to the Clarkesville matter. I cannot tell you how thankful I am that the question is so settled. Dear papa is like a different person, since yesterday morning. He had made up his mind to leave this place in any case—and he naturally dreaded the necessity of looking for a place—in case this matter had resulted differently. . . .

Give our best love to dearest Ellie. Papa joins me in warmest love to you, dearest boy.

Lovingly   Your   Mother

ALS (WP, DLC).

Two Letters to Ellen Louise Axson

My own darling,   Balto., Oct. 12th, 1884

Enthusiastic for the plan as I was from the first, I confess I had no idea how delightful it would be to receive daily letters from my darling. It keeps me in a sort of glow of satisfaction which drives off all fever of worry that can arise from ordinary mishaps or anxieties. And this morning finds me altogether relieved about the home folks and about myself. Yesterday I was full of the aches and languor which are accepted as the premonitory symptoms of a severe cold; but in the afternoon came a letter from home,[1] and before going to bed I dosed myself with several grains of quinine, so that this morning *all* the aches are fled—heartache and all—and I am as fresh and as cheery as this lovely morning itself. Because of course I've been to the Post Office to fetch your sweet note of Friday night—and why *should'nt* a man be well and content when he knows of the welfare and happiness of all whom he loves? He would need to be cased in a *very* thick crust of selfishness to keep out *such* influences!

Father's letter contains a family *secret*, my little sweetheart, which, as one of the family, you may keep with us until it is made public. The Trustees of the South-Western Presbyterian University, of Clarksville, Tenn., have decided upon the election of Rev. Dr. Jos. R. Wilson to the new department of Theology which they are about to establish (the election cannot be made formal till next Spring) and he will accept. His aptitudes are for teaching even more than for preaching, and the ten years during which he has had charged [*sic*] of that affectionate but uncongenial congregation in Wilmington have quite spent his satisfaction in the work there. He has been aided by the admiration and devotion of the people there to do a great deal for their welfare: but he feels that he has now done all that was in his power and that the rest of his ministry in Wilm. would consist in little more than the composition and delivery of sermons which would be their admiration and delight. There is no concealing the fact that they are a coarse-grained people who need—or at least *want* —pastoral work done amongst them such as a refined scholar, possessed of all a scholar's fastidious tastes and acute sensibilities, cannot do,—such, at any rate, as that sensitive gentleman, my father, felt that he could not much longer continue to do,— and his great desire has been to spend the closing years of his life in teaching. He left Columbia Seminary, you know, because the Gen. Assembly sustained the self-will of the students against the discipline of the faculty, and not because he was at all dissatisfied with his work.[2] He never was so entirely himself—so even in good spirits and so uniform in enjoyment of his class-room duties, —as when he was in Columbia: and I am sure that in taking this chair of Theology about to be offered him he will be putting himself in the way of doing the very best work of his life—if the conditions at Clarksville turn out to be anything like as favourable as they now promise to be. He was not *meant* for a pastor—despite the testimony of his splendid pulpit powers,—but he is of the stuff of which the greatest teachers are made. That is the real meaning of his talents for public speech.

At present the case stands thus: The Directors cordially support his nomination, and it is "probable the Executive Committee will extend to" him "a formal invitation, to be ratified by the Board at their next meeting in June. The election is substantially made already, and only lacks the outward form to be given when the Board shall meet." It would be odd—wouldn't it—if both father and I were to enter upon professorships in Sept. next?

The past week's work at "the Johnny Hop," seems to indicate a year ahead of us much more fruitful of instruction than last year. Dr. Adams is lecturing *much* better, and will be very serviceable to us, if he but keep up his present industry.

I hope that my darling will be scrupulously careful of her health during this changeful weather. I am anxious about the effects of N.Y. climate upon my precious Southern flower. I love you beyond all compare, my own Eileen, and am altogether

Your own   Woodrow.

ALS (WP, DLC).
    [1] JRW to WW, Oct. 9, 1884.
    [2] WW was referring to a controversy that split Columbia Theological Seminary and was a prime cause of JRW's departure from the Seminary to the First Presbyterian Church of Wilmington, N.C.
    JRW became Stated Supply (not the installed Pastor) of the First Presbyterian Church in Columbia, S.C., in February 1871. The Session of the church decided that the congregation needed a pastor as well as a preacher, and JRW resigned in July 1873 after some bitter personal controversy. The congregation had two interim ministers and then called the Rev. John H. Bryson, D.D., in November 1873.
    The faculty of the Seminary, resenting what was in fact JRW's ouster, decided at the beginning of the academic year 1873-74 to hold regular divine services in the Seminary Chapel at 11 a.m. on Sunday mornings, and made attendance by the students compulsory. Some of the students greatly objected to the ruling as an interference with their personal liberty and held protest meetings in the Seminary Chapel. Seven of them were thereupon dismissed. But the members of the faculty were divided, and they agreed to ask the General Assembly for a ruling. That body, meeting in Columbus, Miss., discussed the matter on May 22, 26, 27, and 28, 1874, and voted to uphold the students. JRW then and there resigned his professorship and, soon afterward, accepted a pending call to the First Church in Wilmington, N.C. The Rev. John B. Adger, D.D., another professor at the Seminary, also resigned at once. Samuel L. Morris, *Samuel L. Morris, An Autobiography* (Richmond, Va., 1932), p. 54; Fitz Hugh McMaster and J. M. Bateman, *History of First Presbyterian Church and Its Graveyard* (Columbia, S.C., n.d.), p. 3; *Minutes of the General Assembly of the Presbyterian Church in the United States, 1871-74* (4 vols., Columbia, S.C., and Richmond, Va., 1871-74), pp. 489-90, 492-94, 496-97, 512-13, 523-26, 578-81, 676-77.

Balto., Md., Oct. 13th 1884

Yes, my precious little sweetheart, I am glad to say, the mail *is* taken from the boxes on Sundays, and your note of Saturday evening came this morning instead of disappointing me by wait-ing to join the letter that will come to-morrow.

I don't wonder that you object to adopting Miss Lester's pro-posed Sunday plan of sampling all the churches of the city. That would not only be very unsatisfactory, but, it seems to me, would also be more like sight-seeing and diversion than like worship. I never heard Dr. Paxton, my pet, but I am afraid, from what I have heard, that he is not of the sort to be pleasing to us who love the gospel pure, free from the colourings of *dyspepsia*. I [am] sorry to say that I don't remember the name of the minister father mentioned as "the best in New York" (I shall write and ask him who it was), but I do know my own preference for Dr. William Taylor, and I am quite sure that, if the "Broadway Tabernacle" is not altogether too inaccessible from where you may board, after your final settlement, you would find great satisfaction in attending regularly there.[1]

I have roused the dear folks at home—a note from mother this morning (the servants have been taking vacations and getting sick and the dear lady has been working beyond her strength to supply their places, finding, of course, no time for writing). May I quote a paragraph which concerns us? "How is dear Ellie? I am so glad that she came to us—for now I am *sure* you will be happy in each other. She is very lovely, I think—so intelligent and every way attractive. I trust it may not be long before you shall have your dear little girl all to yourself." She also wants to be told "all about" myself "and dear Ellie," and closes by sending "our best love to dearest Ellie"; which quite agrees with this char-acteristic sentence from father's note of yesterday: "We do hope that dear Ellie (whom we both paternally and maternally love—big) will soon get suited as to boarding." Ah! you little witch, see what you have done to my relations, besides making me to the fullest power of my love   Your own   Woodrow.

ALS (WC, NjP).
    [1] The Rev. Dr. William M. Taylor, minister of the Tabernacle Congregational Church.

Two Letters from Ellen Louise Axson

My darling Woodrow,   New York Oct. 13/84
    Cousin Ben came around yesterday afternoon and *would* have me go home with him to tea. I had already refused to go to din-ner. So I had no opportunity to write last night. Now it is Monday morning, and we are in a rush, of course. We are obliged to be

at the League at nine sharp on Mon. to get a place. So though I had a great deal to say, I must put it all off to a more convenient season. Mr. Shinn called last night while I was out. Much as I want to see him, I am thankful I *was* out. Then he asked for Annie, and she saw him, and was delighted with him. She has done nothing since but tell me what "Mr. Shinn said"[.] But she said it was *"awful"* too, for the shop-girls behaved exactly as we expected,—sat around in a circle, perfectly silent, and *listened.* He brought us all lovely flowers, by the way; is'nt he kind and thoughtful? Good-bye, darling. Excuse haste. With all my heart,

Your own Ellie.

My darling Woodrow,   New York. Oct. 11[13]/84.

Your two letters of the eleventh and 12th, both reached me, as you anticipated, this morning. Am *so* sorry, dear, that you have been feeling so badly, and depressed, but am glad, indeed, to get such cheerful reports in "number two"; and especially to learn that your anxiety about the dear ones in Wilmington was groundless. How does your letter report your mother as feeling? I am *delighted* to hear of the Clarksville professorship. I am sure it will be a pleasant and beneficial change. He is getting back to the work which is evidently congenial to him, beyond all other, and it can't fail to do him good. I *do* hope he will find his surroundings pleasant too. So that was the explanation of Dr. Wilson's curiosity as to the location of Clarksville! Your mother will be glad to have him relieved of that incessant "pastoral work"; will she not? Her patience on the subject seemed to have been pretty well exhausted. I am only sorry that the change is not to take place for a year.

I am very glad too to hear that your year's work at the University has begun so promisingly. I hope Dr. Adams will redeem his reputation entirely with you and the rest of the "fellows."

We are as much pleased as ever with our work, and our surroundings at the League. We are so fascinated with it, that we can scarcely tear ourselves away to go elsewhere. We suffer a good deal of mental disquietude about the disposition of our time, for when we are not at the League we have an uneasy feeling, as though we were neglecting our duty; and yet we would be very foolish not to make the most of our opportunities while in the city. We ought to see all we can in our line,—picture galleries[,] art stores of one sort and another. We spent this afternoon at the Metropolitan [Museum of Art];—the present Loan collection closes tomorrow, so we were just in time. It was very good indeed; I saw, for the first time, specimens of Meissonier, Detaille, Géro—[1]

Oct 14   The light went out just at this point, dearest, and my letter came to an abrupt conclusion; now I have only time to close in haste; so goodbye for the present. Take good care of *your*self, darling. I can't tell you how I feel when I hear you are unwell or low-spirited; I want to see you *so* much that I could almost *fly*—or would like to try at any rate! With truest love   Your own Ellie.

ALS (WP, DLC).
[1] ELA's dash suggests that when the "light went out" she may have been meaning to write "Gérôme," i.e., Jean-Léon Gérôme, a contemporary of the other two artists named.

To Ellen Louise Axson

My own darling,   Balto., Md., Oct. 14th, 1884
As I *would* have said *once* (before I became a grave and dignified student of "world themes"!) I owe "cousin Ben" one for having taken you off to tea and so deprived me of the letter that would have been written, had he been less persistent. But it would be selfish beyond even me to *regret* his compelling you to accept his invitation: because I know what a pleasant variety such experiences must form from the rather dismal round of life at No. 0u.

Are you ever in during the afternoon, my pet, or do your hours at the League run through the whole day? If you are free during the afternoons, I will write to Shinn and ask him to call before instead of after dinner next time—unless you are to move soon, in which case I will suggest that he wait till you have escaped that horde of shop-girls. I am quite sure that *he* will be as eager to escape another such ordeal of public conversation as either you or Miss Lester could be: because he is exceedingly sensitive and must have been terribly embarrassed by such a situation. I don't wonder that Miss Lester was "delighted" with the dear genuine old chap—and I believe, as well as hope, that you will like him as much.

I am doing what is of all things most trying to me: I am steadily journeying through a course of systematic reading—which I pray may not be as interminable as it looks. My recreation for the present must consist in turning aside now and again to read some self-opinionated American political economist for Dr. Ely, or to "cram" a few facts and dates for the examination in colonial history which a few more weeks will bring forth.[1] I wish that I could school my palate to be a little more patient of this dry regimen; but I have not yet seen my way quite clear to that sort of victory over my natural disposition.

I am quite well, though, my darling, and in excellent spirits. Has my little sweetheart gotten rid of her cold yet? Take care of yourself, my precious, for the sake of the love you bear

Your own   Woodrow.

ALS (WC, NjP).

[1] The Johns Hopkins, in 1884, revised its requirements for the Ph.D. degree and stipulated, among other things, that candidates should pass written and oral examinations in one major and two minor subjects. Wilson was preparing for examination in one of his minor subjects, American colonial history. He took this examination on November 15, 1884. See WW to ELA, Oct. 27 and Nov. 15, 1884. However, he soon decided—temporarily, as will become evident—not to take the Ph.D. degree. In seeking his father's approval for this decision, Wilson pleaded the danger to his health from too much work. See JRW to WW, Oct. 29, 1884. He further explained his decision in WW to ELA, Nov. 8, 1884.

From Ellen Louise Axson

My darling Woodrow,   New York, Oct. 14/84

Your sweet little letter of the 13th reached me today at the League,—Annie brought it to me when she came back from lunch. Those kind words from your father and mother made me very happy, dearest. Thank you for sending them; their opinion of me was a subject on which, I assure you, I have had many misgivings, so my heart was very full as I read. How can I ever be grateful enough for all their goodness to me!

It *was* Dr. Taylor of whom your father spoke—I remember now. I went to Dr. Paxton's on Sunday; the pulpit however was filled by someone else—I don't know who.[1] But he gave us a *splendid* sermon on the providence of God. By the way, about a third of it was on the subject of evolution,—a noble argument in it's favour! I was very much impressed,—I think I will turn evolutionist. He said—but I hav'nt time, even if I had the ability, to tell you *what* he said!—he took very high ground however; did'nt stand on the defensive at all.

But I am afraid I must give up trying to write tonight. It is so cold that my fingers are stiff, and almost refuse to obey me. Besides the girls are talking so fast, that I don't know what I am saying—keep trying to write *their* remarks instead. I don't know why it is that I can read for hours, and never hear anything that is going on about me, even when I *ought*, and yet am unable to write at all in the midst of confusion. I do hope you carefully destroy these scrawls, dear. Won't you promise to do so? I should be distressed to think they were being preserved as a memorial against me, for I am confident that there is not a sentence in them that can be parsed, and that half the words are spelt wrong! —to say nothing of the penmanship! I think I will try stopping my ears with cotton when I write, and see if that wont make me feel a little less as though I had lost my wits. Though if you only knew it, dear, I couldn't give you clearer proof of how fully, freely, and unreservedly I love you than my willingness to send you such scrawls. That is an honnour which I only pay my nearest and dearest! I cannot but fear however that, like some other common marks of affection and confidence, it is next door to an insult! I wonder if I belong to the same class with "the man who calls you Tom or Jack, and proves by thumps upon your back, how he esteems you dear"! Did I ever think I would be "sae weil acquaint" with so clever a man as yourself, as to take such *dreadful* liberties!

But fie! how I have wasted my time tonight! Now I really must close, for I have ever so much to do before bedtime. With much love for your dear parents and a whole heart-full for yourself believe me darling now and always   Your own Eileen.

ALS (WP, DLC).
[1] Although the New York papers had announced that Dr. Paxton would preach at the First Presbyterian Church on October 12, they give no clue as to who filled the pulpit in his absence.

Two Letters to Ellen Louise Axson

My own darling,   Balto., Md., Oct. 15th 1884

I must write you what I can *before* lecture time this morning: for Wednesday is my busiest day, and after the work begins (at 10 o'clock) it's next to impossible to find time to write. My spirits this morning are sensibly affected by two things, the Republican majority in Ohio[1] and the biting of a snap which feels very much like winter. Still I don't despair of the weather—not even of the political weather. It may change for the better before November. I hope that my darling is *very* prudent about guarding her health against these changes of weather! You don't say anything more about that cold of yours, pet, and I am very anxious about it.

I am so glad, my little sweetheart, that you *do* go about in the afternoons sight-seeing, &c. It is certainly the best thing to do, and the season will soon change so that anything of the kind will be impossible.

I am quite well and love you beyond all expression.

I[n] great haste,   Your own   Woodrow

[1] The Republicans carried Ohio in the state election on October 14 by what at first appeared to be a plurality of about 16,000. Wilson was obviously concerned about the implications of this for the coming presidential election. As it turned out, the Republican plurality in Ohio was approximately 11,000.

My own darling,   Balto., Md., Oct. 16th 1884

Did you really think that I would promise to destroy those little daily notes which I welcome with so much joy and esteem such treasures, but which you dare to call "scrawls"? Will you destroy *my* notes and all the letters I have written you? If you will, I may consider the proposition to destroy these testimonials of your love, which seem to me the best epistles of their kind ever written! Their sentences *can* face the grammar without shame, and their words the dictionary without confusion, but, even if they could'nt, they'd be beyond all criticism from *me*. They are from my darling and are exceedingly precious in my eyes!

The idea of your *needing* the assurance that mother and father had lost their hearts to you, or of your having "misgivings" on that head! *I* knew that they loved you, and I told you so before, you precious little disbeliever!

Do you think that you will be settled in new quarters soon? I must not put off buying winter clothes later than Nov. 1, and it would be most convenient to make my purchases in New York in person, instead of by order as heretofore—though that necessity never appeared so imperative to me before. Don't *count* on this, but regard it as amongst the possibilities, maybe the *probabilities*, and let me know as soon as your arrangements become permanent. I love you with all my heart.

In *tremendous* haste,   Your own   Woodrow

ALS (WC, NjP).

Two Letters from Ellen Louise Axson

My darling Woodrow,   New York   Oct. 16/84.

Mr. Marvin came around last night, with two young men, cousins of his, and took us to the "Institute Fair." I believe that was the name. I was so "used up" when I returned that I could not write even a line, for of course we were on our feet all the evening and, as it happened, we had been walking most of the day. But this morning I suppose will do as well for the writing. Now I have only a moment, however, for I am busy *packing*! Yes—I actually leave this afternoon! Direct your letters hereafter to *120 West 11th*. I hope it is just *the* place; but time must show. As far as appearances and references go, it is every-thing that could be desired. It is one of those on the "Young Woman's C A" registry; we made enquiries there, and they say it is a splendid place, just the right sort for girls alone. It is a small house—only about fifteen boarders, and Mrs[.] Beattie [Elizabeth Beatty] informed me that she takes "no working! girls, and no retail clerks"; ["]it is strictly first-class!" I like her looks very much; she has a *real* nice, kind face, and good manners. My room is *lovely*, large and beautifully furnished, with two broad sunny windows looking *south*. I occupy it alone for the present, the others—all that is left of them—will probably join me at Xmas, unless I take one of the League girls in with me before. But I must not take time to go into so many particulars now,—I will get no drawing done today.

I will write again tonight. Will have some quiet hours for writing to you now. Excuse haste. I love you, darling, with all my heart and am forever,   Your own Ellie.

My darling Woodrow,   120 West 11th St. New York, Oct. 16/84
Here am I at last, snugly ensconced in my new home,—I *hope settled*, for the winter. So far all is well. I came in this afternoon, so have taken my first meal here; very satisfactory it was, and the people *quite* nice-looking. There are eight ladies and seven gentlemen; two of them are Southerners, Mr. and Mrs. Guerry of Macon Ga. He seems to be one of the pleasantest and nicest here,—hav'nt met her yet, she is sick today,—over the Ohio elections, the rest of them declare! Then there is a nice old gentleman and his wife, and a very pretty lady in black, a widow I think, two English ladies, rather "oldish," with their nephew, an uncommonly good looking young man, two other young men that I don't like and—but this is decidedly a colourless description; I had better wait until I find out some of the characteristics of my neighbours before making a list of them. But, to sum up, you may make your mind easy about me; I have made a *rice*! in the world;[1] —true, there is an awful rice in expenses too,—but what can't be cured must be endured. Such a time as I have had looking at boarding-houses! I can now sympathize fully with you in your experiences of a year ago. I have been to about two dozen places, trying to find a small room, high up, or a hall room that could be heated; but they say there is no such thing in N.Y.—in this end of it at least. The hall rooms are all unheated and the furnaces,— the pipes I mean—run no higher than the third floor. So at last I was obliged to take this room, which Annie and I thought of taking together,—had partly engaged. Her father was in a desperate state when he first heard the sort of house she was in; telegraphed her to leave at once, and followed that up with the most excited letter I ever read—"if she didn't act promptly he would come on himself and see about it." But Mr. Marvin wrote quieting some of

his fears, and Annie was so anxious to stay on Eva's account—
that he finally wrote that she might remain for the present. If she
came with me we would pay seven apiece here, and they would
pay the *same* at Clinton Place,—and Eva has'nt it to pay. They
pay five apiece now; three in this room would pay 6 each, and it
is ten times as nice as the other. This room with the dressing-
room is large enough for three,—so that if I hold it alone until Eva
leaves at Xmas they will probably join me here; the choice lies
between that and taking a stranger into their room at No. 60.
But I pay *eleven* dollars a week here and that is ruinous [.] I don't
know whether to keep the room for them or not. I can get a room-
mate at once, I think, from the League[,] a very nice-*looking* little girl indeed, but of course she is a perfect stranger and it is a
great risk. What would you advise.

By the way, I didnt tell you what a pretty place this is; it looks
like a Southern house;—vine-covered piazzas across the full
length of each story; rather a large green garden in front, and,
also a large green "back-yard." My room is *stylish* even, with its
brussels carpet and lace curtains, it's marble-topped furniture,
pretty lounge and easy chairs. It has a grate too, as well as the
register, and I can have a fire to *look at* when I wish. And still I
am not happy! I am pining a little for my dear Mrs. Seaman. I
didn't tell you about her. She has a small, select boarding-house
—a sort of family affair,—on 4th Street. The secretary at the
League directed me to her. It is the *prettiest* house, and she is the
lovliest old lady! She is almost beautiful and altogether aristocratic, with her soft grey hair, her quiet, gentle manner, and
her black silk and lace. She seemed to take a sort of fancy to me;
appeared really disappointed when I went today to tell her I
could'nt go, invited me to come and see her, and dine with her,
at any rate; and was *so* sweet, and kind, and motherly that she
almost made me cry,—poor little home-sick goose that I am. It
would be the very place for me, but there are only hall, and
fourth story rooms, and they are as cold as ice; and of course I
could'nt stand it, though for awhile I tried to persuade myself
that I could, I was so fascinated with the lady and her daughters.
But then it was expensive of course—ten dol. for those cold rooms.

Well! I think I have given you enough about boarding houses
to last a life-time! This I hope ends the chapter. You know that
awful trunk of mine! The express men who brought it to the
house this afternoon wouldn't carry it up stairs, said they couldnt
be paid to! So two of the young men here have just brought it
themselves, up the two flights of stairs, without even saying "by

your leave" to me! In fact, I had never been introduced to them,—was up here and knew nothing about it. I was so worried! It's enough to kill them. They say they wanted to "try their strength"

But I must bring this stupid scrawl to a close. I am a little lonely here by myself—think I'll go to bed and sleep off the blues. I am glad I am such a good sleeper, it is my great remedy for all the smaller ills that flesh is heir to. By-the-by, you ask about my cold; it is almost well again. I do hope the political weather *will* change before Nov. I dare say it will. Arnt we depending on the good *Republicans* to elect Cleveland? But they might vote their own state ticket as usual, as something apart from the presidential election. What is this reading for Dr. Ely? Have you begun your joint work in great earnest? I have hardly left room anywhere to say that my heart is as full of love for you, my darling, —as is this paper of scrawling. As ever   Your own   Ellie.

ALS (WP, DLC) with WWhw memorandum on env. of second letter, relating to certain constitutional questions, printed at Oct. 18, 1884.
¹ She meant, of course, "a rise in the world." The pronunciation "rice" was a middle-class affectation taken up by ELA, and promptly disapproved by WW, to become a private joke between them. See ELA to WW, Feb. 15, 1885, Vol. 4.

Classroom Notes

[Oct. 16–Nov. 6, 1884]
Inscribed (WWhw) on first page: "Dr. Hall—Oct. 16th, 1884"
Contents:
    WWsh and WWhw notes taken on Oct. 16, 23, and 30, and Nov. 6, 1884, in Professor G. Stanley Hall's course in education.

Five loose pages, with notes on verso of three pages (WP, DLC).

To Ellen Louise Axson

My own darling,   Bluntschli Library [Baltimore], Oct. 17th, 1884
    I have just received your note of yesterday morning telling of your move to new quarters. Packing again! You poor little inhabitant of a trunk! How much extra room did you have this time? Enough for everything *and* the "love of a cloak" purchased since the last achievement of packing? You have answered the question of my last letter before hearing it. I am *so* glad, my pet, that you have at last escaped from No. 60 to quarters which promise so much better things. I fear that my little queen will be lonely at first in her pretty room with the South windows: but if it be at all possible (and I think it will be) I shall dispel her lonliness as much as I can, in the course of a couple of weeks or so—unless she thinks that the only effect—the only *abiding* effect,—of such a visit would be to leave her more lonely than ever.

I trust that my darling will turn over a new leaf in one respect when she gets settled in West 11th Street. I have been disturbed by such confessions as these in her correspondence: "I did not go down to breakfast"; your letter. . . . which Annie brought me when *she* came back from lunch." This can mean nothing but that you are *not* making it a point of conscience to take care of your health by going regularly to meals—and my opinion is that you deserve a scolding for that same. *Please*, my pet, don't go without any of the regular meals of the day. You risk your health more seriously than you know by doing so—little as you may be moved by hunger. Wont you promise me "not to do so any more"? I shall be very uneasy until you do.

I shall write to Shinn at once and tell him to call at your new address. I don't suppose that there is any danger *there* of another such parlour ordeal as he and Miss Annie had to endure at No. 60.

You say that "all that is left" of your little crowd will, possibly, join you again at Xmas time. Do you mean that some of them are disgusted and determined to leave, then?

I am to read the third of my essays at the Seminary to-night[1]— "to set a high standard of work for the new men," says Dr. Adams' blarney—it is the one, you may remember, on "Revenue and Supply," the driest of the lot. I am rather anxious as to how it will "take," because I know how much the new-comers will expect of a "Fellow." I read the two first last year, and Dr. A. now wants the rest in order, at intervals through the year.

I am quite well—hurried, as usual, but in excellent spirits—and every day more in love with the sweetest little woman in the world, my matchless Eileen, whose love *constitutes* my happiness. Good-bye, my darling, your notes are *such* a source of comfort and delight to me. With all my heart,

Your own   Woodrow.

ALS (WC, NjP).
1 See the Minutes of the Seminary of Historical and Political Science, Oct. 17, 1884.

From Ellen Louise Axson

My darling Woodrow,   New York, Oct. 17/84.

I have made up my mind tonight to make a bold and vigourous attack upon the vast array of correspondence which lies in so threatening a fashion, before me; and I suppose I had better prove the strength of my resolve, by denying myself and writing but a few lines to you. But that, some how, is a very hard thing to do; my use of those words "a few lines" is certainly farcical. I wonder at my own "cheek" in writing them at all! But everything is comparative in this world, so they are but a few lines compared with what I would like to write; you have no idea how hard it is for me to keep from overflowing into a second sheet every night. By-the-way, I think its "real mean" in you not to promise to burn them. *Of course* I would'nt destroy yours—nor would I ask you to destroy mine if they looked like yours. Suppose I say that I won't write every night unless you promise? What would you do *then*? I would say it if I wasn't afraid it would cost me too dear;—for I suppose, in that case, you would refuse to write daily to me. (Excuse this cut in the paper, it has just made itself known.) Oh, darling, how happy I am to think you are coming! or at least that your coming is "amongst the probabilities." I am afraid, now that the idea has been suggested, I can't help counting on it somewhat. I shall dream of it by night and by day,—shall fairly *live* on the thought. Am so glad you told me *now*, that I may have the pleasure of dwelling on it as long as possible. Surprises are very charming, it is true, yet, after all, they cheat people of some of the sweetest joys of life,—the joys of anticipation. Shall you come the *first day* of Nov? We will have a very pleasant, quiet time in this boarding-house I think—a very different experience from our last. I am even more pleased than on yesterday with my new quarters. It seems to be everything that could be desired. I am very well and in excellent spirits tonight. Isn't the weather lovely? We—four—have been on a long tramp up B-way this afternoon to Reichard's gallery[1] and to a water-colour exhibition.

Good-night, dear love, With all my heart

Your own Eileen.

ALS (WP, DLC).
[1] Gustav Reichard & Co., 226 Fifth Avenue.

From the Minutes of the Seminary of Historical and Political Science[1]

Seminary, October 17th 1884.

Meeting called to order at 8.10 P.M. Dr. Adams in the chair. Minutes of the previous meeting read & corrected. The principal paper of the evening was read by Mr. Wilson—a portion of his work on Congressional Governme[n]t entitled: "The House of Representatives: Revenue and Supply." It was listened to with interest; & it is to be regretted that no abstract has been furnished for insertion in the minutes.

Dr. Adams made a few remarks on civil service reform & reported that a monthly journal on the subject was about being started in Baltimore.

An article on the House of Lords, sent by Mr. Freeman was referred to Mr. Gould for report next meeting.

A card from Mr. Bryce referring to his studies in Italy on the war between the Goths & Eastern Empire was read. . . .

Dr. Jameson brought in the schedule for the year's reviews of periodicals, & also reviewed "A Study of the Parliament of Paris & Other Parliaments of France" by Miss Jane M. Bancroft, of the Northwestern University, Evanston, Ill.

Owing to the lateness of the hour other reports were postponed till next meeting. . . .

Meeting adjourned at 10.10.

Walter B. Scaife   Sec. pro. tem.

¹ The members of the Seminary of Historical and Political Science for the academic year 1884-85 were: Dr. Herbert Baxter Adams, Albert C. Applegarth, T. Alexis Berry, Leigh Bonsal, Jeffrey R. Brackett, George P. Coler, Davis R. Dewey, Albert E. Egge, Dr. Richard T. Ely, Andrew Fossum, Henry B. Gardner, Elgin R. L. Gould, Edgar Goodman, William P. Holcomb, Dr. John Franklin Jameson, John H. Johnson, Charles H. Levermore, William H. Lichty, Robert F. McMahon, Charles N. Morris, John C. C. Newton, Enazo Ota, Nathan Powell, Daniel R. Randall, Adoniram J. Robinson, Shosuki Sato, Walter B. Scaife, George E. de Steiguer, Frederick M. Taylor, Woodrow Wilson, Julian Wood, and Thomas K. Worthington.

A Memorandum

[c. Oct. 18, 1884]

Vs. Mr. *Curtis*: If you talk of amendments, the only question should be: What is the Pres. What is he *for*?—not how make new the old machinery wh. does not recognize him as what he is[.] Proof: How *soon* the El. Com. came to naught.

Human nature a part of every Const

Not *all* of human n. allowed for in the mechanical contrivances of ours. What a hold has *machinery* on the thoughts of men. It dies harder than essences.

No one likely now to question greatness of members of Con. 1787—partly because they were great—but perhaps principally because they have been *voted* so

WWhw memorandum on env. of ELA to WW, Oct. 16, 1884.

To Ellen Louise Axson

My own darling,   Balto., Md., Oct. 18th/84

The rush of lectures is over for the week and so I have a little breathing space in which I can write to my darling without the threat of an immediate engagement to call me away. I have just received your first letter from 11th Street and my heart is full of its words. Oh, my precious little sweetheart! How desperate it makes me to think that you are lonely when I would give anything in the world to be with you! The idea of your being alone and homesick in New York while I am alone and homesick in Baltimore! The idea of our needing each other so much, and yet being obliged to consent to an indefinite waiting for each other! For *my* "home"-sickness is a longing—which I can sometimes hardly endure—for the home of which you shall be queen. I want you —I need you—and I shall never be happy or more than stoically content, by force of forecasting the future,—until I have my darling "all to myself," as dear mother says.

But I trust that, when the strangeness of the place wears off and her acquaintance ripens with the people in the house, my pet will not feel the pain of her loneliness with anything like the keenness that it must have now. I am so glad that your fellow-boarders seem such nice people: for it is quite safe to have a house acquaintance, to talk and exchange courtesies, with people with whom you are thrown in that way. One don't need to know their antecedents or their *outside* characters to go that far with them, and is consequently quite out of danger so long as one keeps within the world which one has in common with such neighbours—the world of boarding-house intercourse.

I don't know what to advise you, my darling, about taking a room-mate from amongst your League acquaintances. Of course it is very desirable that you should relieve yourself as soon as possible of some part of the expense of rooming alone—eleven dollars is *very* heavy; and seven would be quite as little as you could expect to pay for agreeable accommodations anywhere—: but it would be exceedingly risky to take in somebody of whom you know nothing at all; because, once made, such an arrangement is very hard to escape from. It's a partnership for which there is no comfortable dissolution; and, if I were in your place, I should be very sure, from other and more trustworthy evidence than manner or appearance that the person was in very truth a lady before yoking myself to her in any such intimate fashion. A mistake would be distressing, if not fatal, and no caution in the matter should be foregone. I know what hard rules I am laying down, because I know how next to impossible it is to know whether a person will be an agreeable, or even endurable, room-mate until the experiment is actually made,—and it may be that my own observation and experience, having in such matters concerned only men, may not have qualified me to judge of such matters with reference to the other sex. But I know that you, my pet, have generally roomed alone, as I have; and, tho' I am quite sure that two women could endure each other, under necessity, with less friction than two men could, I am anxious above all things not to have you take any step which *might* make your winter an unhappy or even uneasy one. Loneliness would be better: and to endure the expense (if possible) till Xmas would be preferable. It may be, however—is *that* the truth, my darling?—that you do not find Miss Lester a congenial room-mate, and would *rather* take in some-one else? I know very nice—some delightful—persons whom I should prefer not to see all the time or at all hours, who don't wear well; but there is such a thing as bearing those ills we have rather than flying to others that we know not of.

But that's enough of thick-headed, inconclusive advice for one letter! I wish I could be of some *use* to you, instead of simply "darkening counsel"!

I read at the Seminary last night for an hour and a quarter— and my audience looked as tired as I was when I got through. They applauded (to wake themselves up) and Dr. Adams praised, but what a dose it was! Seriously, I think I made a very favourable impression; the work bore evidences of *thoroughness,* anyhow, though it was *not* entertaining, and so may have evinced capacity which was appreciable; but of course I can't tell what my auditors thought. They have voted me a bore for aught I know!

I am well and in tolerable spirits: but tell me, my love, how I am to get along, loving you as I do and yet separated from you as I am, during the long winter that is coming. It don't seem possible to my heart!

It makes me very happy, Eileen, to know that you have such snug pretty quarters. If you will tell me that you are content, nothing shall disquiet me—except the thought that you *can* be content without   Your own   Woodrow.

ALS (WC, NjP).

From Ellen Louise Axson

Mr. Woodrow Wilson, 8 McCulloh St   New York, Oct. 18 1884.
               Come tonight

                                                    E. L. Axson

Tel. (WP, DLC) with WWhw figures on env.

To Ellen Louise Axson

My own darling,   Balto., Oct. 22nd, 1884

It was *terrible* to have to come away! I did'nt know *how* hard it was till the parting was over. I wont say that the pain of separation was greater than the joy of being together—because it was'nt. That joy is beyond all measure, is worth all that can be paid for it. But the leave-taking *is* a *big price*. I felt desperately forlorn as I sped away from the great city which contains my treasure. And I was brought away with such unrelenting vigor that one might have imagined that the railroad authorities knew the temptation I was under to turn back and were determined to give me no chance to do so. We made never a stop between the outskirts of Jersey City and the outskirts of Philadelphia, making those hundred miles in two hours! After passing Philadelphia, we abated our dignity a little and condescended to stop at several of the larger towns by the way; but the whole distance was made at a gallant speed. I was at home in time to go to bed early, and this morning I am quite myself again—except that I have a miserable sickness at my heart, which you may be able to explain.

After leaving you, I went up to 23rd St. to pay for the eyeglasses I had ordered, and then back to the Metropolitan [Hotel], which I reached just in time not to miss my lunch. When lunch was eaten, I had time enough left to pay my bill and seek the ferry.

I made a pretty "close shave" in money-matters, by the way. I spent more on my purchases than I had expected and so reached home with just 35¢.! I'll allow a more liberal margin next time[.]

Did you go to the League in the afternoon?—and will you go to prayer-meeting at the *Scotch church*[1] this afternoon?

Oh, my darling, my precious, matchless little sweetheart—*why* can't I tell you how passionately I love you? You *know*—don't you? You are all the world to me—the world is nothing to me without you—nothing but a loveless duty-mill. I love you and shall ever love you beyond and before all else, and shall every day be more than ever   Your own   Woodrow

ALS (WC, NjP).
[1] The Scotch Presbyterian Church, at 53 West 14th St. in 1884.

Two Letters from Ellen Louise Axson

My darling Woodrow,   New York, Oct. 22/84.

As my notes to you, though written at night, are always mailed on my way to the League, it occurred to me that on this occasion I had better wait until the last moment before writing it; that it might have a little more *perspective,* as it were. I hope you are feeling bright this morning, dear,—not too much fatigued by study and lectures following so closely upon your journey. I am making a brave, and not altogether unsuccessful, fight against the blues! by keeping *very* busy;—not giving myself time to *mope.* I rushed off to the League as soon as I had finished lunch;—after four Annie and I went up to Goupil's gallery—23st [sic] St[1]—where we staid as long as we could;—reached home at dusk, and after dinner wrote a long letter to Uncle Henry, and then read the new "Century [Magazine]" which Mr. Goodrich[2] had loaned me until bedtime.

But ah, dear one, I hav'nt the art to make myself believe that I am not lonely without you[.] However busy I am, or interested in other things, I can't forget to think about you, all the time. I could as soon forget to love you; and you know I do love you, darling, with my very heart of hearts. I wish I could prove to you how much. But it is nine o'clock now, and I ought to be at the League. Excuse haste

With truest love   As ever   Your own Ellie.

[1] Goupil's Gallery of Paintings, 170 Fifth Avenue, corner of 22nd Street.
[2] Arthur Goodrich, representative of Houghton, Mifflin & Company in New York, who, as subsequent letters will reveal, became considerably more than a casual friend of Ellen's. Wilson had probably just met him at the boarding-house, hence Ellen's cryptic reference to him in this letter.

My darling Woodrow,   New York Oct. 22/84

As I think it highly probable that you will feel irresistibly impelled to go to sleep over the following pages, *I* feel it proper to say in advance that no offence will be taken, on that account; and also to explain the cause;—or rather to state an *inexplicable* fact.

There seems to be some curious soporific influence abroad tonight, and I am perfectly sure that this note is going to catch the infection. I came in at five and went to sleep before dinner,—after dinner I immediately went to sleep again; and I have already gaped fourteen distinct times since I took my pen in hand. This is a fact so unexampled in my experience that, what-

ever you may think to the contrary, it is well worth recording!
That palace which we visited this afternoon must have been an
enchanted place. We have just been to "Cottier's,"[1] the branch of
the great London firm, you know;—wonderfully polite people,
they are! A very nice young man took us in charge, and exhibited
and explained everything as carefully as if we were millionares,
though we were particular to explain to *him* that we were *not,*
and that we did not propose to invest *very* largely. It is the most
splendid *business* house I ever saw or imagined. Even Tiffany's
isn't so beautiful, because at Cottiers the furniture and the various articles of vertu in different rooms look as though they were
put there to stay. Every thing is in perfect keeping, so that they
are exactly like well furnished rooms in some superb home. The
permanent arrangements too—walls, ceilings, stained-glass windows, &c. are magnificent. And everything is so tastefully—so
artistically arranged. Well, that visit is literally the only thing
which has happened since I last wrote, that is to say, since this
morning! There is no news, except that I have found out the
name of the poetical athlete[,] it is "Donaldson." Also there are
a number of new scholars at the League, and one of them is a
dwarf, and the most dreadfully deformed person I ever saw;—he
is deformed in every direction! Oh, it is so pitiful! Poor little soul!
I hope he can draw ten times better than any of us.

Good-night, dear, I think I will close this and go to sleep
again[.] I am anxious for tomorrow to come, so that I may have
a letter from you. Do you know I actually want to see you again!
It seems *so* long since you went away! Curious, when I shut my
eyes—or when I don't shut them for that matter—I can see you
"as plain as can be." I can hear the very tones of your voice, I
can watch your smile come and go—why shouldn't that suffice
me. Bodily presence, under such circumstances, would seem to
be a luxury rather than a necessity. But who is satisfied with
the mere *necessities* of life? We are all poor unreasonable creatures.

Best love to your dear parents, and for yourself a love better
than the best, from   Your own   Eileen.

ALS (WP, DLC).
[1] Cottier and Co., decorators, 144 Fifth Ave. and 324 West 26th St., New York.

To Ellen Louise Axson

My own darling,   Balto., Md., Oct. 23rd, 1884
    I have just received and read your sweet note of yesterday

morning, and, like all that you write to me, it has filled my heart quite full of the sort of delight which I derive from your *kisses*, from all demonstrations of your love. Oh, how precious these little notes are! How desolate and unendurable the loneliness would be without them!

I am quite well, my pet,—quite rid of the slight fatigue which I felt during yesterday—though grateful for this little pause in the rush of lectures which gives me leave to turn to my precious Eileen in deed, as it were, as well as in thought.

I wont *advertize* my selfishness, little sweetheart, by *saying* that I am glad that you can't escape from missing me, work you never so hard—I will say simply that "misery loves company," and that I am delighted that my brave little lady *can* work off her loneliness in part, and that she has, in Miss Annie, so congenial a companion with whose aid to wile away discontent.

But this is all that is *possible* to-day, my pet. This is only a *love* note. It cannot carry as much love as I want to send: but you know how much I love you and how entirely I am

Your own   Woodrow.

ALS (WC, NjP).

From Ellen Louise Axson

My darling Woodrow,   New York Oct. 23/84.

Your sweet little letter reached me this morning at the usual time, and was, perhaps, even more than commonly welcome. I was longing so for some word, because I knew it would help the ache which the parting had left in my heart. Ah, yes! that pain of parting *is* a heavy price to pay for being together, but not too heavy for such joy as that of meeting. I for one am willing to make the bargain, and pay the price as often as may be—let the consequences be what they will. I have been a foolish girl to-night, I am afraid. I have been nursing my woes to keep them warm. It is one long hour from dusk to dinner; and instead of lighting the gas and buckling down to something, I lay the whole time in the darkness, thinking of you, until I could almost have cried out for the sound of your voice;—strange! when you have been gone some time, that sort of brooding is one of my greatest joys, not-with-standing my longing to see you, face to face, but when the separation is recent, I feel the difference too keenly.

I am very glad that, in spite of your break-neck speed you reached the end of your journey safely, and not altogether insolvent! That *was* a "close shave,"—but perhaps in your mind it only served sweetly to recall old Princeton days, with their similar experiences. With regard to the Scotch church;—there is a sequel to that joke, which I must not forget to tell. I have now established my cleverness beyond question. I *did* go yesterday, and,— the church was still *there*, it hadn't been spirited away again like Aladdin's palace—but *there wasn't any prayermeeting*! "Service on Sunday at *4* P M. Weekly lecture on Wed. evening at 8 P.M." was what the tablet said "as plain as could be"! I had simply read it wrong as the car hurried me past! So I fear I must give up my prayer-meeting idea altogether. Have you seen the last vol. of Froude's Life of Carlyle. *I* hav'nt and don't propose to; but here is a choice extract—from the "Diary" which I have just culled from the "Nation." Speaking of Gladstone, Carlyle says "he is a representative of the multitudinous *cants* of the age and in his religious, social, moral and political life one of the contemptiblest men I ever looked upon,—a spectral kind of phantasm of a man." Was there ever such a precious pair of idiots as Carlyle—when he tries to be—and Froude![1]

Good-night darling, I *must* stop and write some duty letters to-night. Believe me, dear love, *you* are all the world to *me*. What would I do without you? I cannot even imagine now. Fortunately it is a question that need no answer, except the old one that I am *forever*

Your own Ellie.

ALS (WP, DLC).

[1] ELA quoted from an editorial comment in "Summary of the Week's News: Foreign," New York *Nation*, XXXIX (Oct. 23, 1884), 345. The quotation was garbled. See James A. Froude, *Thomas Carlyle, A History of His Life in London, 1834-1881* (2 vols., New York, 1884), II, 361, 383.

To Ellen Louise Axson

My precious little queen, Balto., Md., Oct. 24th, 1884

It seems here as if winter had made up its mind to delay no longer but to be about its business at once. We have fire in the furnaces for the first time: and I am glad that I did not defer my purchases of clothing. Of course it is cold in New York too? I think that my darling will enjoy a Northern winter more than she now expects to—it is so different from, as well as so much colder than, the corresponding season in the South.

I came very near being found out by Shinn after all! I found a note from him awaiting me here on my return, asking me to attend to something for him which had, he said, to be seen to on *Monday* at the latest! Fortunately it was not too late, as it turned out, to arrange it on Wednesday, however, so that I escaped the necessity for an explanation[.] I shall write to him to-day, if possible—after lectures.

I called last evening, with Wright,[1] upon Mr. and Mrs. Levermore—Levermore is the other Fellow in history, you know—and enjoyed a queer mixture of pain and pleasure. It was pleasant to see a young couple happy in each other and cosily fixed in a pleasant suite of rooms, and to meet so unaffected and agreeable a person as Mrs. L.; but, alas, there was another caller there who got Levermore into an argument—and, of all things, an argument about "the war"!—and about a quarter of an hour had to be spent in letting L. weary himself out in walking around his dreary circles of sophistry! That's where the *pain* came in. I did not find out much about Mrs. L.—she had to be quiet while her husband talked—except that she is nice looking and apparently sweet-tempered.

I wish that I *could* have gone with you to Cottiers, my darling— it must be very beautiful. I wish, too,—but what's the use wishing! I must be content for the present with doing what I've been doing ever since I left you—living over in minutest detail the days we've spent to-gether, from the very first. Those three days which began this week (and which already seem at least a month away!) are six now; and, if I go on dreaming of them day and night, they will stretch over all the long time which must intervene before I see you again. Ah, my darling, how your pretty caresses, and all our intercourse—including even Dr. Taylor's[2] sermon—come back to me to make my joy new again! Your love fills all my thoughts and you are part of my very life! With unbounded love,   Your own   Woodrow.

ALS (WC, NjP).
    [1] Charles B. Wright, a graduate student in English who also roomed at 8 McCulloh St.
    [2] WW and ELA must have attended the Tabernacle Congregational Church on Sunday, October 19, 1884.

From Ellen Louise Axson

My darling Woodrow,   New York, Oct. 24/84.

Yours of the 23rd reached me this morning true to time, and has been speaking to my heart all day, and finding there a faithful echo—"oh, how precious these little notes are" to *me*! How desolate and unendurable this lonliness would be without them! They furnish a daily supply of sunshine, for my private benefit, quite apart from the public programme as announced in the weather bullitins.

I too am very well and in good spirits tonight. The day has passed just as usual. Nothing special has happened, but something is *going* to happen in which I am a good deal interested. The vacant hall room has been taken by another art student,—a girl. Don't know where she studies yet, maybe at the League, for all I know. Of course, I await her coming with deep interest. It would be charming if she should turn out to be "real nice," "perfectly lovely"! &c. &c.

But I must make haste to say "good-night," my darling for I am very busy this evening.

> "I love thee, I love but thee,
> With a love that shall not die
> Till the sun grows cold,
> And the stars are old,
> And the leaves of the Judgement Book unfold!"[1]

With all my heart   Your own Eileen.

ALS (WP, DLC).
[1] Bayard Taylor, "Bedouin Song," from *Poems of the Orient*.

To Ellen Louise Axson

My own darling,   Balto., Md., Oct. 25th/84

I am going to make this a letter-writing day, because I have so many letters to write—most important, one to dear father to ask his advice about reading for a "PhD" this year, a question of mental hygiene—but you shall have the first letter, partly because I want to mail it earlier than the rest, but principally because I can't help it—I *want* to send you a love message before I do anything else!

Were you irresistibly impelled to write these last notes of yours as you did, little sweetheart, or are you studying the art of so writing to me that I shall be made altogether beside myself with love and delight? Has it been through calculation or through impulse that you have written to me in just the way that I have so often coaxed you to adopt in talking to me? Why, my darling, there never were such sweet little letters as these! They confess without reserve all the symptoms of my Eileen's love for me, as she never confessed before[.] They tell me *how she knows* that she loves me:—they open her heart and her life to me as she never opened them before, and so make me feel that I am indeed her own—admitted to secrets which none but a lover may know:—they—well, in a word, they fill my heart to overflowing. It may seem a little thing, my darling, but do you know that you never before told me *what* you thought and wished about me when I was absent? You have often told me that you were always thinking of me, but you never—oh well, you know what I mean: all I can *say* clearly is that you have now found out how best to delight me

I have just received a letter from Shinn, which I enclose because it concerns you almost altogether. I sent him your new address yesterday,[1] and I will try to drop him a line to-day to say that he will be pretty sure to find you out except after dinner, so that he need not try again in the day time.

Have you seen the poor little dwarf draw yet, my pet? I hope too, with you, that he can draw "ten times better than" the rest of you! That reminds me, by-the-way, that I have been chuckling all week over that delightfully human and commonsense bit of philosophy of yours about the unfortunate circumstance that the best artistic gifts seem to be superfluously given to the best-looking girls at the League. Don't it move you to remorseful regret that you are perfecting yourself in your art only to throw it away on me? Ought'nt the pretty artists, who have talent and don't need husbands, to sacrifice themselves to justice and hand the boys over to the plain damsels who need them? Of course there is the difficulty that they [*sic*] boys probably would'nt consent to be 'handed'; and I, for one, am a believer in the doctrine that the loveliest daughters of men were *meant* to charm and win in marriage the sons of men—but these objections don't quite kill the philanthropic argument which stands for the affirmative of the question. Tell me, love—you know more about girls than I do—is'nt it so that the plain girls whom men can't love are often, if not generally, disinclined to love men? However much of the woman and the woman's characteristic affections they may have—is'nt it true that they seldom "fall" in love by an irresistible impulse? Or, does this only *seem* to be so because the consciousness of being unattractive to men drives them within themselves and disposes them to cynicism? You were *made* to win somebody—anybody you might love; but they are made not to win, are'nt they? To come down to thinking in instances: do you think that Miss Anna Harris is *really* as indifferent to men as she seems to be? For my part, I like Miss Anna, and feel that she could attract if she would: but her manner is *hard* toward men and she makes me feel that nothing could induce her to believe in me or confide in me. How different it was when I first met *you*! I used to think 'how this little lady can love if she will, if she but find anyone worthy!' 'What a sacred and boundless treasure has been, or is to be, found by some fortunate man!' And oh! my darling, to think that *I* found it! How shall I ever be able to show how I prize it? I have adopted the only plan I know of: to give in return for it all that is purest and best in my own heart, and to spend freely for my Eileen the best energies of the life of

Her own   Woodrow.

ALS (WC, NjP). Enc.: C. H. Shinn to WW, Oct. 23, 1884, ALS (WP, DLC) with WWhw and WWsh notes on env.
    1 This letter is missing.

To Charles Howard Shinn

Balto., Oct. 25, 1884

Yes, my dear fellow, that *was* a comedy of errors about the calling on Clinton Place—one of the chief errors being mine in not letting you know of the change of address as soon as ever I knew of it myself:—and this crossing of our letters is quite as comical![1] You need not fear that Miss Axson will think that you have been discourteous: she will understand perfectly. You could'nt be expected to find her new place by inspiration.

I enclose the official receipt from the Journalists' Club. It came to me by mail this morning. I suppose that its coming means that Shriver[2] has seen to the whole matter, the withdrawal of your name as well as the payment of the money; but I shall make sure of that by asking him as soon as I can see him.[3] "Sally" Shriver, you know, is an old Princeton acquaintance of mine. He was a well-known *butt* at college.

At the Seminary last night we had a *census* talk from Jno. C. Rose, the *Nation*'s statistical critic, associate editor of Abell's *Sun*, and "Baltimorean Gladstone" (as Adams called him)—a very interesting fellow, with a fine intelligent face.[4] Of course we had, too, the usual "model" reviews of Magazines by Jamieson, Adams, and Ely—but I wont pain you by recalling *that*.

Have you seen Froude's latest volumes on Carlyle? I was thinking of buying them, but have been discouraged by this sentence in a letter from Miss A (who is a great admirer of Carlyle's *works*): "Was there ever such a precious pair of idiots as Carlyle—when he tries to be—and Froude!" This after reading extracts from the new volumes. With much love,

Yours in driving haste,   Woodrow.

ALS (WP, DLC).
    1 WW is replying to C. H. Shinn to WW, Oct. 23, 1884, ALS (WP, DLC).
    2 John Schultz Shriver of Baltimore, College of New Jersey, '78.
    3 Shriver had presumably taken care of the details of Shinn's withdrawal from the Journalists' Club of Baltimore.

⁴ See the Minutes of the Seminary of Historical and Political Science, Oct. 24, 1884, for mention of John C. Rose of Baltimore, who read the principal paper. It was a criticism of that part of the seventh volume of the Census of 1880 relating to evaluation, which, Rose asserted, overestimated the rate of increase in the national wealth. A. S. Abell was founder and, in 1884, owner of the Baltimore *Sun*.

From Ellen Louise Axson

My darling Woodrow,   New York, Oct. 25/84.

It is so late now, that though I have a great deal to say, even more than usual, I am afraid I must *try* and put it all off 'till tomorrow. I had just taken up my portfolio in order to write, when the girl appeared at the door and announced "Mr. Hopkins to see you, Miss." Who? thought I!—running over in my mind all the Hopkins clan in Sav., and finding now [none] who would have any excuse for calling on me. Mr. *Hopkins*? Yes, Miss,—Mr. *John* Hopkins. I began to guess then, and, with much inward laughter, went down stairs and found as I expected *Mr. Shinn*! He has just left after a *delightful* visit. I like him *extremely*. He is so genuine,—so charmingly enthusiastic, and natural. But why, pray, should I tell *you* what he is? He is just what you know him to be, and what I expected. I am so glad to meet him at last; he has been twice to the other house[,] the second time did not see any of the girls, and could not learn my address. He says he heard from you today. By the way, are you in earnest about my keeping your visit a secret? I had to be almost deceitful tonight in order to do it. I am going to the theater with him Monday night. And what did I say about him in one of my letters? He says he has a copy of it in your hand-writing, but he wouldnt tell me what it was!

I am afraid my note of today will be delayed in reaching you dear;—when do they *generally* reach you, by the way? I was busy with Mr. Morton all the morning; and as he came very early— before nine o'clock—I had'nt time to mail it until I went to the League after lunch. I have actually gotten that picture off my hands, at last, and altered to his satisfaction. I added twenty years to the poor woman's age in as many minutes. And now good-night. I love you darling, I love, love *love* you! As ever

                              Your own   Eileen.

ALS (WP, DLC).

To Ellen Louise Axson

My own darling,   Balto., Md., Oct. 26, 1884

You get a *big* dose of it Mondays when my letters double, don't you? Don't it trouble you on Sundays to think how you are going to catch it next day? Last Sunday, of course, you were relieved of that apprehension because you had *me* and could be reasonably certain that I would not write to you while I was in the city; but to-day there is no such circumstance to reassure you. Is it *possible* that it is only *one week* since we went to church together? There *must* be some mistake about it! It must be that time is something altogether subjective, altogether independent of the movements of the heavenly bodies. Unless I have been dreaming, it is only four days and a half since I left New York, reckoning by the revolutions of the earth; but I am quite sure that, reckoning by my feelings, by the movements of my heart, it has been as many weeks! Surely Christmas will never come at this rate, if I am to go on in this way, longing for my darling as if my heart would break, and feeling that time *drags* unendurably so long as I am away from her! I am afraid there's no help for it: the longing and the loneliness increase instead of growing less. The only thing to be done is manfully to avoid the ungratefulness of *discontent*. That at least is possible, and *ought* not to be a very difficult thing in my case, "seeing as how" *some* day I shall be permitted to take my darling and keep her with me always. If I can't wait for that, I don't deserve it! Still you perceive that this solution of the difficulty rests upon a very subtle distinction. It places me in a very uncertain region—somewhere between content and its negative, discontent. We'll put it thus: I can't be *happy* without my Eileen, but I *can* be cheerful and above repining.

I account it an extremely fortunate circumstance, little sweetheart, that you don't get tired hearing me say these things over and over again; because if you *did*, I *should* be discontented. My love is so great for my darling that I *can't* keep silent about it; and it is so constantly manifesting itself in the same ways that I must speak of the same things again and again. What a terrible thing it would be if we *did* get tired of this subject! It is the only subject that will last us all our lives and never wear out. Love is the only thing, apparently, that is perennial. It seems the surest token of our spirituality and immortality[.] Its light is like the light of the sun, not only illuminating but purifying as well, and it would be as unnatural for us to grow weary of it, after once we had experienced its real glory, as for us to wish the sun blotted out from the heavens.

The principal event at the Seminary meeting on Friday evening was an address, on some features of the last census, by a young man whom Dr. Adams called the "Baltimorean Gladstone."

He has one of the most pleasing faces I ever saw, open, earnest, clear-cut in lines of intelligence: and I was interested in all that he said because of the thorough grasp he so evidently had of his subject. He is, as I said, a 'young man,' but he has already won a reputation for ability in analyzing and reading the meaning of statistics which has given him an acknowledged place of authority as critic in that line. The *Nation* refers all its statistical criticism to him. Mr. Rose is a lawyer by profession, but an editor by practice, being associate on the staff of one of the principal dailies here. It is certainly one of the best features of the Seminary that we have through it an occasional opportunity of receiving such infusions of non-University blood into the veins of our student life. The *risk* is that it may often be, as it has sometimes been in the past, very inferior blood.

Be sure to tell me, my love, how the new tenant of the hall-room turns out. I sincerely hope for your sake that she *will* be "lovely" and altogether companionable.

I wrote father a letter yesterday whose length will certainly make him wonder. Sixteen pages! and fourteen of them about the Ph.D.—a regular discourse on the *pros.* and *cons.* of cramming.

I am quite well, my darling, and in reasonably good spirits. I love you, oh! I love you with my whole heart—with all the force of my nature, and cannot but be always   Your own   Woodrow.

ALS (WC, NjP).

From Ellen Louise Axson

My darling Woodrow,   New York, Oct. 26/84

I don't know whether I can compose myself enough to write intelligibly tonight. I can but try however. I have just come from church, and I am in a most elevated and rapturous state of mind. It was "the Church of the Heavenly Rest"![1]—and the music *was* heavenly. I never heard anything like it. It was choral singing, of course; there was one little boy who had a voice like an angel —and there was one such *grand* bass too. I never heard anything so magnificent as some of those chants and anthems.

I have been out since before ten this morning, and feel very dissipated in consequence, in spite of having been twice to church. Mrs. Marvin wrote yesterday asking us all to meet them at their church—Dr. Reed's—and take dinner with them afterwards; I wish people would ask us on some other day than Sunday! But we went; and dined with them at the Murrey Hill Hotel, where they live. It is a superb hotel, the finest—save one—that I ever saw. We got a magnificent view of the city from the observatory too,—the first time I have ever had a bird's-eye view of it. We could see the water around three sides of it, and the long range of the Orange Mountains in the distance. We had a delightful day altogether. Mr. & Mrs. Marvin are the dearest old people imaginable. He is just as kind and warm-hearted as he can be. Seems heartily to enjoy making others happy, and to be always happy himself,—in short he is a delightful "old boy"—a phrase which may sound disrespectful, but it is'nt so intended and it suits the case exactly. His wife is his first cousin, and she must have been a *very* pretty girl; in fact, she is pretty still, with her fresh complexion, her soft waving grey hair, and the deep dimples in her cheeks;—then she is so little and dainty and sweet.

Mr. Marvin strongly advises the girls to join me here, and Annie is coming tomorrow to see about it. I have actually invited them *all* to come if they want to. I think we can put up with four in a room until Xmas. It won't be so bad here, because there are two large windows and a big dressing-room. At any rate I will put up with it, for I believe *three* is better than *none*, all things considered. It is just a case of too much of a good thing. I want *a* room-mate very much. I didn't exactly *crave* more,—but lo! "a troop cometh"! I don't know either whether they are coming or not, it depends on Mrs. Beatty's "terms"; tomorrow will show. The other girl is coming tomorrow too. We art-students "and things" are fairly going to take the premises! I am sorry for all these married people and old! bachelors.

Did you ever read "Beyond the Gates"?[2] If you hav'nt,—*don't*! I have just been doing so, and have been so scandalized, that if it hadn't been Mr. Goodrich's book, I should have hurled it into the fire—the *grate*, I mean! Heaven deliver us from a heaven like that! a heaven where people are sad and sinful, and weary and weak;—a heaven where there are all the old struggles, and disappointment and unrest, with the pleasant additional feature that it is all to be *eternal*. Here when things, either within or without, go wrong, we can, at worst, remember that "the *end* cometh." "All things must pass." I take back my former advice; you really ought to read certain chapters of it, just to see what people are capable of. I had heard of some episodes in it, but I had no idea of their full enormity. It is the story of a woman who had been, in early youth, separated from her lover. Though she is in heaven —so-called—she is, of course, as unhappy about it as ever. So one day, as she is wandering about, reflecting upon her lonely and wretched condition, she hears, in a house hard by, Mendelssohn playing his "Wedding March" to a party of people who had been deaf-mutes upon earth! Where-upon she sinks on the ground a heap of misery; and just at that juncture the lover appears on the scene. He had married some one else by-the-way;—so her first question is "where is *she*?["] He answers,—"she is on earth and *of it*,—another fills my place. I do not grieve to yeild it. Come!" And that is the climax—the conclusion—I may say, of the whole book! Is'nt that something more than ridiculous? "The Gates Ajar"[3] is'nt a circumstance to this. Miss Phelps has made great progress since then. Indeed the names of the two books indicate that very clearly. She now seems to be a sort of "inspector-general" of the celestial city. But I do'nt know why I should go so deliberately to work to render you as *disgusted* as myself! Do people crave sympathy in *those* feelings as well as others?

The end of the second sheet! and I did'nt know it,—was just turning the page to go on writing; now I suppose I must say "good-night." Since you like kisses I will send one, just on your name at the first of this letter! I will also enclose, in the letter, my *whole heart* or would do so if I had it in my keeding [*sic*]. But it has long since gone that way of its own accord; it has passed beyond my control. With truest love   Your own   Eileen.

ALS (WP, DLC).
¹ Protestant Episcopal, at 551 Fifth Avenue.
² Elizabeth Stuart Phelps, *Beyond the Gates* (Boston, 1884).
³ Elizabeth Stuart Phelps, *The Gates Ajar* (Boston, 1869).

To Ellen Louise Axson

My own darling,   Balto., Md., Oct. 27, 1884
I must deny myself this morning in the matter of letter-writing because I must begin at once to "bone" (as they say here) for that examination in colonial history. Our "quiz" did not come off last week, but was postponed till *next* Wednesday, at my suggestion. I will be without excuse this time, and so must be 'well up' on the chosen topics. Unhappily, those chosen topics are not of the most exciting sort. Colonial history, so far as this examination is concerned, is taken to begin with the discoveries of Columbus and the Cabots, and to embrace all the important American voyages of the Spanish bucaneers, the French explorers, and the English traders which took place before ever an Eng. colony was established or thought of on the continent. You can imagine, therefore, what dreary annals we have to familiarize ourselves with. We are expected to have a speaking acquaintance with even

the monkish map-makers of the thirteenth and fourteenth centuries. Altogether, it's a sort of study, first of all, of what might be called *pre-historic* America[.] But I need not bore *you* about all this. I am sufficiently bored for both of us. Not that I am not interested in these things, but that I find the school-boy task of cramming for examination increasingly irksome. I find my interest choked by the anticipated necessity of being answerable to an examiner for an exact knowledge of the innumerable dry particulars of the subject.

So you have seen Shinn at last. I am *so* glad that you like him so much, my love. I was quite sure that you would, though. No one who likes genuine open-heartedness and inartificial feeling could help liking Shinn, even if he were not the bright entertaining fellow that he is. And you are going to the theatre with him to-night? Where, my pet? I am so glad!

No, in spite of Mr. Morton, your letter reached me at the usual time, a little after 9 A.M. These precious little notes come generally soon after breakfast while I am writing to their author.

Ah, my darling how I love you, how desperately I miss you. You are my little queen, my blessed little sunbeam, my all, and I am forever   Your own   Woodrow.

P.S.   Here are the words of yours of which Mr. Shinn has a copy in my handwriting: (Sav,, Feb 18 [1884].)

"Please give Mr. Shinn my best thanks for the dainty little card, and the good wishes it bears. What one can I send him in return for them all? 'The best wishes that can be forged in his thoughts be servants to him.' The card is indeed *very* pretty, and I appreciate his sending it exceedingly. Somehow I feel an especially vivid interest in Mr. Shinn, and regard for him,—more than for any of your other friends of whom I have heard you speak. I suppose, to go somewhat out of my way in search of a selfish reason, it may be because he has happened to get 'mixed up' a little in *our* affairs, and so seems a wee bit my friend as well as yours."

I wish you could have seen how immensely pleased he was when he read it.   Lovingly,   W.

ALS (WC, NjP).

From James W. Bones

Dear Woodrow   Rome Ga Octo 28/84

I must apologize for not answering yours of 9th sooner but I have been crowded with business both at the mill & the farm this month. Besides I got my papers very much scattered last Fall & this summer in moving about so that I have had difficulty in getting them together. I also had to write to Dorsey on one or two points. I believe however I am now prepared to answer your points understandingly. You are correct about my error in valuation of the 80 acres (W½ NW 1/4 1.17.7.). Not having the papers upon which we made partition with me I trusted to my memory & it was at fault. The amt due your aunts Est should be $400. instead of $500.

And now as to the tax list. The rule in Nebraska is to assess the tax on whoever owns the land prior to April 1st. The *E½ NW 1/4 11.17.8* & the W½ of NE 1/4 11.17.8. were sold to Sheldon in Sept 1882 by contract & you took his contract in the partition[.] The Estate was liable for the tax assessed on this land in 1882 under the rule as *it* was the owner when tax was levied. The NW 1/4 12.17.8 was sold to Munger by contract at about same time as sale was made to Sheldon or shortly after & the 1882 tax had to be paid by estate. You took Mungers contract also in the partition. As to the E½ NE 1/4 11.17. that 80 was taken by me in the partition but I think it is described in the deed of partition as the W½ NE 1/4.11.17 (my copy of the deed is in Dorseys hands, having been sent to him some time ago & not yet returned) whereas the W½ NE 1/4.11.17 was sold to Sheldon in Sept. 1882 as above. Either Dorsey made mistake when he sent the list upon which we divided or you made mistake in drawing the deed. I believe this covers all the points made by you in your letter

The inclosed letter of Dorseys explains quit claim deed to I R Lee. I presume his statements are correct but I will not execute quit claim as Trustee until I hear from you. This land was not on the list of lands turned over to me by your uncle Thomas & I have no doubt was sold by your Uncle William as stated prior to the war. If you see proper to have your mother & father execute the deed, have them do so & let it be sent to Dorsey. I will then do same as Trustee for my children.

I also inclose Deed for your father & mother to execute to Miss Mueller as per Dorseys letter sent. This 40 was sold to her in early part of 1882 in May I think for $1000. You will find the amt credited to Estate June 10/82. For some reason I did not give her deed at time but only bond for title. My impression is Dorsey lent her the money to buy the 40, & did not wish her to have deed until her debt to him was paid. At all events the estate got the $1000. & Mrs Mueller is entitled to her deed. Please have the matter attended to as early as you can & send Dorsey the deed. I have sent mine as Trustee

Your affc Uncle   J. W. Bones

ALS (WP, DLC). Attached to WW to J. W. Bones, Oct. 9, 1884.

From Ellen Louise Axson

My darling Woodrow,   New York, Oct. 28/84.

It is half past eight now, and this is "Mr. Brush's day," so I must content myself with a few words now, and "have out my say" tonight. I reached home so late last night—quarter of twelve —that I was obliged to leave my writing for morning. Yet it wasn't too late for me to perform the usual ceremony with which I conclude the evening,—viz., reading over your letter of the day very slowly and carefully, with many pauses—for meditation. As there were two letters yesterday, that process occupied a good deal of time, quite enough, I admit, to have enabled me to write a letter, if I had chosen; and if I had been unselfish I suppose I should have done so. But then there is something so much more deliberate and premeditated about *beginning* to write a letter,—it was too late, not for the act, but for the *resolve*.

It was odd that I received yesterday morning a letter from you enclosing one from Mr Shinn,[1] and in the afternoon a note from Mr. O. enclosing one from *you*.[2] I think I had better send you, mine from him now, to make the electric chain complete. I had a delightful evening,—but I really *must* not stop to tell about it now. Good-bye, until tonight. Yesterday was a very happy day for me dear, because of those two sweet letters. They are real treasures. It is you who must have studied well the art of writing them,—I seem, as I read them, to be ever finding in my heart new depths of love for my darling.   With all my heart,   Your own Ellie.

Excuse this *awful* looking thing I write at a gallop.

ALS (WP, DLC).
  [1] WW to ELA, Oct. 25, 1884, enclosing C. H. Shinn to WW, Oct. 23, 1884, ALS (WP, DLC).
  [2] C. H. Shinn to ELA, c. Oct. 27, 1884, ALS (WP, DLC). He enclosed WW to C. H. Shinn, Oct. 25, 1884.

To Ellen Louise Axson

My own darling,   Balto., Md., Oct. 28, 1884

I have just received and read your sweet letter of Sunday and have kissed my own name at the beginning of it in a way that would have convinced an on-looker, not in the secret, that I was the most extraordinarily egotistic man in the world. Ah, my precious little bewitcher, you have a most wonderful instinct for saying and doing just the things that will most delight me! Since you too like kisses, Miss, I send you six, brimful of love, here on your own sweet name, Eileen—I did not accurately count the number: I guess it was nearer *twice* six; will you take them all?

It was exceedingly diverting to compare—to collate—the two accounts I received yesterday of Shinn's Saturday night call. After dispatching my note to you, and after the subsequent cramming of dates which I indulged in here in my room till about midday, I went over to the University to read in the Bluntschli until dinner time, and found in "the office" *two* letters from Shinn, one of them written Saturday afternoon,[1] saying that he was about to go over to 11th St., and the other penned in wild enthusiasm at 11 P.M. of the same day,[2] just after his return from 120, and made up of a sort of rhapsody on my "rare good fortune," in winning so charming a lady. You made a tremendous impression on the dear old enthusiast, my darling; and I can't sufficiently express my satisfaction at so propitious a beginning to your friendship. He is genuine to the bottom, and I know that it will be easy for you to add to the liking which you have accorded him for my sake as warm a liking for his own. I am quite sure that he is unlike anybody you ever met before, so that one who likes him *must* like him for his own sake. I hope you had a delightful time at the theatre last night, my pet. I thought of it all the evening—even while I was at the Halls', where I called for the first time since my return. My favourite, Miss Jennie, was not at home, and her oldest sister, Miss Belle, entertained her other sister, Miss Laura (Dr. Woods' sweetheart) and me for the greater part of the time with a minute rehearsal of the plot of Julian Hawthorne's "Archibald Malmaison," in full retribution for my briefer recital of the story of the "Giant's Robe." An odd way of spending the time, was'nt it? And yet we got in a good deal of talk about people and politics besides.

Ive made a stern resolve to go steadily through the round of visits I owe, including even those which were owing all last year; and last night I made a beginning—at the pleasant end, so as to get my hand in for the difficult tasks ahead. To-night I expect to call on the Woods, and—then the deluge!

Since I have loved, and been loved by, you, my darling, I have been able to appreciate as I never did before the exact place which friendship occupies in one's life, as distinguished from that love which only one person in the world can accept and return in the case of each one of us. Even to my most intimate friends I turn the same side that I turn to the world. My intercourse with them is freer, less artificial, much more of the heart, than the intercourse I hold with the rest of the world, but it, after all, differs from this latter in degree rather than in kind. It's just Browning's idea that I am beginning to appreciate:

> "God be thanked, the meanest of his creatures
> Boasts two soul-sides, one to face the world with,
> One to show a woman when he loves her!"[3]

When Shinn talks to you about me (if he does) don't you feel that there is a part of me that he don't see at all—which only *you* see or ever have seen? And yet I have probably shown him as much of myself as I have ever shown to a friend. Friends, take them at their best, are outside of my individual, my secret, my inmost, life. You alone, my little queen, are part of that. You alone may know me altogether, at my best and at my worst. You alone may look my heart full in the face and see without reserve the lineaments which others may only guess at. And *this*, my Eileen, is *the* delight of my love for you. I did not know what it was to live until I found you for whom to live, in whom to live. Not even the precious, the inestimable love of my mother gave me so much as a foretaste of this joy. This is *why* you are "all the world to me"—and yet this proves that very phrase a poor, lying phrase, because you are to me what not all the world could be, you are the keeper of all my heart secrets, you are the queen of my very life. You are the one person in the world whose heart is mine, who stands *with* me, as against the rest of the world. Ah, my darling, my darling, what would I be without you!

But this is scandalous—what am I learning about colonial history and the early discoveries all this while? Eileen, I *love* you, and am altogether   Your own   Woodrow.

ALS (WC, NjP).
   [1] C. H. Shinn to WW, 6 p.m., Oct. 25, 1884, ALS (WP, DLC) with WWhw and WWsh historical notes on env.
   [2] C. H. Shinn to WW, 11 p.m., Oct. 25, 1884, ALS (WP, DLC).
   [3] From Browning's "One Word More."

From Ellen Louise Axson

My darling Woodrow,   N.Y. Oct 28 1884
   I am sorry to hear to what dry diet you are being condemned of late,—am not surprised that you find it not altogether agreeing with you. It must be rather trying to be ordered to "eat what is

put before you, and ask no questions"—a very good rule, I dare say, for children, who are sure to choose unwholesome things, but for grown people who are supposed to have learned from experience what is good for them, not altogether desirable. I can imagine how impatient you must feel under these examinations. That Ph.D. is a very valuable possession I presume,—is it not?—but I see you will be obliged to pay a good price for it. What do you think you will do in the matter? Of course you have not decided, but to which side do you incline?

Mr Shinn tells me that he thinks of going to Baltimore soon, and he means to tear you away from dear Dr. Adams and bring you back with me for a few days;—poor unsuspicious fellow! he thinks that we have had such a long separation—since the very first of Oct!

I did'nt tell you what a pleasant time I had last night. We went to the Union Square Theatre and heard "French Flats." It is a *very* funny account of the quarrelling and love-making going on among the lodgers in the several stories. Each scene is laid on a different floor. There is about as much hide and seek in it as in the "Private Secretary"; but it is by no means so good as that. After it, that reckless youth *would* have me go to Mallards[1] for cream,—and that was the cause of our getting back so late. He had his pocket full of family photographs which he had brought to show me, and he wanted to go to some place where he could exhibit them. What a wonderful family it is! All of them—sisters and cousins and aunts, seem to speak Greek and Hebrew and Sanscrit &c. &c. as a matter of course. As for "Millicent"—what a woman! *what* a woman! ! Speaking of Mr. Shinn reminds me of Minnie Hoyt. It seems that Florence Young, writing home to Ella, mentioned his first visit. At a tea at Mrs. Bunting's Ella read the letter, and she says that Minnie, who was one of the guests, spent all the rest of the evening raving about Mr. Shinn,—trying to make them understand what a wonderful man he was! There's "naivete" for you! By the way, I think Mr. S. himself has a good deal of that charming quality.

Wasnt it provoking that Mr. Marvin too should have asked me to go to the theatre last night of all others—when I know so few people and of course have such rare opportunities for going. The other girls went—to the Bijou and Mr. S. sent them all flowers too—though of course he knew nothing of their engagement. He said he was "flush"—that was yesterday, though; I am afraid he *isnt* flush today. I have crowded my sheet as usual, and left not half room enough to tell you how much I love you, dear heart.

But a whole sheet is about as inadequate for *that,* as one corner of it. Our distance from the sky is practically the same, whether we are on the ground or the gatepost. Good night my love, my life, Your own Eileen.

ALS (WP, DLC).
¹ Ellen probably refers to Maillard's, a fashionable confectionery shop.

From Joseph Ruggles Wilson

My dearest Woodrow— Wilmington [N.C.], Oct 29 1884

I have been thinking a good deal, and even anxiously, over the contents of your recent letter—that which touches upon the advisability of aiming at the PhD. You argue so fully and so fairly the pros & cons, however, that I feel as a judge might who has both sides before him ready to his hand. Your dear mother & I—for it takes the two of us to constitute a complete court—have concluded to advise you against the PhD course—for the reason which you yourself so clearly present, viz: it will jeopard if not undermine your health, and no advantage can compensate for even such a *risk.* As to how far "marketable" you now are, or shall be by June next, this must be decided by your professors, together with the open or openable chances. You ought, however, at once, to put yourself up to the highest bidder, those same professors being the auctioneers. Or, if not these, select some others. Meanwhile, be not *anxious*: only wakeful to the slightest touch of opportunity.

What as to your book? You have written nothing thereanent. . . .

We are both well and our love for you is as great as you can wish.

As usual I am pressed for time and so hurry off this brief note. God bless our beloved one is our constant prayer.

Your affc Father.

ALS (WP, DLC).

To Ellen Louise Axson

My own darling, Balto., Md., Oct. 29, 1884

It is *far* beyond my usual time for writing. My time ever since breakfast has been filled *full* with engagements, and this is literally the first pause there has been. I shall have to trust to an afternoon mail's carrying this to you so that you may receive it at the usual time. If I have another such day of crowding engagements, I shall be tempted to neglect some of them rather than run the risk of disappointing my darling even as to the *hour* of my letter's arrival[.]

What an odd note, that of Shinn's which you enclose in to-day's sweet little epistle! How unreserved, how characteristic! If there is any one social drawback to Shinn it is that he makes one feel that he is letting *all* of himself out in what he says. There is no place for the attractive impression of *reserved* power of expression and feeling. But that, of course, is no detraction from the delight of sincerity and enthusiasm, nor does it stand in the way of his capturing one's sympathy and friendship. *He* is certainly *"sui generis."*[1] One likes him because he brings *variety*, because he is so little like the rest of the world, so little tamed by conventionality or shaped by custom, as well as because he is genuine and thoughtful and affectionate.

To-day, my pet, is completed the slow week which has gone since I returned from that delightful trip wh. seems so far away. *Is* not time sluggish!

> "Ah, Love, but a day,
> And the world has changed!
> The sun's away,
> And the bird estranged;
> The wind has dropped,
> And the sky's deranged:
> Summer has stopped."[2]

But there comes every day, in the hands of a dull leaden-faced postman, who dreams not of the rich things he carries, a message of love from the little lady whose love is life to me, and so long as sluggish time brings these treasures I *will* not fret, but will hope and will go on learning the sweet lesson of loving until my love is perfect enough to be worthy of my Eileen, my precious darling.

Don't forget, my pet, to give my love to the dear ones in Savannah whenever you write—and to dear little Eddie when you write to M[innie Hoyt]. I shall send my love for myself to Stockton.

Nothing has happened since my last, except the call at the Woods' (not worth recording); I am pretty well and in good spirits; but before everything else, I am

Your own Woodrow.

ALS (WC, NjP).

[1] This comment was evoked by the following portion of C. H. Shinn to ELA, c. Oct. 27, 1884, ALS (WP, DLC): "The bond that unites us [Shinn and Wilson], and necessarily includes thou also, is *sui generis*, is a full and loyal sympathy and at-one-ness."

[2] From Browning's "James Lee's Wife."

From Ellen Louise Axson

My darling Woodrow   New York, Oct. 29/84.

Our new boarder, Miss Mosely, has been spending the evening chatting with me here in my room,—has just left. She came to the house yesterday, but I did not make her acquaintance until to-day. She *does* work at the League, and in my class! that is, in the afternoon; in the morning she is in a private studio—Mr. Satter-lee's. I like her very much; at least I think I do! She isn't the sort of person of whom one forms very positive impressions, all at once—or whom one must either like or dislike intensely at first sight. She is a rather pretty little brunette with lovely dark eyes; and is a perfect lady in manners and appearance,—indeed I think she has an unusually sweet, modest, quiet manner, and a soft, low voice—a remarkable voice for a native of Michigan. She is from Grand Rapids—teaches there, and is to be here only two months,—I am sorry to say. I think it probable that we will be very good friends.

Friends!—that word reminds me, of what indeed I had small need to be reminded, your letter of today and it's contents. Ah, indeed there *is* a mighty difference between friendship, the wel-come guest of the heart[,] and love, it's lord! No one values or believes in friendship more than I. No one has greater reason to do so;—it is one of the most precious pusessions of life,—but love is life itself,—or becomes so as soon as it is given any part in it. Friendship is a very simple thing and easy to be understood, but love is the greatest of all mysteries; mysterious in it's origin as well as in its nature. How strange to think that but a short time ago, it was not even dreamed of by me—and now it *is*,—and must be forever, the very life of my life! Ah darling, however much of love you may give me, I can never be in your debt. You are literally in *all* my thoughts, for there is never a moment in which I am not distinctly *conscious* of you. You may trust me to keep those heart-secrets well, my darling, even as my own. We *do* stand *together*, as one person, and the world must stand aside. I *will* tell you,—because it is *true*,—how very happy it makes me to think, that great current, the world, which must always sweep between *friends* and cause their lives, though not their hearts, to drift apart, will have no power over our fate; that we will, in truth, make the voyage *together*, face to face as well as heart to heart.

And now dearest goodnight,

ALS (WP, DLC).   As ever   Your own   Eileen

From John Hanson Kennard, Jr.

My dear friend,   New Orleans, Oct. 29th, 1884.

I was extremely sorry not to see you to say good-bye to you and receive your farewell blessing before I left Balto. . . .

I was thoroughly heated tho' I assure you when I read Cable's letter in the Nov. Century called "We of the South."[1] It made me wrathy to see the petty meaness of the man. His defense of his scalawagism reads to me very much like an afterthought. Read it please and see how it strikes you. Could you not find time, my dear friend, to write a short strong letter striping Cable's jacket for him. He richly deserves it, and next to the pleasure of administering the lash to him myself it will please me most to have you deal with the little man. . . .

Very truly, Your friend,   J. H. Kennard Jr.

ALS (WP, DLC) with WWhw notation on env.: "Ans. Nov. 18, 1884."
[1] George W. Cable, "We of the South," *Century Magazine*, XXIX (Nov. 1884), 151-52. Cable was defending a conviction that he had expressed earlier in his story, "Dr. Sevier," which had been printed serially in the *Century Magazine* from November 1883 to May 1884. Southerners, Cable wrote in "We of the South," could be justly proud of their struggle during the Civil War. However, the time had come when they could honorably concede the justice of the Union cause without diminishing their "perfect manhood" by the "weight of a hair." The "doubtful doctrine" of secession never had been really accepted by large numbers of Southerners, and many of those who had believed in the right of states to secede had not advocated its indiscriminate exercise. In any event, Cable went on, secession was not the South's "actual cause." That cause was the defense of slavery, which the "whole intelligence of the South now admits . . . was an error in its every aspect."

Two Letters to Ellen Louise Axson

My own darling,   Balto., Md., Oct. 30, 1884

It *was* a great pity that you should have been invited to go to the theatre by two different persons for the same evening, though I am glad that, since you had to miss one, that one was the Bijou. The only "bijou" companies I ever saw gave entertainments which were far from being edifying. A stage full of young women with scarcely any clothing on is not an improving thing to look upon, even when strange lights and gorgeous scenery combine to reproduce fairy-land. But I may be stupidly off the track, as usual. The Bijou to which Mr. Marvin took the young ladies may be something quite different from what I suppose—may be an unexceptionable place

I must not stop now, my pet, to answer your questions about the Ph.D. &c., because this is, as you know, one of my hard-driving days—a day for only a few lines in which to tell you that I

am well. I know that you will excuse the scantness and emptiness of the note for the sake of the unbounded love which to
[it] is meant to carry to you from

Your own   Woodrow.

My own darling,   Balto., Md., Oct 31 1884

Yesterday Mr. Wright and I, in obedience to a sudden impulse
of curiosity, went down to the rooms of the Y.M.C.A. and attended the afternoon session of the Woman's Congress. We
viewed the remarkable assembly from the gallery, where we
found a corner in which we might be free to compare opinions
as one after another the good things of the programme were
brought forth. Barring the chilled, scandalized feeling that always comes over me when I see and hear women speak in public,
I derived a good deal of whimsical delight—mixed with not a
few instructive suggestions as to character and the like—from the
proceedings. Mrs. Julia Ward Howe was in the chair—a most attractive, motherly old lady, born, apparently, to control rather by
affection than by the exercise of presidential authority—but possessed of less mother wit, I should say, than round, jolly Mrs.
Cheney[1] who rolled herself on to the platform to make the only
natural, spontaneous, graceful remarks that relieved the stiff,
self-assertive tone of the proceedings. The only noticeable 'orator'
who spoke from the floor of the body was a severely dressed person from Boston, an old maid of the straitest sect of old maids.[2]
Not trousers and a Prince Albert coat could have made her more
manly in her bearing. She was a living example—and lively commentary—of what might be done by giving men's places and
duties to women—a very dialectic Amazon!

I enclose the programme[3] in order that you may read the queer
address to the people of Balto. which it contains. What an odd
mixture of deprecating explanation and almost defiant self-as-
sertion! I had to re-read it before I perceived what it was that
gave it so unpleasant a flavour. It is the half-expressed fear that
towards them there will be a repression of the "natural hospitality" of Baltimore—a fear which, I believe, has proved quite un-
warranted.

But enough of that for the present, for I have just received
and read a sweet letter from New York which makes it impossible
for me longer to keep away from the constant topic of my
thoughts, my love for its author. Ah, my darling, how I wish that
I could hold you in my arms just one moment to tell you in kisses

what I think of these sweet responses, these precious confessions, which have come in reply to my letter about friendship. My love, my life, my lovely little sweetheart! How unspeakably happy it makes me to read these precious secrets of your heart. You *are* mine forever, my pet, and I am in everything

Your own   Woodrow.

ALS (WC, NjP).

¹ The Baltimore *Sun,* October 30 and 31 and November 1, 1884, and the *Baltimore American,* October 30 and 31 and November 1, 1884, both reported that Mrs. Ednah D. Cheney of Massachusetts read and commented upon papers at the sessions of the twelfth congress of the Association for the Advancement of Women on October 29 and 31, 1884, but neither newspaper mentioned her participation in the sessions on October 30.

² Although the newspaper accounts mention by name several participants at the congress from Massachusetts and Boston, it is not possible to identify the "old maid" with any certainty.

³ It is missing.

From Ellen Louise Axson

My darling Woodrow,   New York, Oct. 31/84.

Mr. Donaldson is coming around tonight to take us to the Republican parade,¹ so I must make haste to write before I go, lest there should'nt be time after my return. Mrs. Guerry is rather shocked at my going to swell the enemy's crowd, but I have never seen *any* parade yet, so I am not particular. I dont want all the "shows" to come and go without having a peep at them. I am not ashamed to show my colours however. Mr Heiler has given me his Democratic badge to wear. How glad I will be when the suspense is over, and *somebody* is elected. Alas! I fear, I fear there will be little cause for gladness! I did'nt know I *could* become so wrought up over politics. I feel exactly as though some great catastrophe was threatening us all,—or at least as though *something* tremendous was about to happen. What *will* we do if we are defeated? I am afraid there won't be any Democratic party left. Perhaps *both* parties will collapse,—*killed* by their own wickedness! "The wages of sin is death,"—and parties *must* receive their rewards in this world, since they have no hereafter.

I like Miss Mosely, more and more, she is *very* sweet. I am tempted to invite her to room with me during her two months stay;—though I don't know that she would care to do so;—her room is by no means so comfortable as this, but she has it all to herself, for about the same price she would pay for half of this. The other girls decided not to come until Xmas because they must pay a dollar a week more here. I am rather glad; four in this room would be dreadful.

I have joined the sketch class this afternoon, and am *delighted* with it. It meets from half past four to half past five every day,—one member posing for the rest in fancy costume. It is great fun—*not* the posing but the sketching;—and nothing could be of more service to us. I have intended to join all along, but there were *so* many places I wanted to visit in the afternoons;—and besides I was afraid to apply for admission. Then the *rule* is that we must submit a sketch from life, and I had no one to sketch. We practiced on Florence a number of nights, but not with much seriousness. After I came here I grew desperate for a model, and finally decided that there was no help for it, I *must* sketch myself. So you might have beheld me, on several successive afternoons, deeply engaged in that cheerful occupation. I didnt know how ugly I was before. I think I must send you an assortment of them, that you may see how I *really do* look. But I must make haste to close, or I won't be ready when called for. Give my love when you write to your dear parents, and believe me my darling, with all my heart   Your own   Eileen.

ALS (WP, DLC).

¹ There was a large parade in New York in honor of the Republican presidential candidate, James G. Blaine, on the evening of October 31, 1884. District Republican clubs and other political and civic associations from New York and nearby cities participated. The parade proceeded down Fifth Avenue from approximately 53rd Street to 38th Street, along 38th Street to Madison Avenue, and thence to Madison Square, where it was reviewed by Blaine. The Republican *New York Tribune*, November 1, 1884, reported that there were 60,000 marchers; the Democratic New York *World,* for the same date, estimated only 25,000.

From the Minutes of the Seminary of Historical and Political Science

Bluntschli Hall   Oct 31st 1884

At a regular meeting of the Historical and Political Science Association held Oct 31st 1884 Dr Adams was in the chair and twenty members were present.

Mr. Levermore reviewed the last number of the Archivo Storico Lombardo and two numbers of the Revista Storica Italiana. Mr Wilson reviewed the last number of the Revue de Droit International and the Bulletin de la Société de Legislation Comparée for July. Mr. Dewey reviewed several of the minor American journals viz:—The Granite Monthly, the Bay State Monthly, The Pennsylvania Magazine of History, the Magazine of American History, and the Southern Historical Society Papers. . . . Mr. C. H. Shinn a former member of the Seminary was present and after being introduced by Dr Adams gave an excellent outline of his paper (which will be published in the next number of the Historical Studies) on The Land Laws of Mining Camps. . . .

The Seminary adjourned shortly after ten o clock.

T. K. Worthington   Secretary

To Ellen Louise Axson

My own darling,   Balto., Nov. 1, 1884

It made my heart beat very fast to find a telegram from somebody awaiting me yesterday when I came from lectures. Of course I thought of all that might have happened in New York and tore it open with a good deal of suppressed excitement—and it *was* from New York; but Shinn was the signer: he was to leave for Balto. on the 10 A.M. limited express. Since three o'clock yesterday, therefore, we have had him here in his old room like old times. He will stay until Tuesday—he *must* be back in season to *see* the election in New York. He told me of his having carried off your fan Monday night after the theatre. He has innumerable calls to make amongst his friends here so that I shall not see very much of him, I am afraid; for I too shall necessarily be very busy reading for the examination next week. I can, however, enjoy the fresh breeze of enthusiasm—and campaign talk—which he brings with him.

I conclude, my pet, that, since you have said nothing more about the young ladies at No. 60 joining you, the project has come to wreck on Mrs. Beatty's charges. Is it so—or does the negotiation only hang fire? Such an immigration would put an end to those cosy readings on the lounge under the gas-light.

I am sorry to hear that you think of adding the evenings to your work at the League—no, I wont say that, either, because you must know better than I can what would be most advantageous under the circumstances. But it is evident that there is not the same necessity for your doing so that there is in the case of Miss Mosely, who has only two months to give to the work there. I cannot think, at any rate, that evenings given to rest, to diversion, or to a change of work can be in any sense "wasted." I should say, rather, that the[y] were saved, and that a whole day of work of one kind—from breakfast till bed-time—was such a day as only *necessity* could justify. I suppose that a young lady from Michigan would be a sufficient escort on the streets after nightfall—though your description of Miss Moseley does not give much countenance to that view of the case—and there may be an argument in the fact that Miss M., for whom the time is short, cannot go without *your* escort; but these considerations would not make me happy in thinking of my darling's being out without protection after dark. I may seem over-anxious about your safety in the great city, my darling, and it may be that I am over-esti-mating the dangers: but I don't think that I am, and my intense anxiety must be excused, if not justified, by the fact that you are my greatest treasure, that my happiness depends upon your wel-fare, that my life is inextricably and irrevocably bound up in the fortunes of my Eileen, and that anything that might overtax her strength or jeopard her safety in any way is just so much of a weight upon my heart. I know, therefore, that my darling will not think me foolish when I beg that she will not make this new arrangement except for very imperative reasons.

Yes, my pet, I have seen McCarthy's "Four Georges."[1] I am reading the first part, which has been issued in the Franklin Square. Mr. McC. indulges in a good deal of *padding,* in the shape of entirely irrelevant references to all sorts of odd bits of incident in fiction, as well as to very distant analogies in history, but the result is certainly a story of unflagging interest—which is said to be at the same time of trustworthy detail—and his histories are in small danger of being neglected. They are rare good pieces of literature

Have you seen the announcement of Hamerton's new book—the complementary piece to his *Intellectual Life*—on *Social Inter-course*[?][2] We must see that, sooner or later.

I am glad to hear such delightful news about dear Eddie—and the success of "*our* picture"—as you tell it and account for it—is even more gratifying, if possible, than the success of *your* pic-ture. I am proud of my darling's skill in her chosen art, and *her* success gives me purer, more genuine delight than any I could have myself. My love for her has made my admiration for her rare gifts as it were a part of itself: so that, if I may be a part of her work, even in her thoughts, there is an added weight of satisfaction in my pleasure at her successes. Your cousin *is* an amazingly shrewd guesser. I suspect that it is because in such cases her *heart* does the guessing.

May I confess to you, my darling, that I have been fighting against the blues all morning? I can confess anything in my Saturday letters, because I can give the antidote in the Sunday letter which is to overtake it. Perhaps you have not seen enough of me yet to find out just how foolish I am: but you will discover that when I confess that a very frequent cause of despondency with me is an overwhelming doubt about my ability to do anything worth doing. Now and again I lose all faith in my own talents and am possessed of the conviction that I am nothing better than a dull fool, with a vain knack for counterfeiting thought, and am ashamed that anyone should admire me. Of course I could not confess this to anybody but you. I should be taken to be doing that most contemptible of all things, courting a contradiction, "fishing for a compliment"! But I can own to my Eileen, who loves me and therefore has faith in me, that I often absolutely *suffer* under a sense of being a *humbug,* pretending that I possess mind and really possessing nothing but the skill of concealing the absence of it—or, at best, possessed of only a single mental muscle, and for the rest utterly without sparkle or versatility, a heavy one-sided creature unable to find the single hole in life into which he might be made clumsily to fit. Perhaps it is not quite exact to call these the blues: it is better to say that I am filled with a sort of supreme self-indignation, or self-pity, as a man whose education, so far, consists in being able to express clearly the poverty of thought that is in him. I have studied the art of expression without being equally careful—possibly without being able—to have something to say. I blush to see other men less pretentious and more solid, more real— But I must not work the thought into feverishness by trying to force it into language—I must not presume too far upon my assumed Saturday privilege. I must wait for to-morrow to come with its return of my comfortable normal conviction that I may, if I find work, be an ordinary useful man—or, mayhap, of my occasional conviction (or delusion), brief but enjoyable, that I have a message for the world and the ability to deliver it.

My darling need not distress herself because of my folly in manufacturing such doubts out of the desire to be something different from what I am—a brilliant instead of a merely serviceable man. It does me good to confess. It helps to bring me back to my senses. And the *privilege* of confessing to you is like a cool, refreshing breeze, to blow away the clouds that oppress and stifle me. It is thus that you are my life, my darling. Your love is my life. It is the sunshine I most need in my darker moods. It is fast making those moods impossible. When you are with me to chase them away with a smile and a caress they *shall* be impossible!

With a score of kisses for my lovely, my precious little sweetheart,   Your own   Woodrow.

ALS (WC, NjP).

1 Justin McCarthy, *A History of the Four Georges,* Vol. I (New York, 1884). WW seems to have been answering a missing letter from ELA of c. Oct. 30, 1884.

2 Philip G. Hamerton, *Human Intercourse* (Boston, 1884).

From Ellen Louise Axson

My darling Woodrow,   New York Nov. 1./84

I was much entertained by your description of the "Woman's Congress," and also by the *very* graceful! address to Baltimore. I should like to have been with you,—to have heard some of those "representative women in medicine, the pulpit, and the law." I don't know either, whether I should have enjoyed being there or not; sometimes those things amuse me, and sometimes I am too indignant to see the funny side. How *can* they make themselves so absurd,—and worse than absurd! I know some of them are as *good* as can be, and I suppose they must be clever,—above the average; and yet how absolutely *senseless* their conduct. Why is it that cleverness is so apt to unsettle a woman's brains? Is'nt there room in our poor heads for both common sense, and uncommon?

I wish you could have been with *me* tonight. I am *sure* you would have been amused. We attended a lecture at the League by Mr. C. T. Turner, the artist,—on composition. It was delicious in it's way! Mr T. is an excellent artist but no speaker,—doesnt pretend to be. I never saw anyone so absolutely unaffected; he has *no* manner, no style whatever. He is as simple and artless as a child, and as unembarrassed,—as unconscious of self, It was a sort of thing that you could'nt help laughing at, and yet it was *excellent*. He had something to say and he *said* it, he knew exactly what he was talking about; and he went about in a most honest straight-forward fashion. He is a fine sturdy Anglo-Saxon, squarely-built, with ruddy complexion and a big red beard—nothing of the traditional artist about him. Indeed there is only one of the crowd who *is* the ideal artist, in appearance. He is a superbly made young fellow about six feet three with a head and face that reminds one of Byron. He is Byronic in other respects too,—wears a blouse and picturesque hair, and has a high and mighty expression. I don't know the name of this young hero—of the melodrama.

But I have seen none of them whose face lights up so finely with intellect and genius as Mr. Brush'; he has a singularly interesting face, and he is a very interesting man[.] By the way, he is *engaged*. It is quite a pretty little romance. He met her at the league where she was a student last year in the antique class. Now she works in his studio. But it grows late and I *must* close. I love you darling, more than life, and am now and always

                    Your own   Eileen.

ALS (WP, DLC).

To Ellen Louise Axson

My own darling, Balto., Md., Nov. 2, 1884 4.20 P.M.

Shinn has been with me ever since church this morning so that this is the first moment I have had for writing. We have been sitting up here in my room since dinner doing what my conscience does not approve of, but what you will see to have been almost inevitable under the circumstances. We have been reading the *Times* and *Herald* of this morning and canvassing all the possibilities of next Tuesday. I am exceedingly hopeful, though so anxious as to be thankful that there is to be only a day or two more of suspense. Only my profound trust in an over-ruling Providence will keep me from the deepest despondency, my darling, if Cleveland should be defeated. God only knows what will be our political destiny if the Republican machine should triumph again!—6.25 P.M.—I am fated, my love. Two visitors, old Princeton friends, came in and have just released me. There's no telling now when this letter will reach you.

Of course you must send me those sketches of yourself—the complete set. Why that is the very thing I have been wanting for I know not how long, but have hesitated to ask for, because— well *because*: for once I must fall back upon the "woman's reason." If you have made an "ugly" (!) picture of yourself, Miss, you have been indulging in caricature, and should not have been admitted in the class. Do you suppose that I have seen you *only* with the eyes of love and don't *know* that you are the lovliest little lady in the world? Please dont forget to send the sketches. May I keep them as treasures?

This is a miserable excuse for a note—when I *wanted* to write a letter, but I must let it go as it is in order that it may have a *chance* of getting to you to-morrow, for it is meant as an antidote to something written yesterday. Forget *that,* my pet, except in so far as it proves your lover possessed of that sort of vanity which makes a man bemoan the fact that he cannot in his inmost heart think as highly of himself as he would like to think. It is a chapter in his character, which you should understand. The best thing about him is that he can and does love you with all his heart. Your own Woodrow.

ALS (WC, NjP).

From Ellen Louise Axson

My darling Woodrow,   New York Oct. [Nov.] 2./84.

How pleasant it is to come up here and have a quiet chat with you, after talking so much, all day, with other people. I have spent the evening gossiping with the boarders,—discussing Carlyle and Emerson with Mr. Goodrich and Miss Mosely below stairs, and Bob Toombs and Ben Hill with my sweet neighbour, Mrs. Jenkins, above. She is the lady whose husband is away & I have seen more of her than the rest, partly on that account. They have all invited me to their rooms but her's is the only one to which I care to go. She is a beautiful and lovely woman;—by all means the most attractive here. Her place evidently is, and has always been, in "the first circle." She has a charming manner,—it is a singular combination of timidity and sweet gracious dignity. I fancy she was exceedingly shy as a girl. She seems to have spent all her married life in travelling, has been "everywhere," and knows "everybody." She has met all our prominent Georgia statesmen—hence the discussion over Hill, Stephens, and the rest. She has spent several summers in N.C. at Warm Springs and Asheville, has ascended the Black Dome three times—indeed I don't know any picturesque spot in America that she has'nt visited. Though very enthusiastic about it all, she is tired enough of travelling now, and wild to keep house. But her husband, who is a splendid looking fellow, I imagine from his picture, is a perfect Arab. They seem to be "uncommonly devoted," and, I have no doubt, have lovely times together. They spent about six hours a day this summer, in a boat on Lake George, he being an ardent deciple of Isaak Walton. By-the-way, she knows a number of my Georgia friends.

I am beginning to think that the world is a small place after all. Everywhere, you meet someone whom you know, or who knows your friends. A curious instance of that has just happened to me. It appears that Miss Mosely's brother, who seems to be a prominent member of the Presbyterian church in Grand Rapids, invited a young minister, Mr. Caldwell,[1] to visit that church. He staid at their house, and he and Miss M. became very good friends. Now he has turned up in New York, and, calling on her, made the discovery that he knew all about me. And I know as much about him. He is an own nephew of the Rev. J. M. M.[2] His father is a lawyer in Greensboro N.C. and I went to school with his sisters in Rome. One of them was a *very* intimate friend of Jessie Bones. Is'nt it queer that I should meet him and in this fashion?

He is a delightful young man, with a frank, bright, handsome face and cordial manners[.] Though very much in earnest about his work, he has'nt much of the clerical air,—perhaps because he studied law, and has'nt quite recovered from it!

He took us to Dr. Storr's[3] church this morning, and to Dr. Hall's[4] this afternoon. We heard two *splendid* sermons. Dr. Hall was at his best, so simple and yet so impressive, so earnest,—so *good*! We had quite a nice trip to Brooklyn,—walked over the bridge on our return, my first view of it. Is'nt it *grand*? And is'nt the view from it magnificent? Good-night my darling. I am just a little tired, so instead of writing to you any more, I believe I will lie on the lounge and *think* of you a bit. With truest love, I am as ever   Your own   Ellie.

ALS (WP, DLC).
    1 The Rev. Robert E. Caldwell, then twenty-six years old, who had just been graduated from the Union Theological Seminary in Richmond, Va., and was about to assume the pastorate of the South Franklin, Ky., Presbyterian Church.
    2 Perhaps she meant the Rev. Dr. Joseph B. Mack. No Presbyterian minister, northern or southern, to whom she might have been referring at this time had initials J. M. M.
    3 The Rev. Dr. R. S. Storrs, pastor of the Congregational Church of the Pilgrims, Brooklyn.
    4 The Rev. Dr. John Hall, pastor of the Fifth Avenue Presbyterian Church.

To Ellen Louise Axson

My own darling,   Balto., Md., Nov. 3, 1884 10 A.M.
    It is odd that one should be affected more by seemingly trivial things than by the greater things by which they are surrounded: but of course it depends upon what is revealed by the small circumstances. For instance, much as I am interested in Mr. Brush, in the Byronic giant, in the unconscious lecturer; much as I desire a recital of everything that affects or interests you; much as I delight in your charming descriptions of the people and things about you—for they are charming, my pet, in their sweet womanly humour, and taste, and insight—two things in your letters of last week have dwelt with me almost to the exclusion of all the rest. Will you be amused or simply pleased when you hear that the chief of them was the picture of a sweet little lady "curled" cosily on her "dear little lounge" beneath the gas light reading—and the other a less distinct picture of that same bewitching person busily sketching her own features for the sketch class. Can't you guess *why* I picked out these things to think about, and of the two preferred the former? Why, simply because they were pictures of you, of your private life. They gave my imagination something to take hold of. Having never seen either your room or the League

studios, I of course find it difficult to form any distinct picture of your occupations from day to day, and any touch that draws the veil ever so little is what I watch for most eagerly. Some time, little sweetheart, when you have an odd interval of leisure into which no more serious occupation will fit, wont you draw me a ground plan of your room with the position of the different pieces of furniture?

I shall look for those sketches of yourself with eagerness.

I am glad, very glad, my darling that you are in the sketch class because I know how much you wanted to be in it. Remember, Miss, that when *you* pose you must tell me all about your costume &c. Would it be possible for you to get one of the best sketches made on that occasion, for a gentleman here in Baltimore who is interested in that branch of art and would give anything he has for a sketch—a good sketch—taken on that particular day?

But I must stop writing and do some studying while Shinn is out calling.

Perhaps it is not necessary after offering certain testimony given above, to say that my life is wrapped up in my love for my precious Eileen—that thoughts of her are my constant joy. Do you think that you know how much I love you and how entirely I am

Your own   Woodrow.

ALS (WC, NjP).

From Ellen Louise Axson

My darling Woodrow,   New York, Oct. [Nov.] 3/84.

Alas! it is half past ten, and I am only just free to write you. And I had so much to say too, I felt as though I would like to talk to you all the evening. Really, instead of being friendless in the great city, I am getting to have too many friends! It is again Mr. Caldwell who has occupied me tonight. Just after lunch today I went at his request to introduce him to Annie and Florence, who were also his sister's school-mates. He is a charming young fellow. I don't think I ever saw anyone so *eager* to do a favour; he had expected to leave today, but has decided to remain until Thursday for no other reason but to take us sight-seeing; or so he *says,* and I suppose it would be worse than ungrateful to disbelieve him. We are going tomorrow to see an ocean steamer &c. &c.; and he is urging us to take under his escort our much talked-of trip up the Hudson. We had given it up because we could'nt reach home until after nightfall. I hope the time given to "diversion" *is'nt* altogether "wasted"! But it looks something like it; and I seem to be getting quite "gay"! I was in luck this afternoon, had an invitation to the "art reception" at the Metropolitan. Of course a reception in that sense is simply an invitation to the "private view" on the opening day. This autumn's exhibition is of very special interest on account of the splendid collection of pictures by Mr. Watts. R. A., which have just been brought from England; —as a loan. There was great opposition in England to having such valuable works, many of them public property, sent over the water. But the negotiations have at last been successful; and it is a rare opportunity for art lovers here. The pictures—but I really *must* not begin on the pictures now—it is too late. A word, my love, as to your fears for my health and safty in the matter of night work! I appreciate your thoughtful care on my account, dear, and I *won't* make a practice of working at night. I have thought of going occasionally, when I have lost time, in "diversion" in the afternoon[,] to make it up; do'nt you think that would be a good idea? I am inclined to think, Sir, that you *do* "overestimate["] the danger; because everybody that I meet here,—the girls at the League, for instance, who are as nice as can be, some of them of the first families—regard me with unmitigated wonder and amusement when I express any hesitation about going out at night. We went alone to the Sat. night lecture, the first and only time in my life that I ever did such a thing. I was'nt afraid at all, but I felt *awfully* ashamed. But it seemed necessary. It would certainly be a pity to miss all the lectures of the winter,—they have them once a week,—because of that three minutes walk over brilliantly lighted streets. By the way, Mr. Marvin thinks it all right. He laughs at our "country" idea of N.Y. as such a dreadful place, says it is the *safest,* he knows of, in which to bring up children either boys or girls. I hope you understand, dear, that I don't say all this in the spirit of argument, but simply to reassure you, to console you with regard to our "unprotected" condition generally. If you still think I ought not to go, even to the lectures, I won't do it; for it is a matter in which I think you have a right to be consulted.

I am glad you have had such a pleasant visit from Mr. Shinn[.] I imagine that you *have* had plenty of "campaign talk["];—am glad you sympathize in that matter. And to think that tomorrow is *the* day! But no! I will try *not* to think of it, and get myself worked up to fever heat.

My darling, how I have longed to be with you today that I might at least try to help you conquer that despondency. You a dull fool, indeed! with a vain knack for counterfeiting thought! I am afraid I must laugh at you, sir, for how can one argue over such remarkable propositions! Why, I know, and everyone else knows, and you know too, when you are in your right mind, the kind, and the quality of work for which you were sent into the world; for which you have been armed and equipped, for which all your life, even in it's earliest relations, your home training has been a preparation. Yet I can readily appreciate your state of mind. I suppose everyone has their "ups and downs" of feeling, and *must* have as long as human nature and human life remain unchanged. And I believe that the more sensitive and highly organized the nature, the more violent and extreme are these "sudden thrills of fire and frost." It is a penalty you pay for superiority. That stolid tranquillity and content, one sometimes sees, is, I suppose, one of the compensations, alas! how poor an one!— for the dull, and narrow life of the lower classes;—the classes that are really lower, I mean, in range of thought, and hope, and aim, and feeling. But as for yourself, darling, try to look on the bright side of *yourself* as well as of circumstances[.] I'll pledge my life it's the *right* side!

Ah me, I *must* close—much against my will. I have scarcely begun. With all the love that you want, I am as ever,

Your own Ellie.

ALS (WP, DLC).

To Ellen Louise Axson

My own darling,   Balto., Md., Nov. 4, 1884 9.05 A.M.

I have just seen Shinn off, having asked him to "give my regards to my friends in New York when he sees them, and to make as good a report as possible at No. 120." I was *very* sorry he had to go so soon. I have enjoyed his visit immensely, tho' my own necessary preparations for examination and his diligent call-paying gave me only a few hours of his company. I did not tell him of my run up to New York. Nothing led up to or suggested it, and I could not *volunteer* to hurt his feelings. It would hardly have been possible to make *him* see it as anything but a wilful cut—a deliberate breach of friendship—and I did not care to put that between us unless candour and honesty compelled. If it had been what it would seem to him, I should have told him of it: but since it certainly was not that, I shrank from having him think it so.

You may imagine what my feelings, my anxieties, are to-day,

my pet. This is a crisis in my own fortunes, because the result of to-day's vote must decide in large part the character and aim of my political writing. I don't intend to think much about the election till this evening, however. I shall read diligently all day, and then, about half past ten to-night, go down street with my friend Dr. Woods to watch the returns. What time I get to bed must depend upon circumstances—not till morning if the news comes in rapidly and continuously. I shall be a very wobe-gone creature if standing in the street all night should bring me only the assurance of defeat!

I have just received your Sunday letter, my darling. I am de-lighted that you are making so many pleasant friends at Mrs. Beatty's, and that you have had the opportunity of hearing Dr. Storrs and Dr. Hall under such agreeable circumstances. That *must* have been peculiarly pleasant, your meeting with young Mr. Caldwell. New York is certainly *the* places for surprises and round-about happenings of that sort. The world is like a wheel, small at the *centre*.

I wish I could make my letters as interesting as yours, little lady, but my life is as uneventful and as uninteresting as possible —and I can at best give you only a dull chronicle of feelings and opinions. Are you content with that? Is your imagination strong enough to make something out of nothing?

With truest love, Your own Woodrow

ALS (WP, DLC).

From Ellen Louise Axson

New York, Oct. [Nov.] 4/84

No my darling, I was not amused—exactly—but "simply pleased," and something more than pleased, by the revelations in this morning's letter. What was there in that little letter to make the tears come into my eyes;—almost to draw forth a little sob or two? —there was nothing sad about it! And so a grave student, even when most deeply engaged in "world themes" can take time to think and care for such trifles as those, when they concern the woman he loves! In very truth he *must* love her,—even "to the level of every day's most quiet need." I think I must ask you a question which you asked *me* a few days ago,—so that if you think it foolish, you can't blame *me*! "Were you irresistibly im-pelled to write as you did, or are you studying the art of so writ-ing?" Has someone,—some *woman*—been telling you just the things that will most touch a woman's heart? You see we are foolish creatures—we women—and so have been disposed from time immemorial to attach great importance to little things, little proofs of love, little marks of tenderness, and thoughtful care. Perhaps not more importance than do others though—nor more than they deserve, for life is made up of little things. We can't, and we don't receive all its joys and its blessings in one great flood. Happiness, if it comes at all, comes, I think, in the wake of those "sweet observances," comes softly, quietly, day by day, "as the gentle dew from heaven."

But it is near eleven, and I must be a good girl tonight and go to bed betimes, for I have been up late for several nights past. Miss Mosely and I have been having a private sewing circle this evening. At least it very much resembled one, both as regards the work of our fingers and our tongues, for we have been busily gossiping about the Art League and art leaguers. By-the-way you did'nt *really* think those sketches were worth seeing!? I tore them all up long ago except one unfinished one which I kept—for its delightful absurdity. I never *really* thought of *keeping* the things! I will be sure to draw the "ground plan" you wish! Goodnight dear love, with all my heart,

your own Eileen.

I wonder what you are doing tonight! Are you taking part actively in the election? Are you taking things coolly, or are you in a fever of excitement, I am trying as much as possible not to *dwell* on it today, since we can *do* nothing, but only wait. I believe now we will win, don't you?

ALS (WP, DLC).

Notes on a Lecture in Professor Morris's Course on the Philosophy of the State

Nov. 5, 1884

(Dewey)[1]

Rousseau was the most famous advocate of the social contract theory, but not the first. It is to be found in Locke, and even earlier in Hooker. R. differs from Hobbes in his opinion of the original man. R. says that he was neither good nor bad; H. that he was bad. R. held also that at first society must be formed by unanimous consent, not by majority. Criticisms upon this view to be found in Spencer "Man and State" last chapter.

Spencer

1. Principles of Sociology 2 vols.
2. Study of Sociology (International Series)

3. Man vs. the State
4. Social Statics—the first volume I read. It is very different from his later works. It appeared in 1854. His later expressions have been much more suggestive and true. There is the same essential thought, however.

We can find in S no profound acquaintance with previous philosophic thinkers outside of England—a school which follows one general type. The school ignores Greek and German philosophy. Therein is the sensational theory of knowledge—quasi-physical philosophy, recognizing only physical phenomenon. It is characterized by the philosophic skeptic. Locke held that we know only phenomenon, not substance. Hume logically carried this farther and said that we know neither mind nor matter, but only a series of phenomena. The Mills repeated the same story.

In *conception*, therefore, there is nothing new in S's philosophy of "the unknowable." We know of matter and motion; matter-phenomenon of unknown substance: motion-phenomenon of unknown force. Everything centers in redistribution of matter and motion.

The differential from homogeny into heterogony is the whole history of society. When the maximum of evolution is reached then the movement towards dissolution takes place towards homogeny again. The real proportion of one to the other determines present condition. Both are taking place at the same time.

S. is really a much broader man than his theory.

Transcript of WWsh in notebook described at Oct. 8, 1884.
    1 It was almost certainly Davis R. Dewey, not his brother John, who gave this report in Morris's course.

To Ellen Louise Axson

Bluntschli Library [Baltimore], Nov. 5, 1884 11.10 A.M.
My own darling,
You may imagine how profoundly thankful I am for the apparent result of the election. I say 'apparent' because of course we are as yet far short of confident assurance of victory. But all the indications point to Cleveland's election and I hear no *claims* of success for Blaine. It *seems* as if our hopes were abundantly realized, my darling, our prayers for the country answered. If so, a great cloud is lifted from my heart and I can turn to my work with unanxious zest.
I am *very* tired, having been out of bed till three o'clock this morning, standing in a dense yelling crowd, and am painfully

dragging myself through lecture hours as best I may, with the hope of an early chance for rest.

I have just received your Monday-night letter, my pet, How can I sufficiently thank you for its sweet comforting words of cheer and confidence! I *will* try, my precious, to "look on the bright side of myself." It is altogether the wisest thing to do: and it ought to be easy with such help as I get from my darling's unfailing love. And yet it is terribly hard work to thaw out this present "frost" of despondency about my gifts, their character and amount. The *facts* really seem to be against me—on the side of knowledge at least, if not on that of capacity for using it if I had it. After all, however, it *ought* to content me that I can fit myself for useful labour and can faithfully do my best without any special concern as to whether that best will be remembered outside of my own family or beyond my own generation. The whole matter revolves about the question, Is it right to foster a longing to do immortal work and to encourage a conviction of the possession of power to do it; or should one school himself to content with mediocrity and with a prospect of mere ministerial work? Of course, with such content supreme, the highest sort of enthusiasm must be thrust out to die. But how is one to know that he has strength enough to go as far as such enthusiasm sees in its visions of new worlds of thought? How is one to tell a castle in the air from a sober, achieveable purpose? These are the questions that vex my thoughts—and which I *allow* to vex them in the face of my determination to *do* simply what my hands find to do, and to let the perfect performance of that be the present rule of achievement. That is the rule of commonsense; but I am not confessing commonsense: I am confessing my*self* to *you*, who will not think me a mere doubting, weak-kneed fool for my pains. I shall *act* as if I had no doubts: but I can let my darling see, the while, what my feelings are, what my inner history is. She is next my heart—she is absolute mistress of it, its light and life—and confessions which, if made to *any*body else, would seem morbid and enervating, may be made to her without any seeming of the sort. Who can ever estimate the joy that thought gives me!

Later, No. 8 McCulloh St.   1.25 P.M.

Of course, my darling, you must not allow my, possibly overwrought, apprehensions to stand in the way of your attending the weekly lectures which are part, and so important a part, of the privileges of the League. I am glad that Mr. Marvin can take, after the experience he must have had, so rose-coloured a view of New York; and I will not stop to defend, by the opposite testimony of other residents of the great city, our too timorous country ideas about what it is safe and proper for ladies to do. I should be very sorry, however, to see the *practice* of Southern women change in this particular matter of going out at night. You need not feel *"ashamed,"* my pet, to go wherever it is necessary to go after dark without male escort: and I would not for the world express any wish as to your choice of occasions. I am more than willing to trust altogether to your discretion in that matter. I am surer that you will do only what is right and prudent and maidenly than that I could give you any useful advice about what may be the best *rule* to follow. It was not my fear that you would do anything indiscreet that led me to utter a word or two of warning, but only my anxiety that my darling should be safe beyond even a peradventure, and my preference for the young lady who *does* look upon it as something extraordinary and justifiable only by necessity to go out after night-fall without male escort. Do you ever have to go *alone*, my darling?

I am so glad, little sweetheart, that you have an invitation to the loan exhibition, to see the great Watts pictures and the rest. I had heard of the exhibition and was wondering if you were to have a chance of seeing it. How I wish that I might take Mr. Caldwell's place in escorting you sight-seeing! But, since I cant, I am *very* glad that he is exerting himself so in your behalf. He must be a thoroughly nice fellow—not merely serviceable but in himself enjoyable. I should like to send him my regards.

But I must not write any more now. I am going to close with a queer, an unexampled request, at which I know you will laugh— unless you should happen to see that it is a little deeper than laughter. I am going to ask you to put as much *expression* of love as you (conscientiously!) can into your letters. It is that which is the sunshine which is deadliest to the frosts of mood that sometimes lie upon me when I grow tired or discouraged. I know how absurd it *sounds* to seem to suggest thus what you shall write about—and I do not want to make any such suggestion. It would ruin those delightful notes of yours to have them written according to anything but the inclination of the moment. But you will understand what I mean. Whenever my darling has any special thoughts of me at the time of writing, will she not tell me what they are, just to humour the unbounded love of

Her own   Woodrow.

ALS (WC, NjP).

From Ellen Louise Axson

My darling Woodrow,   New York Oct. [Nov.] 5/84.

I wonder how much you have done today in the way of preparing for examination! Not much, I imagine; it is hard enough to settle down to manual work, and I should think brain work would be simply impossible. The League has been completely demoralized,—enacting on a small scale the scenes going on outside. What a mighty drama it is! and how glad I am that I am here to see it! There is something in it all very powerfully to excite the imagination, as well as the rest of one.

I should like to have seen you this morning when we thought everything settled—how did you bear it? I was never so beside myself, in my life;—and it was correspondingly hard not to go to the opposite extreme, when reverses seemed to be coming. But at last accounts it seems almost certain that they won't win—*honestly.* Mr. Shinn has just left. T'was rather comical,—a crowd of us, coming up from dinner had paused in the hall for a last word, and in our excitement had lingered, I don't know how long, comparing papers &c.,—some of us on the lower stairs and some just at the front door. The bell rang, but it failed to disperse us—nobody heeded, until the maid had thrown the door open and there stood Mr Shinn, just in our midst! After making a nice little visit, he proposed that I should walk with him down town, and witness, for myself, some of the scenes he had been describing,— which I did, to my great satisfaction. It was just what I had been wishing to do. What a sight it was! I will never fail to remember vividly these days; though I will be glad enough when they are over;—I should think that everybody—every man—would be *ill,* when it does end[.] I havn't seen one that has any voice left, to speak of, now; a very natural circumstance after standing all night long in the pouring rain, and shouting with all the power of their lungs. I hope it did'nt rain in Balt., or if so, that you changed your programme for the night. I would'nt sit up all night for *any* party. As you may imagine, I have been more excited than ever since reading your morning's letter and finding to my surprise that you—that we—have some personal stake in the the [*sic*] matter. But after all, I dont believe things will be as bad as they have been, even if we are defeated. As Mr. Shinn says, this has cleared the atmosphere wonderfully. The moral effect of such a victory as theirs, would be all most as great as a defeat. And then, there will now be an organized independent party, with plenty of work for young men of intellect and principle, and some hope—some encouragement in working.

Good-night, my darling—and pleasant dreams.

With all my heart   Your own   Eileen.

ALS (WP, DLC).

To Ellen Louise Axson

My own darling,   Balto., Md., Nov. 6, 1884 12.25 P.M.

I verily believe that the letters you write are the sweetest, the most perfect love letters ever written! They show, in everything they contain, two things, the two things that are surest pledges of our continued happiness: that you have found me out and love me as I am, and that you are willing to let me find you out, that my love may have leave to attain its perfection. Are you convinced of my love for you, little sweetheart, because I care for the smallest circumstances of your life and surroundings? Why, I did not tell you the half of that! I don't know that I *could* tell you much of those constant efforts of my fancy to follow you through your daily doings, and especially to see you when you are alone, when maybe you are thinking of me. I like to think that nobody's thoughts but mine are allowed to follow you there, that their coming, were you conscious of their presence, would not disturb your privacy, but possibly only make it the pleasanter. And you see, my winsome little lady, when you tell me what you do in that privacy, when you open to me, as you do nowadays, your secret, central love-thoughts, when you admit me to your heart of hearts, you do the very things that fill me with unspeakable delight—because then I know that I have the love—just the sort of love—that I need. Then I know that you consciously and freely identify yourself with me. Why, the simple fact is, my darling, that I have been given a great power of love, *and love you*. And, inseparable from such love as ours—which far transcends the love of brother and sister—there is the tenderest love for even the humblest trifles in the life of its object. I would'nt accord a moment's belief to the professions of a man who did not love the flower his promised wife had worn, who could not dwell with pleasure upon thoughts of the simplest and most homely of her occupations, or who could think any part of her life too insignificant to interest him!

The conflicting reports about the result of the election have kept me desperately uneasy and I have had very little rest: but it seems all right now and I shall have a chance to behave myself better.

I was sincerely disappointed about those sketches, my pet. I would have given a great deal to see them.

Did you go with Mr. Caldwell to see "an ocean steamer, &c"?

With a heartful of love, my precious Eileen,

Your own   Woodrow.

ALS (WC, NjP).

From Ellen Louise Axson

My darling Woodrow,   New York Nov. 6/84.

How I wish it was only eight o'clock, and I had the whole evening before me. I think I would spend it all in writing you, I have so much to say. But it is nearly eleven instead; I have been so unfortunate as to be "engaged" again; and as I was up late last night, and it is also very cold in this room, I ought really to write but a page. So I must leave the answer to your sweet letter of this morning for another time. How good of you, darling, to write it, in the midst of your work and excitement! You may be sure I appreciate it. When will your examinations come off? I do hope, when they are over, there will be some comparative rest for you. What have you decided about working for the degree?

We have been forming a "reading club" this evening!—an occupation which has prevented my writing sooner. Mr. Goodrich, the Houghton & Mifflin man, originated the idea[,] appointing tonight for the first meeting and Mrs. Jenkins and Mrs. Heiler have come into it with us,—three young people. We met in Mrs. Jenkins pretty room and have had a very pleasant evening; and Mr. G. is jubilant at the success of his scheme. He confided to me that he had intended leaving at the end of the month, the house was so dull, but now that we girls have come, things have brightened up, and he means to stay! Mrs. Beatty ought to know & acknowledge our efforts on her behalf. But I am breaking my resolution about writing. Your letter, dearest, suggests many things—things which lie very near to my heart. But they *must* wait—I have only time now to say that I love, love *love* you as my own life—and better—and am forever

Your own   Eileen.

ALS (WP, DLC).

To Ellen Louise Axson

My own darling,   Balto., Md., Nov. 7, 1884, *1.10* P.M.

The anxiety connected with the election *has* been telling upon me very seriously. I have not been able to study *at all* since Tuesday, and have been at all hours in the midst of the yelling, fighting crowds around the newspaper offices, waiting in vain for trustworthy returns. It has been a weary, distracting, heart-wearing business; but at last there seems to be some sort of certainty. Everything was at stake; but we have won. And that means something very definite for those of us who mean to write upon the principles of administration, who mean to try to be the expounders of the right philosophy of practical politics. It proves that the nation is so earnestly intent upon cleansing the public service that not all the power of the strongest and most unscruplous political "machine" that ever existed under free institutions can withstand its will: and those who write upon administrative questions can feel that they are addressing a public eager to be put in the right way of realizing its awakened moral desires and purposes. The election of Blaine would have been cold steel to the *hopes* of reformers: and without hope there can be no active interest. The moral effect of *nearly* electing Cleveland would have been as nothing in comparison with the moral effect of quite electing him. Indeed failure yesterday, for instance, when everybody saw that Cleveland was the real choice of the nation, would, I think, have been more *crushingly* demoralizing than an utter rout. It would have meant simply that no success *by the ballot* was possible: that government by the people was a sham. It is more demoralizing to have success wrested from one than to have it *won*. It is *right*, under such institutions as ours, to yield to the will of the majority; but it is ruin to yield to the power or to be defeated by the fraud of the minority. I cannot think, therefore, with you and Mr. Shinn, that "the moral effect of such a victory as theirs would be almost as great as a defeat." I should be quite as hopeful as he under defeat: but defeat would altogether change the organization and purposes of the new party (if such it be now) which is to bring our politics back to health and good repute. Overthrow is a much ruder task than achievement; and a party which became crystallized for the purpose of overthrow would not be fit for the execution of great comprehensive plans. We are fortunate in having overcome our enemies *before* we became organized *for that purpose*. Our *sympathy* is thereby established and we are free from the embarrassing necessity—the impossible task—of converting an army of conquest into a parliament of legislators. I am glad that the new party, to be, did not have time to unite on a negative principle: "turn the rascals out": but that they have been forestalled in *that* union by a chance to unite on the lasting positive principle, put good men in *and* keep them to *these* lines of conduct upon which we, "acquainted with each others principles" and "bound together by common opinions, common affections, and common interests," maintain to be the only true lines of conduct for the public servant. Shinn and I can cooperate in opposition; but it is doubtful if we could cooperate in any constructive policy. When the end in view is the defeat of an enemy's forces the means are quite sure to be evident and beyond dispute; but when the end in view is the establishment of new practices you must first decide upon what practices you want to establish and then—a no less difficult matter—upon the means of establishing them. It was much harder to establish and maintain the Federalist party than the Republican: and it is much harder to keep life and harmony in the Liberal party of England, which is the party of progressive purposes, with a head full of plans, than to preserve them in the Conservative party, all of whose energies are devoted to *opposing*, to standing still. But, dear me! I did not intend to bore you thus! I intended to say only, that now we can make a party out of *free elements*, whereas we might, four years from now, have had first to break up a party of opposition in order to set the elements free for combinations having a different purpose. And I beg you to consider this as against the view that defeat might have been almost as advantageous as victory.

Fortunately we were misinformed: the examination in colonial history is to be held, not to-morrow, but a week from to-morrow. I should be in a sorry plight if it were to-morrow. I can think of nothing as yet but the politics which constitute *present* history.

The excitement and fatigue of the week have left me quite nervous; but otherwise I am well, and my spirits are good, though *sober*. My feelings are too intense to be gay. But running through all the moments, thrilling me with quiet joy and shaping every mood, reassuring me with all the sweetest promises of hope, is my love for my Eileen, my queen, my darling.

Your own   Woodrow.

ALS (WP, DLC).

From Ellen Louise Axson, with Enclosure

My darling Woodrow,   New York Nov. 8 [7]/84

Mr. Caldwell called tonight to tell us good-bye as he leaves at twelve o'clock for Frankfort Ky. his new home. We went around to hear Dr. Deems' Friday night lecture;[1]—so that now it grows late, and I must hasten to make the most of the few remaining minutes before bedtime. Yes; we went to see the ocean steamer, *but not* the *ect.*! We had intended going to Greenwood, and some other places, but the two stormy days prevented. On Wed. he went with the other girls up the Hudson, making the visit to the steamer first. I accompanied them so far, and then came back to the League. I had already been up the Hudson, and did'nt care to spend time and money going again.

I wonder how much longer this suspense is to last! Wouldn't it be dreadful if there should be a repetition of 76, the whole thing unsettled for months? Was there ever anyone so desperately wicked as Jay Gould?[2] What an outrage that one private citizen should wield such power in a free country. People are talking *war* on all sides; they say there was very nearly a riot last night and that the militia are ordered out today.[3] Truly, these are stirring times. I rather enjoy it, in spite of my anxiety; and I hope you are doing the same. Perhaps all this excitement will help to scatter those mists of despondency, which have been so unreasonably surrounding you. You dear foolish fellow! I think I must advise you to study the principles of evidence,—I am afraid you are not a good lawyer! *What* testimony, think you, *would* be sufficient to convince you of your own powers? I am sure you have all that anyone—any *young* man, whose life work is before him, rather than behind, could possibly have. If you want proof from within, suppose you adopt Carlyle's definition of genius,—"a faculty for taking infinite pains"! That would give you a standard by which you could determine *accurately* just how much you possess! *Really*, those *are* very hard questions you raise; but it *is* surely right to foster high ambitions! Is'nt it said that, "not failure but low *aim* is crime"? Yet it could'nt have been intended that the effect of a high ideal, of any sort, should be to make us miserable or despondent. Thus in *another* conflict, we must ever strive to be "perfect even as He is perfect," but we are not to go mourning all our days because our best efforts in that direction must always end in failure;—on the contrary we are to "rejoice evermore." I suppose a good rule—if one *could only* follow it!—would be to do one's best work for love of *it*, and it's *object*, calmly yes, *contentedly*, leaving the result, as it affects *oneself*, to an overruling providence. Do you think that kind of contentment fatal to "the highest sort of enthusiasm"? *I* know that it is possible to be enthusiastic for many things without even wishing to be great in them. There are causes—and yours is one of them—so great in themselves, so well worth "infinite pains," that it is *glorious* to be allowed to serve even in their ranks, to work for them in the humblest capacity! And even adopting, for the sake of argument, your own view of your abilities, just think how much more than most of us you can accomplish for those great ends! for truth and justice,—for wise and enlightened government; and as a professor, how much you can do in the manufacture of wise and enlightened *men*. But bah! I am growing didactic! I did'nt *mean* to be, and yet I am going to make the matter worse by enclosing a few lines of *very* didactic poetry. I have time only to add, my darling, how happy it makes me to be allowed to share all those thoughts and feelings, to know that I am not excluded from that inner history. I would find it difficult to tell you just how deeply, how intensely, I sympathize, with you, in all that you tell me of yourself. You are, indeed next *my* heart, —absolute master of it;—and you sway it at your will. I love you, dearest, more than tongue can tell and am forever,

Your own Ellie

ALS (WP, DLC).

[1] The Rev. Edward M. Deems, pastor of the Westminster Presbyterian Church, New York.

[2] The *New York Times* and New York *World* both printed news articles on November 7, 1884, charging Jay Gould and his Western Union Telegraph Company with holding back and manipulating the presidential returns, especially those from New York State. The *New York Times* repeated the charge in its editorial columns on November 7, asserting that Gould had actually hoped to throw the election to Blaine by fraud in return for future favors. The New York *World* charged in an editorial on November 8 that Gould had been trying to influence the New York stock market.

[3] A crowd gathered around the Western Union building at Broadway and Dey Street on the evening of November 6, 1884, and rushed the doors, shouting "anathemas against Jay Gould" (*New York Tribune*, Nov. 7, 1884). The police soon broke up this mob. Later that evening, a similar incident occurred at the New York *Herald* building. There was considerable excitement in the city on account of the still undecided presidential election and much jostling and roughhousing between crowds of Blaine and Cleveland supporters gathered to watch election bulletins. However, there seems to have been no serious rioting. All available policemen were on duty to prevent violence, but the militia do not seem to have been called out.

ENCLOSURE

"The path of duty is the way to glory;
He that walks it, only thirsting
For the right, and learns to deaden

Love of self, before his journey closes
He shall find the stubborn thistle bursting
Into glossy purples, which outredden
All voluptuous garden-roses."

Clipping (WP, DLC), from Tennyson's "Ode on the Death of the Duke of Wellington."

To Ellen Louise Axson

My own darling,   Balto., Md., Nov. 8, 1884   9.40 A.M.

I have just read your little note of Thursday evening, written after the reading club. I am very glad, my pet, that you are finding so many pleasant ways of spending your leisure time. It would have proved a very lonely business to have continued as you began, keeping to your room after dinner. I hope, however, my darling, that you will adhere very strictly to your resolution to go to bed early every night. You cannot *keep* well otherwise. If you have'nt time to write after getting to your room, or after being released there by your lady visitors, by all means postpone my letter till after breakfast, or even till lunch time, the next day. I would rather wait till the afternoon delivery for a few lines written then, than feel that the note received in the morning had been written in time stolen from your rest.

I am so glad, little lady, that you had an opportunity to see the great crowds in N.Y. during the election excitement. It is indeed a time worth remembering—such a time as will not soon be seen again—and you could not have had a better or more pleasant guide and escort than Shinn. I have not heard from him since he left—I suppose the election excitement has rendered letter-writing so far impossible for him.

I am to go out this evening to my friend Woods's house to meet Dr. [James O.] Murray, the present Dean (and therefore, it would seem, the prospective President) of Princeton.[1] He is to preach here to-morrow and is to be the Woods's guest during his stay. He is professor of English literature: a very poor professor, our class used to think, but a very fine one, present opinion says. I go only because Dr. Woods insists that the Princeton men should show Dr. M. such attention as is possible. Hiram knows that I have no more use for the man than he has, and that in accepting his invitation I am giving the strongest possible proof of friendship. I would go out of my way *not* to see Murray; but I would do almost anything to please Hiram.

As for the degree, my pet, father advises me not to try for it:

and, since his advice coincides with my own coolest judgment in the matter, I have concluded to make no special effort in reading for it. It is probable that I shall pass no more examinations, therefore, after the one of next week. I am quite sure that I shall profit much more substantially from a line of reading of my own choosing, in the lines of my own original work, than I should from much of the reading necessary in the Ph.D. course—though my *inclinations* will take me through the most important topics of that course. The difference will be that I will read, *outside* of the prescribed lines, a great deal that will be of infinitely more service to me than the volumes of another sort which I should perfunctorily peruse, to the mortification of my own tastes and desires, were I to goad myself to the tasks heaped upon the degree candidate. Do you approve? You certainly have a right to be consulted, because it is probable that a degree would render me a little more *marketable* next June than I shall otherwise be[.] That is the only fact that has made me hesitate about my determination in the matter. On the ground of mental and physical health there is but one side to the question. Both would be jeoparded by a forced march through fourteen thousand pages of dry reading. But I must put myself up to the highest bidder at the end of this collegiate year: and it is probable that I would fetch a bigger price with a Ph.D. label on me than I can fetch without. It's a choice, apparently, between pecuniary profit and mental advantage—with the mental sacrifice perhaps small enough to allow one to *think* of risking it. Tell me just what you think about it, darling. I *want* your advice, my little sweetheart. You are nearer to me than anyone else in the world. I want you to feel about all my affairs that they are yours as much as mine. Eileen, never forget that I am *absolutely dependent* upon your love and sympathy, and that by withholding any of your thoughts about me and my interests you are to that extent withholding the sympathy which is all in all to me. I would rather have one word of love from you than a chorus of applause from all the world. With a love that is greater than the heart that holds it,

Your own   Woodrow.

ALS (WC, NjP).
¹ In fact, President McCosh did not retire until 1888.

From Ellen Louise Axson

My darling Woodrow,   New York, Nov. 9/84.

I was so sleepy and tired last night, that I thought it would perhaps be more satisfactory to postpone writing my note until this

morning, since it's being Sunday would ensure me the opportunity. But I have been so lazy, that now it is almost time to dress
for church, and I can write but a few lines after all. However, it
does'nt matter, as I write again tonight.

Mr. Shinn called last night—made a delightful visit. He is very
sure of our victory now, says there are some ugly things still
about the situation, but there is no doubt that it will end as it
should. To steal the election now, would be too desperate a game
for anyone to attempt. As for Jay Gould, he would be *hung*, he
came very near it the other night, and being a coward he promptly retreated—*nominally*.[1] Mr. Shinn says, few knew how near the
city came to a terrible riot. I read him what you had to say on
the subject and he was much interested—he had previously asked
me if you had much to say about it—and *what*. By the way, when
I said "such a victory as theirs" I did'nt mean a *stolen* victory,—
I don't suppose the moral effect of *theft* can ever be good. Both
Mr. S. and myself meant, in *that* connexion, an *honest* victory,
but a small, pitiful one,—a few scores or hundreds of votes say—
which was all that seemed possible for them. I am sorry our triumph is'nt more imposing. But then, of course, we must count
the majorities which we had to overcome; and as you say even a
small victory is infinitely better than even a small defeat, because
it secures the *power* to accomplish greater things in the *near* future. I think all that you say of the third party, *splendid*!

But I *must* close for the present, more anon. I love you darling
more than life, and am always and in every thought

Your own   Eileen

ALS (WP, DLC).

1 The New York *World*, November 7, 1884, reported that crowds watching
election bulletins posted outside the buildings of the *World* and other city newspapers on November 6 uttered threats against Jay Gould. The *New York Times*,
November 8, 1884, reported that there had been "ugly demonstrations" on November 6 in which Gould was denounced. The *World* itself appeared to be trying to stir up anti-Gould excitement in a brief editorial on November 7. But
there is no evidence that Gould was ever in any serious danger or that he fled
from the city, as Ellen intimated.

To Ellen Louise Axson, with Enclosure

My own darling,   Balto., Md., Nov. 9, 1884   *1.15* P.M.

Fortunately for the credit of my own understanding, it did not
need your sensible and loving letter of advice to convince me of
my weak folly in the matter of those idle questionings about my
own talents which came with the moods of last week. I have returned to my normal senses now, and shall strive not to stray
from them again. I have in my mental mechanism somewhere a

weight of commonsense which is generally sufficient to keep my thoughts at their proper balance. It is only when I handle that mechanism roughly out of impatience at its small capacity, that this weight gets displaced. I doubt it's not so much morbid intro-spection as the influences of the atmosphere in which I live here that explain my unhealthy states of mind. A man who wants to put fresh thought into the minds and fire into the purposes of his fellow-men of the everyday world naturally feels stifled in a thick, scientific atmosphere. He lives in uneasiness when he realizes that every person and every thing about him is intending to make a mere student of him. A mere student can make himself under-stood only by students. He thinks the thoughts and speaks the dialect of a class, a caste; he can touch neither the sympathy nor the interest of the community at large, which is made up of un-studious people of plain, workaday opinions and simple, practi-cal, unlogical, hand-to-mouth judgments. If one sees men only through and in books, he sees only *simulacra*, walking qualities, labelled emotions, catalogued feelings. If he lives all his life in a room, if he feels more at home in a library than in conversation with his carpenter, if he understands latin better than the senti-ments of his coachman, if he would'nt turn from his constitu-tional history to watch the games of light-hearted children, he is, to the fullest extent of the meaning of each one of these 'ifs', un-fit to have anything to say to his fellow men. The whole effort of University life is to make men interested in books and in the re-mote interests which books discuss; to make them technically ac-curate; to make them prefer Greek accent to correct English pro-nunciation. And it is this spirit against which I struggle. I want to be near the world. I want to *know* the world; to retain all my sympathy with it—even with its crudnesses. I am *afraid* of being made a mere student. I want to be *part* of the nature around me, not an outside observer of it. John Wilson[1] had a great deal to say because he was a splendid animal; he admired and celebrated virtue because he could be tempted by vice. An ascetic could never become, by any ingenuity of training, an effective tem-perance lecturer: Jno B. Gough[2] was a drunkard. Milton lived apart from flirting girls, constructed an ideal love—and wrote pamphlets in favour of divorce. Carlyle could not understand a man who did not have dyspepsia. It's not so much eloquence as "fellow-feeling" that makes Henry Ward Beecher attractive to all classes of hearers. Disreali knew nothing about the true principles of politics: but he knew *men*—especially House of Commons men. Calhoun read the Constitution as the schoolmen read Aristotle—and the world ran over all his doctrines. Burke lived too much with books to know what the French Revolution meant. And so it goes everywhere. You'll never find in a *cloister* a fulcrum for any lever which can budge the world! Here's the problem, then: How get fresh air in this world of book-research? how learn to ride a live horse by practicing on a hobby-horse? How discover by reading heavy books the quick, direct, certain way to inform and influence men who read only entertaining books which touch with a practiced hand their own ordinary lives— books which can be understood without any conscious effort? I want to write books which will be read by the great host who don't wear spectacles—whose eyes are young and unlearned! I don't care how much contempt may look upon my pages through professors' glasses!

But I must leave room to tell you of the discovery I've made. I've found out that, when I've been calling, or have been attending lectures, or have been anywhere away from No. 8,[3] and turn my face once more homeward towards my little den here, I feel *as if I were coming back to you.* Somehow you have become inseparably associated with this little room which you have never seen. You are the home of my thoughts and so you have gotten mixed up with this home of my body. So strong is the impression that it actually makes me feel sad and doubly conscious of my loneliness not to find you here!—as if I *expected* you to be here! Ah, my darling, what better proof could there be of the lack there is in my happiness? I do *not* find my Eileen at home! My precious, when shall our hopes be realized! With a very full heart,

Your own   Woodrow.

ALS (WC, NjP).

[1] John Wilson, 1785-1854, professor of moral philosophy at the University of Edinburgh and regular contributor to *Blackwood's Magazine.* He was generally considered to be a man of great talent and sensitivity but lacking in good judgment and a sense of proportion.

[2] John B. Gough, 1817-86, reformed drunkard, temperance lecturer, and author of many books.

[3] No. 8 McCulloh St.

E N C L O S U R E

"I arise from dreams of Thee
In the first sweet sleep of night,
When the winds are breathing low
And the stars are shining bright:
I arise from dreams of thee,
And a spirit in my feet

Has led me—who knows how?—
To thy chamber-window Sweet!
The wandering airs they faint
On the dark, the silent stream;
And the champnak [*sic*] odors fail
Like sweet thoughts in a dream;
The nightingale's complaint
It dies upon her heart,
As I must die on thine,
O beloved as thou art!"[1]

WWhw (WC, NjP).
[1] From Shelley's "The Indian Serenade." The champak is an Indian tree of the magnolia family.

From Ellen Louise Axson, with Enclosure

My darling Woodrow,   New York, Nov. 9/84.
I think I have had too much dissipation in the way of church going today; I have been three times, and to Hoboken besides! I have heard Dr Patton *twice*![1] Can you wonder I am "used up"! We had a missionary sermon this morning, and it was really fine; but this afternoon, he out-Pattoned Patton. It was all about "metaphysical certitude"—whatever that may be. I ought to know,—for he used the phrase at least a dozen times,—but I don't! It was the most intensely logical and the most intensely chilling production I ever heard. The man has no more warmth about him than a iceberg, I wonder he don't freeze himself to death; but I suppose icebergs don't suffer from cold. It is very amusing to hear the scornful way in which he speaks of people who allow *sentiment* to influence their opinions! You will wonder why I heard him twice; I went in the morning because I didn't know he was going to preach, and I went in the afternoon because there was no time to go elsewhere;—we got back from Hoboken just at four. I went tonight to hear Dr. Deems, and liked him rather well; one is'nt likely to go to sleep under his preaching;—and what a grand congregation! There is a heartiness, an enthusiasm in the crowd and the service that is inspiring. I think now I have "been around" as much as I please, and am ready to settle on somebody,—only I *must* hear Beecher;[2] though Mr. Caldwell thinks it a sin to listen to him on Sunday. I am going to try and get a sitting in Dr. Taylor's church. My friend Mrs. Raymond who has one herself says a season ticket, so to speak, for the gallery, can be had for a very few dollars.

I found Helen about the same—didnt see her, of course. She was desperately low last week & they had no idea that she would live over Sunday but she rallied again; Janie has been very sick since she went to Sav. but she is better now—her lungs are all right, however.

Miss Mosely, who, by the way, I like better all the time, has a cousin visiting her, at present; a nice clever independent woman, of uncertain age. I like her very much, but I wish she was where she belongs—in Chicago. Miss M. and I arranged, a week ago, to room together as soon as this cousin who was expected to spend [a] few days, should have come and gone; and now she has decided to stay a month at least, and perhaps as long as Miss M. herself and as of course they can't both stay any length of time in that hall room, they are going to change their boarding-house. Is'nt it *too* bad? I shall miss her so much; and I seem to be fated about a room-mate; she would have been just the one, for she is as sweet as can be, and they are evidently *very* nice people. I believe I will ask my dear friend Mrs. Powell to room with me, she is miles away from the League, and needs very much to change. She is an accomplished singer and *banjo* player,—and we would have "high old times" here every night. By-the-way, I never told you about Mrs. P.[,] that most curious of Southern productions, but she is a big subject, and I am too tired to begin on her now, will save her for my next, will *begin* my letter with her, so that I won't forget. But now I *must* close. I don't think I have spent the Sunday profitably, with all my church-going—got up late to begin with, so that I was off to church as soon as I had finished setting my house in order—dinner almost as soon as I returned; after dinner talked to the boarders 'till half past two, then off to Hoboken, then to church, and back again at half past five. There *was* one quiet time then before tea, during which I made myself very comfortable and cosy, lying in the darkness thinking, not Sunday thoughts exactly, but thoughts of *you*; though the two are *not* incompatible. You see dear, I have now gotten back to my normal condition, and find my greatest pleasure in that sort of thing,—in dreaming day-dreams of *somebody*, I mean, in recalling how good and strong and pure he is,—how tender and true, —how great in heart, and mind, and soul,—and how much I love him! You would laugh to see how I deliberately *settle down* to think of you, as if I was'nt doing it all the time! but it is a luxury to give one's *whole* mind to it. It is as much an act of self-indulgence as if I sat down to read a novel,—and a great deal more.

Did you ever read some verses by Coleridge called "Something

Childish but very Natural"? I remember I once thought the first part of the title *exactly* descriptive of the poem; now I think the last part equally true,—it *is very* "natural." I think I must copy it and send it to you. Good-night, dear heart, I hope this will find you well and rested from the fatigue and excitement of this last week, and in good spirits—filled with a "sober joy["] at the brightening prospects before us,—for the country and *yourself*. Believe me, darling, with *truest* love.

Your own Eileen.

Have you heard from Houghton & Mifflin yet? I've got to pose in that *horrible* sketch class on Wed. They [words missing] but I begged off on account of the [words missing].

ALS (WP, DLC). Letter damaged.
    [1] Dr. Francis L. Patton preached twice at the First Presbyterian Church on November 9, 1884.
    [2] The Rev. Dr. Henry Ward Beecher, pastor of Plymouth Congregational Church, Brooklyn.

E N C L O S U R E

Something Childish but very Natural (S. T. Coleridge)

> If I had but two little wings
> And were a little feathery bird
>   To you I'd fly, my dear,
> But thoughts like these are idle things
>   And I stay here.
>
> But in my *sleep* to you I fly—
> I'm *always* with you when I sleep
>   The world is all one's own!
> But then I wake, and where am I?
>   All,—all alone!
>
> Sleep stays not, though a monarch bids.
> So I like to wake before 'tis day;
>   For, though my sleep be gone
> Yet while 'tis dark one shuts one's lids
>   *And still dreams on.*

ELAhw (WP, DLC).

To Ellen Louise Axson

My own darling,   Balto., Md., Nov. 10, 1884 9.15 A.M.
    With the opening of another week I am ready to go seriously to work again. I must read now for the rest of the week as if I

had never heard of such a thing as an election of a President of the United States; as if I cared for nothing beyond the walls of my room: as if my heart were wrapped up in what happened two and three hundred years ago, when the Woodrows were all in Scotland, and the Wilsons had never a thought of leaving old Ireland. For these six days at least I must be a "mere student."

I went to see Dean Murray on Saturday evening, according to promise, and, *contrary* to resolutions formed beforehand, went twice yesterday to hear him preach.[1] His voice sounded so familiar from the pulpit that I imagined that I was in the college chapel once more and almost went to sleep as of yore. The Dean is a good preacher—an excellent sermonizer—but he has not a spark of originality. He expresses his ideas as probably half the educated portion of the race would express them. One can fancy that, if there were a catalogue of current ideas, they would be set forth in it much as he sets them forth. His discourses affect me somewhat as I suppose the sound of distant cannonading would. I know that something considerable is going on, but I see no execution done, nobody wounded, and I am satisfied that I am myself quite out of range!

I have just received your note written Sabbath morning. I have a shrewd suspicion, Miss, that if your notes are *always* to be crowded into the smallest corners of your leisure time, the repeated postponements of what you have to say will result in tremendous arrears too large to handle. I am sorry that I failed to convert you from your first opinion about the moral effects of an honest but narrow victory for Blaine on the prospects of a new party: but I suppose Shinn had the advantage of being on the ground to reinforce his position as against the distant fire of my letter.

Of course I had no reference to a *stolen* victory on the part of the Republicans

I hope that you are having the same delightful weather in New York that we are extracting vigour and delight from here. Everything invites to out-of-door exercise, and it seems a genuine outrage on the nature that has been given us, this unkind necessity to spend the time with books, instead of in the sunshine! Still, some of the bracing influences of the air penetrate within even my little den with its single window, and I must content myself with that.

With a heartful of love,   Your own   Woodrow

ALS (WC, NjP).
[1] The Rev. Dr. James O. Murray of Princeton preached in the morning and evening on November 9, 1884, at the Eutaw Place Baptist Church in Baltimore.

From Ellen Louise Axson

My darling Woodrow,   New York, Nov. 10/84.

I am late *again* tonight, in consequence of this "reading club" arrangement, so I will take your advice, and write but a "few lines"! now, leaving the answer to your sweet letters of today for a more convenient season!

I am very glad to learn that you are in good spirits again, for I was not a little concerned at your depression; I dare say your having finally decided the matter of the degree will be of service to you; and it will be better still I hope when you get through the examination, and feel that "there's an end on't["] forever. You ask my advice on the subject; but I feel too incompetent, darling, to venture upon any,—I don't know enough about it;—yet I *do* know quite enough too, for I know that you and your father will be sure to reach a wise and far-sighted conclusion. Indeed if both your mental and physical health would be really "placed in jeopardy" by the course there would seem to be but one decision *possible*.

So you are rather "out" with university life! Well, well I wonder if it too, like crowded routs—and marriage!—is one of those affairs "where those that are out, wish to be in, and those that are in, wish to be out"! How the students who can't reach it long for it, and bemoan their want of "intellectual sympathy"! and yet a student "enjoying those privileges" can give any number of strikingly wise and weighty reasons against it! It serves to strengthen my faith in a proposition which I am very anxious to believe but which I am often more than inclined to doubt,—the proposition viz. that there is some sort of compensation, as well as some sort of drawback, in every lot in life. If I hadn't some *little* faith in that theory, I believe I should be utterly miserable about my fellow-mortals. I think all you say in connection with the University exceedingly true and good. Am not at all surprised that you find it, in many respects, unsatisfactory. But I *must* close. Those were *beautiful* lines dear that you enclose in this letter, many thanks for them. And that was a sweet little discovery of yours, one that moved me deeply,—one too that I know all about, for it is even so with me. *Any* place in which I and my heart are much alone together must be forever associated with *you*. I *am* there dearest in heart, in spirit, as I am sure you too are here, for sometimes I feel *so* near to you, that I can scarcely believe all that long distance is between us. With all my heart

Your own Eileen.

ALS (WP, DLC). WW made a copy of part of this letter on his Caligraph.

To Ellen Louise Axson

My own darling,   Balto., Md., Nov. 11, 1884 12.15 P.M.

Before going into the remote recesses of South Carolina annals, I must respite myself from the Rhode Island, N. Carolina, and New Jersey expeditions, already accomplished since breakfast, long enough to write my precious little sweetheart a few lines.

Those stanzas of Coleridge's which came in this morning's letter, my love, are a great deal more "natural" than childish—if I am to judge by the experiences I've had during the last sixteen months. They are *lovely*—all the more so because my darling adopts and endorses them.

I am glad that you think of getting a sitting at Dr. Taylor's. That would certainly be my choice.

I am afraid that my darling *is* dissipating a little too much in *some* way—or else working too much—for every letter I have received for a week past has confessed that she was very tired, too tired even for writing to me. Please be careful, little sweetheart. It makes me *very* anxious to know how constantly you are overtaxing your strength.

Unless Miss Powell turns out, under the light of a full description, very different from what she seems in the dimness of a few hints, you will certainly "catch a Tartar" by concluding a partnership with her. I hope most devoutly that Miss Moseley's relative will relent and go back to Chicago.

No, my pet, I have'nt heard a word from H. M., & Co., though it is now five weeks since I sent them my *mss.*[1] They are either considering the matter with unusual care or have rejected the thing and forgotten, amidst the election excitements, to return it. The only *certainty* is that I am very anxious and have suspended all definite expectations in the matter.

My darling, I was in earnest when I asked you to get for me one of the best of the sketches to be made of you on Wednesday. Will you, if it does not require *too* great a sacrifice of your feelings? No, Eileen, I take it back (not the wish but the request). I did'nt think at first what a selfish demand I was making. Forgive it, and put it down to my stupidity in not seeing what a delicate—or rather indelicate—task I was setting you.

What delight the last sentences in this sweet letter before me have given me! Does Eileen, my little queen, *really* think of me that way? I wish I knew some of those "day-dreams." It would be the endeavour of my life to lead my darling to their realization.

I have *love* enough to do it—God grant that I may get, through the influences of my love for her, those traits of goodness, of tenderness, of purity, and of strength, which her loving heart now ascribes to me! May I be worthy of her—and may I be as capable of noble life as I am of love for her. Some day, darling, you will know how entirely I am

Your own   Woodrow.

ALS (WC, NjP).
  [1] See WW to ELA, Oct. 7, 1884.

From Ellen Louise Axson

My darling Woodrow,   New York, Nov. 11/84.

I have so many odd stiches to do tonight in the way of preparation for my "Kate Greenaway" *pose* tomorrow, that I really must try to write a short letter, especially as,—but I *won't* mention "reading club" a third time by way of excuse! As this was Miss Mosely's last night, we decided to have another meeting close upon the last, and an very pleasant time we had too! No formality or stiffness whatever. Mr. Goodrich read from Bret Harte's stories, while Miss M. and I sketched her cousin and Mrs. Jenkins. She Mrs. J. is perfectly lovely! and so is Mrs. Heiler!! and so is *Mr. Goodrich*! ! ! his lovliness consisting in the fact that he is going to take me to see Irving and Ellen Terry. To go out with a boarding-house acquaintance is'nt exactly what I should have anticipated doing; but it has'nt taken a whole month, by any means, to obtain satisfactory evidences as to Mr. Goodrich's character and antecedents. He is a thorough gentleman, born & bred,—of good old Mass. puritan "stock"; one who has been most carefully trained up in the way he should go. He is quite a young fellow,—only finished, at Andover last year—fresh and unspoiled, yet very intelligent, entertaining and well-read. You would have been amused the other night, when he asked me to go to hear Irving; he was very awkward and embarrassed; and as you will readily understand I liked him all the better for it—"Miss Axson, would you object?—may I?—ah!—I would—er—like so much to ask—if I only *dared*!—for the pleasure of taking you, &c!"

I begin to hope that your argument in favour of "Cabinet Government" will fall upon ears more ready and willing to hear and heed than you have supposed. The "Nation" seems to be strong on that side, and several times of late has treated the subject more or less at length; as for instance in the number before me where I read that something—"is one of the innumerable instances of the necessity of stronger executive government, of a responsible

Cabinet, who, backed by the country"–&c.[1] But I mus'nt–indeed I am not likely to forget–this "posing["] business. It hangs over my head like a nightmare. I wish I had never joined the horrible class! I love you darling,–I love you with all my heart, and it is ever my greatest joy that I am

Your own   Eileen.

ALS (WC, NjP).

[1] From a review of Edward Stanwood, *A History of Presidential Elections* (Boston, 1884), in the New York *Nation*, xxxix (Nov. 6, 1884), 403.

From Wilson's shorthand notes taken in Professor George Sylvester Morris's course, "The Philosophy of the State"

Notes on Professor Morris's Lecture on Herbert Spencer

Social Statics (earliest work)   Nov. 12, 1884

The first principle of political philosophy is "Every man has freedom to do all that he wills provided he infringes not the equal freedom of any other man." (page 103) This is held to follow from the "divine idea" or the divine will, which is the greatest happiness of mankind. Results also "from man's constitution, considering him as a congeries of the faculties." This first principle is now held to be superior to and the sanction for all other laws.

"Considering society as a corporate body, we may say that man when he first enters into it has the repulsive force in excess, his condition has been that of perpetual antagonism" (197). "Now in proportion to the repulsive force subsisting between atoms of matter must be the restraint required to keep them from exploding" and this restraint is found in the sentiment of veneration, reverence for power, loyalty, or hero-worship. ["]By this feeling it is that society begins to be organized and where the barbarism is greatest there is this feeling [*] strongest." "Universal selfishness" another expression for these repulsive forces of the atom. This is "a survival of the tribes by original man." ["]Hence, we still require shackles, rulers to impose them, and power-worship to make those rulers obeyed["] (199). The Russian soldiers, in the view of Mr. S. are thus governed when they pray for the Czar as "our God upon earth."

Man has the "right to ignore the state" because this right follows from the first principle: because he can do so without infringing upon others' freedom. (207) Further, "legislative authority can never be ethical, must always be conventional merely" (208). "All infliction of pain is in the abstract wrong" (207) for instance and this legislation does. The right to ignore the State is defended (214) as "similarly the right to exercise all the faculties." Pages 208 and 209, implies the truth of the social contract theory, which S. has also very severely and justly criticized.

"To the rightly constituted man all external help is needless, detrimental even. The normally developed character asks no artificial aids" (251).

The duty of the State ["]to protect men in the pursuit of those things which afford satisfaction to the faculties" ("Man is a congeries of faculties"). "This is the same thing as to maintain his rights." (254)

Man vs *The State.*

With regard to the first principle: (15 and 16) ["]the liberty which a citizen enjoys is to be measured not by governmental machinery under which he lives but by the relative paucity of restraints—and that the actions of such machinery is not compatible with liberalism if they put more restraints upon him than necessary—that is[,] more than *negative* restraints."

With regard to restraining influence necessary to keep the original atoms from exploding (the sentiment of veneration, power-worship) 98: "Mere love of companionship prompts men (primitive men) to live in groups.["] 79, 80: Considered H[obbe]'s postulate of the state of war and expressly refuted it. 44: "Small undeveloped societies where for ages complete peace has subsisted," where, though government is incomplete, there is peace and *generosity*, etc. This is an advance towards the *organic conception* of the state of Aristotle and H[egel].

The change, however, is not complete. A distinction is made between what may be called the natural and social man and *Government*. *Government* usurped[,] has imposed shackles[;] so here (44) "It is unquestionably true that Government is begotten of aggression and by aggression." In brute force there is of course no ethical philosophy.

106: As before, "In a popularly governed nation the government is simply a committee of management." This management is not of course an ethical function. It is a mere mechanical one.

Summary—Analysis

1. The *individualism*, analysis in the purely mechanical conception of society. Brought out very strikingly in some of the quotations given. He even likens man to atoms of matter. [Atoms, by the way, can not, consistent with the definition, explode].[1] It is impossible to have repulsive without attractive force. You cannot *think* repulsion without attraction.

Hegel says that the highest duty of the citizen is to be a member of the state. S. that he can do without the State, if normal and perfect. "The individual has combativity and moral quality only insofar as he is a member of the state." Hegel. Sp. is not now so extremely individualistic. He says, at the head of one of his chapters in his Sociology, that the "state is an organism." But if the state is an organism man is not complete without it, anymore than a part of the body is complete separate from the body. Still Sp. comes back again and again to the principle that society exists only for the individual, as a means to an end—the end is the individual. He is still individualistic.

There is of course a great deal of truth in this view. The social organism is of higher grade than the physical organism and has its life in diversity and individualism amongst members. *Government* does exist for the individual and for him alone—but the "State" is not synonomous with "Government." The state is not a mechanism. Sp. philosophy is that of evolution and his philosophy of the State is a special illustration of that. The philosophy of evolution is a philosophy of mechanism. But it is constantly maintained that it is really a theory of organic life. This is deeper view of matter—a spiritualist and philosopher must say this more and more—this is Sp. advanced—his direction at least.

Transcript of WWsh in notebook described at Oct. 8, 1884.
1 WW's brackets.

Two Letters to Ellen Louise Axson

My own darling,   Balto., Md., Nov. 12, 1884

What would I not give for one loving kiss and one look of love and full-eyed confidence from you this morning before I go to lectures! What a wonderfully transformed and beautified place my little den would be, if my darling stood in it at this moment as its queen and mine! Do you know, Eileen, that this is the shape my longings are ever taking? I need your loving *presence*—and I believe that one secret of the need is my desire to be the one person in the world to whom you shall look for care and love and full companionship. I want to take care of you. What I lack above all things else—speaking from a selfish point of view— is some duty that will make me forget to be anxious about myself. If I had to live for you from day to day, if you were the centre of my home and of my work, I could forget all about myself and be perfectly happy. As it is I feel like only *half* a man —lacking that home-life for which I was made. This lack don't make me unhappy with an *u[n]manly* discontent, of course; but I feel all the while as if I were waiting for my *real* life to begin. I know and am all the time conscious that this service of the heart which is so freely yours cannot be complete and perfect until it is suffered to manifest itself in a service of loving care and ministration—a service of the *life*. *That* is *my* constant daydream, darling: to live for you, not as I am doing now, by giving you all my love (that does not satisfy me), but by giving you all my best energies in every direction, by making a happy home for you, by being such a husband as you deserve and my love prompts me to be. It actually pains me to realize that your friends in New York are not even my acquaintances, at the same time that I take a real delight in knowing that you are so happy with them. It is just my heart's desire that you should have no life apart from mine. It is not jealousy, of course, but a lover's eagerness to *possess* his treasure—his impatience with every proof that she is still unidentified in life with him. *Maybe*, little sweetheart, you can understand without explanation what I mean. At any rate, I am quite sure that you will not wonder at the confession, but will take it into your heart for what it is, just additional proof of the passionateness of my love for you, the loveliest little maiden in the world, my darling, *my* Eileen. Remember, as you work at the League to-day that there is somebody who is thinking of you, wishing for you, passionately loving you,

Your own   Woodrow.

Biological Room, J.H.U.

My own darling,   Balto, Nov. 13, 1884 8.45 A.M.

It lacks a few minutes of lecture time, so I will begin my note here and finish it in "the Bluntschli," if necessary. This is the day on which I am most lectured at—scarcely a moment of *leisure* is given me before dinner for my usual chat with my little sweetheart—I can't even go to No. 8 for my letter from her till after 12 o'clock. Just at this minute I am waiting for Dr. Hall to begin his weekly talk on pedagogics.[1] I attend not only because I am to be a pedagogue, but because I find Dr. Hall one of the most interesting and suggestive men [at] the 'Varsity. He is full of ideas and has a pleasant, straightforward, man-of-the-world's way of imparting them. I do not quite like the idea of a nine o'clock exercise—it is too soon after breakfast to settle down to note-taking—but one can stand it once a week, for the sake of hearing one of the University's best men.

I think you misunderstood my argument about the effects of University life, little sweet-heart. The objections which I urged do not come under the general proposition under which you try to bring them: that all occupations, all lots in life, have their drawbacks. For a man whose wish it is to perfect himself in the physical sciences or in technical scholarship—for the chemist, the biologist, the philologian, or the classicist—and such men constitute the vast majority of University students—the Hopkins has, I am sure, *no* drawbacks, save only those which are characteristic of *every* human institution. But this majority creates the *atmosphere* and sets the methods of the place: and *that* it is which makes *me* uncomfortable. My chief interest is in politics, in history as it furnishes object-lessons for the present—the University professor's chief interest is in the accurate details of history—in the precise day of the month on which Cicero cut his eye-teeth—in past society for its own sake. At least that is the tendency—towards scholasticism. Knowing *how* and *why* I like to read of past times, you can see that for me the *specializing* mania of life here has its *special* drawbacks. But I have no time for an argument—or for anything else but a message of overflowing love for my precious Eileen, whom I love with all my heart.   Your own   Woodrow.

ALS (WC, NjP).
   [1] WW's notes on four of these lectures are described at Oct. 16, 1884.

From Ellen Louise Axson

My darling Woodrow,   New York, Nov. 13/84

I am ashamed to say, after your letter of yesterday, that I did not write last night because I was too "tired"! I think it was because I was too *lazy*, rather; for I lay on the lounge to read a little after dinner and ended by going so fast asleep, that I could scarcely rouse myself enough to do with half shut eyes a little necessary sewing before I went to bed. We *had* been rushing about the town enough to perhaps excuse me a little. As soon as I had gotten back to the League after lunch, we went up to the Academy[1] exhibition, now open, stood two hours on our feet before the pictures, then rushed back to the League, which is quite a distance, you know, to be in time for the sketch-class. But you must not worry, dear, about my being tired; I am not *too* tired!—just tired *enough*, to be ready for sleep at ten o'clock, and to have a comfortable sense of having earned it. Of course, we are working hard, but that is just as it should be. I am sure I am not overtaxing my strength, for I am just as well as can be. Who could help being well in such lovely weather. I am very glad we have fine weather now, for all the exhibitions are just open; the "Metropolitan," "the Academy," and the "American,"[2] and we, of course, must be going out to them quite often. The League students are admitted free to all of them,—isnt that nice?

I didn't pose yesterday,—must do so today—got a reprieve of one day by exchanging with a girl who had an engagement for this afternoon.

Pray excuse this stupid scrawl. I write in desperate haste. Ah darling, I love you very, very much! Every hour I am longing for you; when I am enjoying this lovely weather as it should be enjoyed, in the open air, or visiting the gallery, or doing *anything* pleasant my constant thought is,—ah if *he* were only here, how happy I should be!

With all my heart   Your own   Eileen.

ALS (WP, DLC).
  [1] The National Academy of Design, 53 E. 23rd St.
  [2] The American Art Association, which held its exhibitions at the American Art Galleries at 6 E. 23rd St.

To Ellen Louise Axson

My own darling,   Balto., Md., Nov. 13, 1884 6.10 P.M.

I shall not have time to-morrow for more than a hasty note, so I prefer writing now, for the nonce, rather than then, in order that I may write leisurely. I don't like to give my darling tag-ends of my time—just the scraps which nobody else wants or claims. My object is to arrange it so every day that I may set aside a certain time as *hers*: and it is only on Thursday mornings that I find a chance half-hour in "the Bluntschli" or the Biological Room the only time I can command before dinner for the purpose. To-morrow is an exceptional day—a day full of class appointments and at the same time *the day before examination. Its* chance half-hours must be given to a diligent cramming of *dates*.

All through this week of imperative reasons for staying in-doors we have been having the most bewitching weather imag-inable—days full of a glorious warmth and light of sunshine and yet with a certain keen breath of winter in the air which quickens the blood and braces the frame as nothing else can. It has been pure torture to be kept shut up in a room over a book! To-day I've been cheated even of my usual "constitutional"; because from four to six we of last year's Glee-Club were engaged in the divert-ing task of hearing *candidates* sing. We need five or six new men to fill the vacant places, and this afternoon we were reaping the fruits of the advertising we've been doing recently for a few basses and a good many tenors. Whew! *what* singing some of them did do! Three or four of them had capital voices, but the rest developed every degree of absurdity, from the startling style of the street-singers of the Salvation Army to pitiful little squeaks too painful to be ridiculous. The best of the lot has a most re-markable way of swelling his throat out like a frog's—a really portentous sign of muscular exertion.

I fear one member of the Glee Club has led me astray. He has induced me to consent to join a Musical and Dramatic Club of young ladies and young gentlemen, which meets about once a month at private houses to amuse itself to the top of its ability. So far, I know only one of the members of the Club (besides my Glee Club friend); but if she be a fair specimen of the rest I will not repent of my membership. She is both bright and very pretty. It would doubtless be rash, however, to expect the other fair members to come up to the same standard. It remains to be seen, therefore, whether or not I shall make by the venture. I con-sented to join simply because I feel that I shall be the better for relaxation of the sort offered. I love company, and an informal organization such as this is, will afford me an opportunity of meeting a lot of jolly people with the greatest economy of time—to take them in a lump, instead of spending all the evenings of the week in calling upon them one by one.

I am delighted, my pet, that you are to see Irving and Ellen Terry—and you will see them *twice*, wont you? When Shinn was down here he told me that he had promised to take you to see the great pair when they should arrive. Did I misunderstand? Did he say nothing to you about it? By-the-way, if Shinn is to keep you of his opinion in politics rather than of mine, I think I shall have to ask him not to see you any more, lest I become jealous of his influence over you! Which is taking it for granted, of course, that he would regard my wishes in the matter. I do not think that he has quite so high an opinion of me as I have of him: so maybe he would prefer the pleasure of seeing you to the satisfaction of heeding me!

I am sure that you will think, my darling, as I do, that Mrs. Terry is *infinitely* better than Irving—at least if you see them in parts anything like those in which I saw them—namely, Hamlet and Ophelia. His strut is almost as execrable as his pronunciation. She is beyond comparison the finest actress I ever saw. Ah, Eileen, what would I not give to see her *with you*! I envy Mr. Goodrich *with all my heart*! Would'nt *you* rather go with me than with him?

Yes, little lady, I think the *"Nation" is* on our side in the matter of Cabinet Government. Mr. [E. L.] Godkin is an Englishman and knows whereof he speaks on such subjects.

So Miss Moseley has spent her "last night" at No. 120? I am *very* sorry, my darling. I wish you could have kept her. And now? Is Mrs Powell to come?

Of course I thought of you, my little queen, before the Sketch Class yesterday afternoon. It *must* have been a great trial, pet!— and yet I am unsympathetic enough to wish that I could have seen you! since I can't have one of the sketches.

Eileen, I love you with all my heart. You are my pride and my joy, my darling, and it is my strength that I am altogether

Your own   Woodrow.

ALS (WC, NjP).

From Ellen Louise Axson

My darling Woodrow,   New York, Nov 13/84.

Your sweet letter of yesterday morning came to hand at the usual time, and has been filling my heart all day,—making it overflow with love and tenderness for the dear writer. All that I can say, darling, is that your words have found a full echo and answer in *my* heart. How often have *I* felt that, much as I love you now, true love in its fullness and completeness ought to be something more than a matter of feeling, that it can never be quite perfect until it becomes a *service* of love. It is for that I long more than for anything else,—to *do* something that will *prove* how much I love you. I too, want to take care of *you*!—yes, darling, and I want to be taken care of *by* you!—perhaps that is saying most of all for *me,* with my foolish pride and sensitiveness and independence (so-called). Even my own father could hardly have conquered it and *me* so completely as you have done. Ah, dearest, I love you very, very much, everything that you say and do seems to increase that love. Yet love you as I will I can never give you more than you deserve,—my noble, my great-hearted lover. I have sometimes fancied I would like to tell you, in words, just what I think of you! and then I laugh at my own absurdity, and at your probable disgust if I should be tempted to do such a thing; since, not *flattery* alone, but even the most *honest* opinion on such subjects must be expressed delicately to be acceptable!

Well, I *did* pose today! and I must tell you all about it because I need sympathy though I don't deserve it. The beginning of it was that I made a perfect simpleton of myself by going to the American Art Gallery, and spending three hours looking at the pictures,—very tiresome work, as you know! I knew I ought not to do it, when I was going to pose, but Miss LeConte asked me to go with her, and that was such a treat that I could'nt refuse, as it was probably my only chance. So I went, getting back just in time to dress,—and of course, tired. But the first quarter passed all right,—only I thought they had certainly forgotten to call the "rest," and that it was a half hour,—the pose lasts for an hour, with *rests* at each quarter. It was'nt so bad in some respects as I expected; it was dreadful, for three or four minutes, to stand there in that glare, with forty people staring at one, but by the time I had forgotten all about them, and was thinking of many other things—*you*, in fact, and matters connected with you; which was not a good idea, for how could I do that without smiling softly all to myself, and, in so much, departing from the proper rigidity? But I wander! When the second quarter began I found that the "rest" had'nt rested me, I was very tired, and grew more so, then I began to get cold, and colder, then a clammy perspiration broke out upon me, then things began to turn around, and then it all grew perfectly dark. I didn't faint however, I did *not* faint! I heard some one say something and there was a little confusion, but I stepped off the platform myself, and then I was sitting on a bench with my head in a girl's lap, and they were putting water on my face, and doctering me with salts and camphor; and Miss Arnold was talking, of *course,* in a very loud voice. "*Oh*! never was so frightened in my life" I heard her say, my heart's all in a flutter! did you see how she staggered?—thought they would'nt reach her in time,—looked like a ghost, &c. &c. And I was *so* ashamed of myself, and disgusted, for if there is anything I *do* hate it's a "scene." But at least I had the satisfaction of learning that I was'nt the first one, by any means; there have been any number of cases in other years. But I never did such a thing in my life,—and to be considered a *fainting character*! I would almost rather have gone to crying and sobbing, as a girl did week before last. It was on that account that I insisted, after a few minutes, that I was all right and could go on with it, with the understanding, of course, that I was to sit down as soon as necessary; so I stood ten minutes, when I felt it coming on again, and stopped; after that I posed seven or eight minutes and then told them *I* had finished. By-the-way I have a sketch for you! There was'nt much trouble in getting it, 'tis frequently done. I merely dropped a hint to one of the young men, who is a sort of a friend of mine, and he turned it over readily. It is'nt good, but he was the only one, except Annie[,] that I cared to ask and her's is worse. I will send it as soon as I get some pasteboard for doing it up. It is'nt one of the little pencil sketches, but a charcoal. But I *must* stop.

With best love.   Your own   Eileen

Our dear Helen has passed away at last; they left for Sav. early this morning. I received a note to that effect last night. Was sorry I did not get it in time to go over,—have seen none of them since Sunday. But of course there was nothing that I could do, and no one but strangers to me, left. She has suffered so terribly that one cannot but be glad for her dear sake. I doubt not that even for her nearest & dearest the bitterness has passed long ago.

ALS (WP, DLC).

From Melville R. Hopewell

Dear Sir   Tekamah, Neb, Nov. 13   1884
    I have received from Jas. W. Bones a Release of the C. A. Jack mortgage. I now send N.Y. Draft to your order $193.50

Exchange	50
Recdg[1] Release of mtge	1.00
My charges	5.00
	——————
Total to apply	$200.00

Your tax for 1884, is now due, and becomes delinquent Jany. 1, 85, and if not paid by that time there will be a penalty added of 5%. Shall I pay same from bal due on above note. It will all be paid by that time.

Truly &c   M. R. Hopewell

ALS (WP, DLC) with WWhw notation on env.: "Ans. Nov. 17/84."
    [1] i.e., recording.

From Ellen Louise Axson

My darling Woodrow,   New York, Nov. 15/84.

I have lingered at the breakfast table so long to hear Mr. Brigham give a synopsis of General Gordon's speech last night,[1] that now it is almost nine o'clock & I must scribble for dear life to make connections. Gen. Gordon's speech, by the-way seems to have been excellent. I am glad he came to N.Y. at this juncture, he appears to have a great deal of tact,—a fine courtesy; he can speak of vexed questions truthfully, and yet in a way that will wound nobody's feelings. He seems to think that now for the first time the war is indeed *over*, for *all*; it was over for the *soldiers* long ago, he adds!

And so Cleveland *is* elected in very truth! Now that the Tribune has given in, I begin to realize it. I have *known* it for some time but I could'nt *feel* that it was so;—we *can* know a good many things without feeling them, just as we can *feel* things without knowing them!

By-the-way,—I won't stop to trace the association of ideas—it would'nt pay;—what do you know about the "Society for Ethical Culture" and Felix Adler?[2] Mr. Brush belongs to it, and so does a pretty, *young* girl in our class. It is said that they don't believe in a God, or even in the immortality of the soul. What a terrible faith, or no-faith! and the idea of a young *woman* adopting it!

I see, dear, just where the trouble lies, for *you*, in the University atmosphere, and that it is a *special* trouble; I was only talking nonsense before! But I must end here,—excuse haste. We are going this afternoon to Mr. Chase's superb studios.[3]

I went to bed at *nine*! last night! What do you think of that?

How I wish you were with us. I love you, darling, more than life, and am as ever   Your own   Eileen.

ALS (WC, NjP).
    [1] General John B. Gordon spoke at Irving Hall in New York on November 14, 1884, under the auspices of the "Irving Hall General Committee." He reassured his listeners that the recent Democratic victory did not portend any revolutionary changes in national policies and said that there was no reason to distrust either

the Democratic party or the "Solid South" which supported it. Cleveland's election, he went on, marked "a new era of good will between the sections, of purity of administration, of peace, progress and prosperity for our whole country." *New York Times*, Nov. 15, 1884.

2 A leading spirit in the founding of the Society for Ethical Culture in New York in May 1876.

3 W. M. Chase, American painter, whose studios and gallery were at 51 W. 10th St.

To Ellen Louise Axson

My own darling,   Balto., Md., Nov. 15,'84   3.15 P.M.

The examination passed off this morning without any serious casualties, and my mind is free from *that* source of anxiety. And what better preparation for examination could there have been than the sweet letter I received just before setting out for the University! Despite the alarm which I felt at the description my darling gave, in the last part of the letter, of her distressing experience in posing before the sketch class, I went to my hated task with as light a heart as ever made work easy, because of the love which revealed itself in those first pages, which were so full of my Eileen's heart-secrets. My darling! Every fresh declaration of your love thrills me as if it were the *first*. I cannot hear you say too often that I am before all the rest of the world in your heart. And when my little sweetheart confessed that she wanted to be taken care of by me, she confessed the very thing which was of all things that which I most wanted to hear from her sweet lips; because *I* know that that *is*, for her, "saying most of all"! Why, my little queen, ever since I read that letter this morning all the care seems to have gone out of my life, leaving only joy!

And yet I was very sober and not a little disturbed as I read of my pet's distressing breakdown in the posing. You need not feel ashamed, my darling, at having seemed weak to the class: it must need iron nerves and accustomed muscles to go through such an ordeal, and no one could think the less of a sensitive woman for breaking down under it. I think that either fainting or sobbing would be quite excusable under the circumstances. But, my little lady, you *did* overtax yourself needlessly, proving quite conclusively that you *need* me to take care of you. You disarm me by saying yourself that it was foolish to tire yourself out so completely beforehand; but I can beg you again, my precious, to be very careful *not* to do anything beyond your strength and thereby endanger your health. Have you felt any ill effects from the faint? Did you feel as well as ever next morning? It was very unwise to go on with the ordeal after having once broken down, because then of course the weight of *apprehension* was added to the rest and the strain thereby increased just when you were least able to bear it. I sincerely trust that your turn is not likely to come often at posing. You can, of course, stand it much better next time: but it will always be a serious tax upon you: and I shall be very uneasy until I learn that you are quite yourself again.

It was *very* sweet of you, my pet, to get the sketch for me which you promise to send, and I shall prize it very highly, even if it is'nt good. It will have a sort of painful interest for me now that I know what my darling suffered while it was being made— or was it the product of the first quarter of the hour, when you were thinking of me? Ah, my little sweetheart, what *can't* you do for me simply by loving me! I know that your love, like mine, waits for the time when we can render each other all the services of love before it can become perfect; but *now* you can render a *service* of love by just such sweet assurances of love as these which this letter lying open here before me contains. You don't know, maybe, Miss, what a change comes over my work when the mail brings me such messages as these from you. And yet you *do* know that my life is wrapped up in you and my happiness dependent upon your sympathy. So long as you love me, my darling, I am sure of success.

I wish that I could see you just for a *little* while, Eileen—of *course*, I am always wishing that; but at this particular time there are so many special things, all of them small but all having a keen interest for me, about which I would like to talk to you. I would scarcely know how to put them into words—and, if I did, I should hesitate to do so *in writing*. They are little nothings that must be saved for my darling's *ear*. Will you take six more kisses here on your name, Eileen, from

Your own　Woodrow.

ALS (WP, DLC).

From Ellen Louise Axson

My darling Woodrow,　　　　　　　　　New York　Nov 15/84

I have but just returned from an "Art reunion" at the League,— quite a pleasant affair,—a sort of an exhibition of *artists and* their work. There were some very good things on exhibition, and the rooms were lovely. It was held in the rooms of the Antique class, but our rather dingy and dusty old studios were completely transformed with rich hangings of plush and brocade, Turkish rugs &c., to say nothing of the paintings themselves, the bright colour of which made such a contrast to the casts and the severe drawings which belong there.

They turned us out this afternoon to prepare for the "show," and of course we made the most of it, in the galleries. We went to Mr. Chase's studios first; and they are superb. There are three of them, full of all sorts of rare and beautiful things, and all so artistically arranged, that the rooms are as much *pictures*, as any on canvass;—more so indeed than most of Mr. C's, for I don't admire his paintings much. From there I went alone to Goupil's, where I spent the rest of the afternoon in a state of quiet rapture, chiefly over one picture, a marine by Richards.[1] He is the one, you know, whose water is said to be the *wettest* ever painted. We saw one by him at the Corcoran, and admired it very much; do you remember? But it was by no means so good as this. This is simply wonderful, I never saw such a *luminous* effect in any picture; and obtained so simply too. Just think I have spent four afternoons this week in galleries. I think Mr. Brush gave us all a start in that direction the other day by lecturing us roundly about working so hard. He said we were merely dulling our senses by so doing, and it was our duty to go to these places, and educate our *feeling*, so to speak, as well as our fingers. Whereupon we all left immediately for the Academy[.] But I dare say that, when the pleasant weather no longer tempts us, and these special exhibitions close, we will relapse. I am so glad you have joined the musical and dramatic club,—you need the relaxation, and I am sure you will enjoy it. Social gatherings where there is some object, some programme to be carried out, are always the most delightful, if they be entered into with spirit. I hope you found enough good basses and tenors to keep the Glee Club up to its former brilliant standard. What a pity that it should have sustained such heavy losses! But that is the trouble with college society,—it lacks stability! So this is the examination day at last— and by this time it is all over! I give you joy. And now I must say "good night sweetheart[.]" I love you, darling, I *love* you,—I say that very often, don't you grow tired of hearing it? But I don't forget "to love you also in silence with my heart."

Your own   Eileen

ALS (WC, NjP).

[1] William T. Richards, American marine painter. Studied in Philadelphia, France, Italy, and England. Represented in permanent collections of Philadelphia Academy of Fine Arts, Metropolitan Museum of Art, Corcoran Gallery of Art, and Schaube Gallery, Hamburg, Germany.

From James W. Bones

Dear Woodrow　　　　　　　　　　　　Rome Ga. Nov 15th 1884

Yours of 8th was received & I am glad my explanation as to taxes was satisfactory. I inclose my note as Trustee for $502.60 to your mother at 6 mos with interest at 8%. From present outlook as to sale of balance of the land I see no possibility of my paying the money sooner. If I can I certainly will. I trust therefore your dear mother will be as patient with me as she can. The investments I have made here for your aunts estate are good & as soon as I can close out the rest of her Western land I will have the childrens property in good shape both as to present income & future increase in value.

As to the quit claim to Lee I was so satisfied as to the correctness of Dorseys statements that I sent quit claim as Trustee some days before your letter came. It appears that Lee has sold the land & purchaser wants title perfected as much as possible. The parties are waiting anxiously for the paper from you & I hope you will forward it at once.

With love to the dear ones at home when you write

Your affec uncle　James

ALS (WP, DLC) with WWhw notation on env.: "Ans. Nov. 27/84."

To Ellen Louise Axson

My own darling,　　　　　Balto., Md., Nov. 16, '84　10 A.M.

The more I think of that scene of Thursday afternoon in the sketch class the fuller does my heart get of tender sympathy for my precious little sweetheart. What would I not have given to be there to care for her and sympathize with her at the time! Ah, my darling, how I love you! and how it hurts me to think that you must go through such experiences alone—without any benefit from the boundless love and tenderness which my heart holds for you! What do I think of your going to bed at nine o'clock on Friday night? I think that it was an exceedingly prudent and sensible thing to do, my pet, in view of the fatigues of the day before. Have you felt no ill effects from the posing?

There is one passage in your letter of Thursday night, little lady, to which I must make special reply. You say that you have sometimes refrained from saying in your letters things that you have fancied you would like to tell me, lest you should "disgust" me! And don't you know, Eileen, what my love for you means? Everything that comes from your heart meets with instant response and acceptance in mine. Nothing that *you could* say would "disgust" me. It is my greatest *desire,* as regards our correspondence, that you should say just anything and everything you fancy you would like to say—even to putting into words what you think of me! I can imagine my taste revolting if you were to say *conventional* things to me, if you were to say this, that, or the other thing because you thought policy or politeness constrained you to do so—because I cannot imagine your doing anything of the kind!—but nothing that comes from your heart, nothing that is prompted by an impulse to open your whole mind to me, *can* seem to me unnatural or in bad taste. You need never pause to speculate, 'What will he *think* if I say what I am tempted to say?' Just remember that *I love you with all my heart,* and that nothing that is in your heart can offend me, if it be born of your love for me. Speak to me, darling, as to your other self. You have'nt any of that foolish dread of me that Miss Minnie had, have you? You are not apprehensive of my criticism? If there were anything in your sweet letters to criticise, *I* should'nt find it. I esteem much more highly your opinions than my own: and I am yours, darling, in *everything.* I have found out what it is to be happy since I have been   Your own   Woodrow.

ALS (WC, NjP).

From Ellen Louise Axson, with Enclosure

My darling Woodrow,   New York Nov. 16/84.
    Well! I have at last heard Beecher! This was such a lovely day that we thought if we were ever to take the journey to him now was our time; this delicious weather makeing us rather glad of *any* excuse for a long walk; and we did enjoy extremely the walk over the bridge, &c. Beecher was very much what I expected—not quite so eloquent perhaps,—but part of it *was* beautiful, part was laughable and a good deal was heterodox. It was worth going, if only to hear the singing. The first hymn especially was magnificent. It was Luther's great hymn of the church militant,—"Ein feste Burg ist unser Gott"; and it certainly was inspiring when the chorus, joined by the great congregation, making one mighty volume of sound, burst forth with the grand old battle-song! I intended going this afternoon to the First church to hear Dr. Hodge of Princeton,[1] but I was such a lazy girl that I missed it,—went to sleep after dinner, and didn't wake up in time. Is he a good preacher? It is a great name.
    You ask what I will do now that Miss Mosely has gone, and if

Mrs. Powell will come. No, I did think of writing her, but not very seriously, for it is only a few weeks now before Eva leaves, and the other girls will join me. So I think it will perhaps be best now to wait for them,—certainly it will be most "obliging" to them. If Mrs. Powell came it would of course be for the winter. But she would be quite a pleasant room-mate, for no one could be more kind-hearted and good-natured. She is the greatest of favourites with everyone at the League, where indeed, she has filled a very useful position, for she is extremely sociable, even free-and-easy, and she has done wonders from the first towards making us all good friends together,—putting things on an easy friendly footing. She is like Sidney Smith, "a good amalgam." I must not forget that I promised to tell you all about her. I proposed doing so by way of *warning* to you, as a sort of object lesson, a companion picture to that of Mrs. Perkins. *This* Mrs. P. is a Southern girl,—from Ala.,—has been married *seven* years, and is now twenty-three!—is a rather pretty brunette, with splendid, great dark eyes. She is very quick and bright, and ambitious, in many ways, is taking, for instance, some course of study at which she works until twelve o'clock every night; then she has a splendid voice and has been accepted as a member of the chorus in the Thomas orchestra,[2] where she gets fine training, and a good salary besides. But her artistic proclivities are the strongest; she has made up her mind that she will be a "sure enough" artist, and has come here for a *seven-years course*. Think of it! is'nt that astounding? Her husband and little four-year-old boy are left, in the meantime, to their own devices,—she says she has promised them three months of each year! The queer part of it is that she seems perfectly devoted to them, talks of them all the time;—but then true love isnt a mere matter of *feeling*, as poor "Professor" has doubtless discovered, though she has'nt. I mustnt forget to mention,—for it points the moral finely,—that he is a *professor*, of mathematics in some Ala. college—and I think he must be a *saint* besides. We girls were expressing our opinion on the subject, to *her* of course, with the perfect and refreshing frankness which her character and conversation justified;—we didn't see how she *could*[,] we did'nt *understand* it! "Oh," she said, ["] the explanation is quite simple! I married a *very unselfish* man, and I myself am *very* selfish! that's all!" So you see what dangers threaten the peace and comfort of the unfortunate men who meddle with embryo artists. You see how rash you have been, how little judgment and foresight you have shown! Had'nt you better reconsider? To contemplate the fate of Mr. Perkins and Prof. Powell ought to make you quake with fear.

Annie and Florence went yesterday to the Irving matinee,—got in for fifty cents, and sat in the peanut gallery! They say it was full of nice ladies, several League girls among them. They were wild with delight over it. I go on Friday, the first night on which they play "Merchant of Venice." Of course I was most anxious to hear "Hamlet," and we were waiting for it, but we see no announcement of it, so we have given it up. After all, if Ellen Terry is so much the finer of the two, perhaps it is best as it is, for Portia is a better character than Ophelia. No, I had no idea, Mr. Shinn thought of taking me there! had even forgotten that Irving was mentioned, though I remember *that* now. It is *very* kind in him to think of it, Mr. Shinn is too good to me. But I don't propose to be of his political opinions by way of showing my gratitude. I told you, sir, that I thought your little essay on the political situation *first-rate,—exceedingly* just and true. So did Mr. S. himself, for that matter. It was only the following sentence to which I wished to reply, because I thought you misunderstood me. "It is more demoralizing to have success *wrested* from one than to have it won. It is right . . . to yield to the will of the majority; but it is ruin to yield to the power, or to be defeated by the *fraud* of the minority. I cannot think, *therefore*, with you and Mr. Shinn, that the moral effect of such a victory as this is" &c. Of course from that *we* thought *you* thought, *we* meant a victory by fraud! What a complication! tis equal to the case where the young man ventures to kiss the girl because he thought, she thought, he thought she slept!

My subscription to the "Nation" ran out not long ago, and to save myself a little trouble, I ordered it again through a news dealer, and see how it comes directed to me now!—equal to "Y-&-." for "Wyandotte"! I came across this old "wrapper" just now while looking for that letter of yours from which I wanted to quote, so proceed at once to enclose the superscription.[3] I have been so exercised over politics, &c. that I have constantly forgotten to scold you as I intended, and as you deserve, for sending me all these stamped envelopes! It was bad enough before, when you sent them with stamps printed on them, but to go carefully to work and paste them on, one by one, seems so much more *deliberate* an insult! You ought to be ashamed of yourself, sir, and if you ever do such a thing again I'll—tear them all off!

Ah well, I must close this long scrawl, unwillingly though, for I am in a loquacious mood tonight; perhaps because I have held such long imaginary conversations with you this afternoon, and with all my heart so yearn to make them *facts*. This has been my first quiet Sunday afternoon for many weeks and I have really enjoyed it,—naturally since I have spent it all with *you*, darling. You are *my* pride and joy, dear heart, and I have no words to tell you how I love you, what you are to me, or how entirely I am

Your own   Eileen

[1] The Rev. Dr. Archibald Alexander Hodge, Princeton Theological Seminary.
[2] An orchestra and chorus directed by C. F. Theodore Thomas, a musician of German birth who was important in the popularization of symphonic music in the United States and active in the musical life of New York at this time.
[3] This enclosure is missing.

E N C L O S U R E

"And wilt thou have me fashion into speech
The love I bear thee, finding words enough,
And hold the torch out while the winds are rough,
Between our faces to cast light on each?
I drop it at thy feet. I cannot teach
My hand to hold my spirit so far off
From myself—me—that I should bring thee proof
In words of love hid in me out of reach
Nay, let the *silence* of my womanhood
Command my woman-love to thy belief."[1]

ELAhw (WC, NjP).
[1] Part of the thirteenth of Elizabeth Barrett Browning's *Sonnets from the Portuguese*.

From Albert Shaw

My dear Colonel: Minneapolis. Sunday. Nov. 16. '84.

The important journal with which I have the honor to be connected,[1] prints in large headlines this morning *"The End" "Grover Cleveland Elected President of the United States"*—and much more to the same effect. We were not going to admit it till the last county had formally made up its returns. But now we admit it, and we feel better. We have dwelt on the matter so long and so assiduously that it will relieve us to change the subject. The country will of course go to the dogs; but as all we have is invested in this country, and as most other countries appear to be going to the dogs too, we will just stay right here and go to the demnition bow-wows along with the rest of the boys and girls. Minneapolis desires to say that it will be a very cold day when she can't stand as much foolishness at Washington as any other large American metropolis.

Gracious! but how you hot-bloods of the South would hate me if you could but have my editorial scrap-books over night and read what this trenchant stub pen has written about your ill-governed and domineering section of the country and about your abominable old Democratic party. I have given you all Jesse—for $35 a week and promise of an advance. Now I will turn me to less harassing themes. I have carefully abstained from mailing papers to the boys. Why should I desire to shatter friendships which I prize? You and Yager are Southrons, and Democrats by the law of heredity; Shinn is a mugwump by force of circumstance and temporary environment; Jameson is a mugwump by the accident of birth and the fact of a Massachusetts training; Levermore is a "contrairy cuss" and trains with the Mulligan guards[2] just to spite me. You're a wretched, bad lot politically, and while the campaign was on I couldn't safely compromise myself by having communications with any of you. Again let me say, I'm glad it's over. . . .

I wonder how you are coming on with your essays. I expect them to make a sensation, and I am proud of my acquaintance with their author. By the way, I haven't sent you a copy of Icaria;[3] but I'm going to. The copies I had at first melted away somehow, I don't know exactly how, and I keep meaning every day to write to New York for some more, but neglect it. Will get around to it soon. . . .

I trust that Adams and Ely are not bothering you with any of their petty school-boy methods, and that you are spending a pleasant year in ways which you most approve. . . .

Now, Colonel, I shall be sore disappointed if you cut me off your list of correspondents for my irregularity, negligence, and general worthlessness. I am a delinquent and dull correspondent; but I want to hear from you. So be magnanimous.

Please give me a little inside account of things.

Yours most Sincerely,   Albert Shaw

ALS (WP, DLC) with WWhw notation on env.: "Ans. Nov. 28/84."

[1] Shaw was at this time an editorial writer on the Minneapolis *Daily Minnesota Tribune*.

[2] Probably a reference to the "Mulligan letters" affair which had plagued Blaine's campaigns for the Republican presidential nomination in 1876 and 1880 and for the presidency in 1884. Shaw seems to have meant that Levermore had joined forces with Republicans who believed that the Mulligan disclosures made Blaine unacceptable as a leader.

[3] Albert Shaw, *Icaria, a Chapter in the History of Communism* (New York, 1884).

To Ellen Louise Axson

My own darling,   Balto., Md., Nov. 17, 1884   10 A.M.

For the first time the carrier has failed to bring me a letter from my darling. I shall not allow myself to become anxious, however, unless the later deliveries of the day also fail me. I am more apt to be concerned at not hearing just at this time than I should have been a few days ago, because that faint at the sketching class has made me very uneasy lest a continuance of such fatiguing occupations as visiting the galleries, and Mr. Chase's studios, should prove too much for my darling's strength. I know of nothing more fatiguing than just that sort of sight-seeing, and nobody who is not either unusually robust or long hardened to such exertion can be expected to stand it very long. I hope that my pet will be careful not to overdo the thing.

Now that the examination in colonial history is behind me, I am settling down to the task of reading for Dr. Ely's book.[1] I have already, this morning, made a considerable journey in an extraordinary "Introduction to Political Economy" by a garrulous old chap much esteemed as a professor at Williams College in Mass.[2] He "has the absolute by the wool" in a manner which is intensely satisfactory to himself, and which must be deliciously ridiculous to everybody who reads him. And yet he is the most popular of American text-writers, and men all over the country expound his "Elements" with straight faces! I shall have to say very little about him, if I am to keep laughter out of my sentences. I have Bagehot's delightful "Literary Studies" just at hand here on my table, so that I can turn to him for relief when I have exhausted my patience with "these tedious old fools." The poison might be fatal if I did'nt have an antidote within easy reach!

I know very little, and can find out very little, about Felix Adler and the Society for Ethical Culture. I believe, however, that their creed is *non*-Christian rather than *anti*-Christian—or rather that they have no *creed*, shutting out *belief* altogether, as you say. I doubt if they are actively, agressively atheistic. They simply leave revelation out of their calculations, following a sort of hand-to-mouth method of investigation. They'll believe when they see. But I will try to find out something more definite about them.

I love you, my darling, more than tongue can tell. You are the sweetest little woman in the world—and yet, despite that fact, I think that you were intended for plain me—on the principle, no doubt, that people are intended for those whom they can make most happy, those whom they can bind to themselves as you have bound   Your own   Woodrow.

ALS (WC, NjP).
  [1] See the following Editorial Note.
  [2] Arthur Latham Perry, Orrin Sage Professor of History and Political Economy in Williams College.

EDITORIAL NOTE
WILSON'S RESEARCH FOR A
"HISTORY OF POLITICAL ECONOMY IN THE UNITED STATES"

Wilson's letter to Ellen Axson of November 17, 1884, just printed, signaled the beginning of his research for his section of the projected collaboration with Dr. Ely and Davis R. Dewey. Wilson's subsequent letters mark well the progress of his work.

He wrote to Ellen on November 20, 1884, that he had completed work on Arthur Latham Perry; and his letter to her of December 9, 1884, indicated that he was then reading Francis Bowen. Only four days later, as his letter to Ellen of December 13, 1884, makes clear,

From Wilson's shorthand notes for a "History of Political Economy in the United States"

he had moved on to Francis Amasa Walker. There are no further references in his correspondence to specific authors. However, he wrote to Richard Heath Dabney on February 14, 1885, that he was "wading" through three political economists. He wrote to Ellen on March 12, 1885, that he was coming in sight of the end of his research and would soon begin composition of his section. The last reference to note-taking is in his letter to Ellen of March 15, 1885. He had apparently substantially completed his research by March 27, 1885, when he delivered a report[1] on his work to the Historical Seminary.

Wilson's notes, descriptions of which follow immediately, reveal not only the exact scope of his research, but his method as well. Ely had asked Wilson to cover American political economists since Henry C. Carey; perhaps Ely also suggested the authors Wilson should cover. However that may have been, Wilson seems first to have jotted down various bibliographical references and brief extracts in the pocket notebook described below. Having made what seems to have been his start, he then systematically worked through each author, writing in a larger notebook, also described below, brief digests of works as he read them. He interspersed quotations that he thought he might use and, occasionally, added observations of his own. To this notebook he also transferred certain references from the pocket notebook selected, presumably, for their usefulness.

For example, he wrote, after reading the first chapter of the 1883 edition of Arthur L. Perry's *Elements of Political Economy*: "Remark: This historical introduction affords the best means of judging of the exact position of Perry in the history of the science. It shows just his attitude toward the historical school, and, by constant iteration, just wherein he considers himself a holder of new doctrines." Or, to cite another example, Wilson wrote after reading Amasa Walker's *The Nature and Uses of Money and Mixed Currency*: "Great strength expended, *in the use of a very scientific statistical and historical method*, in the discussion of 'Mixed Currency' ('promissory notes issued by individuals or corporations legally authorized to do so, in excess of the actual specie held for their redemption.') His position is, that such a currency is not governed by the laws of value (demand and supply, i.e.), but its expansion is always in excess, because it creates speculation and a feverish demand: then *contraction* takes place, from any cause that affects credit (e.g. adverse balance of trade; demand for specie; stringency; suspicion). Gives tables and diagrams of 'Mixed-Currency Fluctuations.' Considering *inflation* the irresistible tendency, and, consequently, the inevitable result of a currency of this sort, he discusses at length the manifold evils of an inflated, a really inconvertible, paper currency. This Prof Walker's *hobby* (See *ante*, p. 17½ under '3.')"

It is interesting that Wilson wrote down—on a loose page inserted in this notebook—only one brief quotation from William Graham Sumner, who was just then becoming prominent as a political economist and the leading American social Darwinist. The quotation was from pages 168-69 of Sumner's *What Social Classes Owe to Each Other*, which had been published in 1883.

Wilson read, analyzed, and assimilated the large body of writings described below between mid-November 1884 and mid-March 1885, while attending for most of this period a heavy schedule of lectures. These two research notebooks reveal his rapid development as a researcher able to digest complex and varied materials with speed and confidence. His section for the "History of American Political Economy" is printed at May 25, 1885, Volume 4, with an Editorial Note.

[1] Printed at March 27, 1885, Vol. 4.

Pocket Notebook

[c. Nov. 17, 1884]

Inscribed on first page, following 1884 printed calendar, WWhw list
  beginning: "Am. Pol. Econ."

Contents:

WWhw and WWsh reading and bibliographical notes on various
authorities and sources in American political economy relating to
WW's projected collaboration with Richard T. Ely and Davis R. Dewey
on a history of American economic thought.

Pocket notebook (WP, DLC).

Research Notebook

[c. Nov. 17, 1884–c. March 27, 1885]

Inscribed on cover (WWhw): "Woodrow Wilson" and on flyleaf
  (WWhw): "Woodrow Wilson *Nov. 1884*"

Contents:
  (a) WWsh and WWhw digests of, quotations from, and comments
      on:
      Francis Bowen, *American Political Economy* (New York,
        1870).
      Arthur Latham Perry, *Political Economy* (18th edn., New
        York, 1883). Title simplified from *Elements of Political
        Economy* of earlier eds.
      Julian M. Sturtevant, *Economics, or the Science of Wealth*
        (New York, 1883).
      William Graham Sumner, *What Social Classes Owe to Each
        Other* (New York, 1883).
      George Tucker, *Political Economy for the People* (Philadel-
        phia, 1859).
      Henry Vethake, *The Principles of Political Economy* (Phila-
        delphia, 1838).
      Amasa Walker, *The Science of Wealth: A Manual of Political
        Economy, Embracing the Laws of Trade, Currency, and
        Finance* (student's edn., Philadelphia, 1875).
      Francis Amasa Walker, *Land and Its Rent* (Boston, 1883).
      Francis Amasa Walker, *Money* (New York, 1883).
      Francis Amasa Walker, *Political Economy* (New York, 1883).
      [Nathaniel A. Ware], *Notes on Political Economy, as Ap-
        plicable to the United States. By a Southern Planter* (New
        York, 1844).
      Francis Wayland, *The Elements of Political Economy* (Bos-
        ton, 1866).

  (b) WWhw bibliographical references to:
      Francis Bowen, *The Principles of Political Economy Applied
        to the Condition, the Resources, and the Institutions of the
        American People* (Boston, 1846).
      James Tift Champlin, *Lessons on Political Economy* (New
        York, 1868).

Montague Richard Leverson, *Common Sense; or, First Steps in Political Economy, for the Use of Families and Normal Classes, and of Pupils in District, Elementary, and Grammar Schools; Being a Popular Introduction to the Most Important Truths Regarding Labor and Capital* (New York, 1876).

Arthur Latham Perry, *Elements of Political Economy* (New York, 1866).

Arthur Latham Perry, *An Introduction to Political Economy* (New York, 1877).

"Perry's Political Economy," New York *Nation*, II (Feb. 1, 1866), 146-47.

George Tucker, *The Laws of Wages, Profits, and Rent, Investigated* (Philadelphia, 1837).

George Tucker, *Progress of the United States in Population and Wealth in Fifty Years, as Exhibited by the Decennial Census* (Boston, 1843).

George Tucker, *The Theory of Money and Banks Investigated* (Boston, 1839).

Joseph Tuckerman, *An Essay on the Wages Paid to Females for their Labour; in the Form of a Letter, from a Gentleman in Boston to his Friend in Philadelphia* (Boston, 1830).

Amasa Walker, *The National Currency and the Money Problem* (New York, 1876).

Amasa Walker, *The Nature and Uses of Money and Mixed Currency, with a History of the Wickaboag Bank* (Boston, 1857).

Amasa Walker, *The Science of Wealth: A Manual of Political Economy. Embracing the Laws of Trade, Currency, and Finance* (Boston, 1867).

Francis Amasa Walker, "American Agriculture," *Princeton Review*, IX (May 1882), 249-64.

Francis Amasa Walker, "The Law of Rent in Its Relations to the Irish Land Question," *International Review*, XII (Jan. 1882), 52-69.

Francis Amasa Walker, *Money in Its Relations to Trade and Industry* (New York, 1879).

Francis Amasa Walker, "Principles of Taxation," *Princeton Review*, VI (July 1880), 92-114.

Francis Amasa Walker, "The Wage-Fund Theory," *North American Review*, CXX (Jan. 1875), 84-119.

Francis Amasa Walker, *The Wages Question; A Treatise on Wages and the Wages Class* (New York, 1876).

Francis Wayland, *The Elements of Political Economy* (New York, 1837).

Research notebook (WP, DLC).

From Ellen Louise Axson

My darling Woodrow   [New York, Nov. 17, 1884]
    After the volume which I wrote last night, my conscience tells

me that I ought to make tonight's note short and devote my energies to answering some of my other letters. But when I am so
unwise as to begin with you, it is very hard to leave you for some
one else, especially when there are two such sweet letters as those
of today to be answered. No, dear, I have felt no ill effects, beyond a slight headache the next day, from the posing affair. You
must not feel concerned any longer about it; and the class is so
large, that my turn will come very seldom indeed,—perhaps no
more. Just think! one of the young men fainted last year—a great
strapping fellow. Is'nt that delightful? I was really charmed to
hear it. We had this afternoon the lovliest figure we have had
yet,—a fairy in white and sea-green with butterfly wings! and I
could'nt sketch her, because I was obliged to go to the tiresome
old perspective lecture, which we have now every Monday afternoon. This was our second; we had only the a.b.c.'s last week,
but now we are getting deeper into it, and I have been, this evening, busy working problems in "orthographic projection"! Such
a bore! it is so mathematical, and scientific, and mechanical, and
unimaginative, everything, in short, that is supposed to be especially distasteful to artists, and women!—so to those that are
both, it must be *doubly* distasteful.

How I wish, and I wish, my darling, that we could be together
just for that "little while," that I might hear all those small, special things that can't be put into writing. How impossible it is to
"keep up" in our correspondence, with our life, even by the most
industrious writing! No, darling, I have *not* that dread of you
that Minnie had; I am not afraid of your criticism,—as these
scrawls which I am constantly sending abundantly show,—because I have no appearances to keep up with you. Before all else
I want you to know the *truth,* to see just what a foolish little creature I am. I know *now* that such knowledge won't cause you to
love me less, or it would have had that effect long ere this, for
there has been no lack of sincerity in our dealings with each
other. And if you will only love me all *must* be well with me. For
the rest, though your approbation, is more precious to me than
that of all the world beside, your praise sweeter to me than ought
else, except your love, I am too low in my own esteem, especially
when I think of myself in connection with you, for your criticism
to gain any sting from wounded pride. Ah darling I love you[,]
I love you as my own soul, why can I not be, for your dear sake,
all that I wish to be—all that your love ought to be!

Good night dear love. With all my heart   Your own   Eileen.

ALS (WC, NjP).

To Ellen Louise Axson

My own darling,   Balto., Md., Nov. 18, 1884   10.05 A.M.

If yesterday, with all its sunshine and warmth, was dreary and miserable for me because it brought no letter from you, to-day, despite its clouds and biting winds, seems to me bright and cheery because of the *two* delightful letters I have just received. I suppose you must have gone to the box after the single mail collection on Sunday: for these two letters started at the same hour yesterday morning. And such letters as they are! It's enough to put a chap like me quite beside himself with delight to get such sweet assurances of love and tenderness as these, my darling! Do I "grow tired" of hearing you say that you love me? Why Eileen, my little sweetheart! Do you think I shall ever grow tired of happiness? It is your love that constitutes my happiness. Do you think that a man who is capable of loving with all his heart can ever grow tired of proofs of love from those who are dearer to him than his own life—or, above all, from her who *is* his life? Why do you suppose that I have so often asked you to repeat just that simple declaration, which contains all? Don't talk nonsense, my little queen! I shall not grow tired of that sweet declaration— my heart will never cease to thrill at those precious words, "I love you, darling, I *love* you"—until—until you treat me as Mrs. Powell treats that weak "Professor"—so long, that is, as I can believe that the words speak truth! You were wishing for the time to come, my darling, when you could *prove* your love for me through some service of love—and you know that my life waits for that time as for the first season of its perfection—but in the mean time, love, remember this, that your *words* are present proof to me: for, if I know anything of my Eileen, I know her sincerity, I know that her professions are *true*—that I might safely stake all that I am and all that I hope to be on them. If I wished for those professions because I thought them *necessary*—because I needed to be reassured—their repetition would turn my heart cold; but, as it is, my happiness seems somehow to turn upon that repetition, because I know that my little sweetheart declares her love again and again from very fulness of heart, and because she *knows* what a delight it is to me to hear her say these things.

Who wrote these beautiful verses you have sent me, my darling? They are so like yourself—so true to your own "silent womanhood"—that I could believe that *you* had written them, but for the quotation marks!

Ah, you arch mischief you, what do you mean by drawing such

nonsense out of the cases of Mrs. Perkins and Mrs. Powell and calling it a "moral"! I should like to have you near enough to administer a lecture to you—in the shape of *kisses,* which, interpreted by a few whispered words, might reconvey to you the knowledge that I love you *and believe that you love me*—a fact which, I think, Miss, you will agree with me in saying, quite precludes any personal application of this otherwise instructive moral!

And you have a lecture for *me,* have you, because I indulged myself by sending a second package of directed envelopes! Oh, you inconsistent little woman! You have hardly finished warning me of the danger and folly of the *un*selfishness you suppose me to possess before you turn about and begin to rate me for being so *selfish*! Was'nt it the bargain, Miss, that I should have the privilege of assisting you in carrying out this scheme of mine, of daily correspondence, by supplying you with directed envelopes —so that all that you would have to do on busy days would be to write a little note and seal it up? It's much too late to go back on the contract. If I am *not* lawyer enough to perceive the true weight of evidence, I remember some of the legal principles regarding oral agreements. But I am not disposed to be uncompromising. If you object to stamps which I have pasted on, I will send the stamped envelopes, with pleasure. You need not think, however, that I am like Prof. Powell even enough to give up *this* right! It wont be easy to tear the stamps off of the government envelopes! What a dear proud little girl you are! But it is'nt a matter of pride with you—is it?—to keep me from feeling my identification with you until the very hour in which we shall go to the altar together—in which formal sanction shall be put upon our real union.

I wrote to Stockton last night, my pet—an astoundingly stupid letter, which, I am afraid, managed to conceal the warm affection with which it was written. I feel as if he were my brother already; but I did not know how to tell him so.

It is six weeks since I sent my *mss.* to H. M. & Co.—what do you suppose they have done with them?

Eileen, my matchless little sweetheart, I love you with all my heart—that heart which is yours to keep always as your own, because its possessor is   Your own   Woodrow.

ALS (WC, NjP).

From Ellen Louise Axson

My darling Woodrow,   New York, Nov. 18/84

I have been having quite a treat tonight! Mr. Goodrich brought up for my inspection the famous "Rubaiyât" of "Omar Khayyâm" —and Elihu Vedder,[1] which H. M. & Co have just gotten out. I was wild to see it, for I have read and heard of nothing else, it seems to me for weeks past; it was at the "Art Reunion" on Sat. night, but there was such a mob of young men around it all the evening that I barely got a glimpse of it. Mr Goodrich has been trying to obtain possession of it for some time; he brought the poem up and read it to me several nights ago. The original drawings are to be on exhibition at Houghton's next week.[2] It certainly is a most original and beautiful work—one that fully justifies the verdict that it is "by far the most important work of it's kind which this country has produced." Indeed, it can hardly be compared with other illustrated books, it is so entirely different— it is art of a so much higher order. I really believe that, after all, Vedder has more genius than any other American artist; he is not merely a great workman, like so many French artists, (though "his art *is* of the largest and most robust type"!) but he is equally great on the intellectual and imaginative sides. It seems a pity—does it not—that such noble work should be expended on such a heathenish poem!—that he should add any attractions to such miserable philosophy. Why could he not have chosen a subject worthy of his art?

I have been to see an old Sav. lady this afternoon, Mrs. Naphew; she boards at the same house with Mrs. Peck[,] one of the League ladies, and hearing of me through her, very kindly called on me a few days ago. She belongs to the Foley-Habersham clan,—is a kind-hearted old lady; seems inclined to take me under her wing! is bemoaning the fact that she can't "have me in the same house with her," theirs being full. I would rather like to go, myself, for it is a *beautiful* place, is kept by a *lovely* Augusta lady, she says; nearly all the boarders are Southerners, and they have "Southern cooking"!

I am afraid you have plunged without even so much as the necessary pause for rest, into a still greater task than your last; how many thousands of pages will *this* force you to read? I suppose you will be busy about it all the rest of the winter? I hope, dear, that you will find it pleasant and interesting work. Good night darling. I love you so much that I can even hope I was "intended for you" by right of that love. At any rate I feel very much at home in your heart—as if I belonged there. With all my heart   Your own   Eileen.

ALS (WC, NjP).

[1] *Rubaiyat of Omar Kayyam, The Astronomer-Poet of Persia, Rendered into English Verse by Edward FitzGerald with an Accompaniment of Drawings by Elihu Vedder* (Boston, 1884).
[2] At their establishment at 11 E. 17th St.

To John Hanson Kennard, Jr.

My Dear Kennard: Balto., Md., Nov. 18, '84.

Hurrah for Cleveland. I tell you, my dear fellow, 'twas a glorious victory, won against John Kelly and the whole intrenched force of officeholders. Why can't we shake hands across this distance? It's a genuine nuisance that we can't be together, if only for a few minutes to woopover [whoop over] this electrical change in the political atmosphere. As for my single self, I have been trying to adjust my senses to the fact that for the first time since in or about the year in which we were born the Democrats are actually coming into office.

And I think, my dear Kennard, in view of this ge-lorious fact we can afford to forgive the sins of one Cable.[1] I am not the man to answer his little effusion in the *Century*. Folks would say "Who's Woodrow Wilson? How do we know whether he represents the South or Southern sentiment any more truly than Cable does? Let some Southerner speak whose name and fame we know." Besides, I think that you have, in past at least, misunderstood Cable's meaning. I hope you have. I hope that my interpretation is the true one. In speaking of the overthrow of the Virginia Company[,] Doyle (alas, as you see by this, I've been deep immersed in Colonial history), says: "There, as so often in history, our feelings are all enlisted on that side whose defeat we must nevertheless deliberately believe to have been productive of good." That is just where you and I stand with reference to the war between the States. We know that the South would have been ruined by success; in other words, that the preservation of the Union was for the best: that it was politically right. And this is very like what Mr. Cable's language may naturally be read to mean. He warmly professes "pride in our struggle and in all the noble men and women who bore its burdens"; he is ready to admit that secession was wrong. If he stopped there and did not say "morally" wrong there would be little in his piece that I should feel like condemning except the supercilious tone in which it is written. He is, of course, a fool for his pains. He is setting up an impossible standard. It is easy and cheap now to point out that the war was a mistake, but it is perfectly plain that we (Cable included), would fight it over again if placed once more in the same circumstances. Of course I don't need to explain to you that I am not defending Cable. I am simply endeavoring to point out as clearly as may be why I don't think it necessary to attack him, supposing that I were the proper person to do so. I don't think that you need fear that anything that he may say will do much harm. Unfortunately the Northern mind is not susceptible of being convinced on such points. If any one says what falls in with their opinions they assent: if the most esteemed and best accredited man in the country asserts the contrary they are satisfied that he is mistaken. Why make gossip, therefore, by spreading one's self forth in a *Century* "open letter"? Give Cable rope enough and he will hang himself and so save us the trouble: for he is trying all sorts of things for which he is conspicuously unfit and that must be the beginning of the end with him as with everybody else who does the like.

As I said, parenthetically, above, we have just come out of a tremun-Dous soaking in Colonial history. The examination took place on Saturday last, and a very fair, sensible examination it was. Adams gave out five topics and told us to choose, each man for himself, one from the number and spend the two hours in writing an informal essay upon it. That's the sort of examination I like. But it wasn't the sort I had expected: and I went in crammed with one or two hundred dates and one or two thousand minute particulars about the quarrels of nobody knows who with an obscure Governor, for nobody knows what. Just think of all that energy wasted! The only comfort is that the mass of information won't long burden me. I shall forget it with great ease. . . .

We are just now enduring a nice chill dose of sleet, after several weeks of the finest weather imaginable; but I'm so busy that I manage to be quite independent of weather. I am never so busy, however, my dear fellow, that I can't find time to think very often and with strongest affection of one Kennard of New Orleans. There would be lots of fellows to send love, if anybody knew what I was writing up here in my little den.

As ever,   Your sincere friend.   Woodrow Wilson.

Printed in the New York *Sun*, April 18, 1933; elision in the printed version.
1 See J. H. Kennard, Jr., to WW, Oct. 29, 1884, and note 1 to that letter.

Notes on Professor Morris's Lecture on Herbert Spencer

Nov. 19, 1884

(2) [Spencer] terms society an *aggregate*—any number of bodies brought together, whether they naturally belong together or not. An organism is not actually an aggregate, it is essentially a *whole*. This idea admittedly opposed to organic integration. See Jones pages 190-4.[1]

(3) The kind of causation which needs to be studied, which can alone be studied, is *natural* causation. This is displayed among human beings socially aggregated. "The lines of least resistance" are filled by the congeries of the faculties which constitutes each individual. Desire *does* act in just this way, and if desires were the only things to deal with, the view would be entirely true. As it is it is only partially true. This view is of course an extremely important one, for after all that remains true, that philosophy and all science advance as the search after causes. A thing is not explained when it is secret. Locke however seems to mistake description for explanation.

What does S. understand by natural causation? He understands *physical* causation. "Physical causation is invariable sequence" says Mill. Kant points out that it means succession according to rule. "Law of order" says Huxley. All notion both of power and of purpose is excluded. It is expressed intention not only of these philosophers but also of the pure physicists to make known these laws by which we come to any knowledge of power. This exclusion is not perverse; it is necessary and proper in the work of the mathematician—the ideal physical science. But if this view be adopted in science with which we are now dealing this sort of causation is *no* causation but only quasi-causation. We are merely finding out the matter of half sequence or rather leaving out the main question as to the powerful causes of things. This is *all* that is involved in the questions to be considered.

(4) We have the state, or government (not distinguished by S.) represented as keeping always an aggressive attitude to the individual, and thus foreign to him. "Government is begotten of aggression and by aggression." "Ethics of government originally identical with the ethics of war, that is aggression." Pages 44, 45 of "Man and State." His later years have suggested to him the necessary distinction between state, as possibly found in the nature of man, and *government*, or the *machinery* of government.

(5) S. tries to find basis of sovereignty and finds it in *unanimous* will of people and may, significantly, devote itself to that

which the unanimous will of the people desires. Freedom, and protection of property are the things which this universal will desires. The state is founded in law and its object is the essential will of man, of that which is the nature of man to will. This idea furnishes another point of approach between S. and Aristotle and He[gel]. The only difference is that Aristotle and Heg. find it possible to define law and freedom in a *positive* way, whereas S. defines it in a negative form.

(5) The nature of the state remains a means for individualism. The state is purely a means, individuals are the ends. Jones points out that this is inconsistent with the idea of organism. The unity is just as essential as its multiplicity. The *body* is as important as its members.

Transcript of WWsh notes in notebook described at Oct. 8, 1884.
    [1] Morris was referring to Henry Jones, "The Social Organism," in Andrew S. P. Pattison and R. B. Haldane (eds.), *Essays in Philosophical Criticism* (London, 1883), pp. 187-213.

Notes on Professor Ely's Lecture on Bimetallism

November 19, 1884.

Is Bi-met desirable? It is because
(1) It is necessary to provide *good* money in sufficient quantities, to prevent violent fluctuations, and to avoid the contraction of prices so disastrous to the economic life of the active nations of the world. There *must* be a contraction of prices without bimetallism. All arguments against contraction of prices are arguments for bimetallism. A contraction of prices embraces the relations between the past and present, and as these relations are a chief part of economic life, prosperity is dependent upon them. Rents, rates, etc., do not readily change, but prices change quickly and suddenly—hence the embarrassment of falling prices in agricultural produce, for instance. The cost of tillage, too, remains pretty much the same, or tends to increase. Not all expenses can be reduced in a short time. Then, too, there are outstanding debts. The ideal to be sought for is an absolute stable standard of value. It is of course impossible to find this, but may not there be a near approach to it by means of an international double standard? Take Jevons' illustration of 2 reservoirs.
Study these periods:
    Period following introduction of gold as monometallism (1816) in England.
    Period following discovery of gold and large increase in circulation of the world (1850-1873).

Nov. 19, 1884.

Is Bi-met. Desirable? It is —

(1) [shorthand notes]

1 Jevons 162 [shorthand]

[shorthand] *(1816)* [shorthand]

[shorthand] *(1850-1873)*

[shorthand] *1873*

From Wilson's shorthand notes taken in Professor Richard T. Ely's course in finance and taxation

Period following demonetization of silver in Germany and in the United States in 1873.

1809-1849 The estimated rise of gold, 145% (Jevons) also a great fall in prices during these years. 1797 the Bank of England had suspended specie payments. Not until after 1810, however, did a serious depression set in.

After the discovery of gold in California and Australia (49-50) a great rise of prices, of rents, of value of farms.

1873-'80 A recurrence of phenomena following 1816.

(2) We have reason to suppose that it is not sufficient to maintain existing stock of money. We want more than we have. The reasons for this supposition are numerous:

(a) The expansion of commerce, because there must be more or less cash used in transactions of commerce.

(b) Growth of countries, like the United States and Australia.

(c) Settlement of new countries. Notice absorption of gold by the West and by this country.

(d) Opening up new regions.

It seems probable that we have gone as far as is prudent in the use of paper, of bills of exchange, etc. They are necessary, but can they be carried much further? There must be a certain amount of coin somewhere in existence in order to make this operation safe.

Our paper currency does not at all diminish the amount of coin. There seems to be very little disposition on the continent of Europe to extend the use of checks, etc. France has a much larger store of coined money, in proportion to population, than any other country. Is it not possible that this explains however that France is less liable to crisis than are other countries with less money. There was a large accumulated treasure in France when the country needed it for payment of war indemnity. It is probable that it is good policy for the country to put a large amount of its resources into coined money. Facile circulation is accompanied by an increased need of money. Travel has increased wonderfully and travel is paid for in cash. Look, besides, at the payment of employee wages in cash. (See Poor's railroad manual for the statistics of this). 1883 one billion passengers moved one mile in the United States at a cost of 2.40 cents per mile. We have been spending on railroads 1 million dollars for every working day in the year. Transfer of more than 2 millions sterling for railroads in the world. Estimate of *de Lavelaye* [Laveleye].* Why 15½ to 1 rather than another?

This ratio is that which obtains in almost all parts of the world; having been adopted by Germany, the ratio of France and in all countries of the Latin union. There is a tradition of long-established ratio. Most gold and silver of the world have been coined on the basis of that ratio. 1878 legislation is the only thing standing in the way in this country. We have far less silver than there is in France or Germany. Recoinage,[1] if universal, would be productive of vast ills. Is a question of convenience and economy.

Progress of Opinion: 6 years ago everybody thought gold monometallism possible: now there is universal recognition of the impossibility of it.

* Pamphlet on "International Bimetallism." *19th Century*, April 1882[:] article against bimetallism by Lord Sherbrooke ["What Is Money?"]

Transcript of WWsh in notebook described at Oct. 8, 1884.

[1] Wilson wrote "recoinage" in shorthand, but it seems clear that he misheard the phrase that Ely used, "free coinage."

To Ellen Louise Axson

My own darling,   Balto., Md., Nov. 19, 1884 1:10 P.M.
This is the worst time of the day in which to write a letter—just before dinner, when a chap is too hungry to be in the best of talking humours. But there's no time of the day when I don't feel

like going to my darling. My letter-writing does constitute a sort of going to you, in almost a literal sense! Since you confess holding constant imaginary conversations with me, my pet, I might as well confess that I not only let my imagination carry me to your side whenever my duties let me off for a single moment from the *necessity* of thinking about other things, but when I sit down to write a letter to you my love for you so possesses my whole mind, so dominates all my faculties, but it is only by a conscious effort that I can write about anything else. I could as easily think about the Ptolemaic geography while holding you in my arms as about anything but our relations to each other while writing you. Thoughts of you, and of all that makes me love and admire and prize you, fairly fill my heart to overflowing at such times. I can think of you then only as my promised wife, and forget altogether that, like other people, you like news, and playful comment, and personal tid-bits in the letters you receive. My feelings just take the bit between their teeth and bolt with me. Taking shelter behind this explanation, I shall *pretend*, therefore, that, if it were not for this fact, I could write letters to my darling which would be quite as *interesting*, as well as quite as loving, as those she writes to me. As it is, I must take comfort in the hope that my letters claim the homage of her love as surely as hers claim the homage of my love *and admiration*. But, if you wish, I'll try to turn over a new leaf, and make a practice of indulging in disquisitions such as my recent political argument—which so impressed *me* that I had forgotten how I had constructed it—had forgotten where I hung its 'therefore'—and so thought that my darling was disagreeing with the whole of it, in the same breath in which she pronounced it "splendid." I imagined that I had been ingenious enough to construct an argument which was "splendid" without being *convincing*—a man-of-war which was admirable but unseaworthy!—a feat which would naturally cause me some chagrin.

Have you forgotten, little lady, the plan of your room that you were going to draw me?

I love you, Eileen, my sweetheart!

Your own   Woodrow.

ALS (WC, NjP).

From Ellen Louise Axson

My darling Woodrow,   New York, Nov. 19/84.

We have just been having an excited time below stairs over Blaine's Augusta speech,[1] which Mr Brigham has been reading, amid endless interruptions from Mr. Goodrich and myself. Poor Mr. G.! I am sorry for him, his idol is broken, he confesses that he has no more use for Blaine; he is mortified, disgusted! To think that he should so stultify himself,—that he could make such a speech after all those fine professions in the letter of accept-ance. He (Mr G.) is more indignant than I. I think it too ridicu-lous for anything but laughter,—I hope it is too ridiculous to do any harm,—but who knows! One thing seems to be certain, if it does'nt do *great* harm, it's author will be deeply disappointed. It was spoken as he tells us both "purposely and instinctively"; and the purpose and the instinct are equally disgraceful to him. But bah! why should I fill my letter with *him,* of all people.

I have been up in the "head class" today, for the first time, and am "carried away" by it. It is *so* much more fascinating than the work from the antique. I don't believe I ever told you about my being promoted to the life class. It happened on election day, and I was too absorbed in politics to write of such trifles. I think —though it *is* rather a bore to write so much about one's own affairs,—that I must tell you all about it, because I don't know anything that will give you such a good idea of the League and the League girls,—or of what it is, that makes life and study there, so charming. They had all been begging me to apply, for some time, on the strength of the very nice things, which Mr. Brush was good enough to say about my work. At last, I did a head of Homer which they all made a tremendous fuss about, in-sisting that I *must* send it up. I told them they were beside them-selves; I would do nothing of the sort; for only *one* had been admitted from our class, and even Miss Avery, who had so much experience, who had risen regularly from Cooper's, and who had studied in the League manner from the beginning, had been re-fused. But they continued to urge me, and, at last, finding me still stubborn, Mrs. Powell declared that she would *make* me! I laughed, asking her how she would go about it; and there the matter ended, as I *supposed.* But two or three days after, Thomas suddenly appeared and presented me with a roll of paper. While I was wondering what it could be, Mrs. Powell said behind me in a rather *scared* voice—"thats—thats *my* doings, it's your Homer; I *stole* it, and made out your application for the head class!"; and while I gazed at her in speechless amazement, she went on to explain that she hadn't intended me to know anything about it unless I was admitted, but Thomas had been too quick for her. "But" she said ["]run up to the postoffice and get your ticket, I *know* it's there." "*Ticket,* indeed!" said I, "catch me looking for imaginary tickets! I would'nt make myself so ridiculous." With that, one of the other girls rushed frantically from the room, and a moment later came back, waving the ticket in triumph. They actually *had* admitted me! Then such a time as followed. Mrs. P. embraced me fervently and repeatedly, declaring that it was the "lovliest thing that ever happened," and all "our set" crowded around and made great rejoicing. When you remember that none of these girls or boys were "in" themselves, or had any hope of being admitted soon, you will begin to see why I think the League delightful. Mr. Brush also as well as the whole class of seventy, seemed to be interested and, of course, amused at the manner of my entrance. Indeed, it is one of the regular League jokes now. That was, as I said, more than two weeks ago, but I hav'nt cared to go up until today,—havnt felt prepared, was afraid they would turn me out again. How often I have laughed at myself for thinking of applying at *first* for the head class, and have congratulated myself on the sudden spasm of terror, which led me to decide on the Antique;—"because" I thought, "I want to work there a month, *anyhow*, so it will be safer just to apply for that, and settle the other after." But one never knows how or where one stands until they get to headquarters[.] True, I know now much better than I could have known before, that I could have gone into any class I chose at the Academy, and held my own respectably; but though I knew the methods of the two schools were different, I couldn't realize *how much* I had to *unlearn*;—and that, you know, is always harder than to learn. The Academy and Miss Fairchild had but one rule, viz., to work with both eyes open, and put in everything you see as carefully as possible.[2] But at the League you must always look at the model with your eyes half shut,—you must be BROAD, above all things,— you must understand "the *nothingness* of nature"! We must leave out quite as much as we put in, and there's the rub,—for most of us invariably leave out the wrong things, and put in the wrong! After all, though I am a convert to League principles, I am glad I learned the Academy way too, for practical reasons. One's "patrons" might object, if we represented their friends with only one eye and half a mouth, one side of the face being simply a *broad* shadow!

But oh dear, what a dreadfully stupid letter I have written; pray pardon me. And I have made it so long too, that I have left myself no time for many other things that I had to say, suggested by your sweet letter of this morning,—the sweetest ever written, it seems to me. But at least, I have room for "the simple declaration which contains all." I love you,—I love you more and more all the time, I *do* repeat it, darling, because I *must*, from very fulness of heart. I am not afraid to have you stake all that you are on *that*; "if it be falsehood and upon me proved, I never writ,—and no man ever loved."

Good night, dear love,

As ever   Your own   Eileen

ALS (WC, NjP).

¹ James G. Blaine spoke to friends and neighbors in Augusta, Maine, on the evening of November 18, 1884. He attributed his defeat in the recent presidential election to the Democratic vote of the "Solid South." Blaine said that this meant, in effect, that the country was being dominated once more by a southern white minority since southern Negroes, while being counted for purposes of determining electoral votes, were prevented from voting by "reckless intimidation" and even "violence and murder." Depriving the Negro of the vote, Blaine went on, would result in his economic degradation, and his wages would soon be no better than his subsistence as a slave. Blaine concluded by waving the "bloody shirt": leaders of the Confederate "Rebellion" were behind the Democratic victory in 1884. James G. Blaine, *Political Discussions: Legislative, Diplomatic, and Popular, 1856-1886* (Norwich, Conn., 1887), pp. 466-71.

² ELA had studied earlier at the National Academy of Design in New York, probably during the academic year 1881-82. For references to her earlier stay in New York, see her letters to WW of March 10, April 15, July 28, and Oct. 5, 1884.

To Robert Bridges

My dear Bobby,   Balto., Md., Nov. 19/84

It was cruelly hard luck that I should have been looking for you in New York at the very time that you were looking for me here!¹ I was disappointed enough when Pete told me you were out of town: but when I got back here and found that at that selfsame time you were here with Hiram waiting for me to turn up, I was fairly *mad* that things should have gone so elaborately wrong. I had but a single day to spend in New York: so, as soon as I got there I posted over to Brooklyn to fetch my friend Shinn and together we started out for the *Commercial Advertiser* and the *Post* offices. But as soon as I had found Pete he told me that you were away—and the telephone confirmed him. I almost wished that I had stopped in Balto., and not gone on to New York—I wished so altogether afterwards. Though I went on an exceedingly pleasant errand, there was no necessity for me to go.

I went to escort Miss Axson, the young lady to whom I am engaged. She is to spend the winter studying at the Art League— on 14th St. I should be delighted, Bobby, if you could find time some evening to call on her: and I know that *she* would be equally pleased, for she knows pretty much all that I know about "Bob. Bridges." Her address is No. 120 West 11th St. It seems rather strange to me that you don't know her already! There would seem

to be some necessary fitness in a fellow's best male friend knowing the lady who is nearer to him than all the rest of the world:
and one of the first things I thought of when Miss A. decided to
study in New York this winter was that that might bring you two
together—*should* bring you together, if I was to have any say in
the matter. I hope, old fellow, that our *homes* wont lie so far
apart that you can't get to know all about her housekeeping when
she becomes Mrs. Wilson!

I got a letter from Charlie Talcott during the summer[2]—in
answer to one I had written him long before on the subject of
my engagement[3]—in which there occurs this characteristic passage: "That question of yours: 'Did you ever think seriously on
the subject?' is open to grave objections. In the first place it is
leading; and then again it is highly improper. You, who have
received the soft answer of assent, and, being out of the woods,
may whistle, should be very careful how you examine your sensitive friends who have not yet submitted their cases. Suffice it to
say, that I have not yet 'acted in spite of myself and in the teeth
of all discretion'; but when I do act it will probably be in that
way."

I have not answered that epistle by the way. I was hard at work
all summer completing a series of essays which I began here last
winter—and the first three of which won me the Fellowship I
now hold. It's the same old thing—Committee government—but it's
worked up in very different shape from that of the essays with
whose presentation to the publishers you took so great and and
[*sic*] such unselfish pains. As you are no doubt prepared to hear,
I am glad now that you did not find a publisher for me. The
essays were crude then—at any rate the new ones are less crude,
besides being entirely different both in form and in purpose. I
leave out all advocacy of Cabinet government—all advocacy, indeed, of *any* specific reform—and devote myself to a careful analysis of Congressional government. I have abandoned the evan-
gelical for the exegetical—so to speak!—and the result is something very much more thorough and more sober, as well as more
valuable and more likely to be acceptable if published. I shall
attack the Boston publishers first this time (Houghton, Mifflin,
& Co.), and, failing with them, may decide to storm some of the
New York men in person. I send you one of the University circulars containing an outline of two of my chapters.[4]

I am somewhat better satisfied with the conditions of work
here now that my standing in the University is established: but
I am none the less anxious—eager—to get a chair somewhere and

get into permanent harness. It don't pay to be all one's life a pupil; and, though I am as little a pupil and as much my own master here as I could be anywhere as merely a student, I am constantly anxious about the uncertain future. I want "a place"! Maybe you will see an additional reason for my wish if you go around to 11th St.

What do you think of my friend Shinn—I am curious to know because he struck *me* "all of a heap" when I first saw him. It takes a good while to take him all in; for he is certainly *sui generis*!

Wasn't Buck Williamson's death[5] shocking! He was the last man in the class for whom I should have anticipated suicide! But it's high time to turn in. With much love,

  As ever, Your sincere friend Woodrow Wilson

ALS (Meyer Coll., DLC).
[1] WW is referring to his trip with ELA from Wilmington to New York. After leaving ELA at her boardinghouse on October 3, 1884, WW had sought out his friends, as he goes on to explain here.
[2] C. A. Talcott to WW, Sept. 4, 1884, ALS (WP, DLC).
[3] WW to C. A. Talcott, July 5, 1884.
[4] Printed at July 1, 1884.
[5] The Rev. Henry S. Williamson, who died on Nov. 12, 1884.

To Ellen Louise Axson

My own darling, Balto., Md., Nov. 20, 1884 11.20 A.M.

I wrote to Bob. Bridges (of the *Evening Post* and *Nation*, you know) last night, and of course told him of your being in New York and asked him to try to find time to call on you. If there be any two people in the world whom I would rather bring together than any others, those two are you and Bob. Bridges. You know more about Shinn than about any of the rest of my friends: but that has been because my life has been with him during the period of our intimate correspondence. If I have any *best* friend in the world, that friend is Bob. Bridges. His relations with me have been like your relations with Miss Rose [Anderson], though our friendship does not, like yours, date from childhood. I have for a great many years felt towards him as towards a brother: and if we have drifted apart of late years it has been only because of the necessity which has separated our *lives*. It has never weaned my heart from the dear, genuine old Scot. None of Bob. is on the surface: but the deeper you dig the finer the ore. He and Charlie Talcott and Hiram Woods were the *real* friends whom college life gave me for an inspiring possession: and if I keep any friends, I shall, before all others keep them. I was keenly disappointed to find Bob. out of town when I went to New York as your escort: and you can imagine how much was added to that disappointment when I returned and found that at that very time—that very day—he was here in Balto. looking for me! You know I *neglected* him, as well as Shinn, on my next visit to N.Y.—my love for a certain young lady making me selfishly forgetful of all the claims of friendship—so that, if you please, you will not mention that visit to *him*, if you can avoid it conscientiously. Alas! alas! the toils of a single wilful misdeed!—according to the immemorial custom I cast the burden upon the woman who (this time unconsciously and innocently) tempted me! It's *too* bad that I should have to give over all the trouble of concealment to you. If you have *any* objections, darling, rebel and throw me over to the tender mercies of the Scot without compunction!

There is an interesting syllogism, my darling, which might, by judicious quotation, be formulated thus: "Before all else I want you to know the *truth*, to see just what a foolish little creature I am"; "there has been no lack of sincerity in our dealings with each other"; "I have no appearances to keep up with you." (Miss Axson.) "The more you discover your true self to me the more I love you." (Mr. Wilson.) "Therefore, the more foolish he finds her the more he will love her" (Some dispassionate and judicial third person.) Chorus: "How happy their lives will be!" Ah, my little bewitcher, if your welfare depends on my love for you, you are the most fortunate little woman in the world; if, as this sweet letter of Tuesday night says, you "feel very much at home in my heart—as if you belonged there," never did little woman have a home more entirely and singly her own than you have!

Hurrah for the young man who fainted at posing last year! That *was* "delightful," that you should have such substantial precedent!

I haven't dared to count the number of pages I shall have to read before I can commence writing on the American Economists. I'll tell you next Spring when It's all behind me! In the meantime I rejoice in *progress*. I have finished *one* author. May the rest be as easy to master!

But I must end this! Such indulgence is very improper for my busiest day! My darling, I love you more and more every day—and consequently, alas! *need* you more and more every day. But that need itself is a blessing, is an education in feeling. When I do get you I will know what I have gotten and *why* it would be impossible for me to be anything but

ALS (WC, NjP).   Your own   Woodrow.

From Ellen Louise Axson

My darling Woodrow, New York Nov 20/84.

Who do you suppose has suddenly made her appearance in New York? Why, Cousin Hattie! She and Mr. Ewing came this morning to see me; I missed her, of course, so I went this afternoon, to the St. James, to see her—and missed her again! Too bad! was'nt it? I am wild to see her; have no idea what has brought her here so unexpectedly, but it is a very delightful "happening."

You don't know how cosy and comfortable I feel tonight. I actually have a *fire*! think of it! The register has warmed the room enough until last night; but I *was* cold last night, and I thought best to inform Miss Beatty of the fact; so when I came in from the League, the whole room was aglow with the cheerful blaze. It made me feel *good* all over; what a difference it does make! I really can begin to call this *home*, now that I have that warm, bright face to greet me. But even without the fire, I have learned to love this little room, and to feel at home in it. It has become dear to me chiefly because of it's associations with *you*. I might at one time have felt it incumbent upon me to explain that phenomenon, but you have taught me that such explanation is unnecessary; you can understand without it. Why shouldn't it be associated with you? There is your picture, to begin with, looking down upon me, and there is also a much better picture—a *speaking*! likeness always visible to my mind's eye,—and best of all, here is, no image at all, but your very self, ever present, in my heart of hearts—ever consciously present;—much more truly present than any of those whose images happen to be painted on the retina of my eye, or whose voices sound in my ear.

Do you actually mean to *apologize* for *your* letters, my darling? If so I fear I must repeat your own good advice—"don't talk nonsense," please! I am not pining for "news" in the least,—I find your letters a great deal more *interesting* and *admirable* than you can *possibly* find mine, so I beg that you won't make any change on *my* account, but will continue your present style until *you* grow tired of it. I am *sure* that no one ever wrote such sweet letters, before; they are more precious to me than gold, they are my very life.

With truest love I am, my darling, yours forever, Eileen.

It is very odd that "Houghton" &c don't write you. Why dont you write and inquire? I dare say the election has had a great deal to do with it. It has caused so much confusion and preoccupation in all departments.

ALS (WC, NjP).

To Ellen Louise Axson

My own darling,   Balto., Md., Nov. 21, 1884   *11.15* A.M.

If ever anybody deserved a scolding, you deserve one for having kept from me for two whole weeks the story of your promotion to the "life class"! The idea of your letting the excitements of election put it out of your head to write to me about what interests me more immediately and more deeply than any political event that has happened or *could* happen—my darling's success in her chosen work! And if you are to adopt the creed, Miss, that to write about oneself—no matter whether the letter be written to one's lover or not—is to write a "dreadfully stupid letter," I must account myself bound to exclude from my epistles all mention of the affairs, small or great, which make up my life—unless they have in them the interest of concerning other people as well as myself: a practice which I have not hitherto felt bound to observe. Why, darling, this is the most interesting letter I ever read, and my heart is full to overflowing with delight at my pet's singular success, achieved in spite of herself! Nothing could have made me prouder of you than I was already, my gifted little sweetheart; but this story of Mrs. Powell's bold stratagem and its gratifying result has revealed to me better than anything else could have done the conditions—the delightful conditions—of your work at the League, and the fact that you are loved and appreciated there as you should be. And what, do you think, could have given me greater satisfaction and joy than that? Why, I should rather have had that happen than see my book published, my darling! But let me tell you that only women could have conceived and executed such an unselfish scheme or have taken such delight in its success. This is not saying that your *fellow* students may not rejoice in your promotion: they are quite capable of entire unselfishness in that. But the *beauty* of the scheme seems to me to lie in its illustration of the sweetest side of woman's nature. Ah, my darling, what must you think of me, if you supposed that the details of this story could be tedious to me! It has pleased me vastly better than any success I ever achieved myself. And you had'nt told me a word about "the very nice things which Mr. Brush was good enough to say about your work." I insist, Miss, upon your repeating every one of these "things" that he said, in the very next letter you write! If you persist in keeping from me the particulars of your life at the League, I shall suspect that you have'nt read the letters I've been writing you, in so many of which I have plead, both indirectly and by direct appeal, for just such details—the details that are inseparable from *you*, which concern nobody but you, which have you for their centre—and which, consequently, I love.

But really it's a shame that I should scold when the scolding humour is only on the surface, my heart being full of nothing but gladness. Maybe, if you could have watched my face as I read this letter lying here before me, you would'nt have kept away from my side for fear of a scolding! If there be ever any play of expression on my long, grim visage, there must have been something in it then that would have invited you—and tempted? you—to come very close. I cannot tell you as to that, but I know that there were tears in my eyes, such as come there only when my heart is fullest of joy and tenderness. My darling, I wish I could send my love to Mrs. Powell and to the young lady who ran upstairs to the "post-office" to get the ticket.

I was very much interested in what you had to say, my pet, about the difference between the methods, and canons, at the Academy and at the League. I wish, though, that the League authorities would replace that astounding phrase, "the nothingness of nature" with one that has some evident meaning. Of course I can't suggest a better myself—because one has to know what a term means before he can offer a synonyme—but surely a better could be invented by a member of the Society for Ethical Culture! —unless, indeed, their *habit* be vagueness of thought. It seems to me that Miss Fairchild and the Academy people simply translate nature *literally*, whilst the League artists prefer to translate it freely and often even *metaphorically*—to take only its suggestive parts and dwell on them, leaving the imagination of the beholder to complete the picture. As a Philistine, I should say that the *true* method lay somewhere between these two extremes—somewhere between too clear detail and too broad shadow. Practically, I'll adopt and admire the style my darling chooses. She shall be my art mistress, in addition to the other elements of her rule.

I love you, my precious: I love you with a love which has become, it seems to me, the motive power of my life and of my ambition. I am in every thought, and try to be in every act

Your own   Woodrow

ALS (WC, NjP).

From Ellen Louise Axson

My darling Woodrow,   New York, Nov 22/84

If you remember that I was to see Irving and Ellen Terry last night, you will know without being informed why I postponed my writing until this morning. Oh! it was *glorious!*—the lovliest thing I ever saw or imagined is certainly Ellen Terry!—or at least Ellen Terry's acting. Irving is very great as Shylock,—in some parts he is *terrible*,—he is positively blood-curdling; still the mind instinctively turns back again and again to Portia. And the costumes and scenery were so perfectly lovely too, no picture could have been more perfect in colour, in composition, in the whole effect, than each and all of their "scenes";—it was *more* beautiful than a picture,—it was as beautiful as a dream!

Was'nt it odd that we should have happened to have seats just *next* to Miss Mosely and her friends—not even a single chair between; and Cousin Hattie and Mr. Ewing were only half a dozen seats away! And was'nt it odd too that I should have had *two* invitations to hear Irving last night? You remember that was my experience the last time I went to the theatre;—"quite a coincidence!["] Cousin Hattie sent me a note, by Mr. E., yesterday asking me to dine with them and go. I couldn't very well accept even the first part of the invitation on account of my engagement with Mr. Goodrich, so I hav'nt seen her yet, except for a moment after the play; as she was herself engaged yesterday,—invited to a "lunch." But I am going up this morning at ten, and we are to make "a day of it." And as it is a good deal after nine now, I must make haste to close. Am sorry that I *must* wait to answer your sweet letter. I hope Mr. Bridges *will* come to see me, I am very anxious to know him,—I love you darling better even than you know, and I am for all my life   Your own   Eileen

ALS (WC, NjP).

To Ellen Louise Axson

My own darling,   Balto., Md., Nov. 22, 1884   11.30 A.M.

Here is an extract I have just hit upon and which I know you will appreciate and enjoy, as a supplement to certain chapters in Hamerton's *Intellectual Life* which you will doubtless recall. This is more vivacious than Hamerton because it is from an essay on Shelley by my master, Bagehot—the most vivacious, the most racily real of writers on life—whether the life be political, social, or separately intellectual. Of the first Mrs. Shelley he says: "We should conclude that she was capable of making many people happy, though not of making Shelley happy. There is an ordinance of nature at which men of genius are perpetually fretting, but which does more good than many laws of the universe which they praise: it is that ordinary women ordinarily prefer ordinary men. 'Genius,' as Hazlitt would have put it, 'puts them out.' It is so strange; it does not come into the room as usual; it says 'such things'; once it forgot to brush its hair. The common female mind prefers usual tastes, settled manners, customary conversation, defined and practical pursuits. It is a great good that it should be so. Nature has no wiser instinct. The average woman suits the average man; good health, easy cheerfulness, common charms, suffice. If Miss Westbrook had married an everyday person—a gentleman, suppose, in the tallow line—she would have been happy, and have made him happy. Her mind could have understood his life; her society would have been a gentle relief from unodoriferous pursuits. She had nothing in common with Shelley &c."[1] This is a long quotation to burden a short letter with, but I know that you will not begrudge it the space. This is the only way in which I can even come near to realizing the luxury of carrying the best, most suggestive, passages of my favourite authors to my best loved companion. Of course the explanation of Shelley's mistake in this unfortunate marriage is simple. Mistake was inevitable when he chose to marry a girl because her beauty had won his fanciful love at first sight, and because her name was Harriett—a name of tender associations with him because it was borne by a cousin whom he had loved but whom he had lost— to another man! When a man marries off-hand he can't count on anything as certain, except extreme danger. It's like *dying* off-hand and blindly running the chances as to climate in the next world. But to marry thus is just what the man of genius—especially if his nature drives him in straight lines of simple impulse, as Shelley's nature did him—is exceedingly likely to do, and his only protection is to be found in the rule which Bagehot points out: that an essentially ordinary woman is not likely to want him! "Some eccentric men of genius have, indeed," continues Bagehot, "felt in the habitual tact and serene nothingness of ordinary women a kind of trust and calm. They have admired an instinct of the world which they have not—a repose of mind they could not share. But this is commonly in later years. A boy of twenty thinks he knows the world; he is too proud and happy in his own eager shifting thoughts, to wish to contrast them with repose. The commonplaceness of life goads him: placid society irritates him. Bread is an encumbrance; upholstery tedious; he craves excitement; he wishes to reform mankind. You cannot convince him it is right to sew, in a world so full of sorrow and evil."[2] This is obviously a fair description of the state of mind of most 'boys of twenty,' those without genius as well as those with—so they be ever so little awake to intellectual interests. The problem of choosing a life-companion is, therefore, a *serious* one for everybody out of the 'tallow line,' though there's more tragedy in it for the genius than for lesser folk. Perhaps it is fortunate for the race that there are so few geniuses in it. The average man would be monstrously uncomfortable if the wife of his bosom were of this rare make—no less uncomfortable, I take it, than a woman would be at the incomings and outgoings of a husband who was afflicted with the disease of being unlike anybody else she had ever known or heard of, and consequently altogether, hopelessly, unaccountable. The frequent mistakes that are made, by the wrong matching of less extraordinary people, are probably due to the fact that intellectual young men—even more than intellectual young women—see very little of general society; are kept apart until they reach the most susceptible age, and then thrown into associations which ensure their falling in love with the first pretty woman they meet. The boy who from the first is free to live with the other sex and is not taken from them for any long seclusion in school or college cloisters, has much the best chance to make a safe marriage. There *ought not* to be any great difficulty in the choice for anybody, one is inclined to think. Is not *every*one more sensitive to the faults of those whom they love than to the faults of others? Apparently the fault-finding faculties are sharpened rather than dulled by love.

I remember the time, Eileen, when I read Hamerton's chapters on marriage as affecting the intellectual life with great disquietude. I was oppressed by all the possibilities of mistake, somewhat terrified by the impossibility of any provident provision against danger. I knew the strength of my own impulses—the power of love that was in me, the ruling power of my nature—and I realized that mistake was *ruin*, happy choice, salvation. *Everything* depended on the selection I should be allowed to make. Is there any wonder, then, darling, in the fact that I am now so happy? Hasn't a man a *right* to feel happy who knows that his heart's fortune is made! We have been very fortunate, my little queen. We have had unusual opportunities for gaining experience in each other's dispositions, for reading each other's hearts. Everything that has happened since that blessed 16th of September has gone to make it impossible that there should ever be any realization of the sweet, unselfish, puzzling, baffling fear that day urged by the lips I that day kissed. I did *not* know my darling then as I know her now: but my later knowledge of her has proved nothing but that she is what I then thought her. And the little lady who wrote the letter which I received this morning must surely be satisfied with *her* part in the bargain. You wouldn't dare, Miss, to *talk* to me thus, as you write! There's no telling what I wouldn't do. Kisses and caresses would stop the sweet words from coming: I wouldn't for the world stop *them*, they are too precious! and yet how could I keep *from* taking you in my arms and overwhelming you with kisses? Will you try the experiment next time I see you—just to test my self-restraint? I would make almost any sacrifice to hear my shy little sweetheart talk that way—to have her tempt me both with words and with those precious *looks* of love and confidence! It would be worth any number of weeks of this tedious hermit life. My darling! I wonder if you have any conception of the joy your love gives me— of the *gayety* of spirit with which I look forward to the time when you shall be mine, by the law of the land as well as by the law of love!

I am so glad, my darling, that "cousin Hattie" has turned up so delightfully! Give her my love, please. I suppose you saw Ellen Terry and Irving last night?—and of course you'll tell me all about it? With all the love of all my heart,   Your own   Woodrow.

ALS (WC, NjP).
    ¹ Walter Bagehot, "Percy Bysshe Shelley," *Literary Studies* (2 vols., London, 1879), I, 105.
    ² *ibid.*, pp. 105-106.

From Ellen Louise Axson

My darling Woodrow,   New York, Nov. 22/84

I *hope* you will be able to read my note of this morning, though if you can't, it is of no consequence, it wasn't worth reading. I don't think I could have made it out myself—if I had taken time to look over it,—I scribbled in such haste in order to keep my engagement with Cousin Hattie,—and after all I was late; but fortunately she was just as late herself,—was barely ready for me when I did arrive. I have had a delightful day with her; we went shopping &c in the morning, then went back to a late lunch, after which we spent the rest of the day, lying down,—taking a good long comfortable talk. How I wish you knew Cousin Hattie! She is so *lovely*, that she makes everybody love her,—even the clerks in the stores I tell her!—judging from today's experiences. Her sweet, gracious manner does seem to impress and conquer the worst of them. They have just come North for a little frolic; will be here but a few days. Her baby was sick all summer, and she had quite a trying time of it, so now that he is perfectly well, Mr. Ewing made her leave them all with Allie, and come off for change of scene and recreation.

Mr. Shinn called last night while I was out; am sorry I missed him as he has such a long journey over here. He left me the Xmas Harper and another of his quaint notes, in which he expresses *his* regret, and informed me that I am a "blossom-maiden"! &c. &c. &c. Oh, you men! You men! how you do idealize us! It is very lovely in you, I am sure; it "illustrates the sweetest side of"—man's "nature"! but it is unfortunate too, for how can you escape disappointment, when you are brought face to face with the sober realities of every-day life? It seems to me I am very ill-fated in that respect, someone is always saying such absurd things to, or of me,—leaving me with the pleasing reflection that I am an unmitigated fraud. They don't treat everyone so unkindly! Some—Janie for instance, they manage to love for sensible and *true*, not imaginary reasons,—because she is a "real nice girl," "a fine girl," or "a jolly! girl." But it seems that before people can love me, they must first endow me out of the storehouse of their own brains, with the necessary lovable qualities! But after all it is a small matter to me what they please to say or think of me. *They* may call me an angel, or a fairy, or a witch, or a salamander! What care I as long as *you* know and love the *woman*—and I believe you do. If I thought you loved "that maiden in the tale, whom Gwydion made by glamour out of flowers"![1] I should be desperately jealous of her! I want you to love *me*. But all this tirade is'nt aimed at poor Mr. Shinn and his comparatively unoffending little note,—so pray don't tell him; —it is only *suggested* by that, and sundry other recollections.

My darling, I think our friend Mrs. Powell would be somewhat surprised if she knew that two people had been almost *crying* over her little stratagem and its merry conclusion! I think I had some cause for tears. As I think of it again—of your letter I mean, or in short,—of *you*!—my heart is almost too full even now for any thing else,—far too full for words! My dear, dear love!—I said before that I would like to tell you what I thought of you but did not dare, but I think the truer reason is that I *can't*[.] All the words I might use fall so far below my thought that I reject them with utter scorn; they can't even serve my turn for lack of better. I didn't think *any* man could be so perfectly lovely as you, my darling! I shall have a higher opinion of all men for your sake, though I don't believe there was ever such another. How could I think you would care so much for that story. Of course I know that you are interested in what concerns me, that you would be glad to know that I had been promoted—but that you would like such a rigamarole about it! It seemed *very* stupid and silly in me to be telling what "*I* said and *she* said and they said"! After all, perhaps we women do the men we love injustice, while meaning just the contrary, heaven knows! in not judging them more by ourselves. It seems that you are interested in all that concerns me in the same way, and to the same extent, that I am interested in all, great and small, that concerns you. But that isn't what I would have expected because your affairs are of so much more consequence than mine; the latter seem to me,—and how much more ought they to you,—a mere by-play in comparison—hardly worth mentioning. Good night dear heart. With truest love

Your own   Eileen.

ALS (WC, NjP).
¹ From Tennyson's "The Marriage of Geraint."

To Ellen Louise Axson

My own darling,   Balto., Md., Nov. 23/84 *1:10* P.M.

I *thought* that you would be charmed by Ellen Terry's acting. Irving has very great talents; but surely Ellen Terry has genius. He has *made* himself an actor by force of study and of character; she has perfected her voice and carriage for the evident uses of nature. Could anybody but Joe. Jefferson be as natural as she— as perfect a part of the thought of the play? Irving *plays* his part —and plays it often with wonderful power; but she *is* the person of her rôle. *Can* you think while watching her that this is Miss Ellen Terry, the greatest living English actress? Is it not *easy* to keep alive through most of the play, while watching him, the consciousness that this is the famous Henry Irving? There's manifest fortune for the lady in these facts, because, as Portia, she is much more lovely than her much-married self. By-the-way, she doesn't look old enough to have a daughter almost ready to take the stage, does she?

If you "made a day of it" yesterday with "cousin Hattie," my darling, I know that it must have been a very happy day for you. I am *so* glad that you are having this unexpected pleasure. Don't neglect to give her my love.

My friend Hiram (Dr. Woods) had a few friends to tea last evening, and of course I was of the number. Equally of course, I had a good time. The company was constituted of the most congenial elements, and the supper was superfine—what more could be desired? His home is one of the two in Balto. where I feel perfectly at my ease: and of course no social enjoyment is like that which is free and unconstrained. Somehow the artificial requirements of *formality* take all the spirit out of me and make me a bowing machine prolific of conventional speeches—cold compliments and safe, colourless remarks.

Is it your purpose, my little sweetheart, to work altogether in the "head class" hereafter? Who is the artist in charge in that class, and what is the exact nature of the work? You see, my love, I am anxious to follow you as nearly as I can in your studies. I should even like to know, from day to day, if you could think to mention them, the subjects upon which you are engaged. I don't believe that you know, Eileen, what a keen interest I take— or *could* take—in such details. I have the sincerest sympathy with your present studies for various reasons: first and foremost, of course, because they are yours; but scarcely less because I have always had, and been conscious of having, a great store of (potential) enthusiasm for just such occupations and accomplishments. I have never suspected myself of possessing artistic talents, it is needless to say, but I have always known myself capable of entering into the artist's feelings and of understanding his delights. I have always reverenced the power of artistic creation above the power of poetic creation. I suppose that it would be idle for me to hope ever to be an orator if I did *not* have these artistic sympathies. It has been one of the peculiarities—one of the few grave misfortunes—of my life that I have hitherto *known* least of the two things that move me most, poetry and painting. My sensibilities in those directions seem to me like a musical instrument seldom touched, like a harp disused. I tell you all this, my darling, to emphasize the declaration that *everything* you choose to tell me about your work will have a manifold interest for me. I love the artist and I love her work.

Have you never gotten the card board in which to wrap the sketch of yourself you were going to send me, little lady? I have been expecting it anxiously every day; and I am afraid that you will forget to send it. It would be a sore disappointment to me to lose it now!

And do you really enjoy my letters so much, my little queen? If so, it can be for only one reason—because you love me and know that every word I write means that I love you. If my letters have a charm, that must be the secret of it. They come direct from my heart, and come thence without reserve. Since I am thinking all the time as I write how much I love you, I suppose that they must read like one continuous declaration of love, for one who can read with her heart's eyes between the lines which she reads with her lovely brown eyes of sense. How I love those eyes, my darling! What sweet secrets have come to me from their depths! How they fill my waking and haunt my sleeping thoughts! There's no other face in the world so sweet as thine, my Eileen. One loving kiss from your lips, one loving look from your eyes, my beauty, ought to be sufficient earnest of the supreme happiness they promise. Is it necessary, then, to say that the man to whom those eyes have freely given up their secrets, and to whom those lips have been surrendered, is heart and soul

Your own   Woodrow

ALS (WC, NjP).

From Ellen Louise Axson

My darling Woodrow,   New York, Nov. 23/84.

Here is one letter to you lying sealed before me now!—a fact which however shan't prevent my writing as usual tonight. I am so sorry that I failed to get it mailed today, all the more so, because it was unnecessary. I left the house in such haste this morning—having an engagement for church with Cousin Hattie,—that the letter was forgotten, but, I thought, "it will make no difference, for the letters are not collected until afternoon, and I will mail it as soon as I get back from church," but I did'nt get back until night. Cousin Hattie insisted upon my staying with them, and though I hesitated to do so—on account of that letter!—I concluded that I *must*, as my opportunity for being with her was so short.

We went to hear Dr. Taylor, and had a magnificent sermon. His text was one which just suited him,—"Ye are luke-warm,"—and positively the man was like an old Hebrew prophet. I shall never forget it.

How is it that I have heard nothing of Dr. Woodrow's case of late? I am so out of the way that I know nothing, see no papers. I am *so* sorry to hear from Cousin H. of the Synod's action—too bad, too bad![1] They are committing the folly of passing judgment on a matter they don't know anything about. What will Dr. Woodrow be likely to do next?

But it grows late and I must make this note short. If Mr. Ewing isnt imperatively summoned home by business, he is going to stay over until Thursday, and in that case I am to go with them on Wed. night to hear Irving and E. T.! in *Hamlet*. Is'nt that delightful. I love you, darling, I love you more than life; indeed you are become my life and I am in every heart-throb

Your own   Eileen

ALS (WC, NjP).

[1] The Presbyterian Synod of South Carolina, meeting in Greenville, October 22-28, 1884, after listening to many speeches, including one very long one by Dr. James Woodrow himself, and after much parliamentary maneuvering, adopted a resolution reading: "*Resolved*, That in the judgment of this Synod the teaching of Evolution in the Theological Seminary at Columbia, except in a purely expository manner, with no intention of inculcating its truth, is hereby disapproved." The Synod then by rising vote adopted a resolution expressing its confidence in and admiration for Dr. Woodrow. It was, in spite of Ellen's remark, "a complete victory for Dr. Woodrow and the Board of Directors [of the Seminary]," as the Columbia *Southern Presbyterian*, October 30, 1884, said. For reports of the Synod's meeting, see *ibid.*, Oct. 30 and Nov. 6, 1884.

To Ellen Louise Axson

My own darling,   Balto., Md., Nov. 24th, '84 10 A.M.

They must have changed the hour of Sunday collection from the box in which you mail your letters: for another Monday has brought another disappointment to me in the shape of no letter from my darling. I wont be *anxious* this time, as I was last week, but I can't help feeling a little less like working—a little downhearted. This week is to be a sort of holiday week for me, as regards class exercises, and so I have set out upon a steady six-days' reading in English constitutional history. There is to be a Thanksgiving recess of three days (Thursday, Friday, and Saturday) so that Wednesday will contain all the lectures I shall have to attend this week. I could occupy the free field thus afforded me very advantageously in further pursuit of the thoughts of American political economists; but I'm tired of them, and, by way of recreation, have set about hunting down heavier game. I ride no lesser beast than Stubbs[1] in the chase.

This morning's mail *did* bring me a letter from Stockton: and I have enjoyed it hugely. It has the three rare attributes of naturalness, matter, and sense, and makes me all the more eager to perpetuate the correspondence. I am anxious that he should like me as much as I like and admire him.

I hope, my darling, that you did not have such a day of gusts and pelting rain as we had, yesterday: for of course you were with "cousin Hattie." But maybe it wouldn't be a great misfortune to be kept quietly indoors with her:—maybe the rain suited right well with you[r] preferences.

I am looking forward to a rather trying ordeal this evening. The Hopkins Literary Club desire me to be their first critic this year as I was last, in order that they may again start as it were under my auspices! Ahem! quite a compliment to be sure: but one which involves the hardest of all tasks: the task of criticising other men's speaking and adding to that, for yourself, a speech about nothing in particular, which must, nevertheless, *seem* to be about something. Such work needs a special inspiration such as one can't expect to have more than once or twice in a life-time—such, consequently, as I do not expect to be vouchsafed to-night.

What a delight it is, my darling, to be able to turn thus, if only for a few moments, from Stubbs to you! What a supreme delight it will be when I shall *really* have you to turn to from my books! Will you be very kind to me when I am tired, and ready to laugh at me when I am cross? What questions to ask of my matchless little sweetheart! I will cure them by saying, *I love you* and am forever   Your own   Woodrow.

ALS (WC, NjP).
    1 Wilson was referring either to William Stubbs's *English Constitutional History* (3 vols., Oxford, 1883), or to his *Select Charters* . . . (4th edn., Oxford, 1881), or to both. Copies of both works are in the Wilson Library, DLC.

From Ellen Louise Axson

My darling Woodrow,   New York   Nov 24/84.
    Your two delightful letters reached me this morning and have been filling my head, *and* heart all day; many thanks for both. Many thanks also for the very interesting and suggestive passages from Bagehot. I would like to read the essay on Shelley, both to obtain in full his very sensible views on "the intellectual marriage," and also to see what he has to say in defence of Shelley for it would seem to be to some extent an apology for him. What a very keen observer he—Bagehot—is! And what a very fortunate thing it is for the world that it *is* so largely regulated by the law he points out; a most natural law too,—for everybody knows that "birds of a feather flock together"; and the rarer sort, of which there are not enough to make "flocks," dwell apart—to themselves. It is a cheering reflection, from one point of view, for it shows that the poor helpless men of genius are not *utterly* unprotected, after all. Yet it is, for me, a very uncomfortable reflection too, if it be absolutely essential to the happiness of an extraordinary man that his choice should be an extraordinary woman; but I won't tease you with such talk now, when it will do no good;— and after all I am not quite as "ordinary" as the type Mr. Bagehot describes, for she, it seems, is too essentially commonplace even

to *appreciate* or understand anything above the average—I can and *do love* you, my darling, beyond the common.

"And love, mere love, is beautiful indeed—
And worthy of acceptation[.] Fire is bright,
Let temple burn or flax. An equal light
Leaps in the flame from cedar-plank or weed.
And love is fire . . .
And what I *feel* across the inferior features
Of what I *am* doth flash itself, and show
How that great work of Love exhances [enhances] Nature's"[1]

I have been trying all day in vain, to recall what I wrote in my letter of Thursday night which I would'nt *dare say* to you. I have no idea what it could be; I can't be expected to remember my scribblings so long as that. I remember reading long ago what professed to be a thoroughly true and tried receipt for writing "a perfect love-letter"! It was "to begin without knowing what you mean to say, and finish without knowing what you *have* said[.]" So far as that rule goes, mine are all right. But—to return a moment to the subject, I won't be "dared" in that fashion, sir,—when you come, if you can tell me what the words are—perhaps I might be able to repeat them after you!

Mr. Ewing—or Cousin Robert I should say, according to orders—charged me with a message for you, dear, which I proceed to deliver for what it is worth. He wants you, or your influential friends, or both, to write to Col. Henry Preston Johns[t]on,—a son of Albert Sidney—president of the University in New Orleans. It seems that somebody,—Mr. Toulane,[2] I think,—has left a large fortune for the purpose of improving and enlarging that college in any way its managers think best. Mr. Ewing says that this Mr. Johnson, who controls everything, was his professor at the "Washington and Lee," and that he puts a very high value upon the science of political economy,—takes an especially keen and deep interest in it himself. So Mr. Ewing thinks that if someone suggested to him the propriety of establishing a chair of political economy and then put him on the track of a brilliant young professor to fill it, he would be properly grateful for the wise and timely advice, and would act upon it immediately! How does the idea strike you? Cousin Hattie and Mr. E. feel a very great interest in you, darling. Cousin H. is still harping on her last summer's idea,—"oh! if he could *only* come to the Vanderbilt [University]!" "I would give *anything* to get him there[.]" "Yes" says Mr. E. "so would I,["]—"or at least," he adds, laughing, "I would give five hundred dollars in a minute, and all my influence." There is no such chair in that University either.

I meant to answer your questions about my work, my teacher, &c. but I have left myself no time tonight, so all that must wait. I can well believe, dear, that you have a store of potential! enthusiasm for such things;—moreover *I have* long suspected you "of possessing artistic talents," a suspicion which was confirmed by your mother's statements. I only wish for your sake—and also for my own, that I had half as much for music.

I love you, darling, with all my heart. Both my eyes and my heart have given up, not only their secrets, but *themselves*, I am freely and altogether your own   Eileen

ALS (WC, NjP).

¹ From the tenth of E. B. Browning's *Sonnets from the Portuguese.*

² Paul Tulane, merchant and philanthropist, born near Princeton, N.J., May 10, 1801. He established a retail and wholesale trade in dry goods and clothing in New Orleans and New York. Acquired a large fortune and, after living fifty-one years in New Orleans, retired to Princeton. In 1882 he made the first of several substantial gifts to the University of Louisiana, a state institution in New Orleans. It became the independent Tulane University of Louisiana in 1884. Tulane's gifts to the university totaled more than a million dollars before his death in Princeton on March 27, 1887.

From Janet Woodrow Wilson

My precious Son,   Wilmington N.C. Monday [c. Nov. 24, 1884]

We have gotten the papers signed &c at last—and I have addressed the "warranty deed" to Mr Dorsey, as you directed—and enclose you the quit claim—also as you desired. You are very sweet not to complain of my remissness in writing. You know that it [is] not for want of *love* for you. . . .

By the way, I want to ask you what you wish done with *your* furniture & books? I want to get Josie to help me to pack your books, when he comes home. Dont fail to tell me about this in your next, please dear. I will write again this week and tell you all about our plans as far as we have been able to make them. And I am *very anxious* to hear about *your* possible plans. O that we could live together. I cant help hoping that it may be in the future. You have said nothing about dear Ellie in your last two letters. Is she still satisfied with her quarters? and does she keep quite well? I wish she could find time to write me a wee note, at least! Give her warmest love from us both. I am so glad you are hearing from each other every day—it is such a comfort to you both—and to me to know of it.

Josie may be home next week. It will be very hard to let him go away again! But I know it is the best thing for him. Will you run over to see Ellie on Christmas? How nice it is to be so near her!

Good bye for a few days. My next will be less hastily written I hope. Papa joins me in love inexpressible for our darling boy. Wonder if you realize how dear you are to us!

Lovingly yours   Mother

ALS (WP, DLC) with WWhw notation on verso of letter: "Ans 11/30/84."

From Melville R. Hopewell

Dear Sir—   Tekamah, Neb., Nov. 24   1884

Note of Chas A Jack Pr— int from Aug 10, 81 to Nov. 10, 84—	$300.
3 yrs. & 3 m @ 8%	78
	$378.
Paid & Remitted	200
Bal	$178.
Int. 1/3 m—	.40
Recording Release of mtg. retd	1.
	$179.40.
Charges—	3.00
Draft inclosed less Exchange—	$176.40

It is customary for the parties holding a mortgage to pay for the Release, but strictly speaking, he is not obliged to do so. Hence I refund the 1.00

Truly &c   M. R. Hopewell

ALS (WP, DLC) with WWhw notation on env.: "Ans Nov 27/84. *Draft sent to Wilmington.*"

To Ellen Louise Axson

My own darling,   Balto., Md., Nov. 25th/84 9:30 A.M.

I have just received you[r] two sweet letters of Saturday and Sunday. Pray, Miss, if "all that tirade" about the misjudgments of men concerning women was *not* aimed either at me or at "poor Mr. Shinn," who *was* the immediate object? Something stronger and nearer than mere recollections, and the suggestions of Mr. Shinn's note, must have been the moving cause of two such warmly worded pages! But maybe this is inquiring into those things which you have more than once declared to be none of my business!—what other men have said of and to you. That is the only direct wound you have ever inflicted upon me, my darling!

Yes, my precious, you are right: it *is you* that I love, you the woman—the woman who can give her whole heart to me and whom I can love in a way that will satisfy the utmost longings of that heart, whom I can cherish and serve with all of my nature that is best and purest! I couldn't love an angel or a fairy: but I have *enthroned* the woman I love. She seems to me—nay, I know that she is—the sweetest, loveliest, most lovable of her sex—the only one who *could* be my queen, mistress of my complete homage; and you must know by this time, my darling, that I could not say more, were the language a thousand times as rich as it is in words of love, or a hundred-fold more at my command! It is because you *are*, not an angel, but a woman—just the woman that you are—that you have won me and now have my fortunes in your hands.

Well, I made my speech last night, and my auditors actually seemed delighted. I could not have been more flatteringly listened to or more heartily applauded. This does not argue much for the taste of the Hopkins Literary Society. It is, indeed, only another way of saying that its members are young and haven't heard many speeches from men who enjoy speaking as an intellectual exercise. That's the secret, undoubtedly, of what little success I have had as a speaker. I enjoy it (speaking) because it sets my mind—all my faculties—aglow: and I suppose that this very excitement gives my manner an appearance of confidence and self-command which arrests the attention. However that may be, I *feel* a sort of transformation—and it's hard to go to sleep afterwards.

I am still hard at work on Stubbs, but none the less in good health and fair spirits.

Ah, my darling, what would the world be without you and your sweet love! I am sure that I shouldn't care to live if you didn't love me and want me to be   Your own   Woodrow.

ALS (WC, NjP).

From Ellen Louise Axson

My darling Woodrow,   New York, Nov. 25/84
I have surely struck a streak of luck at present! Who do you think is coming to New York now? Uncle Tom and Aunt Sallie![1]

He will be here tomorrow, to remain two or three days perhaps[.] And it will keep Cousin Hattie a little longer too, since she meant to stop over there a day or so, but will now spend them with Uncle Tom here instead. I am just back from the St. James; I resisted all temptation yesterday, and remained resolutely at the League all day,—in fact, since I had to get seats in *two* classes in the morning, and attend the pe[r]spective lecture in the afternoon it was absolutely necessary. But this afternoon I played truant, and we all three went up to the Metropolitan to see the Watts collection; and afterwards I dined with them, so I have had a lovely afternoon and evening.

Our school is closed too on Thursday, much to my satisfaction, for of course as both Uncle Tom and Hattie will be here, an opportunity for shirking work with a clear conscience will be welcome. Am glad *you* are to have so long a recess, though you don't seem inclined to spend it in a very gay and festive fashion. Is this excursion into English constitutional fields a part of your University work proper; or is it made with reference to some of your own private projects? I mean, have you any special object in view in this *special* reading? How are things going at the University now? Any more satisfactorily than before? Is Dr. Adams fulfilling the promise he seemed to hold forth of better work on his own part? What would I not have given to hear you speak last night! to see you pose as "professor of things in general" and "nothing in particular"! You must be sure to tell me all about it,—what you *did* talk about and what other people said of it. On this point, you see, I have more respect for other people's opinions than for yours.

Ah love, how I wish you could turn in very truth from "Stubbs" to me for a few moments, that I could look even for *so* long into the beautiful eyes that *I* love; I would promise almost anything for that. Even without that I will with great cheerfulness make the promise for which this letter asks. There are three simple words which include all such promises,—do they not, darling? I love you,—and I would do anything to make you happy.

With all my heart,   Your own   Eileen

ALS (WC, NjP).

[1] The Rev. Thomas A. Hoyt and his second wife, Sadie (or Sallie) Cooper Hoyt.

From Houghton, Mifflin & Company[1]

Dear Sir: Boston, Nov. 26th, 1884.

Our examination of the manuscript of your work on Congressional Government, which you have recently sent us, has confirmed the favorable opinion which we formed of the first chapters some months ago, and we shall take pleasure in publishing the book at our own risk, and paying you the usual royalty of 10 per cent on the retail price of all copies sold. If this will be agreeable and satisfactory to you, we will at once draw up and forward the contracts for publication to you, and place the work in the printers' hands. We estimate that it will make a volume of about 350 pages similar to the volumes in our American Statesmen Series.

Yours truly,
Houghton, Mifflin, & Co.

WWhw copy (WP, DLC) in env. from Houghton Mifflin with WWhw notation:
"Ans. Nov. 28/84."
  [1] WW kept this copy for his files. He sent a WWT copy to ELA on November 28, 1884. Perhaps he sent the original to his parents.

From Ellen Louise Axson

My darling Woodrow,   New York Nov. 26/84

Of course I could not write last night, as I did not get back from the theatre until quarter of twelve, so I must write a hurried line this morning and try and do better tonight. I had a *glorious* time!—"you have been there yourself" so I need not explain. I didn't like Irving's Hamlet *at all,* at first, but it seemed to grow better as the play advanced,—perhaps we grew more accustomed to his peculiarities,—two or three of the scenes were *magnificent*! And the Ophelia was *exquisite* beyond description. What do you think! as if the play scene was not thrilling enough of itself, they took the pains to supplement it with an accidental excitement! As the king and the court rushed off the stage one of the soldiers dropped his torch very near some of the curtains, and then went off leaving it there! Of course, the curtain blazed up, and then such screaming as there was in the audience, a few hundreds rushed for the doors, and it seemed for a moment as if a panic was inevitable. But they smothered the fire immediately, and the simpletons came back, looking very much ashamed of themselves. You should have heard Cousin Hattie, in her excitement, crying to the people—"keep your seats! keep your seats!" I could do nothing but sit and laugh at her—and them.

I told you I believe that Uncle Tom was coming yesterday. As I came rushing home from the sketch class (it is perfectly dark now at half past five, and I almost *fly*—think I make the distance in a minute and a half!) I saw on our dark street a great figure looming up in the distance & I knew at once that it must be him, no one else is so tall. He had come, for the second time, to take me up with him to dinner. So we had quite a family party; and of course I spend today with them too. I wish you knew Uncle Tom, he is just "too lovely for anything." But I am spending too much time in writing. I am so glad, dear, that your speech was such a success,—but it was just as I expected. Oh dear I am perfectly *wild* to hear you speak! I'd rather hear you than Booth! Excuse haste—I love you darling with all my heart and am always and altogether　　　　　Your own　Eileen

ALS (WC, NjP).

Two Letters to Ellen Louise Axson

My own darling,　　　　Balto., Md., Nov. 26th/84 *11:15* A.M.

So you wont take my dare, and want to know what it is that you are challenged to repeat to my face? I think that I can recall to your mind a certain description of a cozy room with a new-made fire in it—seeming sweet and homelike to you because of "its associations with *you*"—and a certain attempt to tell me *how* I was always with my darling! Do you remember writing some such passages? and do you think that you will risk the consequences of *talking* to me that way when we are together next? I don't think, my darling, that you can have any conception of the delight I experience when you declare your love without restraint, letting me into the mood of the moment at which you write. Where you are, Eileen, is my home; and ought it not to delight me to know that your heart finds its home with me. I have a very distinct conviction, my love, about our intercourse with each other: I have not from the very beginning of our engagement urged you to make repeated confession of your love simply because of the supreme joy I derive from such confessions, in whatever form they come, but because I believe that our happiness depends upon a thorough knowledge of each other's ways of thought and of feeling. Mr. Tedcastle never talked more thorough nonsense, in my opinion, than when he announced the conclusion that his marriage with Miss Beville had been quite safe—quite assured of a happy issue—because he had watched and studied her for some years before proposing to her. That's a good way to get a *friend,* or a housekeeper—but it's not infallible for getting a good wife—unless one be a Dutchman who seeks in a wife only a housekeeper and cook with whom life will be tolerable. You can discover the disposition in that way, but not the *wifely heart.* That is discoverable only by the interchange of love and by the freest interchange of the most sacred confidences. Miss Beville, you know, for all the long intercourse that came before, discovered her love only after she became Mrs. Tedcastle: and your dear friend Mrs. Killough had an exactly similar experience. Some poor women make an exactly opposite discovery—not to speak of some poor men. The secret seems to me an open one. Every woman who holds her accepted lover at arm's-length—compelling him to be satisfied with a mere *promise* of complete surrender—runs this risk and constrains her lover to run it. What did Mr. Beckwith know of Miss Fairbanks? The whole of her heart, all of her true nature, her true self, remains for his future discovery. There are young ladies who admit the men to whom they are engaged to no closer relations than those of a confidential friend. They repel every caress, and if they kiss at all, kiss only with cold lips. Such women are courting a terrible danger. The period of engagement is the only period at which lovers can find out their fitness for each other: and, *therefore,* I think, apart from all the natural inclination and impulse of love, that during such a period they ought as far as possible to live together in the *spiritual* union of husband and wife. Of course, my darling, it goes without the saying that I didn't think of any of these things when I was courting you. I didn't seek your promise in order to satisfy myself afterwards that you were the woman I wanted. The thing sounds monstrous even in the denial! What I did I did simply because I couldn't help it. It was an imperative heart-instinct that brought me to your feet. But, my love, our intercourse since then has furnished the *proof* that we did not mistake our hearts—that we *had* found our true destiny. Could ten years of close *friendship* have revealed us to each other as these fourteen months have done? You have confided in me, and I in you, as we will confide in each other when we are married. There remain no essential discoveries to be made then. We shall love each other better and better—if that be possible—but for the same reasons. Ah, my darling do you wonder that I delight so in your free confidences, when each one of them contains a reflection of the woman I love—when each one of them proves you to be the woman my heart discovered and shall ever cling to—the woman I have lived to meet and to marry, that I might, after that live to make her happy? I shall live to find new ways of making love to you! Are you agreed?

There's one passage in this morning's letter, my darling, that I want to answer. It expresses a regret which I've often seen in your mind—and as often wished to drive away—the regret that you don't share my tastes for *music*. My little queen—I don't say it for your sake only, but because it's the *truth*—that lack will not *at all* affect the joy of our home life. I have weighed that question and count that loss as nothing compared with the gain of having *you* as you are for my own loving, gentle, helpful wife. With a heart overflowing with love,   Your own   Woodrow

Balto., Md., Nov. 27, 1884   10:20 A.M.

Yes, my darling, you certainly *are* in luck! and I am so glad. It makes me *very* happy to know that you are having such a delightful time with those who are so dear to you. How queer it seems that my precious little sweetheart, who is so near and dear to me, who seems always to have belonged to me, should have relatives whom I don't even know! By-the-way, little lady, would you like to be a near neighbor of "uncle Tom's"? An interesting experience I had yesterday suggests the question. Just before lecture,[1] Dr. Adams came to me and asked me if I wouldn't come into his office a moment and "meet some persons who were interested in me and in historical work." I went; and was introduced to Miss Carey Thomas[2] and Dr. Rhodes.[3] Miss Thomas is a daughter of one of the Hopkins trustees, is a graduate (a Ph.D.), I understand, of a German University, and is head, or "Dean," of the faculty of Bryn Mawr College, of which Dr. Rhodes, a prominent "*Friend*" of Philadelphia, is a trustee. You never heard of Bryn Mawr College? Well, neither did I until a very few weeks ago. The fact is that Bryn Mawr College has not been started yet. A wealthy "Friend" of Phila., recently deceased, left $800,000 for the establishment of an institution for the higher education of women, to be conducted under the auspices of the Society of Friends—or at least under the direction of certain members of that Society whom he named as executors and trustees—but to be non-denominational in its teachings and government. Being forbidden to use anything but the interest of the bequest, the trustees have been using the income which has accrued since the founder's death in the erection of the necessary buildings at Bryn Mawr near Philadelphia. But they have also been gradually getting a faculty together and perfecting their organization with a view to opening the college next Autumn. They are of course choosing their teachers with great care because each teacher chosen will, of course, have to lay the foundations of his, or her, department—will have to *organize* it, and give it direction and plan. You understand, then, the object of the introduction in Dr. Adams's office. Bryn Mawr is to have a department of history and the Dean and trustees are in search of some one fit to organize it. My lecture was about to begin, so Miss Thomas simply invited me to lunch at two o'clock in order that Dr. Rhodes might have an opportunity to talk with me. Miss T. was not at lunch herself, but I had a really delightful talk with Dr. R. He is every inch an "Orthodox Friend," and I was "Thee'd" at a great rate: but he is a genuine, earnest, intelligent man, and I enjoyed talking with him, notwithstanding the novel nature of the interview. The Doctor's object was, not so much to discover what I knew as to get a key to my character and an insight into my views on certain points which he considered vital. He was glad to find that I believed that the hand of Providence was in all history; that the progress of Christianity was as great a factor as the development of philosophy and the sciences; and that wars were to be justified only by necessity: and he was careful to ascertain my views as to personal religion. What will come of the interview I can't tell. He gave me his address, asked me to think over what he had said as to the kind of position offered and to write to him within two or three days, accompanying my letter with a statement of the courses of study I have pursued, &c. In the meantime, he supposed, Miss Thomas would want to talk with me and would want to have me meet Mr. Francis King, another of the trustees. There are several things that would make a position at Bryn Mawr very advantageous for a youngster who wants to gain a reputation and make his work tell as soon as possible. To work there would be to work under the eyes of the Hopkins. Miss Thomas is a daughter of one of our most influential trustees, Dr. Jas. Carey Thomas, and Mr. Francis King is a trustee of the University as well as of Bryn Mawr.[4] Indeed the University is very largely under the control of the same "Friends" to whom the government of the college is entrusted. And, aside from that, these "Friends" are amongst the wealthiest and best families of both Baltimore and Philadelphia. Reputation made under their auspices would be reputation *well-placed*, so to speak. At any rate to serve them would be to serve enlightened masters. I don't know what chances there may be for my election: but I should certainly accept any offer from them that included salary enough for us to live on. Before the negotiations go any further, tell me what you think, my darling. I have told you all the essential facts that I know myself— so *please* don't plead insufficient information, but write as my Eileen, my pledged wife. Should I meet Miss Thomas again, I will give you my impressions of her. I know now only that she seems altogether attractive. Altogether, it was a queer experience, wasn't it?

I am ever so much obliged to Mr. Ewing, my pet, for his interest in my fortunes—all the more because that interest really means devotion to *you*. The Mr. Tulane who made the gift to the University at New Orleans was a Princeton man—a *resident* of Princeton, I mean—as eccentric a hermit as ever puzzled his neighbors, and I knew of this disposition of his money; but I did not know who was in authority at New Orleans or what plans the money was to be used to promote. Mr. Ewing's suggestion is very valuable, as well as very kind, and I shall see what useful friends father may be able to find in New Orleans who would be likely to exert themselves in my behalf.

I *think*, my love, that I can safely agree to the proposition that you are "not quite as ordinary as the type Mr. Bagehot describes"! Oh, you dear, delightful, incorrigible little goose! Why *will* you persist in making me out an "extraorindary [*sic*] man"? If you *wont* be convinced, I think that I can point out a way to comfort yourself by disproving your own inferiority. Since it is evident that you overestimate my abilities—it is at least demonstrable that you quite *appreciate* me. But no ordinary woman *can* appreciate an extraordinary man. Therefore you must be quite as extraordinary as I am! Q.E.D. Besides, my precious little sweetheart, there's no surer proof of the entire fitness of a woman for the man to whom she gives herself than that her love *satisfies* him. It's not the quantity alone, but quite as much the *quality* of love that makes it *sufficient* for the needs of the natures on which it is bestowed: and if your love is of the *kind* I want, then are you mine indeed, my darling, and we were meant to make each other happy. And you yourself will admit—wont you, little queen?— that your love for me *is* of that kind. *I* know that it is: because I know that it satisfies even my great, overmastering, tender love for you. What more complete demonstration could there be? May I say, darling, that we are already, in heart, man and wife? Does my Eileen feel *identified* with me? If she does—and I believe she does—she ought to put away these misgivings. Oh my darling, my darling! How shall I ever prove my love for you!

What a brilliant discoverer you are, Miss! One's mother and

one's sweetheart combine to testify that he possesses "artistic talents"! What better proof could there be? I believe that I *do* love art better than you love music, my little bewitcher,—indeed I know that it has great fascination for me—but you need not fear that you[r] husband will be your rival with the pencil!

I love you, darling, with all my heart.

Your own   Woodrow

Stubbs is in the regular Univ. course, my darling, and is not connected with my private work.

ALS (WC, NjP).

  [1] In Professor Adams's course on the history of politics. Adams lectured on November 26, 1884, on Aristotle, Cicero, and Augustine. See the WWsh notes for that date in the first classroom notebook described at Oct. 8, 1884.

  [2] Martha Carey Thomas, born Baltimore, Jan. 2, 1857. Attended Howland Institute near Ithaca, N.Y. A.B., Cornell University, 1877; studied at The Johns Hopkins University, 1877-79; Ph.D., University of Zurich, 1882. Appointed Dean and Professor of English Literature at Bryn Mawr College, 1883, and did much of the work of gathering a faculty before the opening of the college in 1885. Second President of Bryn Mawr College, 1894-1922. Died Dec. 2, 1935.

  [3] James E. Rhoads, born Marple, Delaware County, Pa., Jan. 21, 1828. M.D., University of Pennsylvania, 1851. Gave up medical practice after suffering stroke in 1862 and thereafter devoted himself to philanthropic and educational work. Worked with freedmen in the South after the Civil War and, as secretary of the executive committee on Indian affairs of the Society of Friends, was concerned with missionary and educational work on Indian reservations. Edited *Friends' Review*, 1876-84. Named one of the original trustees of Bryn Mawr College by its founder, Dr. Joseph Taylor. Named first President of Bryn Mawr in 1883 and served until 1894. Died Jan. 2, 1895.

  [4] He was, actually, chairman of the Board of Trustees of Bryn Mawr College.

From Ellen Louise Axson

My darling Woodrow,   New York, Nov. 28/84

  If you find my notes, for the last day or so, unsatisfactory, you have yourself to blame for it, Sir! You it was who gave me orders not to sit up late to write them! and of course if I write in the morning I am hurried, for I *ought* not to steal much from the precious morning hours in the head class. The "pose" is from nine to twelve, so that at this very time—so late am I this morning,—the model is "placed," and the golden moments are slipping away. I had a delightful day yesterday, with my friends. We went to the Metropolitan Museum and several other places—had a *very* thanksgiving dinner, and then a nice long cosy evening together. They all leave today, much to my regret, though it is better for my work! Uncle Tom is very anxious for me to spend the Xmas holidays with him, and I think perhaps I will. But I *must* not be tempted into writing a letter; hope to do better tonight

  With a heart full of love, believe me, my darling, as ever

Your own   Eileen

ALS (WC, NjP).

To Ellen Louise Axson

My own darling,   Balto., Md., Nov. 28th '84   12:15 P.M.

As you will see by the enclosed letter from the publishers, I have some exceptionally good news this morning for my Eileen, and I know that she will be as happy as I am about it. They have actually offered me as good terms as if I were already a well-known writer! The success is of such proportions as almost to take my breath away—it has distanced my biggest hopes. The letter came this morning with yours, my pet. The enclosed is a copy, so you need not take the trouble to return it. There is not much doubt about the terms being "agreeable and satisfactory" to me, as I shall let them know at once

But, little lady, I have a secret for you: I should rather, a hundredfold rather, have the love contained in the *other* letter that came this morning than have my writings *competed* for by all the publishers in the country! It is that love—*your* love, my precious little sweetheart—that makes this first success sweet; because you may share it and you will be glad! *That* is what makes me happy!

I have a favour to ask of you, my darling, and that is that you will write to dear mother—and to sister Marion. If you can't find time otherwise, I will give up two days for them—provided only that you don't take two *consecutive* days. It would gratify dear mother so much if you would write *her* a love letter, as her daughter. She loves you, my pet, very much, asks about you in every letter, and is always sending messages of love to "dear Ellie."[1] You may be able to guess how much I have set my heart upon your writing, when I am willing to forego two of the letters which are so precious to me!

Do you *really* want to know what I talked about to the Literary Society, my pet? Why, I talked, first of all about the debate, of which I was critic, and then about *oratory*, its aims and the difficulties surrounding its cultivation in a University, where exact knowledge overcrows everything else and the art of persuasion is neglected on principle—just a corollary, you see, from what I was writing to you about the other day. Oratory must be full of the spirit of the world: that spirit is excluded from University life. I doubt whether I could recall much of what I *said*; but that was the subject.

Dr. Adams is very anxious to have me go to Bryn Mawr; and I shall write the best letter I can to Dr. Rhodes to-day or to-morrow.

I love you, darling, more than life: my sweetest hope is to make you happy!   Your own   Woodrow.

ALS (WC, NjP). Enc.: WWT copy of Houghton, Mifflin & Co. to WW, Nov. 26, 1884.
    [1] e.g., JWW to WW, Nov. 24, 1884.

From Ellen Louise Axson

My darling Woodrow,   New York, Nov. 28/84

I have just been having some interesting conversation with my Quaker friend below stairs, Mrs. Wright, of Phil. I was anxious—owing to my deep interest in the higher education of women!—to learn something of Bryn Mawr and the new college there! So she has been telling me all about it,—about the beautiful village and buildings, and the wonderful "Dean" Miss *Martha*! Carey Thomas, whom she knows very well indeed.

This is a most interesting letter of yours, dear, and has certainly given me a good deal to think about today. It looks very much as though you were going to have the *opportunity* of deciding for or against Bryn Mawr. There would seem to be many things in it's favour. It's connection with the Johns Hopkins, it's situation, the character of it's trustees and supporters—and Mr. Rhodes— seem all to be delightful. And perhaps the greatest circumstance in it's favour to my mind lies in the fact that you would be the *first* professor,—that you would enter on the work untrammelled by precedent. It would give you more opportunity to do as you please,—to carry out your own views. The work of organizing[,] while, I should think, more difficult, than the mere carrying on of another's plans, must be also much more interesting and inspiring. I should imagine, too, that it would be a more important work—one involving greater responsibility,—and therefore one which would gain a higher reputation for him who did it well. *But* do you think there *is* much reputation, to be made in a *girls school*—or an it please you, a "woman's college"? Can you be content to serve in that sort of a institution? That is the *only* objection to the plan in my mind, but I must confess it seems to me a very serious one. Can you bring yourself to feel thoroughly in sympathy with that kind of thing,—with the *tendencies* and *influences* of such an institution? Can you, with all your heart, cooperate with the strong-minded person who controls it? The "*Dean*"! how ridiculous! If they are going to have "prudes for proctors, dowagers for deans" it would be more consistent to follow Tennyson's scheme[1] to the bitter end and exclude men altogether

—on penalty of death! Seriously, dear, I fear you would find it very unpleasant to serve, as it were, under a *woman*! it seems so unnatural, so jarring to one's sense of the fitness of things— so absurd too. I may be very silly to say so, but it seems to me that it is rather beneath *you* to teach in a "female college";—that last is a "vile phrase," but it suits me—at present! However as you perceive, I am merely telling you how I *feel* in the matter; these are not matured, deliberate settled *convictions* on my part. If you are *sure*, after careful reflection, that it is the best thing for you to do,—if *you* are *entirely* satisfied and pleased with the prospect, you need not fear but that *I* will be equally pleased and satisfied. I am only anxious, my darling, that your impatience for a position of some sort may not lead you to decide hastily in fa- vour of a disagreeable one.

I enclose an article about Ed Brown[2] in which your [you] may be interested because *I* am—very deeply. You know I told you he was running for solicitor. It seems to have been a great triumph for Ed. The boy is very clever;—without having anything really remarkable about his mind,—that *I* have discovered. I have never heard him speak,—he has just the right combination of qualities to ensure success, of the conspicuous kind.

I will also try tomorrow to send that sketch. I have not sent it before because I really did not know how to get it mailed, as it would not go in the box and the office was *so* inaccessible. But I have now interviewed Thomas at the League, and he says he will mail it for me. And by the way I did Mr. Harwood great in- justice, when having merely glanced at it, that first night, I said it was a poor sketch. It is a *very* good sketch when looked at from the proper distance. Being in charcoal, it of course has'nt the del- icacy of a pencil sketch, but it is much more satisfactory because of it's richness of tone. Mr. H. is one of the advanced pupils, in the life class, and he succeeds in getting the general character of his model, and the pose—the attitude—better than almost any. As usual I have reached my limit with dozen of things of the *utmost* importance! still unsaid. And now I have only room to say that I love you darling more—infinitely more—than life and I am in every heart-beat   Your own   Eileen.

ALS (WC, NjP).
    1 ELA is quoting from the Prologue of Tennyson's *Princess* (1847), of which a new illustrated edition, which appeared in 1884, may have caught her eye.
    2 Her cousin, Edward T. Brown. The enclosure is missing.

To Ellen Louise Axson

My own darling,   Balto., Md., Nov. 29, 1884   9:50 A.M.

I have written my letter to Dr. Rhoads; and now it remains to be seen whether or not they will invite me to join the gathering faculty of Bryn Mawr.

I am sorry, my pet, that you had your friends with you so short a time. It was delightful to think of your having such a happy time with them. Your work could afford to stand still for a little while under the circumstances. And you are going to spend the Christmas holidays with "uncle Tom"? That will be a delightful arrangement for you, darling, and I am glad for your sake that it is to be so.

My Thanksgiving "vacation" has been a week of about the hardest work I've done in a twelvemonth. Steady reading always demands of me more expenditure of resolution and dogged energy than any other sort of work: and it, consequently, tells upon me sooner. But hard work is more of a necessity with me at such a season as this than at any other time: because it is the only effectual defence against desperate loneliness. My *inclination* would be to spend this, as all other holidays, in "a *very* gay and festive fashion"; but the festivities of Thanksgiving are *family* festivities and a chap who is away from his family is of course shut out—as I believe I observed a year ago.

Yes, my love, things at the University continue to go at a considerably better pace than last year and Dr. Adams has come out in a decidedly better light; but signs of a collapse are not wanting, and I am afraid that, so soon as lecture material gives out, we shall return to the old hodge-podge system of last "semester." Still, there wont be the element of bitter disappointment that there was then, and I can take whatever comes with comparatively undisturbed equanimity.

Life here is full of mild surprises such as the one represented by the enclosed notice. Why this season should be chosen and why the Biological Laboratory should be fixed upon as the place for such a reception is, and must I suppose remain, a mystery. But the graduate students will doubtless attend, to see what's up. These receptions are delightfully, elaborately dull affairs; but courtesy constrains us to go to them, and make at least a show of enjoyment.

I feel a little tired and low-spirited this morning; but I am quite well, and I can't stay long in the blues when that is the case.

The one thing that never changes with me, darling, is my love for you.   Your own   Woodrow.

ALS (WC, NjP). Enc.: printed invitation to a reception for graduate students from the trustees of The Johns Hopkins University.

From Ellen Louise Axson

New York, Nov. 29/84.

This is indeed exceptionally good news my darling that your letter of today brings me! Hurrah! hurrah! and once again hurrah! I have been—metaphorically—crying "hurrah" all day,—have been literally "so happy I didnt know what to do." If the letter had only come one day sooner!—then I could have announced it to a whole tribe of relations, and in so doing found a vent—a saftyvalve—for my pent-up feelings of excitement and delight. I can't tell you, dear, how glad I am, or how proud I am of you. Was there ever a more complete success! What of all that talk we have been hearing all our lives, about the weary struggles of young authors, however gifted, to obtain their proper recognition? If *this* is a specimen, you won't find the life of an author such a thorny path as some of it's followers would have one believe. Your first book accepted by the first publisher applied to,—the best in the country;—and such splendid terms offered! It is too lovely for anything. I don't believe any young man in America ever had such a brilliant triumph. How proud and happy your dear father and mother will be! I should like to have seen her when she heard the news. If you are not specially anxious to do so, don't write to Mr. Shinn about it. He is coming here the first of the week and I want the fun of telling him. It would be a great relief to my feelings to tell *somebody*! I was actually tempted to tell Mr Goodrich, the Houghton and Mifflin man, but didn't of course, fearing it would for some reason be indiscreet. *Dear* Houghton and Mifflin! how I *love* them!

After all, such treatment being just what you deserve, is only what might have been expected, just what I should have *fully* expected, if I had not heard it so often repeated that, "the publishing business, like all others, is merely a matter of dollars and cents"; and that "books of that order are not a paying investment, the public they address being, comparatively, small"! You must tell me what your father and mother say on the subject. Did you send your dedication with the Mss?[1] That is going to be one of the nicest things about it all.

I am an [sic] truly ashamed, dear, that you should have occasion to request me to write to your mother;—has she been saying anything about my not writing? I believe I have meant to write every night almost since I came to New York;—but every night some spell seems laid upon me which prevents my doing *any-thing*, worth while. I never put the evenings to so little account in my life. Regularly as I come up from dinner I think "I am surely going to do it this time,—but I am *so* tired I absolutely *must* lie on this lounge and rest a little, first"—and then before I know it, I am fast asleep from sheer fatigue and there's an end on't. Everybody is angry with me for not writing,—everybody except dear Auntie [Louisa Brown], kindest and most sensible of women; she says, "I don't expect to hear from you this busy winter;—to satisfy the claims of Grandparents, brothers, and *lover*! is is [*sic*] as much as you will have time for;—uncles, aunts, and friends must be patient and wait." I positively *will* write to your mother tomorrow, come what may. And now good-night, dearest, I love you more than tongue can tell, and I am more proud of you than tongue can tell,—though not more than I have *always* been. Whatever successes you may have, they *cannot* cause me to believe in you *more* fully than I have done from the first. As ever,

Your own Eileen.

ALS (WP, DLC).
 1 WW had apparently already told ELA that he was going to dedicate the book to his father. See also WW to ELA, Dec. 1, 1884, quoting this dedication.

To Ellen Louise Axson

My own darling,   Balto., Md., Nov. 30th/84

Your sweet letter of Friday night, with its earnest protest against Bryn Mawr, has given peremptory pause to my conclusions upon that matter. I think that, had it come twenty-four hours sooner, I should have withheld or altered very materially the letter I sent yesterday to Dr. Rhoads—not because I had not thought a great deal about all the objections you urge: but because those objections derive additional, if not decisive, force as coming from *you*. But the letter I wrote Dr. Rhoads commits me to *candidacy* at least, and should the position be offered me, my only way of escape would lie through the question of *salary*, about which nothing definite has yet been said.

I was mistaken when I said that Miss Thomas was at the head of the college. She is Dean, but Dr. Rhoads is President; and there are to be several men in the faculty—amongst others one or two of the very brigh[t]est who have gone out from the Hopkins. Dr. Adams seems to think that an appointment at Bryn Mawr would be an exceptional honour, especially in the department of history, since several of the best known of the young teachers of the country—such as Wm F. Allen, the historical critic of the *Nation*[1]

—have been spoken of for the post. Whatever else it might be, the position would *not* be *beneath* me, my darling—you may rest quite easy on that point—and I would not be under a woman, so far as I can learn, but my own master, under Dr. Rhoads. The Dean is, I suppose, the disciplinary officer—necessarily a woman in a girl's school.

I have none of the same objections to a school such as that to be opened at Bryn Mawr that I have to a *co-educational* institution: and the question of the higher education of women is certain to be settled in the affirmative, in this country at least, whether my sympathy be enlisted or not. The only query for *me* personally is, do I wish—can I afford—to take a hand in it? As applied to the instance in hand, that query is affected by the only alternatives that offer. One possible alternative we have seen to be a chance to teach, in New Orleans, that branch of my studies in which I take least interest, namely, political economy. Another alternative is a position here—at a salary of about seven hundred and fifty, or at the outside one thousand, dollars—some two years hence in the department of administration. I have already told you more than once the conditions of teaching here in a subordinate position. The general alternative is to go very far away from these eastern centres of educational work and from the great libraries which alone contain adequate materials for original writing.

So much for the negative side of the question. The positive side—not to restate what I pointed out in my last letter on the subject—is that at Bryn Mawr I should probably receive a very comfortable salary (I am prepared to refuse anything less than two thousand dollars); should have more leisure than here or elsewhere for private study; should have opportunities to lecture in Philadelphia and eventually here (if Dr. Adams' plans and promises are made in good faith); should have leisure to learn *how* to teach before seeking a more conspicuous place where the conditions of work might be less favourable; and should have plenty of *congenial* work. It is not my purpose, you know, my darling, to spend my life in teaching. It is my purpose to get a start in the literary work which cannot at first bring one in a living. I should, of course, *prefer* to teach young men—and if I find that teaching at Bryn Mawr stands in the way of my teaching afterwards in some man's college, I shall of course withdraw. But Dr. Adams did exactly the same thing before coming here—he was first of all professor at just such an institution, Smith College in Mass.—and, besides, beggars cannot be choosers. Leave out of sight the fact that this college is to be for women, and it is evident that there could not be a better berth for me than just there. The whole question, therefore, is reduced to this: do I think that I could gain the objects of my ambition in teaching women? The question as to whether it will be *agreeable* or not, I leave out altogether. I could do my duty fully without fretting, provided my ultimate object is not interfered with or postponed meanwhile.

I intend to call on Miss Thomas to-morrow morning for the single object of telling her just the lines in which I purpose doing my best, my special, work, and if she thinks my purposes in any degree incompatible with the work that will be expected of me at Bryn Mawr, she can prevent my appointment.

My anxiety to do what is best in this matter has cost me both sleep and ease of mind. I have not attempted to argue away your objections: they stand with a force of their own whatever is said. I have merely desired to point out other considerations which to a certain extent—perhaps altogether—counter-balance them. And if my darling, after further consideration, continues to think that the position I have consented to seek is one which she should be sorry to have me accept, I will at once and without hesitation withdraw from the candidacy. I will not take, contrary to her choice and judgment, this first step that we shall take together!

I am sincerely glad, little sweetheart, that "cousin Ed." has had the triumphant success indicated in the clipping you sent me, and I have no doubt that he entirely deserved it. His rise has certainly been wonderfully rapid. At this rate he will win a national reputation long before any of the rest of us! He seems to have just the sort of talents which make his pace in the race easy whilst ours is laboured. And, if you have read him aright, success is not likely to hurt him.

Don't fail to tell me, darling, just when your Xmas holidays are to begin, and the date on which you will leave for Phila. It can't be much more than three weeks distant now.

I am not feeling very well to-day: but that's no matter so long as I am not positively sick—and I am far from that as yet.

I love you Eileen, with all my heart. You are my trusted counsellor, my sweet comforter, my darling, my queen, my everything.

Your own   Woodrow.

ALS (WC, NjP).

¹ William Francis Allen, Professor of Ancient Languages and History, University of Wisconsin, who wrote editorial notes for the New York *Nation*.

From Charles Howard Shinn

Dear brother mine—   [New York, c. Dec. 1, 1884]

You deserve a scolding—you dearly beloved Reprobate for not telling me abt your book & the B. M. College scheme—both of which I get from a letter from Adams. I have been quite unwell in this homeless city—colds &c.—but the news is good as a feast. How glad I am for both of you. Believe in you—my sister & brother friends? I should say I did. And yet, if you never amounted to anything I should feel just so—should love you no less. I wonder if we *must* live apart? Can't the world for once give a man the desire of his heart, after having a few times choked him off? In other words, can't "fate" arrange it that thou and I shall happily and busily dwell in the same circle—and help each other thus? I want you with all the definiteness of purpose and steadiness of affection that ever ran from heart to heart. Only one person— that shy, fair lily-maiden, thinks oftener than I, that you are coming to N.Y. pretty soon. Woodrow—I like to talk news, but I "despise" to write it. This isn't meant to be a *newsy* letter. . . .

Love to Worthington. I think of him oftener than of anyone else of our set. Its his charming personality.   C.H.S.

ALI (WP, DLC).

From C. H. Toncray

                         Farmers and Merchants National Bank.
Dear Sir: Fremont, Neb., 12-1-1884

Yours containing deed to hand.
Thanks.
                         Respectfully,   C. H. Toncray, Cashier.

Hw and printed postal (WP, DLC).

From James E. Rhoads

Dear Friend,   Philadelphia, 12 Mo. 1, 1884

Thine of the 28th. ult. with its enclosures, is at hand. The tenor of the letter and the statements given with it are satisfactory. We were aware that thy studies had been directed in special lines, and shall be prepared to expect that thou will need time to perfect thy knowledge of General History. In teaching History, as in the case of any other wide subject, the methods adopted and the order of procedure should, to some extent, be peculiar to the Instructors.

In arranging a course in History we shall have the best thought of such men as Dr. H. B. Adams, C. K. Adams of Univy of Michigan[1] & Profr. Allen of Univy of Wisconsin, as embodied in the courses they have published, and Dr. H. B. Adams would doubtless aid by his advice, so that I think there is no cause for serious anxiety on this account.

From our conversation and from the testimony [of] others, I feel assured that the moral and religious lessons of History will in thy hands be used to fortify a wide and comprehensive yet well defined faith in Christianity. Dr McCosh has lately written that the questioning now (and always) going on respecting what has been heretofore taught as religious truth, will have two issues: one an abiding in or return to what will be very much the old faith; the other entering on a bolder and more unsparing skepticism than any that has preceded it. To give room and time for all honest inquiry, and yet to render aid in forming right conclusions upon vital topics of belief and duty, is the part of every Instructor; and because the department of History can be used so effectively on the right side I have felt the more solicitous that it should be so used.

The Executive Committee of the Board of Trustees will meet within the next two weeks, when thy application will be laid before them with a favorable recommendation.

On all accounts I am glad to learn of thy marriage engagement, and congratulate thee heartily upon it.

With regard sincerely thy friend   James E Rhoads

ALS (WP, DLC) with WWhw notation on env.: "Ans. 12/3/84."

[1] Charles Kendall Adams, Professor of History, University of Michigan, soon to become president of Cornell University and later of the University of Wisconsin.

To Ellen Louise Axson

My own darling,   Balto., Md., Dec. 1, 1884   10:35 A.M.

How shall I thank you for the sweet letter you wrote on Saturday night! My success with the publishers is not worth half so much to me as your delight in it. One ounce of love is worth many tons of literary reputation: and one word of *your* love is sweeter to me than anything and everything this world can afford. My darling! I am so glad for *your* sake that Houghton, Mifflin, & Co. accepted my *mss*! I trust that their action means an *opening* for me: if so, all that goes through that opening hereafter shall be made better by reason of the inspiration of your love. You shall make my success

Of course, my pet, you may have the "fun" of telling Shinn; to save his feelings from the suspicion that I have withheld the news, though, you better say that I left it to you to tell.

No, I did not send the dedication with the *mss.*, but with my letter accepting the terms offered. Do you know how the dedication runs? "To His Father, the patient guide of his youth, the gracious companion of his manhood, his best instructor and most lenient critic, this book is affectionately dedicated by the Author." Do you like that, my darling? I want it to be a surprise to dear father, and so shall leave the secret to be revealed to him and to dear mother by the book itself.

No, my precious, mother has not complained of not hearing from you: but she is constantly asking about you, begging for news from you—and I knew what her heart was really waiting for. I copied your account of that delightful Powell episode and sent it to her.

My darling, it frightens me to know that your day's work so tires you out. It ought not to be so. You must surely be undertaking too much. You spend all day over indoor work, and take no *regular* outdoor exercise: is not that the truth, my pet? I find two hours every day in the open air scarcely enough: and I am quite sure, darling, that *nothing* can justify the slightest risk to the health. If you overwork yourself this winter, little lady, you jeopard both your own happiness and mine. Don't say, Miss, that I don't practice what I preach. I take "lots" of exercise and recreation—I don't work more than six hours a day—and the only thing that ever breaks me down is over*worry*.

My mind is more at ease to-day than it was yesterday about the Bryn Mawr matter. I shall expect you to be quite candid about it. If you disapprove, I will withdraw without a misgiving: if you approve, I shall be confirmed in the opinion that I have so far acted for the best. I have written to father asking his advice. Of course, my darling, I know your loyalty: I know that you are ready to acquiesce most heartily in any course I may decide upon. But the conditions you have so far proposed are a little too hard. I *cannot* be "*sure* that it is the best thing for me to do," for it is quite possible that waiting would bring me a still better opening somewhere else; nor can I be "*entirely* satisfied and pleased with the prospect," since I cannot realize what the conditions of the work are to be until they have ceased to be in prospect. I know, however, that I should be sufficiently in sympathy with the work to do my part earnestly and with pleasure; and I am convinced that, if the salary be large enough to leave *some* margin for books and an occasional trip to Balto. and Washington, there will be better opportunity there than elsewhere for original work: and, after all, it's my *writing*, not my teaching, that must win me reputation.

There is another point, little sweetheart, which enters into the case. I must avail myself of the first good chance of permanent self-support in order to relieve father. His salary will be much less in Tenn. than in N.C.—the congeniality of the work being with him the determining consideration—and I cannot get my own consent to draw any longer upon his resources. The Fellowship can't last long: and while it does last is a slim support.

But enough of business. I shouldn't trouble you before your time!

I love you, darling, beyond all power of speech. I wish you could know what an inestimable blessing your love is to

ALS (WC, NjP).　　　　　　　　　　　Your own　Woodrow.

From Ellen Louise Axson

My darling Woodrow,　　　　　　　　　New York, Dec 1/84.

Well I did after all write to your mother instead of yourself last night, though I did not intend doing so; that is to say, I meant to write to *both*;—but Mr. Goodrich and I became engaged after tea in such a deeply interesting *quarrel*, that before I knew it, most of the evening had passed, and I had time to write to but one. But I won't put you off without a line,—only you must excuse it's being a very hasty one.

I have just read your two letters—yesterday's and todays. You must not attach too much importance to what I said about Bryn Mawr, darling. They did not even *pretend* to be "words of wisdom";—it was hardly more than the expression of my *prejudices*,—and I don't think I have *very strong* prejudices; I am quite open to conviction; in fact I am already about convinced. Of course, it's being a school for women *must* remain an objection[.] But I think you are right,—the advantages—especially those affecting your other work—*do* counterbalance that one draw-back. Then too what you tell me in this letter, does put a better face on the matter. You have a man for President! Good! that makes it less *disagreeable*. Then my chief fear was that it's effect upon you[r] *reputation* would be *bad* rather than good,—that if it made you *any* reputation, it would be of a sort you would'nt *want*. But if Dr. Adams and all the world that *knows*, have such a profound respect for Bryn Mawr and the "higher education of women," and consider the place such a prize, it must be that there is no ground for that fear. But I *must* not let myself go more deeply into this at present: I am *distressed* dear to hear that you are unwell, and *low-spirited* too! I fear that means that you are *seriously* unwell. A young author must be feeling *very* badly physically, to have "the blues" in the first flush of his triumph. I am afraid you have been working too hard again. I earnestly hope tomorrow's letter will bring me better news.

Well I didn't put you off with a line after all, excuse haste. With truest love I am dear heart, as ever

Your own   Eileen.

ALS (WP, DLC).

From Joseph Ruggles Wilson

My precious Woodrow—   Wilmington [N.C.], Dec 2, 84.
Your letter conveying draft for $175.05 came to hand this morning.

I am not ashamed to report that we fairly cried for gladness when we read about the certain and most flattering publication of your book. Somehow, though, given as I am to rather gloomy anticipations, I more than half expected this upshot—for the book is possessed of the rarest qualifications for success. We heartily congratulate you, darling, upon this event, almost unprecedented in the history of American literature—considering your age and unknownness and the high character of yr. publishers. And we are equally glad because of yr. prospect of a situation. Yes you would do well to accept such a position as you describe. It is a beginning, at any rate, and will admirably suit Ellie. Urge the matter all you can, we implore you. It will place you in the *North*, it is true but at its centre which is also the centre of intelligence and of facilities for special study.

I write in haste and excitedly but with more thankfulness in my heart, to the blessed God, than I have felt for a long while.

Josie is at home, and we feel comparatively rich, therefore, again[.] He is well and happy.

All send oceans of love,   Your affectionate   Father

ALS (WP, DLC) with WWhw notation on env.: "Ans. 12/4/84."

From Ellen Louise Axson

My darling Woodrow,   New York, Dec. 2/84.
I was prevented from writing last night by company, so must

again try to content myself with a hurried note this morning. Have just read your sweet letter of yesterday. You don't say in it how you are feeling—except that your *mind* is more at ease; I hope I may truly gather from that, that you are better in other respects; but I am still uneasy; you must be sure to tell me to-morrow.

I think the dedication charming. Am glad you are going to keep it a secret at present. It will be a delightful little surprise. Have you heard from them—your parents—yet, since the book was accepted? How long does it take to publish a *book*? When will it probably be out? If the Bryn Mawr matter falls through, it will help you get a place; won't it? All you say on that point is very sensible, and of great weight;—of quite enough, I freely grant, to over-balance any prejudice against the teaching of women. How does the case stand at present, by-the-way, as to your father's going to Tenn. Is it finally settled? I was asking Cousin Hattie about Clarksville—in an incidental way,—and she says its a lovely place, and has a delightful climate. It seem[s] that it is very near Nashville.

I hope you received the remarkable looking roll I sent you Sat. I made *two* attempts at writing your name on it, hoping that be-tween the two, the postman could make out enough letters to send it in the right direction. I can't write, under the best of cir-cumstances you know,—not on the smoothest of plane surfaces, and when I attempt it on a cylinder the result is farcical! By the way I forgot to tell you that the *dress* in that sketch is one which has a *history*. It is the one which a certain young gentleman of my acquaintance once informed me was "the prettiest gown he ever saw"! In short it is the (remains of the) one I wore at Ashe-ville,—with the waist and sleeves abbreviated to make it look more "Greenawayish." You see, I hold on to the poor old thing; I have a tender feeling for it. But I *must* close now—more tonight. I love you my darling with all my heart and am forever,

Your own   Eileen.

ALS (WP, DLC).

Two Letters to Ellen Louise Axson

My own darling,   Balto., Md., Dec. 2, 1884   10:05 A.M.

I am quite well this morning and the "blues" are altogether dispelled. It *was* unreasonable, I confess, to be low-spirited so soon after hearing of Houghton and Mifflin's decision about my *mss*; but then you must remember that I am constituted, as regards such things, on a very peculiar pattern. Success does not flush or elate me, except for the moment. I could almost wish it did. I *need* a large infusion of the devil-me-care element. The acceptance of my book has of course given me the deepest satisfaction and has cleared away a whole storm of anxieties: it is an immense gain every way. But it has sobered me a good deal too. The question is, What next? I must be prompt to follow up the advantage gained: and I must follow it up in the direction in which I have been preparing to do effectual political service. I feel as I suppose a general does who has gained a first foothold in the enemy's country. I must push on: to linger would be fatal. There is now a responsibility resting upon me where before there was none. My rejoicing, therefore, has in it a great deal that is stern and sober, like that of the strong man to run a race. The light-heartedness comes in when I think of the delight I have been able to give my darling. *You* are my *joy*, my pet. Your love is the effectual sunlight in my life. I couldn't—tried I never so hard—keep from smiling both with lip and heart as I look at this sketch that I have pinned here before me on the wall. It is lovely: the more I look at it, "from the proper distance," the better I like it. I owe Mr. Harwood a debt. Oh, how I love that little lady! It is strange that I should be so moved by a *picture*—and that a mere sketch—but, after all, it isn't the beauty of my little sweetheart that moves me—I admired her before I loved her. But I know the heart that lives in the depths of those eyes; I have learned the sweetest of lessons from those lips. I know why the picture moves me so. I *love* this little lady and she is mine. We two are to spend our lives in loving and helping each other. What would you think of me if I *could* look at this image of her coldly? Why, I would give my life for that sweet little maiden there in the picture: I will give my life *to* her. If you knew her as I do, you would understand why it is that I am

Her own   Woodrow.

ALS (WC, NjP).

My own darling,   Balto., Md., Dec. 3, 1884 1:15 P.M.
   What was my surprise to receive yesterday afternoon a note from Shinn wanting to know why I had not told him about my book and about Bryn Mawr! Dr. Adams had written to him about both—about the latter, apparently, as if it were quite as finally settled as the former! I was *very* much vexed that *you* should have been so anticipated and that the Bryn Mawr matter should be so freely spoken about before it had really taken shape. I

wrote Shinn explaining how my seeming neglect had come about.

I don't know when the book my [may] be expected, my pet. I have no means of estimating the length of time that it will take to print it; but I should suppose that it need not be delayed beyond the first weeks of February.

Yes it may be said to be certain that dear father will go to Clarksville. He has been notified officially of his nomination by the Executive Committee of the Board of Trustees—and that is considered equivalent to election.[1]

At Bryn Mawr the Executive Committee *elects*, and Dr. Rhoads writes me that that Committee will meet within a couple of weeks and that "my application will be laid before them with a favorable recommendation"—which means, I suppose, that I will be elected. But he says nothing about the possible amount of *salary*: and, since it would be very awkward to "kick" on that point after election, I am contemplating the immediate composition of a diplomatic epistle on that head.

I *thought* that there was something strangely familiar about the "hang" of that skirt in the sketch, and now it is explained: it *is* "the prettiest gown I ever saw"—a gown for which I have a queer sort of tender regard. I hope that you will keep it *always*, my darling! It would seem to my mind something very like sacrilege to destroy it or dispose of it! And the fact that it is the dress worn by the sweet, the lovely, little maiden here in the picture before me is just so much more added to the value of this sketch, which did not need anything additional to recommend it. But I've told you as best I could how I feel about this picture—I wish I could tell you in *some* sort of fashion what I think of the little lady who posed for it. I believe, with you, that actions speak louder than words—*and I have given myself to you*—but then, when one's heart is full to overflowing with love, it is very hard not to be able to give that love adequate expression—and such is the condition of   Your own   Woodrow.

ALS (WP, DLC).
  [1] JRW to WW, Nov. 15, 1884, ALS (WP, DLC).

Two Letters from Ellen Louise Axson

My darling Woodrow,   New York, Dec 3/84

How I wish you had been in New York—with me—today! I have been to two *such* interesting exhibitions. The first, this afternoon, was Prang's[1] display of the prize Xmas cards—the original paintings, you know. The contest was not thrown open to the public this year, but twenty-two of the leading artists in America were invited to compete. There are only twenty-two paintings therefore, and they are almost all *good*,—some of them are *exquisite*. Three or four of the League teachers are among the competitors, so of course we are much interested in the result,—though I should'nt give any of them the first prize.

The other exhibition, which I attended tonight, was a still greater treat. It was at Houghton and Mifflin's, and consisted of the *original* drawings of Elihu Vedder, for his great work the "Rubaiyat." There are almost forty of them so they constitute quite a picture gallery in themselves. They are to be on exhibition all this week, for invited guests;—of course Mr. Goodrich took me. I saw the "edition de lux" too, which is about as fine as the original drawings—it only costs one hundred dollars! How I wish you could see them! They are wonderful things; and the more one looks at them the more one sees in them.

But at any rate, you will see the great Watts collection, and that is the greatest art-treat you will be likely to have until you go to Europe! There are about twenty portraits of distinguished men among them, John Stewart Mill, for instance, Robert Browning, Matthew Arnold, &c. &c., so that the subjects are as interesting as the treatment. There were *never* more wonderful portraits painted! the man's—the subject's whole character and career are represented,—the very soul of him seems caught and held on the canvas! The "Nation" says that "if he had never painted anything but portraits, he would still be one of the greatest artists of this or *any other* age!"[2] So you perceive *they* alone are worth coming to New York to see! You note my object in all this,—I mean to hunt up all the holiday attractions of the city and describe them in glowing terms, to see if they won't tempt you hither! I think I must tell you about the *lovely dolls*! at Macy's, and the *be-utiful* show in his windows,—fairies in cockle shell coaches drawn by butterflys, and swans, &c. &c!

When *do* you think you can come?—when do *your* holidays begin and how long do they last? I don't think we have but one day, so that I am doubtful about going to Phil. on account of the loss of time. I couldn't stay but four days at the longest,—Xmas day, which comes on Thursday, and the three following. I don't know whether the trip would pay, but I am afraid Uncle Tom and Aunt Saidie wouldn't like it very much if I backed out now. My plans depend somewhat on yours; be sure to tell me, please as soon as possible how long your vacation will be, and how you propose to spend it! But I must say good-night dear, for it grows late—was late when I began. With more love than words can tell, I am my darling as ever   Your own   Eileen

Please excuse this exceptionally bad scrawl, which I can scarcely read myself. But I am hurried and sleepy too!

1 Henry Prange, stationer, 833 2nd Avenue.
2 "The Watts Exhibition, I," New York *Nation*, XXXIX (Nov. 20, 1884), 445-46.

My darling Woodrow,   New York Dec. 3/84
Who do you suppose called on me last night while I was out? Mr. Bridges. I found his card this morning. Isn't it *too* bad that I should have missed him? I am exceedingly disappointed. And I have missed Mr. Shinn *twice* of late; I am really very unfortunate in that respect. I had some other callers yesterday whom I was sorry to miss, viz. Mrs. Seaman and her daughter. Mrs. Seaman is the sweet looking aristocrat with whom I was so tempted to board,—for whose sake I tried so hard to pursuade myself that *cold was hot*! She came to the League to find me out several days ago, but I was at lunch. Though she saw Annie Lester, she didn't leave her name and I have been wondering who the stranger could have been. It is certainly exceedingly kind in her to take so much trouble,—unless as Mr. Goodrich suggests, she has a vacant room now! *I* reject that idea with scorn.
We are all—at this house—overwhelmed with grief at present, because our two nicest ladies are leaving. Mrs. Guerry starts to-night for Macon, where she will spend two months; and Mrs Jenkins leaves next week for New Orleans—will spend the winter there, and of course we will see her no more. She is *my* special friend, and I really feel blue over losing her. Her husband has come for her; and he is almost as nice as herself! I am very glad you liked Mr. Harwood's sketch. I think it is quite good; certainly one of the best that was made. By the way, I have just gotten my "unlimited" ticket to the sketch class, to my extreme surprise, for my sketches are dreadful—not to be compared for a moment, to scores of others who are kept indefinitely "on trial";—it is very ridiculous. But I suppose it is because I am in the head class, and so they take for granted that I know more about sketching than I choose to show! That dear, delightful Mr. Brush grows lovlier every day!—he said so many nice things to me yesterday that he quite took my breath away. My work was "very fine," and "first-rate,"—"*very strong* and yet delicate," "*ex-*

ceedingly interesting"—showing great "feeling" and "understanding" &c &c! ! He almost made me believe that if I worked—say—
forty years I could learn to paint! But it would take that long,
and I fear would'nt pay for the trouble!

I am indeed delighted, my darling, to learn that you are "quite
well this morning," and in good spirits. The effect of your great
success upon you is, after all, very natural,—very comprehensible,
even without that fine figure with which you explain it. I hope
your pleasure and satisfaction in your triumph won't be any less
than it is your right to feel, because they wear a sober guise and
bring with them serious, earnest thoughts.

But I must try and close now for I have other letters to write,
and I have been running about so much this afternoon, shopping,
that I am already sleepy. Have been shopping chiefly for other
people, but have done a little on my own account too[.] I have
bought the *sweetest* little doll, with big brown eyes and golden
curls! She is sitting on the bureau now, with her head tucked
on one side, and both arms stretched out to me like a baby when
it wants to be taken;—and she looks so sweet that I am obliged
to jump up and kiss her every now and then. She is intended for
Maggie, but I have bought her betimes so that *I* may enjoy her
until Xmas! But I *must* stop—I had better have done so on the
last page, before showing myself a *perfect* simpleton! Good-night,
my darling. I wonder what you are doing at this moment! I am
always wondering *that*—always trying to follow you in your in-
goings and outcomings. If I only had that magic mirror, which
gave visible answers to all those heart-questions. Yet it would
be tantalizing to be "so near and yet so far"! So after all it is
better that the mind's eye should be the only mirror until there
is no need of such mirrors,—until "I do not think of thee—I am
too near thee." I remain as ever, my darling, with truest love

Your own   Eileen.

ALS (WP, DLC).

To Ellen Louise Axson

My own darling,   Balto., Md., Dec. 4th/84   11:30 A.M.

My plans for the holidays depend upon a very unromantic, but
none the less imperative, consideration, namely, upon how much
money I can save for my trip. My vacation extends over nearly
two weeks, beginning on the afternoon of the 24th and running
till the morning of the 5th of January; but, alas! according to
present prospects I cannot afford to spend all that time in New
York. Besides, my little lady, you have yourself suggested a limit.

You cannot afford to lose more than two days in addition to the one given by the League: and it is quite evident that you would lose more than that if I were to stay beyond the four days! So, you see, putting these two considerations together, I can hardly decide for myself what my stay will be. A month ago I hoped to be able to be with you the whole of the two weeks of my vacation—and possibly I might have done so had I not gone to New York to buy my winter clothes—but, as it is, I must stay only so long as my money and your leisure hold out. If you go to Philadelphia, I shall of course ask permission to follow you there: but "uncle Tom and aunt Saidie" would probably deem me a nuisance if I were to try to be with you a great deal of the time—would probably have no tolerance for a monopolist, and I should have to discipline myself to seeing you as seldom as my heart could stand. It was for this reason that I said that I was glad "for your sake," that you were going to spend the holidays in Phila. I wasn't going to be selfish enough to put my own desires into competition with a scheme which would involve such a delightful change for you. You *ought* to get away from New York for a little vacation if you possibly can: and in determining your plans I *want* you to leave *my* claims for the present out of view. *No* sacrifice is great in my eyes which secures your welfare; and though I know what you would say—I know that you would be happier with me than with "uncle Tom and aunt Saidie," or anybody else— still I am sure that a visit to Phila. would do you good, and I want you to go if you think that you would enjoy the trip.

And did you really think, darling, that you would have to tell me of all the art exhibitions and the holiday sights to allure me to New York! Why, my heart is in New York all the time! And if I go there it will be to see *you*, my precious little sweetheart! The other "attractions" will be as mere dust in the balance. If you and the Watts collection were next door to each other and you couldn't go with me to see it, I certainly would not give the Watts collection a thought—except as you might talk about it! Why, my darling, I have been living for this long month past on the anticipation of being with you at Christmas time. Nothing else could have beguiled the weariness of the weeks; and the pain it gives me to know that even that visit must be cut short is greater than I care to confess, being a man and supposed to possess that divine power of *waiting*, and of resting calm in assured hope, which only real men can boast. *Such* disappointment seems a *cruel* hardship! But we know that it is not: that our circumstances are in this sense made for us; and I mean to do what is at once Christian and philosophical, to make the most of the days that I *can* spend with my darling, without any more rebellion at their shortness than is compelled by the large gift of the "old Adam" that I have received. If my Eileen's heart is as eager as mine for leave to keep me longer—if it is as sore as mine at parting—a few days will be almost as rich in delight as several weeks could be! It is her love that makes me happy; so that if she wants me to stay, I can come away without a broken heart! How long would you *like* me to stay, my darling?

Here is the way in which the news was received at home, my pet (dear father *loquitur*) "I am not ashamed to report that we fairly cried for gladness when we read about the certain and most f[l]attering publication of your book. Somehow, though, given as I am to rather gloomy anticipations, I more than half expected this upshot—for the book is possessed of the rarest qualifications for success. We heartily congratulate you, darling, upon this event, almost unprecedented in the history of American literature—considering your age and unknownness and the high character of your publishers."

He is strongly in favour of Bryn Mawr. "It will place you in the *North*, it is true, but at its centre, which is also the centre of intelligence and of facilities for special study." He also thinks that the place "will admirably suit Ellie"! He don't know Ellie's opinions, does he?

I am aware, Miss, that I've been writing you a great many prosy sentences about business of late; but you have forgotten how to read my letters—and me—if you haven't discovered them to be the sentences of *love* letters all the same. And that isn't altogether dull business—is it?—which so vitally concerns yourself because of its influence upon the fortunes of

Your own   Woodrow.

ALS (WP, DLC).

From James E. Rhoads

My Dear Friend   Philadelphia, 12 Mo. 4.   1884.

Thine of the 3rd. just at hand. Thy question is a most proper one, and I did not state what we proposed to offer because I wished to think over the matter carefully. I recognize fully, too, thy reasons for desiring a sufficient salary. We have then concluded to offer $1200 a year for two years, without distinct promise as to the future, but with the hope that by the time this period has elapsed we may be able to offer a larger salary, & ultimately have thee occupy a Professorship. In order to carry out a more definite system than we could otherwise do, we offer to those who have never had experience in College teaching the title of Associate; to those who fulfil their term of engagement, we hope to be able to offer an Associate Professorship, & ultimately as I said above, to offer a Professorship.

I state all this frankly, and and [sic] yet, as thee will see it is incumbent on me to do, I can make no *promise* direct or implied as to the future. I do express what we *hope* to be able to do.

Please let me hear from thee if this will be satisfactory or otherwise. Boarding can be had at Bryn Mawr at reasonable terms, or we can rent to thee a cottage on the College premises at $350 a year.

With much regard, thy sincere friend   James E. Rhoads

ALS (WP, DLC) with misc. WWhw notations on env.

From Ellen Louise Axson

My darling Woodrow,   New York Dec. 5/84.

Once again I have been obliged to postpone my writing until morning—this time until lunch. Am sorry, for I have *so* much to say today, and I don't know now when I will have an opportunity to say it. We—Annie Lester and I—are going tomorrow afternoon to Clairmount, or something of that sort, to spend Sunday with Miss Brown and Mrs. Brown. They came to see and invite us a week or so ago. Annie saw them, I did not. This afternoon I am to go up to Clara Blisse's.[1] There seem to be a good many interruptions to my work of late. Clara's wedding invitations are out, she is to be married next Thursday. I am glad your father is pleased with the Bryn Mawr prospect; his opinion serves still further to reassure me. By the way, did you write to him about New Orleans? Would'nt it be a good idea to make a few inquiries in that direction, before you make final arrangements? Or would you rather teach girls at the *North* than men at the *South*? Perhaps, for the sake of your other work the former *is* preferable.

Many thanks for the quotations, from his letter, about your book, which you may be sure I enjoyed. I have dwelt so much in fancy upon their delight in your triumph.

But time flies, and I *must* close! More tonight,—about our Xmas plans, &c.

With truest love, I am, my darling, now and always
                                              Your own   Eileen.

ALS (WP, DLC).
¹ ELA's cousin, Clara Bliss, was about to marry a Mr. Andrews. See ELA to WW, Oct. 5, 1884.

To Ellen Louise Axson

My own darling,   Balto., Md., Dec. 5, 1884

I am delighted to hear of the exceedingly complimentary things Mr. Brush has been saying about your work—chiefly because it gives me a better opinion of him than I had before, and because of the pleasure and encouragement it must have given you—not at all because I wasn't quite well aware already that such judgments were the only true ones as regards my darling's work. I had supposed, from little things you had told me about Mr. Brush, that he criticised upon the rather small, and altogether mistaken, principle of stinting praise, and I am glad to know that really good work *can* extort enthusiastic commendation from him. Besides nobody needs such commendation more than my little sweetheart; and it will do her lots of good, if she will only *believe* it. You have a most unreasonably humble opinion of your own gifts, my little queen, and I hope that Mr. Brush will be able to convert, as well as to gratify, you. And, if, Miss, *I* am possessed of artistic talents, as you amiably pretend to believe, ought not my unqualified admiration of your work to count for something? It ought at least to mitigate your surprise at your reception of an "unlimited" ticket to the sketch class. By-the-way, my darling, is there any law to prevent your sending me one of your sketches? I want one *very* much. Will you humour the wish?

I am to dine this evening with Miss Martha Carey Thomas. She will, I fear, find me in a somewhat grim humour: for I have just received a letter from Dr. Rhoads saying that the salary to be offered is $1,200, which by dinner time I shall have decidedly declined to compete for. They must offer me *some* inducements to go to Bryn Mawr—not a meagre stipend which would be barely enough to live on, and leave absolutely no margin on which I could collect a small library and make our escape from B. M. in the Summers. They would not value me if I were to 'let' myself cheap: so that, unless they choose to increase the offer considerably, the negotiations are at an end. If my book makes any sort of a hit, it ought to give me prestige enough to get something better than a $1,200 position. I am not in a position to make terms with them, and father's urgent approval of the idea of my going to B. M. inclines me to take a very moderate sum: but I could make more than $1200 at some other trade.

I love you, my precious Eileen! I love you with all my heart.

Your own　Woodrow.

ALS (WC, NjP).

From Ellen Louise Axson

My darling Woodrow,　　　　　　　　　　　New York Dec. 5/84.

Mr. Shinn has just been here, and for once I did not miss him. He has just left, at ten minutes past eleven! Poor Miss Beatty. I couldn't help laughing at her, and yet I have been on pins for the last hour. She sat on the sofa staring at us and looking so utterly wretched all the time. But I begin to think that is her *normal* expression of countenance. She told Mr. S. that she did not think life was worth living! Mr. S was very full of interesting talk on many subjects;—and he also read me extracts from his book, and a long and remarkable letter from his sister. What do you think she is urging him to do in this letter, at some length and apparently in all seriousness? Merely to pursuade you and *me*! each to write a series of articles for the "Overland" about the old and new South! You are to furnish the philosophical—the abstract portion, and I, the "concrete." Truly she must be daft, "much learning has made her mad"[.] Mr Shinn thinks of going to Cal. in a couple of weeks on business connected with the "Overland"—will be gone perhaps a month & will probably go by way of the South,—to New Orleans &c. The people out there have been "bull dozing" his sister because she went for Cleveland. And the people here have been treating him in the same fashion. His uncle in Maine who had invited him to Thanksgiving, wrote that after what had happened they did not care to see him! and the Tribune sent back an accepted article on the same ground. Talk about intimidation in the *South*!

I am very much divided in my mind, my darling, about your Xmas visit. I hardly know what to wish, but I think I had rather have you *all to myself* in New York. I couldn't see half as much of you as I would wish in Phil. and whenever I thought how few the days were, and how little I was getting out of them, I should be *so* impatient that I shouldn't enjoy either you or Uncle Tom. And yet I want you to meet Uncle Tom, and I would like *very* much for you to be in Phil—at least one day. And then it would be hard to wait any longer than is absolutely necessary to see you. It is a hard question; do just as *you* prefer, dear: either spend those four days with us in Phil. or wait till I return to New York. I come back I suppose on the 28th your birthday—wish I could see you that day. And by-the-way there's the Watts collection! We must not forget it. I am very anxious for you to see it.

Excuse haste. I love you dearest with my very heart of hearts and am forever   Your own   Eileen

ALS (WP, DLC).

From the Minutes of the Seminary of Historical and Political Science

Bluntschli Hall, December 5th, 1884.

. . . Dr. Adams, in speaking of original work of that most profitable to the seminary, to individuals and to science, announced the speedy publication of several books by members of the histcal dep't, as Mr. Wilson, Mr. Shinn, et al. . . .

Meeting adjourned shortly before ten o'clock.[1]

1 Entry lacks secretary's signature.

To Ellen Louise Axson

My own darling,   Balto., Md., Dec. 6, 1884 11:05 A.M.

I dined with the "Dean" last evening and had a very interesting experience. When I arrived she was critical and a whit superior; when I left, she had quite admitted my intellectual equality and was ready to defer to me in everything. Finally, she seemed really to enjoy hearing me talk. Her critical temper had all melted into sympathy: and she was anxious to know if I would come to Bryn Mawr if the Trustees were to offer me such and such a salary—for I had told her that I had written to Dr. Rhoads declining twelve hundred. I think that they *will* offer me more, with a prospect of an advance both in academic rank and in salary at the end of two years—and such terms would undoubtedly be better than I could expect to make elsewhere at present, since I am known to have had no experience in teaching and must submit to be taken *on trial* at first.[1]

I shall write to father about the New Orleans matter to-day. The difficulty is that the Bryn Mawr matter is to be decided in less than two weeks: so that steps should be taken for negotiations in N. O. only after I shall have refused, or been refused by, the Phila. folks.

It goes without the saying, my darling, that I would a *great* deal rather teach *men* anywhere, and especially in the South, than girls at Bryn Mawr or anywhere else: but there is no winking the fact that good literary work will be much more noticed and much more noticeable in the North than in the South and the advantages for making my special work tell are likely to be almost *infinitely* better at Bryn Mawr—that is, in the centre of the east—than at any other institution at which it would be possible for me to find a place for teaching *only* my specialties.

I hope, my pet, that you are not having such weather in New York to-day as we are having here—for such a dreary rain as this might seriously interfere with your trip to Clairmount. Where is Clairmount? Is it far out of town? I hope that my darling will enjoy herself there! How I wish I were going with you! But that's a wish I make whenever I hear of your going *any*where: it's just part of the great wish which is all the time filling my heart, the wish to be with you, my little queen, my matchless little sweetheart, whom I love so passionately and so entirely.

Your own   Woodrow.

ALS (WC, NjP).

¹ The following extracts from the minutes of the Executive Committee of the Bryn Mawr Board of Trustees for December 12, 1884, reveal the decision and recommendation of that body following Wilson's talk with Dean Thomas on December 5:

"They also agreed to recommend the appointment of Woodrow Wilson B.A., as Associate in History for a term of two years to date from 9 mo. 15, 1885, at a salary of $1500 a year. . . .

"He has assisted Prof. R. T. Ely in the preparation of a 'History of Political Economy in the United States,' and has now in press a work on 'Congressional Government,' which will appear within a year, and which Dr. H. B. Adams of Johns Hopkins University asserts, will be a highly valuable contribution to historical knowledge.

"He has been very highly recommended by Dr. H. B. Adams of Johns Hopkins University, where he is now a fellow, as to his unusually good literary faculty, as a successful student in History, especially in Constitutional History of England and the United States, and as a man of honorable personal character. Woodrow Wilson is a member of the Presbyterian Church, and throughout his student life has upheld a reputation as an earnest Christian. The President in personal interview has been confirmed in the very favorable opinion of him expressed by Professor H. B. Adams. . . .

"They also recommend that Woodrow Wilson B.A. be appointed Associate in History for a term of two years at a salary of $1500, to begin on the 15th of Ninth month, 1885. . . . We believe he will be a valuable member of the faculty." From "Minutes of the Executive Committee of the Board of Trustees of Bryn Mawr College," 1884-94, bound ledger book (PBm).

These and following extracts from the minutes of the Executive Committee are printed with the kind permission of President Katharine McBride of Bryn Mawr College.

From Ellen Louise Axson

My darling Woodrow,   New York, Dec. 6/84.

As you perceive, I am not at Clairmount, after all, tonight. The weather is so dreadful that I backed out—and am very glad

I did, for it is storming furiously now. In truth, I was glad to find an excuse; they only asked me for politeness—I only accepted out of politeness; now they have done their duty in inviting me, & I have done mine in finding a suitable excuse, and we are happy all around. I really did have enough cold and sore throat to make it imprudent for me to take the trip in this weather. It wouldn't have been worth mentioning under ordinary circumstances, but it was quite enough to serve as an *honest* excuse. I was sorry to let Annie go alone,—indeed I got all ready so that if she seemed to mind it very much, or to think I was treating her shabbily I could go. But she let me off very kindly.

Is it one of my absurd productions made in the sketch class, that you want me to send you, dear? I assure you they are altogether uninteresting. It would be quite ridiculous to send them about the country,—but I am sure you are welcome to them! *I* have no use for them after I do them! I will show you the whole sketch book, when you come. Perhaps you would like me to send you the one of the young man for whom I have a great weakness— because he reminds me of *you*! his face is the same shape, and his mouth and nose suggest yours. Don't know his name, as he isn't a regular Leaguer, but has been coming, for a short time, to the sketch class only.

Yes! I must have given you a wrong impression of Mr. Brush. He is one of the kindest, most encouraging teachers I ever saw, has said a great many cheering things to me, from the first. I think he, is in *every* respect, one of the *best* teachers I ever saw; and I only wish we had one like him in the head class. But I suppose it would be unreasonable to expect *two* like *him*. I am so disappointed in Mr. Freer, that I think of leaving the morning head class, and trying Mr. Weir, in the afternoon class. I think Mr. F is the *poorest* teacher I ever saw! One gets *nothing*—absolutely nothing from him, not an idea, not a suggestion; it is a perfect farce to call it instruction; and it makes us rather impatient when we are paying so much for our lessons, $12.00 a month. But it is'nt poor Mr. Freer's fault at all, he simply *can't talk*; I never saw one make such desperate and unavailing efforts to express his ideas. The trouble is, that, while he may be, as they say, "artistic to his finger tips," he has, *I* think, very little mind. In that respect he is quite the opposite of Mr. Brush who is really an intellectual man,—if he does talk about the Noth,— but I won't vex your soul again with that phrase. At any rate *it* is the *only* foolish thing I ever heard him say; his remarks are always singularly clear, forcible, and to the point; one can't help understanding. One of the girls took a study made in the head class to Mr. *Brush* for criticism, and she got more from him in five minutes than she would have learned from Mr. Freer in weeks; and so did I, merely by overhearing, though it wasn't my picture. I think one of Mr. Freer's difficulties is extreme shyness; he is a comical looking man, a very large blonde, bald headed, spectacled, and exceedingly awkward. He looks like a big school-boy when he comes into the room; his arms are always slightly crooked and held away from his sides, as though he had paint on his hands and was afraid of soiling his clothes, and he always sits down as though he had'nt the least idea whether it was a high stool, a low stool, or the floor, that he was going to strike. But he has a pleasant, bright smile, that lights up his face delightfully. I forgot to mention that he is *very* deaf—as well as dumb,—which of course makes matters a great deal worse.

I am sorry, dear, for the sake of your peace of mind, that there is such a serious hitch in the Bryn Mawr negotiations. I think your course is altogether wise and right; it will do you no good, in any respect, to undervalue yourself so much!—but I have no doubt it will all turn out for the best.

Speaking of colleges, Mr. Shinn left this article,[1] which I was to read and then cut out and send to you; don't know why—it is'nt particularly brilliant—rather a dry statement of facts.

But it is high time for me to say "good-night." I love you darling more—infinitely more than life, and want to see you ah! how much! As the holidays draw nearer I grow constantly *more* eager to see you, less able to be as patient as I ought under the separation. Time is a very erratic old person in his movements—sometimes he flys, & sometimes he creeps. He is creeping now, at a snail's pace.

With truest love believe me darling, as ever,

Your own   Eileen.

ALS (WP, DLC).

[1] Perhaps she did not send it to WW.

From Melville R. Hopewell

Dear Sir   Tekamah, Neb, Dec 6 1884

Yours at hand & noted. As requested I send you a list of taxes on your lands—as I suppose them to be—amounting to

the sum of	$100.21
Charge	1.
Total	$101.21

You will notice that the taxes for 83. have not been paid on 120. acres, in sec 22-22-11, & 80. acres in 27-22-11. I do not know whether this land fell to you or not, but it was a part of the Bones Estate, on which they paid tax in 1882. I do not know how or why I did not report it in 83. If it is your land—the amt above will pay all tax to date as I understand it. but if it is not yours, you can send the amt nec[e]ssa[r]y to pay, on what does belong to you.

Very Truly Yours, M. R. Hopewell

ALS (WP, DLC) with WWhw figures on env. Att: WWhw note listing taxes for 1882 and 1884.

To Ellen Louise Axson

My own darling,   Balto., Md., Dec. 7, 1884

So you *are* going to Phila. after all—and you leave me to decide what *I* am going to do. Well, I am as much 'divided in my mind' as you are: but I suppose there's only one way to decide. It will be a sad disappointment to me not to spend Christmas day with my darling—as I've been dreaming delightedly of doing ever since I knew she was going to be in New York—and it will be rather a dismal business spending the day here alone again; but it is best that I should not go to Phila. I would be able to see only enough of you there to tantalize me. And yet, little sweetheart, have I the right to take just so many more days from your work? If you are willing to have your vacation extended, isn't it possible that you will allow yourself to be persuaded to stay longer with "uncle Tom"? I notice that you say only that you "suppose" you will return to New York on the 28th, and you couldn't plead the call of work with a very straight face when you were intending only to prolong your holiday with me. Maybe, though, if I were to say that I would pass through Phila. on the 28th you would promise to join me? It is probably best that I shouldn't make a point of meeting your uncle this time; because, truly as I am delighted that you are to get away from your boarding house for a little while, I can't help feeling slightly ag[g]rieved that he has spoiled my Christmas for me by claiming the little lady who is all the world—and more—to me and who alone could make the season a happy one for me by her presence. He is doubtless guiltless of all thought of me—and therefore of all thought of harming me—in the matter; but it's true, all the same, that I grudge him the privilege of having you at Christmas time. It is an odd distinction, I know, and one hard to see: but it is not hard to *feel* it. So far as *you* are concerned in arrangements which disappoint me of what I most wanted—so far, that is, as they contribute to your enjoyment—I am sure I have not a selfish thought: on the contrary I am glad for my darling's sake; but there, I confess, my unselfishness ends. I haven't a bit of kindly feeling for "uncle Tom and aunt Saidie"—and I shall have to read far into another volume of Stubbs on Christmas day in order to drive out hard thoughts about them. I'm not a bit of a saint. My only redeeming trait is that I *can* love with all my heart, and therefore *cannot* begrudge *anything* to those I love because I cannot have a share in it, or must suffer because of it! It isn't pleasant or convenient to have strong passions: and it is particularly hard in my case to have to deal with unamiable feelings; because the only whip with which I can subdue them is the whip of hard study and that lascerates *me* as often as it conquers my crooked dispositions. I hope that none of my friends—and much more none of my enemies!—will ever find out how much it costs me to give up my own way. I have the uncomfortable feeling that I am carrying a volcano about with me. My salvation is in being loved and—but, dear me! how I am wandering from the subject, our plans for the holidays! After all, my precious, *I* can't decide when or how my visit shall be made. I can only say that I don't want to go to Phila., if any other arrangement can be made. You haven't told me yet whether you can spare as many days as I can take after you get back from your uncle's—and everything must depend on that.

Oh, my Eileen, how my heart longs for you! Try, my little sweetheart, to love me as much as you can: because I know that you *can* love infinitely, and it seems to me that only infinite love can satisfy me—can satisfy my love for you. There surely never lived a man with whom love was a more critical matter than it is with me! With *all* of your love life will be easy and full of sunshiny promise of the highest, worthiest success: without all of your love life will be hard beyond endurance and full only of irksome duty grimly done, like prison labour. I dare not think what would become of me if your love were to be taken away from me—and yet I wonder at myself for telling even you these secrets—these bottom-secrets—of my nature! Surely a man loves the woman to whom *all* his heart is open! Pride plays so prominent a part in my disposition that probably my companions would not more than suspect *some* change, were my *heart* to die. But pride has no place in my dealings with you, my darling! If there be any treasures in my love, they are yours—altogether yours. You are not a 'companion': you are *mine*—are you not, darling?—my heart's mistress, my sweetest comforter, my promised wife! Do you *think*, little lady, that you can be happy living with *such* a chap—so given to odd moods—so prone to break out suddenly in unnecessary self-revelation? Say again that you love and trust me with all your heart and I will ask no more such foolish questions. I love you as nobody could love you but

Your own   Woodrow

ALS (WC, NjP).

From Ellen Louise Axson

My darling Woodrow,   New York, Dec. 7/84

I wonder if Baltimore and New York are apt to be of the same mind in the matter of weather? I hope so,—I hope you have had just such a peaceful sunny Sabbath as ours. It has been a perfect day; after the storm last night, the air has been wonderfully fresh as well as soft and balmy. I did not imagine that December in the North ever brought such days,—days "wherein it is enough for me not to be doing but to *be*"! And of course, as every-body knows, such days are twice as sweet when following "a day of storm, and wind, and rain"; I suppose that is one reason why storms, of all sorts, are sent. We *need* contrast—light and shade— in this life at least; we must be strangely changed not to miss them in the other. I have often wondered how and why it will be happier because "there is no night there."

I have been, at *last*, to the Scotch Presbyterian Church, and heard a sermon which I liked exceedingly on the text, "Our citizenship is in heaven." Dr. Hamilton[1] has a fine face, and a pleasant one. I think perhaps I will go there regularly, now that I have fallen out with Dr. Taylor. I did not tell you about that,—is all Uncle Tom's fault, the result of something he told me,—and which I wish he had kept to himself! Did you know that Dr. Taylor advocates marriage between white people and negroes? Uncle Tom himself heard him speak on the subject in a public meeting here in New York. He told a long story about one fresh from Africa, who was educated in Scotland, and in conclusion, he said, "and the best of it all was that when he went back to Africa he took a good and fair young Scotch wife with him"! Now is'nt that perfectly disgusting? I can't get over it, though I have tried; I went to church resolutely last Sunday saying to myself, "I will conquer this feeling,—it isn't a thing that affects his piety.["] But it was "no go"; I could'nt forget it a moment, the services did me no good. It was'nt that I was *angry* with him—he might have abused the South for an hour and it would have made no impression upon me, I should not have enjoyed his sermon one whit the less; it is not a matter affecting *us* in the least, but only the *man himself*. How can one respect a person holding such disgraceful, such disgusting views. But bah! Why should I fill my letter with this? And yet I do want to know you[r] opinion on the matter—and if you think me *very* wrong to let it affect me so strongly.

But the gentlemen Mr. Goodrich and Mr. Brigham entrapped me tonight so that now the evening has passed and I must cut short my letter. How much I have wished for one from you today, dear. It is very tantalizing to think that it is in the office and I can't get it on Sunday too, the very day when one wants it most— has most time to dwell on it. But I try to make up for the loss by re-reading all the letters of the week. However, I have already told you, what happy times you and I have together on these quiet Sabbath afternoons. Goodnight my darling, I love you, ah, *how* I love you! With all my heart.   Your own Eileen.

ALS (WP, DLC).
¹ The Rev. Dr. Samuel M. Hamilton, minister of the Scotch Presbyterian Church, New York.

To Ellen Louise Axson

My precious Eileen,   Balto., Md., Dec. 8th 1884
I feel like writing you a regular love-letter to-day. My heart seems even fuller than usual of you this morning: and my letters of late have been so full of business—my letter of yesterday was so full of myself—that I am going to take leave to-day to fill *this* letter with you. You must admit that it is only reasonable to let a fellow now and then talk his full of the subject which constitutes the main tide of all his thoughts, and, therefore, you can't grumble at my occasionally putting nothing *but* my love for you into what I write for your eyes. And the letter I received this morning gives me a fair pretext: it tells me some of the things I've been wanting to know about your surroundings—about poor ridiculous Mr. Freer and the rest—and it makes a little suggestion about the slow pace of time at present which exactly coincides with my own impressions on the subject. Time varies his paces, it seems to me, according to the standpoint from which one watches him. He does seem to *fly* when I compare his progress with mine in my *work*: but he certainly goes more slowly than any conceivable creeping when I consult my heart's desires. I want him to bring my darling to me, and it seems an age since

the last time he vouchsafed me a glimpse of her. Why am I so impatient? I know very clearly: and can tell you if you would *really* like to know. Because my darling's presence is the only thing that can conquer my restless discontent. When she is with me I feel a sort of serene power—a sort of preparedness for any undertaking—a pervading, blessed sense of completeness—such as I never feel when I am separated from her. When she is away there is forever a great *lack* haunting me: I feel as if my work must wait for her coming: I know that when I shall have a home made bright by her love and sympathy all my powers will be at their best and clearest. My heart cannot be in my work because it is all the day with her and she is not yet identified with my work. A man's work can't prosper, the time must seem unendurably slow and without reward, when his heart is desperately hungry, his life only half a life—the fruition of his love yet to come! If you need me as much, darling, if you feel the same lack, there's no need that I should describe the feeling any further. You are my 'good spirit,' my pet. Your love drives all my morose humours out, ere they are fairly lodged: it seems to sing an unceasing song of delight to my heart. What would—what *could*—I be, if I were not   Your own   Woodrow.

P.S. Yes, little sweetheart, it *is really* one of your "absurd productions made in the sketch class" that I want to see—and none could suit me better than the one of the fellow who resembles me! Heaven help him! How unfortunate! I wont let you off. One of your sketches will seem almost like a wee bit of yourself—and may serve to allay my impatience for the coming of the holidays, if only for a few hours or a few moments,   Lovingly   Woodrow

Is the sore throat gone—or does the cold still hang on?

ALS (WC, NjP).

From Ellen Louise Axson, with Enclosure

My darling Woodrow,   New York Dec 8/84
    Oh dear me! I wish and I *wish* for the twentieth time, that I had never promised Uncle Tom to spend Xmas with him! It would be *so very* much nicer to spend it alone with you. I don't know why I promised, except that I had no good excuse to offer and it would have seemed to them unnatural and foolish in me to refuse. But I am sorely tempted now to write and back out, for the more I think of it the harder it seems that we can't spend Xmas *day* together,—that you should be "so near and yet so far"!

Yes, Uncle Tom *did* think of you. He said when he asked me, "I suppose Mr. Wilson will want to be with you, but he can come to Phila. as well as New York." But I see we are agreed to disagree with him on that point; it would be infinitely more satisfactory for you to come to New York; and you need not concern yourself about the further waste of time, I shan't consider it wasted. I want you to stay, dearest, just as long as you conveniently can, and no longer,—I won't complain about the *length* of your visit! —and (heroic resolution) I will try not to complain of it's *brevity*!

I certainly will promise to join you if you pass through Phila on the 28th,—had thought of that plan myself. I will leave the city on the 28th *at the farthest*—had thought of returning to N.Y. on the 26th, but that wouldn't pay; and would deprive me of one of my chief inducements for going,—the treat of hearing Uncle Tom preach. I wish you could hear him. I should think you would feel a special interest in going to Phila. now;—I do. Don't you want to go out and inspect Bryn Mawr? Will the trustees probably hold their meeting before Xmas? I hope it will all be settled soon, for the sake of your mental health,—that you may be freed from worry and anxiety about it. I should like to have been a spectator at the interview between you and the fair Dean! It must have been as good as a play. The idea of any *woman* assuming airs of superiority over *you*!—or any *man* either, for that matter!

Ah darling, if you only knew how those self-revelations which you wonder at yourself for making, cause my heart to glow within me; how at every word it leaps up to answer yours, you would no longer call them unnecessary. When it is a question of *loving* I am not afraid to stand by your side, my darling, and pledge you, heart for heart,—we are equals there. I love you just as much as you want me to; I *am* yours *all* yours. And I not only think, sir, but I *know* that I can be happy with "such a chap," so long as the chap himself is happy. And shall I give you *"all"* my love? Shan't I save a wee bit for any one else? In truth, I often fear that I am in danger of doing that very thing, or something like it, that my love is making me selfish. I am so absorbed in you; my heart turns so constantly, so persistently toward yours, that sometimes it seems to me I scarcely take time to *think* of anyone else. A-propos of this, I will send you a little poem which you probably won't like; they are so emphatically *woman's* verses;—but I hope you will at least appreciate as you should, my exhausting *effort* on your behalf, in copying it! With truest love I am my darling forever,   Your own   Eileen.

ALS (WP, DLC).

A Woman's Answer

"I will not let you say a woman's part
Must be to give exclusive love alone,
Dearest, although I love you so, my heart
Answers a thousand claims besides your own.

I love—what do I not love? earth and air
Find space within my heart, and myriad things,
You would not deign to heed are cherished there
And vibrate on its very inmost strings

I love the summer, with her ebb and flow
Of light and warmth and music, that have nursed
Her tender buds to blossoms . . . and you know
It was in summer that I saw you first.

I love the winter dearly too . . . but then
I owe it so much; on a winter's day
Bleak, cold and stormy, you returned again,
When you had been those weary months away.

I love the stars like friends; so many nights
I gazed at them when you were far from me,
Till I grew blind with tears . . . those far-off lights
Could watch you, whom I longed in vain to see.

I love the flowers; happy hours lie
Shut up within their petals close and fast
You have forgotten, dear; but they and I
Keep every fragment of the golden past.

I love too, to be loved; all loving praise
Seems like a crown upon my life—to make
It better worth the giving, and to raise
Still nearer to your own the heart you take.

I love all good and noble souls;—I heard
One speak of you but lately and for days
Only to think of it, my soul was stirred
In tender memory of such generous praise

I love all those who love you, all who owe
Comfort to you; and I can find regret
Even for those poorer hearts who once could know
And once could love you, and can now forget

Well, is my heart so narrow,—I who spare
Love for all these? Do I not even hold
My favourite books in special tender care,
And prize them as a miser does his gold?["][1]

ELAhw (WP, DLC).
[1] In Adelaide A. Procter's *Legends and Lyrics, Second Series.*

To Ellen Louise Axson

My own darling,   Balto., Md., Dec. 9, 1884   1 P.M.
Mr. Bowen (one of my new intrusive friends, the American political economists)[1] is very interesting, but he is cold-blooded: he discusses marriage from the *economic* standpoint, as intimately connected with the question of *wages*, and it is, therefore, an *immense* relief to turn from him for a little while, to give one's *heart* a chance to think a bit. Wages *have* a most uncomfortable, imperious way of commanding the question of marriage: but so does the body incommode and often dominate the heart: and that does not disprove or throw the slightest doubt upon the conclusion to which everybody who *has* a heart must accede—that the body was made for the heart, not the heart for the body. Marriage isn't in any *true* sense an *economic* question. I mean to marry my darling—provided she continues of the same mind as at present!—simply and only because I love her with all my heart and need her at every turn of my life, and not because I expect some day to earn more money than I shall need for my own support. Oh, you dear little bewitcher, you! Do you think it's fair to thrust yourself into all a fellow's studies so? How can he understand political economy when he is dreaming of a pair of soft, loving brown eyes that he loves? How can he take notes intelligently at lectures when his thoughts are forever running back to words in the morning's letter? How can he follow sensible Mr. Stubbs in his judicious observations when he is thinking of a little artist in New York who has taught him that there's more wisdom and instruction in loving than in all the books ever writ? He is always remembering her caresses and looking forward to her presence; how can he remember when Crecy was fought or hope to comprehend the German Reformation? The only hope for him is to be with her always; because these thoughts will not interfere with—they will help—his studies when the element of *anxiety* and lack and loneliness is taken out of them. Her presence will sweeten all the courses of his life. My private opinion is that he was *meant* to belong to somebody, by that highest

law of property, the law of *love*: was meant to have somebody to spend his life for—and yet was meant to be taken care of by a woman's aid, a woman's tact and sympathy. He needs to be loved and believed in with that unbounded, unquestioning love and belief which only a woman can give—which it is a woman's glory to give, even when she gives it unworthily! My darling I love you: Do you begin to know how *much* I love you, how much you can be to   Your own   Woodrow.

ALS (WC, NjP).
  1 Francis Bowen, 1811-90, editor of the *North American Review*, 1843-53; Alford Professor of Natural Religion, Moral Philosophy, and Civil Polity at Harvard University, 1853-89; author of numerous books on philosophy, religion, history, and political economy.

From Herbert Baxter Adams

Sir: Baltimore, Md., Dec. 10, 1884
    I have the honor to inform you that you have been elected a member of the American Historical Association. If this election is agreeable to you, it will gratify the Executive Council to receive through the Secretary your letter of acceptance. The accompanying constitution states the conditions of membership and the purposes of the Association. The address of the Treasurer is given above.

                    Respectfully, H. B. Adams
                                   Secretary of the American
                                   Historical Association.

Form LS (WP, DLC). Encs.: printed "Constitution of the American Historical Association" and reprint of editorial "A New Historical Movement," New York *Nation*, xxxix (Sept. 18, 1884), 240.

To Ellen Louise Axson

My own darling,   Balto., Md., Dec. 10/84
    How I wish I could give you as many kisses as you would take for that sweet, that perfect, love-letter that came this morning. My darling! I *know* that you love me: why, then, do I take such supreme delight in reading these declarations, in receiving these proofs, of the fact? When you fill a letter with words of love, as you have done this one, you change the whole course of my life for the day. Every ordinary thing seems to throw off its ordinary form and to repeat to me that you love me! I go about my work under a strange sort of excitement, which gives my spirits an unwonted elasticity! Could there be better proof, little sweetheart, of the part you play, and must always be able to play, in my life?

If you can "be happy with 'such a chap,' so long as the chap himself is happy," you are sure of *some* happiness, my darling: for he will be happy so long as you love him. Your love *constitutes* his happiness and, however much other things may harass him, by reason of his exceedingly thin skin, he will always be happy in *that*. He will doubtless worry a good deal over his work—though it is his earnest resolve to try *not* to do so—but he will always be able to throw off such worries at his wife's bidding. Her sympathy, her smiles, will infallibly cure such ills of the mind.

Tell me, my pet—where did you get these verses? I think them *exceedingly* sweet. As coming from you, they are all the sweeter because they *are* woman's verses. Yes, Miss, I do want *all* your love! You can give it to me and still love others: just as I can give you all mine and still love the dear folks at home as much as ever: Because they do not seem to me the same thing at all—the love I give them and the love I give you! I seem to have a separate heart—or, maybe, an *inner*, a heart of hearts—that I give to you; and so there is no comparing the two loves. *I love you as my promised wife*—and that contains the whole secret!

No, darling, I would not have you back out of your promise to go to Phila. I *want* you to go, and enjoy yourself as if there were so [no] such chap as myself—and then I will come to you—on the 28th, unless something prevents.

Yes, the Bryn Mawr matter will be settled before Xmas, I believe

I received the proof of the first pages of my book yesterday—which looks like progress!

I had intended to say something about Dr. Taylor, but I haven't left myself time to-day.

Good-bye, my darling, my matchless Eileen. I love you with all my heart and am altogether   Your own   Woodrow.

ALS (WC, NjP).

From Ellen Louise Axson

My darling Woodrow,   New York Dec. 10/84

I had so many things to do last night, that I was forced by the lateness of the hour when I had finished to postpone writing until morning in consequence of which I can now send you only a few hurried lines in answer to your sweet letter of yesterday. I don't believe anyone ever wrote such sweet letters as yours, my darling, and I am sure that no others were ever more deeply prized. Yes, darling, I *do* need you all the time, I *do* feel that life is incomplete without you,—I almost seem to myself to be waiting for life—my true life—to begin! And yet though I know the feeling so well, there *is* need that you should describe it, whenever your heart prompts you, because I *love* so to hear you say that you need me, that I can help you, that my love will make a difference in your life. In short—was there ever greater selfishness!—it makes me happy to hear that you can't be perfectly happy without me! And yet not for the world would [I] have you *un*happy, you know. But I *must* close, good-bye for the present. What would, what could *I* be if I were not   Your own   Eileen.

ALS (WP, DLC).

To Joseph Ruggles Wilson

My precious father: Balto., Md., Dec. 11, 1884
I must send the enclosed tax-bill, just received,[1] at once because it ought to be paid immediately. Please make out the draft for $101.21, to cover the $1.00 "charge" of the agent in Tekamah. You will see why the amount is so much larger this year than last. Several parcels of land are added which were then carelessly omitted, and we have to pay the 1883 arrears. I never thought to examine last year's bill to see whether we were charged *enough*. I have not the receipt for 1883 with me (Dode can find it amongst the estate papers in my desk—probably in one of Hopewell's envelopes from Tekamah) but it would be well to test Hopewell's correctness by seeing whether the tracts in question really *were* left out. They are the last three on the bill enclosed: N.E. S.E. & W²S E, 22, 22, 11, and N.W. of N.E. & S.E. N.W, 27, 22, 11. I will, of course, require an explanation of all discrepancies from the agent himself. But the 1st of Jan'y is the limit of time for payment, and if there were the omissions mentioned in last year's bill, you had better send the $101.21 to me as soon as convenient. Otherwise subtract $17.05.
I am quite well, and in good spirits.
Please tell me your plans as to *time* of moving to Tenn. Will it be before the Assembly, or not till after the publication of the Minutes?
The Bryn Mawr matter is hanging fire; but I shall probably have *some* report to make within the next week.
With unbounded love to all, In haste,
                    Yr. dev. son   Woodrow
ALS (WP, DLC).
1 M. R. Hopewell to WW, Dec. 6, 1884.

To Ellen Louise Axson

My own darling,   Balto., Md., Dec. 11, 1884

I have, of course, been thinking a great deal about what you reported the other day about Dr. Taylor; and yet I don't now know quite what to say. It is not made clear in your letter whether he made a speech whose object was to advocate the intermarriage of the races in the South, and wherever else they are similarly situated, or whether the story about the negro who married a Scotch wife was incidental to the discussion of some kindred subject. If he favours miscegenation of blacks and whites as a desirable or tolerable solution of the social question in the South, or a general intermixture of African and Aryan blood as a thing to be wished for anywhere that the two races come into contact, both his moral judgment and his political judgment are radically and utterly unsound, and, a whole province of good sense being thus cut off from his mind, the soil of the rest of it may be expected to bring forth only a rank growth of weeds. If, however, there be nothing in what he said of this sort except an inference from that harmless story, he stands in my estimation just where he stood before. He has never seen the negro as we have seen him, and he may be excused with easy charity for having manufactured an Othello-Desdemona romance out of such material as he had—a fine African, whom he idealized, and a callous Scotch girl who probably could stand the life she chose well enough.

I don't know yet, my pet, whether I want to go to Phila. or not for the purpose of making a visit of inspection to Bryn Mawr. Even if I am elected (at something more than $1200, and promise of an advance) I think that, under the circumstances, the scheme will keep. I can inspect Bryn Mawr and hear your uncle another time, when neither will interfere with what is now my uppermost wish, to have my darling all to myself for a few days! If it should be decided that we are to go to Bryn Mawr next year, why then you can get "uncle Tom." to take you out to see the place—can't you?—and I will hear your report, and be satisfied.

My darling, there could be no sweeter answer to my love-letters than this brief note of yesterday. You see, you didn't have time to put anything but love into it: and so, short as it is—and fervently as I wished it longer—it is like a complete song to my heart, filling it with all sorts of answering notes of gladness and love. Ah, my precious, your love is everything to

                              Your own Woodrow.

ALS (WP, DLC).

From Ellen Louise Axson

My darling Woodrow,   New York, Dec. 11/84

I seem to be a little unfortunate this week about finding opportunity for writing "sure enough" letters; I don't like, at all, to put you off with hurried notes so many days in succession,— though they *are* all that is necessary for the fulfillment of my promise! Writing to you however doesn't happen to be a work of *necessity* or duty, but is altogether a labour of love,—not to say an act of self-indulgence! I told Minnie that I could'nt write to her or anyone else because I am always writing to *you*, that I have so very little time for writing to anyone, that the whole of it is no more than is required for you! So she says I must tell you that we are "the most selfish people she ever knew"!

I will try and send you today the sketches you are so foolish as to want; one of the famous old Algerian model in all his native toggery, and the one of "the fellow that looks like you." Remember however that I didn't say the *sketch* looked like you, otherwise you may receive a shock! Yet it *is* a likeness of the young man too;—while my sketches are so bad as to drapery, they generally "look like" the model. That is the trouble with the drapery, —I grow fascinated working on the face, spend most of my time over it, and scratch in the rest.

Speaking of models, I am very much interested in the one we have this week in the head class, a fine old gentleman with "a good grey head." He is blind; and the most interesting part of it is that he lost his sight from a wound received in *our* army! He is from Charlston S.C., and "has seen better days";—is reduced to his present business by reason of his blindness. He grew quite excited when he heard my name was "Axson[,]" that was "a Charleston name[,]" could I be "related to Judge Axson." Charlie Axson was his captain in the army, &c. &c. So of course he and I struck up quite a friendship.

He is the only really good model we have had. I often wonder what can be their principle of selection in choosing models—certainly not *beauty*. Last week we had the most disagreeably ugly girl I have seen lately, her mouth was *sickening*, and she kept it open all the time. The week before that we had a rather pretty little French Canadian—Frances Dubois. But the first week's model was the worst of all—a most villainous looking creature. As one of the girls said, he looked as though he might be cursing us all the time. I was in rather bad company that week; for in the antique class at the same time I was doing a head of *Nero*! But I am spending to much time in writing. This is Clara Bliss' wedding night, so I may not be able to write tonight again[.] Last night was Mrs. Jenkins last evening with us; which explains my not writing then. Good-bye, for the present. I love you, my darling, I love you more than life, and I *do* believe in you, and trust you altogether—how could I do otherwise—towards one so worthy of love and faith.

Give my love to your dear parents. How is your mother's health now? As ever   Your own Eileen.

ALS (WP, DLC).

To Ellen Louise Axson

Balto., Md., Dec. 12, 1884

Have you noticed, little sweetheart, that we have been "out" in our *dates*, in laying our Christmas plans? The 28th will be Sabbath: I must join you on the 29th. I am *so* anxious to see you that I was actually *distressed* for a moment upon making this discovery. It *seemed* like a day's postponement of our meeting! I shall do everything in my power to make those days from the 24th to the 29th seem short: because the other men in the house are going away on their trips on the 24th and I will be left to my own devices. I can probably cheat my arch enemy, loneliness, of his prey by being all the time very busy about *something*—whether that something be Stubbs or long walks.

That was a very interesting experience of yours, my pet, with the grey bearded model sent you from the war times. I should think that your opportunities to study *new* models from week to week would be one of the most attractive features of your work: for every figure, and every face, however ugly in itself, has a suggestion of character and of possible life-experiences about it. I would much prefer even an occasional cut-throat, such as you describe, as a subject than be obliged to see the same men and the same objects every day. Ordinary faces, so to say, *wear out*. I have scanned the features of the men I see daily at the University until most of them have seemed to *fade*. I can no longer find anything in them, or imagine new things behind them. Their expressions are *exhausted*, and now recur in a weary round that tires me. It is the vividness of these impressions and the reality of these fatigues that have led me to say that I have a share in the artistic temperament. A new *type* of face, ugly or beautiful, has a sort of fascination for me, and I often catch myself staring at very common, as well as at very attractive, faces, in the street cars and on the streets. Still it is the study of the characters which the forms suggest, rather than of the forms themselves, that influences me.

I hope that my darling had a delightful time at her cousin's wedding last night. Will the bridal couple leave for Europe at once?

I think that dear mother's health is better, my love. I don't hear from home very regularly now. They are already busy beginning to get ready for the move to Tenn. "Dode" is at home for his holidays.

Little lady, when I see you, and have you in my arms, maybe I can think of *some* words—or some action—which will tell part of the love you have won from   Your own   Woodrow.

ALS (WC, NjP).

Two Letters from Ellen Louise Axson

My darling Woodrow,   New York, Dec 12/84.

As I believe I told you, last evening my cousin Clara's wedding "came off,"—and it was the cause which prevented my writing. I found the affair very entertaining, as it was my first experience of a city wedding. It was at the "Church of the Holy Communion," for Mr. Andrews, being one of those Episcopalians, who don't think anyone but a "priest" has a right to perform that ceremony, Clara yielded her woman's privilege, and deserted her own church and pastor. But, I think people who marry at thirty ought to do it more quietly; it would be more becoming to them; Clara who looks very well, almost pretty, in her ordinary dress, was positively ghastly in her white satin and veil! However I forgot that as you don't know these queer cousins of mine, their performances won't amuse you as they do me.

And so you actually have begun to receive the proof-sheets of your book! That *is* rapid progress. I am *delighted* to hear it,—had no idea the thing could be pushed through so quickly. Your book will catch up with Mr Shinn's, at this rate. The verses you ask about are by Adelaide Proctor, Barry Cornwall's daughter, you know.

Yes, darling, I *am sure* of a *great deal* of happiness, I know that right well. If we have learned the *secret* of happiness as well as we think,—if we have reduced it to so simple a problem, making it dependent upon one thing alone, and that something under our own control, viz. our love for each other, it will be strange indeed if we are *not* happy. For the rest, we will learn to laugh together at the small vexations of life, and to bear its *real* troubles with serene faith. Do you think that you can show a *manly* resemblance in one respect to Bayard Taylor's noble ideal woman, who was

> "of spirit brave—
> To bear the loss of girlhood's giddy dreams;
> . . . . spurning that which seems,
> For that which is, and as her fancies fall,
> *Smiling*: the *truth* of *love* outweighs them all."[1]

Now don't evade the question by saying you don't deal in "fancies"! There are none so wise as to escape them altogether. I love you darling, with *all* my heart, I will,—I do give you *all* my love, and I am forever   Your own   Eileen.

[1] From Bayard Taylor's "A Woman," in *The Poet's Journal*.

My darling Woodrow   New York, Dec. 13[12]/84
I have just received, tonight, from Sav. a letter giving such sad, sad news;—our dear Dr. Thomas is dead! You know how fond we *all* were of him;—Grandfather says he feels his death as if he had been his own brother;—and he was such a true, warm friend of ours. Though, indeed, he was universally beloved; the whole city mourns for him. Grandmother says she never saw such a funeral. It will be a terrible loss to the place,—and he has gone just in the prime of life! He died very suddenly of pneumonia in Washington, where he had stopped on his way to a convention in Baltimore.

Was interrupted just here by a visit from Mr. Bridges, who has just left. I like him *exceedingly*;—and I like his *face so* much more than I expected!—why, I think him really good-looking! there is so much character, intelligence, manliness, in it. That picture you had of him is a perfect parody.

Another coincidence, you know when he called before I had gone with Mr. Goodrich to the Vedder exhibition at Houghton & Mifflin's; and he too went there from here. Of course he didn't know where I had gone, but when I came into the room tonight he "recognized" me as he said at once, and almost immediately asked if I was not there that night. Well, I *did* have the pleasure of telling him about your book!—many thanks for not writing him yourself. But it was'nt half the fun it would have been to tell enthusiastic Mr. Shinn. He was *very* glad to hear it, but he takes things coolly; he actually makes me cool and prim myself, for fear he will be shocked, if I am at all impulsive!

I have had my second lesson from Mr. Weir today and have decided that I like him very much. *His* remarks are certainly to the point, almost as much so as an epigram. He is as *concise* as he is *precise*; I don't think he spends fifteen minutes over the whole class, but for all that, he stays long enough to give each of us something worth remembering. He is much less encouraging than Mr. Brush,—judging from what he said to the others. Of course, being a new scholar, I could'nt expect anything but a scolding;—he did say, however, that he thought I would "make it" or "come it,"—I forget which. His method, I am glad to say, resembles that of Mr Brush in many points and is very different from Mr. Freer's; the latter is too much of an impressionist for me, he is always telling us to "slash into it"; but the others insist most of all on "*severe* study." Mr. Weir is very pleasant though brusque in his manner,—in appearance he is decidedly German —without being a decided blonde;—he has a big rough head, and a big round body, very shaply except that it is too flat on top, brown curling hair, and a smoothly shaven face with very "cleanly" cut lips. He looks very much like a picture I once saw of Martin Luther—when a young man.

But it is more than time for me to close. I love you dearest with my heart of hearts. Your letters fill *my* heart always "with answering notes of gladness and love[.]" I think it may be considered proven that our little confessions don't fall upon unappreciative or unresponsive ears!

> "Our hearts ever answer in tune and in time, love,
> As octave to octave and rhyme unto rhyme, love."

With truest love,   As ever, Your own Eileen.

ALS (WP, DLC).

From Joseph Ruggles Wilson

Wilmington [N.C.], Saturday, [Dec.] 13th [1884]

Dearest Woodrow—

I write a hasty note enclosing receipt of last year which you can examine at yr leisure—and also draft for $101.21, as you request. *Is* there no way by which to dispose of that land & thus save so great annual expenses? This takes the last dollar I have in bank except 6! The Church is some 3 months behind.

With great love   Your affc   Father

ALS (WP, DLC).

To Ellen Louise Axson

My own darling,   Balto., Md., Dec. 13, 1884   2.45 P.M.

Prof. Francis A. Walker last year published a "Political Economy"[1] which is lying on the table here at my elbow saying 'peruse me'; but Prof. Walker can wait—I want to talk with my darling a few minutes[.] Ah, little sweetheart, you're up to your old tricks again, are you? You want me to declare that when my "*boy*hood's giddy dreams" are dispelled, and all my present fancies have fallen, I will have a "spirit brave" enough to be smilingly content with a plain, unromantic truth of loving? Don't you perceive, Miss, that you are in such demands simply *going back to the beginning*? They are reflections of the same mood, and of the same sentiments, that a certain little woman exhibited with very vivid blushes on a certain 16th day of September. Suppose you translate Mr. Taylor thus: 'Do you think you'll have the courage to love your wife as much as you love your sweetheart?' That depends upon how I love my sweetheart. I don't love her as I would an angel; I doubt if I could love an angel—and if I did, I couldn't *hug and kiss* an angel. I love my sweetheart, in the first place, because she is a true, sure enough little *woman*; in the second place, because she loves me, and loves me with a love that can satisfy mine; in the third place, because she can sympathize with me in everything, and has the sweet, loving, womanly ways that most rest and cheer me; and in the fourth place, because by some charm which I do not pretend to explain or name she has imprisoned me in her heart beyond all hope of reprieve. There! Are'nt those plain, matter-of-fact reasons: and do you really think that they are reasons which wouldn't fit the case of a wife—which suit only the dream-claims of a sweetheart? Oh, you dear, irresistible, unreasonable little woman[.] I faithfully promise not to flinch when my numerous fancies about my very mysterious little sweetheart go to pieces and to be smilingly—I'm willing to say *joyfully*—content with the simple fact that I love her and that she loves me. For, after all is said, that's the source of all my joy now. Do you think that I am still loving Miss Ellen L. Axson? Not a bit of it! I've found somebody I like much better than I did her:— somebody who confessed to me that she delighted in my kisses; somebody who calls me 'darling' as if I belonged to her—somebody to whom I *do* belong and who has given herself to me, my own Eileen!   Your own   Woodrow.

ALS (WC, NjP).
[1] Francis A. Walker, *Political Economy* (New York, 1883).

Two Letters from Ellen Louise Axson

My darling Woodrow,   New York, Dec. 13/84

We have had another "art reception" at the League tonight, from which I have just returned somewhat tired and very sleepy, —too sleepy to write much of a letter I fear,—but I will try and do better tomorrow. The reception was *very* pleasant, but just like the last, so I need not describe it;—the most interesting thing was a splendid collection of photographs taken directly from the old masters.

By the way, I have heard nothing more of your *club*—is it a success? do you enjoy it? how often do you meet?

Yes, I do find the study of the changing models very interesting. In fact, you have mentioned the reason why work from the life is so much more fascinating than any other; it is not a "counterfeit presentment," of any sort, before you, but a *living soul*—one's thoughts are kept as busy with him as one's fingers. I am kept constantly wondering and speculating over those "possible life-experiences," trying to imagine what his thoughts and feelings are, —trying to grope my way to some comprehension of his character and fate. In short, it is a study of human nature—as well as of art, —always an interesting study. In the city I suppose we must make "human nature" take the place of that other more beautiful nature from which we are in great measure walled in. And while, I must confess, that it does'nt arouse within me as much enthusiasm and delight, it *does* excite an equal interest. And though it is true that many faces "wear out" for us, it is equally true that many others which we began by thinking altogether commonplace develop constantly new points of interest as we learn to know them; and if I once find anything truly attractive to *me* in a face, it *never* wears out. I am sure to like it always more and more.

I too am "distressed" to find that I am not to see you for a whole day longer! Not until your birthday has passed! It is too bad! I wish Uncle Tom had never asked me to Phil. I assure you I am still sorely tempted to write and tell them I can't spare the time for the visit. Don't be surprised if you hear that I have done so. But it is very late, and I must make haste to close. I love you darling more—infinitely more—than all the world besides, and I am as ever   Your own   Eileen.

My darling Woodrow,   New York, Dec. 14/84

Winter seems to have begun in earnest at last; and this is a typical December day, clear, crisp, and cold; but very pleasant too, because it has been a "still day"; and I am like Whittier, I don't mind the cold so much, "if thereby the very winds are frozen, and unable to flap their stiff wings." I have been again to the little Scotch church, have about determined to settle down upon it; it is cosy and home-like, much more so to me, of course, than the great fashionable ones,—and besides I save car-fare by going to it! Such a sad thing happened there today—a very pretty young girl was seized with an epileptic fit, I suppose,—something of that sort,—and was carried out uttering low, heart-rending cries, and struggling desperately. I hav'nt been able to get her out of my mind all day.

I was surprised to hear that your father and mother are already preparing to leave Wil. I thought they were not to leave until next fall; has the plan been changed? I am very glad if it is so, for I think the sooner the better for your father. I suppose that when they do move, Josie will stay at home and attend the University? What a comfort that will be to your mother! Or, has he become so fond of Bingham—and his uniform!—that he won't be willing to leave?

How is it, dear, that you don't tell me about Dr. Woodrow? I hear all sorts of rumours, and I am very anxious to know how the matter stands. Mr. Bridges was asking me if he was your uncle. He thought he must be from the name. He is strongly on your uncle's side,—has written a little article recently on the subject.[1] I have been much troubled at the reports he gave,—which were however not very clear or definite.

I am hoping you will have an opportunity to see the Vedder drawings, after all. The exhibition at Houghton's is over; but they are to be for some little time at the American art rooms with the "black and white" exhibitions of the Salmagundi Club,[2] which has just opened. The end of my sheet! and it is too late to begin another now. I love you, darling, with all my heart, and I have no words to tell how much I long to see you. "How shall I charm the interval that lowers between this time and that sweet day of grace?" Believe me, dear love, as ever   Your own   Eileen.

ALS (WP, DLC).

[1] The "article" was probably an editorial note which appeared in the New York *Nation*, xxxix (Dec. 18, 1884), 513. It referred to the dismissal of Dr. Woodrow and the consequent resignation of two of his colleagues and viewed the controversy as a welcome sign that southern institutions were at last being aroused by some of the issues agitating currents of world thought.

[2] The Salmagundi Club was a sketch club organized by several artists and their friends in 1871. From 1879 through 1887 the club sponsored Annual Black and White Exhibitions held either at the American Art Association Galleries or the National Academy of Design. In 1884 the exhibition was at the Academy of Design and not, as ELA thought, at the American Galleries. See also ELA to WW, Dec. 17, 1884.

From Robert Bridges

Dear Tommy: [New York] Dec 15 84

I have been trying to catch time for a letter to you but it is no use, and I will have to be content with a few short lines now.

I want to tell you that I have called on Miss Axson as you requested and was delighted. I can congratulate you most heartily on your choice—and do not doubt that you will find all the intelligent sympathy in your work which you need.

I am so glad to hear also, that such a good firm will publish your book. It will be launched under favorable auspices, and I have no doubt will attract the attention of intelligent men. I have just finished writing a few lines about it for my column in *Life*.[1]

For myself, the world wags fast and furious, unrestingly—and I do not have time to stop and think. Pecuniarily I do well. My book work I like well, and have become intensely interested in the political game. Now and then I have a longing for my old days of idealism, and write accordingly. I think you will recognize some of it in a Christmas sketch which the *Commercial* will publish on Saturday....[2]   Your friend   Bob Bridges

ALS (WP, DLC) with WWhw notation on env.: "Ans."

[1] "Droch" [Robert Bridges] wrote a brief advance notice of *Congressional Government* which appeared in his column, "Bookishness," in *Life*, IV (Dec. 25, 1884), 361.

[2] R. Bridges, "A Lily of the Field: A Christmas Sketch," New York *Commercial Advertiser*, Dec. 20, 1884, Supplement.

Two Letters to Ellen Louise Axson

My own darling,   Balto., Md., Dec. 15, 1884

I must content myself with a very brief note to-day. I have had all sorts of interruptions crowding upon me this morning—errands to go, business letters to answer, proof to read, &c—so that I have had scarcely a whole half-hour for study, when I needed many whole hours. When duties press I must deny myself pleasures—even my chief pleasure, which is writing to my darling.

But, after all, a short note can tell you as well as a long one could, that I love you—love you increasingly every day—that you are a sweet presiding spirit in everything I do—my darling, my matchless Eileen. Would you want a bigger love-message than this, that you [are] all in all to   Your own   Woodrow.

My own darling,   Balto., Md., Dec. 15, 1884

I was *very* much distressed to hear of Dr. Thomas's death! I know just how you all esteemed him and what a blow, consequently, his loss must be to you. It is very sad, my darling, and you have my fullest sympathy. I feel the death of your friends almost as if they were mine: and I had a special interest in Dr. Thomas because I had met him and had heard you talk so much about him.

The enclosed clipping [about the Woodrow case][1] represents some very disquieting news that *I* have heard recently. So far I know *only* what this item contains. I have yet to learn the particulars, and the probable outcome of the affair.

I am glad that you saw Bridges this time, my pet, and I am *delighted* that you like him. Bobby is the finest fellow—and one of the ablest—on the continent, and will make a great name for himself some of these days if he can manage not to become a mere newspaper machine. His original, primal forces are magnificent, and must make themselves felt unless he is compelled to harness them to the daily press for life. But the dear old Scot must have changed much since I saw him, in 1882, if he is as cool and unenthusiastic as you found him! He must have been embarrassed: I have no doubt he was: he was made for long wear, not for first impressions. There's plenty of genuine warmth in him, though it's a white heat that never sputters and has no sparks of manner. In short, Bobby is a Scotchman—has ne'er a Celtic characteristic about him. So am I, for the matter of that: and yet you don't think that *I* should be shocked by any display of impulsiveness, that you ought to be cool and prim with me! Or, *do* you? Sometimes I have had a faint suspicion that you did! I suppose I shall hear from Bobby now, and receive his impressions of *you*. Shall I tell you what they are? I was just about to write to him about the acceptance of my *mss.*, in spite of the fact that he had not answered my last letter. For, if any of my friends had a *right* to know of my fortunes in that line, the friend who had the first and highest right was Bob. Bridges[.] If I haven't told you why already, I'll tell you when I see you: it's too long a tale for a letter.

I am glad that you have gone from Mr. Freer to Mr. Weir (do you say 'Vire'?): because evidently the change is eminently satisfactory to my little queen: she has found the sort of teacher she wants. You have described these two men so well—so vividly—that I feel quite as if I had seen them. I have caught myself several times laughing at queer, innocent, helpless, demented Mr. Freer. Maybe the poor chap can't talk because he don't know the "American slanguage" as well as Mr. Weir does.

The sketches didn't come, my pet: did you send them?

I heard a sermon this morning that has left me in a slightly bad humour. We are having just now in Balto., as a successor—perhaps as an antidote—to the 'plenary council' of which we have just gotten rid, a "centennial" Methodist convention, and all the pulpits to-day are of course full of Methodist brethren. At Dr. Leftwich's we had Dr. Vincent of Chatauqua,[2] who gave us, in a big declamatory voice, a discourse *about* the Bible. He knew a good deal besides "Christ, and him crucified," and justified the Bible to us in a ponderous, hammer-and-anvil style till I was sorry I had gone to chu[r]ch: because the man spoke too loud to allow a man quietly to think his own thoughts. The pews were at the mercy of his pitiless fire of blunt sentences: and I had to content myself with hoping that the rest of the congregation were not suffering as much as I was. But enough of Vincent: he's tired me enough already!

Two weeks from to-day you will be in Phila.—wont you, my darling?—and two-weeks from *to-morrow*! But I must not think of that: it makes the time seem interminable!

My too frequent appearance before the Hopkins Literary Society has brought me into a scrape. They wanted to revise their constitution and got me to make them a speech as to the best plan to be pursued. I agreed, and put notions into their heads which led to the drafting of a *new* constitution; and of course *I* had to draft it; the committee accepted my draft out of hand; and now nothing will suffice them but another speech upon its adoption, in the meeting to be held to-morrow evening.[3] It's a nuisance and looks like a waste of time; but I really want to see the society succeed and they are almost absolutely helpless when left to themselves in such matters as this of a radical constitutional change. They are altogether without experience, and seem to lack even some of those instincts of self-government which most of our race possess. They are mere children in trying to conduct a meeting.

I love you, darling! I am absolutely unhappy without you. A speedy end to our separation is fast becoming indispensable to

Your own   Woodrow.

ALS (WC, NjP).
[1] The clipping is missing, but it concerned the following events: A reorganized Board of Directors of the Columbia Theological Seminary on December 10, 1884, took notice of the fact that the Synods of Georgia, Alabama, South Carolina, and Florida, which controlled the Seminary, had disapproved of the teaching of evolution in the institution. The Board voted, eight to four, to ask Dr. Woodrow to resign. He declined and requested a judicial investigation or trial. The Board then requested Dr. Woodrow to appear before it. When he refused, the Board then voted to remove him from the Perkins professorship. Dr. Woodrow appealed to the Synod of South Carolina, and that body ruled that the dis-

missal had been unjustified and unconstitutional. F. D. Jones and W. H. Mills (eds.), *History of the Presbyterian Church in South Carolina Since 1850* (Columbia, S.C., 1926), pp. 169-79; the Columbia *Southern Presbyterian*, Dec. 18, 1884, and Oct. 29, 1885.

The case was afterward fought out in judicatories, all the way to the General Assembly of the southern Presbyterian Church. Letters and notes in future volumes will follow the course of this controversy.

2 John Heyl Vincent, Bishop of the Methodist Episcopal Church and founder of the Chautauqua educational movement.

3 WW's constitution has not been found. It was adopted by the student membership on December 15, 1884. It turned the Hopkins Literary Society into a completely new organization named the Hopkins House of Commons, modeled on the British House of Commons. A speaker, elected twice a year by the membership, was to appoint a prime minister from the majority party in the House. The prime minister would choose a foreign secretary and a home secretary to assist him. These officers were required to take a position on every issue before the House. If they were defeated by a vote of the membership, the speaker had to appoint a new prime minister from the ranks of the victorious opposition. Bills were to be introduced and put through all the forms of a deliberative assembly before a final vote.

Wilson probably modeled these provisions upon those found in his constitution for the Georgia House of Commons (see Vol. 2, pp. 288-91) and in his earlier constitution for the Liberal Debating Club at Princeton (see Vol. 1, pp. 245-49). Wilson also used, *mutatis mutandis*, the constitution of the Hopkins House of Commons as the model for his later constitution for the Wesleyan House of Commons, printed at Jan. 5, 1889, Vol. 6.

The Hopkins House of Commons was to survive only until 1892. Wilson came from Princeton in 1891 to address the House in an attempt to revive student interest. See Langdon Williams to the Editor, Nov. 16, 1885, New York *Nation*, XLI (Nov. 26, 1885), 445; John C. French, *A History of the University Founded by Johns Hopkins* (Baltimore, 1946), pp. 265-67; and Hugh Hawkins, *Pioneer: A History of the Johns Hopkins University, 1874-1889* (Ithaca, N.Y., 1960), pp. 277-78.

From Charles Howard Shinn

Dear Woodrow—   [New York] *Monday* [Dec. 15, 1884]

Time is precious. I am going to Cala. soon, to see how I can help my sister best. I have R.R. passes from Norfolk. If I can secure Old Dominion St[eame]r passes also, I shall not see any of you. This I regret very much—& still hope that I can pass thro' Baltimore. As soon as I read the rest of my book-proof I shall start. Will you please find out for me the exact address of our New Orleans J H. U's of the recent past, as I shall be there a few days? Is there anyone in Nashville, or in Memphis, or in Mobile, that I want to see?

Things happen in a marvelous way for me. I don't know what the outcome of this journey will be—but I think it will do some good in many ways—& I shall gratify my dear mother. . . .

My dear, it is midnight, let me say adios.   Charlie.

ALS (WP, DLC).

From Ellen Louise Axson

My darling Woodrow,   New York, Dec 16/84

I went out to dine last night, and when I returned found the room too cold for me to dare sit in, with my cold; so I was obliged to postpone writing, and now, I have barely time for a hasty line. I dined with my nice boarding-house friend, Mrs. Seaman. Her daughter came last week to invite me for Thursday, but that being Clara Bliss' wedding night, they postponed it to Monday. By-the-way, when I returned their call I found that Mr. Goodrich was partly right!—they *did* have another warmer room vacant which they wished me to take! It is a "swell" place in every respect! We had a superb dinner, everything first-class from the turkey down! —too much of a good thing for me,—or rather for my purse! The boarders do seem to constitute one family there, and it is quite a pleasant circle. One—a very pleasant young Englishman—who has been there a long time, escorted me home. He says they are charming people, the sort one often hears about but seldom sees (he thinks,) people who have really "seen better days." So you are already beginning "to teach the young idea how to shoot"!—have consented to be foster-father to the Literary Society. They do seem to be making pretty heavy demands upon you; but I have no doubt it is an interesting work, and certainly a good work.

No, I could'nt get those miserable sketches off that day, and then I forgot all about them again; *perhaps* I can send them to-day. I am so very, very sorry about the troubles at the Seminary! This was about what Mr. Bridges told me. Do you know who else resigned, among the faculty? The idea of the Synods raising such a dreadful disturbance about such a small matter!

No darling, I don't mean to "go back to the beginning." I *am* sure you will have the courage to love your wife as much as your sweet-heart. But I like to hear you state your position, as you have done in this letter in such an eminently satisfactory manner!

When I say I believe in *you* altogether, I mean that I believe in your love too, which is a part of you. I believe that it is in the deepest sense, *true-love*—made of the stuff that wears. Ah darling have I not every reason to believe all this of your love? have I not every reason to love you in return, with all the strength of my nature? Believe me, dear love, as ever

                    Your own   Eileen.

ALS (WP, DLC).

To Ellen Louise Axson

My own darling,   Balto., Md., Dec. 16, 1884

I am not surprised that you have wondered at my not having said anything about uncle James Woodrow: but the explanation is very simple: I have known nothing to tell! I have heard literally *not one word* about the affair since I left home, except what was contained in the newspaper item I sent you a day or two ago, and what I concluded from your reference to what your cousin, Mrs. Ewing, had told you! This is very extraordinary, I admit. It is more than extraordinary; it is distressing, because I have, of course, been anxious beyond measure to learn how things were going in the matter. But the dear folks at home have always had an odd way of taking it for granted that I had heard all the home news: and this autumn they have been prevented by various things from writing more than an occasional note. I have not heard even the rumours to which you refer, my pet: I wish I *could* tell you something definite! If what the clipping I sent you says is true, the trustees of the Seminary have, at the bidding of the Synods, not only eaten their own words but put themselves utterly in the wrong, and the Seminary in immanent jeopardy of ruin. They have left uncle James the moral as well as the controversial advantage. They cannot do him any real injury. Distressed as I am at the turn things have taken and at the thought of the terrible anxiety and pain uncle James must have suffered; I cannot help seeing that the victory really lies with him, and that the *disgrace* of the affair falls upon the Church. That is the terrible part of it. You may be sure, my darling that I will tell you everything I hear.

My silence about the Musical and Dramatic Club is explained in the same way. There have not been any meetings as yet, so far as I know—and, besides, I did not become a member, after all. The gentleman who invited me to join was kind enough to make an arrangement for me which suits me very much better than membership. I am to be invited to the plays and other entertainments of the Club without having any of the duties of a regular member. They are to have their first entertainment next Friday evening, and I am expected to put in an appearance after the meeting of the "Seminary"—which is always the first claimant on Friday evenings.

No, little lady, the home folks have not changed their plans as to the time of moving to Tenn. They are not to go before Spring; but the task of packing a whole houseful of books and furniture

is so vast, and the preparations to be made for moving, so innumerable, that they a[re] beginning the packing now, so that, if
possible, they may complete their arrangements by easy stages.
It would break dear mother down utterly to put the whole thing
off until it had to be done all at once. Yes, the best thing about
the prospect of their living in a University is that they can keep
Josie with them. It made me very blue to think that they might
have to be left without any of us winter after winter. Rather
than have had that, I should have set up a private school or
found *some*thing to do in their neighbourhood so that we might
be with them.

My love, I hope that you *wont* recall your promise to go to
Phila. I want you to have as long a holiday as possible—and the
little while I could stay with you would not be long enough. The
two put together will be just about the vacation you ought to
have: and, besides, there will be a greater *variety* in going to
Phila. Half the value of vacation is lost if you have to take it
amidst the same surroundings in which you do your work. If you
can have a jolly good time at your uncle's, I'll promise to be a
good boy and not think about myself a bit more than is good for
me. I know my love for you well enough to promise that Christmas day and my birth-day shall not have a cloud for me if I know
that *you* are happy. There are certain anxieties all the time haunting me about your life in New York; I can't get rid of them or
forget them for a moment. But I wont be anxious while you are
at "uncle Tom's," and I will come myself and escort you back to
the great city.

Oh, my darling, my little queen! I hardly dare trust myself to
think how much I long to see you. When I think of all that you
are and can be to me—when I think how different my life would
be if only you were my companion and helper—I grow savagely
discontented with my present *maimed* existence! I *cannot* be patient: I can at most only endure with a feint of cheerfulness. Of
course I haven't left my senses or changed my character so far
as to feel any rebellion against the wise God who governs our
lives: but there *is* misery in this terrible heart-lack, even though
the misery is made sweet by the knowledge of my Eileen's love
and lack of me! That knowledge is my constant delight. *You*, my
darling, are the strength and delight of   Your own   Woodrow

ALS (WC, NjP).

From Joseph R. Wilson, Jr.

My darling brother: Wilmington, N.C. Dec. 17th '84.
I am sorry to say I am not going back to school next session.
Father will have to leave about the 1st of April to go to Augusta
to have his teeth fixed. If I go back I will be obliged to come back
to mother when father leaves so I would only stay about two
months and a half at school. The present plan is that I shall recite my Latin and Math. to Mr. Morrell. I am very sorry I cannot
go back to Bingham because I like it ever so much. Please tell me
what you think of this plan.
I did not pass my examinations as it was not necessary that I
should do so as I am not going back next fall session (or next
session either I am afraid)[.] I got home about two weeks before
school closed. All of the boys are at home now, so I expect to have
a nice time Christmas. I have not time enough to write a letter
this afternoon as "bug is red"[1]
I enclose receipt you asked for, and hope we have it right this
time. Will write in a day or two.
We are all sorter so so and love you a big heap, and send a little heap in this note   Your loving bro.   Joseph.

ALS (WP, DLC).
    [1] Perhaps this was a family saying.

From Janet Woodrow Wilson

[Wilmington, N.C., Dec. 17, 1884]
We all have been so upset by the accompanying excitement of
the public announcement[1] of your father's plans that I have been
unable to write even to my darling far away boy—and I have
rested with satisfaction in the idea of your being not entirely dependent upon letters from home, but I need not tell you that we
constantly think of you with love inexpressible. Will write in a
day or two—   Lovingly   Mother

ALS (WP, DLC). Written on J. R. Wilson, Jr., to WW, Dec. 17, 1884.
    [1] Wilmington, N.C., *Morning Star*, Dec. 11, 1884: "We learn from the *Pres-
byterian* that Rev. Joseph R. Wilson, D.D., of this city, has signified his willingness to accept the call of the authorities of the Southwestern Presbyterian University to the Professorship of Theology in that institution."

From Joseph Ruggles Wilson

Dearest Son—
            Wilmington [N.C.], Wednesday—[Dec.] 17th [1884]
I am very sorry that your spirits are not always at the top notch.

It is to be feared that, superior as yr temperament is to mine in many respects, your tendency to the "blues" is not a very great improvement upon that of the present writer. Fight ag't this as ag't your greatest foe—and fight to conquer.

What I now write especially for, however, is to ask your help. I am expected, it seems from a letter yesterday received from Dr. Waddel, that I am expected to deliver my inaugural at Clarksville in June *next* (the 3d or 4th thereof).[1] Now, please put your good brain to work, to assist me in making the needful preparation. I am to discuss Theology in a general way I suppose—to show what it is, what it does as a study, and, particularly, how it falls into a *University* course. Think of an outline, for me: please. Don't put me off with saying, "Well you, my father, know best, &c. &c." For I don't. And besides I shall desire to do something *extra* and *unusual*.

The people here are quite taken aback by the news—published in the papers—of my prospective break with them:—and they say all sorts of nice things about both me & your dear Mother, which they *ought* to have said before. And, then, they blame the session for its course toward me in that matter which you are conversant with: the report of the same having gotten wind in some way[.][2] This will I fear lead to division and other trouble, by-and-by if not soon. Yet no one blames me; on the contrary appreciate my forbearance, &c.

Josie has just written you he tells me: and has sealed his note. So I send this by itself, on same day.

How dearly we love you, and how greatly we admire you, I need not say,   Your affc   Father

ALS (WP, DLC).
    [1] *Inaugural Address Delivered Before the Board of Directors of the S.W.P. University, in June, 1885, by the Rev. Joseph R. Wilson, D.D.* (Clarksville, Tenn., 1886).
    [2] An interesting but mysterious allusion.

To Ellen Louise Axson

My precious little Sunbeam,   Balto., Md., Dec. 17, 1884
    Does it delight you so to hear me say that our marriage will make a change in my life—a change from anxiety to contentment, from loneliness to sweet helpful companionship—that you will be all in all to me as my wife? Then maybe, Miss, it will please you just a little bit to know that your love makes a vast difference in my life every day now: that I have only to turn to your sweet loving letters to receive cheer such as nobody in the world but

you could send me. It seems to me as if these love-messages which so fill my heart to overflowing changed the very aspect of nature, and all the details of my work seem full of echoes of them. When I am feeling unwell or fagged out, or in any way out of sorts, I have but to recall my Eileen's loving words and to dwell for the thousandth time on those times when I have seen in her face promises on which I would stake my life, and everything seems easy to do: I seem to be given on the sudden new energies and renewed confidence. Ah, little lady, I hope that I play as large a part for good in your daily experiences as you play in mine! I have a name to conjure with that works wonders.

I received a short letter from Bobby this morning, little sweetheart, in which he says, "I want to tell you that I have called on Miss Axson, as you requested, and was delighted. I can congratulate you most heartily on your choice—and do not doubt that you will find all the intelligent sympathy in your work which you need." My sympathetically "cool and prim" little darling seems to have made quite an impression on the old Scot, beginning with the impression her *face* made upon him at the Houghton exhibition.

So you have learned *my* trick, have you, precious, and interrogate my love only to draw me on to "state my position"? Well, Miss, I haven't the slightest objection to stating my position just as often as you wish—as is abundantly proved by the fact that I frequently state it without being asked. My "position" is simply this, that I love you with all my heart and can't be a happy man until I may love you as my wife in addition to loving you as my sweetheart: for *that* can never be supplanted by the other. You will always be my sweetheart; but you will be my wife too—and the two loves shall make you the most loved little woman in the world. May *I* continue to be *your* sweetheart, when I am your husband?

I am so much distressed to hear of your *cold*, darling! Is this the *same* cold? How long have you had it? Please be very careful of yourself, as you love   Your own   Woodrow.

ALS (WC, NjP).

From Ellen Louise Axson

My darling Woodrow,   New York, Dec. 17/84

You will begin to think me very "gay" indeed I am afraid, I report so regularly every morning that I was "out" or "engaged" the night before, and therefore could not write. Last night it was the

Salmagundi sketch club. Mr. Goodrich proposed to take me, and, I was very glad to go in the evening on account of the saving of time. I can really enjoy pictures more at night, when I am freed from the uneasiness about my work, and can examine them in a more leisurely fashion. This is a charming exhibition; so much better than the more pretentious one which it succeeds,—that of the Academy, proper. The Salmagundi Club exhibits in the Academy rooms.

Have just received and read you[r] sweet letter of the 16th. And pray, dear, *what* are those "certain anxieties" which are all the time haunting you about my life here? I assure you, darling, there is no need to be anxious; I am perfectly safe and comfortable;— and moreover I have found a valiant protector! to whom in view of said "anxieties" you ought to be very grateful. I allude, of course, to that "verrie parfait, gentil knight," Mr. Goodrich! He is my devoted champion—in a strictly platonic sense,—and is, in many ways, of the greatest service to me. Some ten days ago, there came a new man to the sketch class, not a regular Leaguer, but an outsider,—an amateur; one who was old enough to know how to behave him[self] too, for he was about forty. However, it pleased him to take special notice of me, and after the class, he joined me on the street and without so much as "by your leave," walked all the way home with me. I happened to tell Mr. Goodrich about him and he got up a great indignation over it, and ever since has been calling for me at the League and escorting me home—says he is going to do it all winter. It is very unnecessary at present, for the man in question was only there one night; he informed me that he was from Boston, and was only passing through the city then, but would be back in a few weeks; and as his business would keep him here most of the winter, he thought he would join the class and get some experience in sketching. But I did not mean to write so much about the old "crank," but simply to show you how well Mr. G. keeps watch and ward over me. Ah! I think I know what you would say about him! Past experience has shown me the turn your thoughts are apt to take on such matters. But you are altogether mistaken. Mr. Arthur Goodrich and I are running the *platonic* schedule, as I said above,— and we are going to run it successfully. True, my former experiments in that line were not brilliant successes, but those were Southern boys,—it is different with the cool-headed New Englanders. Certainly if there is anything in plain speaking, he *ought* to understand me;—though it is true—I *might* speak even *more* plainly, for—"One only passion unrevealed—With maiden pride the maid concealed." But the circumstances don't render it necessary to repeat *that*.

But I must make haste to close. I love you, dear heart, more than tongue can tell, I want you. I need *you* every-day and all day long. Ah, how I long to be near you when you tell me that my presence will make so great a difference to you, that it will satisfy your heart-hunger! I cannot bear to think that my darling suffers from even a "*sweet* misery"! Believe me, dearest,

Yours always and altogether   Eileen.

ALS (WP, DLC).

To Ellen Louise Axson

My own darling,   Balto., Md., Dec. 18, 1884

I am glad that you did tell me about your experience with the impudent fellow who thrust himself upon you as an escort from the League. It was scarcely from such a quarter, however, that I expected annoyance to come to you. I do not wonder that you felt helpless in the matter; but surely, my darling, it would have been possible to dismiss him peremptorily. Even if he was formally introduced to you in the class, no acquaintance so formed would have warranted his so much as *asking* the privilege of escorting you home. The case had scarcely any point of difference from a similar presumption on the part of a street adventurer. He simply went upon the presumption that you would not exercise your right of dismissing him. Oh! *why* am I condemned to live thus separated from you, at a virtually inaccessible distance! If I had been there, I should certainly have offered the fellow the alternative of never speaking to you again or taking a thrashing. To call the puppy a "crank" is to put a very mild interpretation on his deliberately insulting conduct. I know too much of men to be able to accept such a view of the affair: and I think that you are apt to err very gravely on the side of lenient judgments and of making light of such adventures.

Well, I have given the Hopkins literary society a new name, and a brand-new constitution of my own composition. I even wrote a set of by-laws for them, and presided over the meeting at which they adopted all the new methods. They have fallen in with my plans with remarkable unanimity: it remains to be seen how they will operate them. It will require some parliamentary talent to infuse real life into the "Hopkins House of Commons."

It is characteristic of my whole self that I take so much pleasure in these proceedings of this society. It reminds me of the time when I piloted a new constitution to adoption in the society at the University of Virginia.[1] I have a sense of power in dealing with men collectively which I do not feel always in dealing with them singly[.] In the former case the pride of reserve does not stand so much in my way as it does in the latter. One feels no sacrifice of pride necessary in courting the favour of an assembly of men such as he would have to make in seeking to please one man. But shaw! you *can't* be interested in all this personal stuff!

I have another examination to-morrow—this time upon Dr. Ely's lectures on Commerce; not a very formidable ordeal, but one for which I must be making some further preparation.

Are you too having a genuine snow-storm?

I love you, darling. I love you with an intense, eager, all-absorbing love that has made me altogether

Your own   Woodrow

ALS (WC, NjP).
[1] For the Jefferson Society; printed in Vol. 1, pp. 689-99.

From Ellen Louise Axson

My darling Woodrow,   New York, Dec 18/84.

I have just received and read your sweet letter written yesterday. Yes, darling, I am *sure* that you do play as large a part for good in my daily life as I can possibly play in yours. What would I do on such days as these—all darkness, and gloom, and chill,—if I did not have those letters to surround me with brightness and warmth. They furnish the whole day's supply of sunshine; they enable me to start right and in good spirits in spite of the uncongenial weather. Oh dear, I wish I did not love sunshine and warm weather *quite* so much! I wish the cold agreed with me better, and did not make me *quite so* cold and "shivery"—but how foolish to write so! You see this room is at freezing temperature, —my hands are almost too stiff to write—and "out of the abundance of the heart the mouth speaketh."

It was very kind in Mr. Bridges to speak so of me, but he only does it out of good nature, for I felt curiously embarrassed that night,—quite tongue-tied, in fact, and I talked like an *idiot*! I *must* stop darling, much against my will, for it is too cold to write. I love you, dearest, I love you more even than you know, and I am altogether,   Your own   Eileen.

ALS (WP, DLC).

To Ellen Louise Axson

My own darling,   Balto., Md., Dec. 18/84   9.25 P.M.

I shall be so busy to-morrow, with lectures, the examination on commerce, &c., that I think I better write to-night while I am sure of a little leisure for the purpose. I have read my notes on Dr. Ely's lectures, for the examination, until my eyes have grown painfully tired of the pencilled short-hand—and my mind weary of the statistical desert; and generally nothing rests me so much as writing to you. How *could* writing to you be *hard*? I don't have to guard what I say to my darling: I can write with perfect freedom and confidence; and when one can do *thus* what he wants to do, it ought to be easy. If I had to ponder and weigh everything I said to you, for fear that you might misunderstand it; if I had to phrase my meaning circumspectly lest you should take offence, this daily letter-writing would be daily torture. But you are the only person in the world—except the dear ones at home—with whom I do *not* have to act a part, to whom I do *not* have to deal out confidences cautiously; and you are the only person in the world—without *any* exception—to whom I can tell *all* that my heart contains.

I believe that I am only just beginning to appreciate fully the consequences of all this. One of these consequences, which has once and again been forced upon my recognition, is that I am more affected by your opinions than by those of anybody else. With everybody else I am willing that it should be a matter of 'give and take': if I cannot convince them that I am right, I am willing that they should differ with me as widely as they will: it's simply a question of mastery. But I have found to my cost that it isn't so when *you* reject my judgments and opinions, when *you* set my conclusions aside as overwrought or foolish. I will not undertake to name or to analyze the difference. I am quite sure as to what it does *not* arise from, but I can't say now what does cause it. It does not grow out of anything so small as *pique* that you should not always think me right. I have no special *amour propre* as regards my own judgments: I am quite conscious of being extremely fallible. Nor does it spring from a desire to rule your opinions except by reason: I have never found it agreeable to deal with persons who invariably agreed with me. But I have long had the habit of recognizing my own feelings quite frankly—without any attempt to hoodwink *myself*—and I can't make an exception, if I would, in the case of this feeling that takes hold of me when my Eileen prefers other conclusions to mine. Maybe, if the matter were probed to the bottom, it would be found that there was a wee drop of jealousy in the feeling: because these other conclusions may be *somebody else's*. It's odd that circumstances should be able to play such tricks with character. I am quite sure that I don't want to be thought perfect by *any*body: and equally sure that I don't think myself particularly wise; and yet when *you* wave my opinions aside as foolish or exaggerated I—but *what* stuff I am writing! I know that you are sweet enough to indulge me by saying that you *like* me to drift into these moods of self-revelation, but I musn't presume too much upon the implied invitation so long as I am condemned to confine myself to letter-writing: because this pen of mine has no sort of facility in expressing these secret things. It has become confirmed in a habit of formal statement which makes it a most clumsy hand at conveying delicate shades of thought. And while writing to you I am forever making futile, and therefore absurd, attempts to put into words things that clearly were not meant for any such medium—but should be kept for the fuller vocabulary of that other language which lovers know how to *speak*, though not how to *write*.

Eileen, my little queen, if I tell you of a present I want you to make me on Christmas, will you promise it? I want you to write me—and mail, if you can, so that it will reach here on Christmas-day—a *love-letter* pure and simple—that is, a letter containing nothing *but* love. I shall need it on Christmas day. Don't put into it anything that you think you will have the courage to *say* to me with your own sweet lips—unless you will consent to *repeat* it when you see me—because the love *speeches* you make to me are too precious to my heart to be made fewer in number; but put into it *every*thing that your heart prompts you to tell me and that you think you have *not* yet the courage to use to invite my kisses! Ah, my darling, what gift can be compared with the gift of your love and a special renewal of that gift made in your own words will be the most priceless Xmas present I could receive!

Good-night, precious. I shall dream of you all night unless some unusual cause break in upon a long course of precedents.

Your own   Woodrow.

P.S. Don't fail, little sweetheart, to let me know in abundance of time what your address will be in Phila. and just when you expect to start.

Not a syllable from Bryn Mawr yet.   Lovingly, W.

P.S. No. 2   I had meant to say something about Mr. Goodrich,

in answer to your letter of this morning; and, though it *is* very
late, I will even now add a few words while the matter is on my
mind. You were quite right in your forecast of my opinion on the
subject of his attentions to you: I do *not* believe in the possibility
of the "platonic schedule" *at all.* Of course I have *perfect* faith
in your discreetness; but you must remember that he is in ignorance of your engagement, and that not the broadest hints conceivable can make him "understand" so long as you continue to
wear your ring as you have been wearing it. Not to wear it on
the significant finger is in effect to *conceal* our engagement, my
pet, and nobody can be expected to understand hints in the face
of the testimony of his senses. Your faith in the power of the
New England climate to change human nature may be well
founded; but I think that it would be very much fairer to me if
you would wear your ring as an engagement ring. You know it
was my earnest request from the first that you should do this. I
have not insisted on it before because I hesitated to press a point
made principally on my own account; but now I trust that my
darling will see fit to observe my wishes in the matter, if she has
not done so already.

   With a heart full of love,   Your own   Woodrow.

ALS (WC, NjP).

From Charles Howard Shinn

Dearest Woodrow—   [New York, c. Dec. 18, 1884]
   Tis done—the R.R. passes *secured* & enough newspaper cor-
r[espondence] to pay, & more than pay all my expenses. Besides
this I have assurance that I shall be welcome back in the newspaper offices & this is much.
   I want to be told about your plans[.] Do you come to N.Y. &
when. Day & train. Did you go to Phila.? If so when & address?
I can't comfortably leave this side o' the continent without a word
from you & a sight of you. Called on Miss A. a few days ago—
but did not find her in[.] Tell all the boys about my bonanza &
romantic continent circling (Im to return by the N.P.R.R.[)].
                                        C.H.S.

ALI (WP, DLC).

From Albert Shaw

My Dear Wilson: [Minneapolis] December 19. 1884.
   I write hastily to say how glad I am that your book is coming

out so soon and under circumstances and auspices so satisfactory all around. You will get a great deal of credit, and quite a handsome number of 15 cent pieces as royalty. If true merit were duly rewarded in this unfriendly and ridiculous world, you would make more money than Blaine is getting out of his book.[1] But true science has her compensations that the vulgar, mammonseeking world know not of, etc. etc. I am not writing a Sunday editorial and I will swing off of this topic. Really I am certain that your essays will have wide attention, and I do not believe that their fame will be ephemeral. Further, I think they contain the "potency and promise" of "more to follow."

I am glad the election is over. There are other subjects that I like better to write about. I am touching up the railroads this evening. We are having a tough time out here this winter over high rates and crushed markets for grain. Those reciprocity treaties are a big subject.[2] Their bearings are legion and it is difficult to select an attitude. I am espousing the policy of favouring, cautiously, the Spanish treaty. I think it will benefit the country —at least this section of it. But I do not expect to see the treaty ratified. For an infinite variety of the most contrary reasons, nearly all the papers in the country are opposing it. The South acted very badly in the Senate on the Dakota question.[3] Do you not think that the territories have certain unwritten constitutional rights as to admission? I think it clear that they have. Dakota is very populous & in a highly civilized and orderly condition. I wish such questions might not be treated in a strictly partisan manner.

One of my pleasantest daily tasks is that of looking through the exchanges. By spending half an hour or an hour a day in running through the editorial pages of the leading papers North, South, East and West, one gets a fine and broad view of the state of public sentiment. I really like this work very much. If I could only have four or five months off every year for other pursuits, I should be satisfied. Of course this business is the most exacting & exclusive in the world.

Tell Wright that his letter was my foremost social and recreational diversion for a whole week and a half. I don't have any fun up here at all. That's the truth. Everybody is too anxious for dollars. Those who do have fun are not my sort. *Ergo*, I can't consistently rejoice with those who do rejoice. Not being disposed to join the mourners, or the speculators, I am thrown in on my own resources. Tell Wright, further, that I will communicate with him directly before many days. I hear that you, Levermore and

Dewey are great swells in the department and that the new men are what we newspaper folk call "chumps." Good night.—

Albert Shaw.

ALS (WP, DLC).

¹ The first volume of James G. Blaine's *Twenty Years of Congress: From Lincoln to Garfield* (Norwich, Conn., 1884) had just appeared.

² Secretary of State F. T. Frelinghuysen had signed reciprocity treaties with Spain and the Dominican Republic on November 18 and December 4, 1884, respectively. The treaty with Spain provided for a reduction in American duties on sugar and tobacco in return for the free admission into Cuba and Puerto Rico of a number of American agricultural and manufactured products. The treaties were submitted to the Senate on December 9 and 10, 1884, but encountered strong opposition, particularly from Democrats and various commercial interests. They were never brought to a vote, and President Cleveland withdrew them.

³ The Senate had passed a bill for the admission of South Dakota on December 16. The vote was along strict party lines: 34 Republicans in the affirmative, 28 Democrats in the negative.

Two Letters from Ellen Louise Axson

My darling Woodrow,   New York, Dec 19/84

The first *snow* of the season has fallen today;—filling me with the old childish excitement and delight, which I suppose I will never quite out-grow;—which I have certainly brought unchanged so far from the old times when it was the signal for a general holiday, and the maddest of frolics. I would rather like a frolic with it now. For after all, I am very childish still in many respects; I begin to despair of myself,—to think I am one of those people who will never be quite "grown-up." And in that case, how can I manage to grow old gracefully? how can I acquire that imposing dignity of manner, which gives one's character "weight," and inspires respect. And yet perhaps the unfortunate circumstance that I am likely always to remain, in some of my feelings, a child or at least a "young person," will enable me, with even greater confidence, to promise that you shall always be my *sweet-heart*; that I will never cease to regard you with the eyes of my youth. At any rate, I *know* that I can make that promise safely. Whatever else you may become to me, the old feeling cannot be *changed*, it can at most only be *added* to. I had a sweet letter from Cousin Hattie last night, in which, after asking about you,—when you are coming &c.,—she goes on to say that I think I am very happy now in my love, but that by-and by I will look back upon this time, when I thought I loved so dearly, as having been but ["] a very small beginning"! I wonder if all that is true! It is hard to believe; yet she ought to know if anyone does, for it seemed to be a remarkably severe case with her from the first. However, she is kind enough to add that she doesn't wish "to

pour contempt upon this period, which is very sweet and lovely"
—but simply to "encourage" me "for the future"(!)

You ask about my cold, I believe. Yes, it is the same one but
it has'nt been bad, except for two or three days. I was rather
used up with it last night, but I went to bed early,—being too
"head-achy" even to write you,—and slept off a great part of it,
and it is better today, except that I have lost my voice;—not a very
great loss, it won't "break me up" as much as it would Patti, for
instance! I hope that you keep well in spite of the many changes
of weather.

Good-night, dearest. Give love to your parents when you write,
—am sorry they are to be "torn up" all winter.

With truest love, believe me, darling, as ever

Your own   Eileen.

My darling Woodrow,   New York, Dec. 19/84.

If you please, sir,—or even if you *don't* please—you may, can
and *must!* make your arrangements to be here on Xmas day!—
for I have written to Phila, making my excuses, and explaining
how well-nigh impossible it is for me to leave New York at present. I feel as though a weight had been taken off my mind, since
I settled it so. I found myself constantly less and less inclined to
take the trip; it was exceedingly inconvenient for many reasons,
—and it was'nt worth the trouble,—the tremendous undertaking
for instance, of getting myself and my luggage to the depot and
on the train, all alone. Oh, I have any number of good reasons
for not going, and if it makes you "feel bad" to think that I backed
out on you[r] account, I will cheerfully give the prominence to
them whenever you are about! To tell the truth I feel as if some
strangely delightful and unexpected good had befallen me, only
because I have myself written a letter which will, I hope, bring
you to me a few days sooner! Isn't that strange? I can think of
nothing else but that;—he is coming—coming!—next week he will
come! How much sooner that seems than week after next! But
at present I must not think of it any longer but go to sleep, and
dream of it instead, for I had a whole budget of letters to write
tonight, and it grows quite late.

You naughty child to say that I can't be interested "in all this
personal stuff"! You deserve a good scolding for that; and you
should have it too, if I thought you meant what you said. But you
know as well as I do, sir, that the "personal stuff" is the very
thing in which I am *most* interested. And I have found all this

about the society especially pleasant to hear. But I *must* close, with truest love, believe me, darling, as ever, Your own Eileen.

ALS (WP, DLC).

To Ellen Louise Axson

Balto., Md., Dec. 20/84 11.15 A.M.

What sweet things you say to me in your letters, my darling! My letters "surround you with brightness and warmth" and "furnish the whole day's supply of sunshine," enabling you "to start right and in good spirits in spite of the uncongenial weather"? When I read these sentences in the precious little epistles that come to delight me every day, I feel as I suppose a man must feel who has suddenly come into such a fortune as he has long eagerly wished to possess, and with which he thinks he can do all the great things his heart has devised. Here am I who have been waiting all these long years for the love of someone to whose happiness I could devote my life, and I have been given more than I dared to hope for. I have been given the perfect love of my Eileen, the woman of all the women in the world to whom I can render perfect allegiance: the woman whom I knew the world contained, but thought Fortune too niggardly to give me. If I can give my darling happiness—if my love can make her life a life of sunshine—I have found the blessing I had thought to seek in vain! I believe that I am not altogether selfish, that I am capable of considerable self-sacrifice in some directions, and therefore I think that I *could* possibly have made some other woman happy if I had not found you. It would be impossible for me to live *alone*, without home companionship: and it would be equally impossible for me to marry any woman to whose happiness I could not devote myself. But, if I had not found you, I should simply not have known what real love was: I should have gone all my life long mistaking homage and loyal affection for it, and wondering why I was not satisfied. When I found you I found asserting itself within me a new self whose presence I had never recognized before. I had admired other women: I had imagined myself in love with other women, because I had discovered in them such womanliness, such tenderness and sympathetic intelligence, as made me think that it would be delightful to live with them. But I was always able to study them from an attitude of almost dispassionate criticism. I saw their faults very distinctly and felt mildly amused by them: I thought that my love for their possessors was proved by the fact that I could regard these faults with that lack of annoyance, that pity, which one feels in regard to the shortcomings of a sweet child. The feeling was just one side of that instinct of protection which I suppose every man feels towards women. In short, I never forgot *myself* in dealing with other women. There was always a sort of self-protective *aloofness* in my intercourse with them. There was a part of my mind and my heart which I kept to myself, and felt that they had, and could have, nothing to do with: which must, so far as they were concerned, have *always* been kept to myself.

But once, by what seemed a chance, I discovered my real heart. I found a little lady who moved me as I had never been moved before; whose eyes told me, almost from the very first, that there was nothing in my heart which she could not sooner or later find out, if she chose; who made me think *her*, instead of myself, the centre of my world—made me forget my*self* altogether in the one absorbing occupation of loving her. My separateness from her, so long as it lasted, instead of being a calm vantage ground which I took some pleasure and felt some safety in occupying, was only a source of intense pain. I felt that unless I could gain leave to live for her instead of for myself all that was best in my life would be ruined: because she would have awakened in me that love which a man can feel only once—and which had hitherto slept in me—only to leave it forever unsatisfied and hopeless of satisfaction. My darling, you are the centre and source of my life— that's the sum of the whole matter!

It makes me miserably anxious, little sweetheart, to hear that your room is so insufficiently and irregularly heated. No wonder your cold continues and grows worse. *Must* it be so? Is there no remedy? I am afraid of this cold weather: I am afraid that my precious little Southern flower may be injured by it. And, my love, you must *never* sit in your room when it's cold!—not even to write me a *line*—wont you promise me not to? Put an envelope in your pocket and when you get to the League rooms (I suppose it's warm there?) pencil a line on a slip of paper telling me that you are well and love me, and I shall understand and not think of complaining.

And do you *want* to lose that childish impulse which makes you rejoice in the snow and want to play in it? I should be mighty sorry if you did! You would grow too old to be my sweetheart. Since you have loved me I have felt myself developing into a boy (so far as everything but my mind is concerned) even faster than before. We will grow young together and be sweethearts as long as we live. Is it a bargain? With a heartful of love,

Your own   Woodrow.

ALS (WC, NjP).

From Ellen Louise Axson

My darling Woodrow,   New York Dec. 20/84

My cold is troubling me so much tonight, that I think I will try and content myself with a short letter, and go to bed early, like a good girl. Though it will be rather a hard matter to return a short answer to that nice long interesting letter of this morning, a letter too which suggests so many things in the way of question and remark.

In the first place, may I inquire, dear sir, *which* of your judgments and opinions I have been rejecting or setting down as "overwrought or foolish"? I have been trying in vain to recall such a case,—think perhaps if I could find one, I would feel a greater respect for myself as a creature of independent and original thought! But in fact, I have been really amused at myself to see how thoroughly I seem to have become convinced that what you say "is so if it isn't so"!—rather a new state of mind too for me, I assure you, for Papa used to think me a very obstreperous subject,—entirely too much inclined to have opinions of my own, —to decide questions altogether for my own small self. I think we will agree very well about most *subjects*,—indeed the danger is in our agreeing so well that you will be *bored* within an inch of your life! About *people*, and their conduct, the case is rather different, because our dispositions are so different;—in fact, I foresee endless *quarrels* on such matters! You see, as you once said of yourself, you are "nothing if not critical," whereas it is my weakness to think everybody—as well as everything—more or less "lovely";—I am generally *sure* that they *mean* well at any rate. But I am inclined to think, dear, that our differing views on those matters won't do us any harm;—I am sure it will do *me* none. You will make me more sensible and well-balanced in my judgments,—and *yet* I mean to continue as far as possible, to look on the best side of people! Do you know those stern judgments of yours used to frighten me dreadfully?—and you gave me a fresh fright not long ago, by saying that you thought love made one more than ever sensitive to the faults and defects of it's object. Dear me! thought I, what *is* to become of me if he is *more* sensitive to *my* faults than he is to those of others! I had heard all my life that love was *blind*, and thought that my one chance lay in that fact! If you can't be blind you had better bandage your eyes, and *play* blindfold, my dear, for both our sakes! But never mind,—you have promised to *love* me—whatever you see in me, so it is all right. I have the ring on the first finger and will keep it there for the present at least, until it has had time to have all the effect which you think its appearance there will produce. I can't wear it there permanently as I told you, because it is too small for it. It pains me, and makes my finger swell; and by and by if I persisted I should be obliged to have either it or the *finger* sawed off! But what young man was it who told me last summer that I had a *"perfect right"* to keep my engagement secret, and who was so indignant with another young man for his "insolence" in daring to question that right? Good-night, dearest, I love you more than words can tell. I am half wild to get the answer to my last night's letter which will tell me just when to expect you, so that I can begin to count up the hours. With truest love,   Your own   Eileen.

ALS (WP, DLC).

To Robert Bridges

My dear Bobby,   Balto., Md., Dec. 20/84
    Your letter of the 16th [15th] was mighty welcome, and my enjoyment of it was altogether out of proportion to its length. It gave me a glimpse of what you are doing nowadays that I was exceedingly glad to get. But it seems to me, my dear fellow, that you've missed your calling if you've turned satirist "for the most part."[1] Not that I have any doubt about your being able to go into satire with the best. But satire is destructive and has to deliver its lightning in spots. Constructive work is much higher, and I have been living several years under a woful delusion if that is not the sort of work for which you were intended. But I must save that topic for a talk, if we can ever have one. I am coming to New York on the 29th and, if you have gotten off to Buffalo before I arrive, I shall try to stay long enough to have an evening with you after you get back. The length of my stay is to depend upon how long my money holds out, and I should esteem it a great favour if you could send me, on a card, the address of some place, in the neighbourhood of West 11th St., where I can get a week's board at reasonable rates. Of course I don't want you to *look* for a place: write if you happen to know of one, that's cheaper than the hotels.
    I should have told you myself of the acceptance of my book: but Miss Axson "wanted the fun of telling *some*body" and so I left *you* to her. I think that you will agree with me in regarding *this* attempt of mine as *vastly* better than the last, though exceedingly imperfect still.

I am *very* glad that you have met Miss A. and I assure you, old fellow, that I appreciate most highly what you say of her. I quoted that sentence of yours in one of my letters to her; and she replies: "It was very kind of Mr. Bridges to speak so of me, but he only does it out of good nature, for I felt curiously embarrassed that night, quite tongue-tied in fact!" Still, I know from a previous letter how much she enjoyed your visit.

I am glad to hear that you are to get off home for Christmas, because I can imagine how delightful such trips must be to you. My vacation begins to-day and runs till the 7th of Jany, but about half of it must be taken up in clearing off some of the arrears of work which have been accumulating on my hands this "semester"(!)

The Cow sends a great deal of love. As ever
Your sincere friend,   Woodrow Wilson

ALS (Meyer Coll., DLC).
¹ This portion of Bridges' letter was not printed.

To Ellen Louise Axson

My own darling,   Balto., Md., Dec. 21/84
I find that I was mistaken about there being any class-exercises at the University next Wednesday, the 24th[.] The holidays are to *include* the 24th so that my vacation really began yesterday, to run for nearly three weeks. It's hard for me to decide whether I'm glad or sorry. Of course I like to be free to choose my own hours of study: but then, on the other hand, having nothing imperative to keep me here only increases my longing to be with you. Ah, if I could only be off to New York to-night to spend the whole of the three weeks with my darling! We have never yet been three consecutive weeks together! And it seems to me that my little sweet-heart needs me now especially. I have an idea that if I could go on and take care of her for a little while I could find some means of charming away that cold that is making me so anxious and of coaxing back that voice that I love so much! What am I good for, anyhow? Here I am perfectly well and strong, and yet of no manner of use to my darling when she is sick, having to content myself with wishing that I *could* nurse her. Well, well, it shan't always be so: and I *ought* to be able to wait patiently for the sweet time coming.

I wonder if we *shall* love each other as much more after we are married as "cousin Hattie" predicts? It doesn't seem possible, does it? How *can* I feel more identified with my darling then than I do now? Still, if it must come, little sweetheart, I reckon we can stand it! No amount of love can do us any harm, and, for my part, I am willing to let things take their natural course. If that increase of love that is to be expected prove as great a blessing as this first instalment has been, I shall simply be more than ever the most fortunate man in the world. Then, too, my precious, you deserve all the love, and more than all, that could possibly be given you, and to love you more will be but loving you more nearly as you deserve. But what am I to do? There is the quandary! My love for you has already taken complete possession of my heart and life, and, if it is to assert a still greater sovereignty, what is to become of me?

But, after all, darling, I can see how the thing must be as "cousin Hattie" says. Our love *has* grown almost infinitely since our engagement—that's an unquestionable precedent—and as time goes on and we draw closer and closer together till we live but a *single* life, shall we not love more and more perfectly the lovable things we see in each other, and forgive more and more thoroughly the shortcomings, till we shall be absolutely one in everything? When my little sweetheart becomes my wife I shall of course owe her a different sort of homage and service and protection, and maybe she will discover in me then traits that have so far been hidden from her because she did not have a wife's eyes to see them or a wife's ears to hear confession of them. And why shouldn't I go on discovering lovable traits in my Eileen as I have been doing constantly ever since I knew her? I love to think what you shall be to me then, my darling, and what I shall strive to be to you!

The Bryn Mawr affair has broken out in a new place, with somewhat new symptoms. I learned yesterday afternoon, through a note from Dean Martha, that at the late meeting of the executive committee of the trustees "the subject of the historical appointment was deferred until the twelfth of January," and that "Mr. Francis T. King, the president of the Board of the Trustees of Bryn Mawr College, would like very much to have the opportunity of talking with" me.[1] I shall call upon Mr. King at his residence at 5 P.M. on to-morrow, as suggested by D. M., and then and there give him the opportunity for which he longs. I suppose that it is to be a negotiation about salary and that the scheme is to secure me at the lowest figure possible. Unless they offer more than there is any reasonable prospect of my being able to get somewhere else in the East, I don't know what will come of this fresh bargaining. It really seems necessary that I should obtain some position for next year: but it is not yet quite clear to my mind how great a sacrifice I ought to make in order to do so. I cannot afford to hold myself cheap: but neither can I afford to hold myself too dear. The problem is to make them give more than they want to give and yet not more than they *will* give. It's a hard nut to crack, and I am a novice in this sort of diplomacy!

A letter from "Dode" says that he is not to return to Bingham's. The early move now in prospect makes it not worth while: he will have to recite privately to a tutor at home. It's unfortunate that it should have become necessary to break in upon his newly-formed school habits so soon, but it was unavoidable, and it is a great satisfaction to me to know that dear mother will have the comfort of having him at home. The people of the church in Wilmington are in a great state of excitement about dear father's determination to leave. They are terribly 'broken up' over it; because they have all along been intensely proud of having him, though they have allowed themselves to drift into a false assurance that they could keep him without making any special effort to coöperate with him in church work. Their chagrin is now all the greater at finding that they have lost him entirely through their own selfish faults.

Do you remember my injunction, my pet, whenever you write to Savannah, to send my warmest love always to the dear ones there? You don't know what a strong affection I have for your grandparents, for your uncle and aunt and that wonderful group of little ones. I love them all, not only through you and for your sake, but also on my own account; and I have often wished that I had some means of making them realize how *much* I love them all.

I went to the Musical and Dramatic Club after the Seminary meeting on Friday night according to arrangement, and found Miss Jennings' parlours—one of which had been the stage of the evening—full of young ladies and young gentlemen in full dress. It was my occupation thence till about one o'clock Saturday morning to sample various individuals thus disguised. One young lady was very bright and jolly, and we made friends at once; another was very demure and matter-of-fact, and wasn't quite sure she understood all I said; a third nearly giggled her life away at my jokes; a fourth was severely instructive. One young man had known of me and "heard my oration" at the University of Va.; another had a brother who had known me at the same institution, and whom he had often heard speak of me; a third was interested in the Hopkins Glee Club; a fourth was satisfied with letting me know his name and said nothing. Miss Jennings was very gracious—as well as proud of her snowy neck—and hoped that she would have the pleasure of seeing me at other meetings of the Club. So there you have the history of the evening—except that the iced cream was very good and that I had to walk home through a couple of miles of icey streets, meeting an icey wind at every corner!

Since writing these twelve pages, little sweetheart, I have been to the Post Office and gotten your letter of Friday night (probably written just about the hour at which I was talking to the severely instructive young lady aforesaid) in which you announce your intention of disappointing "uncle Tom and aunt Saidie," and summon me for this week. Oh my darling! Is it really so? Am I *really* to spend Christmas-day with my little queen, after all? It's almost too good to believe! Surely the sweet glee in which this merry little note was written must be infectious—or else it is the news and the invitation that it contains that are making my heart beat so fast and my spirits rise so high! I don't know, Miss, whether I shall approve altogether your decision in regard to going to Phila. I shall reserve my judgment till I hear a recital of the "many reasons" which influenced you!—but certain it is that, Providence permitting, I shall have my darling in my arms before the week is more than half gone:—and *then*—then we shall store up pleasure enough to last us till the next time we may be together! Oh my darling, my darling! How passionately I love you—how intensely I long to see you! Thursday seems now almost as far away as the 29th seemed but a few hours ago!

I can't say exactly when I shall be able to start: because this change of plan makes it necessary to crowd several things that I must do before I leave into the next few days. I must let the men in Boston know, for instance, that I shall not be here to receive proofs; I must conclude what negotiations may be necessary with the aforementioned Francis T. King, President &c; I must wait as long as possible to hear from Bridges about a lodging place nearer to 11th St. than any I know of at present, &c. &c. But I shall certainly spend Christmas-day, all of it, with my darling. Are you prepared, Miss, to receive a young gentleman who will feel like being more demonstrative than he has ever been before when once he sets eyes on you again? Will you be ready to give him as many kisses as he wants? Will you do all you can to show him how thoroughly you belong to him? What have I ever done to deserve all the happiness that has been given me? The sweetest little woman in the world is *mine*, and I am to see her and hear her *say* that she is mine. My matchless Eileen! I am afraid I can never make you know how much you are loved by

Your own   Woodrow.

ALS (WC, NjP).

¹ The minutes of the full Board of Trustees of Bryn Mawr College are not extant for this period, but the minutes of the Executive Committee of the Board for December 20, 1884, indicate considerable reluctance by the full Board of Trustees to accept the Executive Committee's recommendation regarding Wilson's appointment. The Executive Committee, in a minute of December 20, 1884, reaffirmed its earlier recommendation as follows: "The subject of a Professor of History as recommended back to the Committee by the Trustees, was again carefully discussed and considered. The Committee finally concluded that they saw no other way but to inform the Trustees, that entering heartily into all the views and feelings of the Trustees, they were unable to bring forward any other name for the place than that of Woodrow Wilson, formerly recommended by the Committee. They therefore recommend that Woodrow Wilson be appointed Associate in History for two years, at a salary of $1500 a year." The response of the full Board was to postpone decision until January and to ask its president to "see and sample" Wilson, "in order that he might be able to have an opinion ready for Dr. Rhoads" (WW to ELA, Dec. 23, 1884).

From Ellen Louise Axson

My darling Woodrow,   New York Dec. 21/84.

I have been writing to your sister tonight, and by reason thereof I fear I must put you off with a short note, for in the meantime my fire, having been made earlier than usual, has gone out, and as I have no more coal with which to replenish, the only resource is to go to bed, early as it is. I was *ashamed* to write to your sister after all these months, so I thought my best plan was to wait a little longer and make Xmas a sort of excuse; dont you think that a good idea? I was really afraid she would think it ridiculous in me to answer a letter after a year's delay!

I woke upon a beautiful world this morning;—we had a glorious snow-storm last night, the first really fine one of the season. I made my way through it to church with immense enjoyment, and then had special blessings called down upon my head by Dr. Hamilton for my self sacrifice in coming through the storm. So I got the praise and the pudding both.

Miss Mosely's vacant room has been taken at last, and by *another* art student!!—as Mr. Finlayson says, "it seems to be an epidemic!" This is a Miss Comstock of Cleveland Ohio, a nice, refined looking lady of perhaps thirty-five. Havn't made her acquaintance yet. She is an Academy student. Another of my dreams has been rudely shattered; I have just received a letter from Rose saying that she can't come on, this winter. I didnt tell you, I think, that I had worked myself into the belief that I could persuade her to come and take lessons in decorative art.

It would be just the thing for her, if she could only afford it—and what *bliss* it would have been to be together here all winter!— I must try and not think about it. Rose says "Réné has gone to Fernandino to spend Xmas, leaving Mr. Beckwith alone in Atlanta; isnt she *mean*?" I think she *is* mean,—uncommonly mean! —their first Xmas together!

My! this room is *so* cold! I must stop at once, pray excuse haste. I can afford now to keep all I want to say until you come, the time is so short. How my heart burns within me at that thought; you are the very light of my eyes, the whole world will grow bright for me when you come. Ah, my darling, my darling I love you with all my heart. As ever   Your own   Eileen

ALS (WP, DLC).

From Charles Howard Shinn

Dear Woodrow.   [New York] Sunday [Dec. 21, 1884]

I sail Wednesday per. Str on Old Dominion line to Newport News. Have pass & *must* be economical as my expenses are frightful of late. You can do much for me socially, as I have to leave without coming to B. Smooth down Wright & Miss Ashton & all the rest. Write me all abt your plans. I cant seem to find out whether you are in Phila or Balt. or what Miss A. is doing. I've written her. Tell Pres. Gilman, Dr. Ely & Jameson & Adams abt my plan. I have no time to write. Let Wright tell Dr. Wood. Give my love to Worthington, Dewey & Levermore. Regards to all the fellows. . . .   Charlie

ALS (WP, DLC).

To Ellen Louise Axson

My own darling,   Balto., Md., Dec. 22/84

It was quite outdoing myself to commit two stupid blunders in a single letter. What I said about the effect produced upon me by your rejection of my opinions *had no special application at all*: and yet I might have known that it would seem to have. It was used just as one way of illustrating the character of my love for you. I don't *want* you to give up your independence of judgment— and, if it were true that you had, the illustration would never have occurred to me. You musn't search for hidden meanings, my darling, in my new devices for telling you that you are more to me than all the world beside. If I have any meaning other than that which appears on the face of what I say, you may trust me to state it plainly.

The other stupidity concerned the ring. Of course I had for the moment *forgotten* that the ring was too *small* for your forefinger. I had no idea of asking you to wear it at the expense of physical suffering. Take it off at once, my pet; and when I come I will have it made larger. Maybe one of your other rings would fit that finger?

I still think, my love, that Mr. Wright was insolent in demanding as a right a knowledge of your engagement: and I have certainly recognized no such right in anybody else. I said that to wear the symbol of our engagement would be fairer to *me*. I have a certain pride in being *acknowledged*; and I think that by such an acknowledgement you would save yourself from such annoyances and disappointments as would result from the failure of promising "platonic schedules." It is altogether an argument for your comfort and *my* rights. I know of no one else who has any rights in the matter.

I am sorry, little lady, that you think it my disposition to look at the *worst* side of people—to take a cynical view of human nature—because I don't think that that is a just view of my character. At least, I hope it is not. I am capable of very unquestioning faith in many of my fellow-men, of an admiration akin to hero-worship in the case of *some*, and I believe that there is a vast deal more good than evil in human nature. I am inclined to credit most men with being better than myself. To lose faith in my fellow-men would be to make of my mental life a mere negation, would be to lose the primal element of that enthusiasm without which a man is dead while he yet lives. I hate a cynic: I despise a sour critic! But, on the other hand, I think it only reasonable to recognize such faults as are discoverable, so long as they are recognized in *sympathy* and not with carping censure—so long as they are not *sought* for from love of fault-finding—that most hateful of all dispositions. And there are some traits of human nature which we are in a sense *bound* to see, simply because they are on the surface—placed as if to be seen! When I declare my utter want of confidence in the possibility of a real platonic affection subsisting between two young unmarried people, for instance, I am simply stating a conclusion which has been forced upon me, not only by observation, but also—and more particularly—*by my own consciousness*[.] Observation has only revealed to me as a *general* rule the law that I found in myself. If a young man and a young woman, both unmarried, find unfailing pleasure in being constantly together, love *must* result in one or both, unless another love intervenes or there is some well-understood circumstance which shuts out hope.

You cannot have been more frightened by my stern, unamiable judgments than I have been by your disposition to place entire confidence in everybody not definitely proved unworthy: and if I have seemed to you harsh, it must have been because I wanted to combat the opposite tendency in you.

However that may be, there is one thing certain—as certain as that I live and love you—and that is that none of my judgments concerning my little sweetheart can ever so much as approach the form of personal censure. If all true love is blind, then mine is blind: and maybe you will accept as proof the fact that I have never seen anything in my Eileen's character that I should like to see changed. I have never made a discovery about her that did not increase my love for her. I not only love but *admire* her altogether. None of my criticisms can ever touch *her*: and she may be absolutely sure that no thought, no impulse, no wish of hers can ever fail to find, not only sympathy, but loving, *entire* sympathy in me—though I be cold and critical towards all the rest of the world. Oh, my darling; *don't* regard me as an intellectual ogre—don't think that my mind and my heart are divorced. Love doesn't *criticise*: it sees and loves the more.

I am miserable about that cold of yours, darling. Are you doing nothing for it? I shall write to you to-morrow exactly when you may expect me. Oh my darling! How I long to see you!

Your own　Woodrow.

ALS (WP, DLC).

From Robert Bridges

Dear Tommy:　　　　　　　　　　　　　[New York] Dec 23 '84

I have only time to reply briefly to your question about a room. It is unfortunate that just at present Harper[1] (of the *Tribune*, a Princeton boy and fellow townsman) is spending a week or ten days at our house with his mother. He is sharing my room, and so I am denied the pleasure of asking you to bunk with me. Parsons goes away to get married and his room is already taken from Jan. 1st. The rest of the house is full. I can only think of 155 West 15th St where Wilder, Felt,[2] and I once roomed. You might easily get a hall-bed-room there for a week, at about $3. Then take your meals as we did around the corner on 14th St at the Hotel Brentwood, or what is better "restaurant" it.

I think Mrs. Sherrill still lives at the old place.

Am rushed to death. Go home tomorrow and to Buffalo next week.   Yours   Bob Bridges

ALS (WP, DLC).

¹ George McLean Harper, born Shippensburg, Pa., Dec. 31, 1863. A.B. College of New Jersey, 1884; Ph.D., the same, 1891. Married Belle Dunton Westcott, May 9, 1895. Employed on *New York Tribune*, 1884. Studied abroad, 1885-87; on *Scribner's Magazine*, 1887-89. Instructor, Princeton, 1889-91; assistant professor, 1891-94; Professor of Romance Languages, 1894-1900; Holmes Professor of Belles Lettres and Language and Literature, 1900-26; Woodrow Wilson Professor of Literature, 1926-32. Biographer of William Wordsworth and author of many works on English and French literature. Died July 14, 1947.

² William R. Wilder and Zephaniah Charles Felt, both Princeton, '79.

From Joseph Ruggles Wilson

My dearest Woodrow—   Wilmington [N.C.], Decr 23, 84

You will please find enclosed my check for $20.00 as a Xmas present in lieu of some useless trinket. This is, indeed, from your dear mother rather than from your cross father. She is worth a hundred of me, anyway.

We are all in usual health, except that your mother has a severe cold, and I have a rheumatic map upon my back with lines running down to my right arm, as a sort of Italy. Am thus unfit to write, &c. &c. &c.

All join me in Xmas salutations and all-the-year-round love.
                                        Your affc   Father

ALS (WP, DLC).

From Ellen Louise Axson

My darling Woodrow,   New York, Dec. 23/84.

I was so *exceedingly* busy last night, that I could not find a moment for writing; and this morning I am even busier, so I *must* try for once really to send a brief note. You observe that I frequently *begin* with that intention,—and my success is certainly conspicuous (by it's absence). My notes *are brief*—as woman's love!

Have just read your sweet letter,—yesterday's—& I must protest again, sir! I did not say you were cynical or inclined to look on the *worst* side of people,—most assuredly I did not *think* it. You look on *both* sides and render a dispassionate and unbiased verdict,—you are severely *just* in your judgments. I simply said, what you had already said of yourself, many times, that you were very "critical." You[r] "attitude" toward the other women with whom you ["]imagined! yourself in love" affords a striking as well as amusing instance of that. But I *must not* try to answer your letter now, for I must send some things off early this morning or they will be to late for Xmas. So goodbye, until day after tomorrow! If I send a letter tomorrow it will miss you, will it not? I am *so* happy to think of it, that I have almost lost my wits—can scarcely attend to my business properly. I love you darling, I love you more than life. As ever   Your own   Eileen.

ALS (WP, DLC).

To Ellen Louise Axson
My own darling,   Balto., Dec. 23rd., 1884
    I am almost too excited to write. To think that this letter is to get to you at most only twenty-four hours before I do! I shall *try*, my darling, to call at No. 120 West 11th Street between four and five o'clock to-morrow afternoon (*this* afternoon, it will be when you read this letter!); but it is possible that this dragging Bryn Mawr business may prevent my starting in the morning as I now intend. Mr. King said yesterday that Dr. Rhoads was expected to be in Baltimore to-day or to-morrow, and might want to see me; and I promised to stay in town till to-morrow evening, if necessary. In that case, I will take the midnight train, as before, [so] as [to] see you as early as possible on Christmas morning. My interview with Mr. King was altogether without significance. He simply wanted to see and sample me, in order that he might be able to have an opinion ready for Dr. Rhoads. What a hateful business it is! My pride will presently rebel altogether and break up the present situation. Why can't these Quakers make up their minds like other people?
    Is [It] was a *very* happy thought, little sweetheart, to make Christmas, rather than her year-old letter, the occasion for your letter to sister Marion. I am *so* glad that you did write to her. It will gratify her exceedingly. She is very anxious to be able to feel that she knows you.
    Yes, my pet, it *was* decidedly "mean" in Mrs. Beckwith to leave her husband so soon and at such a season for a pleasure trip: but I must say that it follows very naturally upon her treatment of him during their engagement. When love is of such a sort, a husband is a mere convenience, if he be so fortunate as to escape being a nuisance. I don't believe in love without *devotion*: and *selfish* love is a contradiction in terms!
    It seems that I am just to miss Shinn. He sails to-morrow. It's

too bad! He writes begging that I come on to-night; but, as you see, that is impossible.

Oh my darling, my darling! How shall I tell you the joy that is in my heart at the prospect of seeing you so soon. Why, my pet, to see you will be to realize the wish that everyday has made stronger since last I held you in my arms—will be to give temporary respite to that passionate longing which can never be altogether satisfied until I may come to you to stay with you, till my sweetheart, my matchless Eileen, has become my bride and has claimed me for life as   Her own   Woodrow.

ALS (WP, DLC).

From Melville R. Hopewell

Dear Sir,   Tekamah, Neb. Dec. 29th 1884

Yours of the 19th at hand—inclosing Dft. $101.21[.] The Draft was payable to your order, but not endorsed by you. I took the liberty of writing your name on the back, and have paid your taxes, and hand you herewith receipts— $100.20
our charges,   1
                                                 _____
                                                    $101.20

The difference in the tax for 1883 & 1884 is most likely due to local tax—for school purposes—these taxes vary in different years —according to tax levied by the school District. State taxes are much lighter for 84 than they have been for some years,

                    Truly Yours,   M. R. Hopewell

ALS (WP, DLC). Encs.: 2 tax receipts dated Dec. 27, 1884.

From Janet Woodrow Wilson

My dearest Woodrow,   Wilmington, N.C. Dec 31st 1884

We received your note of the 28th this morning. It is pleasant to think of your happiness in the society of your dear little girl. I am sure from your saying nothing about it, that you did not receive your father's note with enclosure, before you left Baltimore[.] I am so sorry—for it might have enabled you to prolong your enjoyment a few days longer. I got a New Year's card for dear Ellie—but in looking at it in daylight I dont feel like sending it. If she were not the *Artist* she is, I would not be so hard to please. But you know what advantages we have here in the way of finding anything tasteful. . . . I am not going to make any promises as to *writing* in the future—but will say this much—I *hope* you will not have nearly so much reason to complain of me hereafter. You have been so sweet and good about it. My apology is that I have been quite upset & confused by undertaking to do too much. I will take things more quietly after this. I never meant dear, that I thought you cared less for us all than formerly—merely, that you are not solely dependent upon home letters for comfort. But you understand.

Your father has been troubled for several week[s] with what we think must be *neuralgia*—in his right shoulder and arm. The pain has been very severe at times—but is now less so, and less frequent as well. So that I hope it will soon pass away altogether. Your father had a visit from Mr. Kidder[1] the other evening—when he talked freely with him about his leaving this. Mr. K. is an exceedingly sensible man. He says that it will be a great calamity to the congregation to lose your father—that he has not an enemy in the church or out of it in Wilmington—that the regret at his leaving is universal & deep—that it will be greatly regretted by himself. That he could remain here just as many years as he chose and be sure the people would be satisfied. *But* he advises him *for his own sake* to go. He says he knows that he has not a single congenial companion here—in short the sensible old man knows all about [it]. He is wonderfully sensible & thoughtful. He says the life here must be intolerable to a man of your fathers parts, tastes and acquirements. The interview was a great comfort to dear papa—for he values Mr. K's opinion highly[.] I must not write more now. My trouble is that I cant bear to stop when I once begin.

Did you receive your father's note enclosing cheque for twenty dollars upon your return to New York? We thought much about you dear boy upon your birthday. Josie is very busy enjoying his holiday. He works hard at it.

Love inexpressible to you from us each one. Love to dearest Ellie. Her letter to me was charming. I hope to answer it in a day or two. Lovingly Yours Mother

ALS (WP, DLC).
[1] Edward Kidder, merchant and mill owner of Wilmington, N.C.

From Ellen Louise Axson

Philadelphia[1] Jan. 2/85

What a long, long day this has been, my darling!—the longest, I think I ever spent! I don't know what is to become of me, if it is to grow harder—so very much harder, each time. The parting yesterday was almost more than I could bear. I did not bear it very well! Am sadly afraid that I "moped"! We went just after you left, to that concert at the Academy;[2] which was a very fortunate thing for me, for I felt but little like talking, I can tell you; and there I could sit still and pretend to listen to the music. After the concert, Lily[3] went out to dinner, you know, and I came back and tried desperately to be gay; but I beat an early retreat to my room, on the plea of being tired and here Lily being out, I could be "as wretched as I chose." It is a shame—is it not?—for me to talk of being *wretched!*—that *is* an exaggeration, it is true; I can never be *really* unhappy, I think, while I have the joy "to love and be loved by you." No one, it seems to me, could fail to be happy who was loved by you, and whose sweet privilege,—whose *right* it is to love you in return. Yet there is no denying that the wrench is terrible; —that is the word for it, I think, for all this morning I have felt as though I had been parted from my *life* by some sudden shock. But how foolish in me to talk so!—it will do me no good, and I had best write no more, but try not to think of my afflicted con-dition(!)—Ah my darling, my darling, how I love you! Would that I could prove how much! My poor little heart is scarcely large enough to hold my love, it is full even to overflowing. Be-lieve me, dearest, that I am in every throb of that heart,

Your own Eileen.

Excuse haste. Am sorry to have troubled you with a telegram about the ticket. I knew you would probably discover the mistake but they thought I had better not depend on that.

ALS (WP, DLC).
  1 ELA was visiting the Thomas Hoyts in Philadelphia. WW had accompanied her to Philadelphia and continued on to Baltimore on the same train, taking her ticket with him.
  2 The Academy of Music, now the home of the Philadelphia Orchestra.
  3 Lillian T. Hoyt, daughter of Thomas by his first wife, Mary Harrison.

Two Letters to Ellen Louise Axson

My own darling,   Balto., Md., Jan. 2, 1885   11:55 A.M.
    I am heartily ashamed of myself for having brought your R.R. ticket off with me, and thus given you the trouble of telegraphing for it. Of course I discovered it in my purse as soon as I got here, and was just about to enclose it to you when your dispatch came. You will notice, little sweetheart, that it will not be good after midnight of Monday, the 5th.
    Oh, my darling, I can't tell you how sick I am at heart this morning! It's not a sickness of discontent, but the old feeling of

lack intensified a thousand fold. I am much too profoundly grateful for the sweet privileges of the never-to-be-forgotten week that has just passed to rebel because the discipline of separation must be renewed: but the delights of our recent holiday together have made separation seem all the more desolate and unendurable. But I am not going to dwell on that! A fellow ought to be ashamed of himself for grumbling because he hasn't *all* that he wants, when he has the greatest thing that his heart desires. My darling loves me with all her heart, and that shall suffice me until I have her to tell me so every day. The work and the waiting which must come before my hope receives its complete fruition will but make our marriage day the sweeter when it comes!

Ah, my precious little sweetheart! how shall I tell you what the past eight days have been to me! They have been the happiest days I ever spent. They have given me my darling all over again. They have not so much increased as *confirmed* my love for her by showing me how completely it renews all that is noblest and best in me to be with her, with what unspeakable tenderness it fills me,—with what courage and what a sense of power it endows me to feel the loving presence that is to make my life bright and healthful and strong—that is to keep my mind fresh by keeping my heart young. Oh Eileen, my treasure! I love you! and it is my strength that I love you!

I am *very* tired to-day. I went to the "Jingle party" within a hour and a half after getting in on the train; came home at half-past twelve this morning; read proof till half-past one; went out to mail the proofs, for the early morning collection; and went to bed at two o'clock a worn-out chap. I mean to devote to-day and to-morrow to lazy resting.

My love to all at 1325 [Spruce St., the Hoyt residence]. Good-bye, my darling; I love you unspeakably.   Your own   Woodrow.

My own darling,   Balto., Md., Jan. 3, 1885 11:30 A.M.

I found upon my return that a change had been made in my room here that amounted to a "coincidence." Up to the time I left I had been using a drop-light—a stiff arm from the upper burner —wh. was so placed and so shaded as to make a *screen* quite unnecessary; but when I got back I found that my landlady had bought for my room a student's lamp—such as I had expressed a preference for, and for whose comfortable use in my case a screen is quite indispensable! My darling's beautiful gift to me came, therefore, into immediate use and has already twice made night-reading both possible and comfortable for me. As yet, however, it is something of a distraction, because I am constantly stopping to handle and admire it. You would laugh at me were you to see how often I look at it, and how long. But maybe you could guess *why* I do so. It is not only because it is such an exquisitely tasteful and beautiful thing in itself but also because it is your handiwork —because it reminds me of the precious little lady who made it— my darling, my lovely Eileen. This shall *always* be my study screen.

My darling, lonely as I feel to-day—especially because of the lack of the letter I expected this morning to bring me from you— the effects of my stay with you remain with me so strongly as to make low spirits impossible. They rest upon me like a blessing. I feel like one upon whom all that is fairest and sweetest and no- blest in life has been opened, as a view of surest promise. The future seems to have received a new meaning, and I can't find it in my heart to be any longer so anxious about it as I was. This new taste of your loves seems, by some logic not to be understood, to have made it certain that I shall be offered, before next Autumn, such a position as I want! Ah, my little sweetheart, you are a veri- table witch: your love can transfigure my very nature! But it al- ready seems a long week since I left you in Phila. day before yes- terday!

I received a letter from dear mother yesterday—a nice long let- ter full of home news. She sends warmest love to you, my pet, and says that your letter to her was "charming."

Do you think, darling, that you know just how to get back to 120 after you reach Jersey City? Courtlandt St. ferry is the best to take, you remember, and after you get across, it is the *second*, not the first, elevated road that you come to on Courtlandt St. that you should take to go up town—and you have to cross the street on which it runs to get on the right *side* to go up town to your destination, the 8th St. station. I suppose that these direc- tions are quite unnecessary for a young lady who *can* be so in- dependent when thrown upon her own resources; but possibly they may spare her the trouble of consulting R.R. officials and policemen. How I wish I could return, just to be her escort! If you go around to the League on the day of your return, wont you go to that telegraph office and send me just a word or two telling me of your safe arrival?

I haven't explained to you yet the manner and form of the "Jingle party" I attended, have I? Well, its jingle was the jingle of *rhymes*. Each invited damsel was sent the name of an invited chap, each chap the name of an invited damsel, and everybody was expected to bring with her, or him, some trifle—to cost not more than a quarter nor less than a cent—accompanied with a jingle of her or his own composition, to be presented, through the hostess, to the person whose name she or he had received. Very plain, is it not? These jingles were read aloud by Miss Cunningham and a certain Mister Hamner, and were anonymous to every one but Miss C., who had stipulated for a signed copy of each for herself. Of course I was not included in the programme, not having returned in season to be given a name and time to find a suitable present; but Miss C. made me promise to write a jingle for her collection.

I bought a Ruskin callendar yesterday, of which the enclosed is the first leaf.[1] Were you familiar with the sentence? Isn't it fine?

I hope that my darling is having a delightful time in Phila. You must tell me all you have been doing and seeing there. I've been wondering about it and trying to imagine what you were about: but it's no go: I don't know what "uncle Tom. and aunt Saidie" had planned for your entertainment. Have there been any further developments in the Schufeldt (?) case?[2] You have made me very much interested (for Miss Lilly's sake) in its not coming to anything. Wasn't it rather cruel in "aunt Saidie" to speak of him, and to him, as "the young gentleman who wanted to get married"? Of course it didn't strike me at the time.

But good-bye for the present, my sweet darling. I love you, I love you with all my heart, I love you beyond compare.

Your own   Woodrow.

Love to 1325.

ALS (WC, NjP).
[1] This enclosure is missing.
[2] Apparently an unsuccessful suitor of Lily Hoyt's. She married William White.

From Ellen Louise Axson

My darling Woodrow,   Philadelphia Jan. 3/85.

Your sweet letter with the ticket enclosed came safely to hand this morning, and nobody knows how glad I was to get it!—the letter I mean,—it seemed *so* long since I had seen you!—and what *am* I to do tomorrow without my letter? I will be making Sunday pilgrimages to the postoffice soon, I am afraid. My cousin Minnie, and perhaps also the cousin who sits across the table from me now, if they heard that, or if they knew my state of mind, would mockingly repeat to me those lines once such great favourites of mine, "Blest is the maid whose heart's yet free From love's *uneasy* sovreignty" &c. But that is a great mistake, I have learned better now; I at least, would not for all the world exchange the sweet troubles that follow upon *loving*, for any such negative blessing.

Speaking of Lily,—there *was* a proposal in that room that morning—and there was also a dismissal! And now she says, seriously, that she is *afraid* to tell Uncle Tom the whole truth about it at once. Isn't that dreadful? I don't know what to make of Uncle Tom, he seems demoralized on that one point. I am afraid it is another of the evil consequences of marrying a woman of the world.

Lily sends her kindest regards to you, and says she liked *your* looks extremely "across the room," and hopes to have a nearer view of you sometime this winter. You seem to have won golden opinions from all of them; Uncle Tom is loud in your praise and Aunt Saidie keeps well up with him.

I am enjoying my visit very much indeed. Both yesterday morning and this morning we spent in the house, very lazily and pleasantly,—reading and talking. Yesterday afternoon we "did the town" to some extent,—and a very nice town it is too. This afternoon we went to a matinee—Lawrence Barrett in Robert Browning's play "A Blot on the 'Scrutchon" and a wretched thing it was, I think.[1] I am surprised that our friend Robert should perpetrate anything so poor.

But I am tired of struggling with this pen, it is past my control, and I am sure you will be tired long before you reach this of struggling with the pen-manship;—so goodbye for the present, my darling. I love, love, love you, dear heart, and I am *forever*

Your own   Eileen.

ALS (WP, DLC).
[1] Barrett, a celebrated American actor-manager, had just added "A Blot in the 'Scutcheon" to his current repertory appearances in Philadelphia and Boston, forty-one years after its first production in London. It was not a success in his revival.

To Ellen Louise Axson

Balto., Md., Jan. 4, 1885   2:50 P.M.

Oh my darling, my darling, how shall I answer this sweet, this precious, note that came this morning! Every word in it met a quick response from my heart: because, tho' I have been more than half tricking myself into the belief that I was managing to maintain a sort of content in spite of this newest and bitterest separation by dwelling constantly on the infinite delights of the time we spent together, I have known only too keenly just the feeling my darling describes. It *was* a 'wrench,' my precious little sweetheart, a terrible, heart-breaking wrench, and this is not *life* without you. Sometimes I think that it will be impossible for me to stand the yearning that is in my heart any longer. But, Eileen, my precious, we *have* the joy of loving one another; we have the abundant proof of the eight priceless days we've just spent together that we shall draw closer and closer to each other in the days to come; and you know that, though I cannot be with you now, but must for the present get what good I can out of this lonely labour—which, often dreary, is always a labour of love— I think *all* the time of you: I work, I plan, I *live* for *you*. When *I* get weary or discouraged, or perplexed, or when my loneliness threatens to become desperate, it is an inestimable solace to me to know that you love me—even as I want you to love me, with all the wealth of your love, not a gift of all its treasures withheld; that you think of me with keen sympathy with my work, with a woman's pride and trust in the object of her love, with a woman's loving desire to be by my side, my sweet comforter and companion! Oh, my darling, those are blessed thoughts! And we must not deny ourselves this companionship, poor substitute as it is for what we shall one day have. My heart is in *your* work, my pet —is in all your life, down to its least details; my thoughts follow you through every day's routine. My love is surely of the sort meant for everyday wear, for the *smallest* sympathies and services, as well as for the greatest.

I am not sure that this letter and the one I wrote yesterday will be delivered early enough to-morrow to reach you before you start, but I hope they will, so that I may, in them, accompany you at least by proxy on your journey.

Eileen, my little queen, I love you, I *love* you, and am altogether
Your own   Woodrow.

ALS (WC, NjP).

From Ellen Louise Axson

My darling Woodrow,   New York [Philadelphia], Jan. 4 1885

It is now a quarter of twelve, and as I am to travel in the morning, you will recognize the necessity for writing a short note tonight. Uncle Tom was in one of his best moods tonight, and he kept us all so entertained and amused that we took no note of time. They have their service in the afternoon so that he has the evening at home, and he is particularly brilliant then; I suppose because the reaction has not had time to begin, and the excitement of speaking is still upon him. We had a *grand* sermon this morning, one of the most impressive I ever heard on the text "Choose ye now whom ye will serve." This afternoon to my great disappointment, he did not preach, as the Sunday-school was to have some special New Year exercises. But I really must not write longer;—I leave tomorrow at either eleven or one, am very sorry that I must go for I am having a charming visit. Goodnight, my darling, I love you more, a thousand times more than life; there is no standard great enough to measure my love. As ever,

Your own   Eileen

ALS (WP, DLC). Postmarked Philadelphia, Jan. 5, 1885.

Two Letters to Ellen Louise Axson

Balto., Md., Jan. 5, '85.

Welcome back, my darling, to the dear old boarding house, with its quiet inmates and its sour mistress. I trust that you will find it possible to *stay* there. You *know* what *it* is, and it is like a household of friends to you now. I should be very anxious about the consequences of a move made on other people's recommendations.

I wonder if you are travelling *now* (one o'clock), in order to be back in season for the perspective lecture, or whether you are waiting till after lunch to start? Oh, my darling, what would I not give to be with you now—and always! It has come to seem to me that my proper place is at your side. Our intimacy has ripened so of late as to make stronger than ever the feeling of *relationship* which I have always had towards you since I found out your love for me. I feel that you *belong* to me, by right of love and common interests, that you are in every way nearer to me than those who are nearest of *kin* to me; I catch myself entertaining a sort of surprise that my relations are not your relations; and the general consequence of the feeling is that you are becoming every day more indispensable to me. I am *home*-sick for *you*, Eileen—and I suspect, Miss, from the contents of these two delightful letters that have come from Philadelphia, that *you* are suffering from much the same malady! I feel very selfish when *rejoicing*, as I have been doing, over the precious confessions of these letters, because they are confessions of the *pain* that my departure caused and is still causing you. But I *want* to be literally indispensable to my darling—and 'misery loves company': I can bear my own heartaches more easily when I know that they but answer hers. Oh Eileen, my precious little sweetheart, you don't know what a delight it is to me to hear you avow your love in these sweet, spontaneous forms. My darling! *Do* you need me so much? God bless my little pet! I will live to satisfy that need, little lady. You shall never lack the love you want

You appreciate now, don't you, darling, what I meant when I said that I would hardly dare to go to see you again before I could go to claim you for good and aye? The sweeter and the longer the intercourse, the harder the parting[.] If I hadn't work to do, I don't know how I could pull through these lonely days:— but the misery *is* sweet: I have my darling's love—her whole love —and it is my joy and pride to be   Her own   Woodrow.

My own darling,   Balto., Md., Jan. 6, '85.
I am struggling manfully to get to work and so forget the fresh misery that has taken hold of me because of our renewed separation, but I am not meeting with any very gratifying amount of success—I should not have had any success at all if I hadn't given unwonted leave to my old unsystematic, discursive habit. I have been keeping myself employed at my books by allowing myself to wander at will from one subject to another, leaving each without ceremony so soon as I tired of it in the least. In short, I've been making study a pastime—with the deliberate purpose, Miss, of thinking as little as possible about *you.*

Thank you ever so much, my pet, for the telegram announcing your safe arrival in New York: it was a *great* comfort to me to get it. And now *you* are at work again. Are you trying your best not too think of *me* any more than is unavoidable? Oh my darling! I love you—and I live for the time when this separation shall be ended!

If you heard a "grand sermon" on Sunday, I heard a lecture yesterday which was simply delightful—the best, I think, alike for matter, for style, for manner, that I've heard since I've been at the Hopkins. It was by Mr. Edmund Gosse, "of London, Clark Lecturer on English Literature in the University of Cambridge," and was the first of a course of six lectures on "The Rise of the Classical School of English Poetry in the Seventeenth Century." The special subject of this first lecture was "Poetry at the Death of Shakespeare." I wish I could retail to you all its good points: but they would lose by being taken from their exquisite setting, even if I could recite them. For elegance, beauty, and freedom of movement the style of the lecture was superior to anything I ever heard, and equal to anything I ever read[.] But I must not rush into a rhapsody. I will restrain myself, with the wish that my darling could enjoy these lectures with me. What would I not give if she could! That was my thought all through yesterday's lecture. The worst of listening to a style like Gosse's is that it makes one so desperately dissatisfied with one's own.

There is unquestionably an odd contradiction in "uncle Tom's" character. His daughter afraid to tell him of the temptation she has resisted, and he preaching grandly on the text, "Choose ye now whom ye will serve"—make a picture with a great puzzle in it! He's too lovable a man to have so unlovable a side to his character.

I love you, my darling, longingly, passionately, and I am in every thought   Your own   Woodrow.

ALS (WC, NjP).

Two Letters from Ellen Louise Axson

My darling Woodrow,   New York, Jan 6/85

Yes, here am I once more in the "dear old boarding house!"— and I was so warmly welcomed back by the "quiet inmates" that I was not allowed to write last night, but was forced to put it off until this morning. I had a pleasant journey, and no trouble in finding my way from the ferry, thanks to your clear directions. I reached the house at two o'clock, stopping at my baker's shop for my lunch—two big two-cent plum cakes! As soon as I had disposed of them I went at once to the League, and accomplished quite a good afternoon's work—attending the head class, the sketch class *and* the perspective lecture. We had a splendid pose, —Mr. Harwood as a Laplander—or perhaps an arctic explorer,— in a most picturesque costume. I couldn't miss it altogether, so "Nan" and I staid long enough to make outline sketches, and then rushed up to the perspective.

I have left the "antique," with many regrets, and have had myself transferred to the head class for the season; have been paying there by the month heretofore, so I have nothing to do in the morning at the League. Am going up to the Metropolitan this morning, to see about joining the painting class there,—though I dread taking the journey in this driving rain; it is in the most outlandish place[—]34 st., between second and third Avenues![1] What an undertaking to get there every morning!

I am also going to inspect Annie's boarding house this morning, though it is hardly more than a form, for whether good, bad, or indifferent, I fear I must put up with it. Miss Grace Fairchild came, but accompanied by a friend, another Ohio girl;—so that scheme fell through.

Both your sweet letters reached me yesterday morning, and did indeed accompany me on my journey, for I read them almost all the way up; I wish I could tell you, darling, what treasures your letters are to me. Ah, dearest, you may indeed be sure that you have my whole heart—no smallest portion is withheld. That heart is with you all the time,—in all *your* work—much more, indeed, than it is in my own. Good-bye, my love.

As ever   Your own   Eileen.

That *was* a very fine passage from Ruskin. I hope you will save all the slips for my benefit. It is like having a Ruskin birthday book. Am *very* glad the screen is of use to you.

[1] The school of the Metropolitan Museum of Art was at 214 East 34th St.

My darling Woodrow,   New York, Jan. 6/85

My perplexities about boarding-houses are, I *hope*, over at last, —though I would'nt stake much on it! But at present the matter seems settled. I went to see Annie's house today,—found it quite a respectable place,—the parlour very nice looking; but their room was literally a garret; you can barely stand up straight in it;— indeed Florence Young's head does graze the ceiling, and it has the most comical little windows, about a foot high. There is no register—the room being heated by a little stove; and the furniture of course is of the meanest. I think it would be rather funny to live in such a place, 'twould be in character, for "Bohemians" in the books always live in garrets you know, and art-students are all Bohemians.

However there is no denying that it would be much pleasanter to stay here, for many reasons, the chief among them after all, being the fact that circumstances have forced upon me the conviction that the company of my own thoughts is preferable to that of Misses Lester and Young. But what an unnecessary rig-a-marole I am writing! The long and the short of it is that I am going to stay here; I decided to move and went just now to give Miss Beattie warning. She was much disturbed by it,—though she did'nt blame me, of course;—she gave the other girls a piece of her mind however. She said it was next to impossible to rent a room at this season and asked me what I would be willing to pay. I told her I could'nt afford more than the price for a single room, eight dollars, and, to my great surprise, she said I could have it at that. She wanted me though to be on the lookout at the League for a suitable room-mate, and I told her I would, though I warned her that "at this season" there was scarcely a chance of finding one. Don't you congratulate me on this very agreeable escape from my difficulties?

I went up to the Metropolitan school this morning and was admitted,—will begin work in the morning. They have a pleasant place with rooms fitted up more nicely than ours, as endowed institutions are apt to be;—the Academy in Phil.,[1] for instance is elegant.

I can easily forgive you my darling, for "rejoicing" over the pain our separation causes me because I am equally guilty; I too want to be indispensable to you,—as indispensable as you are to me. Yes I *am* "homesick" for you, dearest. That is the very word; —for whom else should *I* be homesick but for *you*, who are in every way so much nearer and dearer to me than those who are nearest of kin. Is it strange that I should be glad to know that we need each other? I give you vow for vow, my love,—I "will live to satisfy that need,"—that purpose has indeed become my *life*,— my one single aim and end. "You shall never lack the love you want." Do I repeat your words too much? It is because I think no other combination could be so sweet, or express so exactly what I would say to you;—what it seems we would say to each other. Yes, you have my *whole* love my darling, and it is *my* joy and pride to be   Your own Eileen.

ALS (WP, DLC).
    [1] The reference seems to be to the Pennsylvania Academy of the Fine Arts, the first art school in America, founded in 1805.

To Ellen Louise Axson

My own darling,   Balto., Md., Jan 7, 1885
    That was a delightfully full budget of news that came this morning. I like so much to know *every*thing that you do. I can't say, however, that I am altogether satisfied with some of this news. I very much regret the necessity for changing your board-ing house—and, whatever the necessity may be, I trust that you will not go to any place which is either "bad or indifferent." Study in New York has a very great value, which I am not at all in-clined to underrate; but its value cannot compensate for indif-ferent food or for quarters which are not altogether comfortable. It is of the *utmost* importance that in a climate like that of N.Y. one who is not thoroughly accustomed to it should have the best

of all available means for preserving the health; and if you are to be either poorly lodged or meanly fed I shall be miserably uneasy. It would be better to wait, and study in Philadelphia or elsewhere than run such risks. But I am sure that you appreciate these considerations and need not have them urged upon you. A good digestion and unimpaired constitution cannot be preserved in a second-class city boarding house, and six months' enduring now might mean six years suffering in time to come.

You have not told me, my darling, what "the Metropolitan" is which you mean to seek out every morning on 34th St. How are its painting classes organized and conducted? And what or who are the subjects? It will indeed be a tremendous undertaking to go up there every morning! I shall be anxious to learn how my little sweetheart stands it.

Is the cold gone entirely, my precious? Please be exceedingly careful of yourself in this changeable weather.

Yes, my pet, I will send you every day the previous day's slip from my Ruskin callendar, if you wish, since you like so much the sample I sent you. They are not all so good as that first, but they are all excellent. I have destroyed several—the one I enclose was for the 2nd, I think. I was using it for a book-mark.

My darling, you don't know what a thrill of delight the last sentence of this morning's letter gave me. Your heart is in all my work much more than in your own? Ah little sweetheart, how inestimable is the value of the love which you give me so prodigally! What would my work be without it! If my work succeeds, my love, it is because your heart *is* in it—because I am, by sanction of your own so full acceptance,

Your own   Woodrow.

ALS (WC, NjP).

From Ellen Louise Axson

My darling Woodrow,   New York, Jan. 7/85

I have finally accomplished my purpose of going to prayer-meeting at the Scotch church. Mr. Goodrich and I have just returned; we had *such* a pleasant service, Dr. Hamilton is if anything more delightful in his little talks than in his sermons. He announced that he was going to begin a series of Wed. evening lectures on "the great hymns and hymn-makers";—a singular subject for prayer-meeting; is it not? But doubtless one that attracts Dr. H., for I think he himself has the poetical temperament; he is a great lover of beauty of all sorts. And he is rather romantic;

—as Mr. Goodrich expresses it "he is a regular 'loony' on the subject of 'love' "; he is always letting drop some simple but pretty allusion to it, as it were in spite of himself. Mr. G. begs to be allowed to take me to the course, and I am very glad of the opportunity to go.

Am glad you are having such a delightful treat in the way of lectures—oh dear! what *wouldn't* I give to hear them! Your account of them fairly tantalizes me. They *are* public lectures I suppose? Women are admitted?

Yes there does seem to be a certain contradiction about Uncle Tom, but I hope it isn't as bad as it seems. I can't believe he is *really* serious at heart in what he says on that matter; for like Uncle Rob, he always said a great deal that he didnt mean! By-the way, I had a sweet letter from him yesterday, in which he sends his warm regards to you and tells me again how much he likes you.

Many thanks for the sweet note from your sister.[1] I will ask the postman about the letter.[2] But, perhaps she has not *sent* the letter to 23rd St., but was merely asking you if that was the right address?

This was my first day at the Metropolitan. I like it very much so far;—will tell you all about it some other time;—too late now to begin. I spent almost! the whole day there, this being a holiday at the League. They are having a great time there tonight and as they wanted to prepare they gave us to understand that our room was better than our company. The occasion is the presentation of the great Harper prize—a three years course abroad—which was won, you know, by one of the League men, Mr. Major. They have made it a permanent fund by-the-way,—an art scholarship,—to my great satisfaction, for I am sure that one of my friends, Mr. Patter or Mr. Day, will get it next time. They are the most gifted students at the League and they will be just ready for it when it next falls due.

Pray excuse this *scrappy* letter. I discovered last night, that I had no paper left but odds and ends, but forgot to lay in a fresh supply today.

I am very glad that you are taking your studies somewhat easily for a time; to take a sort of half-holiday like that occasionally will be, I am sure, of *great* service to you. Only three lines more in which to say "goodnight," I must cut short my adieus. I love you my darling, "I love you, with the passion put to use, in my old griefs, and with my childhood's faith";—and I am forever   Your own Eileen.

ALS (WP, DLC).
¹ Marion W. Kennedy to WW, Jan. 2, 1885, ALS (WP, DLC).
² Marion, in her letter to WW, had intimated that she would write to Ellen at her old address. At the bottom of that letter, Wilson wrote, "You might ask the postman, Eileen, if he can not get for you the letter that went to 23rd St. W." See also Marion W. Kennedy to WW, March 20, 1885, Vol. 4.

From William F. Ford

Dear Sir,   Bradstreet's. New York, Jan 7th 1884[5]
I have been drawn to you by your studies of Congressional affairs and if at any time you could give me a paragraph on congressional matters which would be of interest to the public I will be glad to hear from you.¹   Yours truly
                         Wm F Ford
                         Editor

ALS (WP, DLC) with WWhw notation on env.: "Ans." Postmarked Jan. 7, 1885.
¹ Wilson seems to have responded negatively to this request. Ford wrote again on February 19, 1885, and Wilson responded by sending the article printed at February 24, 1885, Vol. 4.

To Ellen Louise Axson

My own darling,   Balto., Thursday, Jan. 8/85
I have had numerous unusual interruptions to-day, besides the usual Thursday rush of lectures, so that my letter has been crowded into a quite too small corner.
One of the interruptions was of a kind to interest you, I am sure. Just as I was about to come home from lecture to write to my precious little sweetheart, a gentleman came into "the Bluntschli" seeking me, who introduced himself as Mr. Caldwell. He turned out to be the husband of Dr. Palmer's daughter—the Mr. Caldwell who was, until within a few weeks past, professor of Chemistry at the University at Clarksville. He confided to me that he had resigned to avoid being questioned by the Directors upon the subject of *evolution*—he has been drowned by one of the waves from the maelstrome in Columbia—and has come here to study until he can find employment elsewhere!¹ His wife and children are, of course, in New Orleans. An exile for conscience sake is a very interesting subject, and I shall probably have every opportunity to study this specimen as I have secured board for him here at No. 8. These conscientious evolutionists will presently be numerous enough to control Synodical votes. But more of Mr. C. when I know more.
I am *so* glad, my pet, so *relieved* to hear that you are to stay with Miss Beatty! Is it possible, little sweetheart, that you would

have been so rash as to go into that garret with those other girls if Miss Beatty had not so suddenly and opportunely come to terms! I think that, if you had, I should have posted off to New York and, capturing you by main force—if *moral* force would not have served the purpose—carried you off to decent quarters somewhere. What a place! Bohemianism may be lots of fun, my sweet little sophist, and robust men or women who have no other chance my run its risks: but the simple matter of fact is that proper ventilation is a sheer impossibility for three people living in a room whose ceiling Miss Young could touch with her head! You would have had colds for the rest of the winter. I think, Miss, that you *do* need me to take care of you! Ah, my darling, will the time never come when I *can* do so! I long for you with all my heart, my little queen. I love you—oh, beyond all expression, in every thought, with all my heart, with all my *being*. I am every day more than ever   Your own   Woodrow.

ALS (WC, NjP).
  [1] John W. Caldwell, M.D., Professor of Chemistry at the South-Western Presbyterian University in Clarksville, Tenn., who, according to a statement issued by Chancellor John N. Waddel, had taught theistic evolution and resigned quietly after his views were "disallowed." Columbia *Southern Presbyterian*, Dec. 4, 1884.

From Ellen Louise Axson

My darling Woodrow,   New York, Jan. 8/85.

Many thanks for your sweet letter of this morning with it's good counsel and it's thoughtful care for my well-being. It makes me very glad for *your* sake as well as my own that the matter is finally settled. I have told you before, my thoughts and feelings with regard to the interest you show in all my little affairs; but my darling must not identify himself with my concerns,—my very small perplexities—to the extent of being anxious or uneasy;—they are,—or *were* rather, since they are a thing of the past,—by no means worthy of *that*. By the way I have found a delightfully easy way of getting to the Metropolitan[.] I simply walk across to 4th ave and take the car;—at 32nd St, I believe, I am presented with a transfer ticket to a little car bound for the 34th St. ferry, and it winds about and in and out until it puts me down at the door of the school, so I have scarcely more walking to do than in going to the League.

Such a terrible thing happened at the League today! You know, they had an entertainment there last night, and as usual there were many beautiful things on exhibition. They had not been removed today, and Miss McMillan knocked down and broke into a score of pieces "Saint Geodens' " beautiful bas-relief,—one of his greatest works![1] The girls have done nothing all day but stand about weeping and wringing their hands. But Miss M. went, of course, to tell him and he was extremely kind about it;—it was only the plaster cast, gilded, and could be readily replaced.

But I am very sleepy this evening and must say good night betimes—if I can. It seems hard to say "good-bye" even in a letter. That reminds me of some verses I read, not long ago, and a story connected with them,—a *very* slight story certainly, since it is simply the story of a *look*(!) Once upon a time I met a certain young man of my acquaintance on the street, he seemed much surprised, and proceeded to inform me that he had been thinking of me at that very moment;—and by-and-by, it pleased him to tell me his thought,—he was "thinking of how I had 'looked[']" when he read some certain lines to me a short time before. Then though he could give me no clear account of the "look," he insisted, like Pharaoh with his dreams, that I should tell him *why* I "looked so!"—what it meant! Of course I told him that I could not do that until I knew *how* I looked; but naturally I too was set a-thinking somewhat uncomfortably about said look!—wondering what it could have expressed, or seemed to express. By the way, the young gentleman did'nt know at the time about my little weakness for you. I wonder if *you* could throw any light on this mysterious matter! If you ever come across the lines, read them and see. They are by T. B. Aldrich and are called "Palabras Cariñosas."[2] But what *unmitigated* nonsense I am writing! Now I *must* say "good-night,"—and believe me, my darling, in every thought   Your own   Eileen

ALS (WP, DLC).
    [1] Augustus Saint-Gaudens, the famous sculptor, who was then teaching at the Art Students' League.
    [2] Thomas Bailey Aldrich, "Palabras Cariñosas," a poem.

To Ellen Louise Axson

My own darling,   Balto., Friday, 9 Jan., 1885

Is this paper of too documentary a size to suit your ladyship's tastes? I love *variety* in everything—especially in the things I have to use every day—and so I had this paper cut for me in a size which should be neither "note" nor "letter." You probably wont object seriously to anything which promises to add to the length of my epistles, in coöperation with the habit of running on at least to the complete filling out of a sheet.

Do you know that each day when I sit down to write to my little sweetheart my first thought is, 'what would she like me to talk about?' 'Shall I tell her about Dr. Hall's amusing lecture on Fröbel and the kindergarten or about Mr. Gosses delightful informal talk about the poet Gray? Shall I interpret for her my thoughts about contributing something of value to the literature of administrative science, confessing, as a droll side-play, my perplexing doubts as to just the field that science covers? Shall I begin right away to repeat my declarations of love for her, or shall I compel them to wait until they *will* come in at the last lines? Shall I write of what I am thinking or of what I am doing, of my anxieties or only of my satisfactions? Shall I confess that I have a headache or shall I say nothing about such subjects?' You see, Miss, my idea about letter-writing is, that one should write altogether for the gratification of one's correspondent and not at all for one's own, when there is no necessary topic of business or advice to be discussed; and my difficulty in dealing with the little lady whom I am now addressing is, that I have not been able to find out which of the various kinds of letters I have written her she likes best. She would probably insist that she liked them all equally well; but that don't seem to me possible, and I have often wished for one wee hint of her preference. I have already confessed the temptations under which I labour. I am inclined to go round and round again in the circle of love-language. Like Dr. Hamilton, I am "a regular loony on the subject of love." Not that I haven't a very good reason for being so. Love has worked wonders for me. The love of the dear one's at home kept my disposition from souring when I was a youngster, and prepared my heart when I became a man for that supremely great love which has come to make my life both possible and complete. Love is the greatest—incomparably the greatest—fact of my life. Without it, my heart would starve and my mind become parched and arid. By means of it, one little maiden holds all my fortunes in her hands, to do with them what she will. And I am happy in her power! It would ruin me to have it otherwise. I trust her with all the faith ever given to man to spend; I love her with all the love ever given to a single man to bestow; I have found the end of restlessness, the solution of doubt, the perfection of hope, the sweetest gifts of happiness in making myself

Her own   Woodrow.

ALS (WC, NjP).

From Ellen Louise Axson

My darling Woodrow,   New York Jan 9/85

I have been so busy tonight, that now it grows late and I must try and content myself with writing a short note: I am trying—not very successfully so far—to turn over a new leaf,—to be an early bird, for it is so far to the Metropolitan that the mornings are short at the best, and I must get an early start to accomplish anything

Your account of Mr. Caldwell was indeed of interest to me; and I am so *sorry* too, to hear of the trouble; for his sake, and also for the sake of the church. How is it all to end? I fear our poor church will be torn to pieces. I am glad you have found a place for him at your house, hope you will find him a pleasant companion, he will be the first Southerner you have had there[,] will he not? What a pity he can't get a place in the New Orleans institution!

But I must keep my word and send a few lines only, hard as it is. Yes, I am quite well,—entirely free from cold; and am enjoying this beautiful weather hugely. The northan climate is'nt so bad after all. I rather like it, and it certainly seems to agree with me.

I love you, I love you with all my heart, my darling—my *king*! —and in every thought, I am forever   Your own Eileen.

ALS (WP, DLC).

To Ellen Louise Axson

My own darling,   Balto., Saturday 10 Jany., 1885

Somehow I have come, I don't quite know why, to regard Saturday as the day for special indulgences of length in writing to you. Perhaps it's a remnant of the old school-day feeling, that Saturday is by right a holiday, to be freely given to the sport one likes best. It isn't the best day for special letter-writing, though, in this case, because its letter can have no separate jurisdiction of its own. It takes Sunday's letter into partnership, when it comes to be read.

I have just returned from a pilgrimage to the Peabody library, made to find certain lines called "Palabras Cariñosas" by one T. B. Aldrich. I found them, read them and reread them, with a delight which you may interpret at your leisure, and then set myself to understand as best I could a story told with studious omission of any mention of names, time, or place. As I have ventured to reconstruct it, the story is this: Mr. Goodrich met you unexpectedly on the street "once upon a time," and told you—with evidently platonic interest—that he had just been thinking of you, of how you looked one evening when he read you those lines of Aldrich's, and begged you—with evidently platonic intention—to tell him what the look meant. I say 'Mr. Goodrich' for various reasons, but principally because he is almost the only "young gentleman of your acquaintance" whose remarks to you you have not considered too sacred to be repeated to me.

I think I *can* throw a good deal of light on the mystery of that look, if my theory about the time of the above occurrence be correct—and I have studied my darling's wonderful eyes too often to be surprised that their expression on hearing those lines should have lingered long in Mr. G's memory. My own face probably came as near to wearing the same expression as it is capable of coming just now as I read the same lines at the Peabody—and, in view of the history of some recent partings, whose memory lingers in my heart like strains of perfect music, I should not be surprised if my look had in its glad, tender interest something much higher than my features are usually capable of. "Palabras Cariñosas" is, for us, almost like a postscript to that never to be forgotten and always to be loved "Tale" of Browning's. It led me on to these other lines:

> "I have placed a golden
> Ring upon the hand
> Of the blithest little
> Lady in the land!
>
> "When the early roses
> Scent the sunny air,
> She shall gather white ones
> To tremble in her hair!
>
> "Hasten, happy roses,
> Come to me by May,—
> In your folded petals
> Lies my wedding-day."[1]

Ah, my darling, what blessings are in store for me when the time shall come in which we shall not have to say 'good-bye' to each other. I try over and over again to persuade myself that it will not be long to wait—but it *is* long—every day lengthens instead of shortening the time. And in the meantime, Miss, there's no use telling me—except to prove how sweet and unselfish you are—that

I must not identify myself with you to the extent of worrying about the *little* perplexities of your life in New York. That matter of a boarding place was *not* a small matter—and, if it had been, it would have been a great deal more to me than the biggest of my own dull bachelor experiences. Your welfare is my constant thought, my darling, and my love recognizes no differences of size or importance in the elements which go to make up the sum of your comfort and happiness. Nothing is small that contributes to them. And, besides, it makes me *very* happy, my precious little sweetheart, to know that I have the *right* to offer you what counsel and aid I can. It is an inestimable privilege in my eyes to have leave to forget myself in living for you—my chief cross at present consisting in the fact that I can do so little in my darling's service.

I am so glad, little lady, that you have found such an easy way of getting to the Metropolitan—it makes the journey quite a simple affair. I am very impatient to hear all about the Met. so that I may know what you are doing there, and just how you are doing it

Were you hurt, my darling, by what I said about your uncle? It was thoughtless of me to write for *your* eyes a criticism of the uncle you love so much; but I talk to you as I would talk to myself—and I love you so much and with so thorough a sense of identification that I feel that "uncle Tom." is almost as much my uncle as yours—so you must not think that my criticisms argue any lack of affection or respect for those whom you love. They would be sacred in my eyes, even if I couldn't admire them. I know that you *do* understand me in such matters—but often I am a little afraid that I may inadvertently hurt you by a too blunt declaration of opinion. 'Hurt you'! I would rather cut off my tongue than have it give you unnecessary pain!

The Bryn Mawr decision is to be taken on Monday, and I am waiting for it as a criminal might wait for the answer to his appeal for release. If I am elected, the next six months of work will but speed my happiness; if I am left out in the cold, the coming months will simply punctuate my anxieties and the weary waiting. What would I have? I would have *you,* my little queen, whose slightest word of love fills my heart with the sweetest happiness ever given to man to cheer and strengthen him. No indeed, Miss, you can't repeat my words of love too much. If you think they serve best your meaning, by all means use them: you are proving, what I want to believe, that you love me just as you are loved by

Your own   Woodrow.

ALS (WC, NjP).
¹ From Thomas Bailey Aldrich, "Romance," in *The Poems of Thomas Bailey Aldrich* (Boston, 1882).

From James E. Rhoads, with Enclosure

My Dear Friend,   Philadelphia 1 mo. 10. 1885.

It is with great satisfaction that I am able to state that the Trustees of Bryn Mawr College yesterday appointed thee Associate in History in the College. The appointment is for two years at a salary of $1500 a year. Thy letter about the title was received and its suggestions carefully weighed. We felt the force of them, but to have made a change in the title would have disturbed a system adopted after careful deliberation, one which, altho it may at times seem to act unequally, will it is believed, advance the interests of every member of the Faculty, as it is faithfully carried out; and will benefit the college. With reference to the rank of the Department, we certainly desire the Department of History to hold as important a rank as any other. But thou may remember that the Department of Romance Languages at J.H.U. has had at its head a professor with the title of Associate for several years, yet no one doubts that it is an important one in the University.

Enclosed please find a form of memorandum which has been signed by other members of the faculty as they have been appointed.

Knowing so well as I do how sorely thy time and strength are pressed with present duties I would not urge haste about the arrangement of the programme of study at Bryn Mawr, but hope that thou will consult with the Dean, M. C. Thomas about the subject, and make out a schedule as soon as may be convenient. The list of books for the Library, & appliances for the classroom may be made later.

M. Carey Thomas can show thee a plan already outlined for a course in History. Consider it carefully and offer such corrections or changes as upon mature consideration may seem desirable with brief reasons therefor. Thou wilt notice that the History of France has been chosen as the connection between ancient & modern times. This may be modified, but there should be strong reasons for doing so.

With kind regard, thy friend   James E. Rhoads

P.S. Please sign the two copies of agreement—return the one in my handwriting & oblige.   JER.

ALS (WP, DLC).

Agreement between The Trustees of Bryn Mawr College and Woodrow Wilson, A.M.

This agreement made the 10th of First month, 1885, between The Trustees of Bryn Mawr College and Woodrow Wilson, A.M., witnesseth:

That at a meeting of said Trustees held First mo. 9th, 1885, they duly appointed Woodrow Wilson Associate in History in the College for a term of two years, beginning at the opening of the College, 9 mo. 15, 1885.

On the part of The Trustees it is agreed that they shall pay the said Woodrow Wilson at the rate of $1500 per annum for each of the said two years during which he shall be engaged in teaching in the College. And Woodrow Wilson agrees on his part to assist in the organization of a department of History in the College, to give his advice as to the course of study to be pursued by the students in his department, and to indicate the books and periodicals to be procured for it.

He furthermore agrees to use his best skill and ability in teaching the students assigned to him, and to co-operate with the Faculty in promoting the best interests of the College.

On behalf of the Trustees
James E. Rhoads, Prest.

ALS (WP, DLC).

To Ellen Louise Axson

My own darling,　　　　　　　Balto., Sunday, Jany 11, 1885

How hard it is to be satisfied! Sometimes I almost determine that I will *write* no more words of love to you, but only such intimate confidences and such free personal news-telling as would go by right to my darling's ears, as to my only perfect intimate; because words seem such a *mockery* when used instead of the *deeds* in which one longs to speak his love. When I am with you it is a different matter. It is delightful—it is irresistible—to speak words to which the instant response of love comes! But to *write* such things in cold, senseless ink is *so* poor a shift for uttering the heart's feelings! Then, besides, with a monotonous *pen*, one hesitates to use some of the tenderest words of our language, because in writing—even when read by the *heart* at the ear of the mind—they seem to tremble on the verge of *gush*—because they need colouring from the voice to receive dignity and full credence.

But there's no use trying to break the bondage. How *could* I write a letter to *you* with only a word or two of love in it? How my heart leaps when I read the sweet, though often meagre, love-messages crowded into the last corners of your so precious little letters! I learn them by heart often, from sheer repetition of reading them. I linger over them as if their lines traced pictures of the happiness they promise. If what I write gives you half the delight that your words give me, I *can't* forego the practice, unsatisfactory as it is! But there are several items of news for this letter which I must get in before it is too late

The last proofs of my book came this morning—and lie here waiting revision early to-morrow. This seems to mean very early publication, and makes my heart stand still. What, if, when the book is given to the world, the world refuses to accept it!

You will be amused to learn that, at the request of a friend to whom the Glee Club owes return of many favours, I have consented to sing for a few Sundays in a Unitarian church choir. I sang this morning there—and heard a *fine* sermon—a sort of echo from strong New England days.

You will be disgusted and bitterly disappointed to learn that *Dr. Mack* has been elected to fill uncle James's place![1] I hope that the Seminary *will* die, and die soon, if such pestiferous fellows as he are to be put into its hitherto honoured chairs. *He* in the chair of Science and Religion! He knows about as much of the facts of the one as about the true spirit of the other! What *is* to become of our dear church! She has indeed fallen upon evil times of ignorance and folly! But enough of that—my thoughts are too harsh for the pages of this letter.

Mr. Caldwell proves on closer acquaintance a *very* pleasant, though (I suspect) rather unsuggestive, man.

Little pet, your love is my supreme joy. It makes me glad to live, in order that I may prove with what singleness and wholeness of heart I can and will and do return it, how absolutely and gladly I am and always shall be   Your own   Woodrow

ALS (WC, NjP).
[1] As the Perkins Professor at the Columbia Theological Seminary.

Two Letters from Ellen Louise Axson

My darling Woodrow,   New York. Jan. 11, 1885.

As you see, I did not succeed in getting my letter written last night. I was quite tired and sleepy to begin with,—the result of abundant excercise in the high wind;—and immediately after dinner Miss Comstock and I went to hear Mr. Weir's lecture on "Bastian-Lepage,"[1] from which I returned a *great* deal more sleepy! Mr. Weir as a speaker is really excruciating, he hesitates so dreadfully; when neither *slang* nor the cut and dried art idiom will express his idea he is *lost,*—the English language utterly refuses to come to his rescue. Yet the address was interesting in it's way, for Lepage was his intimate friend and he showed real feeling of an honest manly sort in speaking of him. Personal reminiscences of great men are always of interest. Then there were engravings of all his principal works and some excellent original studies, gifts from the artist to Mr. Weir. You know Lepage has recently died.

You do ask a hard question, my dear, when you tell me to decide which kind of letter I like best! I am afraid I *must* insist that I like all equally well; that is I want some of all kinds. I am equally and profoundly desirous of knowing *both* what you are doing and what you are thinking; I *must* know your anxieties, my darling, as well as your satisfactions. I can't do without the confessions of love,—and I want you to confess the head-aches too for the comfort it gives me to feel *sure* that I know *just* how you fare. The best way to settle it, my dear unselfish love, will be to try and write a little for your *own* satisfaction, as well as mine,—that is to write of whatever happens to be uppermost in your mind at the time, whether it be your perplexities or satisfactions,—your own thoughts or Mr. Gosse's. You may be sure that whatever is most interesting to you at the time of writing your letter is the thing I most prefer to read in *that* letter. But time flies, I must close in haste. I wish, dearest, that I could tell you before I close how much I love you, but it is a most vain wish

With all my heart,   Your own Eileen.

[1] Jules Bastien-Lepage, 1848-84, French painter.

My darling Woodrow,   New York Jan. 11 1885.
I have been having a delightful afternoon with—whom do you suppose? Cousin Allie [Hoyt Truehart] and Lily [Hoyt]! I knew that Lily was thinking of coming up, for Allie, who had business which made it necessary for her to spend a few days in New York, had written begging Lily to join her, before I left Phila. So this morning she came for me and I lunched with them at the St. Cloud.

By-the-way, I met a remarkable man there,—a man who says marriage is "a relic of barbarism"! &c. &c. I won't enlarge;—and

the queerest part of it is that he is a Southerner! But Lily says
he is carefully cultivating those views because he has a very fine
position which he must lose when he marries. His name is Dr.
Chambers and he has control of some large sanitarium;—is resident physician.

I have at last secured my church "sitting," and I had good luck
—as usual. I managed somehow or other to get on the good side
of the old sexton so that he gave me one of the best pews in the
church—for an extremely low price. I told him at first that I
wanted a cheap sitting, so he showed me one near the door at
the side of the centre row,—$17.50 for six months. I enquired if
those against the wall were cheaper, and he asked if I did'nt wish
to pay so much;—"no" I said "I can hardly afford it." He asked
then what I *could* afford, and I said I did not want to go about it
in *that* way! "Oh," he said, "its quite right,—quite right that you
should." So I said, "ten dollars!" He meditated a moment, and then
said, "well, I'll show you a seat you can have for ten dollars," and
forthwith marched me to this *splendid* pew—middle aisle not far
from the centre! Is'nt it comical that I should be making my own
terms both at church and here? I think I am getting "real cute."
I defy the Yankee to make any shrewder bargains! And *how much*
pleasanter it is to have a seat of one's own! I already love the
church twice as much and feel as though it all belonged to me,
though I havnt even occupied *my* pew as yet.

Mr. Goodrich has followed my example and is attending the
Scotch church,—says he too is going to get a sitting there. He
does'nt make any secret of the fact that he goes because I go!
Well! I am glad if I can be the means of attaching him to some
church, though I am sorry his motives are so low. But he has
said several little things of late that made me rather uncomfortable, made me fear that he was not quite *sure* that I was engaged; so tonight I told him point blank that I was. He was very
nice and manly about it, said he did know it; and yet he had made
himself half believe that he did'nt. He thanked me for telling
him, and asked if I would still be his friend. I told him, "most
assuredly if he wished; there was certainly nothing in what I
had said which rendered *necessary* any change in our relations."
He said "certainly not[.]" He thought that friendship might be
established on a better basis than ever, because, laughing, I
could be so sure that I was not at all to blame for any possible
consequences to him, he went into it with his eyes open,—at his
own risk;—he only wished to be allowed to gather up the crumbs
under the table! I can't remember all he said, but he behaved

very well indeed;—and now I *know* we can afford to be friends. It is extremely *nice* in him to wish it. And between us two, I am glad he does wish it, because he is pleasant,—I like him—and because—oh base consideration! he is so *convenient!* I am not so ashamed to admit that as I might otherwise be because it is exactly what he says he wants,—he is always begging me to make a convenience of him. Ah, darling, I *will* be glad when I can depend on you alone for escort and protection. Is that a sufficiently frank confession? It has I think always been included in those three words *I love you.* With all my heart   Your own Eileen.

Please excuse the awful scrawl, something seems to be wrong with my pen.

ALS (WP, DLC).

To Ellen Louise Axson

My own darling,   Balto., Monday afternoon, Jany. 12, 1885

Numerous things have combined to engross, perplex, and delay me to-day, and I must, much against my will, beg you to forgive a *very* brief note.

I *can* put one pleasant piece of information into it, however, namely, that my informant was wrong who said that Dr. Mack had been *elected.* He misread a newspaper paragraph which said that Dr. M. was "announced as the probable successor of Dr. Woodrow"—the announcement comes from Dr. M. himself, as like as not. And I ought to have known that the trustees could make no selection.

I am sick at heart for lack of a letter from my darling to-day—and anxious besides. Of course, though, you would have let me know if anything were wrong.

I love you, little sweetheart, I love you with all my heart—my love for you shapes everything that I do, everything that I think—it *creates* whatever small bits of lovable quality, all that there may be that is worth retaining in   Your own   Woodrow.

This haste is hateful. It's tantalizing to have to whisper 'I love you' and then run!   Lovingly   W.

ALS (WC, NjP).

From Ellen Louise Axson

My darling Woodrow,   New York, Jan. 12/85

I have heard tonight from headquarters [through Goodrich]

that a certain "very thoughtful" work called "Congressional Government" will be out on the 20th of this month! Think of it! only eight days! I am so glad, my darling, and *I* am not at all alarmed as to it's reception by the world. Of course I understand that the book from it's very nature must meet with contradiction, that the more discussion it excites the greater will be it's success. The people who believe in Committee government are expected to criticise and oppose your *views*, but that of course is very different from condemning the book. It's friends may watch it start out on it's adventures with high hopes as well as good wishes;—and I may wish you joy once more, my darling, as much joy as I feel over it all. Mr. Goodrich says he is going to bring me a copy wet from the press,—I told him that if he did I would'nt look at it; I wanted to receive it from *you*; but I don't know whether I could resist looking if he had it in the house.

And so the Bryn Mawr matter is to be settled *today*! Well, I can only wish you joy in that too, my darling;—with all my heart I wish that the decision may be satisfactory to you. I am indeed distressed and shocked to learn of Dr. Mack's appointment to Columbia! It looks very very badly in every respect. How *could* Dr. Mack consent to take the place after having been *the* most active person in getting Dr. Woodrow removed! the very one who began all the trouble! Of course he did not work against Dr. Woodrow in order to obtain his place, but it has exactly that appearance. I was'nt aware that he even *pretended* to know anything about science. Oh! it is a shameful thing from beginning to end.

Yes, darling it *is* "hard to be satisfied"! I know right well how poor a shift are words for uttering the heart secrets. But remember, dear, that is only true of the words we *write*. Those that I *read* seem anything but a "mockery"; "they have the very sound of *truth*" perhaps because they don't depend for their meaning altogether on the "cold and senseless ink,"—because I read them with a *true* and manly voice always sounding in my ears,—because I seem the while to be learning all their meaning from the eyes I love,—those *true* and tender eyes. Try to think how instant will be "the response of love" when the words are *read*, how at every word my heart leaps forth to answer. I am glad that you too like "Palabras Cariñosas";—and where did you find the other dainty little lines? Are they too from Aldrich? Your reconstruction of my tale was quite correct, I didn't imagine that I had veiled it in very deep mystery

Goodnight, dear love,—darling your love is *my* supreme joy. I live and am happy because I am altogether and forever,

Your own   Eileen.

ALS (WP, DLC).

To Ellen Louise Axson

My own darling,   Balto., Tuesday morning, Jany. 13, 1885

Your two letters of Sunday came this morning. I need hardly say that I was intensely, almost painfully, interested in your account of that critical interview with Mr. Goodrich, and that I accept it as a fresh proof of your love for me. You acted just as I should have expected, like a pure, true-hearted, noble woman—the woman that I trust as unreservedly as I love her!

I wish I could stop there, and say nothing more about the affair: but I can't—I can['t] act a lie to you—I can't pretend that I am satisfied that the difficulty is solved. On the contrary, it seems to me that the difficulty has just begun. My darling, I am quite sure that you know that I have nothing of that temper which delights in saying 'I told you so'—I would a *great deal* rather have it turn out that *you* were right than that I was. But it *has* been proved in this case that the continuance of that "platonic friendship" upon which you were counting was impossible under existing circumstances; so that I am sure that you will be less disinclined to accept my view of what must *now* take place. Mr. Goodrich virtually declared that he was already in love with you when he begged that he should still be allowed the intimacy of a friend, *notwithstanding* your engagement. He used the usual *formula* even, and there could have been no other meaning in his words—since your engagement was *of course* no bar to ordinary friendship. But he told you more than that, my love. He told you that he had been allowing his love hope notwithstanding the fact that he already knew that you were engaged. What else *could* he mean when he said that "he had made himself half believe that he didn't" know of your engagement. So that, after all, your relations are scarcely changed at all by the brave, modest, womanly course you took to warn him. He begs for a continuance of the same privileges as before, simply acquitting you beforehand of all "blame for any possible consequences to him." He goes "into it with his eyes open, at his own risk;—he only wishes to be allowed" &c. Goes into *what*, Eileen? Goes into an intimacy which, he already knows, must result in his falling the more deeply in love with you. Engagement is not marriage, my little sweetheart, and honourable men who would not court a wife, see sometimes neither wrong nor utter hopelessness in courting a lady who is engaged—in this age of easily broken engagements, when the old and true idea of their essential equivalence to the additional, but not more sacred, vows of marriage is no longer allowed vogue. At any rate, if Mr. G. were to count it an advantage that you have at least an inkling of his feelings towards you, and were to build upon that fact and upon the opportunities of the five months' intimacy promised him a vague, half-allowed, though desperate *hope*, he would not be denying the world's experience, though he *would* be proving himself utterly blind to my darling's opinions and character.

Pardon me, my pet, if this very plain speaking seem to you harsh. I have written as I have because I think that it will be helpful to you to hear a man's view of the case—and because I know no better way of proving the absolute faith I have in you. I am pointing out the things which I know that you, from sheer purity of heart, wont see; but which seem to me only too clear. And I don't speak of them as a preface to any advice. *If your eyes are open*, I know that you will do just what is right. If you think it prudent to see Mr. G. as intimately and accept his escort as constantly as before, I shall have no thought of objection—though I shall pity him, and fear that he wont derive much benefit from the church services. The same freedom of intercourse as formerly will certainly be attended with very great risks; and even all your woman's tact will not suffice to make it easy to make "a convenience" of him. Don't think me cold and caustic in this matter, darling,—just believe me, please, and credit me with possessing a little worldly wisdom. I want to protect you a little bit *now*, if I can—and this seems to me *such* a plain case.

I have heard from Bryn Mawr, little lady![1] I have been elected "Associate" in History for two years at $1500 a year. This is the lowest rank, and men who are no older than I, but who have received their degrees and had a single year's experience in teaching, are put in the grade above; but I have no substantial grounds for objecting to that. There will be no real subordination. "Associate" means nothing. There is to be but one instructor in history and he is to be the head of the department, of course. I suppose that there can be no question about the advisability of my accepting the offer. Small as it is, it is quite as much as I have any reason to expect would be offered me elsewhere. I have written to father about it, and shall tell Dr. Rhoads that I will take a few days to consider the matter.[2] And now, what say *you*, my little queen? You have the first right to be consulted, and your judgment in the matter is more vital to me than any one else's can be. Would you be altogether satisfied to have me accept? The election for 'two years' means that at the end of that time, my services in the mean time having been satisfactory, I would be promoted to the next rank, "Associate-Professor," and to a larger salary. Tell me without reserve *exactly* what you think, my darling. You are now, and always shall be, my chief counsellor.

Just to think, Miss, that, instead of being a protection to me, you actually expose me to danger. I have just been told by Miss Nellie Woods that one of the most charming young ladies of her acquaintance said that 'she was so glad Mr. Wilson was engaged, because she could be just as nice to him as she chose.' I found out that it was the young lady who gave the "Jingle Party"—and thus was enabled to understand the marked and delightful cordiality with which she received me when I made my "party call." Quite a comical situation, isn't it? Can you imagine why a young lady should wish to be cordial with me?

I received a card to-day informing me that, without the slightest warning, I had been elected—or rather that I am invited to become—a member of the " 'Eight o'clock Club,' which meets at No. 40 Mt. Vernon Place on alternate Monday evenings." I am not told what the "Eight o'clock Club" is or does, but enclosed was a card bearing the legend, "Compliments of Mrs. Edgeworth Bird," and I recollect calling upon Mrs. Bird,[3] in response to an invitation she gave me at one of our University receptions upon the strength of the fact that she knew all about me—and everybody else that had ever lived in Georgia. She was a Miss Baxter—of Athens, I think, and seems to know not only all Georgia but all the South as well. She is vivacious enough to know all the world—at least to be 'hail-fellow-well-met' with it. She may be the patron, the chaperon of the Club—or it may be composed altogether of middle-aged people like herself—think of that and W.W. a member! I shall make enquiries before returning polite reply to "Lydia Crane, Secretary."

But, little lady, I'll run on all day at this rate—and I haven't broached the real subject of my letter yet! Can you guess what that is? *Can't* you? Is there no immediate consequence to my acceptance of the position at Bryn Mawr? If I decide that in the affirmative—as I shall, if you and dear father approve—there is something, you know, which *you* will have to decide! Why, my darling, my heart beats so at *thought* of that decision that it is actually hard for me to write about it! My darling, my precious

Eileen, wont you be thinking of ways to make it possible in June? Midsummer would hardly be feasible, and Bryn Mawr opens on the 15th of September. We wouldn't want to make the first weeks of our married life correspond with the first weeks of college work in a strange place, would we? I can't plead yet for any particular time, because I don't know definitely the plans of the dear home folks—but you know what my wishes are—what I *will* plead for, with all my heart in the prayer, if it be not utterly impossible. Oh, my darling! How shall I tell you of the flood of exultant, tender, passionate feeling that comes in upon me at thought of so near a fulfilment of the sweetheart [*sic*], the holiest, the strongest, the most selfish and most *un*selfish wish of my life. I *cannot* wait for anything but an imperative necessity—that is wherein I am selfish —I long to give myself, *all* of myself, to my darling's constant service—that is wherein I am *not* selfish—I want—I want *you*, my little queen, my precious little sweetheart, my promised wife! Ah, Eileen, wont you take *very* soon

Your own   Woodrow?

ALS (WC, NjP).
   1 J. E. Rhoads to WW, Jan. 10, 1885.
   2 WW wrote to Dr. Rhoads that same day, as J. E. Rhoads to WW, Jan. 15, 1885, reveals.
   3 Who lived at 40 Mt. Vernon Place.

From Ellen Louise Axson

My darling Woodrow,   New York, Jan. 13/85.
   Your sweet note of yesterday afternoon reached me tonight. Am *so* sorry that mine was delayed and that you have been anxious in consequence. I was afraid it would be too late for the postman. It shan't happen again. It hurts me to think that I should haved caused you disappointment or anxiety for no *really* good,—no sufficient reason.
   And what are the other things that are perplexing and troubling you, my darling? You know that I am to be told of the "anxieties" as well as the "satisfactions," and I can spare one no less than the other. Ah me! how my heart aches to do *something* to help when anything in your letters makes me fancy that all is not well with you, either within or without. I fear sometimes that you try to conceal from me your "ups and downs," from that unselfish but somewhat mistaken idea that you must write altogether for my "gratification." The principle may be right and yet one might be wrong in his application of it, in consequence of holding narrow views as to what will gratify another. But I too must write a brief note tonight in consequence of that inconvenient promise

you exacted, viz., that I should not sit in a cold room; this one is growing colder every moment, and I feel myself in the act of "catching cold," so I must close, in haste. Yes it *is* tantalizing to whisper 'I love you' and then run, but there is no help for it sometimes. I *do* love you, my darling, as the apple of my eye. As ever　　　　　　　　　　　　　Your own　Eileen.

ALS (WP, DLC).

To Ellen Louise Axson

My own darling,　　Balto., Wednesday afternoon, Jany. 14, 1885

What a sweet, what a *precious*, little document that was that I received this morning! It was so full of your love—which is my delight and my strength! And may I not wish *you* joy, little sweetheart, on my Bryn Mawr election? I know that you are glad that it seems about to be decided satisfactorily—but are you glad, Eileen, altogether on my account? Tell me, darling, isn't there a little joy for your*self* in what that election promises us? Oh, my darling, if it is to be—and I don't believe that you will have the heart to refuse me—how am I to wait the six months with even a *show* of patience! But I must not talk of that any more just now. I am so much excited about it that, were I to dwell on it long, I think I should go to New York to-night. I must talk about Mr. Gosse. And there *is* something to tell about him which *can* be briefly told—and which will, I am sure, amuse you. His first three lectures he delivered in evening dress—but he came into his fourth wearing an ordinary walking suit, for which he apologised thus: "Gentlemen and Ladies, I must beg you to excuse me for coming before you in this unceremonious garb, but the fact is that I have but just returned from Washington, where I lost both my baggage and my wife. At one time I was afraid that I was going to lose you too. But happily I am here—and I am so overjoyed at seeing *you* that I assure you my other losses seem quite insignificant!" He has a delightful vein of this un-English humour when he chooses to give it leave!

I am so glad, my pet, that you have secured a little home-place in Dr. Hamilton's church. The sexton is "a brick," and you are a most astute maiden. Will you take the commission, Miss, of securing board for two persons at Bryn Mawr? But there I go again! I swore off from that, didn't I? But how *can* a fellow talk about other things when all the—

I went last night to hear Beecher[1] lecture, and was splendidly entertained for an hour and forty minutes, though he was constantly offending my tastes and denying my opinions. His subject was "The Reign of the Common People" and he sent through it a stream of strong, shallow, noisy, irregular, evident, picturesque, taking talk. Nobody wanted him to stop; nobody failed to admire the skill and popular force of the man; nobody carried away much instruction. He proved that dilute sense may fill a hall with intent listeners; he did *not* prove that much greater eloquence, much stronger reasoning, much more compact sense could not fill it quite as full. Dan'l Webster could have had as great success, but Beecher paid much less for his.

So you *did* enjoy "cousin Allie" this time, did you, little lady? I am always so glad to hear of friends coming in upon you in that way. I know that it gives my darling so much pleasure.

Yes, my darling, "the other dainty little lines" were from Aldrich. They chimed in wonderfully well with my predominant thought—for that thought is always of you and of the sweet promises you have made for love of

Your own Woodrow.

P.S. Yes indeed, little sweetheart, you must wait for the copy of my book which I have so long been promising myself the delight of sending you. I will send you the very first copy I see myself. It would hurt me very much if you were to do otherwise—if you were to receive *my* book, even to examine, from anybody but *me*. Lovingly, Woodrow.

ALS (WC, NjP).
1 Henry Ward Beecher.

From Ellen Louise Axson

My darling Woodrow,   New York, Jan. 14/85

Your delightful letter which came this morning and which lies before me now, has, of course, given me much food for thought all day. In fact the matters of which it treated required such *hard* thinking that I have been giving my whole mind to it, with small benefit, I fear to the business in hand! What a laugh I had this morning at myself and my absent-mindedness! In the first place, instead of getting out when the car stopped at the 32nd St. junction, I deliberately rode on into the tunnel and did not come to myself until I had gotten almost to 38th St., from whence I had to walk back, and all the way to the school. Then when I had finally reached it I could not condescend to stop at our floor, —the third,—but continued resolutely to climb higher and higher until there were no more heights to scale!—until, in short, I had reached the *garret*! Don't you think that something must have *dazed* me?

First, let us dispose of Mr. Goodrich. I thank you, dear, for all you say on that subject. It will be helpful to me to hear a man's view of the case. I *must* accept your view now, I don't dare do otherwise, after having given you already such good right to say "I told you so." I don't deny that I am sorry to be obliged to believe you! sorry to think it *possible* for one of my friends to meditate anything so dishonourable. I can't regard such a thought as anything *less* than that;—and yet perhaps I ought not to use so severe a word; you don't accuse him of more than "a vague, half-formed hope"! and then, as you say, there are engagements and engagements; and he can't know how much I love you. Oh, how *perfectly* preposterous that anyone should *dream* of coming between my heart and *you*! It is easy to perceive the difficulties of the situation both for Mr. G. and myself; and it *will* be best to see as little of him as possible. I shall begin at once to gradually withdraw from the "intimacy"(!) You will understand why I cannot do so abruptly; in the first place, it would be very unkind—even cruel—after all that has passed, and after his *apparently* manly behaviour, and in the second place it would lay me open to the gravest misconstruction; it would make it appear that I had been flirting with him—after a very original fashion truly! but still *flirting*—and that now, that being ended, I had no further use for him, no appreciation of his friendship, but would cast him aside like yesterday's newspaper! But I certainly shan't make a convenience of him,—except—do you think it would be better for me to decline going to prayer-meeting with him? There are several little questions which come in there; I would never make a *standing* engagement with any young man—but you!—for anything but church. But when I think of it, that is the only respect in which I *have* made a convenience of him, except in the matter of escorting me from the League; that I shall stop at once. I have a good excuse for Miss Comstock joined the Sketch class yesterday. I suppose you would'nt advise me to break any special engagement already made?—to see Booth, for instance; that engagement was made some six weeks ago, and he bought the tickets yesterday.

By the way, Mr. G. says he was slightly mistaken,—it is on the 24*th* that your book is to be out. And they had a card from someone in Tenth St. today asking for a copy as soon as possible; I wonder who it was, and if that was the first order.

I am *very* glad, dear, that you have heard from Bryn Mawr,

and that all has ended so well; no, I don't think there is any doubt about the advisability of your accepting, and I shall be altogether satisfied to have you do so. I shall be only too glad to know that your doubts and fears with regard to a situation next fall are to be ended so soon in the year, that for the next six months you may go about your work with a mind at ease,—freed from that uncertainty, which, you tell me, is so much harder to bear than any positive trouble.

With regard to the other matter, my darling, I hardly know what to say, I am asked now to *think* about it, so perhaps I had better think longer before I say anything. Yes, dearest, I will be thinking of ways to make it possible early in the season; but I don't see how it could be. There are so many things, great and small, in the way. Don't you think other people would consider it very foolish and unjustifiable? Would not your own parents think so? You must find out very exactly what they *do* think, for I am afraid you are not a good judge, and I am little better, I am so anxious to please you. It is undoubtedly of the first importance to learn their views, since I suppose you would expect to go to them. Don't you think the two weeks from the first of September to the fifteenth would be enough? Or are you obliged to be at Bryn Mawr earlier? But I will say no more about it now,—except, my darling, that amid the tumult of feelings which these thoughts excite, *one* thing seems clear;—if the way were quite smooth I would be glad to decide on June,—and not *altogether* to please *you*,—because *you* wish it,—though that is, of course, by far the strongest reason. Ah me! my poor little heart and hand are both in a flutter as I write this, but I will write it bravely—all the same, —because it is *true*,—because every day makes seperation harder, because it is only half living to live without you. I love you dar-ling—and I am now and forever   Your own   Eileen.

That is a beautiful passage from [Ruskin's] "Sesame and Lilies";[1] —but alas! how unworthy, how ashamed of myself it makes me feel! Ruskin would have us "as wise as serpents and as harmless as doves." Would that we could reach his ideal!—then we would be *angels*! but Eve was made of the same clay as Adam; we have all the same human nature,—and I am not sure, after all, that it is unfortunate.

ALS (WP, DLC).
    [1] Apparently enclosed in WW to ELA, Jan. 13, 1885. It is missing.

To Ellen Louise Axson

My own darling,   Balto., Thursday morning, Jany. 15, 1885

Do you really want to know about all the things that trouble and perplex me, even to the headaches, as well as about my satisfactions—about my 'downs' as well as about my 'ups'? Yes, I know that you *do*, my darling; because latterly I have made a discovery that is the sweetest I *could* make, namely, that I can in most things that concern us two read your heart by reading *my own*: and I know that I should be very miserable if I suspected that you were concealing even the smallest perplexities of your daily life from me. You may be sure, therefore, darling, that I will conceal nothing from you that is greater than a momentary shadow, or an instant's twinge of pain. It would be sheer cruelty for me to tax your sympathy by writing every day of the petty things that have annoyed me. I am, you know, an absurdly sensitive creature. A disagreeable interview, an unpleasant sight on the street, a casual discouragement in my work affect me for a time as keenly as many more permanent influences. When you are by me, my darling, my mind shall be as an open book for you to read, and your love shall be sufficient to chase away *all* worry. But why should I trouble you with trifles which will have gone by and been forgotten before you can read of them. I would *shield* you, little sweetheart, from anything that would give you *unnecessary* anxiety. I am *used* to living this hateful, isolated bachelor-life away off from those I love and need, and I have a man's usual pride in giving as little trouble as possible: but my precious little Eileen is *not* used to fighting her own way alone in a great city—should I add the care of somebody else to the care of herself?—no, not even to satisfy that true woman's heart which prompts her to wish to help me in everything. Besides, my queen, I *have* very few anxieties or perplexities about *myself*—what I have seem to spring, most of them, out of the strong prompting of my love for you, which makes all my wishes turn towards constant companionship with you, and all my thoughts towards a care for your welfare and happiness. And these, you know, little lady, are not *unhappy* anxieties. They are fraught with untold blessings. They have a side of unspeakable delight—that delight which comes from a knowledge of your love for me. You need never fear that you will be 'a care' to me: *that* care is what fills a man's heart with strength and blessed joy. Oh, my pet, how proud I am of your love—that love in which I can trust with more assurance of faith than I can put in my knowledge of my*self*!

I wonder what you have been writing to me about Bryn Mawr(?) I think that I know—but I long for to-morrow's letter just as if I couldn't guess! What will I do for joy when *the day* of my life comes. Do you think that you will be composed and firm enough to keep me in order? I know that you could do *any* thing with   Your own   Woodrow.

ALS (WP, DLC).

From Joseph Ruggles Wilson

My dearest son—   Wilmington [N.C.], January 15, 1885.

Your very interesting letter contains matter for reflection, sure enough. My judgment is perplexed quite as completely as is the case with your own. On the whole, however, it seems to me that you had better accept the position which has been offered, although the offer is extended with a half-withdrawing half-grudging hand. As to the salary, it is small, but for the time-being sufficient. As to the relative rank you are asked to occupy in the faculty, it is certainly absurd, but not necessarily humiliating. For, after all, it will depend upon yourself to lift into superior importance the somewhat lowly chair you are asked to occupy: until it shall command the recognition which is at the outset denied to it. At any rate, it is a beginning, whereat, if you shine, your future will amply take care of itself, either at Bryn Mawr or elsewhere. It is worth, therefore, is it not, a fair trial? You will be in the very centre of the country, will have abundant opportunity to make friends, and by your continued writings illustrated by visible degrees of professional success in practical life, there can be nothing to fear. You are not the man whom unpropitious circumstances are likely to keep down. If you ought to rise, rise you must. But a start is always the first necessity: a foothold. How greatly I wish that it had pleased God to open for you a door very different and much larger than this! Yet perhaps you need the discipline of such narrowness, to enable you to show the stuff of which you are made: a stuff which, if it be of the best—as I believe it to be—will bear a good deal of painful pinching and be the better for the hard process. When you set a clock at 6 the hands go up—when at 12 it goes down. My first salary was $400, and never was there a more compressed situation; it prepared me, though, for larger and wider things. Well, your talents are—to say the least—quite equal to mine, and some of your advantages are superior—far—to my earlier ones. Take heart, then, my precious boy. Commence at once your climb even though your ladder seem so short—and it will lengthen as you ascend.

As to your marriage expenses, do not let these be for a trouble to yr. thoughts. Only do not make them more than downright *necessity* may require, and it will be a pity if we cannot discover some way to meet them without anticipating your slender income.

Your dear mother sanctions all I have said—and you may be sure that when such love as ours prompts the step that has been advised—the counsel may be wrong but it cannot be *far* wrong. Of course though, you and dear Ellie must conclusively decide—and whatsoever the decision of you two, may be, it will meet with our complete approbation.

We are well. The church here is in a melted mood over the prospect of our departure; and I tremble sometimes myself in view of what may be before us. But that which is right is bound to be best. So, let God's hand lead us as it shall please.

I need not add that the sweet mother and the sweet brother join me in sending all love to your sweet self—of whom we are as proud as we are fond.

Your father as always.

ALS (WP, DLC) with WWhw notation on env.: "Ans. Jany 17, 1885."

From James E. Rhoads

My dear Friend   Philadelphia, 1 Mo. 15. 1885.
Thine of the 13th just at hand. The principal Boarding House at Bryn Mawr is perhaps half a mile from the College. I inquired lately of the landlady about board, & I presume two rooms could be had with board for two persons for about $18 to $20. a week—certainly the latter, possibly less than the former.

Thine very truly,   James E Rhoads

ALS (WP, DLC).

To Ellen Louise Axson

My own darling,   Balto., Friday afternoon, Jany. 16, 1885
How shall I be able to send such an answer to your letter of Wednesday night as my heart prompts me to send! I haven't *words* to tell the delight with which its sweet contents has filled me—and how else am I to make you understand what I have felt

ever since I read it? My darling! My heart told me that you would say just what you did—and yet it came upon me like a joyous surprise

"First, let us dispose of Mr. Goodrich." Of course I would not have you break with him abruptly, my pet—seeing that you are sweet enough to ask my advice. You could not well get out of your engagement to go to see Booth; but you *could* find reasons for not caring to attend Dr. Hamilton's Wednesday evening lectures any more—could you not, pet?—for you know the standing character of the engagement gives him the privilege of a specially-favoured friend, and negatives whatever else you may do by way of separating yourself from him. It *is* preposterous, my darling, that any one should so much as dream of coming between us—it is something more than preposterous—it would kill *me* to dream of it. But that does not affect the present question, which is one simply of your *dignity*. I *knew* that you would see the propriety of doing as you have determined to do: and I think that you can do it within a very short time without either being unkind or creating unpleasant impressions. My straightforward, courageous, womanly little sweetheart! How passionately I love you, how entirely I admire you!

And oh, my darling, what shall I say to the precious promises of this letter—the promises that my heart stood still to hear and is throbbing beyond all reason at realizing. You may be sure that I will ascertain as fast as the mails will enable me the plans and opinions of the home-folks, so that there may be no obstacle on that side.[1] I would certainly have to go to Bryn Mawr some days before the 15th [of September], to unpack my books and get everything in proper trim for work, if not to conduct examinations; besides which, Miss, there is the desirability of commencing my work there with a cool head and unexcited faculties—which, I assure you, would hardly be possible for me if we had at that time been but two weeks married! But I might as well stop talking—though I can't for the life of me stop thinking—about this subject till we know the *possibilities*. In the mean time it makes me inexpressibly happy to know that my little queen *wishes* just what I do in the matter, that it may be as soon as possible. Oh that I could kiss those sweet lips for that confession! My darling, you don't know how sacred those words of yours seem to me. They are the seal and earnest of just the sort of love I have sought to win from you. And you may be sure that I am already as much yours, darling, as if you had already claimed me. I can never be more entirely   Your own   Woodrow.

ALS (WP, DLC).
¹ In fact, WW had already written to his father about his hopes for a June wedding. See JRW to WW, Jan. 15, 1885.

From Ellen Louise Axson

My darling Woodrow,   New York Jan 16/85

Your charming little letter of the 14th reached me tonight. I was indeed "entertained" by that delightful witticism of Mr. Gosse's, as well as by your fine description of Mr. Beecher's style. Am sorry that I have but a moment tonight for making answer, but I have been extremely busy all the evening, and it is now very late.

No, dear, you may be very sure that I shan't see your book until you send it to me; I should go about blind-folded if I thought there was any danger of Mr. Goodrich keeping his word and springing it upon me unaware!

I must take time to tell you the latest League news; Miss Mehitable Whelphy is no more, she has become Mrs. George DeForest Brush! She came up to the city Sat. afternoon;—he met her, at the depot I believe, and they walked around to the nearest justice of the peace, he don't believe in preachers, you know, and were married,—and thats all! I did'nt even know it in time to go down to the antique room and take a look at him (!) on Tuesday when he came to give his lesson.

But the room grows cold and I *must* not write. Yes darling I am glad for *my* sake too that the Bryn Mawr matter has ended satisfactory. I believe I hinted at something of the sort in my last! Good-night, dear heart,

With truest love   Your own Eileen.

ALS (WP, DLC).

From the Minutes of the Seminary of Historical and Political Science

Bluntschli Library. Jan 16th, 1885

The Seminary was called to order at 8.15 P.M. Dr. Adams in the chair. . . .

The following periodicals were reviewed; Dec. No. of the Deutsche Rundschau by Mr. Steiguer. The review contained little of importance to the Seminary, the most important article being on Wm von Humbolt which was rather personal than political. Nov. & Dec No. of the Journal des Economistes reviewed by Mr. Wilson. Nov. number contained an important article on Bi-metallism, treating the present state of the question; the failure of the last conference; the single conference in Germany, its origin and connection with the general question, the consequence and probable result of the reform. Dec. no. contained an article on Economic Laws, which was an attempt to prove that Political Economy has its natural laws. In the same number there were three important articles on Socialism. . . . Seminary adjourned at 9.25 P.M.[1]

1 Entry lacks secretary's signature.

From Ellen Louise Axson

My darling Woodrow,   New York, Jan. 17, 1885.

I must, much against my will, send only a little message this morning in answer to those sweet letters which lie before me. I had a great deal to do last night, and then I had managed to catch a heavy cold in the storm yesterday and I knew that the best thing I could do for it was to go to bed as early as possible and sleep it off,—which I did to a great extent.

Thanks again for your good advice as to Mr. Goodrich. I won't let my standing engagement *stand* any longer,—will go with him *now* only occasionally, and in a short time I won't go at all. By-the-way, he said yesterday—"oh! I see,—you mean to *gradually* get rid of me!" He is "quite too awfully" sharp! And I am quite as tired of all this sort of thing—of all men but you. I wish they would "lem'me alone"! I was *never!*—(a suspicious looking omission, eh?[ )][1] "fond of admiration"! as the saying is,—at least I prefered that they should not *dislike* me but like me only a *very little*! But now even that bores me, when it doesn't make me rather indignant. What *right* have others to be "making eyes" at me? I belong to *you*. And I cannot tell you, darling "how passionately I love you, how entirely I admire you"! I am sure dearest that you could never have wished for more love than you have won from   Your own Eileen.

ALS (WP, DLC).
1 ELA inserted "*never!*—(a suspicious looking omission, eh?[ )]" above the line after "was."

To Ellen Louise Axson

My own darling,   Balto., Saturday noon, Jany. 17, 1885

I often wonder what the undercurrent of your thoughts was while writing some of the sweet letters that come to me. Do you realize, for instance, when you make such confessions as this of your gladness for your *own* sake at the settlement of the Bryn

Mawr question that you are writing what will make me almost beside myself with delight. When I read such sentences I involuntarily murmur aloud the words of love that my heart prompts me to utter in reply. To think that my shy little sweetheart has come to love me so much that she rejoices in a near prospect of our marriage, and is made brave enough by that love to confess, not only to herself, but to me her wish that our separation may end as soon as possible!

I suppose that you realize, little lady, that to live at Bryn Mawr on fifteen hundred dollars a year will not be like living at the South on that sum. I have been inquiring, of course, about the cost of board there and find that it is just about as high as it is in New York. The place is fashionable and the winter accommodations are not abundant, so that the landladies seem to have everything in their own hands. Don't laugh at me for giving you this warning. I know that my darling will be actually *glad* to make *any* sacrifices for me—so they be made *with* me—but you know the desire I am constantly confessing, the desire to be sure that you fully realize all that will be involved in marrying a very poor, as well as a very plain, man!

I received a long letter from dear father yesterday in which he criticises the Bryn Mawr offer as absurd in distinction of rank and as "extended with a half-withdrawing, half-grudging hand" —but advises me to accept it as at least a practicable *start* in the part of the country where it will be most advantageous to be. "Of course, though," he concludes, "you and dear Ellie must conclusively decide—and whatsoever the decision of you two may be, it will meet with our complete approbation." There is no danger that they will think a certain June wedding "very foolish and unjustifiable," as I shall soon prove to you from their own lips.

I will probably write to Dr. Rhoads on Monday signifying my acceptance of the place offered—and then it will be my delectable duty to call on Dean Martha, to consult about the courses of study to be announced.

I am puzzled to know, my darling, for reasons which I will explain some other time, whether Mr. Goodrich knows *why* you are so much interested in the forthcoming work on "Cong. Govt."— does he? I had not been told by the publishers, strangely enough, when it was to be published. My only information has come through you—though it is now announced in the papers, I believe.

I must not write any more to-day, darling. I am exceptionally busy just now and must take even Saturday for work.

I love you, precious, inexpressibly! How long these seventeen days of Jany have been! How *can* I wait till you can come and take me as   Your own   Woodrow!

ALS (WP, DLC).

From Ellen Louise Axson

My darling Woodrow,   New York, Jan. 17/85.

It is so late and I am so sleepy that I feel tempted, for your sake more than for my own, to postpone writing until the morning. But I recall last Sunday's experience, and how my letter was delayed; and the remembrance warns me that I had best write a few lines tonight even though they are sure to be both stupid and illegible. I have been "house-cleaning" tonight, besides all sorts of other Saturday work;—work to which Sat. morning has been dedicated by the practice of ages; but here all days are alike,—at the League, and as I can't afford to take a weekly holiday for such slight cause, I devote Sat. night to it instead—though it seems comical work for eleven o'clock at night. It makes me think of the old adage about lazy people being busiest ["]when the sun is in the west"! What bibiomaniac was it who had such a cast-iron system of arranging his books, that whenever he bought a new one, all the other thousands had to be taken down and out,—replaced and recatalogued? I remember some story of that sort, with the amusing details of how he made life interesting for his aimiable household. I have a somewhat similar experience whenever I bring home a "study" which strikes me as rather more tolerable than the works of art which already adorn these walls. If you could see me meditating upon the problems it gives rise to, you would be filled with awe at the sight of such intense mental effort. You would involuntarily "tread softly and speak low" lest you should disturb such profound meditations.

By the-way my last study is rather better-looking than usual. We had a *splendid* model this week,—a handsome young Jew. One can really do better work when one has an interesting model, and not such an old hag as we had last week. Mr. Weir gave me quite a shock by praising mine as heartily as Mr. Brush himself could have done[.] He so seldom says anything "*nice*" that I scarcely knew how to take it; I've never heard him speak so to anyone before but Mr. Patter. He is in my head-class now and my Southern friend Miss Stewart is coming soon. Those two will make it almost as pleasant upstairs as in the antique. Please excuse this hasty scrawl. I love you, darling, as my own soul and I am altogether and always   Your own   Eileen.

ALS (WP, DLC).

To Ellen Louise Axson

My own darling,   Balto., Sabbath afternoon, Jany. 18, 1885

I like to use Sundays as stopping places commanding a view of the weeks gone through and take account of the country passed over—and to-day I think that I see behind me a somewhat longer stretch of country than usual. I have at last gotten into something like a swinging, long-distance gait of work, and I hope to make the pace still better from this time on—especially if I can know that an inestimable prize awaits me in June! Mr. Gosse is gone, I have declined the invitation of the "Eight o'clock Club," I shall use my nights as well as my days for regular study—and so, having both more time to use and a fresh purpose of using it, I *may* 'make' my Ph.D. after all. How different my work is now from what it used to be when it was done without *you*! I hope that there are as many lines and lights in your work that represent me as there are encouragements in mine which represent you, my little queen! I feel like telling you about my work because you seem to be so inseparably connected with it—seem to have done so much of it.

I received a letter from Renick[1] to-day hurrahing over the announcement of my book which he had just seen in the *Nation*.[2] He is very generous in his expressions of delight—and *Mrs* Renick "joins him in warm congratulations and kindest wishes." It seems that he was in Phila. on the 1st, attending a convention of his fraternity.

I am sorry, my love, that Mr. Goodrich presumes to annoy you with such remarks as the one you repeat in the little note received this morning. I had given him credit for more tact and manliness. Of course he must see that it is your wish to see less of him than before—and he must know that that wish is altogether womanly and maidenly. If he had the right feelings in the matter, he would see and act upon the propriety of that wish—would acquiesce in without seeming to notice it, instead of taking the vulgar liberty of *teasing* you about it—or *speaking* of it at all. I can't conceive of a *proud* man's doing so.

I am *so* sorry, so much disturbed, my pet, to hear that you have contracted a fresh cold! Be sure to tell me, darling, of its future behaviour—I shall be very anxious to hear that it is gone. It is very sweet in you to observe my wish to be told of every change in your health. I should be miserably anxious if I could *not* know just how you are.

It is your wish, is it not, my precious, to take dear little Eddie with us at once to Bryn Mawr? I ask now that I may be able to make negotiations for board on a definite basis, if it should prove to be advisable to make arrangements as soon as possible.

I wonder if my little sweetheart has been thinking as much of next summer as I have? Have you ridden past 32nd. St. any more, or climbed again to the garret? That was a delightful little episode! I love to think that thoughts of me can sometimes utterly exclude everything thing [sic] from my darling's mind—that her heart is my *home*, with sacred chambers which no one else may enter. Your love is all in all to

Your own   Woodrow.

ALS (WP, DLC).
¹ E. I. Renick to WW, Jan. 16, 1885, ALS (WP, DLC) with WWhw notation on env.: *"Ans 1/19/85."*
² "Houghton, Mifflin & Co. will soon have ready 'Congressional Government: a Study in American Politics,' by Woodrow Wilson." New York *Nation*, XL (Jan. 15, 1885), 55.

From Ellen Louise Axson

My darling Woodrow,   New York, Jan. 19/85

Those people downstairs detained me so long last night that when I finally was able to write, I found my fire at the point of death;—past hope of recovery,—and was obliged, to my intense dissatisfaction, to postpone writing for fear of taking fresh cold. My cold by-the-way does'nt amount to anything, it is almost gone. Now I must postpone again, for you know what Monday mornings are;—I ought to be on my way now. So I must put off answering those two precious letters just received, until tonight, —no! how provoking! I go to hear Booth tonight. But I *will* write, all the same,—if I can get a fire.

I am so glad, dearest, to hear *anything* about you[r] work and especially to hear that you are feeling encouraged, and in good spirits over it. Oh yes, Mr. G. knows why I am so interested in "Congressional Government"! Of course when the papers were talking about it I talked too! Why are you "puzzled to know"? I hope you *will* explain, for I am *curious* to know! Your interpretations of Mr. G's conduct are to me a rather curious lesson in (masculine) human nature! Men *are* queer creatures! are they not? You can never be sure you understand them because their "motives" are so peculiar—sometimes. But I must stop—more anon. I love you, dear heart, more and more everyday, I think. Believe me darling, as ever   Your own   Eileen

ALS (WP, DLC).

Two Letters to Ellen Louise Axson

My own darling,　　　Baltimore, Monday, 12:50 Jany 19, 1885

Dr. Rhoads has become either disgusted or alarmed by my delay in accepting the Bryn Mawr offer. Just as I was thinking of sitting down to write to him saying that I would accept, I received a telegram from him which runs thus: "Please meet at Dr. Thomas at four this afternoon."[1] I can't imagine 'what's up' that could not be arranged by letter—inasmuch as the 15th of Sept., though steadily approaching, is not likely to arrive before a brief correspondence could be concluded; but of course I shall 'meet' at Dr. Thomas's (i.e. at Dean Martha's) to find out what's intended —in case any one else who can tell me should happen to be 'meeting' there at the same time. I *suppose* that the object is to induce me to surrender—and, if that *is* the purpose, I shall of course surrender with very little ado, since I intended doing so anyhow. If perchance they have discovered some one else whom they would rather have, and wish delicately to hint the same, I will withdraw with even *less* ado. But how absurd it is to make guesses about the matter!

Your little letter of Saturday night gives me a very pleasant glimpse of your "house-cleaning," my darling—and you know how precious *any* glimpse of your private doings is to me[.] But pray, Miss, where did you learn that *Saturday* was the proper day for these particular duties of housekeeping? In all the families about whose domestic affairs I have known anything *Mon*day was house-cleaning day. You must have inherited one of the customs of those nations whose sacred day was Friday (whence our superstitions about enterprizes begun on that day) and whose Monday, consequently, was Saturday.

How I should like to *see* some of those 'studies' which so often need rearranging—and how proud I am to hear of Mr. Weir's unwonted enthusiasm over my darling's work. How long is it going to take you, Miss, to get beyond being surprised at such praise, and to recognize the fact that you have a real genius for such work—as real a genius as you have for *loving* perfectly and perfecting the happiness of those you love? Mr. Weir's praise seems to me delightful, not because it was necessary, but because it was *extorted*. And teachers ought to praise more than they do. Their commendation, when it does not evidently come from mere good nature, is the only commendation that really encourages. I believe that I could believe in my own powers more—which would be much to my advantage, of course—if some recognized master of political criticism, like Mr. [James] Bryce or Mr. [Edward A.] Freeman were to pronounce what I had written well done. Somehow the praise of other people—dear to me as it is as a proof of their love or friendship—seems to me utterly inconclusive as to the character of my work. The success I want is the success of thought, and the masters of thought can guage that.

I love you, my precious little sweetheart, oh *so* passionately, with *such* a longing for your companionship! With *all* my heart
Your own   Woodrow

P.S. I kept this letter, my darling, in order to tell you what Dr. Rhoads wanted—and I find that, as it turns out, there is nothing to tell. He simply wanted to assure me that the cost of living at Bryn Mawr was really not a matter to be alarmed about, that ten dollars apiece per week was in fact not *more* than ten dollars apiece. The only definite plan he had to propose was that the College should furnish one of its cottages and rent it, for $425.00 dollars, to us and the two bachelor professors, with whom we might share the expense, and for whom we might have the privilege of keeping house! He is quite sure that living can be made quite inexpensive by a clubbing together of all the households connected with the College in the purchase of fuel and the larger supplies. The College means to buy for the whole college community—if the community desires.

Such arrangements may be regarded as comfortable and convenient by these interesting Pennsylvanians, but I most certainly beg to be excused: and the man who suggests that my darling undertake housekeeping, under such communistic conditions, for three men[,] can't possibly know what a fool I think him! It is the desire of my heart that she should keep house for *me*—that we should have a home of our own; but we certainly will not have a home that is *not* our own. This man evidently don't understand the art of persuading me to accept $1500; but I am afraid that I shall have to accept it anyhow.   Lovingly,   W.

ALS (WP, DLC).
  1 The telegram is missing.

My own darling,   Balto., Tuesday afternoon, Jany 20, 1885

Monday and Tuesday are the hardest days of the week for me, because the absence of University engagements from them makes it imperative that all the reading should be done in them which the rush of University engagements on other days of the week precludes: and no busy filfilment of appointments is half so fatiguing as a steady strain of attention to books. My busiest days are in the middle of the week, my hardest at the beginning of the week. I could wish that it were otherwise. A single lecture each day would afford a restful interruption, a grateful variety, and, at the same time, leave several hours available for reading—and by such adjustments a fellow might escape the fagged, jaded feeling that comes after two days of hard reading. I don't know that much harm comes of such fatigue, however. There is a sort of grim satisfaction in tiring one's mind out, if it be only to prove one's mastery over natural disinclinations. I feel a much greater affinity for the busy rush and the practical talk of the outside world that don't read than for the noiseless, level, monotonous talk of a book, whose life seems inseparable from a seat indoors. These bright, inviting days, with their crisp air and their alluring sunshine tempt me every moment to throw down these heavy volumes and run out into the glories of the open air. But a man can't find *all* the necessary food for thought in the streets of a great city, or even in the free inspiration of the noble country-side. To be a heeded, a trustworthy, a conscientious thinker nowadays, one must dig in books. He can't find history anywhere else; he can't understand present experience unless he knows the experience bound up between the senseless covers of ponderous books or recorded on the faded faces of old manuscripts; so that he *must* focus all his senses in his spectacles, and strive to forget that he was not meant to sit all day in a hard chair at a square table, pouring all his energies out in deciphering stiff print. There's duty in drudgery as well as in love and in laughter. It's quite as necessary for the Christian to work as for him to be glad. If he finds himself now and then quite worn out, he deserves sympathy, but not release. Fatigue may bring low spirits—but that's probably his own fault—certainly not the fault of the work. In short, if a man does not find duty agreeable, he does not deserve gratification. When fagged out, as I am to-day, loneliness and a keen longing for the sympathetic companionship and the gentle ministrations of the one I love most in the world steal a march on me and take complete possession of me before I can rally to defend myself; and I laugh at myself for not being man enough to do my very small amount of work without feeling the need of petting and encouragement! Poor little boy! he ought to be patted and sung to sleep by his nurse—and whipped in the morning when he is stronger!

 With infinite love,   Your own Woodrow.

ALS (WC, NjP).

Two Letters from Ellen Louise Axson

My darling Woodrow,   New York. Jan 20/85.

Why, oh why! did you extort that unfortunate promise from me as to sitting in cold rooms? You see how it works! It was as I feared, too cold and too late to write last night after my return. Indeed, it is almost as cold now, but I *must* sit in the sunshine long enough to write a *little*.

Oh! I am perfectly beside myself over Booth![1] I never saw anything so finished, so absolutely perfect!—he *never* overdoes his part,—there is no ranting, no mouthing, no staginess of any description. There was in it all such "exquisite *rightness*" as Ruskin says. One would scarcely have wished a single gesture or inflection other than it was. And he really had a good support for once; —Charles Barron, Blanche Thomson, and Annie Clarke. Last night was his first in N.Y. this season; and such an ovation I never saw before; the people cheered for a quarter of an hour before they would let him begin, actually standing up the better to give him "three times three." But this won't do! I must stop short.

Where is the notice of your book in the "Nation"? I looked through all the papers for a month yesterday, and I could not find it;—mean to look again today, for I *must* see it.

My dear, are you *sure* that you "fully realize all that is involved in marrying a very poor as well as a very plain" girl? "Dont laugh at me for giving you this warning" but I want to be certain that you grasp the situation *fully*! Yes, I think I realize the difference between the North and the South in the matter of expenses; my experience this winter has taught me that. But of course it will be all right as far as I am concerned,—provided *you* are not to be made anxious or kept worried over those matters. But of all this, more hereafter; I must close now. Remember darling, that I love you with *all* my heart and am forever

Your own Eileen.

[1] As Iago. See ELA to WW, Jan. 22, 1885.

My darling Woodrow,   New York Jan. 20/84 [1885].

No, I have not past 32nd St. again, or climbed to the garret, but I did still worse today,—I forgot my purse, and was obliged to walk *all* the way! However it was a delightful day, so I rather enjoyed it; I was most lucky to discover my mistake before getting on the car, 'twould have been dreadful to have been caught there. Of course I borrowed five cents to return! I did not tell you that

I have found a girl at the Metropolitan who was in Rome for a long time last fall,—a year ago, I mean—and who knows "everybody" there. She lived in Atlanta for several years and is a "bosom friend" of Mrs. Seaborn Wright,—"Moore & Marsh's" daughter, you know! Her name is Miss Farnesworth, and she is a very bright and pretty girl,—a decided leader in the little society at the "Met."

So you go back to the old Scandinavian system,—do you?—to prove that Monday is the proper day for house-cleaning? Well! I don't know how to get even with you except by going back in *my* turn to "Moses and the prophets"! Was it not decreed in the law that the day *before* the Sabbath should be "a day of preparation" that everything might be pure and clean "without spot or blemish" in honour of the holy day; and also in order that there might be nothing left to do on that day?

Dr. Rhoads certainly seems anxious to secure you for Bryn Mawr, showing what is apparently a very kindly interest in your affairs. I have no doubt he is a very good-hearted old man whether his advice be good or not. I wonder dearest if you—or I either—have indeed realized as we ought what we are about. Ah me! you speak of marrying in *June*, but I fear!—I fear I should do you a great wrong to marry you at all soon! that I, even *I*, who love you so— would be binding heavy burdens grievous to be borne and laying them on your shoulders,—burdens which no love could remove or make light. You say the board is ten dollars a week! Why, that is higher than New York, for here while one can certainly pay *ten*, if one chooses—one can also get it for *seven*; but that is the trouble with "suburban retreats"; one must submit to city rates without the power of choice which the city so abundantly affords. It is absurd to locate a college at a fashionable resort. Think of Davidson with its twelve dollars a month for board! You would be obliged to pay a thousand for board alone;—and then other things! Why "washing" alone, at city rates, would be a hundred or so more. And where, darling, is the margin for your books and necessary journeys to Washington &c?—and where, above all, is that ease and quiet of mind without which it would seem to me well nigh impossible for one to do intellectual work. I have often wondered that the average minister succeeds half as well as he does, harassed—tormented—as he always is by the struggle to make both ends meet. How could I bear to see you so, and to know that, say what you would, it was *my* fault!—that I had bound upon your feet, not "wings," but "*chains*." Such a thought would break my heart. My only *comforting* thought is that I too can work, and will, if I can find the work to do;—and yet I must confess to myself how uncertain a thing that would be, under the circumstances, —how many contingencies surround such plans.

You see how hard I am trying to be perfectly frank with myself, to see things clearly and definitely. And of course my love for you demands that I should be equally true and frank with you,— I know that there is no danger of your misconstruing anything I say,—I am perfectly sure of that, in spite of the unaccountable embarrassment which I feel in raising these so necessary questions. And after all I can't be very clear or definite in speaking to you because I don't know *what* to do or say. Oh if I only had a mother to tell me!

I fear I have already said a great deal to hurt you, my darling, —I, who would rather die than give you ever so little pain, but you must forgive me,—it is all for love. I think I have scarcely a desire left except to make you happy,—to learn what is truly best for that end.

Believe me my dear love, always and altogether,

Your own Eileen.

I feel that I have been very wrong not to think of all this before; but I did not know the facts until yesterday and I find I did *not* realize them until this morning.

ALS (WP, DLC).

To Ellen Louise Axson

My own darling,   Balto., Wednesday afternoon, Jany. 21, 1885

The 'notice' of my book in the *Nation* is merely an announcement of it from the publishers, in the "Notes" of the number for Jany 15.—not at all worth looking for.

I am *so* glad that my darling has had a chance to see the great Booth—and I think that I enjoyed her enthusiastic words about his acting as much as she could have enjoyed the play. By-the-way, my pet, you did not tell me what play it was. Was it Hamlet?

I am glad that I *did* extort that promise about not sitting in cold rooms. It results in losses to me which I feel very keenly, but no price is too great to pay for my darling's health.

I have received a couple of curious letters as a result of my essay at authorship. The editor of "Bradstreet's," the leading economic weekly, "has been drawn to me" by my studies of Congress, and hopes that I will feel at liberty to speak of congressional matters occasionally through his columns.[1] And one Chas. H. Fitch "hopes that my forthcoming work on the machinery of legislation will supply a satisfactory basis" for some vague "codification of official proprieties," which is his hobby, enclosing in his letter several newspaper paragraphs written by him on the subject for the *Evening Post* and other papers![2] The "Bradstreet's" man, Wm F. Ford, seems to have *read* my essays—how or where there's no imagining, unless he be one of the H. M. & Co's "readers."

If you are having the same glorious weather that is making all Baltimore smile, I hope that that cold of yours is getting ashamed of staying, if it be not altogether gone. I have been reading the last three days with a keen consciousness that out-of-doors the world was radiant with sunshine and full of an air that is like nectar to the lungs—and such a consciousness has not made Mr. [George] Bancroft seem a very charming writer. Imagine a fish in the stale waters of a close, dark tank hearing the cool, silvery plash of free sunlit waters just outside his prison-walls, a frisking horse in his cramped stall smelling the pastures outside and catching now and again from thence the ringing notes of his stable-mate's frisking neigh, or a bird denied all sight of the green boughs whose rustling is always in his ears and all part in the joyous flight of the free wings that he knows to be in the air, and —No, that will hardly do—it's 'most too poetical: Imagine, instead, a man who loves to walk compelled to tread a mill and you will have formed a sort of conception of what it has cost me to read, read, read when the open air so tempted to aimless roving through its bright spaces. It's not so much one's self as other people that one enjoys out-of-doors on days like these—the bright eyes, the elastic step, the rosy cheeks, the easy energy of everybody one meets fill one with a sort of joy in other people's living that can be experienced at no other time. One feels like saying, 'Yes, I know: *is'nt* it nice! Let's take a *long* walk!'

With a heartful of love,   Your own   Woodrow.

ALS (WC, NjP).
   [1] W. F. Ford to WW, Jan. 7, 1884[5].
   [2] Charles Howard Fitch, sociologist and economist. His letter is missing.

From Ellen Louise Axson

My darling Woodrow,   New York Jan. 21/85.

I am sadly afraid from today's letter that someone is overworking himself again!—overtaxing his strength, as he certainly *is* his spirits! Of course a *certain* amount of weariness does one no harm, it only makes rest more pleasant,—sleep more sweet, especially if it is attended by the quiet satisfaction which comes from the consciousness that one has done a good day's work. But fatigue which goes to the point of exhaustion is another matter, and a very serious one,—I fear that is *over*-fatigue which is sufficient to leave one so jaded and depressed. The powers that be, at the University, seem to have succeeded in devising a peculiarly unfortunate programme for the weeks. Such an unequal division of one's labour—such long stretches of the same kind of work,— I have noticed is apt to be bad for almost everyone. Almost all people need variety in their day. True I don't! I *hate* to change! but I observe, for instance that almost all the students at the League, prefer to do different sorts of work in the morning and afternoon, or if they can't do better to at least work upon different casts. I think, dear, that whether it is "in the programme" or not, it would be better for you to make more "restful interruptions"—to take some sort of brisk vigorous exercise whenever you feel yourself getting "fagged out." I wish you could take some regular exercise apart from mere *walking*. That does'nt break your train of thought enough, it is no medicine for the mind; you need *diversion*,—something to warm your blood,—horseback-riding, fencing, boxing!—can't you devise something of the sort?—and manage to get really interested in it?

But I must write only a little note tonight, for I have been to *prayer meeting*! and I have still much to do before I have earned my night's sleep! I love you, my darling, "with my heart, and my soul and my duty, and my life and my living and my uttermost power[.]" Believe me as ever,   Your own Eileen.

ALS (WP, DLC).

To Ellen Louise Axson

Balto., Thursday afternoon, Jany 22, 1885

No, my precious little sweetheart, I was not hurt by anything contained in the loving and womanly letter that came this morning: I *could* not misunderstand my darling, and I *want* her to tell me everything that is in her thoughts concerning the question which is now all-important for us. Oh this hateful paper! What would I not give to be able to *say* what I am compelled to *write*! The only thing that disturbs me in your letter, precious, is that *you* should be so much distressed about the decision of this question. You may be sure that I have thought over the matter often and most carefully, with an eye to its *business* side alone, as it was clearly my duty to do—and, after such views repeatedly taken, I can say, without hesitation and without bias from sentiment that there would, in my opinion, be nothing *imprudent* in our going to Bryn Mawr on $1500 a year for two years. In the first place, it will *not* cost us ten dollars per week apiece necessarily. That is the outside figure supposing that we took *two rooms,* of equal size and convenience. Dr. Rhoads mentioned that as the highest sum named for board and room for one person. It is like the eleven dollars that you paid at first for your room at Mrs Beattie's. It was only in making sport of Dr. R. that I put the cost in the light I did. It was very thoughtless in me to forget the effect it might have upon your mind. I have not had any correspondence with the boarding-house keepers at Bryn Mawr, all my information coming through Dr. R., but their charges would be unlike any I ever heard of if they demanded twice as much for two persons as for one.

But, suppose they do, what then? I admit that, a thousand dollars being paid out for board, no margin would remain for books or for the necessary (?) journeys to Washington; but I think that enough would remain for our other necessary expenses: and I am sure that there is something that is more needful for my success than books and trips to the capital, namely, peace of mind. *That* will come to me, not with abundant means, but with *you!* I am not saying this, darling, only as a lover: I am simply putting into words a deep, deliberate, rational conviction—a conviction which antedates my acquaintance with you: for I knew then that I could never have true peace of mind until I found the companionship which I have since found in your love!

How does the case stand, then, with me? If I am to spend another year without you, it will be simple prudence to decline the Bryn Mawr offer, and spend that year *here.* I would only break myself down by undertaking the responsibilities of such a situation alone. Pecuniary anxieties, should I be weak enough to yield dominion to them, could not torment me half so much as the double burden of novel responsibilities and loneliness. The reason I asked, in one of my recent letters, about your plans concerning dear little Eddie was, that I wanted to have a definite correspondence with the Bryn Mawr landladies; and, if I found that their charges were beyond the capabilities of $1500, it was my intention to decline the position there.

It is hardly possible for me now, however, to withhold my decision any longer—I have already been quite too slow about arriving at it—and I shall sign the two-year contract in the full assurance that it will be quite possible for us to make satisfactory arrangements.

Of course I shall not do this to "force your hand," my precious little queen. I want to leave you absolutely free to make your own decision: my only desire is to *help* you in this, as in all other things. Take counsel of your *heart*, darling, not of your fears. And, above all, have no fears for *me*! Your love, if you will share my fortunes with me, *can* "remove and make light" *any* burdens of circumstance. Have you so little faith in love that you think the inconveniences of imperative economy, which can have in it no actual *want*, enough to outweigh it with me? You talk as if a salary of $1500 must plunge us into positive discomfort. It *would* make me miserable to know that I had married you only to make you feel the trials of actual poverty. But the salary promised will be enough for us to *live on* for two years—and it will be enough to preclude all necessity for your turning your talents again to money-making. I should feel it as a cruel humiliation if I found that I had not relieved you from that necessity, that I had offered you a support which I was not able to give you! Why, little lady, I am not *at all* of your creed in this matter. I believe that it gives love *wings, not* chains, to lay upon it the necessity for self-sacrifice—and the sharper the sacrifice, the longer and stronger the wings! If such love as ours needed any cement, it would be the best *policy* to get married on a very meagre income.

This is quite like the Asheville argument! I haven't for a moment doubted what course would be best for *me*: the only difficulties I have to meet arise from your solicitude on my account! *I* can tell you what to say and to do, my precious. Oh if my love could only suffice for you, taking the place even of that mother's counsel for which you long! If it be *possible*, darling, let me—oh let me!—fill even that place in your heart. You will make me *happy*, Eileen, by marrying me—I cannot be happy until you *do* marry me. Nothing can compare with the pain of separation from you. I speak that which I know, and I speak it with all solemnity, knowing all that is involved, when I say that your companionship is more essential to my *ambitions* than the books I cannot yet own or the journeys I cannot take. My first need is *you*—these things come *far* behind! I shall have the privilege of ordering for the college library the books most necessary for my use in teaching: and the Phila. libraries contain all that I shall *need* for any special studies I am likely to find time to make in term-time during those first two years—and, if I wrote "Cong. Govt." without visiting Washington, much more can I write upon the science of administration without doing so! But, whether or not, I shall have all the facilities necessary for efficient *teaching*—and at my age I can afford much better to let my special writing wait than to let our marriage wait! Original work cannot make me happy; but *you* can! And what I cannot do with your companionship and love, I certainly cannot do *without* you!

And now, my darling, you have my answer to this sweet letter that has brought so many tears to my eyes. We will not do anything rash. If it be *necessary* that I should wait—even till Christmas time—I will do it, and nobody (not even my little sweetheart —unless her heart tells her) shall know what it cost me! But, if it be *not* necessary—if a marriage in June be *possible*—I *cannot* wait—I *will* not wait for anything but my Eileen's consent! I know, my darling, that your chief desire is to make me happy—and, since that is so, you must let me be the *judge* of what will make me happy. I *could* not deceive you, my Eileen! So you must take my word implicitly, and let fear and anxiety be swallowed up of love. Love does not make me lose my head: and, if you cannot trust my judgment upon this question, you cannot trust it upon any.

With unspeakable love and tenderness,

Your own   Woodrow.

ALS (WC, NjP).

From Ellen Louise Axson

My darling Woodrow,   New York Jan. 22/84 [1885]

As I came up from dinner tonight Mr. Goodrich asked me to wait a minute as he had something to show me—a new edition of Holmes poems. I did so and when he came down he had two books. One of them he put in my hands and through the little slit in the paper cover I read "Congressional Government"! I dropped it like a hot plate, and told him what I thought of him for bringing it after I had told him expressly that I did not wish him to do so. But he seemed highly amused at the success of his trick. However I made him take it away at once without opening it, so I hav'nt really *seen* it. One can scarcely be said to have seen a man at all when one has seen only the back of his head for a second! This was one of two copies—the first—which came from Boston today.

I am very much pleased with Mr. Wm. F. Ford,—and his letter. It is quite a nice compliment that he should have read your book and taken such decided action upon it *already*—before people are supposed to know anything about it. Do you feel disposed to address the public "through his columns occasionally." I should imagine that the public one would reach by that means would [be] a very large, and a very solid one.

No, we have not been having such deliciously tempting weather as you describe. It has been too cold and windy; today the thermometer is at "8 above," but it is pleasant not-withstanding—bright and bracing. My cold, by the way is altogether gone.

I did not tell you what play I heard? It was "Othello" with Booth as Iago—a rather unfortunate selection I think. But Mr. G. was determined to take me to the opening night; and I went, under protest, for I had already an engagement for "Hamlet" next week. Both engagements were made long ago. I look forward with keener delight than ever now to seeing the "Hamlet," for I am simply *wild* over him—Booth. I would go to a matinee also, if he only acted in Shakspeares plays then. But I have been writing a lot of duty letters tonight, and the consequence is that now it is long past eleven and I am so sleepy that I can scarcely keep my eyes open, so I *must* close. I love you darling, and am now and forever,   Your own Eileen.

ALS (WP, DLC).

From Joseph Ruggles Wilson

My precious son—   Wilmington [N.C.], Thursday—22nd Jan. 85

We received a message on Monday afternoon—from Annie—to tell us that dear little Jessie was "very ill." Your mother and Josie went over to Columbia the same night. On Tuesday Josie wrote that she was thought to be "a shade better." This morning a letter came from yr mother with particulars. The disease is "inflammation of the brain with other complications," and "George is not at all hopeful as to the result." The probability therefore is that we are to lose this sweetest of children. God grant that it may not be so! I know what your feelings will be when you get this gloomy news. But if you hear nothing from me for a day or two, you may argue favorably from my silence. The doubt must be promptly decided, one way or the other. Meanwhile, neither you nor I can do anything in the way of help, except by our prayers.

As to *our* plans, on which *yours* may somewhat depend, I can write nothing definitely until I shall have consulted with your mother who will probably arrange for a couple of months' board —April & May & a part of June—in Columbia.

In talking over your affairs, mother and I have thought of this:

—of presenting you for a marriage gift the note for $500.00 which you hold from yr uncle James Bones. Therefore, you had better arrange with him at once for its payment, informing him of the nature of your necessity, which is imperative. If the note be not yet due, you might offer to forego interest to date, and to *pay* interest up to the time when the cash is to be called for.

I enclose a piece that appeared in this morning's "Star" that may amuse and possibly gratify, you for a moment.[1]

Love to dear Ellie when you next write.

Your affc   Father.

ALS (WP, DLC).

[1] It was a clipping from the Wilmington, N.C., *Morning Star*, Jan. 22, 1885, quoting an announcement of the forthcoming publication of *Congressional Government* in the Raleigh, N.C., *State Chronicle*, Jan. 20, 1885. The *Star* added a word of commendation of its own. WW sent this clipping to ELA on Jan. 24, 1885.

To Ellen Louise Axson

My own darling,   Balto., Friday afternoon, Jany 23, 1885

You offer a great deal of good and very sage advice about overstudy and the need of exercise in the little note that came this morning, and I am very much obliged for it all. Constant reading probably *does* jade me a little too much, and a more liberal allowance of "restful interruptions" would certainly be great gain so far as my health for the time-being is concerned. But I think that the work is telling on me a little just now only because I have never before held myself down to the systematic performance of set tasks, and that my body and mind will both accommodate themselves to the novel discipline within a few weeks. But, in any case, the reading has to be done, whether I can reduce the friction generated by resisting habits and inclinations or not; and my little sweetheart must not trouble her head too much about it. There is not much danger of the harm done being either very great or very permanent. I will promise not to carry it to the breaking-down point. As I have said so often before, the wear and tear comes in only with loneliness and worry—one reason, among many, why I know that the help and companionship of a loving wife are more necessary to me a thousand fold than a private library or means for travels of investigation—provided the only woman whom I *could* marry will consider it no too great sacrifice to accept for my sake a very scant living. I shall be rich in her, if she feel not poor in the possession of me and little else. I must ask of her the sacrifice once discussed by two young people walking homeward on a railway track.

I have been, very naturally, thinking a good deal of late about the practical details of our life at college next year—I mean as regards my work (for my thoughts have been very selfish)—and there seem to me to be several very simple, feasible, and delightful plans by which you can give me the best possible aid merely by doing, as my proxy and for my benefit (you see how selfish I am!), such reading as you delight most in doing. I shall have to work away unceasingly in one or two rigid specialties; my little queen can find out for me what is going on in the world, what subjects are commanding most space in the magazines (for the library will contain them all), what is being written that would be suggestive to me; can recite to me the plots and read to me the choice parts of the best novels of the day, and fill my too prosy brain with the sweetest words of the poets; can, in short, keep my mind from dry rot by exposing it to an atmosphere of fact and entertainment and imaginative suggestion. We will purvey for each other in separate literary fields, if my darling is pleased with the idea, and she may add to her talents in the great art which she already excels in that other equally great accomplishment of making pictures for the mental eye of the man who loves her with all his heart and adores her with all his manhood,

Her own   Woodrow.

ALS (WC, NjP).

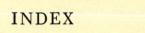

INDEX

NOTE ON THE INDEX

THE reader is referred to the Note on the Index to Volume 1 for a statement of general principles and practices for this series, including the treatment of Wilson's Marginal Notes. The alphabetically arranged analytical table of contents eliminates duplication in both contents and index, of references to certain documents, like letters. Letters are listed in the contents alphabetically by name and chronologically for each name, by page. The subject matter of all letters is, of course, indexed. The Editorial Notes and Wilson's writings are listed in the contents chronologically by page. In addition, the subject matter of both categories is indexed. The index in general covers significant references to books and articles in text or notes, but does not furnish bibliographical information or cover routine documentation. Footnotes and descriptive-location notes are indexed. Page references to footnotes which place a comma between the page number and "n" cite both text and footnote, thus: "624,n3." On the other hand, absence of the comma indicates reference to the footnote only, thus: "55n2," where the page number indicates where the footnote appears. The letter "n" without a following digit signifies an un-numbered descriptive-location note.

An asterisk before an index reference designates identification or other particular information. Re-identification and repetitive annotation have been minimized to encourage use of these starred references. Where the identification appears in an earlier volume, it is indicated thus: "*1:212,n3." Thus a page reference standing without a preceding volume number is invariably a reference to the present volume. The index will usually supply the fullest known forms of names of persons of more than casual interest, and, for the Wilson and Axson families, relationships as far down as cousins. Persons referred to in the text by nicknames or shortened forms of names, can be identified by reference to entries for these forms of the names.

A sampling of the opinions and comments of Wilson and Ellen Axson covers their more personal views, while broad, general headings in the main body of the index cover impersonal subjects. Occasionally opinions expressed by a correspondent are indexed where these appear to supplement or to reflect views expressed by Wilson or by Ellen Axson in documents which are missing.

"Abe," see Brower, A. T. H.

Abell, Arunah Shepherdson ("A. S."), *373,n4

"Academy, the," see Axson, Ellen Louise, Life in New York, National Academy of Design

Academy of Music, Philadelphia, 576,-n2

Adams, Charles Kendall, *502,n1

Adams, Herbert Baxter, *1:15,n20, *2:391,n1; 9, 26, 40,n2, 110n1, 124,n5, 135, 144, 332, 335n1, 339, 344, 345, 350, 492n1, 501, 502, 504; his praise of WW's work, 172, 360; introduces WW to Miss M. C. Thomas, 489; recommends WW to Bryn Mawr, 518n1

Adams, Henry Carter, *2:391,n1 (where he is incorrectly identified as Herbert C. Adams); 26

Adger, John B., *350n2

Adler, Felix, *436,n2, 446

"Agnes," see Tedcastle, Agnes V.

Allen, William Francis, *498,n1, 502

American Historical Association, 529

Anderson, Anna Morris, see Ely, Anna M. A.

Anderson, Daisy, see King, Daisy Anderson

Anderson, Dr. and Mrs. H. M., 64,n1, *195n1, 259

Anderson, Julie ("Jule"), see McRae, Julie Anderson

Anderson, Rosalie ("Rose"), *2:555,n3; 6,n3, 12, 14, 31, 33n3, 34, 51, 57, 68, 76, 83, 84, 98, 104, 122, 126, 191, 194,n1, 247, 251, 260, 264, 272, 282, 569; engaged to M. DuBose, 13n1

Anderson Street Presbyterian Church, Savannah, *15,n2, 35

Andrews, Clara Bliss, cousin of ELA, *333,n4, 514,n1, 534, 535, 545

"Anna," see Harris, Anna

"Annie," see Lester, Annie

Arkansas Industrial University, see Wilson, Woodrow, Seeking a Position, University of Arkansas

Art Students' League, New York, see Axson, Ellen Louise, Life in New York

Association for the Advancement of Women, 390n1

Augusta Female Seminary, *1:486,n1; 9, 11n5, 94n1

"Aunt Ella," see Axson, Ella Law

"Aunt Emma," see Hoyt, Emily A. R.

"Aunt Flo," see Seay, Mr. and Mrs.

"Aunt Florence," see Hoyt, Florence

Axson, Benjamin Palmer, first cousin of ELA, *2:557n2; *6,n3, 16

Axson, Carrie Belle, first cousin of ELA, *2:557n2; 6n2,3

Axson, Edward William ("Eddie"), brother of ELA, *2:372,n2; 5,n2, 6n3, 160, 161, 176, 188, 216, 225, 296, 297, 306-307, 619

Axson, Ella Law, paternal aunt-in-law of ELA, *2:557n2; 6n3, 8, 31, 77, *142n1

Axson, Ellen, first cousin of ELA, *2:557n2; 6n2,3, 16, 31, 35

Axson, Ellen Louise, fiancée of WW, *2:334,n2; described by WW, to R. H. Dabney, 27, to C. A. Talcott, 231-32; named for two aunts, *2:576, *306; family ties, 162, WW on, 166-67; parents' deaths, *201n1,2; her first letter, 227; requests WW to destroy her letters, 354-55, his reply, 356, her rebuttal, 361; has malaria, 322, a cold, 550

ARTISTIC INTERESTS

criticism, 128-29, 140; "Checkmated," *2:590; 31,n4; drawing and painting: 190, 195, 246, 301-302, 315-16; her "batch of generals" at Savannah, *77,n5; her wish to teach, 162, 171, 175, 187, 203; WW on, 166, 168, 176-77, 184-85, 208. See also Corcoran Gallery of Art; Walters Gallery; Life in New York

LIFE IN NEW YORK

advance plans for: 55, 218, *222,n2, 235

art and artists: sketching, 519, 533; posing, 425, 431, 434-35, 492, 533; teachers, 462, 519, 537

American Art Association, *431,n2, 540n2

American Art Galleries, *431n2, 434, 540n2

Art Students' League, 223n3, 235, 242, 331; ELA's first day at, 336; her description of its methods, 462-63; teachers of, compete in Christmas card contest, 509

Chase, William Merritt, *436,n3, 439, 446

Cooper Union Institute, of the Cooper Union for the Advancement of Science and Art, 222, 235, 462; WW on, 242

Cottier and Co., *367,n1, 370

Goupil's Gallery of Paintings, *366,-n1, 439

Lepage, Jules Bastien, *599,n1

Metropolitan Museum of Art, 352,

400, 485, 492; school of, *584,n1, 586, 587, 588, 590, 593, 625
National Academy of Design, 431,n1, 463,n2, 540n2, 551; ELA, a student at, in 1881-82, *2:334n2; *464n2
Prange, Henry, *508,n1
Reichard, Gustav and Co., *361,n1
Richards, William Trost, *439,n1
Saint-Gaudens, *591,n1
Salmagundi Club, *540,n2, 551
Turner, C. T., 395
Vedder, Elihu, *454,n1, 509, 536, 540
Watts, George Frederick, 400, 485, *509,n2, 512
boardinghouses and landladies: 329, 333-34, 347, 357-59, 377, 387, 454, 510, 568, 585-86; WW on: 353, 582, 586-87, 589-90, "those horrid people," 330
churches and preachers: churchgoing as "dissipation," 419, as "entertaining," 535; bargaining for a pew, 419, 600
Beecher, Henry Ward, *419,n2, 441; WW on, 417, 607-608,n1
Church of the Heavenly Rest, *376,-n1
Church of the Holy Communion, 535
Church of the Pilgrims, *398n3
Deems, Edward M., *412,n1, 419
Fifth Avenue Presbyterian Church, 398n4
First Presbyterian Church, *347,n1, 355n1, 441
Grace Episcopal Chapel, 347
Hall, John, *398,n4
Hamilton, Samuel M., *523,n1, 568, 587-88, 592, 607
Madison Avenue Dutch Reformed Church, 332
Madison Square Presbyterian Church, *334n2
Parkhurst, Charles H., *333,n2
Paxton, William Miller, *347,n1, 354,n1; WW on, 351
Reed, Edward A., *332,n1, 376
Scotch Presbyterian Church, *365,n1, 369, 523, 524n1, 540, 587, 600
Storrs, R. S., *398,n3
Tabernacle Congregational Church, 351n1, 370n2
Taylor, William M., *351,n1, 354, 370,n2, 419, 478; ELA on his "advocacy" of inter-racial marriages, 523, WW's reply, 532
Westminster Presbyterian Church, *413n1
See also Hodge, A. A.; Patton, F. L.
plays and actors: ELA would rather hear WW than Booth, 487; Edwin Booth, anticipated, 609, 620; as Iago, 624,n1, 632; *French Flats* at the

Union Square, 384; Henry Irving and Ellen Terry, anticipated, 425, 433, 443, 478; in *Merchant of Venice*, 470-71, in *Hamlet*, 486; WW on, 433, 476

MALE FRIENDS AND SUITORS

105, 163, 169-71, 175. *See also* Mr. Baker; Caldwell, Robert E.; Gailor, T. F.; Goodrich, A.; McRae, Jack; Shinn, C. H.; Stephens, J.; Strider, J. P.; Thornwell, C.; Wright, James

OPINIONS AND COMMENTS

birthdays, 187
"comforters" in bereavement, 207-208
engagements, 170-71; WW on, 178
Episcopalian ritual, 266, 274, 535
evolution, 354
intemperance, 93
lectures, 58
love and friendship, 387
Oxford gowns and hoods, 266
people in general: "men *are* queer creatures," 620, "Eve was made of the same clay as Adam," 610, cleverness in women unsettling to their brains, 395, female lecturers, 46-47, "evil consequences of marrying a woman of the world," 580
people in particular (a sampling): Blaine vs. Cleveland, *390,n1, 407, *436,n1, *461,n1, 516; Jay Gould, *412,n2,3, *416,n1; John B. Gordon, *436,n1; Hannah Whitall Smith, *46,n1. *See also* reading
"whatever is is right," 171, 187; WW's replies, 177, 191-92
WW: writing history, 58, his style, 107, as art critic, 128, his theories of cabinet government, 425-26, "beneath" him to teach in a "female college," 495, his "stern judgments," 562, WW's defense, 570-71, ELA's reply, 572, his need of exercise, 628

READING

a sampling of authors, titles, allusions, and quotations:
T. B. Aldrich, 591,n2
Alice Through the Looking-Glass, 257
Anstey's *Vice Versa*, 299, 306, WW on, 302
Bagehot on Shelley, 480
T. L. Beddoes, 314,n2
Ben Hur, *47,n5, 53
William Black, J. H. Ingraham, *47,n3,4
E. B. Browning, 284, *444,n1, *481,-n1
Coleridge, 421
Froude and Carlyle, *369,n1, 373
Jean Ingelow, *76,n3, 106
Henry James, 59
Frances Kemble, 163n, WW on, 168

Lorna Doone, 47, 218
Jules Michelet's *The Bird,* 65-67, WW on, 80
E. S. Phelps's novels, *377-78,n2,3
Adelaide Procter, *527-28,n1
"Jean Paul" Richter, 306,n1
Ruskin, 47, 63-64, 79, 85, 610
Swinburne, 130
Bayard Taylor, *371,n1, *536,n1
Tennyson, *475,n1, *494,n1
Henry Timrod, *76,n4

VISITS TO

Gainesville, Ga., 296, 297, 299; Lookout Mountain, 255, 259, 260, 265-66; Philadelphia, 492, 509, 512, 516, 521, 525, 530, 559, 567, 576n1; sees L. Barrett at, in *A Blot in the 'Scutcheon,* *580,n1; Rome, Ga., 91, 169, 194; Sewanee, 57-58, 255, 271; Tallulah Falls, 307, 316, 325-26, WW on, 311-12; Wilmington, 58, 264, 324, 329. *See also* Axson, Rebecca R.; and "Bonaventure," "Richmond," "Strathy Hall," Thunderbolt

Axson, Isaac Stockton Keith, paternal grandfather of ELA, *2:547n3; 6n3, 207, 252
Axson, [Isaac] Stockton [Keith] II, *see* Axson, Stockton
Axson, Leila, first cousin of ELA, *2:557n2; 6n3, 16, 31, 35, 76
Axson, Margaret Jane Hoyt, mother of ELA, *2:334n2,3; death of, *201n2
Axson, Margaret Randolph, *see* Elliott, Margaret Axson
Axson, Randolph, Jr., first cousin of ELA, *2:557n2; 5,n2, 6n3, 16, 154
Axson, Randolph, Sr., paternal uncle of ELA, *2:557n2; 5, 6n3, 207
Axson, Rebecca Randolph, paternal grandmother of ELA, *2:334n3; 6n3, 207; her opposition to ELA's visiting Wilmington, 235, WW on, 239-40, 243, 247, 248-50, ELA on, 244-45, 251-52; ELA's dread of parting from, 315
Axson, Samuel Edward, father of ELA, *2:334,n3; removal to Milledgeville hospital, *6n1, ELA on, 7, WW on, 13-14, attending physician at, 49n9; health of, 30, 53, 75, 176, relation of, to ELA's marriage, 166-67,n2; congratulates WW on collaboration with R. T. Ely, 77-78, quoted on WW, 168n2; death of, *201n1, WW on, 200, ELA on, 201
Axson, Stockton, brother of ELA, *2:386n1; 85, 117, 216, 225, 251, 265, 296, 298, 306-307, 453, 479; ELA's praise of, 207; and Davidson College, 207, 307, 318

Bagehot, Walter, "my master," 111, 264; his *Literary Studies,* 446, quoted, 472,n1,2
Baker, Mr., 170, 256
Baltimore American, *209,n1, 390n1
Baltimore *Sun,* 373,n4, 390n1
Banker's Magazine, *135,n1
Beatty, Elizabeth, *356-57, 377, 589-90, 629
Beckwith, John F. B. ("Brock"), *22,n2
Beckwith, Mr., *2:587; *273,n2, 488, 569
Beckwith, Réné Fairbanks, *2:587; *272,n1, 273,n2, 488, 569, 573
Bernard, William H., *1:671n1; 636n2
Berry, T. Alexis, *2:569; 182
"Beth," *see* Erwin, Elizabeth L. A.
Beville, Miss, *2:458,n1; 487
Bingham School, *222,n4, 280. *See also* Wilson, J. R., Jr.
Bird, Mrs. Edgeworth, *605,n3
Blaine, James Gillespie, 336, *391n1, *413n2,3, *445n2, *461,n1. *See also* Cleveland, Grover
Blair, Henry W., his education bill, *135,n2, 144, 158
Blake, John Rennie, *1:31n1; *307,n3
Bliss, Benjamin K., cousin of ELA, *331,n2, 333
Bliss, Clara, *see* Andrews, Clara Bliss
Bliss, Theodore, cousin of ELA, *333,n3
Bluntschli, Johann Kaspar, *2:392n2; 26
Bluntschli Library, The Johns Hopkins University, *2:447n3; 9,n2, 332, 344, 382, 589
"Bob," "Bobby," *see* Bridges, Robert
Boggs, William E., *2:322,n1; 219n2
"Bonaventure," *16,n4, 141,n2
Bones, Helen Woodrow, first cousin of WW, *1:650n6; 9n5
Bones, James W., uncle-in-law of WW, *1:39n4; 9,n5, 88, 91, 98, 169-70, 175, 180, 193, 211, 251, 255, 265; estate matters and loan of $1,000 from JWW, 240, 310, 316-18, 327-29, 342; note for $500 held by WW, 633
Bones, Maria, *2:392; 33,n2
Bones, Marion McGraw ("Mami"), first cousin of WW, *1:487n2; 9,n5, 91,- n1, 193, 207, 211, 233, 255
Bones, Marion Woodrow, maternal aunt of WW, *1:39n10; *see* Woodrow, William, estate of
Boylston, Mrs. J. Reid (Hester), *2:96; *318n1
Boylston, Robert, death of, *318,n1; WW on, 320
Bradford, Gamaliel, *22n1, 247n3
Bradstreet's, 589,n1, 626-27,n1
Bridges, Robert ("Bob," "Bobby"), *1:284,n1; 232, 278, 510, 536, 540,

553; his pen name, "Droch," 541n1; his "Over the Ferry," 199,n3, his "A Lily of the Field," 541n2; WW on, 466, 542

Brower, Abraham T. H. ("Abe"), first cousin-in-law of WW, *2:17n3; 9,n5, 10, 22,n3, 192, 265; takes position in Chicago, 170, 175, 180

Brower, Jessie Bones, first cousin of WW, *1:38,n4; 9,n4,5, 122, 170, 173, 174, 180, 252, 255, 265, 397; asks WW to visit, 192

Brower, Lefoy, *2:372,n1; 9,n5

Brower, Marion, cousin of WW, *2:293,n3; 9,n5, 174,n1, 265

Brown, Edward Thomas ("Ed"), first cousin of ELA, *2:519,n1; *298,n1, 305, 495,n2, 500

Brown, Louisa C. Hoyt, maternal aunt of ELA, *2:402n2; 118n1, 251, *300n1, 498; ELA's middle name after hers, 306; her children, 306-307

Brown, Loula, first cousin of ELA, *306, 308, 315

Brown, Minnie, first cousin of ELA, *306

Brown, Warren A., uncle-in-law of ELA, *2:401,n2; 286, 288, 292, 306

Brush, George DeForest, 336, 344; ELA on his marriage, 615

Bryce, James, *2:547,n2; 362, 622

Bryn Mawr College, see Wilson, Woodrow

Bryson, John H., *343,n2, 350n2

cabinet government, 223-24, 425-26, 433; G. Bradford on, 21-22

Cable, George W., *388,n1, 455,n1

Caldwell, Bessie, *246,n1, 265

Caldwell, Caroline E. Livy, *172n1

Caldwell, John W., *14n1, *589,n1, 593; WW on, 598

Caldwell, Kate Pearson, *171,n1

Caldwell, Robert E., *397,n1, 399, 419

Caligraph typewriter, *2:366,n1; 103, 113, 229, 259, 319, 326, 338n1, 423n

Carey, Mathew, *36

caucus, 112

Central Presbyterian, see Woodrow, James

Century Magazine, 366, 388,n1, 455

Chandler, Janie Porter, *2:453n1; 5, 91, *266,n1, 340, 420, 475; her twenty-five scholars, 76

Chandler, Samuel, *2:527; *268n1

Channing, Edward, *40,n1

Chautauqua movement, *543,n2

"Checkmated," see Axson, Ellen L.

Civil Service Law and reform, 321, 362

Clarke, Joseph T., *125,n7

Clay, Caroline M. Law ("Carrie," "Miss Carrie"), *142n1, 153; WW likens ELA to, 146, 173

Clay, R. Habersham, *142,n3

Clay, Thomas C., *140, 146

Cleveland, Grover, *247,n2, 259, 276, 336, 436,n1, 516; Albert Shaw on election of, 444; WW on, 396, 404, 410-11, 422; WW on effects of Republican victory in Ohio, 355,n1

Columbia Theological Seminary, controversy at, involving JRW, *1:50n1; *349,n2. For controversy at, on evolution, see Caldwell, John W.; Dabney, R. L.; Mack, Joseph B.; Woodrow, James

committee government, 18-19, 21, 80, 111, 224, 602

Corcoran Gallery of Art, 329,n2, 439

Corson, Hiram, *2:662,n1; 72

"Cousin Allie," see Truehart, Alice L. Hoyt

"Cousin Ben," see Bliss, Benjamin K.

"Cousin Ed," see Brown, E. T.

"Cousin Hattie," see Ewing, Harriet Hoyt

"Cousin Robert," see Ewing, Robert

"Cow, the," see Woods, Hiram, Jr.

Dabney, Richard Heath, *1:685,n1; WW to, on ELA, 27, his reply, 164

Dabney, Robert Lewis, *2:564n1; 143, *218-19n1, *242-43,n1

"Daisy," see King, Daisy Anderson

"Dan," "Dan'l," see Webster, J. E.

Davidson College, 172n1, 207, 308n3, 319; WW's homesickness at, recalled, 268

Dewey, Davis Rich, *36,n5, 39, 137,n3, 403,n1, 558; WW on, 50

Dewey, John, *136,n3

Dr. Thomas, see Thomas, James G.

"Dode," see Wilson, J. R., Jr.

Dorsey, George W. E., *2:118,n1; 165, 310, 327-28, 380, 482

"Droch," see Bridges, Robert

DuBose, McNeely ("Mac"), *12,n1, 51, 58, 84, 88, 98, 194,n1, 272; WW's opinion of, 96, 104; ELA's defense of, 106; WW's retraction, 113, 260, 283

Duncan, Martha Deloney Berrien Nesbit, *15,n1, 24, 30, 36, 46, 65

Duncan, William, *17n1

Duryea, Joseph Tuthill, *1:357,n2; 138

"Ed," see Brown, E. T.

"Eddie," see Axson, Edward W.

educational reform, C. W. Eliot on, 42-44

Eliot, Charles William, 42-44, 58; WW on, 45

Elliott, Margaret Axson ("Maggie," "Madge"), sister of ELA, *2:417n1; *118n1, 306, 308; described by ELA, 297; doll for, 511

Ely, Anna Morris Anderson, *343n1

Ely, Richard Theodore, *2:448n1; 335n1, 339, 553; marriage of, *342,n1; WW on, 25, 344; his proposed "History of Political Economy in the United States," with WW and D. R. Dewey: *36,n4, 62,n3, 112, 125, 172, *518n1; WW on, 49-50, 82; ELA on, 39; ELA's father on, 75, 77-78; WW's doubt of continuing, 196, 209, 230; WW's reading for, 446,n1, 467

Emerson, Alfred, *125,n7

Erwin, Elizabeth L. Adams ("Beth"), *2:402n1; 47, 75, 93

estate of William Woodrow, see Woodrow, William, estate of

Ethical Culture Society, see Society for Ethical Culture

Eutaw Place Baptist Church, *422n1

"Eva," see McNulty, Eva

evolution, teaching of, see Columbia Theological Seminary

Ewing, Harriet Hoyt ("Hattie"), first cousin of ELA, *267,n4, 468, 474, 476, 485, 486, 506, 558

Ewing, Robert, first cousin-in-law of ELA, 274, 468, 471, 475, 478; proposes WW for a chair in political economy, 481, WW on, 491

executive, Joseph Story's views on, and WW's, compared, 169,n2; WW on, 223

Fairbanks, René, see Beckwith, René F.

"Fannie," see Hoyt, Frances

federal and state governments, 157, 159, 223

Felt, Zephaniah Charles, *571,n2

First Presbyterian Church, Baltimore, 96,n1

First Presbyterian Church, Columbia, S.C., 172n2, 344n2, 350n2

First Presbyterian Church, Savannah, 107n1

First Presbyterian Church, Wilmington, N.C., 350n2

Fitch, Charles Howard, *627,n2

"Florence," see Young, Florence

Ford, William F., 589n1, 627n1, 631

Free Trade Club, Atlanta, 76,n2

Freeman, Edward A., *124,n3, 622

Friends' Review, *492n3

"Gaddy," see Gadsden, E. M.

Gadsden, Edward Miles ("Gaddy"), *2:324n2; 22,n4, 52, 318; WW on, 321-22

Gailor, Charlotte Moffett (Mrs. Frank M.), *195n1

Gailor, Thomas Frank ("the Prodigy"), 195n1, *268n3; ELA on "his Reverence," 266-67, 273, 285, 299-300; WW on, 269-70, 293-94, 302-303

General Assembly of the Presbyterian Church, U. S. (southern), 128n1, 166, 183; Minutes of, and WW's work on them, 95, 143, 147, 198, 216, 218, 229, 264; ruling of, affecting JRW, 349, 350n2. See also Woodrow, James

Gildersleeve, Basil L., *2:336n1; *125,n7, 273, 286; ELA on, 280; WW on, 283, 289-90

Gilman, Daniel Coit, *1:593,n1; 26, 42, 45, 124, 221, 332

Godkin, Edwin L., *2:74n1; 433

Godwin, Harold ("Pete"), *1:249n3; 25n3, 135, 278,n1, 464; his marriage, *232,n3

Goodrich, Arthur, *366,n2, 377, 409, 454, 462, 509, 551, 587-88, 600, 609-10, 615, 631, 632; ELA on, 425, 616, 620; WW on, 433, 555-56, 594-95, 603-604, 614, 617, 619

Green, Aminta, *2:582; *46,n2, 55, 64, 74, 119, 187, 188

Hall, Dr., *49,n9, 53

Hall, Granville Stanley, *73,n1, 335n1; requests WW as assistant, 205,n1, 311, ELA on, 207, WW on, 430,n1

Hall, Laura, *148,n3, 382

Harper, George McLean, *571,n1

Harris, Anna, *2:505,n1; 75,n1, 91, 163, 190, 226, 372

Harris, J. Rendell, *123

Hartwell, Edward M., *125,n8

"Heathen, the," see Lee, W. B.

"Helen," see Killough, Helen Porter

Hiram, see Woods, Hiram, Jr.

Historical Seminary, see Seminary of Historical and Political Science

Hodge, Archibald Alexander, *1:304n1; *441,n1

Hodgson, Telfair, *280,n1

Hopewell, Melville R., *2:392; *32,n1, 338, 483

Hopkins House of Commons, see Wilson, Woodrow, Johns Hopkins University

Houghton, Mifflin & Co., 366n2, 421, 424,n1, 453, 454, 465, 497, 502; showrooms of, 454,n2, 509, 536, 540

Howe, Annie Wilson, sister of WW, *1:4n6; 215, 632

Howe, George, Jr., M.D., brother-in-law of WW, *1:39,n8; 216, 632

Howe, Jessie, niece of WW, *2:64; illness of, 215, 632, 635

Hoyt, Emily A. Roberts ("Emma"), maternal aunt-in-law of ELA, *323,n1

Hoyt, Florence, maternal aunt-in-law of ELA, *226n1, 256

Hoyt, Florence Stevens, first cousin of ELA, 265

Hoyt, Frances ("Fannie"), first cousin of ELA, *315,n1

Hoyt, Henry Francis, maternal uncle of ELA, *307,n2, 315,n1, 323

Hoyt, Lillian T. ("Lily"), first cousin of ELA, *576n3, 579,n2, 580, 599

Hoyt, Louisa Cunningham, see Brown, Louisa C. Hoyt

Hoyt, Mary Eloise ("Minnie"), first cousin of ELA, *2:496n3; 91, 163, 190, 216, 220, 226, 227, 237, 238, 252, 256, 263, 265, 384, 441, 451, 533, 579; WW's first meeting with, recalled, 109; writes WW of death of ELA's father, 200,n1, 201

Hoyt, Mary Frances Hines, maternal aunt-in-law of ELA, *316n1

Hoyt, Mary Harrison, maternal aunt-in-law of ELA, *268n4, *576n3

Hoyt, Robert Taylor, maternal uncle of ELA, *2:545n1; 207, 219, 251

Hoyt, Sadie (Saidie, Sallie) Cooper, aunt-in-law of ELA, *484,n1, 509. 512

Hoyt, Thomas Alexander, maternal uncle of ELA, *268n4, *484,n1, 485, 487, 509, 512, 521, 523, 576n1, 580, 581-82, 595

Hoyt, William Dana ("Willie," "little Will"), first cousin of ELA, *220,n1, 265

Hoyt, William Dearing, M.D., maternal uncle of ELA, *2:477n1; 176, 201, 220,n1, 237, 251, 256, 265; "my second father" to ELA, 211

Hull Memorial Presbyterian Church, see Anderson Street Presbyterian Church

Huntsville Presbyterian Church (Ala.), *344n2

Independent Presbyterian Church, Savannah, 6n3, 17n2

Industrial University of Arkansas, see Wilson, Woodrow, Seeking a Position, University of Arkansas

Ingle, Edward, 10, 137, 199,n2; WW on, 8-9

International Review, 159,n2

Jack, Charles A., 2:461-62; and estate of William Woodrow, share of JWW in, 338, 483

James, Edmund J., 135,n1

"Janie," see Chandler, Janie Porter

Jefferson Society, *1:576,n1; 553n1

"Jimmie," see Woodrow, James Hamilton

Johns Hopkins University, The, see Wilson, Woodrow

"Josie," see Wilson, J. R., Jr.

Journalists' Club of Baltimore, 373,n2, 3

"Jule," see McRae, Julie Anderson

Juilliard v. Greenman, *158n1

Kennard, John Hanson, Jr., *62,n1, 139n1

Kennedy, Anderson Ross, brother-in-law of WW, *1:66n1; 131,n2, 143, 168n1, 177,n1

Kennedy, Marion Wilson, sister of WW, *1:4n5; 573, 588,n2; on ELA, 167,n1; on WW's style, 99, 118; suggests teaching post for WW, 130-31, 143, 148,n4, 155

Kent, Charles William, *1:588n1; 28

Kidder, Edward, *1:153n1; 575,n1

Killough, Helen Porter, and Mr. Killough, *2:526; *91,n2, 92, 338,n2, 340, 344, 420; WW on, 110, 488; death of, 435

King, Clarence, 194

King, Daisy Anderson, *31,n3, *195n1

King, Francis T., *490,n4, *565,n1, 573

Law, Caroline Matilda ("Miss Carrie"), see Clay, Caroline M. L.

Law, William, *142n1

Law, Willie, *77,n6, 90, 96

"League, the," see Axson, Ellen L., Life in New York

Lee, William Brewster ("the Heathen"), *1:514,n1; 24,n2

Lefevre, Walter S., *1:683,n1; 28

Leftwich, James T., *96n1, 104, 543

legal tender decision of Supreme Court, WW on, 135, *158,n1

Lester, Annie, 246, 336, 352, 353, 357, 360, 364, 368, 377, 399, 443, 510, 585

Levermore, Charles H., *362n1, 370, 557

"Little Auntie," see Walker, Ellen A.

"Loula," see Brown, Loula

"Mac," see DuBose, McNeely

Mack, Joseph B., *171,n2, 217,n2, 227, 237, 257,n2, 398n2, 598,n1, 601, 602

"Maggie," see Elliott, Margaret A.

Marquand, Allan, *1:134n4; 232n3

Marquand, Elisabeth, *232,n3

Marquand, Henry, 278,n1

Marquand, Henry Gurdon, *232n3

Marvin, Mr. and Mrs. Walter, 331, 336, 356, 357, 376; Mr. Marvin, Jr., "cousin Walter's old bachelor brother," 332; "the young Marvin boy," 333

Mayrant, Kate Drayton, *2:284n2; 324, 326n2

McCosh, James, *1:133,n4; 74, 217, *415n1

McLaren, William E., *266,n2

McNulty, Eva, *330,n1, 333, 358

McRae, Jack, 280, 286, 289, 299-300, 302, 315; ELA on, *194,n1

McRae, Julie Anderson ("Jule"), *31,n3, *194,n1
Minneapolis *Daily Minnesota Tribune*, *445n1
"Minnie," *see* Hoyt, Mary Eloise
Minor, John Barbee, *1:583n3; WW asks for reference from, 150-52; warns WW against impractical theorizing on government, 157
Morris, George Sylvester, *335n1, 340
Mulligan, James, letters of, *445n2
Munger, William T., 165,n1, 240, 310, 380
Murray, James O., *1:205n5; 414, 422,n1

New York *Commercial Advertiser*, 278n1, 464, 541,n2
New York *Evening Post*, 24, 25n4, 37, 44,n1, 199,n1, 464, 627
New York *Nation*, 102,n1, 247,n3, 259, 326,n3, 369,n1, 373, 425-26,n1, 433, 500n1, 509,n2, 540n1, 619,n2
North Carolina Presbyterian, *see* Woodrow, James

"Oakdene," home of A. T. H. Brower, 161, 168, 173, 216, 241
Ota, Enazo, *2:553n2; *362n1
Overland Monthly, 75, 82, 159, *213,n1, 278, 516

Palmer, Benjamin Morgan, *13,n1, 589; and academic posts for WW and JRW, 74, 343,n1
Pan-Presbyterian Council, *see* World Presbyterian Alliance
parliamentary government, *see* cabinet government
Patton, Francis Landey, WW on, *114,n3, 138; ELA on, 129, *419,n1
Peabody Library, 593
Pease, Charles H., 165,n1, 240, 310
Pennsylvania Academy of the Fine Arts, *586,n1
Perkins Professor, *see* Woodrow, James
"Pete," *see* Godwin, Harold
Philadelphia *American*, 172n
Phillips, Charles, *1:26n2; 319
Phillips, William Battle ("Bill"), *1:47n1; 319
Porter, Clark, 92, 100
Porter, Helen, *see* Killough, Helen Porter
Porter, Janie, *see* Chandler, Janie Porter
Presbytery of Wilmington, *142,n1
"Prodigy, the," *see* Gailor, Thomas Frank

Raleigh *State Chronicle*, 633n1
Randall, James Ryder, *47,n6
Renick and Wilson, *2:138n1, *2:304

n3; disposal of joint property and pending cases of, 22,n1,2,3,4, 318
Renick, Edward Ireland, *2:96,n1; 619,n1; reports to WW on operations of Treasury Department, 22, 35,n3, 39, 54-55, 102,n1, 188. *See also* Renick, Isabel L.
Renick, Isabel L., *2:324n2; her marriage to E. I. Renick, 318, WW on, 321, ELA on, 324
Rhoads, James E., *489,n3, 498-99, 573, 621-22
"Richmond," estate of Thomas C. Clay, *140-42, 153; WW on, 145-46
"Ridge," *see* Wright, Jacob R.
Rome Female College, 171, 247n1
"Rose," *see* Anderson, Rosalie
Rose, John C., *373,n4, 375-76

Saint Louis Presbyterian, *see* Woodrow, James
Sato, Shosuki, 139, *362n1
Scaife, Walter B., *172, *362n1
Scudder, Horace Elisha, *149n1, 158n, 162
Seay, Mr. and Mrs. ("Aunt Flo"), 31
Seminary of Historical and Political Science, The Johns Hopkins University, *2:447n3; 8,n1, 123,n1, 124-25, 214,n1, 301, 344,n1,2, 373,n4; WW's activities in, 40-42, 135, 172, 182-83, 188,n1,2, 301, 360,n1, 361, 364, 391, 517, 615; participants in debate on education, 135-37; members of, 1004 85, *362n1
Sewanee, Tenn., ELA's friends at, *195n1
Shaw, Albert, *214,n1, 278; on Cleveland's election, 444
Shinn, Charles Howard, *2:662n1; 4, 9, 52, 62, 139, 229, 369, 396, 399, 401, 517, 573-74; WW on, 23, 134-35, 262-63, 433, 466; bond between Shinn and WW, 386,n1; ELA and Shinn, 9,n3, 32, 98, 121, 130, 188, 346, 352, 353, 360, 373, 374, 379, 381,n1,2, 383, 384, 407, 414, 416, 433, 475, 510, 516
Shinn, Milicent Washburn, *2:640n; 213, 516; ELA on, 384
Smith, Gessner Harrison ("Harry"), *28,n3
Society for Ethical Culture, *436,n2; WW on, 446
South, the, and education, 135-37, 217; ELA on its "tragedy," 142; WW on the "old" and the "new," 145-46; Albert Shaw on, 445; and the Civil War, 455-56
South Dakota, admission of, *557,n3
Southern Presbyterian, *see* Woodrow, James
Southern Presbyterian Review, *see* Woodrow, James

South-Western Presbyterian University, 343, 348, 349, 590n1

Stephens, Alexander H., *2:136n1; 228n1, 256, 397

Stephens, John, *227,n1, 236, 256, 263

Stillman, William James, *125,n7

"Strathy Hall," home of R. Habersham Clay, *142,n3

Strider, J. P., *105,n1, 163

Synod of South Carolina, *478,n1. *See also* Woodrow, James

Talcott, Charles Andrew, *1:241n3; 465,n2; on WW's proposals for constitutional reform, 168-69

tariff reciprocity treaties, *557,n2

Taylor, Joseph, *492n3

Tedcastle, Agnes Vaughn, *2:334; 91, 116, 126, 161, 168, 170, 173, 190, 195, 216, 226; ELA on her "perpetual praise" of her husband, 188-89

Tedcastle, Arthur W., *2:334; 91, 139, 188-89, 195, 216, 226; WW on first marriage of, 487-88

Texas University, *see* Wilson, Woodrow, Seeking a Position, University of Texas

Thomas, C. F. Theodore, *442,n2

Thomas, James Carey, *490

Thomas, James G., *6,n2, 48; death of, 536; WW on, 541-42

Thomas, Martha Carey, *489,n2, 490, 498, 515, 517, 596, 621

Thornwell, Charles, *2:471n1; 170, 186

Thunderbolt, *16,n5

Truehart, Alice Louise Hoyt ("Allie"), first cousin of ELA, *267,n4, 599

Tulane, Paul, *481,n2; WW on, 491

Tulane University, *482n2. *See also* Wilson, Woodrow, Seeking a Position

Turpin, Isabel L. (Mrs. James S.), *see* Renick, Isabel L.

"Uncle Henry," *see* Hoyt, Henry F.

"Uncle Randolph," *see* Axson, Randolph, Sr.

"Uncle Rob," *see* Hoyt, Robert T.

"Uncle Tom," *see* Hoyt, Thomas A.

"Uncle Will," *see* Hoyt, William Dearing

Union Theological Seminary, Richmond, Va., *218n1, *398n1

University of Arkansas, *see* Wilson, Woodrow, Seeking a Position

University of California, 155

University of Louisiana, *see* Tulane University

University of the South, 140; Commencement at, described by ELA, 266

University of Texas, *see* Wilson, Woodrow, Seeking a Position

University of Virginia, 143, 151

Vanderbilt University, *see* Wilson, Woodrow, Seeking a Position

Venable, Charles S., *1:584n2; 28

Waddel, John N., *2:74n2; *590n1

Walker, Ellen Axson, "Little Auntie" of ELA, *2:576; 245

Walters, W. T., *55,n1

Walters Gallery, *56n1, 64, 74, 83, 87, 120, 128, 140

Webster, James Edwin ("Dan," "Dan'l"), *1:249n2; 232,n2

Wednesday Club, 132

Wilder, William Royal, *1:253n2; 571,n2

Williams, Talcott, *124,n4

"Willie," *see* Law, Willie; Hoyt, William Dana

Wilmington *Morning Star,* *548n1, *633,n1

Wilson, Janet Woodrow, mother of WW, *1:4n2; WW on, 113; *advice of, to WW on*: diet, 102, marriage, 181-82; health of, 196, 215-16; trip of, to Arden Park, 220, 222; urges ELA to visit Wilmington, 239-40,n1, 249-50; preparations of, to leave Wilmington, 546-47; her share of estate of William Woodrow, 165,n1; loan of $1,000 to J. W. Bones, 240-41; taxes on estate, 537; WW as legal agent for estate properties, 310, 316-18, 327-29, 341-42, 348, 379-81, 435-36, 440, 482, 483, 501, 520-21, 531, 574. *See also* Bones, J. W.; Woodrow, William, estate of

Wilson, John Leighton, *1:440n4; 18,n2, 74, 107, 121

Wilson, Joseph Ruggles, Jr. ("Dode," "Josie"), brother of WW, *1:4n8; 233, 298; at Bingham School, *222,n4, 238, 262, 268-69, 482, 535, 540, leaves, 548, 566; his imaginary navy, 11; Wilmington Bicycle Club, 262,n1

Wilson, Joseph Ruggles, Sr., father of WW, *1:3,n1; 95; on employment for WW at University of Arkansas, 165, 183; proposed as delegate to World Presbyterian Alliance at Belfast, *127,n1, 143; his allowance to WW, 165; Christmas present to WW from JWW, 572; wedding present to WW, 633; appointment of, to South-Western Presbyterian University, 343,n1,2, 348, 349, *548n1, asks WW's help in preparing inaugural address at, *549,n1; sermon of, quoted by WW, 254-55; congratulates WW on acceptance of *Con-*

gressional Government, 505; feelings of Wilmington congregation on departure of, 575, 613

advice to WW on: the "blues," 548-49, hasty marriage, 183, marriage expenses, 613, accepting Bryn Mawr offer, 505, 513, 612-13

See also Columbia Theological Seminary

Wilson, Leighton, *see* Wilson, John Leighton

Wilson, Woodrow, *1:3,n7

AND ELLEN AXSON

consults her on his moustache, 12; grows lock of hair for, 55-56; on constitution for the State of Matrimony, 38, for an inter-State Love League, 248; their first meeting, 108-110; on her part in his fanciful autobiography, 147; on her father's death, 200-201,n1,2; on keeping their engagement secret in Wilmington: "we are proud beyond most folks," 258; on family tradition that WW held ELA as a baby, 305,n3; gift of portfolio to, 329; WW asks Bridges to call on ELA, 464-65, 466; ELA's account, 536, 553; Bridges' account, 541; WW on, 542, 564

advice on: danger of going unescorted at night, 392-93, ELA's rebuttal, 400, WW's reply, 406; danger of street adventurers, 552, of sitting in a cold room, 624; early bed-time, 414; engagement ring as protection, 556, ELA's reply, 563; exercise, 503; flirtation and Platonic friendship, 302-303, 556, 603-604; impropriety of theaters named Bijou, 388; overtaxing strength, 392, 424, 437-38, 446; pronunciation, 359n1; suitable room, food, and roommates, 360, 363, 586-87; ELA on WW's advice, 15, 562; WW on his own advice, 13

marriage: economics of, 528-29, 625; wedding gift of WW's parents, 633; timing of wedding, 167-68, 183, 210-11, 528-29, 605-606, 625

visits, made or proposed, to: Baltimore, 55, 74, 80, 84, 87; New York, 356, 359, 361; Philadelphia or New York for Christmas, 511-12, 514, 516-17, 521-22, 534, 559, 564, 567, 573; Rome, Ga., 210, 214-15, 260; Savannah, 3,n1; Wilmington, N.C., 50, 94-95, 118, 122, 189, 222, 235, 238, 239-40, 243-44, 247, 258, 293, 295-96, 300-302, 307-308, 323-24

BRYN MAWR COLLEGE

first interview, 489-91; serious interest, 493; ELA's cautious counsel, 494-95;

WW applies, 496; replies to ELA, 498-500; sponsors of history department at, listed, 502; WW asks ELA's views, 503-504; her reply, 504; the offer, 513-14; JRW's approval, 505, 513, 612-13; offer declined, 517-18; new terms, minutes of trustees quoted, *518n1, 565-66, *568n1; WW's comments, 515; "not a syllable from Bryn Mawr yet," 555; negotiations, 507-508, 573; WW awaits decision, 595; new offer, 596, *597, 604, 621; WW consults ELA, JRW, 604-605, 612; search for housing, 613, 622. *See also* King, Francis T.; Rhoads, J. E.; Thomas, M. Carey

CONSTITUTIONS

for: the Hopkins House of Commons, *543,n3; the Jefferson Society, 553, n1

GERMAN, STUDY OF

134,n1

HEALTH

4, 8, 11, 12, 18, 68, 199, 214-15, 225, 228, 237; eyeglasses, 365

JOHNS HOPKINS UNIVERSITY

anniversary exercises of, 45-46; WW's fellowship at, for 1884-85, 197, 199, 202, 203, *209,n1, *212-13, 214, 465, his acceptance, 221, ELA's comment, 228; WW's appraisal of his professors at, 25-26; his program of studies at, for 1884-85, 335,n1; daily routine, 622-23; student group, characterized by Albert Shaw, 445; advantages of, 156

organizations at: American Historical Association, 529; Eight O'Clock Club, 605, 619; Musical and Dramatic Club, 432, 546, 566-67; Archaeological Society, 72, WW's report on, 125,n7; English Seminary, 125,n6; Phi Kappa Psi, 28, Maryland Alpha Chapter of, 45,n1; Hopkins Debating Club, known also as the Literary Club, or the Hopkins Literary Society: renamed by WW, the Hopkins House of Commons: *543,n3; WW's constitution for, *544n3; WW as critic for, 479-80, 484; debating activities of, 69, 84, 88; WW's talk on oratory, to, 493

See also Bluntschli Library; Peabody Library; Seminary of Historical and Political Science; Walters Gallery; and, for WW's newspaper articles on the Johns Hopkins, Writings; for WW's dilemma over taking a Ph.D., Self-Analysis

LIFE IN WILMINGTON

122, 204-205, 258, 312-14, 319, 329-30, 349

MUSICAL INTERESTS

glee club at the Johns Hopkins, 4-5, 16-17, 29, 30n, 283, 432; Princeton Glee Club at the Hopkins, 45; the "Star Spangled Banner" unknown to WW, 100, sings it, with effect, 105; declines to join a Methodist choir, 96; sings for a Methodist benefit, 148; sings in a Unitarian choir, 598; comical account of leading singing in Wilmington, 204-205

NAME

"even the T. gone from my name now," 28; nicknamed "Colonel" by Albert Shaw, 214, 444

OPINIONS AND COMMENTS

analysis of Carlyle, Disraeli, Calhoun, Burke, 417-18
art criticism, 120-21, ELA's replies, 128-29, 140
Henry Ward Beecher, 417, 607-608
birthdays, 282-83
bohemianism, 590
Francis Bowen, *528,n1
Ednah D. Cheney, *389,n1
chivalry, 146
choosing a wife, 472-73, 487-88
Christian love, 13
church in Baltimore, a, "first rate preaching and plenty of pretty girls," 96,n1
Civil War, the, 455-56
co-education, and higher education for women, 155, 499-500
education, common school, not a federal concern, 136
Episcopalians, 53
free will and predestination, 177, 191-92
friends, his best: Bridges, Talcott, Woods, 464-65, 466, 542
Edmund Gosse, 583-84, 592, 607
Julia Ward Howe, 389
ignorance, the confession of, 319-20
Thomas J. Jarvis, *275,n2, 276
journalism, 263
marriage, with and without love, 487-89; and economics, 528; miscegenation, 532
opinions, his own "blunt," 595
oratory, 283; memorizing speeches, 103-104, 137-38; influence of, superior to influence of writing, 276-77; female, the "dialectic amazon," 389
politics, 275. See also Blaine; Cleveland
propriety and convention, 248-49
Josiah Royce, *10,n6
Alfred M. Scales, *275n1
C. H. Shinn, 386,n1
self-government, "instincts of," 543
Society for Ethical Culture, 446

Mrs. Alexander T. Stewart, *112,n1
Sunday papers, reading of, against conscience, 396
teaching, general and specialized, 164-65
valentines, 19-21
John Heyl Vincent, *543,n2

READING

a sampling of authors and works read and alluded to:
Thomas Bailey Aldrich, 593-94,n1
Matthew Arnold, 71,n3, 89
"my master, Bagehot," 471, quoted, on Shelley, 471-72,n1
George Bancroft, 627
Beddoes, 314,n2, 322,n1
Ben Hur, ELA on, 47,n5, WW on, 53-54
John Bright, 277
Robert Browning, 383,n3, 386,n2, 594
John B. Gough, 417,n2
Hamerton's Intellectual Life, *2:-344,n1; 393,n2; his Human Intercourse, 393,n2
Henry James, 52-53, 69-70
Frances Kemble, 168
Sidney Lanier, 17n, 34,n1
Lorna Doone, 34, 47, 53, 218, 294
Macaulay, 70
Justin McCarthy's History of the Four Georges, 393,n1
James O. Murray, 422,n1
James Payn, 146-47,n1, ELA's reply, 154
D. G. Rossetti, 288-89,n1, 297,n1, 306
Ruskin, 46, 79
Shelley, 419,n1
William Stubbs's English Constitutional History, or Select Charters, 479,n1
Swinburne, 113,n2, 143-45
Trevelyan, 71n2
Francis A. Walker's Political Economy, 538,n1
John Wilson, 417,n1
Wordsworth, 304, 305,n1,2

SEEKING A POSITION

Tulane University, 481, 491, 499, 517
University of Arkansas, first proposal of, 130-31; WW asks references of professors at Princeton and Virginia, 151, 157, 159; correspondence on, 148, 150, 151, 154-56, 160, 162, 165-66, 167-68, 173, 177, 183, 205-206, 208-209, 213, 214; end of the affair, 216, 221. See also Kennedy, Marion Wilson
University of Texas, 73-74, 81, 134, 143
Vanderbilt University, 481-82
See also Bryn Mawr College

SELF-ANALYSIS

on matters of temperament: congeniality of the academic environment, 5; happiness, 10; love and friendship, 382-83; love, will, and duty, 95; need of love, 270-71, 429, 560-61, 592; headaches, love and manliness, 253-54; selfishness and the "blues," 275; self-doubt and despondency, 393-94, 405, ELA's reassurances, 400-401, 412-13; depression over lack of letters from ELA, 281-82; his fallibility, and respect for others' opinions, 554-55; defense against ELA's saying he takes "a cynical view of human nature," 570-71; his need of privacy, 312; his gregariousness, 432; more effective with groups than with individuals, 553; his own oratory, 484; aspiration, and his impatience to achieve, 20, 37-38, 145, 209, 405; his reaction to his success at the Hopkins, 197, to acceptance of his book, 506-507; his share of the artistic temperament, 477, 534-35; his sensitiveness, 611; homesickness remembered, 262, 268; the loneliness of his mother, 262; the intellectual stimulus of his father, 293; dreams of ELA, 261; apology to ELA for his self-absorption, 308-309
on professional values: choice of constitutional studies, 26, 151, 230-31; importance to early marriage of first teaching position, 154-56, 160, 166-68; further study versus teaching and early marriage, ELA on, 202-203, 210, WW on, 208-209, ELA's summation, 234-35; impatience with "cramming," 144, 353-54, 378-79, 382, with the "mere student," 416-18, 422, with the Ph.D. objective, *353,n1, 371, 376; ELA on, 384, 423, JRW on, 385, Dabney on, 164; decision to drop, 414-15, to continue, 619; inadequacy of specialization, 430; pros and cons of Bryn Mawr, 498-500, 503-504
on writing as a craft: 18-19, 53-54, 59-60, 69-70, 98-99, 264; reading as stimulus for writing, 144; writing as creation, 264; on his own letters, 319; proposal to write for *Bradstreet's* declined, 589,n1; result of Blaine-Cleveland election will "decide . . . the character and aim of my political writing," 402

VISITS TO

Columbia, S.C., 6n1; Wilmington, N.C., 215. *See also* And Ellen Axson

WRITINGS

Cabinet Government in the United States, *1:493; 159,n2

Committee or Cabinet Government?, *2:410n1; 21,n2,3, 24,n1, 25,n1, 75,n1, 91, 159,n1, 168,n1, 231; WW on style of, 99
Congressional Government [volume of 1885], *2:156-57, *2:644n1
composition of (roman numerals designate chapters): proposed titles for, 80; written without visiting Washington, 630; I and II, WW's abstract of, 223; II, 18,n1, finished, 59,n1; III, 83, 94, 98, finished, 103, 106, WW on, 364; IV, 218, 229-30, 243, memo for, 214, finished, 259, 267; V, 267, 270, 282, finished, 301; V and VI, plans and progress, 259, 264, 267, 282; VI, 270, begun, 301, finished, 318
and the publisher: I-III submitted to, 111, 149; WW asks return of I for additions, 158,n1, 162; WW doubts early publication, 301; letter to, 335; finished work sent to, 337; no word from, 424,n1, 453, 468; accepted by, *486,n1, 493; WW on effect of acceptance on opening for a position, 502; proofs from, 530, 598; publication date and announcement, 602, 617, 619,n2, 633n1. *See also* Houghton, Mifflin and Co.
and the Hopkins: chapters read to the Seminary, 172, 182-83, *188,n1,2, 360,n1, 364; Dr. Adams on, 172, 360; Albert Shaw on, 556-57; relation of, to questions of Dr. Ely's project, and of leaving the University, 196; I-III submitted with fellowship application, 205,n1, 465; seen by Prof. Hall, 205,n1
and family and friends: ELA's influence on, 243, 248, 270, 301; ELA rejects Mr. Goodrich's gift of, 631; dedication to JRW, 497,n1, quoted, 503, ELA on, 506; Bridges and, 465, 542, Bridges' advance notice of, 541; rejoicing over acceptance, by ELA: "Dear Houghton and Mifflin," 497, by JRW, 505, 513
Fragment of a Ditty, 287
History of Political Economy in the United States [project abandoned, unfinished], relation of, to plans for *Congressional Government*, 196. *See also* Ely, R. T.
Newsletters from the Johns Hopkins, 24n, 25n4, 37, 199,n1
To E. L. A. on Her Birthday, 178

See also Wilson, Janet W., WW as legal agent for estate properties

Woodrow, James, maternal uncle of WW, *1:42n1; 90n1; *and controversy over teaching of evolution*: publications cited: *Central Presby-*

terian, *257n2; New York *Nation*,
*326,n3, *540n1; *North Carolina
Presbyterian*, *243n1; *Saint Louis
Presbyterian*, *222,n5; *Southern Presbyterian*, *222,n5, *479n1, *590n1;
Southern Presbyterian Review,
*218n1, 237,n1, *243n1; Perkins
professorship and, *218n1, *223n5,
*542,n1, *598,n1; WW on, 216-18,n1,
237,n1, 542,n1, 546; ELA on, 227,
602; action of the Synod in, *478,n1.
See also Columbia Theological Seminary
       See also Wilson, Woodrow, Seek-
ing a Position, University of Texas
Woodrow, James Hamilton ("Jimmie"),
first cousin of WW, *1:576n2; 88,n1
Woodrow, Thomas, Jr., maternal uncle
of WW, *1:39,n1,11. *See also* Woodrow, William, estate of
Woodrow, William, maternal uncle of
WW, estate of, *2:113n1; 33n1;
JWW's share of, 17-18,n1, 165, $1,000
loan from, to J. W. Bones, 240;
share of Marion W. Bones in, 33,
328; share of Thomas Woodrow, Jr.
in, *2:113n1; 328, 341, 380; division
of, and taxes on, 327-28, 380; persons buying lands from, listed, 380.
See also Bones, J. W.; Dorsey, G. W.
E.; Hopewell, M. R.; Wilson, Woodrow, as agent for the property of
JWW
Woods, Hiram, Jr. ("the Cow"),
*1:133n3; 11, 12, 24,n5, 138, 150,
232, 402, 414, 464; engagement of,
*147,n3; joshes WW on his use of
the typewriter, 326-27
World Presbyterian Alliance, third General Council of, 127,n1, 143, 147
Worthington, Thomas K., 28, 206,
344n2
Wright, Charles B., *370,n1, 389, 557
Wright, Jacob Ridgeway ("Ridge"),
*1:412n1; 232,n2
Wright, James, *2:651; *83,n1, 169-71,
175, 185-86; WW on, 178

Yager, Arthur, 137
Young, Florence, 336, 384, 399, 443,
585

923.173
W75p
v.3

Date Due

75629

DEMCO NO. 295